T0388481

THE ROUTLEDGE HANDBOOK OF LAW AND DEATH

The Routledge Handbook of Law and Death provides a comprehensive survey of contemporary scholarship on the intersections of law and death in the twenty-first century.

It showcases how socio-legal scholars have contributed to the critical turn in death studies and how the sociology of death has impacted upon the discipline of law. In bringing together prominent academics and emerging experts from a diverse range of disciplines, the *Handbook* shows how, far from shunning questions of mortality, legal institutions incessantly talk about death. Touching upon the epistemologies and materialities of death, and problems of contested deaths and posthumous harms, the *Handbook* questions what is distinctive about the disciplinary alignment of law and death, how law regulates and manages death in the everyday, and how thinking with law can enrich our understandings of the presence of death in our lives.

In a time when the world is facing global inequalities in living and dying, and legal institutions are increasingly interrogating their relationships to death, this *Handbook* makes for essential reading for scholars, students, and practitioners in law, humanities, and the social sciences.

Marc Trabsky is an Associate Professor at La Trobe University, Australia.

Imogen Jones is an Associate Professor at the University of Leeds, United Kingdom.

THE ROUTLEDGE HANDBOOK
OF LAW
AND DEATH

Edited by Marc Trabsky and Imogen Jones

Routledge
Taylor & Francis Group
a GlassHouse Book

Designed cover image: wildpixel / iStock / Getty Images Plus

First published 2025
by Routledge
4 Park Square, Milton Park, Abingdon, Oxon OX14 4RN

and by Routledge
605 Third Avenue, New York, NY 10158

a GlassHouse book

Routledge is an imprint of the Taylor & Francis Group, an informa business

British Library Cataloguing-in-Publication Data
A catalogue record for this book is available from the British Library

Library of Congress Cataloging-in-Publication Data
Names: Trabsky, Marc, editor. | Jones, Imogen, 1982- editor.
Title: The Routledge handbook of law and death / edited by Marc Trabsky and Imogen Jones. Description: Abingdon, Oxon [UK] ; New York, NY : Routledge, 2025. | Includes bibliographical references and index.
Identifiers: LCCN 2024028989 (print) | LCCN 2024028990 (ebook) | ISBN 9781032303383 (hardback) | ISBN 9781032303390 (paperback) | ISBN 9781003304593 (ebook)
Subjects: LCSH: Dead bodies (Law) | Death. | Right to life. | Human body–Law and legislation.
Classification: LCC K564.H8 R68 2025 (print) | LCC K564.H8 (ebook) | DDC 340/.115–dc23/eng/20240627
LC record available at https://lccn.loc.gov/2024028989
LC ebook record available at https://lccn.loc.gov/2024028990

ISBN: 978-1-032-30338-3 (hbk)
ISBN: 978-1-032-30339-0 (pbk)
ISBN: 978-1-003-30459-3 (ebk)

DOI: 10.4324/9781003304593

Typeset in Sabon
by Taylor & Francis Books

This *Handbook* is dedicated to our friends, Pete and Courtney.
Their loss is felt each day.

CONTENTS

Contents

ILLUSTRATIONS

Figures

Tables

Box

CONTRIBUTORS

Carson Cole Arthur is a Lecturer in Criminology at the University of Law, United Kingdom. His work has been published in the *Crime, Media, Culture, Social & Legal Studies, Law, Culture and the Humanities*, and *Third Text Online*.

Zohreh BayatRizi is an Associate Professor in Sociology at the University of Alberta, Canada. Her main interests are the history of sociological concepts as well as the sociology of death and dying. She is the author of *Life Sentences: The Modern Ordering of Mortality* (2008). She is currently working on advancing a critical, transnational concept of grief with a focus on death and grief among immigrants in Canada.

Belinda Carpenter is a Professor in the School of Justice at Queensland University of Technology, Australia. She is the author of 40 articles and book chapters on issues surrounding death investigation, including the coronial determination of suicide, the impact of inquests on families, and the role of autopsy in a death investigation.

David J. Carter is a Scientia Associate Professor of Law in the Faculty of Law & Justice at the University of New South Wales, Australia. His work focuses on understanding law as a factor in the cause, distribution, and prevention of disease and injury while advancing the fair treatment of those living with communicable disease.

Heather Conway is a Professor at Queen's University Belfast, United Kingdom. She is the author of *The Law and the Dead* (2016) and researches on legal issues around funerals. Heather is a Council Member of The Cremation Society, and current President of the Association for the Study of Death and Society.

Penny Crofts is a Professor in the Faculty of Law at the University of Technology Sydney, Australia. Her current research focuses on organisational wrongdoing, horror, and philosophy. Her books include *Wickedness and Crime* (2013) and *Evil Corporations: Law, Culpability and Regulations* (2024).

Kate Falconer is a Lecturer at the Radical Humanities Laboratory and School of Law, University College Cork, Ireland.

Claire Ferguson is an Associate Professor in the School of Justice at Queensland University of Technology, Australia. She is the author of *Detection Avoidance in Homicide: Debates, Explanations, and Responses* (2021). Claire's research focuses on manner of death determination and concealed homicide.

Caroline Fournet is a Professor of Law in the School of Law at Exeter University, United Kingdom. A substantial part of her research explores the use and importance of forensic evidence in the investigation and prosecution of international crimes as well as in the identification of victims and the building of post-atrocity memory.

Maria Giannacopoulos is an Associate Professor and Director of the Centre for Criminology Law and Justice in the Faculty of Law & Justice at the University of New South Wales, Australia. In 2023, she was shortlisted for the Law, Literature and Humanities Association of Australasia Articles/Chapter Prize for 'White Law/ Black Deaths' and she co-edited 'Imagining Decolonised Law' for *Law Text Culture*.

Sabrina Gilani is a Senior Lecturer in Law and Critical Theory at the University of Sussex, United Kingdom. Her research undertakes a materialist critique of criminal punishment, and she is currently working on a book about posthuman approaches to punishment as part of Routledge's New Trajectories in Law book series.

Jessica Jacobson is a Professor of Criminal Justice and Director of the Institute for Crime and Justice Policy Research at Birkbeck, University of London, United Kingdom. Her research and publications span many aspects of the justice system, and she is currently leading an ESRC-funded study on the coronial process, *Voicing Loss*.

Imogen Jones is an Associate Professor at the University of Leeds, United Kingdom. Her current research focuses on the autopsy stage of medico-legal death investigations, with an emphasis on the values, attitudes, and practices of professionals and the implications of these.

Edward Kirton-Darling is a Senior Lecturer in the School of Law at University of Bristol, United Kingdom. He is the author of *Death, Family, and the Law: The Contemporary Inquest in Context* (2022). His work includes focus on investigations into deaths linked to social welfare and the role of the bereaved in those investigations.

Karolina Kuberska is a medical anthropologist and health services researcher at The Healthcare Improvement Studies Institute (THIS Institute) at the University of Cambridge, United Kingdom. Her research focuses on interdisciplinary approaches to understandings of health and wellbeing.

Desmond Manderson FRSC FASSA is jointly appointed as a Professor in the ANU Colleges of Law and College of Arts and Social Sciences at the Australian National University, Australia. His books include *From Mr Sin to Mr Big* (1993), *Songs Without*

Music (2000), *Law and the Visual* (2018), and *Danse Macabre: Temporalities of Law in the Visual Arts* (2019).

James Martel is a Professor in the Department of Political Science at San Francisco State University, United States of America. He is the author, most recently of *Anarchist Prophets: Disappointing Vision and the Power of Collective Sight* (2022).

Sheelagh McGuinness is a Professor of Law in the Centre for Health Law and Society and the School of Law at University of Bristol, United Kingdom. Her research focuses on health law and reproduction.

Emma Milne is an Associate Professor in Criminal Law and Criminal Justice at Durham University, United Kingdom. She is a feminist socio-legal scholar whose research focuses on criminal law and criminal justice responses to infant killing and foetal harm. Emma is author of *Criminal Justice Responses to Maternal Filicide: Judging the Failed Mother* (2021).

Alexandra Murray is a Research Fellow at the Institute for Crime and Justice Policy Research at Birkbeck, University of London, United Kingdom, where she is working on studies on the coronial process (*Voicing Loss*) and online fraud. She was awarded her PhD in 2022, for research on the subject of invisible disabilities in the Personal Independence Payment assessment and appeal process.

Edward Mussawir is a Senior Lecturer in Griffith Law School at Griffith University, Australia. His interest lies primarily in jurisprudence, and his recent research has focused upon the jurisprudential meaning of animals. His publications include *Jurisdiction in Deleuze: The Expression and Representation of Law* (2011) and *Creatures of Jurisprudence: Bears and Bees as Juridical Species* (forthcoming).

Adina-Loredana Nistor is a Lecturer in Criminology in the Faculty of Law at Vrije Universiteit Amsterdam, Netherlands. She is also a PhD candidate in International Criminal Law at the University of Groningen, Netherlands. Her research explores how cultural differences impact international trials throughout their proceedings, with a particular focus on the International Criminal Court.

Remigius N. Nwabueze is a Professor of Law in the School of Law at the University of Southampton, United Kingdom. He is the Principal Investigator of a Leverhulme Trust grant, under its Major Research Project category, in relation to the project titled 'Modern Technologies, Privacy Law and the Dead' (RPG-2020-048).

Maria Fernanda Salcedo Repolês is a Research and Teaching Associate at the Federal University of Minas Gerais Law School, Brazil. She is a Researcher at the Brazilian National Council for Scientific and Technological Development (PQ-2 CNPq) and General Coordinator of Polos de Cidadania Transdisciplinary Program. Her work focuses on the social effects, rights violations, and damages caused by urban, water, social, and environmental conflicts and disasters.

Honni van Rijswijk is a Senior Lecturer in the Faculty of Law at the University of Technology Sydney, Australia. Honni's research focuses on representations of harm and on developing new frameworks of responsibility for understanding harm, especially harms that are not properly captured by law.

Hamish Robertson is a Senior Lecturer in Health Management in the School of Public Health and Social Work at Queensland University of Technology, Australia. His work focuses on aged care and disability through the lens of geography.

Hannah Rumble is a Research Fellow in the Centre for Death and Society at the University of Bath, United Kingdom. She is a social anthropologist specialising in death, dying, and disposal. Her research includes projects on funeral poverty, the natural burial movement, direct cremation, and bereaved people's experiences of the coronial process.

Rebecca Scott Bray is an Associate Professor of Criminology and Socio-Legal Studies in the Faculty of Arts and Social Sciences at the University of Sydney, Australia. She works at the intersection of law, criminology, and socio-legal death studies, with a focus on issues around death and the dead in law, society, and culture.

Joshua D. M. Shaw is a Lecturer in Kent Law School at the University of Kent, United Kingdom. His current research focuses on 'minor legal literatures' or 'minor jurisprudences' where the materiality of the human body and body parts become a basis for what can be lawfully done with such materials.

Ella Tait is a Queensland solicitor and Bachelor of Civil Law candidate at the University of Oxford, United Kingdom.

Lorna Templeton is a Research Associate in the Centre for Death and Society at the University of Bath, United Kingdom, and a researcher on the *Voicing Loss* study of the coronial process. She has long experience of researching addiction and mental health, focusing particularly on impacts of substance misuse on children and families, and bereavement through substance use.

Marc Trabsky is an Associate Professor and an Australian Research Council DECRA Fellow at La Trobe University, Australia. He is the author of *Law and the Dead: Technology, Relations and Institutions* (2019), which was awarded the Law and Society Association of Australia and New Zealand Book Prize in 2019, and *Death: New Trajectories in Law* (2024).

Joanne Travaglia was a Professor of Health Services Management and Head of School in Public Health and Social Work at Queensland University of Technology, Australia. Her work focused on patient safety, vulnerable groups, and their experiences in health and social care systems.

Stuart Wallace is an Associate Professor in the School of Law at the University of Leeds, United Kingdom. His current research focuses on how human rights law applies in the United Kingdom, particularly to the investigation of deaths and other serious human rights violations.

1

LAW AND DEATH

Mapping the Terrain

Marc Trabsky and Imogen Jones

Introduction

Law and death are inextricable in our world. From capital punishment to euthanasia, cemeteries to memorials, property to inheritance, and homicide to genocide, law is replete with discourses of death. Yet the narrative that law has no time for death continues to be reiterated by scholars who reify law as only productive or repressive of life. Or scholars who ignore the vitality of the legal institutions that encounter death in the everyday, mistaking their vivacious prattle for the monotonous tonality of a mechanical automaton. The fact is that law has always been obsessed with death. Indeed, it is a grave mistake to think that law shuns the dying, that legal institutions turn their back on death, and that legal procedures sequester the dead to the gloomy archives of a bureaucratic office. Death matters to law; in fact, as Robert Pogue Harrison writes, it could be said that law gathers in the places of the dead.[1] And death gains its significance from the legal systems that recognise its existence in the world. We are not suggesting that there is no death outside of law, but rather that without law, death remains in our world undefined.[2] *The Routledge Handbook of Law and Death* calls for death to be taken seriously by legal scholars, and for laws to be understood in their plurality by scholars of death studies.

It is uncontroversial to claim that law has *always* been obsessed with death, because jurists, legal scholars, and philosophers since antiquity have repeatedly questioned the relationship between law and death. In *Justice Miscarried: Ethics and Aesthetics in Law*, Costas Douzinas and Ronnie Warrington analyse themes of law, ethics, and death in Sophocles' *Antigone*.[3] In this play, Antigone defies the law of King Creon of Thebes by

---

1 Robert Pogue Harrison, *The Dominion of the Dead* (Chicago, IL: University of Chicago Press, 2003).
2 We are thinking specifically of the Ad Hoc Committee of Harvard Medical School, which in 1968 created a new legal definition of 'brain death'. Over the last 50 years, many jurisdictions have enacted a legal definition of death through legislation or case law. See Ad Hoc Committee of the Harvard Medical School, "A Definition of Irreversible Coma: Report of the Ad Hoc Committee of the Harvard Medical School to Examine the Definition of Brain Death." *Journal of the American Medical Association* 205, no. 6 (1968): 337–40.
3 Costas Douzinas and Ronnie Warrington, *Justice Miscarried: Ethics and Aesthetics in Law* (New York and London: Harvester Wheatsheaf, 1994). See also Judith Butler, *Antigone's Claim: Kinship Between Life and Death* (New York: Columbia University Press, 2000).

DOI: 10.4324/9781003304593-1

burying her brother, Polynices. She believes that she has a duty to honour her brother through burial, rather than leaving him in the open, prey to animals, and her ethical obligation surpasses the law of the land, even when faced with the threat of her own demise. Sophocles' play – and we could add here the story of Orpheus and Eurydice in Ovid's *Metamorphoses* – defines law in relation to death, whether death is punishment for contravening a law or whether a law is created to regulate the relationship between the living and the dead. In *Metamorphoses*, Orpheus is told of the prohibition of looking back as he leads Eurydice out of Hades, and overcome with passion and in the slither of a moment, he damns Eurydice to a second death.[4] In Douzinas and Warrington's analysis of *Antigone*, law and justice is juxtaposed to argue that in death the ethics of the 'other' calls us to act in defiance of the law. We suggest, though, that it is not only ethics that makes these demands on us. In the face of death, and as we near the twilight of the night, creativity and passion tempt us towards transgressing law.[5]

The legal epistemology of death appeared profoundly in crisis in the seventeenth century. The *Hayne's Case*, which defined the corpse as neither a person nor a thing (*res nullius*), 'but a lump of earth hath no capacity', unnerved jurists, legal scholars, and philosophers with the possibility that law could not comprehend the liminality of death.[6] Francis Bacon, Sir William Blackstone, Sir Edward Coke, and Matthew Hale were but a few common law jurists to question law's incapacity to know when life began and when it ended.[7] This juridical question remained befuddled for hundreds of years, and even though a small number of cases have attempted to make sense of death, some legal scholars argue that law is still dumbfounded by the possibility that personhood persists after death.

In more recent times, legal scholars and philosophers, such as Judith Butler, Robert M. Cover, and Achille Mbembe have examined how law enacts death through its words and actions.[8] Cover writes that interpreting the law occurs in the context of death, and he offers capital punishment as an example of how the word of law authorises death. Butler, on the other hand, takes this argument further by contending that the speaking of law not only authorises but performs death, while Mbembe considers law as one of many possible weapons for creating '*death-worlds*', and following the writings of Giorgio Agamben, keeping the 'other' barely alive in death. Whether concerned, then, with how law understands death or problematising how law is complicit with making death, jurists, legal scholars, and philosophers have examined the entanglements of law and death in our world.

---

4 See Ovid, *Metamorphoses, Books IX–XV*, trans. F. J. Miller (Cambridge, MA and London: Harvard University Press, 1984). For a feminist analysis of the tale of Orpheus and Eurydice, see Kaja Silverman, *Flesh of My Flesh* (Stanford, CA: Stanford University Press, 2009).

5 See Maurice Blanchot, *The Gaze of Orpheus and Other Literary Essays*, trans. L. Davis (New York: Station Hill Press, 1981).

6 *Hayne's Case* (1614) 77 ER 1389, 1389. For a critical analysis of this case, see Marc Trabsky, *Death: New Trajectories of Law* (Abingdon and New York: Routledge, 2024), ch. 4.

7 See further Ngaire Naffine, "But a Lump of Earth? The Legal Status of the Corpse," in *Courting Death: The Law of Mortality*, ed. Desmond Manderson (London: Pluto Press, 1999), 95–110; and Margaret Davies and Ngaire Naffine, *Are Persons Property? Legal Debates About Property and Personality* (London: Ashgate, 2001).

8 Robert M. Cover, "Violence and the Word," *The Yale Law Journal* 95, no. 8 (1986): 1601–29; Judith Butler, *Excitable Speech: A Politics of the Performative* (New York: Routledge, 1997); Judith Butler, *Precarious Life: The Powers of Mourning and Violence* (London: Verso, 2004); Achille Mbembe, *Necropolitics: Theory in Forms*, trans. Steve Corcoran (Durham, NC: Duke University Press, 2019).

The Routledge Handbook of Law and Death offers a comprehensive survey of contemporary scholarship on the relations of law and death in the twenty-first century. It showcases how socio-legal scholars have contributed to the critical turn in death studies and how the sociology of death has impacted upon the discipline of law. In bringing together 34 authors from a diverse range of disciplines, the *Handbook* shows across 24 chapters how far from shunning questions of mortality, a plurality of legal institutions persistently talks about death. Touching upon the epistemologies and materialities of death, and problems of contested deaths and posthumous harms, the *Handbook* questions what is distinctive about the disciplinary alignment of law and death, how law regulates and manages death in the everyday, and how thinking with law can enrich our understandings of the presence of death in our lives.

Mapping the terrain

It would be impossible to even identify, let alone summarise, the vast amount of scholarship on death. What we do here, therefore, is briefly map some of the key contributions that have framed our approach in this *Handbook*. When we began this project, we wanted to provide a space to showcase the importance of interdisciplinary perspectives to law and death. Taking a socio-legal approach is to accept porous boundaries, learning from the humanities and social sciences, new methods, and perspectives.[9] We believe that by challenging orthodox understandings of law, we open ourselves to more rich understandings of the world around us. The study of the interaction between law and death is no exception to this; this *Handbook* showcases the multifarious ways in which our approach towards law can deepen when we take a socio-legal approach.

It is notable that although socio-legal engagement with death is a relatively new field, death emerged as an object of study in the humanities and the social sciences in the nineteenth century. Death Studies, which it is now called, is itself an amorphous discipline, joined by a central theme rather than a cohesive approach. Throughout the twentieth century, the concept of death as a taboo featured in writings of Sigmund Freud, Otto Rank, and Martin Heidegger, which contributed to the formulation of a 'repressive hypothesis' of death in sociology, anthropology, history, and psychoanalysis.[10] Some of the most notable contributions followed this in Elizabeth Kübler-Ross' 'five stages of grief' and Ernest Becker's thesis on the 'denial of death'.[11] Concurrently, philosophical writings on death, its experience and management, and our duties and obligations to the dead also gained traction in the twentieth century. Death manifested as a theme in the twentieth century in the work of Georges Bataille, Maurice Blanchot, Jacques Derrida, Michel Foucault, and Giorgio Agamben amongst others.[12]

9 On socio-legal studies, see Nikolas Rose and Mariana Valverde, "Governed by Law?" *Social & Legal Studies* 7, no. 4 (1998): 541–51.

10 See Sigmund Freud in "Thoughts for the Times on War and Death" and "Mourning and Melancholia" in Sigmund Freud, *On the History of the Psycho-Analytic Movement, Papers on Metapsychology and Other Works, Volume XIV (1914–1916)*, trans. J. Strachey (London: Vintage, The Hogarth Press and the Institute of Psycho-Analysis, 2001); Otto Rank, *Will Therapy* (London: W.W. Norton & Co, 1978); Martin Heidegger, *Being and Time*, trans. J. Macquarrie and E. Robinson (New York: Harper & Row, 1962); Émile Durkheim, *Suicide: A Study in Sociology* trans. J.A. Spaulding and G. Simpson (London and New York: Routledge, 2005).

11 Elizabeth Kübler-Ross, *On Death and Dying* (London: Simon and Schuster, 1969); Ernest Becker, *The Denial of Death* (New York: Free Press Paperbacks, 1973).

12 Giorgio Agamben, *Language and Death: The Place of Negativity*, trans. Karen E. Pinkus and Michael Hardt (Minneapolis: University of Minnesota Press, 1991); Giorgio Agamben, *Homo*

More recently, those who study the sociology of death have reinvigorated the field by challenging the repression of death thesis. Jenny Hockey, Tony Walter, and Allan Kellehear have all contributed to this 'critical turn', reminding us of the social, political, personal, and relational importance of the dead.[13] However, despite this embrace of death as a topic for sociological research, the discipline of law has been excluded or dismissed as unhelpful. Legal institutions have been described as obstructive bureaucrats, and legal processes have been reduced to repressive rules, which serve only to interfere with our ability to be socially connected to the dead. We challenge this hypothesis, for far from being a lifeless set of rules, laws appear in each chapter in the *Handbook* as productive of relationships between the living and the dead. Law's incitement to discourse about death is manifold, whether in coronial investigations, death registration practices, giving voice to the will of the dead, or regulating places and methods of disposal.

There are important exceptions to the absence of the discipline of law in the critical turn of death studies. In *The Work of the Dead*, Thomas W. Laqueur charts the relationships between the living and dead throughout time.[14] This tome is expansive cultural history which, amongst other things, highlights that the care of the dead crosses cultures and law cannot remain indifferent to obligations to take care of human remains. Other examples include Ruth Richardson's historical examination of the rise (and fall) of the anatomists in England and Stephan Timmerman's ethnography of the work of medical examiners in the United States of America.[15] The former is a pivotal work that serves as a crucial reminder that the treatment of the dead has long been an issue of social justice, highlighting the role of law and medicine in promoting these injustices against the poor. The fallout from this period persists as the public become alert to the use and abuse of the dead body in medicine. The latter emphasises the importance of labels in law and medicine, and the difficulties of balancing liberal conceptions of justice, an objective with the inherently social environment in which suspicious deaths occur and are investigated.

Sacer: Sovereign Power and Bare Life, trans. Daniel Heller-Roazen (Stanford, CA: Stanford University Press, 1998); Georges Bataille, *Theory of Religion*, trans. Robert Hurley (New York: Zone Books, 1992); Maurice Blanchot, *The Writing of the Disaster*, trans. Ann Smock (Lincoln, NE: University of Nebraska Press, 2015); Jacques Derrida, *Aporias* trans. Thomas Dutoit (Stanford, CA: Stanford University Press, 1993); Jacques Derrida, *The Gift of Death*, trans. David Wills (Chicago, IL: University of Chicago Press, 1995); Michel Foucault, *Death and the Labyrinth*, trans. Charles Ruas (New York: Continuum, 2004); Michel Foucault, *Speech Begins after Death: In Conversations with Claude Bonnefoy*, trans. Robert Bononno (Minneapolis: University of Minnesota Press, 2013).

13 Jenny Hockey, *Experience of Death: An Anthropological Account* (Edinburgh: Edinburgh University Press, 1990); Tony Walter, *The Revival of Death* (London and New York: Routledge, 1994); Allan Kellehear, *Death and Dying in Australia* (Oxford: Oxford University Press, 2000). See also David Clark, ed., *The Sociology of Death: Theory, Culture and Practice* (Cambridge: Blackwell, 1993); Glennys Howarth, ed., *The Changing Face of Death: Historical Accounts of Death and Disposal* (London and New York: Macmillan Press, 1996); Elizabeth Hallam, Jenny Hockey, and Glennys Howarth, *Beyond the Body: Death and Social Identity* (London and New York: Routledge, 1999); Glennys Howarth, *Death and Dying: A Sociological Introduction* (Cambridge: Polity, 2007); and Elizabeth Hallam and Jenny Hockey, *Death, Memory and Material Culture* (Oxford: Berg Publishers, 2010).

14 Thomas Walter Laqueur, *The Work of the Dead: A Cultural History of Mortal Remains* (Princeton, NJ: Princeton University Press, 2015).

15 Ruth Richardson, *Death, Dissection and the Destitute* (Chicago, IL: University of Chicago Press, 2001); Stefan Timmermans, *Postmortem: How Medical Examiners Explain Suspicious Deaths* (Chicago, IL: University of Chicago Press, 2006).

When considered together, both books examine who has the right to speak on behalf of the dead, and what obligations in law and ethics pertain to this important office.

The contribution of bioethics and medical ethics to highlight the interconnectedness of law and death cannot be understated. The moral outrage and psychological harm suffered when various organ retentions led not only to legal changes but to also a significant body of literature challenging the acceptability of medicine and law's combined refusal to respect the dead as deserving respect. Following powerful public enquiries,[16] Brazier and McGuiness remind us that 'respecting the living means respecting the dead too'.[17] This follows those who engage more directly with law, notably Joel Feinberg,[18] who includes the interests of the dead into their normative frameworks for law. Feinberg challenges readers to, for example, balance the interests of society in destructive cadaveric research such as that involved when the dead are used as car crash dummies, with our emotional sensibilities regarding the dead. Feinberg argues that the dead are a powerful symbol for the living, but falls short of concluding that this is of greater importance than wider societal benefit from the use of the dead.

Furthermore, the twentieth century witnessed wars and atrocities which have, rightly, irreversibly reframed the relationship between law and death. As human rights gained traction amidst national and international concerns, there developed an understanding of the power of the dead in creating and mediating discourse. Of note here is Katherine Verdery's examination of the 'political lives of dead bodies', following the end of the fall of communism in Eastern Europe.[19] Focusing on Northern Ireland, Lindsay Prior also provides a notable examination of the 'social organisation' of death, highlighting the intersection of social, medical, legal, religious, and political responses to death.[20] Jessica Auchter's account of the dead as unavoidable, if ghostly, reminders of exclusionary politics provides further uncomfortable evidence of the power of 'statecraft' to exercise control over our bodies in both life and death. This led her to argue that '[d]ead bodies are considered a problem *for* governance in that they require some kind of management, yet rarely considered a problem *of* governance in that they rarely cause us to reflect on structures of authority and power'.[21] This link between bones, politics, harm, and healing is ever present in the accounts of (forensic) anthropologists as they worked to unearth the evidence of mass killings and disappearances across the world.[22] Against the context of the killing of 2,753 people in the terrorist attacks on the World Trade Center in 2001, Jay

16 *Learning from Bristol: The Report of the Public Inquiry into Children's Heart Surgery at the Bristol Royal Infirmary 1984–1995*, CM 5207 (1) (2001); *The Royal Liverpool Children's Inquiry Report*, HC 12-11 (30 January 2001) [Redfern Report].
17 Sheelagh McGuinness and Margaret Brazier, "Respecting the Living Means Respecting the Dead Too," *Oxford Journal of Legal Studies* 28, no. 2 (Summer 2008): 297.
18 Joel Feinberg, "The Mistreatment of Dead Bodies," *The Hastings Center Report* 15, no. 1 (February 1985): 31.
19 Katherine Verdery, *The Political Lives of Dead Bodies: Reburial and Postsocialist Change* (New York: Columbia University Press, 2000).
20 Lindsay Prior, *The Social Organisation of Death: Medical Discourse and Social Practices in Belfast* (London: Palgrave Macmillan, 1989).
21 Jessica Auchter, "Paying Attention to Dead Bodies: The Future of Security Studies?" *Journal of Global Security Studies* 1, no. 1 (2016): 44.
22 There have been several large funded projects around this, including those led by Elizabeth Ansett and Jean-Marc Dreyfus as part of the "Corpses of Mass Violence" project (https://corpses. hypotheses.org/#:~:text=Bringing%20together%20perspectives%20of%20social,Marc%20Drey fus%2C%20has%20enlighten%20how) and more recently Claire Moon's work on "Forensic Humanitarianism and the Politics of the Grave" (https://humanrightshumanremains.com).

Aronson has been prompted to ask, 'Who owns the dead?'[23] These new ways of causing death in an ever-complex global political world highlight the importance of bringing together our understanding of legal responses with the context in which the dead are created.

The recent past has not only been marked by the making of death and unearthing of the dead. New technologies have changed and extended our relationships with dying, death, and the dead. While sociologists have discussed so-called 'dark tourism',[24] the ability of the dead to be viewed for both good and less desirable reasons has been transformed. The internet, smartphones, and digital photography have all facilitated an environment in which moments of death and the dead can be broadcast, viewed, and shared across the globe. Attempts to ensure that these acts do not come at the cost of the dignity of the deceased and wellbeing of the bereaved have proved challenging for law. Concurrently, digital technology can be invoked to protect these same people.[25] The development of post-mortem computed tomography to 'virtually' examine a corpse and the use of the internet to facilitate remote legal hearings have transformed the way that legally mandated processes impact both on the dead body and on the extent to which legal processes can be adapted to social and cultural needs.

In 'Tales from the Crypt', Desmond Manderson calls for critical analysis of the relationship between law and death. Neither law nor death are '*faits accomplis*', Manderson explains. Death is culturally constructed, and so too are our legal systems. Law's 'cultural facticity, its pragmatic rather than its conceptual approach, brings new insights to the philosophy of death'.[26] Published in 1999, *Courting Death* was a pioneering edited collection, alongside volumes edited by Sheila McLean on euthanasia and Austin Sarat on capital punishment, because it was the first to collate essays from critical legal scholars, who in different ways, 'investigate[d] how death has constituted our selves, and how this mutual constitution is evidenced, articulated and realised by human law'.[27] The volume included chapters on capital punishment, euthanasia, dying declarations, coronial

23 Jay D. Aronson, *Who Owns the Dead? The Science and Politics of Death at Ground Zero* (Cambridge, MA: Harvard University Press, 2016).

24 See, for example, Sara Jones, "The darker side of travel: The theory and practice of dark tourism," *Mortality* 15, no. 4 (2010): 343–4.

25 The conflict in Iraq was a particular prompt of this line of scholarship. See, for example: William Silcock, Carol Schwalbe, and Susan Keith, "'Secret' Casualties: Images of Injury and Death in the Iraq War Across Media Platforms," *Journal of Mass Media Ethics* 23, no. 1 (2008): 36, https://doi.org/10.1080/08900520701753205; Sue Tait, "Visualising Technologies and the Ethics and Aesthetics of Screening Death," *Science as Culture* 18, no. 3 (2009): 333, https://doi.org/10.1080/09505430903123016; Sue Tait, "Pornographies of Violence? Internet Spectatorship on Body Horror", *Critical Studies in Media Communication*, 25, no 1 (2008): 91, https://doi.org/10.1080/15295030701851148; David Campbell, "Horrific Blindness: Images of Death in Contemporary 'Media'," *Journal for Cultural Research* 8, no.1 (May 2006): 55. https://doi.org/10.1080/14797580042000196971.

26 Desmond Manderson, "Introduction: Tales from the Crypt – A Metaphor, An Image, A Story," in *Courting Death: The Laws of Mortality*, ed. Desmond Manderson (London: Pluto Press, 1999), 2.

27 Manderson, "Tales from the Crypt", 2. See Sheila McLean, ed., *Death, Dying and the Law* (Dartmouth: Dartmouth Publishing Company, 1996); Austin Sarat, ed., *Pain, Death, and the Law* (Ann Arbor, MI: University of Michigan Press, 2001); Austin Sarat and Christian Boulanger, eds., *The Cultural Lives of Capital Punishment: Comparative Perspectives* (Stanford, CA: Stanford University Press, 2005).

investigations, burial practices, and exhumations. It emphasised that death is *par excellence* 'the archetype for the exercise of responsibility in our lives':

> Just as our unique self is created by the prospect of death, our death shows each of us what it means to face up to a responsibility. We die: all of us, alone, and without evasion. We cannot escape this fate, we cannot trade or talk or bribe our way out of it. It is something which must be faced by each of us and which no one can address in our stead. That is the essence of responsibility ...[28]

This *Handbook* is indebted to *Courting Death*, for it paved the way for us to bring together prominent scholars and emerging experts from a diverse range of disciplines to write about the inextricability of law and death in the twenty-first century. The increased visibility of death in our world, together with a vigour for an interdisciplinary critical lens, has led to renewed calls for scholarly investigations into how law regulates, manages, governs, and discourses about death. This enthusiasm has generated a multiplicity of publications since the turn of the twenty-first century on, to mention but a few areas, the coronial jurisdiction, control of bodies, the making of death-worlds, inequalities of dying, and marginalisation and power. We believe that we are living in the most opportune moment for a socio-legal examination of the relationship between law and death. And so, to extend Laqueur's statement that, '[t]he dead body matters',[29] we would say that this *Handbook* assumes a responsibility to recognise the role of law in making death matter.

Structure

The *Handbook* has been arranged in four parts under the headings 'Epistemologies of Death', 'Materialities of Death', 'Contested Deaths', and 'Posthumous Harms'. While authors in each part explore a variety of topics that touch upon death, the arrangement of chapters within different parts provides distinctive perspectives on disciplinary alignments of socio-legal and death studies. As we discussed above, the *Handbook* maps the terrain in an emerging field of legal scholarship, and while death has been subject to jurisprudential inquiry since antiquity, it is only recently that scholarly examinations of the intersections of law and death are becoming recognisable as a field of study within itself. The *Handbook* thus offers more than mapping an existing field of knowledge. It aims to curate a field through the arrangement of parts and chapters, which undoubtedly exposes the subjectivity of the editors, as well as the way all handbooks shape the contours of a 'community of practice'.[30] Those minuscule acts of curation and bricolage, at every turn of the editorial process, remain incomplete, for they include as much as they exclude names, voices, places, and stories. We do not intend for this *Handbook* to be an exhaustive description of the interdisciplinary field of knowledge on law and death, but we hope that each turn suggests pathways for further research, and stresses the importance for legal scholars to work alongside and learn from the humanities and social sciences when writing on dying, death, and the dead.

28 Manderson, "Tales from the Crypt", 7.
29 Laqueur, *The Work of the* Dead, 1.
30 For an insightful commentary on the history of handbooks, and their role in creating fields of knowledge in law, see Shane Chalmers and Sundhya Pahuja, "Introduction Practice, Craft and Ethos: Inheriting a Tradition" in *Routledge Handbook of International Law and the Humanities*, ed. Shane Chalmers and Sundhya Pahuja (Abingdon and New York: Routledge, 2023), 1–18.

In Part 1 of the *Handbook*, 'Epistemologies of Death', authors respond to the problem of how law makes sense of death. In previous scholarship, legal knowledge has at best been reduced to doctrinal definitions of death and at worst been dismissed as inferior to the medical discipline. There is a conspicuous absence in the legal discipline of critical examinations of how law creates knowledge of death and how legal institutions govern life and death through relations of knowledge and power. In Chapter 2, Desmond Manderson, in rewriting and modifying 'Tales from the Crypt' from *Courting Death* for the Handbook, reflects on death as the figure and ground of law. Indebted to Jacques Derrida's writings on the 'gift of death', Manderson explores how law requires responsibility to function and how in our encounter with death responsibility becomes possible. Zohreh BayatRizi (Chapter 3) offers a perspective of how law makes sense of death from the discipline of sociology. Far from denying death, law governs mortality through the normative ordering of death, whether timely or premature, just or unjust, normal or pathological. James Martel (Chapter 4) explores legal epistemologies by revisiting the problem of how law bestows personhood on the dead. Both Walter Benjamin and Michel Foucault provide a conceptual framework for thinking about how the authority of the dead continues to act upon the living posthumously, which Martel applies in case studies on the death penalty and exhumations.

Chapters by Maria Fernanda Salcedo Repolês and Edward Kirton-Darling (Chapter 5), Maria Giannacopoulos (Chapter 6), and Marc Trabsky (Chapter 7) focus on how to conceptualise law's role in making (mass) death and letting (individuals) die. The central question in these chapters is in what ways do legal institutions and judicial systems make sense of life as disposable and death as ungrievable. In Chapter 5, Repolês and Kirton-Darling draw on empirical research with communities affected by the Vale dam collapse in Brazil in 2019. They argue that the judicial response to the collapse of the dam reinforces a necropolitics and necroeconomics, which reifies specific lives as disposable and their deaths as ungrievable. Giannacopoulos (Chapter 6) contends that law has an intrinsic death knowing and producing function in the settler-colonial state. Through Irene Watson's concept of 'buried alive' and Achille Mbembe's theory of necropolitics, Giannacopoulos shows that Aboriginal deaths in custody are continuing instances of colonial law's inherent death-making function. In Chapter 7, Trabsky juxtaposes thanatopolitics to necropolitics in conceptualising how legal institutions govern life by letting individuals die. The chapter is interwoven with interludes of an ambivalent death, one that is neither exceptional nor unfathomable, but one that questions legal epistemologies of a quotidian death.

In *The Dominion of the Dead*, Robert Pogue Harrison contends that burial practices are integral to 'the humic foundations of our life worlds'.[31] We interpret 'the act of burying the dead' in Part 2 of the Handbook, 'Materialities of Death', as a legal technology that 'prepares the land for human habitation and makes possible the formation of a place'.[32] Burial practices question how we share our dwellings with the dead and how we attach law to the dead. The laws regulating the disposal of human remains have traditionally been analysed from a doctrinal perspective. Each of the chapters in Part 2 examine how law governs the place of the dead in our world from a socio-legal perspective, whether that place is the grave, morgue, or death chamber. In Chapter 8, Joshua

---

31 Harrison, *The Dominion of the Dead*, x.
32 Marc Trabsky, *Law and the Dead: Technology, Relations and Institutions* (Abingdon and New York: Routledge, 2019), 21.

D.M. Shaw, for example, responds to Harrison's assertion by considering decomposition as both constitutive and 'jurisgenerative' of law's forms. While burying the decomposing body attaches law to the dead, the materiality of 'leaky bodies' creates a spacing of 'non-law' inherent in the formation of law. Furthermore, in Chapter 9, Kate Falconer theorises the graveyard as a heterotopia that fragments legal relations and facilitates social and familial conflict, while Heather Conway (Chapter 10) considers the funeral and memorial as both a site of contestation of the intimate bonds that the living form with the dead and a site of legal management of the materialities of death.

In Chapter 11, Imogen Jones examines the early stages of coronial death investigations. Focusing on the role of care in the treatment of deceased bodies when a medico-legal autopsy is required, she highlights the importance of unseen work in making legal processes function efficiently, while also expressing concern that lack of consistency risks fairness and has the potential to cause secondary harms to the bereaved. Lastly, in Chapter 12, Sabrina Gilani takes readers to the aesthetics of the death chamber, contemplating what the spectacular botched execution can tell us about the constitutionality of capital punishment and how law seeks to govern and control the material processes of dying in the twenty-first century.

Part 3, 'Contested Deaths', examines how legal institutions in England, Wales, and Australia assume responsibility or are derelict in their performance of responsibility when investigating contested deaths. It also explores how colonialism and racism remain embedded in these legal processes and coronial institutions, how the family of the deceased are expected to play a circumscribed role during death investigations, and how the idea of a 'contested' death is both inherent in but also incongruous with the coronial jurisdiction. In common law jurisdictions, coroners are required to investigate sudden, unnatural, violent, and accidental deaths. The legal processes that coroners employ when investigating such deaths are often invisible to the public and alienating for families of the deceased. How these operate differs across jurisdictions and can be superseded by other legal mechanisms such as public inquiries or criminal proceedings where circumstances demands.

In Chapter 13, Jessica Jacobson, Alexandra Murray, Hannah Rumble, and Lorna Templeton chart a shift in the focus of inquests in England and Wales from the past to the future. This highlights the multifarious functions of the coronial jurisdiction, and the potentially negative consequences for the bereaved when the purpose of inquests is ambiguous. With Belinda Carpenter, Ella Tait, and Claire Ferguson (Chapter 14), we shift to Australia, where the potential injustice caused by 'feedback loops' leads to suicides in different racial and situational contexts being subject to altering discourse and definition by coroners. In Chapter 15, Carson Cole Arthur discusses the example of black people killed by the police. He reminds us of the power of legal processes to reinforce and perpetuate racial injustice. Rebecca Scott Bray (Chapter 16) draws on the role of the digital in facilitating open justice to explore the modern relationship between the state and citizens when death is contested.

Chapters by Hamish Robertson, David J. Carter, and Joanne Travaglia (Chapter 17) and Stuart Wallace (Chapter 18) examine the potential, and failure, of legal processes to identify and demand change that could, if done properly, significantly reduce chances of deaths being caused by failures on the part of the state. In Chapter 17, Robertson, Carter, and Travaglia focus on inquiries into healthcare-related deaths. They argue that despite the role of healthcare in these deaths, medicine retains jurisdiction over them, undermining the effectiveness of any redress. While Wallace (Chapter 18) demonstrates that without a tracking and enforcement mechanism, 'prevention of future death reports' risk minimal learning from deaths.

In *The Political Lives of Dead Bodies*, Katherine Verdery reminds us that politics is complex and contextual, and can be engaged in by anyone.[33] While Verdery is writing about the circumstances of the dead body in the post-1990s Soviet bloc, in Part 4, 'Posthumous Harms', we consider how politics permeates our understanding, regulation, and treatment of both the dead and the still-living in the face of death. Each of the chapters examine death – and the dead – at a moment of trauma and crisis. This is due to the circumstances of the death and the social, political, and legal responses to these deaths. 'Posthumous Harms' demonstrates how law may be used to try to manage and order these deaths, which can never eliminate the social and political context in which both the law and deaths occur. In Chapter 19, Karolina Kuberska and Sheelagh McGuiness show how ambivalence in the meaning and experience of death can be caused by the state's attempt to legislate a way to recognise early pregnancy loss. Remigius N. Nwabueze (Chapter 20) charts the potential for harms caused by the taking and publication of posthumous images. By bringing together philosophical exploration and doctrinal analysis, we are reminded of the sometimes difficult marriage of theory and practice in law.

Chapters by Emma Milne (Chapter 21), Penny Crofts and Honni van Rijswijk (Chapter 22), Edward Mussawir (Chapter 23), and Caroline Fournet and Adina-Loredana Nistor (Chapter 24) focus on how law responds to the act of killing, whether that is infanticide, corporate homicide, *ius vitae necisque* or crimes against humanity. In Chapter 21, Milne alerts us to the gendered construction of criminal offences, showing how the 'born alive' rule has been, and continues to be, used to facilitate the prosecution of socially deviant women. Crofts and van Rijswijk (Chapter 22) turn to how law responds to the killing of people by corporations by justifying such deaths as the risk of capitalist pursuits and thus abdicating its responsibility to hold them responsible for committing homicide. In Chapter 23, Mussawir shows that the act of killing does not only feature in the plays of Sophocles and Ovid, as we discussed earlier in this chapter, but is contemplated in Roman jurisprudence in Justinian's Digest in the form of a 'right of life and death' (*ius vitae necisque*) and 'action on poverty' (*actio de pauperie*). In the last chapter, Fournet and Nistor (Chapter 24) reflect on how the International Criminal Court oscillates between a personalised depiction of encounters with death and a dispassionate narration of events when responding to and adjudicating crimes against humanity and other atrocity crimes.

The Routledge Handbook of Law and Death shapes an emerging field of socio-legal scholarship on law and death. It shows how thinking about death can enrich socio-legal accounts of law and how turning our attention to law can enhance sociological inquiries into the presence of death in our lives. In a time when the world is facing global inequalities in living and dying, and legal institutions are increasingly interrogating their relationships to death, we hope that this *Handbook* will make for essential reading for scholars, students, and practitioners in law, humanities, and the social sciences.

33 Verdery, *The Political Lives of Dead Bodies*.

Bibliography

Ad Hoc Committee of the Harvard Medical School. "A Definition of Irreversible Coma: Report of the Ad Hoc Committee of the Harvard Medical School to Examine the Definition of Brain Death." *Journal of the American Medical Association* 205, no. 6 (1968): 337–340.

Agamben, Giorgio. *Language and Death: The Place of Negativity*, translated by Karen E. Pinkus and Michael Hardt. Minneapolis: University of Minnesota Press, 1991.

Agamben, Giorgio. *Homo Sacer: Sovereign Power and Bare Life*, translated by Daniel Heller-Roazen. Stanford, CA: Stanford University Press, 1998.

Aronson, Jay D. *Who Owns the Dead? The Science and Politics of Death at Ground Zero*. Cambridge, MA: Harvard University Press, 2016.

Auchter, Jessica. "Paying Attention to Dead Bodies: The Future of Security Studies?" *Journal of Global Security Studies* 1, no. 1 (2016): 36–50.

Bataille, Georges. *Theory of Religion*, translated by Robert Hurley. New York: Zone Books, 1992.

Becker, Ernest. *The Denial of Death*. New York: Free Press Paperbacks, 1973.

Blanchot, Maurice. *The Gaze of Orpheus and Other Literary Essays*, translated by L. Davis. New York: Station Hill Press, 1981.

Blanchot, Maurice. *The Writing of the Disaster*, translated by Ann Smock. Lincoln, NE: University of Nebraska Press, 2015.

Butler, Judith. *Antigone's Claim: Kinship Between Life and Death*. New York: Columbia University Press, 2000.

Butler, Judith. *Excitable Speech: A Politics of the Performative*. New York: Routledge, 1997.

Butler, Judith. *Precarious Life: The Powers of Mourning and Violence*. London: Verso, 1998.

Campbell, David. "Horrific Blindness: Images of Death in Contemporary Media." *Journal for Cultural Research* 8, no. 1 (2006): 55–74.

Chalmers, Shane, and Sundhya Pahuja. "Introduction Practice, Craft and Ethos: Inheriting a Tradition." In *Routledge Handbook of International Law and the Humanities*, edited by Shane Chalmers and Sundhya Pahuja, 1–18. Abingdon and New York: Routledge, 2023.

Clark, David, ed. *The Sociology of Death: Theory, Culture and Practice*. Cambridge: Blackwell, 1993.

Cover, Robert M. "Violence and the Word." *The Yale Law Journal* 95, no. 8 (1986): 1601–1629.

Davies, Margaret, and Ngaire Naffine. *Are Persons Property? Legal Debates About Property and Personality*. London: Ashgate, 2001.

Derrida, Jacques. *Aporias*, translated by Thomas Dutoit. Stanford, CA: Stanford University Press, 1993.

Derrida, Jacques. *The Gift of Death*, translated by David Wills. Chicago, IL: University of Chicago Press, 1995.

Douzinas, Costas, and Ronnie Warrington. *Justice Miscarried: Ethics and Aesthetics in Law*. New York and London: Harvester Wheatsheaf, 1994.

Durkheim, Émile. *Suicide: A Study in Sociology*, translated by J.A. Spaulding and G. Simpson. London and New York: Routledge, 2005.

Feinberg, Joel. "The Mistreatment of Dead Bodies." *The Hastings Center Report* 15, no. 1 (1985): 31–37.

Foucault, Michel. *Death and the Labyrinth*, translated by Charles Ruas. New York: Continuum, 2004.

Foucault, Michel. *Speech Begins after Death: In Conversations with Claude Bonnefoy*, translated by Robert Bononno. Minneapolis: University of Minnesota Press, 2013.

Freud, Sigmund. "Thoughts for the Times on War and Death" and "Mourning and Melancholia". In *On the History of the Psycho-Analytic Movement, Papers on Metapsychology and Other Works, Volume XIV (1914–1916)*, translated by J. Strachey. London: Vintage, The Hogarth Press, and the Institute of Psycho-Analysis, 2001.

Hallam, Elizabeth, Jenny Hockey, and Glennys Howarth. *Beyond the Body: Death and Social Identity*. London and New York: Routledge, 1999.

Hallam, Elizabeth, and Jenny Hockey. *Death, Memory and Material Culture*. Oxford: Berg Publishers, 2010.

Harrison, Robert Pogue. *The Dominion of the Dead*. Chicago, IL: University of Chicago Press, 2003.

Heidegger, Martin. *Being and Time*, translated by J. Macquarrie and E. Robinson. New York: Harper & Row, 1962.

Hockey, Jenny. *Experience of Death: An Anthropological Account*. Edinburgh: Edinburgh University Press, 1990.

Howarth, Glennys, ed. *The Changing Face of Death: Historical Accounts of Death and Disposal*. London and New York: Macmillan Press, 1996.

Howarth, Glennys. *Death and Dying: A Sociological Introduction*. Cambridge: Polity, 2007.

Jones, Sara. "The darker side of travel: The theory and practice of dark tourism." *Mortality* 15, no. 4 (2010): 343–344.

Kellehear, Allan. *Death and Dying in Australia*. Oxford: Oxford University Press, 2000.

Kübler-Ross, Elizabeth. *On Death and Dying*. London: Simon and Schuster, 1969.

Laqueur, Thomas Walter. *The Work of the Dead: A Cultural History of Mortal Remains*. Princeton, NJ: Princeton University Press, 2015.

Manderson, Desmond. "Introduction: Tales from the Crypt – A Metaphor, An Image, A Story." In *Courting Death: The Laws of Mortality*, edited by Desmond Manderson, 1–16. London: Pluto Press, 1999.

Mbembe, Achille. *Necropolitics: Theory in Forms*, translated by Steve Corcoran. Durham, NC: Duke University Press, 2019.

McGuinness, Sheelagh, and Margaret Brazier. "Respecting the Living Means Respecting the Dead Too." *Oxford Journal of Legal Studies* 28, no. 2 (2008): 297–316.

McLean, Sheila, ed. *Death, Dying and the Law*. Dartmouth: Dartmouth Publishing Company, 1996.

Naffine, Ngaire. "But a Lump of Earth? The Legal Status of the Corpse." In *Courting Death: The Laws of Mortality*, edited by Desmond Manderson, 95–110. London: Pluto Press, 1999.

Ovid. *Metamorphoses, Books IX–XV*, translated by F. J. Miller. Cambridge, MA and London: Harvard University Press, 1984.

Prior, Lindsay. *The Social Organisation of Death: Medical Discourse and Social Practices in Belfast*. London: Palgrave Macmillan, 1989.

Rank, Otto. *Will Therapy*. London: W. W. Norton & Co., 1978.

Richardson, Ruth. *Death, Dissection and the Destitute*. Chicago, IL: University of Chicago Press, 2001.

Rose, Nikolas, and Mariana Valverde. "Governed by Law?" *Social & Legal Studies* 7, no. 4 (1998): 541–551.

Sarat, Austin, ed. *Pain, Death, and the Law*. Ann Arbor: University of Michigan Press, 2001.

Sarat, Austin, and Christian Boulanger, eds. *The Cultural Lives of Capital Punishment: Comparative Perspectives*. Stanford, CA: Stanford University Press, 2005.

Silcock, Willam, Carole Schwalbe, and Susan Keith. "'Secret' Casualties: Images of Injury and Death in the Iraq War Across Media Platforms." *Journal of Mass Media Ethics* 23, no. 1 (2008): 36–50.

Silverman, Kaja. *Flesh of My Flesh*. Stanford, CA: Stanford University Press, 2009.

Walter, Tony. *The Revival of Death*. London and New York: Routledge, 1994.

Tait, Sue. "Visualising Technologies and the Ethics and Aesthetics of Screening Death." *Science as Culture* 18, no. 3 (2009): 333–353.

Tait, Sue. "Pornographies of Violence? Internet Spectatorship on Body Horror." *Critical Studies in Media Communication* 25, no. 1 (2008): 91–111.

Timmermans, Stefan. *Postmortem: How Medical Examiners Explain Suspicious Deaths*. Chicago: University of Chicago Press, 2006.

Trabsky, Marc. *Law and the Dead: Technology, Relations and Institutions*. Abingdon and New York: Routledge, 2019.

Trabsky, Marc. *Death: New Trajectories of Law*. Abingdon and New York: Routledge, 2024.

Verdery, Katherine. *The Political Lives of Dead Bodies: Reburial and Postsocialist Change*. New York: Columbia University Press, 2000.

PART 1

Epistemologies of Death

2

CRYPTIC COMMENTS

Desmond Manderson[1]

In memory of

Dorothea Lange's photograph "Gravestone, St. George, Utah" is uncanny. It reminds us of the frailty of our paltry efforts to memorialise ourselves, our families, our lives, and our place. The forces of nature are indomitable. In time, the most emphatic of our monuments become an empty surface, a blank canvas wind-blasted smooth by time. 'In memory of...', yes, but of whom or what? In the confounding face of death, deliverance becomes effacement, loss becomes lack. Is that not the way with all culture and all memory, finally serving only to remind us that there is something we've forgotten? Lange's image is a muffled cry from the underworld: only the anguished tone, not the contents, remain.

Let us turn from death as an idea to something specific: law and death. Each of the two crucial terms in this conjunction are typically presented as if they were *faits accomplis*. Nothing could be further from the truth. In the first place, we can and ought to study the relationship of law to mortality because death is a cultural invention. Perhaps this seems counterintuitive. The question is not *that* we die but rather that we know we die. Consciousness changes everything. Animals, I suppose, or at least some animals, do not seem to suffer in quite this way. For them it seems that the waters of experience are not contaminated by the prospective loss that death threatens, or the retrospective loss that time accomplishes. But the human animal – and there is increasing evidence that we are not alone in this regard[2] – is different. The shadow of time past and the darkness of death fall over and structure our lives:

> Death works with us in the world; it is a power that humanizes nature, that raises existence to being, and it is within each one of us as our most human

---

1 This work originally appeared as Desmond Manderson, "Tales from the Crypt," in *Courting Death: The Law of Mortality*, ed. Desmond Manderson (New York: Pluto Press, 1999), 1–16. It has been rewritten and modified for this publication.
2 Susana Monsó and Antonio J. Osuna-Mascaró, "Death Is Common, so is Understanding It: The Concept of Death in Other Species," *Synthese* 199, no. 1 (2021), 2251–75.

DOI: 10.4324/9781003304593-3

Figure 2.1 Dorothea Lange, "Gravestone, St. George, Utah," gelatin silver print, 1953. Reproduced
    with permission from the Nelson-Atkins Museum of Art, Kansas City, Missouri, United
    States of America.

quality; it is death only in the world – man knows death only because he is man,
and he is man only because he is death in the process of becoming...[3]

Norbert Elias made a similar point in his study of time.[4] Events will pass regardless of
human intentionality, but the construction of time in a specific way, as a measure, linear,
constant, and abstract, is pure human invention. Time and death, parent and child, are
not the boundless oceans of our experience. They are the fragile boats we humans build
to sail upon it. If so, then our challenge is not just to accept death but to understand its
meaning for us and to appreciate the ways in which human societies, now and in the
past, have developed certain modes of approaching it. This, of course, is the burden of
Philippe Ariès' great work *Homme devant le mort*.[5] We are before death as we are
before the law: subject to it and outside of it at the same time.[6]

    Second, then, we ought to consider the relationship of law to mortality because law,
no less than death, is a cultural artefact – not command but discourse, not sublime and
inflexible authority but a resource in political struggle. Once we accept the cultural

---

3 Maurice Blanchot, *The Work of Fire/Part du feu*, trans. Charlotte Mandell (Stanford, CA: Stan-
    ford University Press, 1995), 9.
4 Norbert Elias, *Time: An Essay* (Oxford: Basil Blackwell, 1992).
5 Philippe Ariès, *The Hour of Our Death/Homme devant la mort*, trans. Helen Weaver (Oxford:
    Oxford University Press, 1981).
6 Georges Didi-Huberman, "Before the Image, Before Time: The Sovereignty of Anachronism," in
    Compelling Visuality: The Work of Art in and Out of History, ed. Claire Farago and Robert
    Zwijnenberg (Minneapolis: University of Minnesota Press, 2003), 31–45.

contingency of both law *and* death, we can begin to think about how they might throw light on each other. The forces and norms of law help constitute the epistemology of death, just as the forces and norms around death help constitute the epistemology of law. On the one hand, then, law governs how we think about death and dying. Take as a simple example the ambiguous treatment of the dead body,[7] which is neither still a person nor yet a thing, occupying some liminal place between the two – or perhaps, even better, occupying already the place of memory that like Lange's image seems to recede like a horizon away from both. On the other hand, death itself governs our lives and social structures, not least in setting the limits of personal responsibility, whether economic, social, or political. The intense debates over questions of intergenerational trauma or colonial reparations are precisely about the relationship between social responsibility and individual mortality. What is at stake is what death puts an end to, and on the contrary what it begins.

There is an ineradicable tension here between two indissociable logics. Law is the collective expression of our belief in the human capacity for responsible action. Law circumscribes, authorises, and enforces responsible conduct. Law is pragmatic, and as Scott Veitch argues, ultimately, it is a code of limitation and finitude; through it, culpability is individualised and limited.[8] But death is precisely that element that lies outside of our control, that marks the dissolution of the possibility of individual existence or choice or decision. It is the moment in which we become utterly vulnerable, our body and our memory entrusted to others beyond all hope of enforcement. Law seeks to control every aspect of our lives, including the manner of our passing, while death is precisely that element that lies outside of our control. So too the legal order is constructed around individual action and responsibility, yet death is precisely the moment at which this 'I' ceases to be. There are two forms of knowledge here: the Apollonian and the Dionysian. The law expresses an epistemology of individuality and control and finitude, while death traces a counter-epistemology of dissolution and transcendence. Notions of responsibility are caught between the mortal logic of law on the one hand and the immortal voice of ethics of the other.

Intermezzo: Dragged under

I don't dream, or at the very least let us say that I never remember my dreams. Perhaps my Apollonian force is so distrustful of any Dionysian urges that it chooses to repress them entirely. I doubt this is a good thing, but there it is; every night a death and every birth 'a sleep and a forgetting'.[9] But often I lie half-awake in the dark, aware of every sound and creak and conscious of a force upon me imposing its own demands. Blanchot, the insomniac for whom night is never black enough, stated:

> If night suddenly is cast in doubt, then there is no longer either day or night, there is only a vague twilight glow, which is sometimes a memory of day, sometimes a longing for night.[10]

7 Ngaire Naffine, "But a Lump of Earth: The Legal Status of the Corpse," in *Courting Death: The Law of Mortality*, ed. Desmond Manderson (New York: Pluto Press, 1999), 95–110.
8 Scott Veitch, *Law and Irresponsibility* (London: Routledge, 2007).
9 William Wordsworth, "Ode on Intimations of Immortality from Recollections of Early Childhood (1804)," in *Selected Poems*, ed. Stephen Gill (Harmondsworth: Penguin, 2004).
10 Blanchot, *Work of Fire*, 336.

Insomnia is a kind of law; a command that overrides your will. In that state of obedience to a law that keeps me awake, as a passive receptacle of night's authority, I do not have dreams; rather, dreams have me. In suspended animation, I suffer an insomniac's fancies. My mother was born with a cowl over her head – a premonition of death but also, they say, protection against death at sea. But for me, the fear of drowning is recurrent. With a certain passive resignation, I fall and slip and sink until the waters close, oblivious or disinterested, over my head. As such images pass uncontrollably across my mind, I feel overwhelmed by a sense of unfathomable impotence. This nightmare does not just take the form of a premonition of death – death itself, I suppose, is indistinguishable from such a nightmare. Rather, it manifests as a moment of terminal irresponsibility, in which I find myself unable either to wake up or to act differently. In death, as in my nightmare of drowning, we are dragged under, come what may. To be alive, again – to come to, in startled astonishment, to the early-morning warbling of the birds – is still to be dragged, but this time back to responsibility. With exhausted relief, I discover that I still have the capacity to decide. I am not yet out of time. Though this discovery is not without its own terrors.

Law's rotting meat

Law and death are creatures of the crypt – a hidden cell or chamber. It conceals and darkens that which it encloses. In every crypt a secret lies. And that secret is, finally, the corpse; either the literal corpse that the crypt entombs or the figurative sense of finitude and mystery it embodies:

> As for the cellar, we shall no doubt find uses for it. It will be rationalised and its conveniences enumerated. But it is first and foremost the *dark entity* of the house, the one that partakes of subterranean forces...[11]

All crypts convey a mystery because they encase an unknowable space, the experience of death that I can never know or touch or feel. But more than this, as Derrida writes, a crypt is not just invisible, a lack of light or negativity; it is a positive darkness that engages actively in the production of mystery.[12] All representations of death are necessarily misrepresentations. Death, therefore, has about it not just an absence of meaning, an ignorance that may be remedied, but a cowl that resists uncovering. It is a negative space that can be mapped only by an inventory of borders or a series of echo soundings in the dark.

From Hammurabi to Napoleon, law, for its part, has always been a matter of codes. A code is an order, but it is a secret order. A dress code, a code of conduct, a code of silence, Code Red,[13] the *Code Civil*. These are arcane practices that likewise resist uncovering. This was Kafka's point in 'Before the Law', of course.[14] The authority of law lies precisely in its ability to conceal itself, to exert power by *withholding*, by remaining unfathomable, by keeping its distance and, therefore, its allure, its obscure desire, its

---

11 Gaston Bachelard, *The Poetics of Space*, trans. Maria Jolas (Boston: Beacon Press, 1969), 18.
12 Jacques Derrida, *The Gift of Death/Donner la mort*, trans. David Wills (Chicago, IL: University of Chicago Press, 1995), 89–90.
13 See the discussion of *The Right Stuff*, dir. Philip Kaufman (1983) in Slavoj Zizek, "Superego by Default," *Cardozo Law Review* 16 (1994): 925–42.
14 Franz Kafka, "The Parable of the Law," in *The Trial* (Harmondsworth: Penguin Modern Classics, 2015).

majesty. As Derrida argues so eloquently in his discussion of that text, 'the inaccessible incites from its place of hiding'.[15]

Very well then, the law is encrypted – it is not to be read but deciphered; it is a mystery – not so much a language to be learned as a ritual to be absorbed. It is hardly surprising, then, that H. L. A. Hart, that most familiar of jurisprudes, worked with the codebreakers at Bletchley Park during World War II, where he was described as a 'natural cryptographer'.[16] Law is an Enigma machine. It is a system of signs hidden behind a system of signs.

Sometimes, like a secret handshake, a password, or a trapdoor, codes conceal the very fact that they conceal. Laws provide us with smooth surfaces that appear to be about what they appear to be about. 'The law which governs Australia is Australian law',[17] concluded Justice Brennan in attempting to cut a Gordian knot through the legal thickets – and the dead bodies of generations of Indigenous Australians – that littered the ground of the *Mabo* case. As Nicholas Mirzoeff said in another context, 'Nothing to see here.'[18] Encryption, which entombs meaning in the dark and the deep, always presents a series of signs on the surface that mislead us as to the signs beneath. What is encoded cannot be read directly. Insight must be disinterred, and that is the true vocation of legal scholars. We are not philosophers or linguists. We are tomb raiders.

Above all, law and lawyers proclaim their omnicompetence. The law has a spatial jurisdiction but absolute authority within it. The law is, apparently, a system of sovereign command. Thou shalt, says the law; thou shalt not. But this is just what has been called (in another context) 'mineralization', 'a hiding place (like the kind insects make of their own body when they feign death)'.[19] This image of an exoskeletal protective shell, a self-made crypt, also has overtones of Kafka,[20] though metamorphosis is not the same as death:

> It is halfway between the two, neither life nor death. The one who has been transformed remains as a memorial example still present within the human community – in the form of a tree, a fountain, a bullock, a flower.[21]

The skeleton of the law, apparently so implacable, is in fact exuviae; a memorial. But 'in memory of...' what? The rotten fleshy matter hidden underneath. It points, by this bluster and assertion of absolute power, to its own encrypted body. The *secret* of law, the vulnerability against which it armours itself, like a cockroach, is its weakness. Law *cannot* instil the responsibility it requires of its subjects. Death on the one hand and our own free will on the other, though opposites in so many ways, are alike in slipping beyond law's grasp. Law's competence and authority are just a shellacked surface; impotence and impossibility are its secret meat.

15 Jacques Derrida, "Before the Law," in *Acts of Literature*, ed. Derek Attridge (London: Routledge, 1002), 191.
16 Nicola Lacey, *The Nightmare and the Noble Dream: A Life of H. L. A. Hart* (Oxford: Oxford University Press, 2004), 93.
17 *Mabo v Qld (No. 2)* [1992] HCA 23; (1992) 175 CLR 1, per Brennan J. para. 29.
18 Nicholas Mirzoeff, "The Right to Look," *Critical Inquiry* 37 (2011): 473–96, 474, 495; the line is originally drawn from Jacques Rancière, "Dix thèses sur la politique," *Aux bords du politique* (Paris: Gallimard, 1998), 217.
19 Blanchot, *Work of Fire*, 252.
20 Franz Kafka, "The Metamorphosis," in *The Metamorphosis and Other Stories*, trans. Joyce Crick (Oxford: Oxford World's Classics, 2009), 29–74.
21 J. Hillis Miller, *Versions of Pygmalion* (Cambridge, MA: Harvard University Press, 1990), 2.

Intermezzo: Searching for justice

A friend of mine – but this was 30 years ago now – was a woman with a sense of justice rubbed red raw. She had just finished her law degree, which left her feeling bitterly disappointed. The desire for justice and the promise of certainty had attracted her to the study of law in the first place, but, of course, it was the first task of legal education to disabuse her of both these ideals. To discover beneath such a sturdy skeleton so much flesh, always imprecise and sometimes touched with the stench of corruption, is shocking. Many people don't ever quite recover from it. Law students, contrary to popular belief, are not natural-born cynics but disappointed idealists. That was my friend. Betrayed by the promises that the legal system had held out to her and never fulfilled. Betrayed by the lack of fairness she encountered everywhere, petty and monumental.

When I knew her, she seemed to be searching, ever more errantly, for some place that would fulfil her desire for belonging and justice. The law was no consolation. She moved to Israel and planned to convert to Judaism, but no sooner had she arrived than her boyfriend abandoned her. Another anchor had proved unable to weigh her down sufficiently. So she floated from place to place and from effort to effort. From London to Montreal to Helsinki, everywhere she went, she felt thwarted and angry. Every endeavour she tried seemed only to exacerbate her feelings of betrayal. Nothing was fair, she said, and she was right. Nothing much was.

Beyond the law

Law is flotsam. It presumes responsibility, and it requires it. Our personal responsibility for our actions is a key organising assumption of the legal system, whether in criminal, tort, or contract law. In *The Gift of Death*, Derrida made the same point about religion.[22] He argued that in the Dionysian world, there can be no responsibility. Ecstasy is not an ethics. In the Dionysian frenzy, there is no sense of 'self' and 'other'; it is this relationship, this difference, that makes responsibility – a sense of obligation or response-ability to the needs of another person – possible. Religion and law alike presume access to an individual, a self whose interests are not the same as everyone else's, and an individual capable of choosing. But this necessity also gives rise to a betrayal. When Moses descended from Mount Sinai holding the Ten Commandments that founded both a religion and a jurisprudence (for in the Old Testament they were indistinguishable), he discovered the people corrupted by false gods, and he reacted with fury. The free will that is the weight of our compact with God also allows the possibility that the people will choose *against* the law, against God.[23] It was the same in the Garden of Eden. To be given the recognition – more, the worship – He craved, God granted Adam and Eve free will, for only a recognition or authority freely given would have been meaningful. But Adam and Eve used their free will not to obey the Lord but to betray Him. Trust is a risky business.[24]

This is an argument with powerful implications in relation to law. Law requires that our choice or decision to act is not based simply on obedience or the following of rules but lies outside it. When the law enjoins us to 'be responsible', it requires that we make a

---

22 Derrida, *Gift of Death*.
23 Yvonne Sherwood, ed., *Derrida's Bible* (New York: Palgrave Macmillan, 2004); Timothy Beal, "Specters of Moses: Overtures to Biblical Hauntology," in *Imagining Biblical Worlds*, ed. David Gunn and Paula McNutt (Sheffield: Sheffield Academic Press, 2003), 171–87.
24 Joshua Neoh, *Law, Love and Freedom* (Cambridge: Cambridge University Press, 2019), ch. 1.

decision about whether or not to obey that must be based on a sense of responsibility that comes from *somewhere else*. Legal responsibility implies individual free will. Without this extra-legality, we would not be behaving responsibly but simply obediently; in other words, we would not be behaving as if we had a choice.[25] But if that were true, if obedience to the law were not chosen but simply followed automatically, then it must likewise follow that disobedience could not be chosen either. Without the concept of freedom of choice, on what grounds could any criminal be considered 'responsible' for their actions? Illegality would be (and it is often argued that it is) predetermined, a function of psychology, or upbringing, or genetics, or tragedy. On what grounds could an individual be punished for acts outside their control?

In short, responsibility is the central concept of the law, and it makes no sense without the concept of free choice, a *decision* to obey, which cannot be justified simply on the basis of what the law says. It therefore follows that the legitimacy of law, the reason we obey it, cannot be found simply by reference to the formal machinery of law. The concept of law *must* depend on a notion of responsibility ultimately derived from elsewhere.

Here, as elsewhere, Derrida echoes Emmanuel Levinas. No normative order can *make* us responsible; on the contrary, it is only by some mysterious unbidden sense of responsibility for others that a normative order can get underway, gain meaning and credibility, in the first place.[26] This sense arises not in response to the demand of an institution but the absolute vulnerability of an other. Ethics, says Levinas, is necessarily *prior* to law,[27] which can neither make us ethical nor survive without it.

The nature of this responsibility is the experience of choosing a decision independently of others, but in a respect that affects another, which is to say, *in response* to them. To be responsible for someone means to accept freely a duty to act in the interests or to fulfil the needs of another, at precisely the moment when those needs or interests are different from our own. Mutual self-interest is not the same thing as responsibility. To say that I have a responsibility towards you is to some extent to recognise that I am different from you, and that I am acting *for* you or on your behalf.[28] This kind of action only comes from a sense of oneself as a distinct individual in relationship with other individuals who are, in turn, distinct from us.

Such a sense of individuality, of difference, of our precious irreplaceability, is relatively modern. Ivan Illich and Philippe Ariès both date this heightened self-consciousness to about the twelfth century:[29]

> I am not suggesting that the 'modern self' is born in the twelfth century, nor that the self which here emerges does not have a long ancestry. We today think of each other as people with frontiers. Our personalities are as detached from each other as are our bodies... This existential frontier is of the essence for a person who wants to fit into our kind of world... For earlier medievals, *person* denotes

25 Jacques Derrida, "Force of Law," *Cardozo Law Review* 11 (1989–1990): 961–2.
26 Emmanuel Levinas, *Otherwise than Being or Beyond Essence*, trans Alphonso Lingis (The Hague: Martinus Nijhoff, 1981); for further discussion, see Desmond Manderson, *Proximity and the Soul of Law* (Montreal: McGill-Queen's University Press, 2007), 51–72.
27 Emmanuel Levinas, *Éthique comme philosophie première* (Paris: Rives Poche, 1998); Adriaan Peperzak, *Ethics as First Philosophy* (London: Routledge, 1995).
28 Manderson, *Proximity*.
29 Ariès, *Hour of Our Death*; Ivan Illich, *In the Vineyard of the Text* (Chicago: University of Chicago Press, 1993), 23–6.

office, function, role, variously derived from the word's origin in the Latin *persona*, a mask. For us it means the essential individual, conceived of as having a unique personality, physique, and psyche.[30]

Following this train of thought, the logic of the law that requires responsibility meets the ethics of death that constitutes it in two ways. First, the psychic frontier that Illich and Ariès identify makes the modern experience of death vertiginous to us, the more awful because what is lost in death is unique. But at the same time, it also makes a sense of responsibility or sacrifice possible at all. Our sense of death and of responsibility are alike artefacts of modernity. Alongside the experience of death as we so fearfully navigate it in the modern world comes a sense of self and, therefore, the possibility of a truly responsive relationship with others:

> For one never reinforces enough the fact that it is not the *psyche* that is there in the first place and that comes thereafter to be concerned about its death, to keep watch over it, to be the very vigil of its death. No, the soul only distinguishes itself, separates itself, and assembles within itself in the experience of this [practice of death].[31]

Second, death is the archetype for the exercise of responsibility in our lives. Just as our unique self is created by the prospect of death, our death shows each of us what it means to face up to a responsibility. We die – all of us, alone and without evasion. We cannot escape this fate; we cannot trade or talk or bribe our way out of it. It is something that must be faced by each of us and that no one can address in our stead.[32] That is the essence of responsibility: the acceptance of an action or decision that must be taken on oneself and that cannot be shirked or delegated. In that sense, one cannot speak of someone dying *for* someone else or *instead* of them. Death is never an exchange. Death is the moment for which all our responsibility prepares us; it is the event in the shadow of which all responsibility finds inspiration. This is part of the value to be found in the way our society understands death. It shows us both the necessity and the possibility of responsible action. It is the figure and ground of law.

As it is generally true that the relationship between law and responsibility takes place in the shadow of the valley of death, in a more specific way with the obligation to bury the dead, it is given its most intense and legal formulation in *Antigone* but of course it long predates it.[33] There is a paradox here. The responsibility of dying and the apparent accountability of burying are at odds.[34] Responsibility, as we have seen, takes place outside the law as a decision, a silence, and a freedom. Accountability requires an explanation of behaviour in terms of the articulation of established reasons, and so the subjugation of a decision to general rules. It demands obedience to formal law and formal practices. But ultimately, the call to burial is silent. It is a mute entreaty to act purely on another's behalf, without any hope of recognition or acknowledgement from the person for whom we act. No one is as powerless as the dead, as unable to demand

---

30 Illich, *Vineyard of the Text*, 24–5.
31 Derrida, *Gift of Death*, 14.
32 Derrida, *Gift of Death*, 41–4.
33 Sophocles, *Antigone* (441 BCE), in *The Three Theban Plays*, trans. Robert Fagles (Harmondsworth: Penguin, 1984).
34 Derrida, "Force of Law", 963–7.

action or to return a favour. From *Antigone* onwards, non-burial has become the epitome of the violation of justice exactly *because* the dead are the most vulnerable, their 'rights' entirely unenforceable except through the freely given actions of another. But our responsiveness in such a circumstance of ultimate dependence *cannot* be accounted for. To whom would this accounting be due? What form would it take?

The image of burial and, more broadly, the idea of responsibility can be expressed in terms of a sacrifice, but as Derrida argues, they can equally be articulated in terms of a gift. In each case, something is at stake that exceeds the idea of self-interest or exchange.[35] 'The moment the gift, however generous it be, is infected with the slightest hint of calculation, the moment it takes account of knowledge, or recognition, it falls within the ambit of an economy.'[36] An example comes to mind: like you, no doubt, I have often walked through cities and had to confront the pleas of beggars on the street. Every act of charity raises the question, why *this* one? Why not the others? Why not all the others? Why a coin and not a note? Why not more? Why not nothing? It is an experience that troubles me. For a long time, I tried to give myself a *law* to obey, a *rule* to follow: some procedure capable of relieving me of the taxing responsibility of having to make a decision, each and every time. But after a while, I gave up these attempts to create for myself a principle capable of justifying in advance my heartlessness or my generosity. No such law is possible. Each act of giving is unique, secret, spontaneous, and inexplicable. There *is* no accounting for it.

Death is, in this sense, the paradigm of the gift, since to die is an experience of personal responsibility so incommensurable and infinite as to be beyond calculation and beyond exchange. But even more importantly, death is the guarantor of all gifts since it is the fact of our mortality that makes possible a gesture that will *not* be eventually rewarded or traded or added up as part of some vast eternal exercise in bookkeeping. Our mortality ensures that some acts of generosity will remain unpaid. Death makes a double line under our life and leaves the ledger never squared.

Intermezzo: Afterlife

The next I heard, my friend had given up practising law and turned to teaching. She wrote me a letter from Finland. It was the middle of winter; not for the faint-hearted. She described the begging, poverty, and drunkenness she saw on the streets, but despite all that, she said she found the gift of teaching reward enough. The day I received this letter, buoyed by her enthusiasm, I phoned Helsinki to find out how she was. She was no longer there. She had quit her job that week and abruptly left the country; consumed, as I supposed and feared, by a sinking feeling that comes in the darkness of a solstice night.

A month later, she wrote again, another, final letter. Its change in tone and direction shocked me:

> What do you think happens when we die? If nothing happens, doesn't it seem completely unjust and unfair that nothing will happen to people who do bad in

35 Here, Derrida's argument (and mine) sets itself against the celebrated work of Marcel Mauss, *The Gift: The Form and Reasons of Exchange in Archaic Societies* (New York: W. W. Norton, 2011). The debate over the adequacy of Mauss's analysis is extensive and cannot be broached here.

36 Derrida, *Gift of Death*, 112.

their lives? Is it right that the just and good die and have the same fate as the bad people? Surely not! ... Even if your academic training still blocks your belief, then I suggest that you think about death. For sure, your death is certain. All your life leads to your death. It's so simple.

It was the brute fact of death that finally drew my friend not just to an idea of God but to its necessity. Only the structure of a conservative faith, enforced by an omnipotent and just God and applied without fail to the dead, seemed to her to make good on the promise, so constantly withheld from her in this life, that the bad will be punished and the good rewarded – if not in this world, then for eternity in the next. Only an afterlife, she came to believe, could redeem justice.

Imagine there's no heaven

And this is where she and I decisively parted company, not just in real life but in spirit and in belief. Acts of justice and compassion cannot, *must* not, be wholly justified. There is no satisfactory *reason* why we ought to respond to the call of the other, this other, any other. It must be a gift. The existence of God, for all the good it may do, seems on the contrary to undermine the logic of the gift. Instead, it very often entails two related concepts. The first is that it ushers in the epoch of the Book, codifying rules on the basis of some justification external to human experience. The Book converts doing justice into a matter of following the law. Responsibility becomes a function of obedience. The second is that it provides for eternal life as a reward for virtue. The promise of the afterlife converts gift into credit, responsibility into accountancy. Such a system of reward and punishment is

> an offering that appears too calculating still; one that would renounce earthly, finite, accountable, exterior, visible wages, one that would exceed an economy of retribution and exchange only to capitalize on it by gaining a profit or surplus value that was infinite, heavenly, incalculable, interior, and secret...[37]

The gift, on the other hand, is the expression of a responsibility to others that takes place *outside* the principles of economy or accountancy. In the same vein, justice is the expression of a responsibility to others that must take place *outside* the structure of legal prescriptions. It is the code beneath the code of law. The explanation for our actions by reference to a rule or a process – which is what law sets out to describe – is a necessary element of social relations, but, in the case of burial, charity, and justice, it is never sufficient. Responsibility is the supplement that law requires for its functioning but cannot constitute.

Death makes *this* justice and *this* responsibility possible. On the one hand, it confronts us with a responsibility that cannot be evaded, and on the other, it puts an end to all thought of economy and reward. It requires of us to take on the responsibility for justice not as part of an economy, a trade, or a calculation but purely for its own sake. Death makes justice possible because it provides the horizon or parameters of a life in which freedom and responsibility are not simply functions of obedience or calculation. But by the same token, injustice and illegality become equally possible choices. Without death, there is neither, only a grey insomnia of passivity, a state of suspended animation that for

---

37 Derrida, *Gift of Death*, 109.

Blanchot is a fate worse than death. This is the consequence of the flight from freedom, from responsibility and from death.

It is too harsh to say that the concept of immortality governed by a system of punishment and reward renders such justice impossible. But religion has left a trail of bloody violence in its wake. It is not just a consequence of certainty, although that is partly true. It is because the rewards for being in possession of the truth now seem to be eternal, and because death – it could be one's own but it could just as easily be that of others – can now be traded off, along with everything else, against some future and much greater prize. That is a terrible risk to run. Without the absolute closure of death, there can be no end to the commodification of life.

One cannot but wonder if there might not be more justice and less arrogance in a world where we humans had a stronger sense of our own mortality. In all this, law is complicit. Law creates institutions, such as nations and corporations, designed to extend life indefinitely. It sustains an economic system based on a fantasy of infinite growth and infinite resources – an immortal planet quite unlike the world we actually inhabit.[38] Law even presents *itself* as embodying a community and a tradition and claims to carry forward that spirit beyond the death of each of us. There is a self-deluding eternity to these manoeuvres. We must be critical of the myth of law as transcendent, immemorial, and certain.[39] Law often provides for human beings the comfort of continuity and thus allows us to evade the logic of the gift. Law often claims a plenary power and thereby denies us the space for responsibility.

Coda

At the end of her last letter, my friend wrote:

I hope you are well and that you will think about everything I have said.

I never heard from her again. I don't know in what country she is living now, or with whom, or how, or under the flag of what mighty banner of justice. I certainly hope she is well, too, and I can honestly say that I have thought long and hard about everything she said.

Encoded, in the crypt, lies the body of law, as mortal and fragile a vessel as any. The secret it conceals is its weakness, but this weakness is in fact its strength. We should not despair at law's impotence but welcome the choice it gifts us. Law requires and allows a supplement. What still makes justice possible, though never certain, in this world, is our freedom and our inescapable responsibility – both our quickening and our death. For my friend, that was not an adequate answer. For me too, as the morning steals the night. But sometimes it is. Eventually, the sun will gutter out. Unfathomable night will return to the earth. Why, then, will we have saved a life? Only to establish a connection without reason in an ethics that allows no opportunity for repayment and no hope of memoriam. What then will remain of justice? No reward, no consequence, no memory. Only the secret act of giving and having given. What then will remain of us when the waters at last close, oblivious or disinterested, over our heads? No gravestone, open and public. Only a crypt, so perfectly concealed that nothing but the trace of an age-old memorial stone remains.

---

38 Of course, the literature on this topic is vast. For a recent contribution, see Nancy Fraser, *Cannibal Capitalism* (New York: Verso, 2022).

39 Peter Fitzpatrick, *The Mythology of Modern Law* (London: Routledge, 1992).

Bibliography

Ariès, Philippe. *The Hour of Our Death/Homme devant la mort*. Translated by Helen Weaver. Oxford: Oxford University Press, 1981.

Bachelard, Gaston. *The Poetics of Space*. Translated by Maria Jolas. Boston, MA: Beacon Press, 1969.

Beal, Timothy. "Specters of Moses: Overtures to Biblical Hauntology." In *Imagining Biblical Worlds*, edited by David Gunn and Paula McNutt, 171–187. Sheffield: Sheffield Academic Press, 2003.

Blanchot, Maurice. *The Work of Fire/Part du feu*. Translated by Charlotte Mandell. Stanford, CA: Stanford University Press, 1995.

Derrida, Jacques. "Before the Law." In *Acts of Literature*, edited by Derek Attridge, 191–216. London: Routledge, 1992.

Derrida, Jacques. "Force of Law." *Cardozo Law Review* 11 (1989–1990): 920–1045.

Derrida, Jacques. *The Gift of Death/Donner la mort*. Translated by David Wills. Chicago, IL: University of Chicago Press, 1995.

Didi-Huberman, Georges. "Before the Image, Before Time: The Sovereignty of Anachronism." In *Compelling Visuality: The Work of Art in and Out of History*, edited by Claire Farago and Robert Zwijnenberg, 31–45. Minneapolis: University of Minnesota Press, 2003.

Elias, Norbert. *Time: An Essay*. Oxford: Basil Blackwell, 1992.

Fitzpatrick, Peter. *The Mythology of Modern Law*. London: Routledge, 1992.

Fraser, Nancy. *Cannibal Capitalism*. New York: Verso, 2022.

Illich, Ivan. *In the Vineyard of the Text*. Chicago, IL: University of Chicago Press, 1993.

Kafka, Franz. *The Metamorphosis and Other Stories*. Translated by Joyce Crick. Oxford: Oxford World's Classics, 2009.

Kafka, Franz. *The Trial*. Translated by Wilma and Edwin Muir. Harmondsworth: Penguin Modern Classics, 2015.

Lacey, Nicola. *The Nightmare and the Noble Dream: A Life of H. L. A. Hart*. Oxford: Oxford University Press, 2004.

Lange, Dorothea. Gravestone, St. George, Utah. Gelatin silver print. 1953.

Levinas, Emmanuel. *Éthique comme philosophie première*. Paris: Rives Poche, 1998.

Levinas, Emmanuel. *Otherwise than Being or Beyond Essence*. Translated by Alphonso Lingis. The Hague: Martinus Nijhoff, 1981.

Manderson, Desmond. *Proximity and the Soul of Law*. Montreal: McGill-Queen's University Press, 2007.

Mauss, Marcel. *The Gift: The Form and Reasons of Exchange in Archaic Societies*. New York: W.W. Norton, 2011. First published 1925.

Miller, J. Hillis. *Versions of Pygmalion*. Cambridge, MA: Harvard University Press, 1990.

Mirzoeff, Nicholas. "The Right to Look." *Critical Inquiry* 37 (2011): 473–496.

Monsó, Susana, and Antonio J.Osuna-Mascaró. "Death is Common, so is Understanding It: The Concept of Death in Other Species." *Synthese* 199, no. 1 (2021): 2251–2275.

Naffine, Ngaire. "But a Lump of Earth: The Legal Status of the Corpse." In *Courting Death: The Law of Mortality*, edited by Desmond Manderson, 95–110. New York: Pluto Press, 1999.

Neoh, Joshua. *Law, Love and Freedom*. Cambridge: Cambridge University Press, 2019.

Peperzak, Adriaan. *Ethics as First Philosophy*. London: Routledge, 1995.

Sherwood, Yvonne, ed. *Derrida's Bible*. New York: Palgrave Macmillan, 2004.

Sophocles. *The Three Theban Plays*. Translated by Robert Fagles. Harmondsworth: Penguin, 1984.

Veitch, Scott. *Law and Irresponsibility*. London: Routledge, 2007.

Wordsworth, William. "Ode on Intimations of Immortality from Recollections of Early Childhood (1804)." In *Selected Poems*, edited by Stephen Gill. Harmondsworth: Penguin, 2004.

Zizek, Slavoj. "Superego by Default." *Cardozo Law Review* 16 (1994): 925–942.

3

BEYOND DENIAL

A Sociological Investigation of the Normative Order of Death

Zohreh BayatRizi

Introduction

Neither death nor law exists in a vacuum. It is already known that the definition of death is historically contingent. People are pronounced dead today who would have been considered alive but in a permanent vegetative state in the past. Conversely, people are considered alive and in need of urgent care today who would have been pronounced dead prior to the advancement of resuscitation techniques. Law is also socially and historically contingent, and its formation and transformation over time reflect changes in culture, economy, racial relations, technology, etc. In the United States (US), a person can be legally dead in New York but alive in New Jersey.[1] When these two contingent phenomena come together, several socio-legal questions arise. At what point is a person legally dead? How is murder different from legal killing? What is the difference between war crimes and the 'normal' conduct of war? Do people have a right to kill themselves? Do they have a right to ask others for assistance in killing themselves? Can we pronounce a disappeared person 'dead' for legal purposes? The moral implications of these questions are significant. A prime example today is the outrage we in the Western world feel over Russian war crimes in Ukraine, which have led to calls for international human rights investigations. The atrocities in Bucha stand out in particular. Yet similar atrocities in Afghanistan and Iraq in the aftermath of the US-led invasions in 2001 and 2003 respectively (including indiscriminate mass killings and rapes by US military personnel) did not make it to most evening newscasts in the US. Nor was the illegality of those wars under international law seriously challenged. The Black Lives Matter Movement has drawn attention to the fact that race is a factor in the death of African Americans in police custody. And even there, it appears that the death of black men has drawn more outrage than black women.[2] There are many such examples domestically and internationally within and across all countries.

---

1 Patrick Jones, "How You Can Be Declared Dead in One State and Not in Another with Bioethicist Dr. L Syd M Johnson." Death Space: Filling the Void [Podcast]. Apple Podcasts, 2021.
2 Kimberlé Williams Crenshaw et al., *Say Her Name: Resisting Police Brutality Against Black Women* (New York: African American Policy Forum, 2015), https://scholarship.law.columbia.edu/faculty_scholarship/3226.

DOI: 10.4324/9781003304593-4

The legal complexity and uncertainty of death is a reflection of the wider cultural and normative complexity that surrounds it. From Gilgamesh's grappling with the meaning of mortality in the world's oldest surviving poem (*The Epic of Gilgamesh*) to Hamlet's tortured thoughts on killing, betrayal, and suicide in Shakespeare's *Hamlet*, to Ivan Ilyich's journey to self-understanding on his deathbed in Tolstoy's *The Death of Ivan Ilyich*, from Buddhist prohibitions on killing to debates over the glorification of violence in contemporary entertainment, we encounter human efforts to make sense of, regulate, and find a place for mortality. And yet this question has remained wide open. This complexity partly stems from the socio-biological ambivalence of death. Death troubles us because we seem to be the only species that can anticipate our own mortality and the only one that has gone to great lengths to come to terms with it.[3] Death brings a host of negative feelings, including sorrow, anger, loneliness, fear, and loss.[4] Too much of it at once and a society can become crippled and chaotic: 'And the life of man, solitary, poore, nasty, brutish, and short.'[5] Yet death is not all bad. It is the ultimate solution to old age, pain, and hopelessness. It is part of the evolutionary guarantee of our survival as a species[6] and a political guarantee of peace and order, enforced as law-preserving violence.[7]

On the surface, what we see is cultural, legal, and normative uncertainty. But somehow we navigate this confusing world, make judgements, and move on. How do we do that? How does our social upbringing prepare us to face, accept, and transcend these uncertainties? What sorts of attitudes towards death (of ourselves and others) does it inculcate in us? This chapter goes beyond 'law' in its narrower conception to examine a wider question that encompasses law: when it comes to death, how do we make sense of right and wrong, normal or abnormal, justified or excessive? How do we form an emotional and moral 'economy' of death that allows us to simply 'move on' from or 'normalise' many instances of death while experiencing outrage and sorrow over others? In this chapter, I argue that one major factor that gives coherence to our divergent responses to death is our perception of it as 'orderly' or 'disorderly'. It is assumed that law creates order. It can. But order implies the existence of a system for making hierarchies and divisions between what is allowed and what is not. What is tolerated and what is not. What is clean, tidy, normal, in its own place, and conforming. We make these distinctions not by studying legal codes or rule books but by acquiring a mental 'disposition' or 'practical reason', to paraphrase Bourdieu.[8] This practical reason is a tacit shared understanding that we bring into various situations and various social fields, from everyday encounters to legal, medical, moral, military, and political fields. The objective of this chapter is, in a sense, to understand how this 'practical reason' forms around death. I begin with an examination of the existing socio-psychological theories on this

---

3 Ernest Becker, *The Denial of Death* (New York: Simon and Schuster, 1997) and Zygmunt Bauman, *Mortality, Immortality, and Other Life Strategies* (Stanford, CA: Stanford University Press, 1992).
4 Elisabeth Kübler-Ross, *On Death and Dying* (New York: Macmillan, 1969).
5 Thomas Hobbes, *Leviathan* (Middlesex: Pelican Press, 1978 [1652]), 186, and Norbert Elias, *The Civilizing Process: Sociogenetic and Psychogenetic Investigations*, rev. ed., trans. Edmund Jephcott (Oxford: Blackwell, 2000), 161–82.
6 Talcott Parsons, Renee Fox, and Victor Lidz, "The 'Gift of Life' and Its Reciprocation," in *The Talcott Parsons Reader*, ed. Bryan S. Turner (Malden: Blackwell, 1999 [1972]), 123–54.
7 Walter Benjamin, "Critique of Violence," in *Deconstruction: A Reader*, ed. Martin Bullock and Michael W. Jennings (New York: Routledge, 2001).
8 Pierre Bourdieu, *Practical Reason: On the Theory of Action* (Stanford, CA: Stanford University Press, 1998).

subject and then present a potential alternative framework for bringing coherence and clarity to our seemingly confusing and eclectic approaches to death and dying.

Decades of denial

The most famous Western scholar to try to bring coherence to 'the history of death' is Ernest Becker. In 1973, shortly before his own untimely death, Becker published his Pulitzer Prize–winning book, *The Denial of Death*. The central premise of Becker's book is borrowed from Freud: 'the unconscious does not know death or time: in man's physiochemical, inner organic recesses he feels immortal'.[9] The self yearns for immortality, yet the body knows it is mortal. Hence the terror of mortality: 'to have emerged from nothing, to have a name, consciousness of self, deep inner feelings, an excruciating inner yearning for life and self-expression – and with all this yet to die'.[10] This terror is perhaps environmentally acquired, perhaps innate – Becker inclines towards the innate.[11] Deeply in denial of our mortality, we become narcissistic – 'hopelessly absorbed with ourselves', desiring self-esteem, wanting to be heroes.

Drawing on insights from several disciplines, Becker posited that human culture and civilisation is an edifice raised to shelter us from the reality of our own mortality. As it turns away from its traumatic confrontation with its finitude, the ego takes refuge in religion, heroism, competition, and cultural and technological production. The symbolic social system feeds our narcissism into immortality. Cultural relativity is nothing but the relativity of 'hero systems', ranging from 'magical, religious, and primitive' to 'secular, scientific and civilized'.[12] Whatever their form, these symbolic hero systems afford people a feeling of 'primary value' and 'cosmic specialness', a hope that in their creations they can 'outlive or outshine death and decay'.[13] The idea that culture as such is produced because of our knowledge of our own mortality was not new; Arendt, among others, had theorised a link between culture and death prior to Becker.[14] In addition, by the time Becker published his book, sociologists had been advancing their own theories of denial for about 20 years. But Becker's 1973 formulation became an instant classic.

In the same year, a court in Leeuwarden, the Netherlands, made a groundbreaking ruling on the euthanisation of an elderly woman by her daughter, Dr Gertruida Postma. The ruling, which gave Postma only a one-week suspended jail sentence, paved the way for the eventual decriminalisation of euthanasia in 2001. The medical profession gradually relaxed its ethical standards to embrace euthanasia more openly. First, it was ruled that the death of the patient is only allowed when it is an inevitable (albeit known and anticipated) side effect of a gradual increase in the dose of painkillers. Eventually, however, physicians, judges, and governments adopted the view that, under certain conditions, death itself can indeed be the primary purpose of a drug administration.[15] Death

---

9   Becker, *Denial*, 2. See also Sigmund Freud, "Our Attitude Toward Death," in *Civilization, Society, and Religion*, ed. Albert Richards and James Dickson, vol. 12 of *The Standard Edition of the Complete Psychological Works of Sigmund Freud*, trans. James Strachey (London: Penguin Books, 1985), 79.
10 Sam Keen, "Foreword," in Becker, *Denial*, xii.
11 Becker, *Denial*, 2.
12 Becker, *Denial*, 4–5.
13 Becker, *Denial*, 5.
14 Hannah Arendt, *The Human Condition* (Chicago, IL: University of Chicago Press, 1958).
15 Zohreh Bayatrizi, *Life Sentences: The Modern Ordering of Mortality* (Toronto: University of Toronto Press, 2008), ch. 4.

became something to accept and even hasten, rather than always deny and postpone. Also in 1973, the US Supreme Court made a historic ruling in *Roe v. Wade*, declaring abortion to be a constitutionally protected right – another move that legally sanctions a form of medically induced death that was previously treated as murder. That ruling has since been overturned by *Dobbs v. Jackson Women's Health Organization* in 2022, and the debate on this matter is again wide open in the US.

Becker's aim had been to give a coherent meaning to the motivations behind our conduct and find the universal force that explains human social action. Alas, before the ink had dried on his book, Becker's theory was undermined by the aforementioned Dutch and US rulings. These rulings – and much else that was going on in and around 1973, including the Vietnam War and the Fourth Arab–Israeli War – showed that whether we psychologically deny death or not, our legal, political, and social approaches to death are much more complicated.

Despite evidence showing that the denial thesis might be on shaky grounds, much of the sociological literature on attitudes towards death is implicitly or explicitly dominated by the denial/acceptance binary (and the related binaries of traditional/modern and religious/secular). In particular, the denial thesis has had a large hold in theoretical and empirical studies on death and dying.[16] While not always using the exact phrase 'the denial of death', sociologists have used a variety of concepts to convey the same paradigm. Kellehear describes the denial of death as a 'significant but fragmented' quasi-theory that 'claims to be the central sociological background and stage for the bulk of our death related behaviour'.[17] According to Kellehear, fear of death, medicalisation of death, and the crisis of individualism are often used in reference to, or as an explanation for, the same phenomenon as the denial of death. Zimmermann and Rodin offer a modified categorisation involving five major bodies of sociological 'evidence' for the denial of death thesis: '1) the taboo on conversation about death; 2) the medicalization of death; 3) the segregation of the dying from the rest of society; 4) the decline of mourning rituals; and 5) death-denying funeral practices'.[18]

In sociology and social thought, the idea that people's relationship to death is changing in the Western world goes as far back as Weber (1919), who noted the inability of rationalised Western science, as the dominant force in society, to give meaning to death.[19] But does this inability lead to denial? Many sociologists seem to think so. Since at least the 1950s, a significant portion of theoretical and empirical sociological literature has been dedicated to showing that societies in general, and modern societies in particular, struggle to cope with death. This struggle is supposedly played out in various ways, but in modern societies it often involves denial, taboo, silence, exclusion, sequestration, and concealment. Often these arguments overlap with other binary conceptions of attitudes towards death, such as 'traditional' versus 'modern' or 'religious' versus 'secular', insofar as 'traditional' or 'religious' worldviews are presumed to accept death and 'modern' or

---

16 Martin Robert and Laura Tradii, "Do We Deny Death? I. A Genealogy of Death Denial," *Mortality* 24, no. 3 (2019): 247–60, and Laura Tradii and Martin Robert, "Do We Deny Death? II. Critiques of the Death-Denial Thesis," *Mortality* 24, no. 4 (2019): 373–88.

17 Allan Kellehear, "Are We a Death-Denying Society? A Sociological Review," *Social Science and Medicine* 18, no. 9 (1984): 713.

18 Camilla Zimmermann and Gary Rodin, "The Denial of Death Thesis: Sociological Critique and Implications for Palliative Care," *Palliative Medicine* 18, no. 2 (2004): 122.

19 Max Weber, "The Vocation of Science," in *The Essential Weber: A Reader*, ed. Sam Whimster (London: Routledge, 2004), 270–87.

'secular' attitudes are presumed to deny death.[20] These arguments have been advanced by theoretical, historical, and empirical studies. The historico-theoretical tradition seeks to differentiate between how societies have dealt with death over large historical timeframes, such as the Stone Age, Middle Ages, or Late Modern societies, often pointing out an increasing trend of denial and silence around death in contemporary Western societies.[21] Conversely, the empirical-ethnographic tradition emerged out of observations of the medical and commercial management of death in contemporary hospitals and funeral homes.[22]

Unsurprisingly, almost from the beginning, the denial of death thesis has faced pushback and criticism from sociologists, who argue that, historically, human societies have accepted and prepared for death rather than deny it.[23] Walter documents the revival of death as a topic of discourse and the revival of traditional and natural ways of dying.[24] Seale argues that the 'social organization for death in late modernity is remarkably active, realistic and death accepting'.[25] Kellehear argues that starting from the Stone Age, human cultures have come up with various ways to deal with and prepare for death.[26] Also, for a society that is supposed to be denying death and treating it as taboo, we seem to be unable to stop talking about it[27] – the present book being a case in point.

The problem with the acceptance/denial binary (and other related binaries such as traditional/modern or religious/secular) is that no matter how nuanced the arguments of each side, at the end we are left with rigid constructions. While these constructions might, at best, capture the cultural macro-currents, they do not tell us much about how people in actual socio-historical circumstances approach death. Therefore, they fall back on using universalistic terms about cultural approaches to death in large historical time frames, such as 'premodern societies', 'modern societies', the 'Stone Age', and the 'Middle Ages'. For instance, Seale offers a reading of history in which people relate to their own death and that of others, first through religious scripts, then modern medical scripts, and lastly late modern fragmented scripts.[28] He seems to assume that while cultural scripts have been homogenous in the 'past', they have become fragmented in late

20 See, e.g., Clive Seale, *Constructing Death: The Sociology of Dying and Bereavement* (Cambridge: Cambridge University Press, 1998).

21 See, e.g., Geoffrey Gorer, "The Pornography of Death," in *Death, Grief, and Mourning in Contemporary Britain* (London: Cresset, 1965), 169–75; Norbert Elias, *The Loneliness of the Dying* (Oxford: Blackwell, 1985); Philippe Ariès, *Western Attitudes Toward Death: From the Middle Ages to the Present*, trans. Patricia M. Ranum (Baltimore, MD: Johns Hopkins University Press, 1974); Philippe Ariès, *The Hour of Our Death* (London: Allen Lane, 1981); Bauman, *Mortality*; Zygmunt Bauman, "Postmodern Adventures of Life and Death," in *Modernity, Medicine and Health*, ed. Graham Scambler and Peter Higgs (New York: Routledge, 1998), 217–31; Philip Mellor and Chris Shilling, "Modernity, Self-Identity and the Sequestration of Death," *Sociology* 27, no. 3 (1993): 411–31.

22 See, e.g., Herman Feifel, ed., *The Meaning of Death* (New York: McGraw-Hill, 1959); Jessica Mitford, *The American Way of Death* (London: Hutchinson, 1963); Kübler-Ross, *On Death*; Zimmerman and Rodin, "Denial of Death".

23 Robert Blauner, "Death and Social Structure," *Psychiatry* 29, no. 4 (1966): 378–94; Lyn H. Lofland, *The Craft of Dying: The Modern Face of Death* (Beverly Hills, CA: Sage, 1978); Talcott Parsons and Victor Lidz, "Death in American Society," in *Essays in Self Destruction*, ed. Edwin Schneidman (New York: Science House, 1967), 133–70.

24 Tony Walter, *The Revival of Death* (London: Routledge, 1994).

25 Seale, *Constructing Death*.

26 Allan Kellehear, *A Social History of Dying* (Cambridge: Cambridge University Press, 2007).

27 Bayatrizi, *Life Sentences*, 5; Lofland, *Craft of Dying*, 92.

28 Seale, *Constructing Death*.

modernity. But what if there never was homogeneity and, instead, attitudes and scripts have always been diverse? For instance, in my native country of Iran, literature dating back over 1,000 years contains a number of cultural orientations towards death: heroic death (in Ferdowsi's epic *Shahnameh*), death as rejoining the universal spirit (in Rumi and other Sufi poets), nihilistic and fatalistic death (in Omar Khayyam), and death as predestination (the mainstream Islamic view and in folktales such as 'The Gardner and Death').[29] This could very well be the case in many cultures.

The politics of death

Another problem with these theories is that they are markedly apolitical and ignore how social and political inequalities, domination, and subjugation affect attitudes towards death. They assume a universal respect for the sanctity of life, reluctance to die, and abhorrence of killing. Yet, on every level, from families to communities, countries, and internationally, the life of some people is treated as more sacred and their death as more unimaginable than others. To make sense of the apparent normative incoherence of our approaches to mortality, we need to come up with a political understanding of death – a type of analysis that foregrounds the relations of power to understand the 'normative economy' of our emotions; that is, the norms that govern which lives we deem cherished, whose loss we find grievable, and which deaths we shrug off as 'inevitable' or 'justified'. This is why it is crucial to also bring in the voice of critical scholars who have drawn attention to the fact that we are not all 'equal before death'. In addition, perceptions of death are not universal across class, race, gender, nationality, ethnicity, etc., and much work needs to be done to delineate the experiences and attitudes of marginalised populations.[30]

Social thinkers have taken several conceptual approaches to analysing how power relations undergird our normative approaches to death. Two approaches stand out: those who take a social structural approach and those who take a cultural approach. Among the first, Agamben, Mbembe, Arendt, Galtung, Farmer, Fassin, Bauman, and Simpson have unpacked the political structures of the power over death and explained how colonial, totalitarian, and capitalist political economic structures have led to the derealisation and dehumanisation of racialised populations, imagined enemies and 'wasted' lives.[31] In particular, drawing on Foucault and Agamben, Achille Mbembe unpacks the practical conditions under which the necropolitical 'power to kill, to let live, or to expose to death' is exercised by invoking the sovereign right to kill under the state of emergency or exception.[32] Mbembe discusses colonialism,

29 Bayatrizi, *Life Sentences*, 50.
30 Steve Conway, "Death, Working-Class Culture and Social Distinction," *Health Sociology Review* 21, no. 4 (2012): 441–9; Glennys Howarth, "Whatever Happened to Social Class? An Examination of the Neglect of Working Class Cultures in the Sociology of Death," *Health Sociology Review* 16, no. 5 (2007): 425–35.
31 See, e.g., Giorgio Agamben, *Homo Sacer: Sovereign Power and Bare Life* (Stanford, CA: Stanford University Press, 1998); Achille Mbembe, *Necropolitics: Theory in Forms*, trans. Steve Corcoran (Durham, NC: Duke University Press, 2019); Hannah Arendt, *The Origins of Totalitarianism*, 2nd ed. (Cleveland, OH: Meridian Books, 1958); Johan Galtung, "Violence, Peace, and Peace Research," *Journal of Peace Research* 6, no. 3 (1969): 167–91; Paul Farmer, "An Anthropology of Structural Violence," *Current Anthropology* 45, no. 3 (2004): 305–25; Didier Fassin, *Life: A Critical User's Manual* (John Wiley & Sons, 2018); Zygmunt Bauman, *Modernity and the Holocaust* (Ithaca, NY: Cornell University Press, 2000); Audra Simpson, "The State is a Man: Theresa Spence, Loretta Saunders and the Gender of Settler Sovereignty," *Theory & Event* 19, no. 4 (2016).
32 Mbembe, *Necropolitics*, 66.

apartheid (South Africa), occupation (Israel), and the 'war on terror' as specific examples. Colonialism is also front and centre in the work of Mohawk scholar Audra Simpson, who argues that the settler state is built on the death and disappearance of Indigenous Peoples, women in particular, and that the colonial 'logic of elimination' and dispossession are responsible for the continued death and disappearance of Indigenous women today.[33] On a different front, Paul Farmer draws on Galtung's notion of structural violence to argue that modern power and economic inequalities underlie the exposure of impoverished populations in Haiti to death.[34] Modern structures are also front and centre in Bauman's examination of the role of the bureaucratic machinery in carrying out the Holocaust, where the division of labour and separation of moral from instrumental reason created an efficient and calculated process of mass killing. Many participants did not even realise their own participation; all they did was create a train schedule or order supplies from one place to another.[35]

Among those who take a cultural approach, Butler reflects on the rise of prejudiced political views in the US in the aftermath of 9/11 and how they portrayed US deaths as grievable and their loss unimaginable, while rendering Afghani or Iraqi lives as unworthy of commemoration and their deaths 'ungrievable'.[36] These Afghani and Iraqi victims suffer from the 'violence of derealisation'; their lives are not real, as if they have never been there, and the typical US audience is not exposed to accounts of their hopes, dreams, and daily lives. This notion echoes Razack's earlier studies of Indigenous deaths in custody in Canada and how attempts to 'improve' the situation only make it worse because of prejudiced attitudes that see Indigenous Peoples as 'flawed bodies always on the brink of death'.[37] In a different context, Doka has used 'disenfranchised grief' as a label for grief that is denied or downplayed because the deceased is not deemed worthy of grief or their survivors are not deemed worthy of sympathy, as has been the case for AIDS victims in the US in the 1980s or women who experience miscarriage.[38] Bauman's work straddles both structural and cultural approaches. In some of his culturally based analysis, he blames modern instrumental rationality and its relentless pursuit of perfection for the fact that many 'imperfect' lives are treated as 'waste' and left to die or intentionally eradicated.[39]

Ordering not denying: Towards an alternative

Let us take stock of the complexities and contradictions discussed so far. Just looking at the current moment in world history, some world denizens can legally arrange their own death through medical assistance, while many others are constantly and unexpectedly exposed to death from structural violence, climate change, wars, racism, and so on, and yet another smaller group of people might find themselves simply condemned to live because they are kept in a permanent vegetative state or on suicide watch. Is there a conceptual category that allows us to understand how death can be both denied and

---

33 Simpson, "The State is a Man."
34 See, e.g., Farmer, "An Anthropology of Structural Violence."
35 Bauman, *Modernity and the Holocaust.*
36 Judith Butler, *Precarious Life: The Powers of Mourning and Violence* (London: Verso, 2004).
37 Sherene Razack, *Dying from Improvement: Inquests and Inquiries into Indigenous Deaths in Custody* (Toronto: University of Toronto Press, 2015), 134.
38 Kenneth J. Doka, "Disenfranchised Grief: An Exposition and Update," in *Readings in Thanatology*, ed. Michelle M. Byers and David W. Kissane (New York: Routledge, 2020), 275–83.
39 See Zygmunt Bauman, *Wasted Lives: Modernity and Its Outcasts* (London: Polity Press, 2004); Bauman, *Modernity and the Holocaust.*

accepted, taboo but also spoken of, postponed yet sometimes also hastened, fought off but also welcome, unthinkable but also deliberately inflicted?

I propose the concept of *ordering*. The important thing to focus on is the (historically contingent) normative order of death, an order that determines not *whether* but *which* death is to be accepted, *which* to be prevented at any cost, *which* to be tolerated, *which* to be ignored, *which* to be silenced, and *which* to be spoken of. Orderly death is ultimately acceptable; disorderly death is prevented or hidden. Mary Douglas famously remarked, quoting Lord Chesterfield, that 'dirt is matter out of place'.[40] The same applies to disorderly death. Cultures do not merely deny death but rather offer ways to *order death*; that is, they create a proper place and context for experiencing death while at the same time trying to contain the psychological, social, political, and economic threats imposed by the unpredictable nature of human mortality. This ordering can involve:

- efforts to postpone death, as in medical treatment of illnesses, but also efforts to hasten it, as in medical euthanasia
- efforts to objectify and shine a light on death, as in autopsies or embalming, but also efforts to hide and silence death, as in prohibitions and taboos in some cultures against taking and/or showing photos of corpses
- efforts to prevent violent death, as in crackdowns on gang wars or terrorism, but also engagement in organised political violence, as in military conflict, drone attacks, and carpet bombing
- efforts to publicise, mourn, and even politically capitalise on some deaths, such as building war memorials or commemorating victims of certain conflicts, but also utter ignorance or denial of other deaths, such as 'collateral damage' suffered by civilians on the other side
- efforts to save lives at any cost, as in vaccine nationalism and hoarding during the COVID-19 pandemic, but also letting others die from the same pandemic or from climate change.

Death as such is not an object of control or prohibition. But unruly death – death that is messy, out of place, and out of order – has to be stopped. The binary distinction between 'orderly' and 'disorderly' deaths is produced and maintained through a set of sub-binary distinctions outlined below.

Timing: A 'timely' death is orderly while a 'premature' death is disorderly. The definition of what is 'timely' or 'premature' has been ever shifting, given the state of medicine, food security, and the prevalence of epidemics and devastating wars. However, a general orientation towards postponement is consistently observed in most societies. In modern societies, public health and medical technology help prevent 'untimely' death, while hospice and palliative care aim to prepare people for death and ease their experience of it when the 'inevitable' time has come. In real life, however, evidence consistently indicates higher rates of premature death among lower classes and barriers to end-of-life care.

Regulation: A 'just' death is orderly while an 'unjust' death is disorderly. This line demarcates legal versus extrajudicial executions, legally authorised medical assistance in dying as opposed to mercy killing, and legitimate killing in battle versus war crimes.

40 Mary Douglas, *Purity and Danger: An Analysis of Concepts of Pollution and Taboo* (London: Routledge and Kegan Paul, 1966), 36.

Medical codes of ethics, codes of war, and penal codes ensure (or at least give the appearance) that when a person is killed, the death is 'deserved' or 'inevitable' or 'authorised', and therefore 'just' and ultimately acceptable. But these regulations can become contentious. We see this in the ongoing contestation surrounding the deaths in police custody of African Americans in the US or Indigenous Peoples in Canada. What police see as justified use of force according to internal police codes of conduct and training begins to appear wholly unjustified against the historical backdrop of colonisation, slavery, and the overrepresentation of certain populations in the criminal justice system.

Risk management: Predictable and 'normal' rates of mortality are manageable and orderly, while sudden spikes in mortality rates, such as during epidemics, are 'pathological' and disorderly because they create economic and psychological chaos. Durkheim's distinction between normal and pathological rates of suicide comes to mind here; the former is expected and conforms to socio-historical trends, while the latter indicates an underlying social problem. Risk management through public health, epidemiology, food and drug safety regulations, and suicide and accident prevention help keep mortality rates low and predictable, and thus orderly. Again, what is 'normal' or 'pathological' is socio-historically defined. In countries where mortality rates are already quite low, reports of even a minuscule statistical spike in mortality risk (e.g., increased risk of cancer from certain pollutants or foods) can be reported in alarming language,[41] while these same countries have sought to export their pollutants to poor countries because, to paraphrase a World Bank chief economist, death is a normal occurrence there, if not from air pollution then from something else.[42] We also saw these double standards in risk management at play during the COVID-19 pandemic, when the World Health Organization was calling for equitable global access to medical supplies based on public health priorities, while many countries were flexing their economic and political muscles to get to the front of the line.

Symbolic ritualisation: Death that is symbolically meaningful and properly mourned is orderly.[43] Meaningless death, dying in vain, dying alone, or corpses that are lost or hard to identify present disorder. Religion has long helped ritualise and give meaning to death – a role now played by psychological counselling. Mourning also helps deal with grief. It can be public or private, as is increasingly the case in modern societies.[44] And yet, as we have seen, grief and commemoration themselves are often politicised, and not every death is treated as equally worth grieving, commemorating, and ritualising. Military or state funerals, war memorials, tombs of unknown soldiers, and mausoleums for political leaders are examples of politicised symbolic ritualisation. Conversely, mass graves, unmarked graves, and 'enforced disappearance' are prime examples of withholding ritualisation. In international human rights parlance, 'enforced disappearance' refers to the abduction and (most likely) murder of individuals without any trace of their bodies or place of disposal. This is a tactic used when there is fear that even the corpse can become symbolically meaningful, often by authoritarian governments, but note that the US Government disposed of Osama bin Ladan's body at a secret location at sea.

41 Jonathan E Fielding, "The Health of Health Risk Appraisal," *The Journal of Health Science Research* 22, no. 4 (1987): 441.
42 Quoted in Vandana Shiva, "The World on the Edge," in *On the Edge: Living with Global Capitalism,* ed. Will Hutton and Anthony Giddens (London: Jonathan Cape, 2000), 114–5.
43 Robert N. Bellah, "Civil Religion in America," *Daedalus* 96, no. 1 (1967): 1–21; Nancy Reeves, "Death Acceptance Through Ritual," *Death Studies* 35, no. 5 (2011): 408–19.
44 Seale, *Constructing Death*; Walter, *Revival of Death.*

Placement: Death has a proper place, at a safe distance from 'us'. Death belongs to others; it happens to others. This, as Freud argued, is one way we deal with the knowledge of mortality. Death that happens to us or those close to us geographically, emotionally, ethnically, and historically is threatening and unacceptable. Disorderly death is death out of place, death that is close to home. In her writings on the US invasion of Afghanistan, Butler discusses how victims of violence who look like 'us' are treated as more worthy of sympathy and grief than strangers far away in Afghanistan who do not share those resemblances and life trajectories.[45]

All in all, the binary distinction between 'orderly' and 'disorderly' deaths and the other sets of binary distinctions that derive from and express it (e.g., 'timely' versus 'premature', 'just' versus 'unjust') are socio-historically contingent. Elsewhere, I have examined and provided detailed empirical evidence for the existence and operation of these binary distinctions.[46] In this chapter, I focus only on the distinction between premature and timely death, which overlaps with the distinction between natural/inevitable and preventable death. The conception of death as a 'preventable risk' historically emerged thanks, in large part, to the development of new statistical techniques for measuring mortality rates and identifying the most common causes of death, including accidents, water contamination, and common diseases.[47] John Graunt, the father of statistics, took death as his topic of interest in 1662.[48] He tabulated in aggregate form the individual cases of death in London, aiming to keep track of how many people died each year, of what cause, at which age, of what gender, and in which parish. This revolutionary technique became massively popular. In the centuries that followed, and with the accumulation and refinement of this type of knowledge, public authorities began to take account of these scientific developments and devised plans to prevent *unnecessary* or *preventable* deaths, as evident in 'medical police' in German-speaking areas[49] and public health commissions in the United Kingdom.[50] Similarly, life insurance underwriters became interested in mortality rates as a useful instrument for predicting mortality risk.[51] Death was slowly reconceptualised as a malleable *risk* against the collective good; that is, a preventable *threat* to the political strength and economic prosperity of the European empires.[52] This history involves explicit public discussion of death, which contradicts the death taboo thesis. But this public discussion has been of a

45 Butler, *Precarious Life*.

46 Bayatrizi, *Life Sentences*, 159–70.

47 Bayatrizi, *Life Sentences*, ch 2.

48 John Graunt, *Natural and Political Observations Mentioned in a Following Index, and Made upon the Bills of Mortality; With Reference to the Government, Religion, Trade, Growth, Ayre, Diseases, and the Several Changes of the Said City* (London: Tho. Roycroft, 1662).

49 Johann Peter Frank, *A System of Complete Medical Police: Selections from Johann Peter Frank*, trans. and ed. John P. Frank (Baltimore, MD: Johns Hopkins University Press, 1976, orig. pub. 1786).

50 Edwin Chadwick, "On the Best Modes of Representing Accurately, by Statistical Returns, the Duration of Life, and the Pressure and Progress of the Causes of Mortality Amongst Different Classes of the Community, and Amongst the Populations of Different Districts and Countries," *Quarterly Journal of the Statistical Society of London* 7, no. 1 (1844): 1–40; James Kay-Shuttleworth, *The Moral and Physical Condition of the Working Classes Employed in the Cotton Manufacture in Manchester* (London: James Ridgway, 1832).

51 Geoffrey Clark, *Betting on Lives: The Culture of Life Insurance in England, 1695–1775* (Manchester: Manchester University Press, 1999), 119–20.

52 Zohreh Bayatrizi, "From Fate to Risk: The Quantification of Mortality in Early Modern Statistics," *Theory, Culture and Society* 25, no. 1 (2008): 121–43.

decidedly scientific nature and might have contributed to the decline of death talk in everyday language and folklore, as identified by Elias[53] and others.

But what of the attempts to hasten death, such as medically regulated euthanasia? Studies of historical developments leading to the legalisation of euthanasia in the Netherlands show that euthanasia was legalised, in large part, due to it being seen as a 'dignified', 'neat', 'controlled', and 'transparent' alternative to the existing practice of either letting patients die a painful and 'undignified' death or letting doctors and nurses secretly euthanise their patients.[54] While undignified death is disorderly because it is meaningless, thus violating 'symbolic ritualisation', secret euthanasia is also disorderly because it is subject to no officially sanctioned codes and procedures, thus violating 'regulation'. Legalised euthanasia, in contrast, is dignified, clean, transparent, and thus orderly.

The notion of ordering is not perfect. It is not meant to be. No one can claim that ordering death explains all aspects of social or legal attitudes towards death throughout history or even in the present time, in all societies or even in one. But ordering has the advantage of giving a coherent meaning to some of the most salient but also most contradictory social mentalities, approaches, and practices regarding death. Ordering is neither modern nor premodern. It is not Western, nor is it Oriental. Rather, it is a common human practice. Available accounts of death management throughout history, especially in non-Western societies, provide empirical evidence of a cross-cultural (albeit not universal) tendency towards ordering.[55] Yet societies differ in how they bring death under order. While in some societies the ritualistic aspects of death management and ordering are more pronounced, other societies are characterised by a greater presence of what Parsons and Lidz call realism and instrumental rationalism.[56] Ritual ordering of the moment of death according to religious teachings or magic might be the oldest still existing practice.[57] Conversely, the instrumental rational ordering of death, which relies mainly on the use of disciplinary and discursive methods such as law, medicine, and bioscience, is a much more recent development. However, although the rational element is emphasised, the ordering of death today in fact consists of a hybrid of rational and ritual elements. So again, such labelling can only be applied with caution.

But why does death need to be 'orderly'? Is it because, as Freud and Becker would have it, death is psychologically terrorising? This possibility has been examined by terror management theory in psychology and also resonates with sociological writings on death denial, death taboo, and the sequestration of death. Terror management theory in psychology is directly built on Becker's denial of death thesis. It breaks Becker's meta-theory into numerous operationally defined and testable hypotheses that take as their point of departure the notion that human behaviour is shaped by the internal death terror and that this terror 'must be quelled through the development of death-denying cultural belief

---

53 Elias, *Loneliness*.

54 Bayatrizi, *Life Sentences*, ch 4. See also John Griffiths, Alex Bood, and Heleen Weyers, *Euthanasia and Law in the Netherlands* (Amsterdam: Amsterdam University Press, 1998) and Rob Schwitters, "Slipping into Normality? Some Reflections on Slippery Slopes," in *Regulating Physician-Negotiated Death*, ed. A. Klijn, F. Mortier, M. Trappenburg and M. Otlowski (Trappenburg: Elsevier's Gravenhage, 2001).

55 Kellerhear, *Social History*, 168; Clifford Geertz, *The Interpretation of Cultures: Selected Essays* (New York: Basic Books, 1973), 158; Bronislaw Malinowski, *Argonauts of the Western Pacific* (London: Routledge, 1922), 490 (cited in Blauner, "Death and Social Structure", 378).

56 Parsons and Lidz, "Death in American Society."

57 Kellerhear, *Social History*.

systems and self-esteem'.[58] Some terror management theory researchers have focused on the regulation of the body and its adornment because the human body itself is a consistent reminder of mortality. For example, Martinez applies Becker's thesis to uncover the codes of death denial in his semiotic study of athletic advertisements.[59] Others have tested the hypothesis that cultural beliefs provide a sense of security and protect against the fear of death, and that when faced with reminders of one's own mortality, people tend to hold more strongly to their beliefs. This hypothesis has been tested in a range of studies looking at cultural conformity, reactions to crime and punishment, in-group/out-group dynamics, social consensus, and aggression against those who challenge one's beliefs.[60] Similar assumptions underlie Bauman's assertion that culture as such is an attempt to overcome the terror of death and Mellor and Shilling's argument that the knowledge of our own mortality erodes our ontological security.[61] In this case, we would be explaining a social phenomenon in terms of an individual, psychological need.

The second option is to say, along with US functionalists, that death, the dying, and the dead represent a danger to society and the rituals surrounding death are meant to manage or prevent this danger. Blauner argues that 'since mortality tends to disrupt the ongoing life of social groups and relationships, all societies must develop some forms of containing its impact'.[62] Geertz observes that in Bali, Indonesia, a dead body has to be buried as soon as possible 'because it is dangerous to have the spirit of the deceased hovering around the house'.[63] Malinowsky also notes that 'death … causes a great and permanent disturbances in the equilibrium of tribal life' in Papua New Guinea.[64] In Durkheim's work on religion, death represents a taboo that has to be ritually managed.[65] Modern societies are no exception in this regard. According to Blauner, these societies contain the social disruptiveness of death through bureaucratisation and routinisation. Hospitals and funeral homes, in particular, help contain and reduce the disturbance caused by death through isolation and orderly procedure.[66] This functionalist assumption is shared by non-functionalist authors; Baudrillard, for example, has noted that the modern political and economic order is built on the containment of death and a strict separation between the living and the dead.[67]

But to accept the notion that societal attitudes to death are characterised as attempts to order death does not necessitate accepting as a precondition or a starting point the functionalist theory that death poses a threat to social order. Nor is it necessary to subscribe to

---

58 Jermaine Martinez, "Codes of Death Denial: Applying Ernest Becker to a Semiotic Study of Athletic Advertisements Featuring Runners," *Rocky Mountain Communication Review* 3, no. 2 (2007): 31.

59 Martinez, "Codes of Death Denial."

60 For a detailed discussion of these studies, see Martinez, "Codes of Death Denial": 29–41; Fenna Van Marie and Shadd Maruna, "'Ontological Insecurity' and 'Terror Management': Linking Two Free-Floating Anxieties," *Punishment and Society* 12, no. 1 (2010): 7–26.

61 Bauman, *Mortality*; Mellor and Shilling, "Modernity, Self-Identity."

62 Blauner, "Death and Social Structure": 378.

63 Geertz, *Interpretation of Cultures*, 158.

64 Malinowski, *Argonauts*, 490.

65 Emile Durkheim, *The Elementary Forms of Religious Life* (New York: Free Press, 1965, orig. published 1912).

66 Blauner, "Death and Social Structure": 384. See also Parsons, Fox, and Lidz, "Gift of Life".

67 Jean Baudrillard, *Symbolic Exchange and Death* (London and Thousand Oaks, CA: Sage, 1993). See also Jean Baudrillard, *The Spirit of Terrorism and Other Essays*, trans. C. Turner (London: Verso, 2003).

the psychoanalytical theory that death causes an internal terror that must be tamed or quelled through a commitment to cultural production. Each, or even both, of these theories might be valid. But regardless of whether death presents a threat, it, like most other bio-social phenomena (eating, sleeping, marriage, sex, reproduction, birth, divorce, etc.), is subject to a social regime of ordering, meant to put it in its proper place. In that sense, and contrary to all previously discussed views, neither death nor its social management is unique. We cannot look at these arrangements and infer from them the 'denial of death'. Nor can we argue that the moral or legal 'justifications' for the unequal distribution of death and grief stem from different mechanisms than those that justify the unequal distribution of food, clean air, security, sexual freedom, or marital rights. As a human bio-social experience, death is subjected to a normative order – an order that is as arbitrary, imperfect, and riddled with social inequalities as any other bio-social experience.

Bibliography

Agamben, Giorgio. *Homo Sacer: Sovereign Power and Bare Life*, translated by Daniel Heller-Roazen. Stanford, CA: Stanford University Press, 1998.

Arendt, Hannah. *The Human Condition*. Chicago, IL: University of Chicago Press, 1958.

Arendt, Hannah. *The Origins of Totalitarianism*. 2nd ed. Cleveland, OH: Meridian Books, 1958.

Ariès, Philippe. *Western Attitudes Toward Death: From the Middle Ages to the Present*, translated by Patricia M. Ranum. Baltimore, MD: Johns Hopkins University Press, 1974.

Ariès, Philippe. *The Hour of Our Death*. London: Allen Lane, 1981.

Baudrillard, Jean. *Symbolic Exchange and Death*. London and Thousand Oaks, CA: Sage, 1993.

Baudrillard, Jean. *The Spirit of Terrorism and Other Essays*, translated by C. Turner. London: Verso, 2003.

Bauman, Zygmunt. *Mortality, Immortality, and Other Life Strategies*. Stanford, CA: Stanford University Press, 1992.

Bauman, Zygmunt. "Postmodern Adventures of Life and Death." In *Modernity, Medicine and Health*, edited by G. Scambler and P. Higgs, 217–231. New York: Routledge, 1998.

Bauman, Zygmunt. *Modernity and the Holocaust*. Ithaca, NY: Cornell University Press, 2000.

Bauman, Zygmunt. *Wasted Lives: Modernity and Its Outcasts*. John Wiley & Sons, 2013.

Bayatrizi, Zohreh. *Life Sentences: The Modern Ordering of Death*. Toronto: University of Toronto Press, 2008.

Bayatrizi, Zohreh. "From Fate to Risk: The Quantification of Mortality in Early Modern Statistics." *Theory, Culture and Society* 25, no. 1 (2008): 121–143.

Becker, Ernest. *The Denial of Death*. New York: Free Press Paperbacks, 1973.

Bellah, Robert. "Civil Religion in America." *Daedelus* 96, no. 1 (1967): 1–21.

Benjamin, Walter. "Critique of Violence." In *Deconstruction: A Reader*, edited by M. Bullock and M. W. Jennings, 62–70. New York: Routledge, 2001.

Blauner, Robert. "Death and Social Structure." *Psychiatry* 29, no. 4 (1966): 378–394.

Bourdieu, Pierre. *Practical Reason: On the Theory of Action*. Stanford, CA: Stanford University Press, 1998.

Butler, Judith. *Precarious Life: The Powers of Mourning and Violence*. London: Verso, 1998.

Chadwick, Edwin. "On the Best Modes of Representing Accurately, by Statistical Returns, the Duration of Life, and the Pressure and Progress of the Causes of Mortality Amongst Different Classes of the Community, and Amongst the Populations of Different Districts and Countries." *Journal of the Statistical Society of London* 7, no. 1 (1844): 1–40.

Clark, Geoffrey. *Betting on Lives: The Culture of Life Insurance in England, 1695–1775*. Manchester: Manchester University Press, 1999.

Conway, Steve. "Death, Working-Class Culture and Social Distinction." *Health Sociology Review* 21, no. 4 (2012): 441–449.

Crenshaw, Kimberlé W., Andrea J. Ritchie, Rachel Anspach, Rachel Gilmer, and Luke Harris. *Say Her Name: Resisting Police Brutality Against Black Women*. New York: Columbia Law School, 2015. https://scholarship.law.columbia.edu/faculty_scholarship/3226.

Doka, Kenneth J. "Disenfranchised Grief: An Exposition and Update." In *Readings in Thanatology*, 1st ed., edited by John D. Morgan, 275–283. Abingdon and New York: Routledge, 2020.

Douglas, Mary. *Purity and Danger: An Analysis of Concepts of Pollution and Taboo*. London: Routledge and Kegan Paul, 1966.

Durkheim, Émile. *The Elementary Forms of Religious Life*. New York: Free Press, 1965. First published 1912.

Elias, Norbert. *The Civilizing Process: Sociogenetic and Psychogenetic Investigations*, rev. ed., translated by Edmund Jephcott. Oxford: Blackwell, 2000.

Elias, Norbert. *The Loneliness of the Dying*. Oxford: Blackwell, 1985.

Farmer, Paul. "An Anthropology of Structural Violence." *Current Anthropology* 45, no. 3 (2004): 305–325.

Fassin, Didier. *Life: A Critical User's Manual*. John Wiley & Sons, 2018.

Feifel, Herman, ed. *The Meaning of Death*. New York: McGraw-Hill, 1959.

Fielding, Jonathan E. "The Health of Health Risk Appraisal." *Health Services Research* 22, no. 4 (1987): 441–452.

Frank, Johann Peter. *A System of Complete Medical Police: Selections from Johann Peter Frank*, edited by Erna Lesky. Baltimore, MD: Johns Hopkins University Press, 1976. First published 1786.

Freud, Sigmund. "Our Attitude Toward Death." In *Sigmund Freud, Volume 12: Civilization, Society, and Religion*, edited by A. Richards and A. Dickson. London: Penguin Books, 1985.

Galtung, Johan. "Violence, Peace, and Peace Research." *Journal of Peace Research* 6, no. 3 (1969): 167–191.

Geertz, Clifford. *The Interpretation of Cultures: Selected Essays*. New York: Basic Books, 1973.

Gorer, G. "The Pornography of Death." In *Death, Grief, and Mourning in Contemporary Britain*, 169–175. London: Cresset, 1965.

Graunt, J. *Natural and Political Observations Mentioned in a Following Index, and Made Upon the Bills of Mortality; With Reference to the Government, Religion, Trade, Growth, Ayre, Diseases, and the Several Changes of the Said City*. London: Tho. Roycroft, 1662. Retrieved from the Early English Books, 1641–1700 microfilm set, 972: 31, no. 14.

Griffiths, John, Alex Bood, and Heleen Weyers. *Euthanasia and Law in the Netherlands*. Amsterdam: Amsterdam University Press, 1998.

Hobbes, Thomas. *Leviathan*. Middlesex: Pelican Press, 1978. First published 1652.

Howarth, Glennys. "Whatever Happened to Social Class? An Examination of the Neglect of Working Class Cultures in the Sociology of Death." *Health Sociology Review* 16, no. 5 (2007): 425–435.

Jones, Patrick. "How You Can Be Declared Dead in One State and Not in Another with Bioethicist Dr. L Syd M Johnson." Death Space: Filling the Void [podcast] 10 June 2021, produced by Patrick E. Jones. 43:53. www.buzzsprout.com/1711186/8676534-how-you-can-be-declared-dead-in-one-state-and-not-in-another-with-bioethicist-dr-l-syd-m-johnson.

Lofland, Lyn H. *The Craft of Dying: The Modern Face of Death*. Beverly Hills, CA: Sage, 1978.

Kay-Shuttleworth, James. *The Moral and Physical Condition of the Working Classes Employed in the Cotton Manufacture in Manchester. Enlarged: and Containing an Introductory Letter to the Rev. Thomas Chalmers, Etc*. London: James Ridgway, 1832.

Keen, Sam. "Foreword." In Ernest Becker, *The Denial of Death*, xi–xvi. New York: Free Press, 1997.

Kellehear, Allan. "Are We a Death-Denying Society? A Sociological Review." *Social Science and Medicine* 18, no. 9 (1984): 713–723.

Kellehear, Allan. *A Social History of Dying*. Cambridge: Cambridge University Press, 2007.

Kübler-Ross, Elizabeth. *On Death and Dying*. 1st ed. New York: Macmillan, 1969.

Malinowski, Bronislaw. *Argonauts of the Western Pacific*. London: Routledge, 1922.

Martinez, Jermaine. "Codes of Death Denial: Applying Ernest Becker to a Semiotic Study of Athletic Advertisements Featuring Runners." *Rocky Mountain Communication Review* 3, no. 2 (2007): 29–41.

Mbembe, Achille. *Necropolitics: Theory in Forms*, translated by Steve Corcoran. Durham, NC: Duke University Press, 2019.

Mellor, Philip A., and Chris Shilling. "Modernity, Self-Identity and the Sequestration of Death." *Sociology* 27, no. 3 (1993): 411–431.

Mitford, Jessica. *The American Way of Death*. London: Hutchinson, 1963.

Parsons, Talcott, Renee C. Fox, and Victor M. Lidz. "The 'Gift of Life' and Its Reciprocation." In *The Talcott Parsons Reader*, edited by Bryan S. Turner, 123–154. Malden: Blackwell, 1999. First published 1972.

Parsons, Talcott, and Victor Lidz. "Death in American Society." In *Essays in Self-Destruction*, edited by Edwin Schneidman, 133–170. New York: Science House, 1967.

Razack, Sherene. *Dying From Improvement: Inquests and Inquiries into Indigenous Deaths in Custody*. University of Toronto Press, 2015.

Reeves, Nancy C. "Death Acceptance Through Ritual." *Death Studies* 35, no. 5 (2011): 408–419.

Robert, Martin, and Laura Tradii. "Do We Deny Death? I. A Genealogy of Death Denial." *Mortality* 24, no. 3 (2019): 247–260.

Schwitters, Rob. "Slipping Into Normality? Some Reflections on Slippery Slopes." In *Regulating Physician-Negotiated Death*, edited by A. Klijn, F. Mortier, M. Trappenburg, and M. Otlowski, 93–108. Trappenburg: Elsevier's Gravenhage, 2001.

Seale. Clive. *Constructing Death: The Sociology of Dying and Bereavement*. Cambridge: Cambridge University Press. 1998.

Shiva, Vandana. "The World on the Edge." In *On the Edge: Living with Global Capitalism*, edited by Will Hutton and Anthony Giddens, 112–129. London: Jonathan Cape, 2000.

Simpson, Audra. "The State is a Man: Theresa Spence, Loretta Saunders and the Gender of Settler Sovereignty." *Theory & Event* 19, no. 4 (2016).

Tradii, Laura, and Martin Robert. "Do We Deny Death? II. Critiques of the Death-Denial Thesis." *Mortality* 24, no. 4 (2019): 377–388.

Van Marle, Fenna, and Shadd Maruna. "'Ontological Insecurity' and 'Terror Management': Linking Two Free-Floating Anxieties." *Punishment & Society* 12, no. 1 (2010): 7–26.

Walter, Tony. *The Revival of Death*. Routledge, 2002.

Weber, Max. "The Vocation of Science." In *The Essential Weber: A Reader*, edited by Sam Whimster, 270–287. London: Routledge, 2004. First published 1919.

Zimmermann, Camilla, and Gary Rodin. "The Denial of Death Thesis: Sociological Critique and Implications for Palliative Care." *Palliative Medicine* 18, no. 2 (2004): 121–128.

4

ANOTHER LAW OF THE DEAD?

Legal Personhood, Death, and Time in Anglo-Saxon Jurisprudence

James Martel

Introduction

When do the dead cease to be legal persons? Do they ever cease to be some kind of person regardless of how long ago they died? In this chapter, I argue that the category of the dead is a highly unstable one precisely because there is no definite binarism between death and life, that the dead retain certain aspects of legal personhood while they lose others, and that this ambivalent set of give and takes changes over time (both in terms of the time since death and the historical period that considers the legal personhood of the dead at any given moment). After providing some theoretical context for how to think about the relationship between life and death more generally, I focus on the law and how it relates to death specifically. I make this further argument in two parts, first looking at capital punishment and the idea that 'death is different' (arguing that it is, in fact, not so different after all, at least not absolutely so) and then I turn to legal wrangles over corpses and the ownership of dead bodies (or lack thereof). In both parts, I turn to United States (US) case law to show that the dead occupy a complicated position vis-à-vis the living. Insofar as every living person will one day be a member of the dead, this is the one category that all living persons can and must relate themselves to (even though we rarely want to do so). Accordingly, the category of death is not easily separated from life. The legal perspectives that engage with thinking and acting upon a law that serves the living and the dead alike are inevitably conceived entirely from the position of the living, who, perhaps equally inevitably, bring their own thoughts and biases into a legal form. Yet the fact that the living are opining on a phenomenon, death, that is, by its very nature, opaque to them, means their conjecture is inherently more esoteric and even metaphysical than the law generally allows, creating a kind of aporia in the law at the very point where the law would very much like to assert full control and determination.

The authority and subversive power of the dead

To begin this inquiry, permit me to briefly engage in some theoretical explanations for why the law may find itself confounded to some degree by the dead. Two theorists in

DOI: 10.4324/9781003304593-5

particular may be of help in thinking about this: Walter Benjamin and Michel Foucault. In his well-known 'Toward a Critique of Violence', Benjamin tells us that the law is inherently violent, partaking in particular in a category that he called 'mythic violence'.[1] The law is mythic, Benjamin tells us, because its authority is not based on real, ontological sources but rather on projections that are inherently theological in form, if not content. Accordingly, the law must be violent, not for the sake of transmitting justice but rather to establish its own existence over and over again (both to itself and the subjects that it rules over). Benjamin contrasted this mythic violence to what he called 'divine violence' (though 'godly violence' might be a more accurate translation). Divine violence is based on a real deity rather than a false one and serves not to promote new truths in the face of false ones but rather to unmake the false truths that have been purported in God's name (or, in some secular works, stand in for God, like the state or nature). On this contrast, Benjamin stated:

> Mythic violence is blood-violence over mere life for the sake of violence itself; divine violence is pure violence over all of life for the sake of the living.[2]

Thus, even as we are reduced to the status of 'mere life' by mythic violence, we are at the same time members of the 'the living', a category that benefits from the way divine violence interferes with mythic violence (including law), creating gaps in the latter's control that allow human subjects the chance to produce laws and judgments of their own.

The category of the living would seem, by definition, to have nothing to do with the dead, but I argue that this is not an absolute and literal category but rather a fluid and capacious one. For Benjamin, the living is what we are when we are left to our own devices, not dominated and violated by the lies of mythic violence. In his 'On the Concept of History', Benjamin made this clearer when he stated:

> The only historian capable of fanning the spark of hope in the past is the one who is firmly convinced that *even the dead* will not be safe from the enemy if he is victorious. And this enemy has never ceased to be victorious.[3]

Here, we can see that, for Benjamin, the dead and the living alike face the same threat. Death does not seal off those who previously were alive from being affected by politics, being able to win and being able to lose. The dead are as vulnerable to the lies and distortions of mythic violence as the living are and, for that reason, can effectively be considered to be part of the living. This is one example of why we should not necessarily think of the dead as absolutely distinct from the living. The line between life and death is not a binarism in that sense but maybe something more like a spectrum. As the dead recede out of memory, they may indeed pass into a kind of non-existence, but until they do, they remain tied up with the same political risks –and the same political opportunities – as those who are still alive.

---

1 Walter Benjamin, "Toward the Critique of Violence," in *Toward the Critique of Violence: A Critical Edition*, ed. Peter Fenves and Julia Ng (Stanford, CA: Stanford University Press, 2021), 57.
2 Benjamin, "Critique of Violence," 57–8.
3 Walter Benjamin, "On the Concept of History," in *Walter Benjamin: Selected Writings vol. 4, 1938–1940*, ed. Howard Eiland and Michael W. Jennings (Cambridge, MA: Belknap Press of Harvard University Press, 2003), 391.

One last notion of Benjamin's that is useful in thinking about the dead and their relationship to and with the living comes from a short writing of his called 'The Storyteller'. In that essay, Benjamin tells us that the power of storytelling, an art that he claimed was dying out, comes in the way that it is punctuated by death. Death gives a regularity and rhythm to life, without which life would be endless and meaningless. Thus, he stated:

> Just as a sequence of images is set in motion inside a man as his life comes to an end – unfolding the views of himself under which he has encountered himself without being aware of it – suddenly in his expressions and looks the unforgettable emerges, and imparts to everything that concerned him that authority which even the poorest wretch in the act of dying possesses for the living around him. This authority is at the very source of the story.[4]

Given that each of us has a certain authority that comes from the fact of our own death, we have here a resource by which to resist mythic violence. Whereas mythic violence seeks to overwrite reality with its own phantasms, the fact of death and our participation in it, whether we like it or not (we usually do not), has the effect of keeping us tethered to material reality. This includes the materiality of our own bodies, which really only becomes apparent to us – and unavoidably so – when we die, when our body begins to rot and change, now immune to any mythical attempts to read it as having this or that meaning. Even before we die, our experience of the death of other people in our lives may also teach us this lesson, but this is a lesson that much of Western society is oriented towards avoiding (burial rites are, for example, a way to safely remove the dead from sight and separate their now dead body from their memory, which remains as it were alive and 'one of us').[5]

In this way, the authority of the dead serves as a resource not only for the dead themselves but also for the living (of which, as previously argued in this chapter, we can consider the dead to be members). Death is a limit on human life and human subjectivity, but in that limitation, death also preserves a space that cannot be overdetermined and cannot be entirely eclipsed by any false projections or forms of centralised control and determination.[6]

In his treatment of the question of the law and death, Michel Foucault made similar points about the limits and potential freedoms that death imposes on human subjects. Foucault famously spoke of the distinction between sovereignty and biopolitics, a change that happened over the course of a few centuries as humankind moved from medieval to modern forms of political and social power. In his lecture series 'Society Must Be Defended', Foucault stated:

> The right of sovereignty was the right to take life and let live. And then this new [biopolitical] right is established: the right to make live and let die.[7]

---

4 Walter Benjamin, "The Storyteller: Observations on the Works of Nikolai Leskov," in *Walter Benjamin: Selected Writings vol. 3, 1935–1938*, ed. Howard Eiland and Michael W. Jennings (Cambridge, MA: Belknap Press of Harvard University Press, 2006), 151. I am grateful to Zachary Reyna for his bringing my attention to this passage in "The Storyteller".

5 For more on this, see Robert Pogue Harrison, *The Dominion of the Dead* (Chicago, IL: University of Chicago Press, 2003), and Thomas W. Laqueur, *The Work of the Dead* (Princeton, NJ: Princeton University Press, 2015).

6 I expand on this argument in James Martel, *Unburied Bodies: Subversive Corpses and the Authority of the Dead* (Amherst, MA: Amherst College Press, 2018).

7 Michel Foucault, *Society Must Be Defended: Lectures at the Collège de France, 1975–1976* (New York: Picador, 2003), 241.

Here, 'making live' indicates a much deeper form of control and penetration than sovereignty ever had, penetrating into all aspects of life (hence biopolitical), wherein 'the ratio of births to deaths, the rate of reproduction, the fertility of the population' and other related matters all become part of the calculation of 'protecting' (but really determining and managing) human life as such.[8] And to speak of 'letting die' refers to the way that the meaning and nature of death itself is transformed for the modern biopolitical society. If, for the state, death is the ultimate threat that it can impose upon its citizenry, from a biopolitical perspective, which takes us well beyond the state, bringing in all kinds of new social actors, death becomes something that eludes the control over the living. As Foucault tells us:

> Death was no longer something that swooped down on life – as in an epidemic. Death was now something permanent, something that slips into life, perpetually gnaws at it, diminishes it and weakens it.[9]

In this way, death represents not the acme of state power but rather its nemesis. To say that the biopolitical order 'lets [someone] die' is more along the lines of that old joke where a dog's owner, faced with a dog that will not obey any commands, says, 'Just lie there. Ignore me.' Letting die in this sense is similarly more of a recognition that biopolitics can never have full control over life precisely because it cannot fully control (much less prevent) death.

In describing this transformation, Foucault was not saying that sovereignty disappears from the world only to be replaced by biopolitics. The need to kill to establish its own power (a need that tracks very well with Benjamin's understanding of the origins of legal violence) remains even as the state and other biopolitical functions have a new understanding of and relationship to death. What perhaps remains in common for the regimes of sovereignty and biopolitics is that when it comes to death, their respective control of it can never be utter. The sovereign, for example, can *only* kill the subject. Once it has done that (a topic I will return to when considering the question of whether, legally speaking, death is 'different'), the sovereign has no further power, and so, if the living subject does not hold life as being precious above all things, the sovereign may lose power over the living and the dead (something that Foucault referred to when he spoke, for example, of the criminal who becomes a folk hero by facing their execution bravely, calling curses unto the king as the executioner's sword is drawn[10]).

In this way, we can see once again that the line between life and death is never absolute and can not result in the state or other forms of control having complete power over the living or dead. It is not the bifurcation between life and death but rather the indistinction between them that is the source of this subversive power for the dead. In short, the dead are not different enough to have no effect on the living. Just as the threat of death is not so utter that it cannot prevent the brave criminal from challenging the state, so too does the fact of death prevent biopolitical power from having a totalising control over the living. For this reason, it does not make sense to exclude the dead from Benjamin's category of 'the living'; the dead are necessary co-conspirators with those who are alive to thwart the attempt to control either group utterly.

8 Foucault, *Society Must Be Defended*, 241.
9 Foucault, *Society Must Be Defended*, 241.
10 Michel Foucault, *Discipline and Punish* (New York: Vintage Books, 1979), 60–1.

Death is not (that) different: *Furman v. Georgia*

Having set out some theoretical models for how to think about death in relation to law, let me turn more directly to the practice of law itself, particularly in the Anglo-Saxon world (and more particularly still, in the US). I begin with a discussion of how the idea that 'death is different', a doctrine that came out of the 1972 US Supreme Court decision in *Furman v. Georgia*, is perhaps not entirely accurate in terms of the way the law treats and engages with death more generally.[11]

The *Furman* decision, in some ways, serves as a milestone in US jurisprudence when it comes to the death penalty, though not necessarily for obvious reasons. The decision of the majority of the justices (there were no concurring opinions; each justice wrote a separate opinion) suspended the death penalty on the grounds that it was 'cruel and unusual punishment' and thus in violation of the Eighth Amendment. Yet that decision was not to last long. A mere four years later, in *Gregg v. Georgia*, the US Supreme Court restored the practice of state executions, using *Furman* as a guide. The claim was that the *Furman* decision only held that the current practice of administering death was cruel and unusual but gave a sense of how the state could kill in a way that conformed to the Constitution (including the Eighth Amendment). This created an entire industry of capital punishment lawyers who worked to administer the complicated mechanism by which death could be legally administered once again. In this way, *Furman* ultimately did not retire the death penalty and could be said to have resurrected it. One reason for the justices ruling against the death penalty in *Furman* was that the penalty was becoming increasingly rare and thus it was relatively arbitrary when people were executed. Paradoxically, *Furman* created a pro–death penalty backlash, and state murder (i.e., administration of the death penalty) subsequently went up quite a bit before eventually returning to the point where it is once again almost as rare as it was when *Furman* was decided.

A key doctrine to come out of the *Furman* decision was the idea that the death penalty is cruel and unusual because dealing death, as opposed to any other form of punishment, cannot be reversed and is truly final. As Justice William Brenner put it:

> the unusual severity of death is manifested most clearly in its finality and enormity. Death, in these respects, is in a class by itself.[12]

If, for example, new evidence came up that exculpated an executed individual, the fact that they had been killed would put them beyond the power of redemption. Further, even if an accused was guilty, Brenner reasoned that death is so ultimate a punishment it is almost inherently disproportionate to any crime:

> our laws distribute punishments according to the gravity of crimes and punish more severely the crimes society regards as more serious. That purpose cannot justify any particular punishment as the upper limit of severity.[13]

11 Much of what follows about *Furman* comes from a conference and then an edited volume that I took part in, entitled Furman at Fifty. I am grateful to Austin Sarat, Linda Ross Meyer, John Bessler, Corinna Lain, Carol Steiker, Jordan Steiker, Sara Mayeux, and Nica Seigel for organising this conference. An edited volume, titled *Furman at Fifty*, based on the presented papers is forthcoming.
12 *Furman v. Georgia*, 408 U.S. 238 (1972), 289.
13 *Furman*, 303–4.

Insofar as death inherently does represent that upper limit, Brenner was arguing that it is not automatic that death should be one of the punishments that the law metes out. Since, as he put it, there are other punishments (such as life without parole) that effectively remove the criminal from public life, these are more in keeping with the principle of proportionality and the 'humaneness' that Brenner associated with Anglo-Saxon law.

To this reasoning, let me make a few points to show how, for all the insistence that death is different, the law once again reflects more of a spectrum than an absolute divide between life and death. Although we are talking about punishment here and not legal personhood per se, the question of the rights of the legal person does arise, for example, in Brenner's concern that killing a person takes away their 'right to have rights', suggesting that the dead, unlike the living, no longer have rights.[14] Brenner agreed that life in prison may destroy a person's 'political existence' but claimed that it leaves their actual existence intact. Another way to say this is that after death, the state has no further access to the deceased person, whether in a negative (punitive) sense or a positive (rights-based) way. Brenner quotes a nineteenth-century proponent of the death penalty as saying, 'When a man is hung, there is an end of our relations with him. His execution is a way of saying, "You are not fit for this world, take your chance elsewhere."'[15]

In saying this, Brenner acknowledged that death, in a sense, removes a person from the law's power (we will see that the Ruggles report, explored in the next section, expressed the exact same concern); thus, that which from the accused's perspective is perhaps the worst possible outcome (the end of their life) is also, for the law, a sign of its own limitations. Foucault's idea that death allows a person to escape from the grasp of biopolitics may seem gruesome in that a person may well not want to 'escape' in that way, but if you look at things from the law's perspective (which, for Foucault and Benjamin, is the only perspective that matters, since the law is only ever concerned with its own anxious status), this is a serious problem.

Recognising this inherent limitation in the power of the law when it comes to death, the law has sought to get as close to death as possible without necessarily killing a prisoner. From this perspective, life without parole (a sentence that has increased massively since the *Furman* decision) is a kind of living death – that is to say, a death (the destruction of the prisoner's political life) where the prisoner remains under the state's command and control. In this case, (physical) death is indeed different in that it ends this power, but it is not utterly unrelated to those punishments that fall just short of it. Further, although death is indeed impossible to reverse, so too is any form of imprisonment in the sense that an imprisoned person can be released but cannot have their lost years of life restored to them.

I should add that Benjamin and Foucault's analyses clash a bit on this matter, insofar as from a Foucaultian perspective, life without parole is the preferred stance of the law because it thereby retains its biopolitical authority, but from a Benjaminian perspective, death is preferred – at least some of the time – since death is what establishes the law's very existence in the first place. In this contradiction, we may see the sources of what has in effect become a kind of zombie life for the death penalty. These days, people sentenced to death in the US are often in a horrible and endless limbo where they are not actually killed but remain in a kind of near-death state, always living under what John Bessler called 'State-sanctioned death threats'.[16] State-imposed executions happen very rarely

---

14 *Furman*, 290.
15 *Furman*, 290.
16 John Bessler, "What Ifs and Missed Opportunities: The U.S. Supreme Court, Death Sentences and Executions, and the 50th Anniversary of *Furman v. Georgia*," in *Furman at Fifty*, 16.

these days, but prisoners on death row live in a constant relationship to their own death, even if the vast majority will die of old age instead of being executed by the state per se.

The indistinction between life and death that we see here is then perhaps less an accident resulting from a vagary of various US Supreme Court rulings but rather an indication of the fact that the law has a deep ambivalence about death. Death is at once (here, again, we see the twin diagnoses of Benjamin and Foucault both clashing and supporting one another) the ultimate – sovereign – power of the state and a sign precisely of the state and the law's weakness and limitation. Given this dual nature, it makes sense that the outcome is not the abolition of the death penalty but rather its ongoing, if highly restrained, existence, hovering as it were in the interface between life and death.

Do the dead own their own (legal) personhood? *In re Widening of Beekman Street* and *Pierce v. Proprietors of Swan Point Cemetery*

The same ambivalence can be seen in court cases dealing directly with the question of the legal personhood of the dead. Here, the issue is again, and above all, the law's own power and right to decide on this and other matters. Perhaps the most important case to cite in this regard is the 1854 New York Supreme Court case of *In re Widening of Beekman Street*. In that case, the City of New York sought to widen Beekman Street, requiring the removal of a segment of a cemetery (80 graves holding over 100 individuals' remains) belonging to the Brick Presbyterian Church in lower Manhattan. The city offered US$28,000 for relocating the graves in that segment, and the relatives of a deceased person buried in the affected area of the cemetery contested who should receive that money. Only five remains were identifiable among the affected graves. The plaintiff, Maria Smith, the daughter of the late Mr Moses Sherwood (who was buried in the affected area) – acting on behalf of herself, her brothers and sisters, and their descendants – claimed that Mr Sherwood's own legal personhood persisted beyond his death and that she was effectively representing his personhood in demanding that she (not the church) be reimbursed for the cost of reburial (i.e., reinterring her father's remains in a new grave, in a locality selected by her, and her father's existing gravesite monument erected over the new grave, with the expenses paid out of the funds being held by the court). The New York Supreme Court ruled in favour of Ms Smith.

As part of this case, a review of Anglo-Saxon law regarding the legal personhood of the dead was commissioned by the court. The review was written by Samuel B. Ruggles, an important lawyer and politician of the time. In his report, Ruggles forcefully rejected the British concept of 'ecclesiastical cognizance' – the legal tradition that gave the church control over all matters having to do with the dead. He cited Edward Coke, the famous British jurisprude, as saying, 'the burial of the cadaver, that is, *caro data vermibus* [flesh given to worms] is *nullius in bonis* [belonging to no person] and belongs to ecclesiastical cognizance'.[17] Ruggles especially opposed Coke's notion that the dead body is nothing but 'worm food', arguing that the dead person, in

17 Samuel B. Ruggles, *An Examination of the Law of Burial in a Report to the Supreme Court of New-York by Samuel B. Ruggles, Referee in the Matter of Taking a Portion of the Cemetery of the Brick Presbyterian Church, in Widening Beekman-street in the City of New-York* (New York: F. Fanshaw Printer, 1856), 42. I engage with this report and the *Beekman* case more fully in James Martel, "Interrupted by Death: The Legal Personhood and Non-personhood of Corpses," in *Interrupting the Legal Person*, Studies in Law, Politics and Society, Vol. 878, ed. Austin Sarat, George Pavlich, and Richard Mailey (Bingley, UK: Emerald Publishing, 2022). I am particularly grateful to Austin Sarat, George Pavlich, and Rebecca Johnson for organising the conference that preceded the publication.

effect, still possesses certain rights, anticipating but resisting Justice Brenner's 1972 claim that the dead no longer had 'the right to have rights'. Ruggles argued that:

> The right to the individuality of a grave, if it exists at all, evidently must continue so long as the remains of the occupant can be identified– and the means of identifying can only be secured and preserved by separate burial.[18]

More generally, for Ruggles, the buried corpse deserved a certain modicum of respect and even a sense of sacredness. The corpse emerges here, much as in *Furman*, as a quasi-person – an idea explicitly evoked in the later *Pierce* case, which is considered below. This issue of less than full personhood is also in keeping with the status of slaves, a legal issue that was very much in the air (to put it mildly) at the time of *Beekman*, here combining what Orlando Patterson called 'social death' with actual death.[19]

The *Beekman* decision as a whole does not truly resolve the issue of the personhood of the dead because, in effect, taking back the power to control the corpse from the church (much of the Ruggles report is concerned with asserting the law's power over that of the church and, more generally, asserting US law over British tradition) gives the power to the heirs of the dead. This leaves the question of the dead bodies' own self-ownership – a hallmark of legal personhood more generally – highly ambivalent.[20]

In Beekman, the dignity and personhood of the corpse were used to undermine the sense that any one group dominated and controlled the corpse, but at the same time, the corpse was never fully given to itself. In this way, the corpse confounds as much as it delimits the power of law in keeping with its complicated status as having an authority of its own (which, as the Ruggles report pointed out, diminishes over time as the corpse effectively dematerialises).

Another important case, *Pierce v. Proprietors of Swan Point Cemetery* (1872), concerned a dispute between the widow and daughter of a deceased man over whether the widow could disinter and rebury her deceased husband elsewhere against the daughter's wishes. The Rhode Island Supreme Court ruled in favour of the daughter. Whereas the *Beekman* case was decided around seven years before the American Civil War, *Pierce* was decided roughly seven years after, with the question of 'owning' bodies of the living decisively settled in favour of the newly minted Thirteenth Amendment. Yet an exception was still made for prisoners, who could indeed be effectively enslaved – the legal foundation of the US modern-day prison labour system, which is full of Brown and Black bodies. Who 'owned' the corpse, however, remained a contentious and unresolved question at the heart of *Pierce*.

The language of the *Pierce* decision reflects this deep ambivalence. The opinion in *Pierce* first acknowledges that the dead body is a '*quasi*-property', a term that perfectly encapsulates the not-quite-a-subject and not-quite-an-object nature of the dead body generally seen in the law.[21] The decision also stated:

18 *In re Widening of Beekman Street*, 4 Bradf (N.Y.) 503, in *The American Ruling Cases as Determined by the Courts; Including the Fundamental Cases of England and Canada; also All Reviewing and Illustrating Cases of Material Value from the Latest Official Report, Completely Annotated*, Volume II (Chicago: National Law Book Co.), 1122.

19 Orlando Patterson, *Slavery and Social Death: A Comparative Study* (Cambridge, MA: Harvard University Press, 1982), 38.

20 *Beekman*, 1121–2.

21 *William G. Pierce and Wife v. Proprietors of Swan Point Cemetery and Almira T. Metcalf*, 10 R. I. 227 (Rhode Island Supreme Court, March Term 1872), in *The American Ruling Cases as*

Although, as we have said, the body is not property in the usually recognized sense of the word, we may consider it as a sort of *quasi*-property, to which certain persons may have rights, as they have duties to perform arising out of our common humanity. But the person having charge of it cannot be considered as the owner of it in any sense whatever. He holds it only as a sacred trust for the benefit of all who may, from family or friendship, have an interest in it.[22]

The decision went on to directly address the question of 'the right to have rights', holding that:

Strictly speaking, according to the strict rules of the old common law, a dead man cannot be said to have rights. Yet it is common so to speak and the very fact of the common use of such language, and of its being used in such cases as we have quoted, justifies us in speaking of it as a right in a certain qualified sense and a right which ought to be protected.[23]

These textual hesitations ('*quasi*', 'strictly speaking … yet') are indications of an uncertain status for the dead – one that cannot and will not be resolved exactly because the dead are different but not *that* different from the living. The dead remain part of the human community (at least for a time) and so are related to 'the living', often in ways that are unexpectedly intimate. Especially in US law, something in the dead body – although it is never specified exactly what – resists Coke's notion of *caro data vermibus*. There is some remnant of the living person in the dead and some anticipation of the dead in the living person. Further, even Coke's formulation speaks to the material nature of bodies, and it is precisely their materiality that is reflected in the idea that, over time, the corpse becomes increasingly less personlike and more of a natural object, going from a '*quasi*-object' to an object full stop.

Conclusion: Another law of the dead?

By way of conclusion, I would like to consider what the law could be like if it had a different relationship to death and the dead; that is to say, a form of law that did not see the dead as either being the proof of its own existence and power or a way to slip out of its grasp. As Benjamin stated in his *Origin of the German Trauerspiel*:

And if it is in death that the spirit becomes free, in the manner of spirits, it is not until then that the body too comes properly into its own. For this much is self-evident: the allegorization of the physis can only be carried through in all its vigour in respect of the corpse. And the characters of the Trauerspiel [the German baroque plays that are the study of Benjamin's book] die, because it is only thus, as corpses, that they can enter into the homeland of allegory. It is not for the sake of immortality that they meet their end, but for the sake of the corpse.[24]

Determined by the Courts; Including the Fundamental Cases of England and Canada; also All Reviewing and Illustrating Cases of Material Value from the Latest Official Report, Completely Annotated, Volume II (Chicago: National Law Book Co.), 1125.
22 *Pierce*, 1127.
23 *Pierce*, 1126.
24 Walter Benjamin, *Origin of German Tragic Drama* (New York: Verso, 1998), 217–8.

Here, Benjamin tells us that the body really 'comes ... into its own' only through the process of dying. In dying, the body returns to its own (rotting) materiality and becomes, in a sense, immune to the kinds of phantasms and projections that are the stuff of mythic violence. The 'authority' of the dead that Benjamin spoke of can be said to result from this immunity. In saying that 'It is only ... as corpses [that bodies] can enter into the homeland of allegory', Benjamin alluded to the way that dead bodies, like allegories, work to resist and subvert the projections of mythic violence, allowing the body, at last, a form of rest. And this subversion works not just for the corpse itself but for anyone – that is, any person who is alive – to place themselves in the path of the dead body and in that way benefit from a similar anti-projective power.

Once again, we see more evidence for why Benjamin's concept of 'the living' necessarily includes the dead. The living (taken in an ordinary sense) need the dead to help keep them from being totalised by mythic projection. In a way, the dead are agents of divine violence (not directly of course, since the dead are not themselves godlike) and help to constitute and produce that community that Benjamin called the living.

If the dead do possess this anti-projective power, we see that rather than being the acme of passivity (a depiction that we see to some extent in the legal considerations of the corpse), they are indeed agents and, we could say further, subjects. If so, in thinking further of the dead as both agents and subjects, what effect would this other way of thinking about the dead tell us about the practice of law?

I do not believe that Benjamin was against all law per se, only mythic law, so what we are really talking about here could be considered a law for the living – that is, a law that includes the dead and those who are alive in a community that engages in nonviolence. When Benjamin talked about nonviolence in 'Toward the Critique of Violence', he did not necessarily mean this in a literal sense insofar as there are times when Benjamin clearly does see a need for violence. But when we recall that the German word 'Gewalt' used by Benjamin, which is translated into English as 'violence', does not just mean physical violence but also something like force or projection, we can see that by nonviolence he was referring to practices that are not redolent of mythic violence. At one point in his essay, he asked, 'Is any nonviolent resolution of conflicts possible?' and he definitively answered: 'Without a doubt.'[25]

A nonviolent law – that is, a law for the living – would not share the insecurity of a law that comes from mythic violence. The reality of a nonviolent law would not be in question because it would be based on collective judgments and decisions rather than mythic projections. Further, it would be anchored in materiality – that is, in the actual bodies that the living and the dead share (a realisation that the living would be aided by the dead in achieving).

Without this existential anxiety, the law would lose its requirement to be violent. It could reflect the kinds of activities that the law (even mythic law) claims to follow – restitution, recuperation, maybe even something like justice. Mythic law is never for the subjects of the law (i.e., for mere life) but only for itself. A law for the living would be entirely and only about the living; it would truly be a law for the people, of the people and by the people (in name *and* practice). Although this may seem utopian, I argue that, in fact, we are always practising this form of law, even as we submit to the vagaries and lies of mythic forms of law. The law of the living, which I would connect explicitly to anarchist forms of law, is, in fact, the edifice holding up the false and violent mythic

25 Benjamin, "Critique of Violence," 50.

forms of law in the first place. If we can take back our own legal practices, then we do not need to reinvent the law (or the world) but simply recognise the law of the living for what it is and let mythic law disappear back into the nothingness that it always was.

Bibliography

The American Ruling Cases as Determined by the Courts; Including the Fundamental Cases of England and Canada; also All Reviewing and Illustrating Cases of Material Value from the Latest Official Report, Completely Annotated. Vol. II. Chicago: National Law Book Co., 1912.

Benjamin, Walter. "Toward the Critique of Violence." In *Toward the Critique of Violence: A Critical Edition*, edited by Peter Fenves and Julia Ng, 39–61. Stanford University Press, 2021.

Benjamin, Walter. "The Storyteller: Observations on the Works of Nikolai Leskov." In *Walter Benjamin: Selected Writings, vol. 3, 1935–1938*, edited by Howard Eiland and Michael W.Jennings, 143–166. Cambridge, MA: Belknap Press of Harvard University Press, 2006.

Benjamin, Walter. "On the Concept of History." In *Walter Benjamin: Selected Writings, vol. 4, 1938–1940*, edited by Howard Eiland and Michael W.Jennings, 389–400. Cambridge, MA: Belknap Press of Harvard University Press, 2003.

Benjamin, Walter. *Origin of German Tragic Drama*. New York: Verso, 1998.

Bessler, John. "What Ifs and Missed Opportunities: The U.S. Supreme Court, Death Sentences and Executions, and the 50th Anniversary of *Furman v. Georgia*." In *Furman at Fifty*, edited by Austin Sarat (forthcoming).

Foucault, Michel. *Society Must Be Defended: Lectures at the Collège de France, 1975–1976*. New York: Picador, 2003.

Foucault, Michel. *Discipline and Punish*. New York: Vintage Books, 1979.

Harrison, Robert Pogue. *The Dominion of the Dead*. Chicago, IL: University of Chicago Press, 2003.

Laqueur, Thomas W. *The Work of the Dead*. Princeton, NJ: Princeton University Press, 2015.

Martel, James. "Interrupted by Death: The Legal Personhood and Non-personhood of Corpses." In *Interrupting the Legal Person* (Studies in Law, Politics and Society, Vol. 878), edited by Austin Sarat, George Pavlich, and Richard Mailey, 103–118. Bingley, UK: Emerald Publishing, 2022.

Martel, James. *Unburied Bodies: Subversive Corpses and the Authority of the Dead*. Amherst, MA: Amherst College Press, 2018.

Patterson, Orlando. *Slavery and Social Death: A Comparative Study*. Cambridge, MA: Harvard University Press, 1982.

Ruggles, Samuel B. *An Examination of the Law of Burial in a Report to the Supreme Court of New-York by Samuel B. Ruggles, Referee in the Matter of Taking a Portion of the Cemetery of the Brick Presbyterian Church, in Widening Beekman-street in the City of New-York*. New York: F. Fanshaw Printer, 1856.

5

DEATHS IN THE MUD

Law and Grievable Lives in Minas Gerais

Maria Fernanda Salcedo Repolês and Edward Kirton-Darling

Introduction

Two hundred and seventy-two people died in the mud that poured out when the Vale dam near Brumadinho broke on 25 January 2019. The released tailings flooded down the valley containing the Paraopeba River, destroying buildings and filling the channel and surrounding lowlands with toxic waste. The families of those who died do not call this event a disaster; they call it a crime. Vale, the mining company responsible for the dam, operates all over Brazil's Minas Gerais, a large, mountainous inland state. The English translation of the state's name, 'General Mines', shows the importance of mining in the state dating back to colonial times. Dotted all over the state are tailings dams, holding vast quantities of the toxic byproducts left over from operations to extract valuable ores. In a separate incident on 5 November 2015, 19 people died when another tailing dam, the Fundão dam near Mariana, failed. Many in Minas Gerais fear that the hundreds who died at Brumadinho and Mariana will not be the last such deaths in Brazil. Their fears are wholly justified; at the time of writing, 63 dams across Brazil are categorised as dangerous by the National Mining Agency, including 41 in Minas Gerais. Three are assessed as level 3: 'imminent rupture or is occurring'.

In this chapter, we explore how the law bears responsibility for the catastrophe that befell the people of Minas Gerais and how legal and political narratives of disaster combined with economic imperatives fail to account for the deaths caused and generate future deaths. Our analysis draws on empirical work undertaken by the first author (Repolês) with communities affected by dam collapses. Academics from the Polos de Cidadania programme at the Universidade Federal de Minas Gerais have worked – and continue to work – with bereaved families, local indigenous communities, and others affected by the dam failure in Brumadinho and other disasters in the state, to seek justice and accountability for the deaths.

In such situations, we argue that law can operate as part of a system of necropolitics and necroeconomics, and an essential part of this is to seek to frame lives as ungrievable.[1] However, we also trace the use of legal mechanisms to resist this. Based on the theories

---

1 Judith Butler, *Frames of War: When Is Life Grievable?* (London: Verso, 2010).

DOI: 10.4324/9781003304593-6

of Judith Butler and Achille Mbembe, our discussion will include the intersections of deaths, law, necropolitics, necroeconomy, and the disposability of life. This chapter comprises three sections. The first section ('The company's emergency support') analyses how Vale, as a market player, reacted to the deaths and imposed financial compensation as the sole form of liability. We argue that this is a way of avoiding responsibility, as the company has complete control over the money and dominates its language, so paying in cash does not necessarily mean taking responsibility for what happened. On the other hand, the affected families and communities demand different forms of compensation that are more sensitive to the need to mourn and recognise the value of human lives lost in such a violent way. We discuss the intersection between those experiences and how the law distributes risk and reward, making past and future deaths good for business. In the second section ('The judicial compensation system'), we examine the judicial system's response and question whether it has delivered justice or repeated the necropolitical and necroeconomic cycles, reinforcing a framing of lives as incapable of being grieved. In the final section ('Families and communities'), we explore the role of the law in making justice for the deaths at Brumadinho and the timid advances of the judicial system in this regard, with a particular focus on examining the importance of the legal relationships between dead bodies (and parts of bodies), public authorities, bereaved families, and the possibility of resistance.

It is helpful to start with an illustrative moment. On 14 February 2019, less than one month after the Vale dam near Brumadinho had collapsed, an investigative hearing opened with the commission's president requesting one minute of silence for the deceased. Everyone in attendance stood up except for Vale's president, Fabio Schvartsman, who remained seated, looking at the floor.[2] At that same hearing, when giving testimony, Schvartsman stated that Vale was 'a Brazilian gem, which we cannot condemn for an accident that happened at its dam, no matter how great the tragedy'.[3] Schvartsman's attitude and comments caused general outrage among those present and motivated the families of the deceased to designate each of the 272 dead as 'the real gems'. Since then, they always refer to the dead as 'our gems'.

A central theme of the bereaved families' argument is that 'accident' should not be used to describe the dam collapse, nor is it a 'disaster' – it is a 'crime'. The struggle over nomenclature emphasises contrasting views on what it would be like to reach justice in a case like this, a justice that includes what is known and how knowledge produces value.

We suggest that the approach of Vale and Schvartsman understands death from dam collapse in Brumadinho and elsewhere as, at best, part of the price of doing business and something that should be avoided if possible. And where such death does occur, it is simply an unfortunate necessity in achieving the essential goal of economic growth. In contrast, as we have argued elsewhere,[4] drawing on Bauman,[5] death in such circumstances results from

---

2 Gabriel Ronan, "Presidente da Vale se senta durante um minuto de silêncio em homenagem às vítimas de Brumadinho," *Estado de Minas. Caderno Gerais*, 14 de fevereiro de 2019, www.em. com.br/app/noticia/gerais/2019/02/14/interna_gerais,1030694/presidente-vale-senta-um-minuto-de-silencio-homenagem-brumadinho.shtml

3 Ronan, "Presidente da Vale se senta durante um minuto de silêncio em homenagem às vítimas de Brumadinho," 2.

4 Maria Fernanda S. Repolês and Edward Kirton-Darling, "Disaster, Place and Epistemic Injustice," in *Sociolegal Studies of Epistemic Injustice in Spaces and Places*, ed. Ceri Davies, Mark Flear, and Dan Wincott (London: Palgrave Socio-Legal Studies, forthcoming 2024).

5 Zygmunt Bauman, *Wasted Lives: Modernity and its Outcasts* (Malden: Polity Blackwell, 2004).

choices made to prioritise continued resource extraction. These choices increase the vulnerability of those in 'sacrifice zones', meaning the resulting deaths are neither accidents nor inevitable tragedies but instead the result of deliberate human action. However, the explanatory frame of these deaths as resulting from accidental disasters and the implication about the lack of human control frames those who die as incapable of being grieved.[6] Such an explanation of their deaths acts to make their lives disposable and capable of being sacrificed.

It is not just the corporate approach that renders death from dam collapse incapable of being grieved; the law is also complicit. The failures by Vale in this context match the refusal by the structures of the legal system to hear the voices of the bereaved and indigenous communities affected by the ongoing disaster in Minas Gerais and illustrate the limitations of official understandings of what might constitute rectification and redress. Taken together, we suggest these acts of framing in the approach of these institutions and systems – of implicitly communicating an understanding of some deaths as less than others – amount to a denial of those affected and the use of power-knowledge to feed the necropolitical and necroeconomic cycles.

The strategies that act to discipline, normalise, and kill in this context are multi-faceted, complex, and interrelating. We set out some instances of the operation of these strategies in the following sections. However, we also discuss families' and communities' agency to resist and 're(exist)' and develop strategies to face the logic of death and claim life, memory, and dignity for their loved ones.

The company's emergency support: The language of necroeconomics

The first measure the Federal Public Prosecutor's Office took through a Term of Adjustment of Conduct signed with Vale a few days after the dam collapse was the payment of emergency aid. As Brumadinho is a small town, many people had relationships with the disappeared and survivors. In this sense, one could speak of an entire city in mourning. The city stopped. All regular activities were interrupted by the intense movement focused on the search for the missing.

This ostensibly exceptional emergency extended for over two and a half years, with Vale paying aid until October 2021. The payment provoked a discussion about definition – about who could claim to be affected by the collapse – with Vale agreeing to pay emergency aid to all people who could prove residency in the municipality or within one kilometre of the Paraopeba River. This decision highlighted an important characteristic of Brumadinho: the dispersed nature of the municipality, encompassing 40,000 inhabitants over almost 640 square kilometres (247 square miles). Therefore, people far from the disaster and its effects received aid. With an average monthly salary of 2.5 of the minimum wage and 33.5 per cent of its population surviving on 0.5 of the minimum wage,[7] the area was flooded with money overnight.

This situation caused divisions because some of the inhabitants directly affected by the loss of their families, homes, or livelihoods continue to mourn; as one interviewee described, 'My life stopped on 25 January 2019.'[8] On the other hand, the population that was not directly affected but saw their income increase due to aid entered a state of

---

6 Judith Butler, *Precarious Life: The Powers of Mourning and Violence* (London: Verso, 2009).

7 IBGE – Instituto Brasileiro de Geografia e Estatística, 2022 (accessed 23 August 2023), https://cidades.ibge.gov.br/brasil/mg/brumadinho/panorama.

8 Polos de Cidadania, Faculdade de Direito da Universidade Federal de Minas Gerais, *Entrevista I.* [January 2022]. Interviewer: Maria Fernanda Salcedo Repolês. Brumadinho, 2022. 1 arquivo transcrição de 18p, 2.

euphoria. A good portion of the money was directed towards weekend parties and bar-becues and exchanging consumer goods, primarily cars and motorcycles, which were proudly displayed around the municipality.[9]

Interviews with relatives of the dead found that the aid money created a climate of illusory prosperity. When reflecting on the situation, one interviewee stated, 'Today, people have a party, but they don't realise that this money will run out. And after it runs out, what will happen? How will these people manage?'[10] She also noted that this artifi-cially provoked prosperity by the injection of aid money does not translate into formal jobs, increased job opportunities, or greater industrialisation or expansion of economic sectors. Thus, it is not true prosperity but an illusion of prosperity. Perhaps more sig-nificantly, the prosperity is disconnected from the cause of the payment. Aid was paid to all people residing in the municipality, not just those who had suffered direct losses, and was thus separated from the loss the dam collapse caused. This caused a sense of dis-respect towards the bereaved,[11] and division within the community in Brumadinho. Far from providing emergency aid, it was money that acted to exacerbate loss and grief, but which could be pointed to by Vale as an act of corporate generosity.

Similarly, the fieldwork by Polos de Cidadania in the Naô Xohã indigenous village in São Joaquim de Bicas, a municipality adjacent to Brumadinho, found another example of this division. The village was not on top of the mud-flooded land, but the breach damaged all access routes to the village. Further, the indigenous people's subsistence economic activities include agriculture and fishing on the Paraopeba River; thus, their entire existence was upended by the impossibility of safely using the river's water after the dam rupture. In addition to this economic issue, the destruction of the river changed their habits, culture, and ways of life.

In response, Vale proposed to pay emergency aid to those affected. A key problem was that Vale chose to do so by relying on the decisions of an anthropologist hired by the company. This individual singlehandedly decided who would receive aid, without any intervention from public bodies and in total disregard of the governmental anthro-pological reports which recognised the rights of the Pataxó Hã Hã Hãe ethnic group in this village.[12]

In Polos de Cidadania fieldwork interviews, people from the village recalled the effects on the community's most prominent religious festival, held in October each year. The 2020 festival took place in a climate divided between families receiving emergency aid and those under analysis by the Vale-hired anthropologist. On the day of the festival, children got into fights, and some refused to participate because some families had used the aid money to buy new clothes for their children while others wanted their children to wear old clothes. As a result, what was supposed to be a celebration of kinship central to the community's daily life turned into an event of great sadness and disunity.[13]

Other interviewees went deeper into the dam rupture's effects on the ways of life of indigenous communities around the river. Further, in these communities' cosmovision, the river is a living being that belongs to the kinship between human beings, non-human natural beings, and non-human supernatural beings. This kinship is part of everyday

9 Polos de Cidadania, "Entrevista I. January 2022," 2.
10 Polos de Cidadania, "Entrevista I. January 2022," 3.
11 Polos de Cidadania, "Entrevista I. January 2022," 3.
12 Polos de Cidadania, Faculdade de Direito da Universidade Federal de Minas Gerais, "Relatório de Atendimento Aldeia Naô Xohã, São Joaquim de Bicas, MG, Entrevistados 1 and 2," 8p, 2021, 1.
13 Polos de Cidadania, "Relatório de Atendimento Aldeia Naô Xohã, Entrevistados 1 and 2," 5.

religious practices in the community. Thus, for the members of these communities, the death of the river is the death of a relative.[14] As Butler reflected, life capable or incapable of being grieved refers to human and non-human beings, for the definition of life itself refers not to some kind of 'right to live', which she criticised as 'an omnipotent fantasy of anthropocentrism',[15] but to the conditions that make lives valuable. In her words:

> The question is not whether a given being is living or not, nor whether the being in question has the status of a 'person'; it is, rather, whether the social conditions of persistence and flourishing are or are not possible.[16]

These few examples of the vast range of experiences of those in communities affected by the dam collapse and broader mining-induced crisis illustrate how Vale's approach has caused division, undermining or ignoring local experience and ways of life. These cases may seem circumstantial as to the ways in which the systems we analyse act as we suggest. However, we propose that they should be otherwise interpreted as the result of lives framed as incapable of being grieved.

The case in point is better comprehended if the framing of these lives is put into a political and economic context to make visible the approach that frames them as unliveable. That is why we turn to Achille Mbembe's definition of necropolitics[17] and the correlated concept of necroeconomics.[18] Necropolitics goes beyond the power to kill; it is about the social and political power to expose the other to death, whether civil, physical, or social. It is a power that subjugates lives to the power of death and makes some bodies available, in limbo between life and death. Drawing on Mbembe's work, Darian-Smith, Haskaj, Lopez, Gillespie, and others have developed the concept of necroeconomics, which refers to death as an essential activity to produce value. The framing we explore in this chapter produces the conditions that make this business possible.

The uses of death by economy and politics in extraction activities such as mining place tailing dam disasters as the business itself – a strategy for expanding and maximising profits. Thus, necroeconomics refers to a model of economic production that sets practices in which companies conduct their business and obtain profit and gains from deaths, making deaths part of their economic growth cycle, perpetuating violence.

An in-depth economic study in a case report produced by Polos de Cidadania[19] pointed out some necroeconomic signs in the Vale dam rupture in Brumadinho. That case report

---

14 Saberes Tradicionais UFMG; Direitos Humanos UFMG, "Curso de Direito à Existência Aula 5," YouTube, 14 de julho de 2021, 2:32:14, www.youtube.com/watch?v=4X6xDPtN_vc, 1:34–1:37:56.
15 Butler, *Frames of War*, 18.
16 Butler, *Frames of War*, 20.
17 Achilles Mbembe, "Necropolitics" (trans. Libby Meintjes), *Public Culture* 15, No. 1 (2003): 11–40.
18 Eve Darian-Smith, "Dying for the Economy: Disposable People and Economies of Death in the Global North," *State Crime Journal* 10, no. 1 (2021): 61–79; Fatmir Haskaj, "Biopower to Necroeconomies: Neoliberalism, Biopower and Death Economies," *Philosophy & Social Criticism* 44, no. 10 (2018): 1148–68; Patrícia Lopez and Kathryn Gillespie, *Economies of Death: Economic Logics of Killable Life and Grievable Death* (London: Routledge, 2015).
19 The research report cited hereafter is the original Portuguese version produced by Polos de Cidadania: André Luiz Freitas Dias and Maria Fernanda Salcedo Repolês, *Dano-morte,Necroeconomia e Dano Existencial no rompimento da barragem da Vale S.A. em Brumadinho, MG*. Belo Horizonte, MG: Marginália Comunicação, 2021. A shorter, English-language version is available at https://polos.direito.ufmg.br/wp-content/uploads/2021/07/ENTENDA-A-NOTA-TE%CC%81CNICA-DO-POLOS-UFMG-PT-ES-EN.pdf (page 17 onwards).

showed that Vale experienced no share price losses in response to the dam failures in Mariana and Brumadinho; any decrease in share value was episodic and short term. In fact, the closure of the mines produced an iron ore shortage that resulted in a significant increase in iron ore prices in the international market. Vale also used expedients to recover its losses, including increasing the volume of papers in the stock market and pressuring the Brazilian government to allow Vale to reopen its business in the Brucutu and Itabira mines and in ports. Specialised international pro-Vale press coverage contributed to maintaining investment flows even after Vale's labour, civil, administrative, and environmental liabilities were verified.[20]

The case report highlighted that the real/dollar exchange rate variation in recent years allowed Vale to reduce costs in Brazil – both production costs in general and those related to indemnities paid for the dam failure in Brumadinho. Profits, however, are measured in US dollars. Therefore, for example, while Vale officially declares that it has paid US$1 billion (R$6 billion) in indemnities, the company reported gains of more than US$5 billion (R$30 billion) in the first quarter of 2021.[21]

All the elements presented here allow for some reflection. While Vale increased its profits after two major breaches of law resulting in mass death, the affected populations, communities, and families suffered worsened conditions and repeated rights violations. The payment of indemnities did not guarantee the complete assessment of their rights for two reasons: (1) the financial value of the indemnities was disproportionately low compared to international standards and when considering the size of the company and magnitude of the harm; and (2) the money paid cannot indemnify damages related to the loss and value of lives. Recognising that lost lives are grievable requires forms of compensation beyond money. The value of life, human and non-human, lost in the dam rupture requires recognisability,[22] that is, the condition to be recognised, since 'recognizability precedes recognition'.[23]

Limiting compensation to a monetary value is convenient for Vale, given that the company's focus is producing profit and so money is the language it speaks. The use of schedules of damages is an essential feature of this.[24] The schedules of damages developed following the dam collapse in Mariana set out the costs incurred following future 'disasters', providing certainty for corporate management. Importantly, these schedules are future oriented and thus not isolated decisions applicable only to this case. Their

20 Dias and Repolês, *Dano-morte, Necroeconomia e Dano Existencial no rompimento da barragem da Vale S.A. em Brumadinho, MG*, 36–44.
21 Dias and Repolês, *Dano-morte, Necroeconomia e Dano Existencial no rompimento da barragem da Vale S.A. em Brumadinho, MG*, 61.
22 Butler, *Frames of War*, 5.
23 Butler, *Frames of War*, 18.
24 There are three schedules of damages for the dam rupture in Mariana. Fundação Getúlio Vargas (FGV) and the Public Prosecutor's Office prepared one each that were never fully applied. A private law firm developed another named Novel, which was applied to specific groups, and ratified by the judge of the case. In Brumadinho, Aedas, a technical consultancy firm designated by the judge, developed an emergency schedule of damages. In the civil lawsuit, there is a promise of the development of a final schedule of damages (not yet completed at the time of writing this chapter). Polos de Cidadania's case report studied a document that Vale presented in the labour lawsuit – a study Vale made after the Fundão dam failure near Mariana that estimated indemnities for lives lost as US$1 million per person. Polos de Cidadania's case report contrasted this with amounts paid in similar cases worldwide, showing the average is US$2.5 million per person. A complete analysis of this issue can be found in Dias and Repolês, *Dano-morte, Necroeconomia e Dano Existencial no rompimento da barragem da Vale S.A. em Brumadinho, MG*, 47–58.

application involves the mining company and insurers calculating risk based on the outputs of this exemplary case. Moreover, the case shows that deaths caused by dam operational failures can be treated as externalities in business since they do not affect profits – in fact, they can turn into profits if well managed. Essentially, this means it is cheaper to continue with the current business model and 'compensate' for instances where deaths occur. The effect is that companies can plan ways to optimise profits and offset losses to such an extent that a major disaster and loss of life caused by the company becomes a source of profit maximisation in a necroeconomic cycle.

The pricing of the cost of death and the provision of emergency support reinforces the necroeconomic cycle. It is a strategy that sees death as part of business. To continue that business, it generates internal divisions, de-characterises ways of life, prevents collective mourning (even individual family mourning), and minimises and devalues the community bases that sustain social groups. However, we contend that it is not just Vale's approach that has produced death across these communities but also failures by the legal system. We turn to explore this in the next section.

The judicial compensation system: Between justice and necropolitics

The first public institutions to arrive at the dam rupture site were the fire department, forensic services, and the police. Public universities, especially the Federal University of Minas Gerais; the federal, labour, and state prosecutor's offices; and the Office of the State Public Defender followed shortly after. The federal and state legislative bodies each opened a parliamentary commission of inquiry to investigate the dam rupture, resulting in two reports.

The state report concluded that Vale, part of Vale's agents and directors, and the TÜV SÜD engineers were liable for environmental, administrative, civil, and criminal damages.[25] It listed several remedial measures and recommendations for public bodies, including the justice system. It also suggested a governance model for organising the remediation process. It ended by establishing measures for the legislative power to improve the relevant legislation.[26] The federal report, from the Federal Chamber of Deputies, similarly concluded that Vale, part of Vale's agents and directors, and the TÜV SÜD engineers were liable for environmental, administrative, civil, and criminal damages.[27]

Both reports concluded there was a connection between the previous dam failure in Mariana and the dam rupture in Brumadinho, and both pointed to an underlying systemic issue related to the current mining exploration model. Both reports concluded that both ruptures were avoidable and that accountability is a fundamental step in rethinking the mining exploration model.[28] All the steps taken after the legislative reports show that public institutions had to respond forcefully to the Brumadinho dam rupture and surrounding issues. As the parliamentary reports stated, this was a highly complex conflict requiring a plural, inter-institutional, and multifaceted governance; an unprecedented case

---

25 Assembleia Legislativa do Estado de Minas Gerais, *Opção pelo risco: causas e consequências da tragédia de Brumadinho: a CPI da ALMG*. (André Quintão (org.) (Belo Horizonte: Scriptum, 2021), 77.

26 ALMG, *Opção pelo risco*, 263, 274.

27 Câmara dos Deputados, *Rompimento da Barragem de Brumadinho CPI da Câmara dos Deputados. Relatório Final* (Brasília: Editora da Câmara dos Deputados, 2019), 227, 226.

28 ALMG, *Opção pelo risco*, 254–5; Câmara dos Deputados, *Rompimento da Barragem de Brumadinho*, 227, 289.

from the point of view of human losses but with an equally tragic antecedent for social, environmental, and dam safety aspects.

After the legislative organs called on the judiciary, the first pronouncement came from the Regional Labour Court on 15 June 2019, approving the agreement between the Public Labour Prosecutor's Office and Vale, which referred to collective and labour insurance damages without prejudice to individual claims. This agreement only covered surviving workers and families of deceased workers with a direct employment relationship with Vale.

On 4 February 2021, the Minas Gerais State Court of Justice (TJMG) established a judicial reparation agreement with Vale and the Minas Gerais state government, with the participation of the State Public Prosecutor's Office and the State Public Defender's Office. The scope is 'the reparation for damages caused by the rupture of dams',[29] as stated on the Minas Gerais state government's official website.

The first problem with the judicial reparation or civil agreement is how it presents itself to the general public through that broad statement. Unlike the labour agreement (made on 15 June 2019), which explicitly stated other potential damages are excluded, the civil agreement does not clearly state whether it provides for other forms of reparation for individuals or groups. Whenever Vale is called upon to take a stand in court, out of court, or publicly, the company states that the civil agreement settles all its debts on the issue. The State of Minas Gerais follows this understanding. In contrast, the people affected, prosecutors, and public lawyers understand that the civil agreement/settlement excludes other individual and group damages and so must be interpreted in the same way as the labour agreement. These disputes fill the Brazilian judiciary with lawsuits. The last survey, conducted in January 2022, by the National Council of Justice, found nearly 5,000 legal actions related to the rupture in federal, state, and labour courts.[30]

Another issue is the use of the term 'mediation' to define the negotiation between the Minas Gerais state government and Vale that led to the civil agreement. Several technical requirements of mediation were absent in this negotiation, and examining the procedural irregularities and their implications enables exploration of how the judicial system can be seen to be part of the necropolitical cycle in this instance. An example is the TJMG regulation[31] requirement to separate judicial and mediation activities. This repeats the requirement in the Code of Civil Procedure.[32] It also requires that mediators take a preparatory course at the Judicial Centre for Conflict Resolution and Citizenship (CEJUSC)[33] and be included in an official register maintained by the office of the third vice-president.[34] Judges who have administrative duties at the CEJUSC must ratify the outcome of a mediation, which is why they cannot participate as mediators.[35]

---

29 This agreement is available at www.mg.gov.br/sites/default/files/paginas/imagens/probruma dinho/ata_acordo_vale_04-02-2021_1.pdf.

30 Conselho Nacional de Justiça, "Observatório Nacional sobre questões ambientais, econômicas e sociais de alta complexidade e grande impacto e repercussão." *Painel de acompanhamento de processos das ações de grande repercussão*, 2022, https://paineis.cnj.jus.br/QvAJAXZfc/opendoc. htm?document=qvw_1%2FPainelCNJ.qvw&host=QVS%40neodimio03&anonymous=true& sheet=shOBSPrincipal&select=LB513,Brumadinho.

31 Tribunal de Justiça do Estado de Minas Gerais (TJMG), *Resolucão n.873/2018*, www8.tjmg.jus. br/institucional/at/pdf/re08732018.PDF.

32 *Código de Processo Civil* [Code of Civil Procedure], Law No. 13.105/2015, www.planalto.gov.br/ ccivil_03/_ato2015-2018/2015/lei/l13105.htm, article 167.

33 TJMG, *Resolucão n.873/2018*, article 8, I.

34 TJMG, *Resolucão n.873/2018*, article 5, VI.

35 TJMG, *Resolucão n.873/2018*, article 8, VI.

The third vice-president of the TJMG holds the presidency of CEJUSC, and one of their administrative duties is to punish mediators when required. Punishments are determined by the third annex of Resolution 125 of the National Council of Justice, the code of ethics for judicial conciliators and mediators, which states:

> Art. 8. Failure to comply with the principles and rules set out in this Code, as well as a final conviction in criminal proceedings, will result in the exclusion of the conciliator/mediator from the respective register and in being barred from acting in this capacity in any other body of the national Judiciary.[36]

Since maintaining the register is one of the administrative duties of the office of the third vice-president, we can infer that this office cannot carry out mediations because it could not punish itself. Additionally, the second punishment cannot be applied to judges in Brazil without complying with the specific dismissal rules for the occupation. Barring judges from acting in the judiciary otherwise undermines the prerogatives of their office, which would be an attack on the judiciary as a power of the democratic rule of law.

Another obstacle lies in article 8: 'Any person who becomes aware of inappropriate behaviour on the part of the conciliator/mediator may make a representation to the Coordinating Judge so that the appropriate measures can be adopted.'[37] In other words, complaints of inappropriate behaviour on the part of a mediator would have to be submitted to the third vice-president. This creates unreasonable situations such as the third vice-president knowing details of the mediation that she/he was a part of. Or the third vice-president being denounced for inappropriate behaviour and being the one who judges this behaviour. In practical terms, the participation of judges in CEJUSC's administrative staff and in court makes it impossible to judicialise a claim if the parties understand that mediation has failed. Article 8, II of the tribunal regulation states:

> II – the conciliator or mediator, the parties and their attorneys are subject to a confidentiality clause, which they will sign at the beginning of the work, and must maintain secrecy concerning what is said, shown or debated in the session, and that such occurrences will not be considered as evidence for purposes other than conciliation.[38]

This raises the problem of conducting the mediation process and then being part of the judging panel in the court case. Strictly speaking, a judge should not know what was discussed in the mediation, which is protected by confidentiality. If there is a risk that the mediating judge will also be the judge who will preside over the case, even on appeal, the principle of impartiality (for the case judge) and the principle of confidentiality (for the mediating judge) are violated. It would be a confusion of attributions that the law and regulations have made a point of separating. However, in the civil agreement regarding the Brumadinho dam rupture, the president and the third vice-president of the TJMG conducted the case without stating in the file that they complied with the legal

---

36 Conselho Nacional de Justiça, *Resolução n.125/2010* – Dispõe sobre a Política Judiciária Nacional de tratamento adequado dos conflitos de interesses no âmbito do Poder Judiciário e dá outras providências, 2010, https://atos.cnj.jus.br/files/compilado18553820210820611ffaaaa2655.pdf, article 8.

37 Conselho Nacional de Justiça, *Resolução n.125/2010*, article 8, § único.

38 TJMG, *Resolucão n.873/2018*, article 8, II.

requirements, and the president of the TJMG ratified the agreement. If those affected disagree with the civil agreement, who can they appeal to?

These procedural and conceptual flaws illustrate a process that fails to listen to the affected population effectively. This failure is the harmful consequence of the formal procedural errors contained in this process. The formal problems are compounded by the testimonies of those affected, whose participation the justice authorities denied at every turn. The mediation hearing process for the civil agreement prevented the affected individuals, families, their associations, and private lawyers from taking part on the grounds that the Public Prosecutor's Office and the Public Defender's Office would represent them. These institutions, in turn, refused to give information to those affected, claiming a duty of confidentiality. Thus, the affected people and families only learned of the terms of the agreement when the court released the information to the media. That does not mean they were passive in the face of the lack of participation. They went to court several times, arguing against their exclusion from the agreement negotiations. These actions resulted in the mobilisation of judicial institutions to hold public hearings and meetings, but never in direct participation in the negotiations or access to information on the terms being discussed. Two documents produced by a large segment of those affected by the Brumadinho dam rupture – the 'Pact of the Affected'[39] and 'Manifesto: Which Reparation Plan Do We Want?'[40] – summarised a large part of their complaints and demands. In Box 5.1 we highlight a few aspects of both documents and list the claims particularly relevant to our discussion in this chapter.

Box 5.1   List of selected claims

The right to full and effective participation.

Documents with language accessible to those affected.

Reparation actions reports should be made easily available to those affected.

Permanent communication channel for complaints and other urgent demands.

Awareness and prevention campaigns to promote and guarantee the continued revitalisation of the banks of the Paraopeba River.

Creation of new rules for companies.

A radical change in the mining model.

A guarantee that the crime will not be repeated.

Concern about Vale's advertising and publicity strategies.

The need to guarantee that the voices and stories of the affected communities are transmitted to the rest of society.

The need to honour the victims of the crime with global testimony of what happened and happens every day in Brumadinho.

Memory and truth.

Source: Compiled by the authors from 'Pacto dos Atingidos pelo Crime da Vale em Brumadinho' (2021) and 'Manifesto: Qual Plano de Reparação Queremos?' (2022).

---

39 "Pacto dos Atingidos pelo Crime da Vale em Brumadinho," 2021, www.ihu.unisinos.br/categorias/608460-a-justica-que-queremos-dos-para-e-com-os-atingidos-pelo-crime-da-vale-em-brumadinho.
40 Polos de Cidadania, Faculdade de Direito da Universidade Federal de Minas Gerais. *Entrevista I.* [January 2022]. Interviewer: Maria Fernanda Salcedo Repolês. Brumadinho. 1 arquivo.mp3 (60 min.) transcrição de 18p, 2022.

It is clear from the list in Box 4.1 that those affected believe financial accountability is not enough to achieve justice in this and similar cases. They demand other rights such as participation, environmental and social wellbeing, respect, memory, and truth. In other words, to use our theoretical references, they want lives that can be lived and mourned, and they also want to break with the necropolitical and necroeconomic cycles that sustain mining. From what we have described of the justice system's actions in relation to the Brumadinho dam rupture and subsequent proceedings, we can ask to what extent the justice system has come close to meeting these demands for justice or to what extent it has served the circulation of necropolitical and necroeconomic cycles. Who benefits from the formal, conceptual, and operational problems of the negotiation process that led to the civil agreement between Vale and the Minas Gerais state government?

In practice, the way the Court of Justice conducts negotiations and the conceptual and technical confusion in the agreement process described above meant that Vale has almost complete control over the negotiation and resulting agreement. The dam rupture's financialisation also extends to the perspective of reparations and compensation. Thus, the market and the state come together to set the cost of the disaster. This pricing reinforces the necropolitical and necroeconomic logic that accepts lives as killable and incapable of being grieved. According to this logic, the harms suffered by or inflicted on these communities are side effects of the mining activity risk that, at most, can be accountably incorporated as an internality but preferably remain an externality. In the next and final section, we discuss the justice system's response from the perspectives of the families and communities searching for justice.

Families and communities: Public grieving, outrage, and justice

In the previous sections, we discussed how the market and institutional responses to the dam rupture in Brumadinho could be interpreted as part of the cycles of necropolitics and necroeconomics. We also argued that these cycles are perceptible in how human and non-human lives are made disposable in the mining territories, making them killable. This section presents examples of how people, families, and communities resist dehumanisation and devaluation of their lives. We focus on the claims that take away the financial aspect of compensation and use the law to make lives grievable.

The first example is the institutional response to immaterial damages. The TJMG priced these damages and included them in the R$37 billion civil agreement, equivalent to about US$7.4 billion. These values are unprecedented for extrajudicial agreements in Brazil but trivial for the affected families and indigenous communities. Recurring speech patterns and phrases among the families of the deceased appeared in their interviews and conversation circles with the Polos de Cidadania field team. A recurrent and particularly noteworthy complaint was that they are still awaiting an apology and a simple message of acknowledgement that their family members died in the dam rupture.[41]

In a lawsuit filed in the Labour Court by family members of the deceased and the Metabase Union, which concerned 131[42] fatal victims who were direct employees of Vale,

41 Polos de Cidadania, Faculdade de Direito da Universidade Federal de Minas Gerais. *Entrevista I.* [January 2022]. Interviewer: Maria Fernanda Salcedo Repolês. Brumadinho. 1 arquivo.mp3 (60 min.) transcrição de 18p, 2022.

42 This lawsuit was filed on behalf of the direct employees of Vale. The Brumadinho rupture killed 131 Vale employees, 120 employees of companies that provided services to Vale, 19 tourists and residents of the adjacent district to the mine, and two unborn children carried by their mothers, Vale employees.

the plaintiffs discussed the *general damage for loss of life* – a modality of non-economic damages disregarded by the above-discussed agreements. This damage aims to compensate for the suffering of the victims on the verge of death. The obligation to pay for general damages for loss of life occurs when the person, still alive, experiences suffering caused by a wrongful act that generates death. It recognises a different situation from the general damage paid to family members for the pain of losing a relative. It is also different from the collective punitive damages covered by the agreement in the Labour Court, which is due to society for Vale's negligence regarding safety, life, and physical integrity in the workplace.[43]

In response, Vale's lawyers asked families to prove whether the person died due to the dam rupture or for another reason. According to them, it was plausible that one of the 131 people who died may have experienced a sudden fatal illness, stroke, or heart attack. That would mean that when the mud hit the person, they were already deceased, thereby exempting Vale from liability to pay the general damages for the loss of life. However, it is essential to note a detail: the mud took 34 seconds to reach the first fatal victims and one minute to reach the mine site cafeteria and Vale's administrative buildings, where most employees were during the dam rupture.[44] The cynicism of Vale's legal argument points precisely to what we want to clarify here: it is directly related to a necropolitical and necroeconomic project. To understand the gravity of this argument, one must read it in light of the families' complaint, recurring in interviews carried out by the Polos de Cidadania team, that Vale's management refuses to call or talk to them, recognising in the foreground that the deceased victims are dead because the dam broke and released tons of toxic mud on them.

One must also put Vale's argument into context in light of families' struggles to have the Forensic Institute register death certificates with the date and time of '25 January 2019, at 12:28 pm' and the cause of death as 'mud burial'.[45] This record, having potential and critical legal consequences, was not automatic because the search for deceased victims went on for months following the dam rupture. In fact, as of October 2023, over four years after the collapse, there are still three victims whose remains have not been found and who are listed as 'missing'. Forensic services explained that there is no evidence of the personalised and individual circumstances of the death of each of the deceased. Given that the tons of mud peeled off skin and crushed bone, the deceased individuals were identified by analysing over 1,000 DNA fragments. Families buried their loved ones in closed coffins containing only an identified fragment.[46]

The Association of Relatives of Victims and Affected by the Collapse of the Córrego do Feijão Dam (AVABRUM) gathers families and survivors of the tragedy. It actively participated in defining a memorial to the victims, built in Córrego do Feijão, the Brumadinho district where the dam was located. On the 25th of each month, AVABRUM organises cultural events, gathering results that can be added to the memorial's collection (Instagram: @avabrum). AVABRUM is currently fighting for an apology and the right to

43 Dias and Repolês, *Dano-morte, Necroeconomia e Dano Existencial no rompimento da barragem da Vale S.A. em Brumadinho, MG*, 4.
44 Dias and Repolês, *Dano-morte, Necroeconomia e Dano Existencial no rompimento da barragem da Vale S.A. em Brumadinho, MG*, 22.
45 Dias and Repolês, *Dano-morte, Necroeconomia e Dano Existencial no rompimento da barragem da Vale S.A. em Brumadinho, MG*, 22.
46 Daniela Arbex, *Arrastados: os bastidores do rompimento da barragem de Brumadinho, o maior desastre humanitário do Brasil* (São Paulo: Intrínseca, 2022).

memory. According to the affected families, acknowledging the general damages of the loss of life is, in this sense, a step towards preserving people's memory and the right to exist and to *re-exist*. [47] For them, Vale's argument that sought to reverse the burden of proof is equivalent to inflicting a second death, a moral death, as if the passage of mud could erase their stories.

To interpret these efforts, we can develop Butler's frames of war. In other words, we can understand the opposed attitudes, of Vale and the judiciary on the one hand and the demands of those affected on the other, as a war of places, of narratives, of who says what the law is, and, ultimately, of who lives and who dies.

The next step in Polos de Cidadania's research is to follow the implementation of the Brumadinho Memorial Museum. There have been recent important victories for the families. In July 2023, after two years of negotiation, AVABRUM concluded a deal with Vale, with the intermediation of the Public Prosecutor's Office, that defines the format of the administration of the Brumadinho Memorial Museum. The impasse in this negotiation was related to Vale's pressure to manage the museum directly rather than just supporting it financially. The AVABRUM families insisted that Vale would only finance the space, guaranteeing its economic sustainability. What was under discussion was the museum's curatorship and which narrative would be central – in other words, how the dam collapse would be framed. In one public speech on the subject, a former Vale employee, a survivor of the collapse who lost her sister, said, 'Vale is going to enter the museum, yes. Not as the beautiful company that honours the victims, but as the criminal that killed with impunity.'[48] In December 2021, when the building was ready, Vale announced its inauguration, against the families' wishes. AVABRUM stopped the inauguration through an extrajudicial representation to the Public Prosecutor's Office, in which the families prohibited Vale from using the names of their relatives or transporting the body fragments, which remain at the Forensic Medicine Institute, to the memorial, where they were to be deposited. In Butler's words, these were parts of bodies with 'invariably public dimensions'[49] and so subject to deep public contestation. Faced with this demonstration, Vale had no choice but to halt its inauguration plans and agree to the families' demands. Thus, the agreement signed in July 2023 covers all the demands and stipulates that Vale will finance the project while also prohibiting the company from any management or curatorial activities. A board of trustees, consisting of three victims' relatives and two independent members chosen by AVABRUM, will carry out these activities.

Going back to the months following the dam collapse, when identifying the deceased victims, the wakes took place in a community hall because Brumadinho did not have a wake hall large enough for hundreds of deceased. These became public events for an entire town in mourning. Vale controlled the wakes and determined the rules for them, and soon ordered that the wakes be limited to ten minutes per person, fearing collective indignation due to the proportion of these rituals.[50] This event is reminiscent of a passage in Butler's book:

> Open grieving is bound up with outrage, and outrage in the face of injustice or indeed of unbearable loss has enormous political potential. It is, after all, one of

47 Dias and Repolês, *Dano-morte, Necroeconomia e Dano Existencial no rompimento da barragem da Vale S.A. em Brumadinho, MG*, 23.
48 Polos de Cidadania, "Entrevista I. August 2023]. Interviewer: Maria Fernanda Salcedo Repolês. Brumadinho. 1 arquivo.mp3 (60 min.)," 2023.
49 Butler, *Precarious Life*, 26.
50 Arbex, *Arrastados*, 128.

the reasons Plato wanted to ban the poets from the Republic. He thought that if the citizens went too often to watch tragedy, they would weep over the losses they saw, and that such open and public mourning, in disrupting the order and hierarchy of the soul, would disrupt the order and hierarchy of political authority as well.[51]

That is an important lesson that one might learn from the struggle of bereaved families, the indigenous communities who lost their relative – the Paraopeba River – and all those affected by the Brumadinho dam collapse. Their struggle for justice, reparation, memory, and mourning is the ultimate expression of life and, therefore, not limited to these people and their personal tragedy. Their struggle relates to a wider struggle to reverse the necropolitical and necroeconomic cycles that insist on placing people around the world in this category of disposable bodies. That is certainly its enormous political potential.

Conclusion

This chapter analysed the legal responsibility for the dam collapse in Brumadinho through the lenses of the legal and political narratives of disaster combined with the economic imperatives that contribute to the generation of future deaths in Minas Gerais. Each section presented one stance on the problem.

First, we discussed the market's response to disasters, signalled by the reactions of Vale, the company liable for the dam collapse in Brumadinho. We presented various case elements to prove that the company is fuelling a cycle of necroeconomics; that is, it counts deaths as part of its business and profit generation. Part of this strategy is to render human and non-human lives in mining territories as non-lives, lives that become killable and not grievable.[52] In this sense, we should not only look at the deaths. Additionally, it is essential to understand the devaluation of life and the attacks on sociability, community, and environmental forms and ways of life; the necroeconomy uses strategies to separate, disunite, and turn one against the other. While people's living conditions deteriorate, Vale's profits grow and its responsibility decreases.

In the second section, we discussed how the judicial system responded to the deaths at Brumadinho and questioned if the judicial system has delivered justice or reinforced necropolitical and necroeconomic cycles. We contend that many of the judicial system's actions reinforced the logic of death. We signalled two main points to prove this. First, the judicial institutions' formal, conceptual, and operational problems and the financialisation of the indemnities both benefitted Vale, which 'speaks' the language of money fluently. Thus, Vale gained control over the negotiation processes. Second, the legal institutions are then trapped in a necropolitical cycle; agreements and lawsuits are used to devalue lives and silence victims.

Based on Butler, we analysed the 'market' and 'state' positions as frames of war. According to Butler:

[O]ne way of posing the question of who 'we' are in these times of war is by asking whose lives are considered valuable, whose lives are mourned, and whose lives are considered ungrievable. We might think of war as dividing populations

51 Butler, *Precarious Life*, 39.
52 Butler, *Precarious Life*; Butler, *Frames of War*; Mbembe, "Necropolitics."

into those who are grievable and those who are not. An ungrievable life is one that cannot be mourned because it has never lived, that is, it has never counted as a life at all. We can see the division of the globe into grievable and ungrievable lives from the perspective of those who wage war in order to defend the lives of certain communities, and to defend them against the lives of others – even if it means taking those latter lives.[53]

We frame the Brumadinho dam collapse case as a war of places, of narratives, of who says what the law is, and, ultimately, of who lives and who dies. Thus, in the third section, we discussed how the affected families and communities resist the system of necropolitics and necroeconomics in Minas Gerais and highlighted the political significance of public grieving and its ability to humanise and define 'liveable lives'.[54]

For those seeking to resist a necropolitical and the necroeconomic approach, the most significant difficulty is collectively creating egalitarian conditions for recognising life as worth living. Meeting this challenge requires ensuring the possibility of mourning the lost lives, whether human or non-human, and providing adequate living conditions for those who live and work in mining and tailings dam areas to be considered lives in the fullest sense, both in their individual dimension and in other complex collective, social, and political dimensions. In the face of the dominance of the systems that produce unjust death, it is a formidable contest for those who wish to find a different path.

In this context, against these cycles of death, the right to memory becomes fundamental. Moreover, the ability of the justice system to listen to these stories and define the killings as legally relevant, reimagining the parameters of justice, becomes an existential imperative. The deaths in the mud at Brumadinho, the deaths caused by refusing to listen to the bereaved and indigenous communities, and future deaths from continued extraction all illustrate how law and the legal system are complicit in the production of death and perhaps point to the possibility of making such deaths capable of being publicly grieved.

Bibliography

Assembleia Legislativa do Estado de Minas Gerais (ALMG). *Opção pelo risco: causas e consequências da tragédia de Brumadinho: a CPI da ALMG* [Opting for Risk: Causes and Consequences of the Brumadinho Tragedy: the ALMG CPI]. André Quintão (org.). Belo Horizonte: Scriptum, 2021.

Arbex, Daniela. *Arrastados: os bastidores do rompimento da barragem de Brumadinho, o major desastre humanitário do Brasil* [Dragged: Behind the Scenes of the Brumadinho Dam Collapse, Brazil's Biggest Humanitarian Disaster]. São Paulo: Intrínseca, 2022.

Bauman, Zygmunt. *Wasted Lives: Modernity and its Outcasts*. Malden: Polity Blackwell, 2004.

Butler, Judith. *Precarious Life: The Powers of Mourning and Violence*. London: Verso, 2009.

Butler, Judith. *Frames of War: When Is Life Grievable?* London: Verso, 2010.

Câmara dos Deputados. *Rompimento da Barragem de Brumadinho. CPI da Câmara dos Deputados. Relatório Final* [Brumadinho Dam Rupture. CPI of the Chamber of Deputies. Final Report]. Brasília: Editora da Câmara dos Deputados, 2019.

Conselho Nacional de Justiça. "Observatório Nacional sobre questões ambientais, econômicas e sociais de alta complexidade e grande impacto e repercussão." Painel de acompanhamento de processos das ações de grande repercussão [Process monitoring panel for high-profile actions]. 2022. https://paineis.cnj.jus.br/QvAJAXZfc/opendoc.htm?document=qvw_l%2FPainelCNJ.qvw&host=QVS%40neodimio03&anonymous=true&sheet=shOBSPrincipal&select=LB513,Brumadinho.

---

53 Butler, *Frames of War*, 38.
54 Butler, *Precarious Life*.

Darian-Smith, Eve. "Dying for the Economy: Disposable People and Economies of Death in the Global North." *State Crime Journal* 10, no. 1 (2021): 61–79.

Dias, André Luiz Freitas, and Maria Fernanda Salcedo Repolês. *Dano-morte, Necroeconomia e Dano Existencial no rompimento da barragem da Vale S.A. em Brumadinho, MG* [General Damages for the Loss of Life, Necroeconomy and Existential Damages in Vale's Dam Rupture in Brumadinho, Minas Gerais]. Belo Horizonte, MG: Marginália Comunicação, 2021. https://polos.direito.ufmg.br/wp-content/uploads/2021/07/Nota-Tecnica-Brumadinho.pdf.

Haskaj, Fatmir. "From Biopower to Necroeconomies: Neoliberalism, Biopower and Death Economies." *Philosophy & Social Criticism* 44, no. 10 (2018): 1148–1168. https://doi.org/10.1177/0191453718772596.

Instituto Brasileiro de Geografia e Estatística. "Population." Accessed 23 August 2023. https://cidades.ibge.gov.br/brasil/mg/brumadinho/panorama.

Lopez, Patricia, and Kathryn Gillespie. *Economies of Death: Economic Logics of Killable Life and Grievable Death*. London: Routledge, 2015.

"Manifesto: Qual Plano de Reparação Queremos?" December 2022. https://guaicuy.org.br/wp-content/uploads/2022/11/Carta_plano-de-reparacao_3.pdf.

Mbembe, Achilles. "Necropolitics," Translated by Libby Meintjes. *Public Culture* 15, no. 1 (2003): 11–40.

"Pacto dos Atingidos pelo Crime da Vale em Brumadinho." 2021. www.ihu.unisinos.br/categorias/608460-a-justica-que-queremos-dos-para-e-com-os-atingidos-pelo-crime-da-vale-em-brumadinho.

Polos de Cidadania, Faculdade de Direito da Universidade Federal de Minas Gerais. "Relatório de Atendimento Aldeia Naô Xohã, São Joaquim de Bicas, MG. Entrevistados 1 and 2" [Service Report Aldeia Naô Xohã, São Joaquim de Bicas, MG. Interviewees 1 and 2]. Transcript, 8 pages. 2021.

Polos de Cidadania, Faculdade de Direito da Universidade Federal de Minas Gerais. "Entrevista I. January 2022. Interviewer: Maria Fernanda Salcedo Repolês. Brumadinho." mp3 recording, 60 minutes. Transcript, 18 pages. 2022.

Polos de Cidadania, Faculdade de Direito da Universidade Federal de Minas Gerais. "Entrevista I. August 2023. Interviewer: Maria Fernanda Salcedo Repolês. Brumadinho." mp3 recording, 60 minutes. 2023.

Repolês, Maria Fernanda S., and Edward Kirton-Darling. "Disaster, Place and Epistemic Injustice." In *Sociolegal Studies of Epistemic Injustice in Spaces and Places*, ed. Ceri Davies, Mark Flear, and Dan Wincott. London: Palgrave Socio-Legal Studies, forthcoming 2024.

Ronan, Gabriel. "Presidente da Vale se senta durante um minuto de silêncio em homenagem às vítimas de Brumadinho" [President of Vale sits during a minute of silence in honour of the victims of Brumadinho]. *Estado de Minas. Caderno Gerais*, 14 February 2019. www.em.com.br/app/noticia/gerais/2019/02/14/interna_gerais,1030694/presidente-vale-senta-um-minuto-de-silencio-homenagem-brumadinho.shtml.

Saberes Tradicionais UFMG; Direitos Humanos UFMG. "Curso de Direito à Existência: Aula 5" [Right to Existence Course: Class 5]. YouTube Video, 2:32:14. Posted 14 July 2021. www.youtube.com/watch?v=4X6xDPtN_vc.

6

COLONIAL LAW AS NOMOCIDE

Maria Giannacopoulos

Introduction

Colonial law has an intrinsic relation to death. Usurpatory, dispossessing, and lacking consent at its foundation, settler-colonial 'law' is born from violence and works to reproduce and repetitively maintain colonial conditions in Australia. In this sense it has a death-producing function that is embedded and active within all aspects of the colonial legal infrastructure. If 'law' is the strongest form of violence, its imposition over other laws is necessarily deathly. This chapter reveals and names the non-consensual and so death-producing features of Australian law as *nomocide* and argues that there is too much at stake to deny the death-producing function of colonial law. This argument is made with reference to the ongoing fight to end Aboriginal deaths in custody within the colonial debtscape by revisiting the *Nulyarimma* challenge and Irene Watson's seminal essay "Buried Alive" more than two decades after it was written.

The 'Aboriginal industry' in the colonial debtscape

The multiple iterations of the Black Lives Matter movement in 2013, 2014, and 2020 have brought global attention to the racialised violence of state policing in the US and to the racist violence entrenched within and enacted by the state's institutions. It may not be well known to international audiences that across the seas from the US, in the settler colony of Australia, there has been an ongoing racialised crisis of colonial law with deathly impacts on Aboriginal lives and lands. And even within Australia, this crisis is still very far from being universally seen, let alone understood as stemming from the legal system itself. In 2000, as Australia showcased racial harmony to international audiences during the Sydney Olympics, Wiradjuri Elder Isobell Coe in an interview with Irene Watson of the Tanganekald, Meintangk, and Boandik First Nations Peoples stated: 'we have never ceded our sovereignty from one end of the country to the other. There has never been any treaty signed.'[1] Coe drew a clear line of causation between the fact that

---

1 Irene Watson, "The Aboriginal Tent Embassy 28 Years After it was Established: Interview with Isobell Coe," *Indigenous Law Bulletin* 5, no. 1 (2000): 17.

DOI: 10.4324/9781003304593-7

Aboriginal peoples did not consent to the imposition of colonial law with the ongoing deaths of Indigenous peoples at the hands of that law:

> In relation to what's happening now I think things have gotten worse. We look at the death rate of our people – it's increased. There's millions of dollars poured into the Aboriginal industry each year, and there is still nothing you know, it doesn't get to the people. There is something like 400,000 Aboriginal people across Australia, and my arithmetic says it doesn't add up. There is something very drastically wrong here. If we all dropped dead tomorrow there would be so many people in the Aboriginal industry who would be out of jobs. We make up a big part of the health system, the welfare system, the gaol system.[2]

Coe's analysis of the rising number of deaths came just nine years after the Royal Commission into Aboriginal Deaths in Custody handed down its 339 recommendations.[3] The Royal Commission was set up in 1987 in response to growing concern about the rate at which Aboriginal peoples were dying in custody and the evasive public justifications provided for those deaths. If non-Aboriginal people had died in custody at the same rate over the same period, the period being from January 1980 until May 1989, this would have equated to nearly 9,000 deaths. Coe's critique remains urgent. Pouring resources into the 'Aboriginal industry' does not work to shift the annihilation of Aboriginal life and land that occurs when sovereignty is exercised from the colonial centre.

In 2023, more than 30 years after the findings of the Royal Commission were handed down, 547 people have died in custody.[4] Alongside this sobering reality, the current governmental funding priority relating to the 'Aboriginal industry' is to commit $336.6 million over two years for the Electoral Commission to deliver a referendum for the purpose of instilling a First Nations Voice into Parliament. This includes $10.6 million to produce information pamphlets for the 'yes' and 'no' cases and distribution of these to all Australian households.[5] As a result of this same budget, the National Aboriginal and Torres Strait Islander Legal Services (NATSILS) have declared a funding emergency. Here at this budgetary level is an opportunity to visualise the death economy of colonial law. The criminal justice system, in particular policing and prisons, are creations and enactments of colonial power. These are institutions of colonial law where Indigenous life is targeted, producing political, social, and often physical death. The Federal budget reveals the austerity applied to necessary services required to ameliorate the harms of these regimes. Currently, this reality is covered over by reformist narratives of constitutional law that are positioned as being above and outside the structural causes for the Aboriginal deaths that occur at the hands of the colonial legal system. The constitutional reform campaign, which ran for over a decade in various guises, culminated in October 2023 with the referendum returning a 'no' vote. Even if the vote had been 'yes', this would not have had the power to decentre a regime of law that has a death-producing function for colonised peoples. This is because the yes/no binary flattened and violently displaced the larger questions of colonial debt and decolonisation that urgently need to be

2 Watson, "The Aboriginal Tent Embassy," 17.
3 Royal Commission into Aboriginal Deaths in Custody, *National Report, Vol. 1* (1991).
4 "Deaths in custody in Australia," accessed 6 February 2024, www.aic.gov.au/statistics/deaths-custody-australia.
5 "Federal Budget of Australia," accessed 6 February 2024, https://budget.gov.au/content/bp2/download/bp2_2023-24.pdf.

reckoned with. The technology of the referendum worked to naturalise the legitimacy of the colonial structure posing the question. This is because both 'yes' and 'no' as available positions are not independent of the system that poses the wrong question and only two possible answers as the path to racial justice.[6] Such law reform campaigns and legal events may not be well known to audiences outside of Australia, yet their relevance to discussions on the death economies of colonial law is profound.

Australia is a country that has been taken for free, and the denial of responsibility for that theft and the unpaid debts it has accrued are reliant upon an imposed colonial legal infrastructure (the nomopoly) that structures and maintains a colonial debtscape. Within the debtscape, the allocation of funding signals the colonial state's priorities. The central priority of the state, expressed through the enactment of patriarchal white sovereignty, is to 'discriminate in favour of itself'[7] even when and because its existence is the effect of colonial theft where land, subterranean earth, and water are rendered freely available for use without payment, compensation, or accountability to Aboriginal peoples. Reform of the colonial legal infrastructure of the Constitution is premised upon the denial of two death-producing realities. These are that Indigenous sovereignty has never been ceded and consent to be ruled over by colonial law has never been granted by Aboriginal people. Although reform of law generally appears as a progressive development, it can obscure what law is constituted by and the work it performs under colonial conditions. This chapter has a focus on two features of colonial law – its usurpatory (nomopoly) and non-consensual (nomocide) nature – that give it an intrinsic relation to death.

'Buried Alive': Usurpation is the work of the nomopoly

In 2003, Achille Mbembe's essay 'Necropolitics'[8] was released, and it spoke to the death worlds of the postcolony. Released a year before was Irene Watson's seminal essay 'Buried Alive'[9] which is perhaps less well known to readers outside Australia but is critical to the study of law and death together. Watson theorises the specific role played by colonial law in producing death economies. This essay, written from the position of a survivor of colonial deathworlds, not only precedes the release of 'Necropolitics' but captures its essence. To be 'buried alive' is 'a form of death in life'.[10] In 'Necropolitics', Mbembe argues that the destruction of human bodies and populations are what 'constitute the nomos, the political space in which we still live' and draws on Hannah Arendt to show the inextricability of the politics of race from the politics of death.[11] Watson situates her theorisation explicitly 'as a survivor of terra nullius, at a time when the Australian state persists with the burial of my living being'.[12] She situates herself as 'one of the voiceless amidst the chaos seeking to write my way out of the rubble that buries'.[13]

---

6 Maria Giannacopoulos, "'We're doing everything but treaty': Law reform and sovereign refusal in the colonial debtscape," *Overland*, 1 December 2023, https://overland.org.au/2023/12/were-doing-everything-but-treaty-law-reform-and-sovereign-refusal-in-the-colonial-debtscape.

7 Aileen Moreton-Robinson, "The possessive logic of patriarchal white sovereignty: The High Court and the Yorta Yorta decision," *Borderlands* 3, no. 2. (2004): 7, www.borderlands.net.au/vol3no2_2004/moreton_possessive.htm.

8 Achille Mbembe, "Necropolitics," *Public Culture* 15, no. 1 (2003): 11–40.

9 Irene Watson, "Buried Alive," *Law and Critique* 13 (2002): 253–69.

10 Mbembe, "Necropolitics," 21.

11 Mbembe, "Necropolitics," 14.

12 Watson, "Buried Alive," 253.

13 Watson, "Buried Alive," 253.

To seek to bury all that survives genocidal violence is the work of the contemporary Australian state and its associated law. This sits both well and uneasily with Mbembe's positioning of the colonial occupation of Palestine as the 'most accomplished form of necropower'.[14] Watson's voice of survival grounded within her own laws of place, works to reveal the importance of seeing death economies of law not as legacy but on a continuum in places where colonial invasion seems a settled matter. Where Mbembe argues that the 'sovereign right to kill is not subject to any rule in the colonies',[15] Watson makes visible how the 'formation of a new social order was founded on the possibility of our disappearance'.[16] Law, Watson explains, is different to the European idea of sovereignty, different in that it is not imposed by force of arms and does not exclude in its embrace; it envelops all things, it holds this world together.[17] The sovereign right to kill and usurp laws of place becomes embedded as rule through colonial law.

In Watson's words, 'as our people were mowed down like flies by gunshots and diseases, we questioned their violation of Ancient Aboriginal laws'.[18] The critical distinction here between the violence that was necessary for the formation of the colonial order and the attempted annihilation of ancient laws of place that 'holds the world together'[19] makes it necessary to ask when seeking to track the relation between law and death: What is 'law' when it is thought in relation to colonisation? In colonial contexts, the meaning of law cannot be presumed to be known, nor can it be assumed to be singular and distinct from violence. Both sovereignty and law are not unitary concepts[20] and yet both are used in colonial societies repetitively and without qualification. It is through usurpation, frontier violence, and dispossession that colonial law comes to appear as the singular 'law'. I have named this usurpatory law *nomopoly*. First laws of place are 'different to the European idea of sovereignty different in that it is not imposed by force of arms and does not exclude in its embrace'.[21] All people, even colonisers, 'come into the laws of place as they come into ruwi, but the greater majority have no sense or recognition of laws of place as they succumb to the idea of sovereignties of state'.[22]

What is being disturbed through these theorisations is the tendency to understand law as singular and as distinct from ongoing violence. In a colonised place, there are at least two forms of law that are irreconcilable but that sit in a power relation that is deathly. Understandings of 'law' that take its singularity for granted are blind to the usurpatory function of colonial law in usurping first laws of place and, in line with this, its death-producing function. The colonial state and its associated laws 'in imposing boundaries does this from a place of power and not law as it draws its imagined lines around the earth's body'.[23] The state creates its 'lines in an attempt to displace laws of ruwi and also to enclose a place, one that is beyond closure, in the same way that the universe and

14 Mbembe, "Necropolitics," 27.
15 Mbembe, "Necropolitics," 24.
16 Watson, "Buried Alive," 254.
17 Watson, "Buried Alive," 255.
18 Watson, "Buried Alive," 254.
19 Watson, "Buried Alive," 255.
20 Stewart Motha, "The Sovereign Event in a Nation's Law," *Law and Critique* 13 (2002): 311–38.
21 Watson, "Buried Alive," 255.
22 Watson, "Buried Alive," 255.
23 Watson, "Buried Alive," 255.

beyond is.'[24] This racialised bordering generates a *deathscape* [25] with a 'necropolitical drive' where death is not incidental but a planned tool of government.[26]

I have coined the term *nomopoly* to articulate the usurpatory nature of colonial law and its positioning as singular legal authority.[27] A nomopoly denotes a monopoly in the creation of *nomos*/law,[28] but in a colonial context it has the added feature of structurally foreclosing the operations of the first laws of Aboriginal peoples by subjecting all to its rule. The absence of a legitimate basis for this subjectification or 'throwing under'[29] is what gives rise to the need for continual policy moves seeking to absolve the colonial legal apparatus for lacking consent to rule. The nomopoly works to foreclose upon the operations of the first laws of Aboriginal peoples structurally and repetitively by subjecting all to colonial integrationist rule. In Australia, as in many other settler-colonial countries globally, law *as* nomopoly imposes a colonial infrastructure over first laws and stolen territories. While the functions of the nomopoly are manifold, one of its key effects is to obfuscate its own death-producing function. But the relation of colonial law to death can really only be invisible to those who are not its direct targets. Watson's embodied account of being 'buried alive' reveals what is at stake, and for whom, when law is thought as separately to death.

In 2022, after the acquittal of a police officer who had been charged with murder for the fatal shooting of Kumanjayi Walker, protestors who understand, see, and feel the full impact of an imposed law said: 'No guns – no guns in our own remote community. We don't want no guns. Enough is enough.'[30] The Northern Territory, which falls under the control of the Federal Government is in the central and central northern regions of Australia, and a large proportion of its population is Aboriginal. Although Rolfe had entered Walker's home in Yuendumu, Walker's country, and fired more than one gunshot ending Walker's life, the Northern Territory Supreme Court would not equate this police killing to murder. Ned Jampijinpa Hargraves, in a statement issued after the colonial court's verdict added: 'We want a ceasefire. No more guns in our communities. It must never happen again. The police must put down their weapons. We have been saying this since the beginning. We cannot walk around in fear in our own homes.'[31] In both these instances the protest calls result at the point where the state entities of the police and judiciary collude to nullify black and Aboriginal deaths. A ceasefire, an end to the war on Aboriginal people, is being called for, yet not everyone within Australia can see the war that plays out through the arms of the legal system. This is because positionality in

24 Watson, "Buried Alive," 255.
25 "The Deathscapes Project" archive, accessed 6 February 2024, https://us16.campaign-archive.com/home/?u=6f3de369e336fc0ecd343cc25&id=eb47e1026a.
26 Jordana Silverstein. "Mapping deaths in custody to dismantle carceral logic," *Overland*, 30 January 2019, https://overland.org.au/2019/01/mapping-deaths-in-custody-to-dismantle-carceral-logic.
27 Maria Giannacopoulos, "Debtscape: Australia's Constitutional Nomopoly," *Borderlands* 18, no. 2 (2019): 116–36.
28 Roderick Macdonald and David Sandomierski, "Against Nomopolies," *Northern Ireland Legal Quarterly* 54, no. 4 (2006): 610.
29 Macdonald and Sandomierski, "Against Nomopolies," 610.
30 "Zachary Rolfe: Policeman acquitted of murdering Aboriginal teenager," *BBC News*, 11 March 2022, www.bbc.com/news/world-australia-60703420.
31 Ned Hargraves, "No more guns in our communities, it must never happen again," *Solidarity*, 11 March 2022, https://solidarity.net.au/highlights/ned-hargraves-no-more-guns-in-our-communities-it-must-never-happen-again.

relation to law and state power can be a powerful contributor to understanding power relations or the thing that makes the brutality of those powers disappear.[32]

Nomocide: The absence of consent and a law that kills

When the imposed nomopoly refuses to engage with its violent origins and the lack of consent at its heart, nomocide is the result. Nomocide is the killing function performed by law in reproducing colonial conditions in contemporary Australia. Australian law lacks foundational consent for its existence, and this is why moves to reform it are so prevalent in the contemporary moment. Not satisfied with its imperialising grip over Indigenous lands and waters, the Australian state and legal apparatus use illegitimately acquired power to seek retrospective consent to legitimise ongoing violence in the present. In thinking about the relation of death and law in this historical moment – a time when the direct link between settler-colonial legal infrastructures of courts, prisons, police, and legislatures and the violation of Indigenous and black lives has been laid bare – it is also necessary to think of who is equipped to speak and who can be heard on this relation.

In 1998, Isobell Coe, along with her husband Billy Craigie, Wadjularbinna Nulyarimma, and Robbie Thorpe, brought an action to the Supreme Court of the Australian Capital Territory to have the crime of genocide recognised in Australian law.[33] The applicants asserted that John Winston Howard (former Prime Minister), Timothy Andrew Fischer, Brian Harradine, and Pauline Lee Hanson had, by introducing into the Parliament and/or securing the passage of the *Native Title Amendment Bill* (1997), committed an act of genocide. The applicants asserted that the failure to enact legislation creating statutory offences of genocide following the *Convention on the Prevention and Punishment of the Crime of Genocide* (1948) also constituted genocide. Justice Crispin said that 'these contentions were obviously somewhat startling' and 'it was not readily apparent how allegations relating to the formulation of government policy concerning land rights and the introduction of a Bill to amend a Commonwealth statute could support charges of genocide'.[34] If Justice Crispin's role is to uphold the nomopoly, it is consistent that he would find these claims startling. It is unintelligible to him that the passing of Native Title legislation and the refusal to generate statutory offences on genocide could themselves have genocidal effects. It was a problem for the colonial court that 'applicants and intervenors relied on the suffering of Aboriginal people generally' even if the 'pain of dispossessed and alienated people was vividly conveyed'.[35] The challenge for death and law scholars in settler colonies is the question of foundation. Seeing colonial law as the effect of usurpation and lack of consent would allow for the protest calls being made in a case such as *Nulyarimma* to be not only intelligible but to allow for the relation of colonial law and death to be fully visible. When the *Nulyarimma* challenge came

32 Maria Giannacopoulos, "Law's Violence: The Police Killing of Kumanjayi Walker and the Trial of Zachary Rolfe," in *The Routledge International Handbook on Decolonizing Justice*, ed. Chris Cunneen, Antje Deckert, Amanda Porter, Juan Tauri, and Robert Webb (London and New York: Routledge 2023), 81–90.

33 *Nulyarimma No.1: In the matter of an application for a writ of mandamus directed to Phillip R Thompson Ex parte Wadjularbinna Nulyarimma, Isobell Coe, Billy Craigie, and Robbie Thorpe (Applicants), Tom Trevorrow, Irene Watson, Kevin Buzzacott and Michael J Anderson (Intervenors)* [1998] ACTSC 136.

34 *Nulyarimma No. 1*, para 9.

35 *Nulyarimma No.1*, para 10.

into court, it was deemed unintelligible because legal expertise in the nomopoly is deemed to come only from those who impose law and not those who are subject to its violent effects. In this way, legal logics that stem from colonial law are deathly.

Because their action was unsuccessful, in 1999 Coe, Craigie, Nulyarimma, and Thorpe sought leave to appeal before the High Court. The excerpt of the transcript of these court proceedings reveals the very deep tension and disagreement about the nature and meaning of colonial law.[36] Coe, who identifies the real and deathly effects of this tension, is powerful and direct in her assertion that the hierarchy of courts to which she has appealed are genocidal precisely because they refuse to recognise the crime of genocide *in* Australian law. She posed a question to the court, one that remains relevant for all scholars, believers, and upholders of colonial law: Where can Indigenous people go for justice? Her question to the judges as colonial law's gatekeepers is structurally incapable of being heard. Justice Kirby was violently dismissive: what is the *substantive* issue, he asked, having refused a recognition of genocide even when recognition is the very thing that would render the issue *substantive*. Coe's response that the undeclared 'war against our people must end' is met with: 'Well, this is a Court of law. We are obliged to conform to the law.' When Coe in turn responds that this is precisely what makes the court 'a party to the genocide', Justice Gummow steps in to shut down the dialogue, ruling that 'no, we will not hear that sort of thing'. The Justices, who embody and uphold the nomopoly, will not hear, or listen, or respond to the call to help stop Indigenous deaths. This was a hearing that they would not *hear*.

The unwillingness to *hear* questions with potential to unravel the illegitimate foundation of the legal system was a key aspect of the much celebrated yet deeply colonising judgement of *Mabo v Commonwealth (No. 2)* less than a decade earlier. In that decision, the High Court overturned the legal fiction of *terra nullius*, correcting the historical record that Australia was not an empty land, but in so doing deemed sovereignty non-justiciable.[37] This refusal to engage with the foundational violence of colonial sovereignty was rationalised by an aporetic logic. The sovereignty held by the colonial state could not be questioned as this would fracture the skeletal principle upon which the entirety of the legal system is premised.[38] The *Mabo No. 2* ruling drew attention to, but authorised a turning away from, the foundational violence underwriting the contemporary legal order. With *Mabo No. 2* ruling on the necessity of looking away from the violent origins of law by deeming colonial sovereignty non-justiciable, the refusal in *Nulyarimma* continued this work by now casting genocide as outside of colonial law's remit. Wiradjuri and Maori scholar Latoya Rule, whose brother died in custody due to 'events of spit hood and positional asphyxia', thinks it 'senseless' that the state would ascribe responsibility to itself for deaths that they argue are 'required for the state to progress its genocide'.[39] But what colonial law, as a powerful arm of the state, does is to invite the complicity of its adherents to act *as though* the legal regime is legitimate, *as though* it has consent to do what it does. Our complicity then requires an implicit enactment of what Justice Gummow explicitly ruled: a refusal to *hear* that colonial law, a law without consent at its heart, produces death.

36 Maria Giannacopoulos, "White Law/Black Deaths: Nomocide and the Foundational Absence of Consent in Australian Law," *Australian Feminist Law Journal* 46, no. 2 (2020): 249–63.
37 *Mabo v Queensland (No. 2)* (1992) 175 CLR 1.
38 *Mabo v Queensland (No. 2)* (1992) 175 CLR 1.
39 Latoya Rule, "Blak Brow: Sovereign Debt," *The Lifted Brow*, 21 December 2018, www.thelifted brow.com/liftedbrow/2018/12/19/blak-brow-sovereign-debt-by-latoya-rule.

When Robbie Thorpe from the Krautungalung people of the Gunnai Nation, a key figure in the fight to have genocide recognised in Australian law was asked about the state of Aboriginal rights in Australia in 2000, he explicitly attended to the question of consent and its link to Aboriginal deaths by law:

> One of our rights being breached is the right to consent. Aboriginal people haven't consented. If you do things without consent, its considered rape. Now, a lot of crimes have been committed against Aboriginal people. There is a history of denial, which has gone on, and these crimes are continuing ... Until they have a treaty with Aboriginal people we can't talk about making laws for Aboriginal people or applying it to them. The treaty will give them that basis of law to do it ... there ain't no future here. My people are haemorrhaging in terms of their lives ...[40]

Thorpe made a clear analogy between the lack of consent that produces state criminality, Aboriginal death, and the disingenuous and racialised concept of consent encoded within Australian law. Thorpe argued that within the logic of colonial law itself, the absence of consent is considered tantamount to rape in relations between individuals. And yet this absence of consent, a consent that would have required Indigenous peoples to be seen as sovereigns in their own right, is the basis upon which the current legal framework is built. Watson takes the question of consent to another level:

> First Nations are many, so would there be one universal treaty or many? Who would represent the Nation(s) in treaty negotiations? Who would determine representation, the state or First Nations? And what is up for negotiation? Could we agree to our separation from and the destruction of our lands? Can the state accept 'no'? If we say NO, how will it roll? It is becoming clearer to me that the idea of consent is itself a white colonial construct; First Nations had no process which could enable consent to our own demise and or extinguishment.[41]

Watson articulates the limits of the notion of consent within the context of ongoing colonial relations of power. With the coloniser centred and continuing to impose itself as nomopoly, any consent-like arrangement that flows from it would set in train arrangements working in line with the extinguishment of Aboriginality. This is because the colonial project is 'about ensuring that the Aboriginal relationships to all things Indigenous are inevitably extinguished' and this 'end of Aboriginality is a form of genocide'.[42] As long as the 'domestic paradigm' kills one law in favour of its own, the law is emptied of justice moving from 'genocide to *juriscide*'. While the term *juriscide* has no extended definition, Watson learned this term from Valerie Kerruish.

Consent, its absence in law partnered with the continual drive to acquire it in law, is the basis for the extension of colonial power in modern-day Australia. Through this absence and presence dynamic, consent is alive and well as a legal technology of

40 Irene Watson, "Talking Up Aboriginal Law in a Sea of Genocide: Interview with Robbie Thorpe," *Indigenous Law Bulletin 5*, no. 1 (2000): 14.
41 Irene Watson, "Aboriginal Recognition: Treaties and Colonial Constitutions, 'We Have Been Here Forever ...'" *Bond Law Review* 30, no. 1 (2018): 13.
42 Irene Watson, "Aboriginal Recognition," 13.

dispossession. It does remain challenging, though, for 'lovers of law'[43] to take the illegitimate basis of Australian law as a sufficient reason to disinvest from its value and to see it as the author of Indigenous death. Nowhere has this challenge played out more starkly than in the constitutional Recognise campaign that culminated in the *Uluru Statement from the Heart* calling for a First Nations Voice to Parliament. This federally funded constitutional campaign, part of what Coe would call the 'Aboriginal industry', ran from 2012 to 2017 and saw $15 million dollars poured into the campaign with a vision to alter the preamble of the Constitution by identifying Indigenous peoples as the First Nations. Had it been successful, it would have been a low-impact constitutional change keeping the colonial power structure locked firmly in place.[44] The referendum council convened by the government for the purpose of canvassing views on constitutional recognition came back with a recommendation to establish a 'voice to Parliament', but this was rejected by settler-colonialists in 2023 as it deviated from the colonial script. At almost every consultation, Aboriginal and Torres Strait Islander participants raised issues of sovereignty, asserting that sovereignty was never ceded, relinquished, or validly extinguished. Participants at some consultations were concerned that recognition would have implications for sovereignty. The re-opening of the question of sovereignty and the law-making power of Aboriginal peoples, albeit within the existing legal structure, is what made the recommendation for a new advisory voice unpalatable. By closing down this recommendation, the government reaffirmed a singular idea of sovereignty without naming that sovereignty as *colonial*. But the remaining challenge, once a lack of consent in colonial law is accepted, is what to make of the strategy of seeking a place at the colonial table and in the structure of law established by a colonial constitution.[45] As Watson has asserted in relation to the Australian Constitution, 'first nations did not consent to this newly constructed and constituted status'.[46]

Perhaps comfortable in the thought that consent applies only between individuals as per the Western doctrine of informed consent, lawyers and law academics continue to trade in and perpetuate the legitimacy of a coercive system when favouring constitutional reform. Constitutional reform is underwritten by the assumption that even if consent for Australian law and the constitutional structure setting out Australia's political, legal, and economic infrastructure was originally absent, it can be acquired retrospectively in processes completely controlled by the colonial system itself. It is in this sense that the category of consent, as the presumed way that societies are governed, is invisibly operating to entrench Australia's colonial order.

Conclusion

In 2019, in Kaurna Yerta (Adelaide) I attended a rally after the police killing of Kumanjayi Walker in Yuendumu while in his home and on his country. Protest placards from the family and community of Kumanjayi Walker read: 'We don't need this Government; we have been governing this place for millennia!' and 'Your laws are killing us'. An

---

43 Maria Giannacopoulos, "Without love there can be law but no justice," *Globalizations* 17, no. 7 (2020): 1085–90.

44 Maria Giannacopoulos, "Can there be a Constitutional solution to dispossession?" *ABC Religion and Ethics*, 26 May 2018, www.abc.net.au/religion/the-uluru-statement-from-heart-one-year-on-can-a-first-nations-v/10094678.

45 Giannacopoulos, "Can there be a Constitutional solution to dispossession?"

46 Watson, "Aboriginal Recognition".

Aboriginal Elder at the rally called out to the police who were surrounding the protestors outside Parliament House on North Terrace: 'This is a peaceful protest. Why do you bring your guns?' A year later, at the Black Lives Matter protest, also on Kaurna Yerta,[47] protestors drew the lines of connection that hold between black deaths in the US and Aboriginal lives in Australia. Samara Fernandez-Brown, the cousin of Kumanjayi Walker, addressed the rally: 'The death of George Floyd has resurfaced a whole bunch of pain for my family and I, and a whole bunch of fight!'[48] The relation between law and death is a live question and cannot be consigned either to history or to theory. This relation is a route through which law in conditions of colonialism can be more fully seen and reckoned with. The criminal legal system must be decentred so that Aboriginal law can come to 'sit on top of whiteman's law' because, says Senior Lawman Murray George, 'our law is the law of the land'.[49] Aboriginal Laws, rightful laws of place 'are not imposed by force of arms and do not exclude in their embrace'.[50] Such law, Watson teaches, 'holds this world together'.[51] A critical legal language is needed, one that has already been largely provided by Indigenous activists and scholars. Usurpation and the absence of consent, the buried yet constitutive features of the Australian nomopoly, produce Indigenous death or nomocide. Nomocide is my offering to a critical legal language seeking to capture the full spectrum of structural violence, annihilation, and extinguishment that flows from a system of law that has no legitimate authority to rule. If the nomopoly continues to be confirmed through mechanisms of reform as is planned with the 2023 referendum, and full autonomy and self-determination of Indigenous peoples denied, then nomocide will only escalate.[52] The price of not disturbing the nomocidal effects of colonial law will continue to be paid as extinguishment of Indigenous life and land.

Bibliography

Giannacopoulos, Maria. "Nomophilia and Bia. The Love of Law and the Question of Violence." *Borderlands* 10, no. 1 (2011): 1–10.

Giannacopoulos, Maria. "Sovereign debt crises, referendums and the changing face of colonial power." *Continuum: Journal of Media and Cultural Studies*, 31, no. 1 (2017): 33–42.

Giannacopoulos, Maria. "Can there be a Constitutional solution to dispossession?" *ABC Religion and Ethics*, 26 May 2018. www.abc.net.au/religion/the-uluru-statement-from-heart-one-year-on-can-a-first-nations-v/10094678.

Giannacopoulos, Maria. "Debtscape: Australia's Constitutional Nomopoly." *Borderlands* 18, no. 2 (2019): 116–136.

Giannacopoulos, Maria, "Your laws are killing us: The death of Kumanjayi Walker and the crisis of colonial law." *ABC Religion and Ethics*, 20 November 2019. www.abc.net.au/religion/the-death-of-kumanjayi-walker-and-the-crisis-of-colonial-law/11722836.

Giannacopoulos, Maria. "Without love there can be law but no justice." *Globalizations* 17, no. 7 (2020): 1085–1090.

47 Walter Marsh, "'Yapa Lives Matter' as a global movement embraces Adelaide," *The Adelaide Review*, 7 June 2020, www.adelaidereview.com.au/latest/2020/06/07/black-lives-matter-adelaide-rally-2020/#.
48 Marsh "Yapa Lives Matter."
49 Senior Lawman Murray George, "Aboriginal Law must sit on top of whiteman's law, because 'our Law is the Law of this land'," *Sovereign Union*, 4 December 2013, http://nationalunitygovernment.org/content/aboriginal-law-must-sit-top-whitemans-law-because-our-law-law-land.
50 Watson, "Buried Alive," 255.
51 Watson, "Buried Alive," 255.
52 Giannacopoulos, "White Law/Black Deaths," 262.

Giannacopoulos, Maria. "White Law/Black Deaths: Nomocide and the Foundational Absence of Consent in Australian Law." *Australian Feminist Law Journal*, 46, no. 2 (2020): 249–263.

Giannacopoulos, Maria. "Law's Violence: The Police Killing of Kumanjayi Walker and the Trial of Zachary Rolfe." In *The Routledge International Handbook on Decolonizing Justice*, edited by Chris Cunneen, Antje Deckert, Amanda Porter, Juan Tauri, and Robert Webb, 81–90. London and New York: Routledge, 2023.

Giannacopoulos, Maria. "'We're doing everything but treaty': Law Reform and Sovereign Refusal in the Colonial Debtscape." *Overland*, 1 December 2023. https://overland.org.au/2023/12/were-doing-everything-but-treaty-law-reform-and-sovereign-refusal-in-the-colonial-debtscape.

Hargraves, Ned. "No more guns in our communities, it must never happen again." *Solidarity*, 11 March 2022. https://solidarity.net.au/highlights/ned-hargraves-no-more-guns-in-our-communities-it-must-never-happen-again.

Macdonald, Roderick, and David Sandomierski. "Against Nomopolies." *Northern Ireland Legal Quarterly*, 54, no. 4 (2006): 610–633.

Marsh, Walter. "'Yapa Lives Matter' as a global movement embraces Adelaide." *The Adelaide Review*, 7 June 2020. www.adelaidereview.com.au/latest/2020/06/07/black-lives-matter-adelaide-rally-2020/#.

Mbembe, Achille. "Necropolitics." *Public Culture*, 15, no. 1 (2003): 11–40.

Moreton-Robinson, Aileen. "The possessive logic of patriarchal white sovereignty: The High Court and the Yorta Yorta decision." *Borderlands*, 3, no. 2 (2004): 1–9.

Motha, Stewart, "The Sovereign Event in a Nation's Law." *Law and Critique* 13 (2002): 311–338.

Royal Commission into Aboriginal Deaths in Custody. *National Report*, Vol. 1 (1991).

Latoya Rule. "Blak Brow: Sovereign Debt." *The Lifted Brow*, 21 December 2018. www.theliftedbrow.com/liftedbrow/2018/12/19/blak-brow-sovereign-debt-by-latoya-rule.

Silverstein, Jordana. "Mapping deaths in custody to dismantle carceral logic." *Overland*, 30 January 2019. https://overland.org.au/2019/01/mapping-deaths-in-custody-to-dismantle-carceral-logic.

Sovereign Union: First Nations Asserting Sovereignty. "Aboriginal Law must sit on top of whiteman's law, because 'our Law is the Law of this land'." Published on 4 December 2013. http://nationalunitygovernment.org/content/aboriginal-law-must-sit-top-whitemans-law-because-our-law-law-land.

Watson, Irene. "The Aboriginal Tent Embassy 28 Years After it was Established: Interview with Isobell Coe." *Indigenous Law Bulletin*, 5, no. 1 (2000). https://classic.austlii.edu.au/au/journals/IndigLawB/2000/48.html.

Watson, Irene. "Talking Up Aboriginal Law in a Sea of Genocide: Interview with Robbie Thorpe." *Indigenous Law Bulletin* 5, no. 1 (2000). https://classic.austlii.edu.au/au/journals/IndigLawB/2000/47.html.

Watson, Irene. "Buried Alive." *Law and Critique* 13 (2002): 253–269.

Watson, Irene. "Re-Centring First Nations Knowledge and Places." *AlterNative*, 10, no. 5 (2014): 514.

Watson, Irene. "First Nations and the Colonial Project." *Inter Gentes* 1, no. 1 (2016): 35.

Watson, Irene. "Aboriginal Recognition: Treaties and Colonial Constitutions, 'We Have Been Here Forever …'" *Bond Law Review* 30, no. 1 (2018): 7–18.

Whittaker, Alison. "Indigenous deaths in custody: inquests can be sites of justice or administrative violence." *The Conversation*, 15 April 2021. https://theconversation.com/indigenous-deaths-in-custody-inquests-can-be-sites-of-justice-or-administrative-violence-158126.

Williams, George, "Race and the Australian Constitution: From Federation to Reconciliation." *Osgoode Hall Law Journal* 38, no. 4 (2000): 643–665.

"Zachary Rolfe: Policeman acquitted of murdering Aboriginal teenager." BBC News, 11 March 2022. www.bbc.com/news/world-australia-60703420.

7

THANATOPOLITICS OF LAW

Marc Trabsky[1]

Introduction

The average life expectancy of a British adult has dropped by at least 13 months since 2015. Researchers blame widespread cuts to healthcare and welfare spending, spiralling costs of living, and increases in dementia, diabetes, and cancer diagnoses.[2] This trend doesn't even include the deterioration of mortality during the recent global pandemic, which appears to have decreased life expectancy, particularly in already disadvantaged communities, not only in the United Kingdom but throughout Europe, the United States, and elsewhere. The facile truism that every generation will live longer than the previous one has been thoroughly debunked. The reversal in life expectancy, or more specifically how it disrupts the fantastical human desire for immortality, reveals a great deal about transformations to the epistemology of death in the twenty-first century. Death is understood today as something that can be mastered, controlled, and manipulated. Governments can put an individual to death by their own hands or through their complicity with others. They often let vulnerable populations die by failing to provide timely medical, social, or legal assistance. They also extend the lives of the most advantaged in society by financing technologies that can only be accessed by the few. Governments routinely invest in the management of life to a point where they allow individuals to die. The recent deterioration in life expectancy is not a catastrophe for the state; on the contrary, it is a problem to be monitored, quantified, and calculated. Whether they create the conditions to edge death ever slightly closer or whether they remain indifferent to the

---

1 This work originally appeared as Marc Trabsky, "Chapter 1: Legal Epistemologies of Death," in *Death: New Trajectories of Law* (Abingdon and New York: Routledge, 2024), 1–13. It has been modified for this publication. The research for this chapter was funded by an Australian Research Council Grant entitled 'Socio-Legal Implications of Virtual Autopsies in Coronial Investigations' (DE220100064).
2 See Denis Campbell, "Rise in life expectancy has stalled since 2010, research shows," *The Guardian*, 18 July 2017, www.theguardian.com/society/2017/jul/18/rise-in-life-expectancy-has-stalled-since-2010-research-shows; Patrick Collinson, "Life expectancy falls by six months in biggest drop in UK forecasts,", *The Guardian*, 8 March 2019, www.theguardian.com/society/2019/mar/07/life-expectancy-slumps-by-five-months.

DOI: 10.4324/9781003304593-8

fatal consequences of their decision making, it is without doubt that in seeking mastery over the vicissitudes of mortality, governments reify the value of death.

In 2022, *The Lancet*, a prominent medical journal, published a wide-ranging report on the paradox of dying in the twenty-first century. The report contends that dying is unbalanced across the world, death has lost its value for society, and vulnerable populations suffer greatly from a lack of investment in end-of-life care. Many people die of preventable conditions, particularly in low-income countries, and they die without access to affordable and timely medical treatment. In contrast, dying in high-income countries is often a protracted process, where '[f]utile or potentially inappropriate treatment can continue into the last hours of life'.[3] Ineffectual medical treatment can be a major cause of health poverty for the survivors of the deceased, contribute to needless suffering for the dying person and their family, and divert indispensable funding from palliative care, which has the potential to improve the quality of dying in the final moments of life. The report exhorts states not only to recognise the 'value' of death, but also to reform institutional death systems to restore equality to the dying process. But to do so they first need to critique the teleological fantasy that they can master death, that science can manipulate death by forever extending life, and mortality, much like nature, is an obstacle to be tamed through technology.

In *Death: New Trajectories of Law*, I write that it is a misnomer to claim that legal institutions have failed to recognise the value of death.[4] Indeed, I offer the idea that death has become subject to a governing logic of economisation, and this wouldn't have been possible without the complicity of legal institutions. Laws are depicted in the book as enabling, if not extending, the concept of economy into domains which were perhaps at one point in time never thought of as primarily economic. The book examines then how the governing logic of economisation suffuses legal definitions of death, legal technologies for death registration, and legal conceptualisations of the status of the corpse. Each chapter is guided by the question of how bio-technological innovation has transformed legal relations between life and death, but also how the legal governance of death has become increasingly inextricable from economic rationality.

The conceptual framework that underpins *Death: New Trajectories of Law* is that since the eighteenth and nineteenth centuries legal institutions govern life by letting individuals die. In this chapter, borrowing from and further extending that schema of governmentality, I offer a theorisation of the quotidian practices of a *thanatopolitics* of law. Law does not subside with death, nor does it shun the dead. Legal institutions adjudicate the liminal horizon between life and death, they are complicit with a governing rationality that allows death, and they are imbued with a responsibility to take care of the dead. This chapter weaves an intimate story of an ambivalent death, tracing its bureaucratic procedures and observing responses from the bereaved, to question legal epistemologies of an everyday death. The death that is narrativised in this chapter is not exceptional, and neither is it unfathomable. Every death is tragic and leaves in its wake unanswered questions and obfuscated memories. If death is not a limit of law but a condition of its possibility, this chapter argues that it is necessary to consider in what ways legal institutions ordinarily let individuals die.

---

3 "Report of the *Lancet* Commission on the Value of Death: Bringing Death Back into Life," *The Lancet* 399 (2022): 837.

4 Marc Trabsky, *Death: New Trajectories of Law* (Abingdon and New York: Routledge, 2024), 1–13.

Interlude

I received the call as soon as I touched down on the tarmac. The call felt strident and insistent, despite having rung only once. It was from an unknown caller, a friend of my friend, who informed me that she died a couple of days ago. The circumstances of her death were ambiguous. They were cobbled together from credit card statements, second-hand knowledge, and handwritten instructions. She checked into a hotel on the weekend, purchased a couple of bottles of champagne, and failed to check out after extending her stay for another night. The hotel porter found her dead, slumped over in the bathtub. Empty bottles of champagne and multiple packets of prescription medicine were found strewn across the room. There was no suicide note, but she left pages of funerary instructions, which subsequently became controversial due to their exclusionary effects.

I sensed in that call the immediacy of law's embrace of death. Law didn't turn away from this death, but rather like the prohibition that forbade Orpheus from looking back, law was always there, observing Eurydice from the shadows. The caller cautiously asked me questions about the legal aftermath of our friend's death. She first asked what happens when a person dies intestate, since it became obvious that our friend didn't leave a will. We then discussed whether a coroner would investigate the circumstances of the death – it is an ongoing investigation as I write – and the legal status of her funerary instructions – which are non-binding in our jurisdiction. Our conversation pivoted towards the minutiae of death in everyday life, and I was astonished by the powerful extent of law's reach. Who is responsible for handing back the keys to her rented apartment? What can be done with her sentimental chattels? Who is responsible for registering her death, closing her bank accounts, and sorting through her books, clothes, and crockery? Of particular importance amongst her friends was her nearly finished thesis, and her notebooks on death and dying filled with ideas about future projects. Law doesn't foreclose this future; rather, it suspends it in uncertainty.

Politics of death

In the final part of the first volume of *The History of Sexuality*, Michel Foucault offers a strident critique of the transformations in the governance of life and death in the eighteenth and nineteenth centuries. He marks this epoch as a turning point between the decline of sovereign power and the emergence of bio-power in the West. While Foucault concedes that human life, as an object of power–knowledge relations, had always been exploited by sovereigns, particularly when expanding their territories, sentencing an enemy to death, or quarantining plague towns, since at least the eighteenth century, humankind began problematising

> what it meant to be a living species in a living world, to have a body, conditions of existence, probabilities of life, an individual and collective welfare, forces that could be modified, and a space in which they could be distributed in an optimal manner.[5]

In other words, life became an object of knowledge, and through the development of human sciences, life was dissected into microscopic components to be observed,

---

5 Michel Foucault, *The History of Sexuality, Volume 1: The Will to Knowledge*, trans Robert Hurley (London and New York: Penguin Books, 1998), 142.

quantified, and manipulated. Insofar as these sciences transfixed humankind, life became a problem for governments, which entailed developing a range of political technologies for managing the vicissitudes of life and death.

Foucault explains in *The History of Sexuality* that an analytics of bio-power consists of a range of political technologies. This includes an *anatomopolitics* of the human body and a *biopolitics* of the population. The former refers to the individualisation of the subject, and the subjugation and docility of the body through practices of examination, discipline, and surveillance, whereas the latter takes as its site of intervention not the individual subject but the population, the 'species body', or human life itself. Bio-power differs from older forms of power insofar as it seeks to incite, control, and optimise life. It also involves the delegation of authority from state institutions, and the distribution of power–knowledge relations into every facet of life, from households to schools, and from markets to clinics. 'Power is everywhere,' writes Foucault, 'not because it embraces everything, but because it comes from everywhere.'[6] In the decentralisation of power and knowledge, a population emerges as both an object of scientific study and a problem to be managed by governments. Foucault makes it clear, however, that sovereignty is not replaced by bio-power, whether disciplinary or regulatory, but rather re-valorised through practices of government that intervene directly and indirectly in the administration of a population. While the modern incantation of bio-power greatly differs from sovereign power – which was overwhelmingly dominated by the spectacle of law's violence – it only does so by reshaping a 'deductive' power over life and death into a 'positive' power to foster, elongate, and maximise life.

This does not imply, though, that death was no longer of interest to states in the eighteenth and nineteenth centuries. Death appears as a contradictory figure in *The History of Sexuality*, where it is simultaneously a remainder of the splendour of the sovereign's power to put someone to death, while also being a limit point of the exercise of bio-power that seeks to elongate life. It even manifests at times in Foucault's writing as a moment of absolute resistance to the concentration of power in the state. Indeed, in *Society Must Be Defended* Foucault remarks that '[p]ower no longer recognizes death, power literally ignores death'.[7] He also contrasts death to mortality, the latter of which power can control, and surmises that 'power has a grip on [death] only in general, overall or statistical terms'.[8] While I have written at length about the statistical value of mortality, it will suffice here to observe that these terse quotations do not give a full account of Foucault's theory of death. It is without doubt that the sovereign's 'right to *take* a life or *let* live' was replaced in the eighteenth century by 'a power that exerts a positive influence on life, that endeavours to administer, optimise, and multiply it, subjecting it to precise controls and comprehensive regulations'.[9] Death was never ignored by power in the eighteenth century, it did not vanish from its grasp in the nineteenth century, and it was not repressed in the twentieth century when bio-power flourished as a dominant arrangement of government. In later writings, Foucault precisely coins the term *thanatopolitics* to account for how political technologies for managing death appeared alongside, intertwined with, and immanent to the governance of life in the modern era.[10]

---

6 Foucault, *The History of Sexuality*, 93.
7 Michel Foucault, *Society Must Be Defended: Lectures at the Collège de France, 1975–1976*, trans David Macey (London: Picador, 2003), 248.
8 Foucault, *Society Must Be Defended*, 248.
9 Foucault, *The History of Sexuality*, 136–7, emphasis in original.
10 Michel Foucault, "The Political Technology of Individuals," in *Technologies of the Self: A Seminar with Michel Foucault*, ed. Luther H. Martin, Huck Gutman, and Patrick H. Hutton (Amherst: University of Massachusetts Press, 1988), 160.

Thanatopolitics is conceptually different from *necro-politics*, which has been widely mobilised across the humanities and social sciences over the last decade. The latter appears in Achille Mbembe's writings as either the opposite, underside, or an extension of bio-power. 'I have demonstrated,' Mbembe writes in *Necro-politics*, 'that the notion of biopower is insufficient to account for contemporary forms of the subjugation of life to the power of death.'[11] He utilises the concept to describe how governments exercise sovereignty over life through the power of death – they decide who lives, who dies, and who to expose to violence – particularly in the context of slavery, occupation, colonisation, war, and genocide. Mbembe is indebted to the work of philosopher Giorgio Agamben in focusing on how the state of exception normalises the sovereign's right to kill. He puts forward the concept of *necro-politics* to explain how

> in our contemporary world, weapons are deployed in the interest of maximally destroying persons and creating *death-worlds*, that is, new and unique forms of social existence in which vast populations are subjected to living conditions that confer upon them the status of the *living dead*.[12]

In other words, necro-power can explain much better than an analytics of bio-power how governments can exercise a 'right' to kill individuals, mutilate and disfigure populations, and, particularly through cultivating and disseminating discourses of racism, create the conditions for social or political death in the twenty-first century.

In comparison to this reformulation of sovereign power, *thanatopolitics* is quotidian in its distribution throughout a population. In Foucault's writings, it is not the antithesis of *bio-politics* but the continuity of its techniques in another direction of life. If it is agreed that death is not repressed, ignored, or banished by state institutions – a point I make in my previous writings[13] – then the experience of dying and the afterlife of the corpse are as much a part of an analytics of bio-power as every other facet of life. This perhaps explains why Foucault is at pains to emphasise how the sovereign's power 'to *take* life or *let* live' is transformed in contemporary times into 'a power to *foster* life or *disallow* it to the point of death'.[14] To put this differently, if *biopolitics* describes the way that governments invest in life, foster it, and manage its fluctuations, *thanatopolitics* denotes the techniques by which governments facilitate or resist death, tolerate or prolong it, or monitor, control, and manipulate its trends. *Thanatopolitics* is not a description of how governments subjugate human beings to terror, violence, or death. Instead, it is a conceptual tool to give an account of how a panoply of institutions harness technologies to allow individuals to die.

This interpretation of *thanatopolitics* is more akin to Lauren Berlant's theory of 'slow death' than Mbembe's description of *necro-politics*. In an essay on causality, subjectivity, and the purported 'obesity epidemic', Berlant defines 'slow death' as 'the physical wearing out of a population and the deterioration of people in that population that is very nearly a defining condition of their experience and historical existence'.[15] Due to Berlant's

---

11 Achille Mbembe, *Necro-politics*, trans Steven Corcoran (Durham, NC: Duke University Press, 2019), 92.

12 Mbembe, *Necro-politics*, 92, emphasis in original.

13 Marc Trabsky, *Law and the Dead: Technology, Relations and Institutions* (Abingdon and New York: Routledge, 2019).

14 Foucault, *The History of Sexuality*, 138, emphasis in original.

15 Lauren Berlant, "Slow Death (Sovereignty, Obesity, Lateral Agency)," *Critical Inquiry* 33, no. 4 (2007): 754.

interests in how the exercise of bio-power creates knowledges of health, and subjects individuals to techniques of normalisation, 'letting die' is not a passive abandonment of life but an active management of the circulation of life and death. My theorisation of *thanatopolitics* in this chapter differs from Berlant's concept of 'slow death' in several instances. First, I mobilise the concept to describe how legal institutions in particular harness technologies to allow individuals die. But second, the term enables me to show how in allowing individuals to die, legal institutions reify the value of death in the world, which is to say they economise the *allowance* of a specific amount of death in any given population. The contrasts I am drawing here between *thanatopolitics* and *necro-politics* is not intended to introduce a hierarchy of concepts. I suggest that both political technologies are theoretically useful for describing how sovereign power and bio-power function, sometimes inextricably, while other times almost separably, in different parts of the world. However, if it is agreed that the potency of sovereign power waned in the eighteenth century, rather than insist on its revival in the form of a totalising power that subjugates life to (social) death, I contend that it was reshaped by bio-power into *a political technology for 'taking life or letting live'*. In other words, I suggest that *necro-politics* is one tool amongst others, available to both state and non-state institutions in the governance of death, whether those deaths are violent or accidental, or expected or sudden. *Thanatopolitics* is another technology of bio-power, however, one that is mobilised by legal institutions in subjecting death to the governing logic of economisation.

Interlude

I often spoke with my friend candidly about death. During the pandemic, we would walk around empty parks, repetitively circling the same square, debating, sometimes ardently, how to categorise the particularities of legal governance during a global health crisis. We discussed whether 'biopolitics' is the most appropriate term to describe a mélange of technologies oriented towards fostering life for some, while also letting others die. Or whether disciplinary power was more useful for describing how legal institutions rendered explicit their jurisdiction in regulating our movements in the cityscape. We presciently discoursed about those deaths that will ensue due to governmental interventions into everyday life. These conversations remain imprinted in my mind. Little did I know, and I still don't know, the effects of those conversations on my friend's decision to end her own life. While we seldom walked after lockdowns were lifted, all I knew was that my friend became dismayed about the exponential increase in the number of deaths that governments allowed.

We never spoke during those walks about the bureaucratic procedures that constitute a coronial investigation. I often wonder whether she understood what would happen to her body after she died. Institutions will be given their due, despite our wishes that they leave us alone. The only contact I had with the coronial investigation into her death was through email. The police officer assisting the court sent a poorly written missive to her friends asking if we wanted to write a statement to help the coroner piece together the circumstances of her life and death. These narratives are important for framing how a coroner memorialises the life of the deceased, and coroners often must negotiate between competing tales of a person when they make a finding on how that person came to live and die. I tried to carefully compose my narrative, mindful of being prosaic for a legal audience, and eschewing any suggestions that institutional forces were responsible for her death. But at the same time, I felt I was betraying my friend, reducing the complexities of her life to a page of itemised 'facts'. I struggled with writing that page, and I veered from noting 'facts' that I felt were important for making a finding of the cause of death to including rhetorical flourishes designed to contradict a simplistic narrative of the life and death of my friend. I realised in that moment, though, how little control I had over how the coroner would produce a legal epistemology of my friend's death.

Technologies of death

It is not only death that affects Foucault in the final part of *The History of Sexuality*. In the pages following his ruminations on the governance of death in the eighteenth century, he sketches out a theory of law, which since its publication has generated much confusion in the legal discipline. Foucault explicitly states that law and its institutions did not vanish with the emergence of the age of bio-power. However, he also insists that law is increasingly functioning as a norm, and legal institutions, mechanisms, and technologies form part of a 'continuum of regulatory apparatuses'. 'This argument for the co-existence, hybridization and mutual inter-dependence of law and norm in societies where government takes the form of the calculated administration of life,' write Nikolas Rose and Mariana Valverde, 'may surprise those who think that Foucault denied the role of law and legal mechanisms in the exercise of modern forms of power.'[16] Indeed, many legal scholars have interpreted Foucault's claim that law has been replaced by the norm as an indication that the former's significance has declined in contemporary life. This line of argument goes on to claim that Foucault erroneously categorises law with sovereign power and neglects to comprehend the local specificities of the force of legal institutions, technologies, and relations.

In 'Norms, Discipline, and the Law', François Ewald unapologetically redeems the function of legal institutions in Foucault's writings. He claims that far from marginalising the status of law or removing it from an analytics of bio-power, Foucault seeks in *The History of Sexuality* to understand how legal institutions, technologies, and mechanisms became reshaped in the modern era. While law is not isomorphic with the norm, Foucault questions, according to Ewald, how law operates alongside or intertwined with a governance of life and death in a 'normalizing society':

> His further commentary makes it clear that the formation of a normalizing society in no way diminished the power of law or caused judicial institutions to disappear. In fact, normalization tends to be accompanied by an astonishing proliferation of legislation. Practically speaking, legislators never expressed themselves as freely or as extensively as in the age of bio-power. The norm, then, is opposed not to law itself but to what Foucault would call 'the juridical': the institution of law as the expression of a sovereign's power.[17]

Misunderstandings of Foucault's writings have tended to suggest that law has lost some kind of essential characteristic, which in the transformation from sovereign to bio-power has been replaced with the norm. However, Foucault does not suggest that the sovereign functioning of law was completely superseded with a regulatory orientation. Rather, he

16 Nikolas Rose and Mariana Valverde, "Governed by Law?" *Social & Legal Studies* 7, no. 4 (1998): 542.
17 François Ewald, "Norms, Discipline, and the Law," trans. Marjorie Beale, *Representations* 30 (1990): 138.

simply contends that 'law operates more and more as a norm'.[18] What he means by this is that law is increasingly organised as a technology of normalisation, and at once harnesses normalising technologies in its functioning. Normalisation, according to Ewald, is a mechanism for the production of norms, standards, and rules:

> Normalization is a means of assigning value that renders absolute standards of perfection meaningless. The good is figured in terms of adequacy – the good product is adequate to the purpose it was meant to serve. Within the normative system, values are not defined a priori but instead through an endless process of comparison that is made possible by normalization.[19]

To put this differently, normalisation is one technique amongst many for disciplining bodies (*anatomopolitics*) and controlling populations (*biopolitics*) – that is, for governing relations between life and death. It is a political technology that in the era of bio-power is indistinguishable from, but not isomorphic with, legal institutions, technologies, and mechanisms. This idea of normalisation as a technology that produces an outcome emerges from Ewald's interpretation of the norm as denoting 'both a particular variety of rules, and a way of *producing* them and, perhaps most significantly of all, a principle of *valorisation*'.[20] Yet Ewald also emphasises the necessity of distinguishing 'between the norm itself and the apparatus, institution, or technique of power that brings it into action and functions according to its principles'.[21] In this chapter, I heed Ewald's warning to not collapse law into the category of the norm. I consider law as an arrangement that consists of institutions, technologies and mechanisms, which together construct norms, deploys norms, and self-referentially, cultivate legal epistemologies through the principle of normalisation.

In previous writings, I conceived of law as a network of institutions, relations, and technologies. I utilised this conceptual framework to write a history of how coroners assumed responsibility for taking care of the dead in the nineteenth and twentieth centuries. In *Law and the Dead*, I took aim at how a governance of death is theorised by Foucault as a *political* technology, insisting upon the specificity of law's institutional formations. Then in *Death*, I broadened my conceptualisation of law by categorising legal institutions as normalising insofar as they distribute law making in more diverse forms, include non-legal claims to knowledge in their epistemologies, and anchor legal technologies in governmental practices. While the idea of the governance of death as both a political and legal technology may be ill-suited to writing a history of the office of coroner in the nineteenth and twentieth centuries, the increasingly blurring of *anatomopolitics* and *biopolitics* in the twenty-first century has resulted in the entanglement of the political and the legal, or, as Rose and Valverde say, the governmentalisation of law. This concept facilitates a critical analysis of how legal technologies are produced by and transform non-legal institutions, and how legal institutions deploy political technologies to produce wide-ranging socio-legal effects in society.[22]

18 Foucault, *The History of Sexuality*, 144.
19 Ewald, "Norms, Discipline, and the Law," 152.
20 Ewald, "Norms, Discipline, and the Law," 140, emphasis added.
21 Ewald, "Norms, Discipline, and the Law," 153.
22 Rose and Valverde write that 'an analysis of law from the perspective of government would turn away from the canonical texts and the privileged sites of legal reason, and turn towards the minor, the mundane, the grey, meticulous and detailed work of regulatory apparatuses ... of all the places where, in the bureaucratic workings of our over-governed existence, laws, rules and

Interlude

There was much discussion amongst her friends about when the coroner would release her body for burial. I would add that most of her friends were vexed, if not incensed, by the delay in allowing our friend's body to be committed to the earth. My friend was intensely secular. She wrote in her funeral instructions that she wanted a natural burial, and she provided precise, meticulous guidelines for how, where, and by whom she should be washed, dressed, and entombed. Her friends were keen to follow her instructions, but there were no communications from the coroner about when her body would be released. Her friends, in the throes of grief, impatience, and anger, asked me for guidance, but I couldn't provide any certainties, only speculation. Legal institutions will not be rushed by the desires of the bereaved when it comes to matters of life and death. I must confess that the questions that swirled in my mind touched upon a legal epistemology of death. I wondered if the coroner was holding on to the body because she didn't fit the archetype of a person who dies by suicide, or the forensic pathologist couldn't discern the precise medical cause of death, or the toxicology reports were delayed due to bureaucratic hang-wringing over what kinds of deaths enjoy priority within the department.

I attended her memorial late due to a medical appointment, but I suspect I booked my appointment for that time because I found it difficult to go to the memorial. The funeral was a separate affair, only accessible to a few, far away from the city. I arrived after the formal proceedings when all her friends, who appeared mournful, yet also somewhat relieved, were drinking champagne. As per the funeral instructions, my friend asked us to drink champagne once she died. Her close friend who washed and dressed her prior to her burial remarked that she was surprised to see an incision along the femoral artery in her neck. I didn't see the incision myself, but I was familiar with this dissection, which would have been done to inject contrast media throughout her arteries when performing a computed tomography angiogram. The purpose of the procedure is to highlight abnormal bleeding in the body, and in our jurisdiction, it requires the permission of the coroner.

I wondered in that moment when I heard about the incision whether law did not merely embrace my friend's death. Law authorised the autopsy of her body, it performed an incision and imagining, and it allowed its release and encouraged its decay. I spoke prosaically about these legal authorisations – I felt detached from the individualisation of my friend's body – and I justified the violence of the dissection as the effect of a time-poor pathologist. I was struck by a response from the bereaved that no matter the legal justification for the incision, it was a grotesque violation of the integrity of her body. I am not sure that my friend would have felt the same way. She strongly believed in the disintegration of her body after death and its entanglement with the earth. Neither a person nor a thing, my friend desired one day to become *res nullius*, which in law is defined as 'a lump of earth hath no capacity'.[23]

Conclusion

In *What World Is This?*, Judith Butler writes that 'letting die' is 'the tacit policy of market rationality that accepts a certain number of deaths as necessary to keep the

standards shape our ways of going on, and all the little judges of conduct exercise their petty powers of adjudication and enforcement': Rose and Valverde, "Governed by Law?", 546.
23 *Hayne's Case* (1614) 77 ER 1389, 1389.

economy going'.[24] While that is undoubtedly an aspect of *thanatopolitics*, and it is the central premise of *Death: New Trajectories of Law*, which focused on how death has become subject to a governing logic of economisation, it is not the only tale that can be told about neoliberal rationality in the twenty-first century. *Thanatopolitics* is neither an exception to the rule, nor is it mutually exclusive from biopolitics. As I have discussed in this chapter, 'letting die' is a quotidian practice of governmentality that is inextricable from 'making live', such that *thanatopolitics* and *biopolitics* are but two sides of a *dispositif* that routinely invests in the management of life to a point where individuals are *allowed* to die. As Stuart J Murray remarks, 'there can be no politics of life – no politics of *making live* – that does not also *let die*. Biopolitics kills, albeit indirectly and in the passive voice. It lets die in the name of life.'[25]

This chapter has shown that law positively embraces death. Its institutions are obsessed with the minutiae of mortality, and with defining the threshold from whence life becomes death. In the aftermath of a death, they impose duties upon the bereaved while assuming responsibility for taking care of the dead. Legal institutions are complicit with the governmental logic of economising death; that is to say, they enable, if not foster, the *allowance* of a specific amount of death in any given population. This is most explicit when considering how governments put an individual to death by their own hands, but it is also as significant when governments ordinarily let individuals die through neglect, omission, or 'slowing down', to quote Berlant. In *Precarious Life*, Butler foreshadows this confluence of 'letting die' and 'making live' by asking us to consider who is grievable. If *thanatopolitics* is immanent in legal institutions, then the question for legal scholars is who is allowed to die, whose deaths count for law, and which deaths are marked by law as grievable.[26] For when faced with the intransigence of *thanatopolitics*, we must not seek to liberate death from legal institutions, but rather inquire into how law counts only some of the dead, and honours only some of the lives, in its complicity with the governmental rationality of 'letting die'.

Bibliography

"Report of the Lancet Commission on the Value of Death: Bringing Death Back into Life." *The Lancet* 399 (2022): 837–884.

Berlant, Lauren. "Slow Death (Sovereignty, Obesity, Lateral Agency)." *Critical Inquiry* 33, no. 4 (2007): 754–780.

Butler, Judith. *Precarious Life: The Powers of Mourning and Violence*. London and New York: Verso, 2004.

Butler, Judith. *What World Is This? A Pandemic Phenomenology*. New York: Columbia University Press, 2022.

Campbell, Denis. "Rise in life expectancy has stalled since 2010, research shows." *The Guardian*, 18 July 2017. www.theguardian.com/society/2017/jul/18/rise-in-life-expectancy-has-stalled-since-2010-research-shows.

---

24 Judith Butler, *What World is This? A Pandemic Phenomenology* (New York: Columbia University Press, 2022), 103.

25 Stuart J. Murray, *The Living from the Dead: Disaffirming Biopolitics* (Philadelphia: Pennsylvania State University Press, 2022), 1. See further Stuart J. Murray, "The Practice of Everyday Death: On the Paratactical 'Life' of Neo-liberal Biopolitics," *Canadian Review of American Studies* (2022), e2021017, http://dx.doi.org/10.3138/cras-2021-017, and Stuart J. Murray, "Thanatopolitics: On the Use of Death for Mobilizing Political Life," *Polygraph* 18 (2006).

26 Judith Butler, *Precarious Life: The Powers of Mourning and Violence* (London and New York: Verso, 2004), 20.

Collinson, Patrick. "Life expectancy falls by six months in biggest drop in UK forecasts." *The Guardian*, 8 March 2019. www.theguardian.com/society/2019/mar/07/life-expectancy-slumps-by-five-months.

Ewald, François. "Norms, Discipline, and the Law." Translated by Marjorie Beale. *Representations* 30 (1990): 138–161.

Foucault, Michel. *Society Must Be Defended: Lectures at the Collège de France, 1975–1976*. Translated by David Macey. London: Picador, 2003.

Foucault, Michel. *The History of Sexuality, Volume 1: The Will to Knowledge*. Translated by Robert Hurley. London and New York: Penguin Books, 1998.

Foucault, Michel. "The Political Technology of Individuals." In *Technologies of the Self: A Seminar with Michel Foucault*, edited by Luther H. Martin, Huck Gutman and Patrick H. Hutton, 145–162. Amherst: University of Massachusetts Press, 1988.

Mbembe, Achille. *Necro-politics*. Translated by Steven Corcoran. Durham, NC: Duke University Press, 2019.

Murray, Stuart J. *The Living from the Dead: Disaffirming Biopolitics*. Philadelphia: Pennsylvania State University Press, 2022.

Murray, Stuart J. "The Practice of Everyday Death: On the Paratactical 'Life' of Neo-liberal Biopolitics." *Canadian Review of American Studies* (2022): e2021017. http://dx.doi.org/10.3138/cras-2021-017.

Murray, Stuart J. "Thanatopolitics: On the Use of Death for Mobilizing Political Life." *Polygraph* 18 (2006): 191–215.

Rose, Nikolas, and Mariana Valverde. "Governed by Law?" *Social & Legal Studies* 7, no. 4 (1998): 541–551.

Trabsky, Marc. *Death: New Trajectories of Law*. Abingdon and New York: Routledge, 2024.

Trabsky, Marc. *Law and the Dead: Technology, Relations and Institutions*. Abingdon and New York: Routledge, 2019.

PART 2

Materialities of Death

8

HUMIC LAWSCAPES

Joshua D. M. Shaw[1]

Introduction

In 1614, in the *Haynes's Case*, the 'dead body' was reportedly described by justices at the Serjeant's Inn as 'being *but a lump of earth [it] hath no capacity*'.[2] The absence of capacity meant that title to a shroud did not vest in the individual wrapped in it, but remained with whom placed the property there. To that, English jurists – Sir Edward Coke, Matthew Hale, William Blackstone – added that the case also stood for another rule: no property in a corpse.[3] For these jurists, the dead body lacked capacity of a different kind, too. Not only did the dead body fail as a subject of rights at common law; it was also not an object suitable as property. Rather, the dead body was of ecclesiastical cognizance alone. But despite what was said at Sergeant's Inn, or how the decision has been interpreted, there *is* capacity; dead bodies have affections that animate lawful relations; have capacity to secrete social effects in the folds, distention, and perforation of decomposing flesh, which impress on the world and congeal as law.

Robert Pogue Harrison claims that our relations with decaying matters, and processes of decay, are constitutive of social and cultural forms.[4] He refers to these relations as the humic foundations of the life-world (the 'humic', in the sense of relating to 'humus' or decomposed materials sediment in the earth). By extending the concept of humic

---

1 This chapter is adapted from my PhD dissertation which was supported by the Social Sciences and Humanities Research Council of Canada as a recipient of the Joseph-Armand Bombardier Canada Graduate Scholarships Doctoral Scholarship. In 2021–2022, I also contributed to the SMART-ART project funded by the Natural Sciences and Engineering Research Council of Canada (CREATE 555425-2021), which partly supported me as I completed my dissertation. The chapter was also a winner of the Austin Sarat Award from the Association for the Study of Law, Culture and the Humanities in 2023.
2 *Haynes's Case* (1614) 77 ER 1389, 1389.
3 Edward Coke, *The Third Part of the Institutes of the Law of England: Concerning High Treason, and Order Pleas of the Crown, and Criminal Classes* (London, 1644), 203; Matthew Hale, *The History of the Pleas of the Crown: Volume 1* (London: T. Payne, 1800), 515; William Blackstone, *Commentaries on the Laws of England, Volume 2* (Philadelphia: J. B. Lippincott Co., 1895), 235.
4 Robert Pogue Harrison, *The Dominion of the Dead* (Chicago, IL: University of Chicago Press, 2003).

foundations from cultural studies to the analysis of law, the jurisprudent may re-encounter the decomposing dead as constitutive of law's forms just as the humic is constitutive of other social or cultural forms. The jurisprudent may notice the law secreted by flesh as it folds, as flesh distends, as it is perforated. Order is framed by movement, composition, and destruction of the body. Flesh contorts, joins with touch, and pulls apart, forming a frame incidental to the body's movement which enables from chaos an expression that obtains a certain sensibility, a sense of the lawful in that order, authority, and meaning are jointly fastened on the earth as the body grazes, walks, dances, plays, or is hawked or dragged.[5] In this space of encounter, abutting bodies, abutting the earth, where limbs, flesh, carbon mingle, is the place where laws form, where habits individuate from this flux of matter and obtain a certain solidity that becomes hard to bend – becomes a path that must be followed.[6] This 'vibrant' body, shedding law with each movement, with each affection,[7] forming grooves in the earth and cortical tissues,[8] has been the subject of study by legal scholars before, especially where that body exists in some recognisably living form (like the embodiment of a woman, of an intersex or racialised person, in cases of disability, pregnancy, among other embodiments),[9] but the jurisprudent can be drawn to another kind of body: that of the dead.[10] Because there *is* movement to the dead, even if we often do not think of it.[11]

The constitutive effect of the humic is demonstrated in how the dead haunt the laws of England and her colonies – common, statutory, and ecclesiastical. In this chapter, I trace

5 Elizabeth Grosz, *Chaos, Territory, Art: Deleuze and the Framing of the Earth* (New York: Columbia University Press, 2008). See, e.g., Olivia Barr, *A Jurisprudence of Movement: Common Law, Walking, Unsettling Place* (Abingdon: Routledge, 2016); Joshua David Michael Shaw, "Confronting Jurisdiction with Antinomian Bodies" *Law, Culture and the Humanities* 20, no. 1 (2024): 94; Marc Trabsky, *Law and the Dead: Technologies, Relations, Institutions* (Abingdon: Routledge, 2019). With respect of play, see Joshua D. M. Shaw, "A Minor Jurisprudence of Play: Becoming Jurisprudents through Play in the *Majora's Mask*," in *Law, Video Games, Virtual Realities: Playing Law*, ed. Dale Mitchell, Ashley Pearson, and Timothy D. Peters (Abingdon: Routledge, 2023), 190–210.
6 Margaret Davies, *EcoLaw: Legality, Life and the Normativity of Nature* (Abingdon: Routledge, 2022).
7 See Jane Bennett, *Vibrant Matter: A Political Ecology of Things* (Durham, NC: Duke University Press, 2009); Anna Grear, "Foregrounding Vulnerability: Materiality's Porous Affectability as a Methodological Platform," in *Research Methods in Environmental Law*, ed. Andreas Philippopoulos-Mihalopoulos and Victoria Brooks (London: Edward Elgar, 2017), 3–28; Andreas Philippopoulos-Mihalopoulos, "Atmospheres of Law: Senses, Affects, Lawscapes," *Emotion, Space and Society* 7 (2013): 35; Andreas Philippopoulos-Mihalopoulos, *Spatial Justice: Body, Lawscape, Atmosphere* (Abingdon: Routledge, 2014); Shaw, "Confronting Jurisdiction."
8 Davies, *EcoLaw*; Grosz, *Chaos, Territory, Art*. Also see Margaret Davies, *Law Unlimited: Materialism, Pluralism and Legal Theory* (Abingdon: Routledge, 2017).
9 See, e.g., Sara Ahmed, "Deconstruction and Law's Other: Towards a Feminist Theory of Embodied Legal Rights," *Social and Legal Studies* 4, no. 1 (1995): 55; Ruth Fletcher, Marie Fox, and Julie McCandless, "Legal Embodiment: Analysing the Body of Healthcare Law," *Medical Law Review* 16, no. 3 (2008): 321; Fae Garland and Mitchell Travis, *Intersex Embodiment: Legal Frameworks beyond Identity and Disorder* (Bristol: Bristol University Press, 2023); Roxanne Mykitiuk, "Fragmenting the Body," *Australian Feminist Law Journal* 2, no. 1 (1994): 63.
10 A variation of the thesis is advanced by Ngaire Naffine in "'But a Lump of Earth'? The Legal Status of the Corpse," in *Courting Death: The Law of Mortality*, ed. Desmond Manderson (London: Pluto, 1999), 95–110. However, Naffine does not develop the thesis with respect of the legal theories with which I am engaging here.
11 See, e.g., Barr, *Jurisprudence of Movement*; Shaw, "Confronting Jurisdiction"; Trabsky, *Law and the Dead*.

such hauntings in one instance: *Gilbert v Buzzard and Boyer*, a case from 1820 dealing with a citation of burial law. With *Gilbert*, the Consistory Court of London – a court of ecclesiastical law – indexed the decomposed corpse to the faltered claim to burial.[12] Once fully decomposed, the grave was no longer occupied, extinguishing any surviving claims to the exclusive use of that plot, and reverting the land to the parish. By tracing the influence of decompositions in this case, describing how decomposing materials can be a constitutive form to law, I suggest that the decomposing body evinces a quality – an 'ontogenetic' and 'jurisgenerative' quality.[13] The constitutive form is, in part, in the fluidity of decompositions, which defies containment, stillness, and stable identities, as it leaks, expands, and spreads.[14] Human remains become excrement, as opposed to dignified and ordered by sepulchre, which stages a spacing of 'non-law'. Likewise, the absence that follows decomposition also factors in the formation of law.

Such a thesis demands a materialist theory of law. Within contemporary jurisprudence, there are varied accounts of how physical matter relates to law, and *vice versa*, drawing disparately from Marxist, new materialist. and actor–network theories, among other strands. But, like critical legal theorists Hyo Yoon Kang and Sara Kendall, my interest in materiality (the stuff, things, objects, etc. that make up the world) attunes to 'the legal meaning or quality of the elements that fabricate law'.[15] Such an attunement requires me to: 'observ[e] how certain elements mobilize and condition legal meaning by simultaneously serving as law's material conditions and as the embodiments of legal matters themselves', and 'investigat[e] the properties of those legal materials', as 'a mode of understanding law's composition and relationality'.[16] Relatedly, Alain Pottage describes materialist enquiry into law as, 'instead of presuming "law"', beginning:

> with a set of raw elements: texts, institutions, statements, gestures, architectural and material forms, formalized roles and competences, and self-descriptions (people often characterize themselves as practitioners or participants in 'law'). And, instead of abstracting to a field, medium, code or rationality in which these elements cohere into 'law', one would explore the ways in which elements are assembled into *dispositifs* [whose networked relations, in duration and place, conduce effects experienced as, or later recognized as, 'law'].[17]

---

12 *Gilbert v Buzzard and Boyer* (1820), 3 Phill 335, 161 ER 1342 [*Gilbert* (1820)]. The case was previously heard in a court of common law and reported as *R v Coleridge* (1819), 2 B & ALD 806, 106 Eng Rep 559. There, the Crown sought, on behalf of Mr Gilbert, mandamus which would require 'the rector, officiating curate, churchwardens and sexton of the parish of Saint Andrew' to effect the burial in an iron casket (560). Five justices unanimously held against the Crown, each stating that the method of burial was of ecclesiastical cognizance alone.

13 See Joshua D. M. Shaw and Roxanne Mykitiuk, "Jurisgenerative Tissues: Sociotechnical Imaginaries and the Legal Secretions of 3D Bioprinting," *Law and Critique* 34, no. 2 (2023): 105. Also see Margaret Davies's discussion of biogenesis and jurisgenesis in Davies, *EcoLaw*.

14 See discussion of 'leaky bodies' in Elizabeth Grosz, *Volatile Bodies: Toward a Corporeal Feminism* (Bloomington: Indiana University Press, 1994); Robyn Longhurst, *Bodies: Exploring Fluid Boundaries* (Abingdon: Routledge, 2001); Margrit Shildrick, *Leaky Bodies and Boundaries: Feminism, Postmodernism and (Bio)Ethics* (Abingdon: Routledge, 1997).

15 Hyo Yoon Kang and Sara Kendall, "Legal Materiality," in *The Oxford Handbook of Law and Humanities*, ed. Simon Stern, Maksymillian Del Mar, and Bernadette Meyler (Oxford: Oxford University Press, 2019), 20–37, 34.

16 Kang and Kendall, "Legal Materiality," 34.

17 Alain Pottage, "The Materiality of What?" *Journal of Law and Society* 39, no. 1 (2012): 167, 181.

As I explain below, I develop a materialist theory of law with the assistance of concepts – principally, Andreas Philippopoulos-Mihalopoulos's 'lawscape' – which enlarge and draw focus to the contribution of spatiality, temporality, corporeality, and affect to the genesis of law and legal meaning.[18] In doing so, a materialist theory of law can re-animate, and trace, the relations that comprise the human dead for law.

A right to be deposited in our parental earth

English doctors of ecclesiastical law claimed all God's creations, upon death and by natural right, were deposited in their 'parental earth'.[19] Ecclesiastical law facilitated that right within the English parish and improved it by associating the right with the churchyard where the dead could lie proximate to prayerful communities interested in their absolution. Burial was a spiritual matter, in that it expressed a fundamental relation with God, and ecclesiastical law reflected this in its formulation of the right to Christian burial. But as laid bare in *Gilbert*, the right so claimed could also assume a material form: it referred to the placement of the body in terms of location and mode, and evoked the process of decomposition in how it related the body to the earth and other matter. *Gilbert* thereby shows how the office of Christian burial factored the process of decomposition, which in turn begins to illustrate my claim that bodily decompositions can matter to law and theory. Principally, *Gilbert* demonstrates that the decomposing body can mediate the transition between legal statuses and the relations that comprise those statuses.

In *Gilbert*, the Consistory Court of London was asked whether churchwardens could refuse to bury a parishioner in an iron casket and insist on the use of a wooden one instead. Alternatively, if the churchwardens could not refuse, could a parishioner be charged more for the burial? Key to the parishioner's argument was that 'the ground once given to the interment of a body [was] appropriated for ever to that body'.[20] A parishioner's right to Christian burial was forever, and so it did not matter whether the casket's material prevented or delayed the body's decomposition (although the parishioner also maintained that iron 'goes to rapid decay' and 'would decay as soon as wood'.[21]) To admit authority to decline materials was to erode the parishioner's right to burial:

> If the imperishable nature of the article is admitted as a ground of objection, where is the objection to stop? It may next be made to the interment in lead. There can be no legal right to reject the material: the churchyard and burial grounds belong to the parish, for the interment of the parishioners; they are vested by law in the incumbent and the parishioners. Every parishioner has generally a right to a place in the churchyard; he has no right to any particular spot; but when death and interment have taken place, then there is a severance of the common property, the general right has become a particular right, there is a legal appropriation of a legal right. Inviolability of sepulture is one of the dearest and most ancient rights of mankind; it is most deeply impressed on all

18 Philippopoulos-Mihalopoulos, "Atmospheres of Law"; Philippopoulos-Mihalopoulos, *Spatial Justice*.
19 Robert Phillimore, *Ecclesiastical Law of the Church of England* (London: Henry Sweet, 1873), chapter 10; also see generally about the ecclesiastical legal history of burial in England in Heather Conway, *Law and the Dead* (Abingdon: Routledge, 2016).
20 *Gilbert*, 1344–5, 1350.
21 *Gilbert*, 1344.

our minds, and embodied in our common forms of speech. In the grave a man expects to be undisturbed; it is his last home; and this, *ut requiescat in pace, usque ad resurrectionem* [that he may rest in peace, until the resurrection] (2 Inst. 489), is considered by Lord Coke as a ground of the parishioners' duty of repair.[22]

The churchwardens replied that '[c]ast-iron would certainly be imperishable', and that its common use would interfere with the rights of parishioners to Christian burial:

> [I]f the mode of burying in iron coffins were resorted to, it would be impossible for all the parishioners to be buried in the church-yard, and they would be driven at considerable expense to purchase additional grounds out of the parish. The right of burial is like other rights; it is not to be so used as to injure others.[23]

Further, the allotment of land for a parishioner's burial was not forever. Rather, church-wardens were only required to ensure 'that the body be kept unmolested until it decays'.[24]

Dr William Scott of the Consistory Court held that a parishioner's right to Christian burial could not be denied outside the canons. The canons generally required the body to be laid to rest and buried in consecrated soil, consistent with those portions of theology concerned with death, God's Last Judgment, and the resurrection (otherwise known as 'eschatology').[25] Once committed, the burial ground could not be put to any other use as the land and the dead were inviolable, for as long as both were identifiably present; limited exceptions provided by the canons were exercised sombrely and with hesitation. Sir Henry Spelman – an English scholar of antiquaries cited by Dr Scott – said in his seventeenth-century tract that 'the very burial of [the] body [...] assigned [a place] to some office of Religion' or *Locus Religiosus*, because:

> the nature of the soil has changed from secular, and, in reverence of this new function, counted to be religious, and now therefore by the Canons nothing may be taken for any more graves there.[26]

To be buried was to finally return the body to the earth and emplace one's soul amongst the safekeeping of the soil to await resurrection.[27] By such a process the land was

---

22 *Gilbert*, 1344–5. Latin translation is my own.
23 *Gilbert*, 1345.
24 *Gilbert*, 1345.
25 The right to a Christian burial was enjoyed by all who belonged to the Christian community; namely, as parishioners to the parish churchyard. Exceptions could be granted to those travelling or itinerant. Those dissenting from the Church were by the nineteenth century increasingly admitted, by statute, into their own burying grounds. See generally Conway, *Law and the Dead*.
26 Henry Spelman, *De Sepultura* (London: Robert Young, 1641), 12. *De Sepultura* concerns clergy exhorting monies in consideration for burial, which was contrary to the canons. The tract reproduces and comments upon canons pertaining to burial.
27 Such eschatology was not universally shared across time or denominations. To suggest the soul could be emplaced in the soil was to suggest it had, or could have, a materiality, which was inconsistent with the theories of some. The eschatology to which I refer to was that relied on, albeit variably, by medieval and early modern ecclesiastics in England who countenanced the ecclesiastical law applicable to the English parish. See discussion in Caroline Walker Bynum, "Material Continuity, Personal Survival and the Resurrection of the Body: A Scholastic Discussion in its Medieval and Modern Contexts," in *Fragmentation and Redemption: Essays on Gender and the Human Body in Medieval Religion* (Brooklyn, NY: Zone Books, 1992), 239–97;

'severed from human property' and returned to God. Since at least AD 750, such a spot was generally the yard surrounding the parish church, when a constitution was imported by Archbishop Cuthbert from the Holy See of Rome that required it.[28] Deviations threatened excommunication, such as Pope Boniface VIII's promulgation in AD 1300 which prohibited the disembowelment of human remains, and their boiling to separate flesh from bones.[29]

The sacred status of the burial spot, and the body emplaced in it, prohibited clergy from exhorting monies in consideration for the service of burial as it profaned what properly belonged to God (as *Locus Sacratus*). Selling land for burial also constituted 'a reaping of commodity out of carcasses of the dead', which presented an impossible commodity in God since the human body was His as *imago Dei*. [30] The ecclesiastical 'office of burial' was devoted to furthering 'the Law of Nature and divine Law [of] bury [ing] the dead', which required clergy to selflessly deposit the human dead in their parental earth and to ensure they remained deposited.[31] Whilst 'no positive rule of law or of religion [...] prescribe[d]' the 'way the mortal remains [were] to be conveyed to their last abode'[32] – such matters instead arose from sentiment and use – the law did provide for a right to burial.

But with respect to the parishioner's claim, Dr Scott complained that the parishioner misconstrued the right to burial, giving it a content unfamiliar to the 'original abstract right' and without due regard for what was 'necessarily involved in it': '[t]hat right, strictly taken, is to be returned to his parent earth for dissolution, and to be carried there for that purpose in a decent and inoffensive manner'.[33] To demand an iron casket may develop out of 'natural feelings' toward the dead, specifically the want to have those remains treated with care, but the right narrowly pertained to being deposited in and returned to the earth (although ecclesiastical law did not prohibit it).[34] Further, the parishioner's argument that 'the ground once given to the interment of a body is appropriated forever to that body' failed:[35]

> [I]t seems to be assumed that the tenant [of the grave] himself is imperishable;
> for surely there cannot be an inextinguishable title, a perpetuity of possession
> belonging to a perishable thing: but obstructed in a portion of it by public

Caroline Walker Bynum, *The Resurrection of the Body in Western Christianity, 200–1336* (New York: Columbia University Press, 2017).

28 *Gilbert*, 1347.

29 William Devlin, "Cremation," in *The Catholic Encyclopedia: An International Work of Reference on the Constitution, Doctrine, Discipline, and History of the Catholic Church (Volume 4)*, ed. Charles Herbermann et al. (New York: The Encyclopedia Press, 1908), 481–3.

30 Spelman, *De Sepultura*, 11. In early medieval England, Christian eschatology permitted different bodily cultures where the dead bodies of saints, and parts thereof, were commodified and exchanged, *because* of saints' proximity to God. There were periods where significant trade was undertaken with respect of relics. However, relics were not practised under the Church of England. See Caroline Walker Bynum, "The Female Body and Religious Practice in the Later Middle Ages," in *Fragments for a History of the Human Body: Part 1*, ed. Michel Feher, Ramona Naddaff, and Nadia Tazi (Brooklyn, NY: Zone Books, 1989), 160–219; Patrick J. Geary, *Living with the Dead in the Middle Ages* (Ithica, NY: Cornell University Press, 1994).

31 Spelman, *De Sepultura*, 3.

32 *Gilbert*, 1347.

33 *Gilbert*, 1348.

34 *Gilbert*, 1350.

35 *Gilbert*, 1350.

authority, the fact is, that 'man' and 'for ever' are terms quite incompatible in any state of his existence, dead or alive, in this world. The time must come when his posthumous remains must mingle with and compose a part of the soil in which they have been deposited. Precious embalmments [sic] and splendid monuments may preserve for centuries the remains of those who have filled the more commanding stations of human life: but the common lot of mankind furnishes them with no such means of conservation. With reference to men, the *domus aeterna* is a mere flourish of rhetoric. The process of nature will resolve them into an intimate mixture with their kindred earth, and will furnish a place of repose for other occupants of the grave in succession.[36]

Accordingly, an iron casket could be requested, but was not guaranteed. If iron was allowed, churchwardens were entitled to charge more to maintain the grounds, since iron was likely to slow the process of decay and thereby delay the plot's reversion to common use of the parish.[37]

Jurisgenerativity of the corpse

At least in my reading, the Consistory Court incorporated the process of decay into legal reasoning. The dead body 'mingle[d] with and compose[d] a part of the soil', which, for Dr Scott, aligned title to a grave with the temporality of the dead body. Title thereby extinguished once the body fully churned and disassembled, and '[t]he process of nature [...] resolve[d] [the body] into an intimate mixture with their kindred earth'.[38] At this juncture, clerical duties to burial were fulfilled, in that no meaningful trace of the person remained, lying vulnerable to disturbance or defilement where it was deposited. The soul was preserved amongst that spot of soil, to await resurrection, as the physical body was taken in by worms, becoming, once again, one with the earth: dust to dust, just as God sentenced.[39] For clergy, upon the extinguishment of title the land became amenable to subsequent use which, in the context of a consecrated churchyard, was restricted to further burials as the land reverted to common use of the parish. If not a churchyard, it would have reverted to a natural state, awaiting appropriation for any lawful use.[40] In *Gilbert*, with consequence to the parish, the iron casket prolonged 'the process of nature' to which title was indexed; however, the body would still decompose and so the title, like the body, was perishable and therefore could not be prohibited. But delayed decomposition, arising from a parishioner's choice of material, entitled the churchwarden to charge more to ensure the churchyard's upkeep over a longer period.

The physical matter of the decomposing corpse – its materiality – functions here as an intermediary between legal statuses where one status and the relations that comprise it become another once decomposition is complete. The material presence of the decomposing dead, and its eventual absence, orders how others – churchwardens, undertakers,

36 *Gilbert*, 1349–50.
37 *Gilbert*, 1354.
38 *Gilbert*, 1350.
39 Worms consuming the corpse is a motif common among discourses on sepulchre in the eighteenth and nineteenth centuries.
40 Prue Vines, "Bodily Remains in the Cemetery and the Burial Ground: A Comparative Anthropology of Law and Death *or* How Long can I Stay?" in *Courting Death: The Law of Mortality*, ed. Desmond Manderson (London: Pluto, 1999), 111–27, 122.

parishioners – lawfully relate to each other and the burial place. The ordering is spatial, in that *Locus Sacratus* excludes others and prohibits conduct at that spot where the corpse is placed. It is also temporal, in that bit by bit the corpse vacates that spot, becoming indistinguishable from the soil, which conditions upon completion further iterations of use. Elsewhere, Marty Slaughter describes that which 'lies outside law', as 'chaos, fragmentation, hybridisation, and decomposition' in contrast to 'law belong[ing] to and creat[ing] an order of things' that connects, unifies, *and* 'survives the individual parts'.[41] Slaughter looks to the cutting up, decomposition, and admixture of bodies and bodily materials as evincing this point of 'non-Law'. Likewise, the decomposing corpse may be said to perform a duration of non-law between two points of law separated in chronological time: the grave site as *Locus Sacratus* exists as an order of things that encases and preserves the dead's repose; and once decomposed that place assumes another order, becoming property again or at least available for such lawful uses. The duration between creates a space of non-law, of chaos, needed to bring about another law where the prior law perished.

That duration also participates in creating the order that follows. Borrowing from Robert Cover, the duration may be described as 'jurisgenerative' in that immanent to its expression is the genesis of normative worlds which supply a sensory and narrative repertoire for law.[42] Cover was writing on diverging constitutional interpretations, far afield from dead bodies, but I think his comments on the formation of an interpretive community, namely through the exertion of an 'insular autonomy'[43] or a 'principle of separateness [as] constitutive and jurisgenerative'[44] can be extended by analogy to the physical matter of decomposition. Cover described the jurisgenerative as akin to 'juridical mitosis', where:

> New law is constantly created through the sectarian separation of communities. The 'Torah' becomes two, three, many Toroth as surely as there are teachers to teach or students to study. The radical instability of the paideic *nomos* forces intentional communities – communities whose members believe themselves to have common meanings for the normative dimensions of their common lives – to maintain their coherence as paideic entities by expulsion and exile of the potent flowers of normative meaning.[45]

Different cultural and institutional configurations thereby proliferate *nomoi* by conditioning people's separation from a prior community – allowing another to intentionally form in contradistinction[46] – or maintain nomoi through apparatuses of enforcement that pre-empt separation.[47] Those worlds suppress the possibility of others in the fact of their unity, as an enforcement of that which is already present or as inspiration toward what is imagined to be.[48] Returning to *Gilbert*, we might see a similar movement at play where a

---

41 M. M. Slaughter, "Sacred Kingship and Antinomianism: Antirrhesis and the Order of Things," *Law and Literature* 4, no. 2 (1992): 227, 228.

42 Robert M. Cover, "Nomos and Narrative" *Harvard Law Review* 97 (1983): 4.

43 Cover, "*Nomos* and Narrative," 26.

44 Cover, "*Nomos* and Narrative," 29.

45 Cover, "*Nomos* and Narrative," 15–6.

46 Cover, "*Nomos* and Narrative," 12–3.

47 Cover, "*Nomos* and Narrative," 13.

48 Robert M. Cover, "Violence and the Word," *Yale Law Journal* 95 (1985): 1601.

prior unity in *Locus Sacralas*, analogous to Cover's Torah, was disembowelled by the appearance of difference divined through the body's decomposition. The integrity of the prior unity channelled through the body in repose was dissolved as the body decayed, setting the occasion for another unity to take place. The movement was repeated with each burial, with each process of decomposition, which nested the space of non-law within a pattern or choreography that formed a superior unity or structure. The difference produced by the jurisgenerative functioned *for* that structure as opposed to against it, enabling a change in state necessary for its performance. Here, that structure was created through narratives of Christian eschatology, of which the parish and the parishioners formed part. An iron casket portended the narrative's destabilisation by protracting the decompositions upon which it relied. The Consistory Court attempted to re-incorporate the jurisgenerative within the higher unity supplied by the eschatological narrative by admitting iron if churchwardens could still maintain the grounds for their holy purpose.

Antinomian bodies

Elsewhere, I have characterised bodily processes as jurisgenerative in that flesh and other viscera necessarily exceed the grids law imposes on the human, creating space in their transgression for different legalities to emerge.[49] I have located these 'leaky bodies' in contests of the medico-legal prescription of death,[50] in speculations of the jurisdictional effects of post-mortem organ and tissue donation,[51] and, with Roxanne Mykitiuk, in appraising the imaginaries that could arise from 3D bioprinting.[52] In these cases, I (or, in the last instance, we) have taken Mykitiuk's argument about 'recalcitrant' bodies and bodily fragments further;[53] the body and bodily parts are not only a corporeal remainder to law's discourses, but also formative spacings for law.[54] Law can be made through the physical processes of bodies – processes which are 'antinomian' in that such bodies test the nomoi they form part of – with new orders forming as nomoi stretch, perforate, and heal over.[55] And like many scars, a trace of that wound indelibly brands the flesh as the new nomos settles. Antinomian bodies, as I have called them, can mediate both law's dissolution and formation, as sinews connecting normative possibilities.[56] The human dead functions similarly: as the integrity of the body falters, the nomos carried by the body does too, transforming, taking on a new figure, with each decomposition. Although, unlike my prior investigations of the jurisgenerative, the antinomian body disappears – it becomes absent or other – which is suggestive of a different form to law.[57]

Marty Slaughter makes a similar observation when counterposing the genealogy of law – the sacred body that is the King's common law – to the 'antinomianism' of decompositions, fragments, adulterations, among other agents of chaos. Law is the binding of 'an individual

49 Joshua David Michael Shaw, "The Spatio-Legal Production of Bodies Through the Legal Fiction of Death," *Law and Critique* 32, no. 1 (2021): 69.
50 Shaw, "Spatio-Legal Production of Bodies."
51 Shaw, "Confronting Jurisdiction."
52 Shaw and Mykitiuk, "Jurisgenerative Tissues."
53 Mykitiuk, "Fragmenting the Body."
54 Shaw and Mykitiuk, "Jurisgenerative Tissues."
55 Shaw and Mykitiuk, "Jurisgenerative Tissues."
56 Shaw and Mykitiuk, "Jurisgenerative Tissues."
57 Regarding the importance of absence to embodiment, generally see Drew Leder, *The Absent Body* (Chicago, IL: University of Chicago Press, 1990).

to a name and gather[ing] [of] dispersed isolated things under a sign', of a filial unity, which 'relates the individual to an order that survives the individual parts'.[58] Slaughter relates metaphors of physical, bodily processes to the law of 'Antinomians', the seventeenth-century movement of protestants that rejected the King's Law, claiming instead that the 'law [lying] within' the individual would, through the achievement of 'inner perfection', allow the King's '[L]aw [to] wither away'.[59] The antinomian position is one of

> an outcast individual without language and syntax, with only a private language, babbling to himself with words that in their detached state are pieces of copper rather than pennies, that have no social meaning and make no contact – that decompose and vanish like the body.[60]

Antinomianism potentiates the fulfilment of chaos, the fulfilment of disorder, through the individual's withdrawal and separateness. But whilst Slaughter's reference to decompositions is metaphorical, I see it as real, materialised in the flesh. The decomposing corpse – as conduit of a space of non-law – works analogously to Slaughter's 'Antinomians', withdrawing from the nomos of the body, creating the possibility of a new nomos as tissues separate, bones disintegrate, and residues mix with the earth.

My claim relates to, but is different from Prue Vines' comments on *Gilbert*, who straightforwardly argues that 'once the body [...] decompose[s] it [...] *disappear[s]*, and the land is no longer a burial ground – it [...] [loses] that character'.[61] Vines continues by saying 'the body is defined as separate from the soil in which it is buried, and after decomposition seems to have legally and culturally "disappeared". The site of burial is then available to be used again.'[62] She contrasts *Gilbert* with practices among Indigenous peoples in Australia, for whom 'the body when [it] decompose[s] would seem not to [...] "disappear[...]" or "evaporate[e]" but [...] merge[...] with the land'.[63] With that comparison, Vines concludes the ecclesiastical legal system, and the common law which has inherited its principles, 'can only conceive of death as personal silence or absence'.[64] But the corpse does not merely evince an absence, nor does it merely separate the body from land; there is a productive quality to the dead, expressed through its relations with others, which Vines leaves undertheorised, in that its process of decomposition bears on, and constitutes a form for, law. There is an architectonics to the corpse, in the sense of a spacing and movement to the corporeal form which grafts on to and creates physical and social space including the law and normativities of such space.[65]

Those architectonics are also elided by political theorist James Martel in his recent analysis of the dead.[66] Martel and I share in arguing that the corpse, especially as it

58 Slaughter, "Sacred Kingship," 228.
59 Slaughter, "Sacred Kingship," 233.
60 Slaughter, "Sacred Kingship," 234.
61 Vines, "Bodily Remains," 122.
62 Vines, "Bodily Remains," 123.
63 Vines, "Bodily Remains," 122.
64 Vines, "Bodily Remains," 122.
65 Henri Lefebvre, *The Production of Space* (London: Blackwell, 1989); also see Shaw, "Spatio-Legal Production of Bodies."
66 James R. Martel, "Interrupted by Death: The Legal Personhood and Non-Personhood of Corpses," *Studies in Law, Politics and Society* 87A (2022): 103.

decomposes, is subversive to the Law and that, through that subversion, participates in authorising another law.[67] However, we appear to differ in how we conceive this subversion taking place. Martel describes the corpse as 'exert[ing] a kind of counteragency', because the corpse – like any object – 'inherently resist[s] projection' of the Law's phantasms.[68] In doing so, he draws on Walter Benjamin to argue that the dead may lack language (at least as humans know it by speech and sound) but nonetheless 'emit "the magic of matter" among themselves', forming a 'material community' of affects which 'rebel[s] against the false names and fetishistic projects – and especially commodity fetishism – to which [humans] subject them'.[69] The corpse as object evinces a limit to law through its unmaking of language – of law's mythic violence – which gives room for other forms of law (or the Law's rearticulation).[70] On the surface, our accounts resemble each other, but there are differences (which, due to constraints of space, require explanation elsewhere). For now, it is adequate to say I see Martel as having a negative account of the corpse (as lack, silence, object, etc.), counterposed to law as belonging only to a symbolic domain, whose relation is achieved principally through a dialectic of opposing forces. By contrast, I attempt a non-dialectical materialism where certain distinctions (absence/presence, subject/object) are not fundamentally opposed to one another, but are generated together on an immanent plane of 'differential elements and relations'.[71] As literary theorist Erin Edwards put it, the '"live human" and "corpse human" part ways, not according to a more traditional divide between vitalism and mortalism but according to different modes of *doing*'.[72] It is through the latter, I think, that the jurisprudent can better sense how the dead have capacities for law without reinscribing the familiar problematics of conventional legal theory.

Toward a materialist theory of law and the dead

The legal status of the human dead has constantly challenged scholars. But I try to overcome the challenge by following Ngaire Naffine and Margaret Davies, who called on jurisprudents to look beyond conventional theories of personality and property.[73] Instead, the jurisprudent should analyse the socio-material conditions through which human bodies, living or dead, take form, inhabit, and obtain meaning[74] – it is in our attention to 'the historical and discursive processes which shape our socio-legal environment', including our relations with the physical and social world, where the legal status and function of the human dead may be understood (or at least understood with different effect).[75] Whilst personality and property are not irrelevant to the common law, they are

67 Martel, "Interrupted by Death."
68 James R. Martel, *Bodies Unburied: Subversive Corpses and the Authority of the Dead* (Amherst, MA: Amherst College Press, 2018), 137.
69 Martel, *Bodies Unburied*, 139.
70 Martel, *Bodies Unburied*, 140–1; also see Martel, "Interrupted by Death."
71 Pheng Cheah, "Non-Dialectical Materialism," in *New Materialisms: Ontology, Agency, and Politics*, ed. Diana Coole and Samantha Frost (Durham, NC: Duke University Press, 2010), 70–91, 85.
72 Erin E, Edwards, *The Modernist Corpse: Posthumanism and the Posthumous* (Minneapolis: University of Minnesota Press, 2018), 6.
73 Margaret Davies and Ngaire Naffine, *Are Persons Property? Legal Debates About Property and Personality* (Farnham: Ashgate, 2001); Naffine, "But a Lump of Earth."
74 Naffine, "But a Lump of Earth."
75 Davies and Naffine, *Are Persons Property*, 184.

mere fragments of a social process – '[n]either [...] possesses a unitary, stable meaning'[76] – and fail to account for all factual elements (like those in *Gilbert*). It is that thesis on which my reading of *Gilbert* necessarily depends. It is also the thesis my reading potentially confirms and elaborates, albeit with a materialist theory of law. By materialist theory of law, I mean to describe law as the effect of a socially imbedded, embodied, and ecologically mediated practice of action that *matters* in experience and existence including that of the non-human.[77] But in addition to confirming and elaborating Naffine and Davies's socio-legal thesis, and in so doing observing how the body's decomposition can factor in the genesis of law and norms, my approach raises a question for a materialist theory of law that warrants comment.

A useful concept to a materialist theory of law is the lawscape, which Andreas Philippopoulos-Mihalopoulos defines as 'the tautology between law and space/matter [that] unfolds as difference' in physical and social existence.[78] The lawscape 'is co-determined with the space between bodies [...]; the space that is produced and is occupied by bodies; the movement of bodies; the desire of bodies; and the withdrawal of bodies for another law'.[79] Bodies which compose the lawscape can be human, non-human, material, and immaterial.[80] The lawscape can be thought of as being 'held up' in social practice, in that physical and social spaces extend from witting and unwitting acts of bodies that converge in place, figuring whom and what belongs in a place and that which is excluded.[81] The lawscape also enfolds time, sustaining durations, flows, and rhythms between and within the practices of bodies.[82] The resulting spatio-temporalities of living flesh thereby exude law, as the lawscape, as they form patterns (and thus normativities) for physical and social action.[83]

With the dead, however, the space between, produced, and occupied by bodies (the cadaver itself, its constituent parts, and that which the corporeal becomes) tends to subtraction in the loss of corporeal integrity and identity, eventually leaving little to no trace – an absence that appears totalising. Here, the body does not so much hold up the

---

76 Davies and Naffine, *Are Persons Property*, 181.
77 See, e.g., Grear, "Foregrounding Materiality"; Alain Pottage, "Introduction: The Fabrication of Persons and Things," in *Law, Anthropology, and the Constitution of the Social: Making Persons and Things*, ed. Alain Pottage and Martha Mundy (Cambridge: Cambridge University Press, 2004), 1–39.
78 Andreas Philippopoulos-Mihalopoulos, "Lawscape," *International Lexicon of Aesthetics* (2020), http://doi.org/10.7413/18258630100.
79 Philippopoulos-Mihalopoulos, "Lawscape."
80 See Gilles Deleuze, *Foucault*, trans. Seán Hand (Minneapolis: University of Minnesota Press, 1988); also see Andreas Philippopoulos-Mihalopoulos, "Law, Space, Bodies: The Emergence of Spatial Justice," in *Deleuze and Law*, ed. Laurent de Sutter and Kyle McGee (Edinburgh: Edinburgh University Press, 2012), 90–110.
81 Sarah Keenan, *Subversive Property: Law and the Production of Spaces of Belonging* (Abingdon: Routledge, 2015); also see Joshua David Michael Shaw, "Transcarceral Lawscapes Enacted in Moments of Aboriginalisation: A Case-study of an Indigenous Woman Released on Urban Parole," *International Journal of Law in Context* 16, no. 4 (2020): 422.
82 Sameena Mulla, "Topological Time, Law and Subjectivity: A Description in Five Folds," in *Law and Time*, ed. Sian Beynon-Jones and Emily Graham (Abingdon; Routledge, 2020). Also see Mariana Valverde, *Chronotopes of Law: Jurisdiction, Scale and Governance* (Abingdon: Routledge, 2015).
83 Shaw, "Confronting Jurisdiction"; Shaw "Spatio-Legal Production of Bodies"; Shaw and Mykitiuk, "Jurisgenerative Tissues"; also see the discussion of biogenesis and jurisgenesis in Davies, *EcoLaw*.

law; rather, by decomposing the body appears to *drop* the law as flesh *wastes* away, *withdrawing* from extant unities of life/law/order.[84] From this vantage, decomposition appears thoroughly anarchic in the total absence of law that it portends – an annihilative spacetime of non-Law.[85] The flesh is atomised, sublimated as autonomous particles that refuse communication with (or at least comprehension by) others, given up entropically to disorder against the unity promised by Law.[86] But in flux, the space between, produced, and occupied by bodies also tends to accretion, creating excess matters and substrates for other things. Those excretions enable new relations as different forms are assumed, and in this way hold up further iterations of lawscapes: as humic foundations for whatever law is to come. Despite Harrison, these humic foundations need not be cultivated as relations of memory, debt, or inheritance (such as in traditions of burial).[87] Rather, relations of the dead are potently multiple, which a materialist theory of law may attune to and shape.[88]

Whilst Philippopoulos-Mihalopoulos's concept of lawscape is abundant with relation – bringing seemingly disparate bodies together on a singular ontological plane to trace the complex entanglements generative of difference in the physical and social world – he emphasises that the lawscape is conditioned by withdrawal: there is an ontological need of all bodies to 'succum[b] to […] ruptures', retreating from the lawscape and turning inward.[89] In turning inward, withdrawal instantiates a duration of non-relation, of a retreat to the law of the individual. The need to withdraw allows for difference, the emergence of striations and separateness in the lawscape, which are fundamental to a lively law that frames, creates, and orders meaningful action.[90] The conditions of withdrawal then shape the desire and attainment of one's return to a lawscape to become part of its atmosphere,[91] where atmosphere is 'the excess of affect that keeps bodies together; and what emerges when bodies are held together by, [through] and against each other'.[92] Decomposition appears not only to imitate the ontological condition of withdrawal, but actually realises it in the flesh, ever widening the reach of annihilation until the remains are physically overtaken and gone. In so doing, decomposition appears to take the thesis of withdrawal to its extreme: the law of the individual (autonomy or 'the capacity to give oneself one's own law by one's own means'[93]) otherwise enabled by withdrawal is evacuated upon the destruction of the physical body, which may be uniquely felt by those for whom that individual's life/law/order was meaningfully affective (for whom awareness of, and care for, the finitude of relation – relative to the place of law – can inaugurate a feeling of loss).[94]

---

84 Jean-Luc Nancy, *Corpus*, trans. Richard A Rand (New York: Fordham University Press, 2008), 105.
85 Nancy, *Corpus*.
86 Slaughter, "Sacred Kingship."
87 Harrison, *Dominion of the Dead*. Certainly, memory, debt, and inheritance are familiar modes of relating to the dead, and often central to the juridification of the earth within common law traditions. See Barr, *Jurisprudence of Movement*.
88 See, e.g., Shaw, "Confronting Jurisdiction."
89 Andreas Philippopoulos-Mihalopoulos, "Withdrawing from Atmosphere: An Ontology of Air Partitioning and Affective Engineering," *Society and Space* 34, no. 1 (2016): 150, 154.
90 Philippopoulos-Mihalopoulos, *Spatial Justice*; also see Grosz, *Chaos, Art, Territory*.
91 Philippopoulos-Mihalopoulos, "Withdrawing from Atmosphere."
92 Philippopoulos-Mihalopoulos, "Withdrawing from Atmosphere," 158.
93 Stewart Motha, "My Story, Whose Memory: Notes on the Autonomy and Heteronomy of Law," *Studies in Law, Politics and Society* 87B (2022): 1, 15.
94 Harrison, *Dominion of the Dead*.

Withdrawal by decomposition may occasion the end of the individual body – at least relative to that lawscape – but it is not the end of law. As critical legal theorist Stewart Motha stresses, law is not only autonomy (of the individual); law is also heteronomy in the sense of the 'presence of an external or different law: of myth, extraneous forces, drives, legal institutions and history'.[95] The law of the other. Even with the destruction of the individual (archive, actor, corpse, etc.), in its wake there seeps a heteronomous carriage whose retrieval from the pits of what is no longer there supplies meaning for new forms. Most clearly, as bodies decompose, excrements 'throw' their presence open, exceeding the body/law of the individual, defying the signs of order and intelligibility incarnate in the human form, enabling the possibility of new worldings, or lawscapes, in the resulting tangle of worms, mycelia, and soil-kinds, among other bodies.[96] But absence too throws itself, felt knowingly or unknowingly on others, whose traces supply 'heteronomous determinants'[97] for future lawscapes.

Conclusion

I close this chapter as I began: with Harrison and the humic foundations of the life-world. Harrison writes that as 'humans dwell, the dead, as it were, indwell – and very often in the same space'.[98] The humic foundations result from this 'indwelling' of the dead among and in the living, forming part of, and structuring from within, institutions of social and cultural life. Importantly for Harrison, this is firstly an ontology *of the dead*, in that 'the corpse [and our disposal of it] is one of the most primordial of human institutions'.[99] Disposing of the dead establishes place, and 'mortalises' time, in a mode of being rehearsed later by statues and gravestones, among other objects, all of which demand awareness of humanity's finitude and memorialisation of and care for what has passed.[100] I do not inherit his thought uncritically. As critical theorist Ewa Domańska observes, Harrison writes in a register that is 'humanistic, anthropocentric, and Eurocentric, essentialist, and Christian'.[101] But I think it is possible to rehabilitate the *humus* in postmodern directions: to, as Erin Edwards put it, encounter the dead as 'materializing (and often decomposing) [...] heteroglossias, necroglossias, and object-oriented *res*glossias that problematize the binary between body and discourse, matter and information'.[102] In the polyphony of the lawscape, the humus can be understood to do more for law than impose (for Harrison), or bemuse and resist (for Martel), or represent silences (for Vines). In a materialist theory, the *humus* participates in the making and unmaking of law, much like other cultural formations, through both presence *and* absence, law *and* non-law, autonomy *and* heteronomy, all of which messily, fractiously, and uncontrollably compose (and decompose and recompose) differentiations within the lawscape.[103]

95 Motha, "My Story." Motha (p. 19) notes resonances between the jurisprudential concept of heteronomy and 'recent strands of new materialist thinking and attention to *affect* in legal studies', like Philippopoulos-Mihalopoulos's lawscape.
96 Nancy, *Corpus*.
97 Motha, "My Story," 12.
98 Harrison, *Dominion of the Dead*, ix.
99 Harrison, *Dominion of the Dead*, 92–3.
100 Harrison, *Dominion of the Dead*.
101 Ewa Domańska, "Necrocacy," *History of the Human Sciences* 18, no. 2 (2005): 111, 117.
102 Edwards, *Modernist Corpse*, 41.
103 Harrison, *Dominion of the Dead*.

As a cadaver is taken up by worms, its material presence – and rights, duties, and powers indexed to the corpse – alters, resulting in changes to how others lawfully orient and relate to a physical and social space. A burial spot may require additional care until the iron-clad corpse falls apart into the soil, becoming fit for re-use once decomposed; decay may effect a pestilence (or, depending on the theory of contagion, a miasmatic atmosphere) that necessitates closing intramural facilities, displacing them without the city limits;[104] sanitation, decency, and the preservation of coronial evidence may require the prompt and secure retrieval, transfer, and storage of the dead prior to an inquest.[105] Concurrent to these changes is the re-composition of physical and social space, and the normative worlds staged in and through that space.[106] But irrespective of the particular lawscapes a corpse challenges and sustains, decomposing bodies resist and open up the lawful as it is spaced through the craft of disposal, potentially authorising novel and different ways of relating to the dead and the spaces they occupy.[107] Here lies the law-scape of the human dead, awaiting use by the jurisprudent attuned to its capacities.

Bibliography

Ahmed, Sara. "Deconstruction and Law's Other: Towards a Feminist Theory of Embodied Legal Rights." *Social and Legal Studies* 4, no. 1 (1995): 55–73.

Barr, Olivia. *A Jurisprudence of Movement: Common Law, Walking, Unsettling Place*. Abingdon: Routledge, 2016.

Bennett, Jane. *Vibrant Matter: A Political Ecology of Things*. Durham, NC: Duke University Press, 2009.

Blackstone, William. *Commentaries on the Laws of England, Volume 2*. Philadelphia: J. B. Lippincott Co., 1895.

Bynum, Caroline Walker. "The Female Body and Religious Practice in the Later Middle Ages." In *Fragments for a History of the Human Body: Part 1*, edited by Michel Feher, Ramona Naddaff, and Nadia Tazi, 160–219. Brooklyn, NY: Zone Books, 1989.

Bynum, Caroline Walker. "Material Continuity, Personal Survival and the Resurrection of the Body: A Scholastic Discussion in its Medieval and Modern Contexts." In *Fragmentation and Redemption: Essays on Gender and the Human Body in Medieval Religion*, 239–297. Brooklyn, NY: Zone Books, 1992.

Bynum, Caroline Walker. *The Resurrection of the Body in Western Christianity, 200–1336*. New York: Columbia University Press, 2017.

Cheah, Pheng. "Non-Dialectical Materialism." In *New Materialisms: Ontology, Agency, and Politics*, edited by Diana Coole and Samantha Frost, 70–91. Durham, NC: Duke University Press, 2010.

Coke, Edward. *The Third Part of the Institutes of the Law of England: Concerning High Treason, and Order Pleas of the Crown, and Criminal Classes*. London, 1644.

Conway, Heather. *Law and the Dead*. Abingdon: Routledge, 2016.

Cover, Robert M. "*Nomos* and Narrative." *Harvard Law Review* 97 (1983): 4.

Cover, Robert M. "Violence and the Word." *Yale Law Journal* 95 (1985): 1601–1629.

Davies, Margaret. *Law Unlimited: Materialism, Pluralism and Legal Theory*. Abingdon: Routledge, 2017.

104 With respect of animal bodies and miasmas, and the institutional response to these apparent dangers, see Marc Trabsky, "Institutionalising the Public Abattoir in Nineteenth Century Colonial Society," *Australian Feminist Law Journal* 40, no. 2 (2014): 169.

105 See Trabsky, *Law and the Dead*.

106 See Andreas Philippopoulos-Mihalopoulos, "Law is a Stage: From Aesthetics to Affective Aestheses," in *Research Handbook on Critical Legal Theory*, ed. Emilios Christodoulidis, Ruth Dukes and Marco Galdoni (London: Edward Elgar, 2019), 201–22. Also see Shaw, "Minor Jurisprudence of Play."

107 With respect of jurisdiction and authorisations of the lawful in instances involving the dead, see Barr, *Jurisprudence of Movement*; Shaw, "Confronting Jurisdiction"; Trabsky, *Law and the Dead*. Also see Shaunnagh Dorsett and Shaun McVeigh, *Jurisdiction* (Abingdon: Routledge, 2012).

Davies, Margaret. *EcoLaw: Legality, Life and the Normativity of Nature*. Abingdon: Routledge, 2022.

Davies, Margaret, and Ngaire Naffine. *Are Persons Property? Legal Debates About Property and Personality*. Farnham: Ashgate, 2001.

Deleuze, Gilles. *Foucault*. Translated by Seán Hand. Minneapolis: University of Minnesota Press, 1988.

Devlin, William. "Cremation." In *The Catholic Encyclopedia: An International Work of Reference on the Constitution, Doctrine, Discipline, and History of the Catholic Church (Volume 4)*, edited by Charles Herbermann *et al.*, 481–483. New York: The Encyclopedia Press, 1908.

Domańska, Ewa. "Necrocacy." *History of the Human Sciences* 18, no. 2 (2005): 111–122.

Dorsett, Shaunnagh, and Shaun McVeigh, *Jurisdiction*. Abingdon: Routledge, 2012.

Edwards, Erin E. *The Modernist Corpse: Posthumanism and the Posthumous*. Minneapolis: University of Minnesota Press, 2018.

Fletcher, Ruth, Marie Fox, and Julie McCandless. "Legal Embodiment: Analysing the Body of Healthcare Law." *Medical Law Review* 16, no. 3 (2008): 321–345.

Garland, Fae, and Mitchell Travis, *Intersex Embodiment: Legal Frameworks beyond Identity and Disorder*. Bristol: Bristol University Press, 2023.

Geary, Patrick J. *Living with the Dead in the Middle Ages*. Ithica, NY: Cornell University Press, 1994.

Grear, Anna. "Foregrounding Vulnerability: Materiality's Porous Affectability as a Methodological Platform." In *Research Methods in Environmental Law*, edited by Andreas Philippopoulos-Mihalopoulos and Victoria Brooks, 3–28. London: Edward Elgar, 2017.

Grosz, Elizabeth. *Volatile Bodies: Toward a Corporeal Feminism*. Bloomington: Indiana University Press, 1994.

Grosz, Elizabeth. *Chaos, Territory, Art: Deleuze and the Framing of the Earth*. New York: Columbia University Press, 2008.

Hale, Matthew. *The History of the Pleas of the Crown: Volume 1*. London: T. Payne, 1800.

Harrison, Robert Pogue. *The Dominion of the Dead*. Chicago, IL: University of Chicago Press, 2003.

Kang, Hyo Yoon, and Sara Kendall. "Legal Materiality" in *The Oxford Handbook of Law and Humanities*, edited by Simon Stern, Maksymillian Del Mar, and Bernadette Meyler, 20–37. Oxford: Oxford University Press, 2019.

Keenan, Sarah. *Subversive Property: Law and the Production of Spaces of Belonging*. Abingdon: Routledge, 2015.

Leder, Drew. *The Absent Body*. Chicago, IL: University of Chicago Press, 1990.

Lefebvre, Henri. *The Production of Space*. London: Blackwell, 1989.

Longhurst, Robyn. *Bodies: Exploring Fluid Boundaries*. Abingdon: Routledge, 2001.

Martel, James R. *Bodies Unburied: Subversive Corpses and the Authority of the Dead*. Amherst, MA: Amherst College Press, 2018.

Martel, James R. "Interrupted by Death: The Legal Personhood and Non-Personhood of Corpses." *Studies in Law, Politics and Society* 87A (2022): 103.

Motha, Stewart. "My Story, Whose Memory: Notes on the Autonomy and Heteronomy of Law." *Studies in Law, Politics and Society* 87B (2022): 1–18.

Mulla, Sameena. "Topological Time, Law and Subjectivity: A Description in Five Folds." In *Law and Time*, edited by Sian Beynon-Jones and Emily Graham. Abingdon: Routledge, 2020.

Mykitiuk, Roxanne. "Fragmenting the Body." *Australian Feminist Law Journal* 2, no. 1 (1994): 63–98.

Naffine, Ngaire. "'But a Lump of Earth'? The Legal Status of the Corpse." In *Courting Death: The Law of Mortality*, edited by Desmond Manderson, 95–110. London: Pluto, 1999.

Nancy, Jean-Luc. *Corpus*. New York: Fordham University Press, 2008.

Philippopoulos-Mihalopoulos, Andreas. "Law, Space, Bodies: The Emergence of Spatial Justice." In *Deleuze and Law*, edited by Laurent de Sutter and Kyle McGee, 90–110. Edinburgh: Edinburgh University Press, 2012.

Philippopoulos-Mihalopoulos, Andreas. "Atmospheres of Law: Senses, Affects, Lawscapes." *Emotion, Space and Society* 7 (2013): 35–44.

Philippopoulos-Mihalopoulos, Andreas. *Spatial Justice: Body, Lawscape, Atmosphere*. Abingdon: Routledge, 2014.

Philippopoulos-Mihalopoulos, Andreas. "Withdrawing from Atmosphere: An Ontology of Air Partitioning and Affective Engineering." *Society and Space* 34, no. 1 (2016): 150–167.

Philippopoulos-Mihalopoulos, Andreas. "Law is a Stage: From Aesthetics to Affective Aestheses." In *Research Handbook on Critical Legal Theory*, edited by Emilios Christodoulidis, Ruth Dukes, and Marco Galdoni, 201–222. London: Edward Elgar, 2019.

Philippopoulos-Mihalopoulos, Andreas. "Lawscape." In *International Lexicon of Aesthetics* (2020). http://doi.org/10.7413/18258630100.

Phillimore, Robert. *Ecclesiastical Law of the Church of England*. London: Henry Sweet, 1873.

Pottage, Alain. "Introduction: The Fabrication of Persons and Things." In *Law, Anthropology, and the Constitution of the Social: Making Persons and Things*, edited by Alain Pottage and Martha Mundy, 1–39. Cambridge: Cambridge University Press, 2004.

Pottage, Alain. "The Materiality of What?" *Journal of Law and Society* 39, no. 1 (2012): 167–183.

Shaw, Joshua D. M. "A Minor Jurisprudence of Play: Becoming Jurisprudents through Play in the *Majora's Mask*." In *Law, Video Games, Virtual Realities: Playing Law*, edited by Dale Mitchell, Ashley Pearson, and Timothy D. Peters, 190–210. Abingdon: Routledge, 2023.

Shaw, Joshua D. M., and Roxanne Mykitiuk, "Jurisgenerative Tissues: Sociotechnical Imaginaries and the Legal Secretions of 3D Bioprinting." *Law and Critique* 34, no. 2 (2023): 105–125.

Shaw, Joshua David Michael. "Confronting Jurisdiction with Antinomian Bodies." *Law, Culture and the Humanities* 20, no. 1 (2024): 94-119.

Shaw, Joshua David Michael. "Transcarceral Lawscapes Enacted in Moments of Aboriginalisation: A Case-study of an Indigenous Woman Released on Urban Parole." *International Journal of Law in Context* 16, no. 4 (2020): 422–442.

Shaw, Joshua David Michael. "The Spatio-Legal Production of Bodies Through the Legal Fiction of Death." *Law and Critique* 32, no. 1 (2021): 69–90.

Shildrick, Margrit. *Leaky Bodies and Boundaries: Feminism, Postmodernism and (Bio)Ethics*. Abingdon: Routledge, 1997.

Slaughter, M. M. "Sacred Kingship and Antinomianism: Antirrhesis and the Order of Things." *Law and Literature* 4, no. 2 (1992): 227–235.

Spelman, Henry. *De Sepultura*. London: Robert Young, 1641.

Trabsky, Marc. "Institutionalising the Public Abattoir in Nineteenth Century Colonial Society." *Australian Feminist Law Journal* 40, no. 2 (2014): 169–184.

Trabsky, Marc. *Law and the Dead: Technologies, Relations, Institutions*. Abingdon: Routledge, 2019.

Valverde, Mariana. *Chronotopes of Law: Jurisdiction, Scale and Governance*. Abingdon: Routledge, 2015.

Vines, Prue. "Bodily Remains in the Cemetery and the Burial Ground: A Comparative Anthropology of Law and Death *or* How Long can I Stay?" In *Courting Death: The Law of Mortality*, edited by Desmond Manderson, 111–127. London: Pluto, 1999.

9

THE GRAVE AS A CONTESTED SPACE

Kate Falconer

Introduction

The cemetery is often described as a heterotopia: a world within a world that is set apart from society by virtue of the rupture in time it represents.[1] Perhaps because of its heterotopic status, the cemetery has been the subject of analysis from many different disciplinary perspectives, as well as several special issues and edited collections – each of which seeks to develop a more interdisciplinary understanding of this unique space.[2] A key insight emerging from this body of work sees the cemetery as a place of conflict. The purposes, and persons, a cemetery serves within its community are the subject of debate and interpretation, the overlapping roles played by these spaces of the dead – as places of mourning, community, history, and commerce – often existing in contrast, if not outright contestation.

Within the wider cemetery context, some attention has been paid to the individual grave as a place of conflict: a place where private grief is performed as public mourning and where the 'rightness' of that mourning is assessed by others.[3] The central contention of this chapter is that the legal framework that surrounds the dead body and its disposal in England and Australia, by seeing the grave as little more than a plot of land that can be the subject of multiple intersecting legal rights, facilitates these social conflicts and actively promotes the grave's status as a contested space.

The law's complicity in the grave as a site of conflict stems from its willingness to establish and uphold a framework of fragmentary legal relations around the locus of the grave. These relations are often unknown and invisible to those who claim some social or familial tie to the site. As the first section of this chapter explains, for example, there exists a sense of entitlement – the sense of having the ability to control the plot and what is placed on, and in, it – shared by visitors to particular graves who see themselves as the

---

1 See Peter Johnson, "The Geographies of Heterotopia," *Geography Compass* 7, no. 11 (2013): 799.
2 See, e.g., Arnar Árnason and Erica Borgstrom, eds., "Cemeteries," Special issue, *Mortality* 8 no. 2 (2003); Jenny Hockey, Carol Komaromy, and Kate Woodthorpe eds., *The Matter of Death: Space, Place and Materiality* (London: Palgrave Macmillan, 2010).
3 See, e.g., Kate Woodthorpe, "Private Grief in Public Spaces: Interpreting Memorialisation in the Contemporary Cemetery," in *The Matter of Death: Space, Place and Materiality*, ed. Jenny Hockey, Carol Komaromy, and Kate Woodthorpe (London: Palgrave Macmillan, 2010), 117.

DOI: 10.4324/9781003304593-11

grave's 'owners', having 'purchased' that grave from the cemetery.[4] Except, from a legal perspective, and as set out in detail in the second section, what has almost always been purchased is nothing more than the 'exclusive right of burial' – a parcel of legal rights that decidedly do not sound in property. Distinct (and distinctly proprietary) rights of various strength do exist in the grave, but these rights vest elsewhere – in the holder of the freehold title to the cemetery in question, and in the (former) holder of the right to possession of the body of the deceased. Thus, we have at least three different legal rights, with potentially three different legal right holders, centred around a single grave.

The third section of this chapter examines these fragmentary legal relations and the conflict they engender. Interpreting the idea of the 'tragedy of the anticommons' developed by law and economics through a critical legal studies lens, this section argues that, in a setting that is already contentious – that is, the cemetery – and in a space that is already deeply imbued with meaning and ritual – that is, the grave – this fracturing of legal relations cements the grave's status as a contested space. At the same time, the manner in which courts resolve those conflicts that arise at the grave provides several important insights into the law's interaction with death and the law of the dead more broadly.

Situating the grave in society

Human beings have been burying our dead for almost 100,000 years.[5] Indeed, it is often said that the burial of our dead is what makes us human – both in the sense of defining our species and identifying it as something *other* to all other species of animal – in the first place.[6] And since this earliest of times, the grave has been a special place for those left behind – a place of memory and of ritual as much as it is a place of grief and loss. This importance gave the grave priority. As Harrison notes, the dead were the first among our earliest ancestors to have a permanent dwelling – that is to say, human beings housed their dead before they housed themselves.[7]

This commitment to the housing of our dead has continued throughout our history, from the ancestral tombs that protected the city in ancient Greece and Rome, to the communal churchyards of late medieval Britain, and on to the garden cemeteries of the modern Global North.[8] And throughout this necrogeographic history, the cemetery has retained its heterotopic status. It is 'the other city',[9] an underworld counter site to the city that has breached the earth to embed itself in the land of the living.[10] In so doing, the

---

4 See Kate Woodthorpe, "Sustaining the Contemporary Cemetery: Implementing Policy Alongside Conflicting Perspectives and Purpose," *Mortality* 16, no. 3 (2011): 259.

5 The oldest accepted burial site located to date is at Qafzeh, Israel, where 15 individuals were buried approximately 92,000 years ago. However, recent claims that an early hominid ancestor – *Homo naledi* – intentionally buried its dead some 200,000 to 300,000 years ago may radically alter this history.

6 This sentiment is occasionally interpreted literally and is sometimes meant as something of a shorthand for a broader sense of disposing of the body in some intentional way (e.g., by cremation or exposure). This chapter limits its analysis to burial.

7 Robert Pogue Harrison, *The Dominion of the Dead* (Chicago, IL: University of Chicago Press, 2003), 38.

8 Thomas W. Laqueur, *The Work of the Dead: A Cultural History of Mortal Remains* (Princeton, NJ: Princeton University Press, 2015) Part II contains a comprehensive history of where and how we have buried our dead.

9 Michel Foucault, "Of Other Spaces," trans. Jay Miskowiec, *Diacritics* 16, no. 1 (1986): 25.

10 Marc Trabsky, *Law and the Dead* (Milton: Routledge, 2019), 21.

cemetery creates discontinuities in the space and time of the living.[11] For the dead, however, it creates its own strange heterochrony. For the dead, the cemetery takes death as its starting point and continues into a quasi-eternity devoted to their dissolution and disappearance.[12]

While the cemetery has always been a heterotopia, our approaches to these places of burial have changed. In medieval and early modern England, for example, parishioners were buried in the churchyard of their local parish as of right.[13] While a fee might be payable for the service provided, and a higher fee might provide the particularly distinguished deceased with a choice burial location within the churchyard – or even within the church itself – generally speaking, to speak of 'rights' in individual grave plots was folly for much of the last millennia. The deceased was laid to rest where space was available, with no guarantee that their own peaceful repose would not be interrupted at some point in the not-too-distant future by the interment of another in close proximity.[14]

The introduction of the modern, urban, secular cemetery in the early nineteenth century, however, brought with it a new commercialism, and the new cemetery corporations realised they could make good money 'selling' plots of land to the future dead – these individuals being able to pick and choose which plot best suited their tastes (and wallets).[15] Laqueur, for example, notes that in these new cemeteries, the dead were seen as requiring the same amenities as the living wanted for themselves: 'privacy, comfort, and the honor of bourgeois life'[16] – all things that could be obtained with the acquisition of the appropriate burial plot, 'his or her own little box for his or her own little personal decay'.[17]

By the 1960s, the ability to 'buy' graves became available to more and more people in the Global North. This was frequently one of the most important purchases a family might make[18] – a fact that remains true today. And as much as in ancient times, the purchase of a grave in the modern world is about giving the individual dead a home that those left behind can visit, a place and a space that belongs to both the dead and the living.[19] In this way, then, the importance of the grave both to the immediate family of the deceased and to the deceased's broader community cannot be overstated.

But family and community can come into conflict at the grave. After all, and as Foucault has identified, an existing heterotopia can function in different ways according to the synchrony of the culture in which it occurs.[20] As noted in the introduction to this chapter, for example, the gravesite is a place where the appropriateness of one's private grief is assessed according to public standards of mourning. Overly long grieving periods in which the bereaved continue to visit and memorialise at the grave of their loved one

---

11 Trabsky, *Law and the Dead*, 21.
12 Foucault, "Of Other Spaces", 26.
13 Laqueur, *Work of the Dead*, 151–5.
14 Laqueur, *Work of the Dead*, 215–38 discusses the cemetery overcrowding prevalent in this period.
15 Laqueur, *Work of the Dead*, chap. 5.
16 Laqueur, *Work of the Dead*, 216
17 Foucault, "Of Other Spaces," 25.
18 Doris Francis, Leonie A. Kellaher, and Georgina Neophytou, *The Secret Cemetery* (English ed. New York: Berg, 2005), 45. The authors note that the grave plot was frequently the first, and perhaps only, piece of property a family was able to purchase. As we will see, in fact, no conveyance of property is carried out in the purchase of a grave.
19 Francis, Kellaher, and Neophytou, *Secret Cemetery*, chap. 4.
20 Foucault, "Of Other Spaces,",25.

can be seen by others in the community as pathological or 'bad' grief, or even as indicating an altogether different emotion: guilt.[21] And this tension between public and private can be particularly problematic for the families of those who die in diaspora or otherwise as a member of a minority community, whose cultural grieving practices can differ markedly from the mourning rituals prevalent in the 'host' society.[22]

Many of the tensions between individual mourners and the wider community exist because of competing senses of ownership within the cemetery. The local community frequently feels as if the cemetery (as a place in and of itself; that is to say, not necessarily as a conglomerate of individual graves) 'belongs' to that community in the sense that the cemetery is a physical representation of local customs and local attachment to place.[23] On the other hand, and again as referenced above, the individuals whose loved ones are buried in a particular grave plot feel a sense of entitlement to do what they like with that plot. This sense of entitlement stems from the idea that the deceased's loved ones, having paid some fee to the relevant cemetery authority, 'own' the grave plot in question.

That these cemetery authorities do in fact use the language of 'ownership' in relation to financial transactions surrounding the ability to bury a body in a particular grave only substantiates this sense of entitlement. Manchester City Council, for example, refers to the 'registered grave owner',[24] and the websites of Leicester City Council,[25] Cambridge City Council,[26] and Birmingham City Council[27] each advise that you can 'buy a grave' in the cemeteries they control. As the next section makes clear, however, the lay conception of 'ownership' that this language invokes can diverge sharply from the meaning and power ascribed to 'ownership' in property law – a divergence that becomes clear at the graveside.

'Owning' the grave in law

The concept of 'ownership' is normatively very powerful. From a lay perspective, it is often seen as allowing the absolute control of a particular resource or other object of property to the exclusion of all others. In law, however, the concept of 'ownership' is ephemeral and fractured, its exact content depending on the precise circumstances.[28]

---

21 Woodthorpe, "Private Grief," 127.

22 Katie McClymont, "They Have Different Ways of Doing Things: Cemeteries, Diversity, and Local Place Attachment," *Journal of Intercultural Studies* 39, no. 3 (2018): 267. The expensive and flamboyant funerals of the Traveller community in Ireland and the United Kingdom, for example, are well known and frequently the subject of (often insensitive) tabloid news. Similarly, the elaborate memorialisation done at the gravesite by members of this community is often commented upon, if not openly objected to. The highly personalised 37-tonne marble memorial erected over the grave of Willy Collins, known as 'the king of Sheffield', in Sheffield in 2020, for example, was the subject of multiple complaints by local residents and ultimately found to be in breach of cemetery rules by the local council.

23 See McClymont, "Different Ways," 267–85.

24 "Graves: Grave deeds, ownership and transfer of title," Manchester City Council (accessed 12 June 2023), www.manchester.gov.uk/info/200032/deaths_funerals_and_cemeteries/5084/graves/4.

25 "Buying a grave," Leicester City Council (accessed 12 June 2023), www.leicester.gov.uk/your-community/births-marriages-and-deaths/funerals-burials-and-cremations/burials/buying-a-grave.

26 "Buy a grave," Cambridge City Council (accessed 12 June 2023), www.cambridge.gov.uk/buy-a-grave.

27 "Buying a grave," Birmingham City Council (accessed 12 June 2023), www.birmingham.gov.uk/info/20210/deaths/383/buying_a_grave.

28 Thomas C. Grey, "The Disintegration of Property," in *NOMOS XXII: Property*, ed. J. Roland Pennock and John W. Chapman (New York: New York University Press, 1980), 69.

Ownership in a legal sense, if it exists at all, refers to the right that gives its holder the highest possible degree of access to and control over an object of property (as opposed to an *absolute, unfettered dominion* over that object, as is commonly believed in non-legal circles).[29] In modern land law, the estate that best approximates this concept of 'ownership' is freehold title (also known as an estate in fee simple).[30] Freehold title is the most common means of owning private (real) property in common law jurisdictions. This being the case, and returning to our particular area of interest in this chapter, 'ownership' of any particular grave vests in the holder of the freehold title to the land into which that grave has been dug. The true 'owner' of any given grave could then be a religious diocese (as was and is the case with many English churchyards), a private corporation, or a local council.

This freehold title allows the titleholder to set the ultimate agenda for what is done with the land in question (subject always to relevant statutory and common law restrictions).[31] But the very nature of ownership at law – fractured and pliable as it is – allows the freehold titleholder to limit their own ability to engage with the land in question in favour of another. So, for example, the 'owner' can allow another to make use of their land, or to profit from it, and so on.[32] And it is here that the exclusive right of burial emerges.

Sometimes referred to as a 'burial licence', the right that is in fact obtained by individuals when they contract to 'purchase' a grave plot in a cemetery is the exclusive right of burial. This right, which may be perpetual or may be limited in duration, provides the right holder with the ability to decide, to the exclusion of all others, which body will be interred in the plot in question. Importantly, this includes the holder of the relevant freehold title, who would otherwise have had the legal ability to make this decision – the freehold titleholder having intentionally limited their ability to engage with their land as they see fit in this respect. The exclusive right of burial also provides several ancillary rights to the right holder – such as the right to erect a tombstone (although the form and content of that tombstone can be limited by the terms of purchase of the exclusive right of burial). Interestingly, it appears that any tombstone erected at the grave becomes the personal property of the holder of this exclusive right,[33] a position that remains unchanged regardless of who has in fact *paid* for the tombstone to be erected.

It is unsurprising that, to a lay outsider, the power to control important matters in relation to the grave – such as who is interred there and how they are memorialised – appears to invoke the exclusive control of an asset or piece of land we associate with ownership. In many jurisdictions, however, this is simply not the case.[34] While the position remains somewhat contested,[35] the generally accepted view is that the exclusive right of burial is nothing more than a contractual licence. This means that, effectively, the

---

29 William Swadling, "Property: General Principles" in *English Private Law*, ed. Peter Birks (Oxford: Oxford University Press, 2000), 1:218 [4.36].

30 Modern land law fails to acknowledge older, deeper relationships with land. In Australia, for example, the land we walk on is the ancestral Country of our First Nations communities. The inherent and deeply spiritual relationship between these communities and their Country creates a sense of self and of belonging for First Nations people that underpins all other dealings with land, and this cannot be overlooked.

31 See Larissa Katz, "Exclusion and Exclusivity in Property Law," *University of Toronto Law Journal* 58, no. 3, (2008): 275.

32 Grey, "Disintegration of Property," 69.

33 See, e.g., *Burial and Cremation Act 2013* (SA), s. 39(1).

34 Cf. the Canadian position: Alan Dowling, "Exclusive Rights of Burial and the Law of Real Property," *Legal Studies* 18 no. 4 (1998): 440–1.

35 See Dowling, "Exclusive Rights," 438–52.

'purchasers' of the exclusive right of burial have done no more than enter into a contract with the relevant cemetery authority (as fee simple titleholder), the terms of which allow these purchasers to engage with the particular plot of land in question in a way that would otherwise be considered a trespass (i.e., by interring a body and erecting a tombstone) in consideration for the handing over of a (potentially quite large) sum of money.[36]

All of this is to say that no property rights whatsoever are conveyed with the purchase of a burial licence. Thus, if we return to Manchester City Council and their references to grave ownership, we find that when you 'buy a private grave', you are in fact purchasing only 'the burial rights for 99 years, subject to extension'[37] – that is to say, no ownership interest in the land itself ever passes and the rights are instead merely contractual.

At times, there are legal reasons for this interpretation of the exclusive right of burial. In churchyards controlled by the Church of England, for example, the incumbent who grants the right of burial may not themselves have a legal estate in the land and are thus incapable of passing title in the grave plot to another[38] – *nemo dat quod non habet*, after all. For the most part, however, the refusal to pass freehold title with the purchase of an exclusive right of burial is one largely based on policy concerns.

Here, we can make a comparison between the exclusive right of burial and the English parishioner's right to a pew in their local church. In the case of the former, the right grants its holder the ability to make decisions about interment and grave adornment but does not provide the right to exclude others from the gravesite,[39] or to use the small plot of land for any purpose besides burial and commemoration.[40] In the case of the latter, the right grants its holder the ability to use a particular pew for divine worship while they reside in the parish, but nothing else.[41] The disadvantages of dividing a church into individual seats held in fee simple on the basis of such a limited and temporal right is obvious, and in the same way, so is the division of a cemetery into hundreds, if not thousands, of individual fee simple graves.[42] Simply put, and as will be explored (albeit from a different perspective) in the next section, it is a remarkably inefficient means of managing a resource such as land.

But freehold title and the exclusive right of burial are not the only rights that exist in relation to the grave. We must also consider the right to possession of the body of the deceased. This legal right is grounded in common law and is of uncertain juridical status.[43] It vests in a particular, identifiable person, giving that person the ability to decide and control the means by which the deceased's body is disposed to the exclusion of all others (as opposed to the ability to decide which body, if any, is interred in a particular grave plot that is enjoyed by the holder of the exclusive right of burial). The purpose of this legal right is to ensure the body of the deceased is decently disposed of, and as a result, the right is generally agreed to terminate at the time such disposal takes

---

36 See Dowling, "Exclusive Rights," 442–4; P. W. Young, "The Exclusive Right to Burial," *Australian Law Journal* 39, no. 2 (1965): 150–7.
37 Manchester City Council, "Graves".
38 Peter Sparkes, "Exclusive Burial Rights," *Ecclesiastical Law Journal* 2, no. 8 (1991): 133, 134.
39 *Smith v Tamworth City Council* (1997) 41 NSWLR 680, 694.
40 See, e.g., *Hoskins-Abrahall v Paignton Urban District Council* [1926] 1 Ch. 375 (Great Britain).
41 Sparkes, "Exclusive Burial Rights," 133.
42 Sparkes, "Exclusive Burial Rights," 134.
43 Kate Falconer, *Bones of Contention: The Right to Possession of the Body of the Deceased as a Property Right*, Doctoral Thesis, Australian National University, 2020. I argue that this right sounds in property.

place.[44] This being the case, if burial is the chosen form of disposal, it has traditionally been held that any remedy for interference with the interred body lies not with the holder of the right to possession (this right having terminated with disposal), but with the holder of the freehold title to the cemetery land and the law of tort via a trespass to land claim,[45] as well as the criminal law.[46] This reflects the view that once a body is interred, it becomes part of the earth in which it is entombed – the body having 'appropriated that part of the soil for its own use'.[47]

If, however, the right to possession terminates when the body is buried, what ongoing relationship can the holder of this particular right have in the grave in which the deceased is interred? The answer lies in the fact that the traditional position just now set out may no longer hold true – at least in Australia. In an important 2015 decision, Justice Robb of the New South Wales Supreme Court held that, after interment of the body and the termination of the right to possession, the former holder of that right gains an irrevocable licence coupled with a grant of interest in the land in which the body is buried.[48] This ongoing and definitely proprietary relationship of the former holder of the right to possession with the land in which the deceased is interred exists so that the peaceful repose of the deceased is not disturbed,[49] and likely lasts until the natural dissolution of the body.[50]

Thus, we have at least three intersecting legal rights at play in the 2.5-by-8-foot incision in the earth that is the grave. The first – ownership in the true, legal sense of the word – entitles the freehold titleholder to control the land of which the grave is a part – to establish a gardening regime at the cemetery, to determine the hours during which the cemetery is open to visitors, and to set codes of conduct for those within cemetery grounds. The contractual exclusive right of burial, on the other hand, entitles the right holder to make decisions regarding the use of the grave in question as a place of disposal – who is to be interred there and how they are to be memorialised. The irrevocable licence coupled with a grant of interest in land, on the other hand, acts to identify the party who holds it as the protector of the deceased's eternal sleep. These rights – and particularly the second and third just now set out – may be held by the same person but are certainly not required to be. And so the grave becomes a locus of fractured and fragmentary legal relations, a state of affairs that, as the next section shows, can only lead to conflict and contestation.

---

44 See, e.g., *Calma v Sesar* (1992) 2 NTLR 37, 41.

45 See, e.g., William Blackstone, *Commentaries on the Laws of England*, 1992 ed. (Chicago, IL: University of Chicago Press, 1765–1769), 2:429: '[t]he parson indeed, who has the freehold of the soil, may bring an action of trespass against such as dig and disturb it.'

46 *R v Lynn* (1788) 2 TR 733; 100 ER 394 (unauthorised disinterment a criminal offence); *R v Sharpe* (1857) Dears & B 160; 169 ER 959 (unauthorised disinterment a criminal offence). The *Land Act 1994* (UK), s. 83 and *Burial Act 1857* (UK), ss. 20 and 21 Vict., c. 81, s. 25 serve as examples of statutory iterations of this principle. The existence of these criminal law provisions arguably provides the broader community with some legal interest in the grave, or at least in the peaceful repose of the body interred therein.

47 *Beard v Baulkham Hills Shire Council* (1986) 7 NSWLR 273, 280. See also *Doodeward v Spence* (1908) 6 CLR 406, 412; *Robinson v Pinegrove Memorial Park Ltd* (1986) 7 BPR 15,097, 15,098–99; *Leeburn v Derndorfer* (2004) 14 VR 100, 106 [25].

48 *Vosnakis v Arfaras* [2015] NSWSC 625 (26 May 2015), [65]–[104], [141]. This discussion makes clear that the irrevocable licence coupled with a grant cannot be excluded by the terms of the contract that exists in relation to the burial plot at issue between the holder of the exclusive right of burial and the relevant cemetery authority.

49 *Vosnakis*, [97]–[98].

50 *Vosnakis*, [96], [143]–[145].

Fragmentation and contestation at the grave

In the previous section, we saw how law establishes and upholds a framework of fragmentary legal relations at the graveside. This section argues that this fragmentation of rights in relation to the grave is an example of the 'tragedy of the anticommons'[51] and that the existence of this anticommons at the grave provides crucial insights into the law of the dead.

In property theory, the conception of fragmented property rights leading to an 'anticommons' emerges from the field of law and economics. Law and economics, as the name suggests, examines law through the lens of economic inputs, outputs and efficiency. In the eyes of law and economics scholars, anticommons property – where too many people have exclusionary rights in relation to a particular asset (usually land), thus limiting the ability of all to make effective use of that land – is simply not efficient.[52] We can make similar claims about the fragmentation of legal rights in the grave – only the efficient use we refer to is not measured in economic terms but rather in human terms, and the tragedy we are concerned with is not the *under*-utilisation of the resource in question but rather the *over*production of conflict and contestation. In doing so, we both move away from the wealth maximisation norm at the core of law and economics that plays an uncertain role in property law and take account of the social relations that critical legal scholars see as missing from law and economics accounts of property law.[53]

By taking this approach, we can see how the fragmentation of legal rights in the grave engenders bitter disputes among the bereaved. The legal right to erect a gravestone – and to determine what is inscribed on that gravestone – held by the holder of the exclusive right of burial, for example, can become a means of challenging family relationships. And so the names of surviving partners and children can be omitted, or misspelled, by the right holder, perhaps in an effort to cement, for eternity, the 'correct' hierarchy of relationships.[54] At other times, the names chiselled in stone by the party with the exclusive right of burial might be calculated to cause distress to other surviving loved ones.[55] In each of these cases, the party with the legal right to erect and maintain a tombstone can use their right to exclude other bereaved individuals from the decision-making process, thus using their fragmentary right in the grave to create conflict.

In a similar vein, those with competing rights in the grave are frequently in conflict with each other. The cemetery authority, as the 'owner' of the land itself, for example, can remove grave ornamentations erected on the grave by the holder of the exclusive right of burial (provided such adornments are not permitted by the contract entered into between the authority and right holder in question). While such actions are almost certain to cause distress and anguish to the bereaved, including the holder of the exclusive right of burial, no legal recourse is available. The prerogative remains that of the freehold

---

51 This term is borrowed from Michael A. Heller, "The Tragedy of the Anticommons: Property in the Transition from Marx to Markets," *Harvard Law Review* 111, no. 3 (1998): 621–88.

52 See, e.g., Norbert Schulz, Francesco Parisi, and Ben Depoorter, "Fragmentation in Property: Towards a General Model," *Journal of Institutional and Theoretical Economics* 158, no. 4 (2002): 594–5.

53 See, e.g., Duncan Kennedy, "Law-and-Economics from the Perspective of Critical Legal Studies," in *The New Palgrave Dictionary of Economics and the Law,* ed. Peter Newman (London: Macmillan, 1998), 2:465.

54 See, e.g., *Escott v Brikha* [2000] NSWSC 458 (26 May 2000).

55 See, e.g., *Boni v Larwood* [2014] SASC 185 (8 December 2014).

titleholder to do with their land as they will. The repercussions of such action, if any, must come about as a result of social pressure rather than legal right.[56]

The holder of the exclusive right of burial can also come into conflict with the (former) holder of the right to possession of the body of the deceased. As we know, following the interment of the deceased, the latter holds a lesser proprietary interest in the grave in question to ensure the deceased's peaceful repose. When the exclusive right of burial allows for an additional interment, then, disputes can arise between the two right holders as to who this right might be exercised in favour of – that is to say, the identity of the corpse that the original deceased will be made to share their grave with. In these cases, threats of exhumation can be made that are distressing to all involved – including the courts, who are loath to see a body disturbed unnecessarily.[57]

Ultimately, and as these disputes show us, legal rules and principles do not represent a recognisable scheme of human association.[58] This is especially true in the case of disputes relating to death, the dead body, and its disposal. In these cases, parties frequently rely not on strict legal rights but rather ephemeral emotional claims. Thus, in the important Australian burial law case of *Smith v Tamworth City Council*, the birth parents of the deceased argued that their status as close blood relatives of the deceased entitled them to be mentioned on his tombstone. While this claim was run alongside more recognisably 'legal' arguments – for example, that the birth parents had paid for the purchase of the burial licence, and this entitled them to have the burial licence, registered in the name of another, transferred to them – the case was, at its core, a dispute about family relationships and societal understandings of those relationships rather than legal property. And the case was decided in this vein also, the birth parents' claim being rejected on the basis that the conscience of the community could not countenance the overriding of the adoptive parents' wishes when the adoption had taken place over 20 years ago.[59]

What can this tell us about the law of death and the intersection of death and law more broadly? We know that death is a social phenomenon, mediated in individual societies by the unique confluence of factors such as access to wealth, communication techniques, religion and family dynamics, politics and policies, medicine, and war present therein.[60] And we have already commented on the social importance of the grave. The dead body is no less a product of its society. The corpse is representative of a particular individual who has gone, that individual having once been part of a particular community that will mourn their loss. At the same time, the dead body is a powerful symbol of mortality and the disorder and decay that follows the extinguishment of life.[61]

We also know that courts have repeatedly commented on the fundamentally social nature of disputes that arise in relation to the dead body and its disposal, expressing embarrassment and discomfort at having to adjudicate pyrrhic family conflicts[62] in which

56 In early 2023, for example, the CEO of a cemetery in regional Victoria, Australia, was stood down following community protest at and criticism of the decision to remove, sometimes by force, noncompliant grave decorations such as solar lights, glass vases, and photo frames.
57 See, e.g., *Vosnakis*, [154]–[155].
58 Roberto Mangabeira Unger, "The Critical Legal Studies Movement," *Harvard Law Review* 96, no. 3 (1983): 565.
59 *Smith v Tamworth City Council* (1997) 41 NSWLR 680, 697.
60 See Tony Walter, *Death in the Modern World* (London: SAGE, 2020).
61 See Elizabeth Hallam, Glennys Howarth, and Jennifer Lorna Hockey, *Beyond the Body: Death and Social Identity* (New York: Routledge, 1999), chap. 7.
62 See, e.g., *Leeburn*, 102 [10].

emotions, rather than legal arguments, run hot.[63] At the same time, in deciding these cases, courts have insisted that '[p]ressures of time, stress and pain add to an already emotional situation where there are no winners and losers, only deeply held and legitimate feelings that are exacerbated by uncertainty'.[64] But, of course, there are winners and losers. The law is not attuned, and indeed cannot be attuned, to death, dying, and the dead body as multifaceted social relationships involving entire families and communities. Instead, when disputes over the dead body, or the ground in which it is interred, come to court, the law requires that conflict conform to the formalities of an adversarial system. These legal conflicts are resolved by establishing a winner and a loser, by distinguishing between the party *with* the relevant legal entitlement and those *without*. The very nature of these conflicts – as *legal* disputes about *legal* rights – requires that there be a victor who triumphs over the vanquished.

The continued acknowledgement of the inherently social and emotional nature of dead body disputes by the courts highlights that the legal rules and principles that make up the law of the dead are inherently contradictory (or, to put it more bluntly, are 'shot through with irreconcilable ideological commitments'[65]). And so we see, for example, the contradiction between an individual right holder having the capacity to decide how, when, and where a particular body will be disposed of to the exclusion of all others – and having the full support of the law in doing so – and the expectation that that individual consult with other interested parties (without being legally bound to do so).[66] These competing principles, pronounced in the same sentence in *Smith v Tamworth City Council*, speak to the law's desire to proclaim a winner (and thus retain its legitimacy as a means of social control) while at the same time fulfil a particular social role – as mediator of a very particular and almost unspeakable form of social discord.

Conclusion

There is a difference between proprietary claims and claims of belonging, although they frequently blend into each other in Western culture.[67] Perhaps nowhere is this more true than at the graveside. This chapter has shown that the fragmentation of legal relations at the grave – the creation and continued acknowledgement by courts of at least three competing rights in the one small plot of land – has created an 'anticommons' in the cemetery. Within this anticommons, the tragedy that arises is not that of inefficient underuse but of the overproduction of conflict and contestation. These three interrelated and overlapping realms of exclusion, often wielded by three distinct right holders, allow for the grave to become a site of legal dispute as well as emotional and social discord.

---

63 Burial disputes involve complex factual issues that are 'the subject of hot debate and much emotion' according to *Meier v Bell* (Unreported, Supreme Court of Victoria, Ashley J, 3 March 1997), 8. Similar sentiments appear in *Calma*, 42: '[t]heir respective legal claims were subsumed by deep emotion'; *Lochowiak v Heymans* ([1997] SASC 6301 (8 August 1997), [8]: '[a] court is, understandably, reluctant to enter into sensitive disputes of this kind which, clearly, involve emotional issues of a high degree'.

64 *Ugle v Bowra & O'Dea* [2007] WASC 82 (16 March 2007), [1].

65 S. E. Salako, "A Critical Legal Study of Property in Land," *Liverpool Law Review* 13, no. 1 (1991): 4.

66 *Tamworth City Council*, 694.

67 Harrison, *The Dominion of the Dead*, 25.

At the same time, this fragmentation of legal relations at the grave provides us with insights into law's interaction with death and the dead body. It tells us that in this context, law attempts to walk a fine line: on the one hand maintaining the requirements of a winner-takes-all adversarial system, and on the other both acknowledging and attempting to resolve the multifaceted and multi-party disputes surrounding death and the dead body that can envelop entire communities. The law's success in this venture can only ever be incomplete.

Bibliography

Árnason, Arnar, and Erica Borgstrom, eds. "Cemeteries," Special issue, *Mortality* 8, no. 2 (2003).

Blackstone, William. *Commentaries on the Laws of England*. Vol. 2. Chicago, IL: University of Chicago Press, 1992. First published 1765–1769.

Dowling, Alan. "Exclusive Rights of Burial and the Law of Real Property." *Legal Studies (Society of Legal Scholars)* 18, no. 4 (1998): 438–452. https://doi.org/10.1111/j.1748-121X.1998.tb00075.x.

Falconer, Kate. *Bones of Contention: The Right to Possession of the Body of the Deceased as a Property Right*. Doctoral Thesis, Australian National University, 2020.

Foucault, Michel. "Of Other Spaces", translated by Jay Miskowiec. *Diacritics* 16, no. 1 (1986): 22–27. https://doi.org/10.2307/464648.

Francis, Doris, Leonie A. Kellaher, and Georgina Neophytou. *The Secret Cemetery*. English ed. New York: Berg, 2005.

Grey, Thomas C. "The Disintegration of Property." In *NOMOS XXII: Property*, edited by J. Roland Pennock and John W. Chapman, 69–85. New York: New York University Press, 1980.

Hallam, Elizabeth, Glennys Howarth, and Jennifer Lorna Hockey. *Beyond the Body: Death and Social Identity*. New York: Routledge, 1999.

Harrison, Robert Pogue. *The Dominion of the Dead*. Chicago, IL: University of Chicago Press, 2003.

Heller, Michael A. "The Tragedy of the Anticommons: Property in the Transition from Marx to Markets." *Harvard Law Review* 111, no. 3 (1998): 621–688. https://doi.org/10.2307/1342203.

Hockey, Jenny, Carol Komaromy, and Kate Woodthorpe, eds. *The Matter of Death: Space, Place and Materiality*. London: Palgrave Macmillan, 2010.

Johnson, Peter. "The Geographies of Heterotopia." *Geography Compass* 7, no. 11 (2013): 790–803. https://doi.org/10.1111/gec3.12079.

Katz, Larissa. "Exclusion and Exclusivity in Property Law." *The University of Toronto Law Journal* 58, no. 3 (2008): 275–315. https://doi.org/10.3138/utlj.58.3.275.

Kennedy, Duncan. "Law-and-Economics from the Perspective of Critical Legal Studies." In *The New Palgrave Dictionary of Economics and the Law*, vol. 2, edited by Peter Newman, 465–474. London: Macmillan, 1998.

Laqueur, Thomas Walter. *The Work of the Dead: A Cultural History of Mortal Remains*. Princeton, NJ: Princeton University Press, 2015.

McClymont, Katie. "'They Have Different Ways of Doing Things': Cemeteries, Diversity and Local Place Attachment." *Journal of Intercultural Studies* 39, no. 3 (2018): 267–285. https://doi.org/10.1080/07256868.2018.1459519.

Salako, S. E. "A Critical Legal Study of Property in Land." *The Liverpool Law Review* 13, no. 1 (1991): 3–19. https://doi.org/10.1007/BF01079303.

Schulz, Norbert, Francesco Parisi, and Ben Depoorter. "Fragmentation in Property: Towards a General Model." *Journal of Institutional and Theoretical Economics* 158, no. 4 (2002): 594–613. https://doi.org/10.1628/0932456022975196.

Sparkes, Peter. "Exclusive Burial Rights." *Ecclesiastical Law Journal* 2, no. 8 (1991): 133–151. https://doi.org/10.1017/S0956618X0000106X.

Swadling, William. "Property: General Principles." In *English Private Law*, vol. 1, edited by Peter Birks, 203–384. Oxford: Oxford University Press, 2000.

Trabsky, Marc. *Law and the Dead*. Milton: Routledge, 2019.

Unger, Roberto Mangabeira. "The Critical Legal Studies Movement." *Harvard Law Review* 96, no. 3 (1983): 561–675.

Walter, Tony. *Death in the Modern World*. London: SAGE Publications, 2020.

Woodthorpe, Kate. "Private Grief in Public Spaces: Interpreting Memorialisation in the Contemporary Cemetery." In *The Matter of Death*, edited by Jenny Hockey, Carol Komaromy, and Kate Woodthorpe, 117–132. United Kingdom: Palgrave Macmillan. 2010. https://doi.org/10.1057/9780230283060.

Woodthorpe, Kate. "Sustaining the Contemporary Cemetery: Implementing Policy Alongside Conflicting Perspectives and Purpose." *Mortality* 16, no. 3 (2011): 259–276. https://doi.org/10.1080/13576275.2011.586125.

Young, P. W. "Exclusive Right to Burial." *Australian Law Journal* 39, no. 2 (1965): 50–57.

10

THE ROLE AND REPERCUSSIONS OF LAW IN CONTESTED FUNERALS AND CONTESTED MEMORIALS

Heather Conway

Introduction

The death of a close relative can trigger a range of intra-familial disputes over the fate of the dead, who become sites of conflict amongst the living. Arranging the funeral is the first pressing issue, as multiple decisions are required in a compressed timeframe. Further down the proverbial line, the choice of memorial can be contentious even if the pressures of time are not as intense. Where either scenario triggers litigation, and consensus or compromise cannot be reached, the law must intervene to end the impasse.

This chapter uses the different legal frameworks that apply here to explore law's management of contested funerals and contested memorials, and how judges navigate the complex relational dynamics at play as different family members stake their claim to 'own' – and consequently control – both the deceased and the narrative of his/her life and primary relationships.[1] While the emphasis is on England and Wales[2] and Australia with their comparable laws, the content is applicable throughout other common law jurisdictions[3] with substantively similar rules and socio-cultural attitudes towards treatment of the dead. Additionally, the chapter draws on literature from the multidisciplinary field of

---

1 As used throughout this chapter, the term 'family' (and any derivatives, including 'surviving relatives') is not confined to the traditional nuclear family. Instead, it denotes contemporary, fluid structures that embrace a range of personal relationships and living arrangements, linked to notions of 'doing' family and reciprocal obligations beyond institutionalised norms. See, e.g., Janet Finch and Jennifer Mason, *Passing On: Kinship and Inheritance in England* (London: Routledge, 2000) and Michael Gilding, "Reflexivity Over and Above Convention: The New Orthodoxy in the Sociology of Personal Life, Formerly Sociology of the Family," *The British Journal of Sociology* 64, no. 10 (2010): 757–77.

2 Although two separate jurisdictions, England and Wales are amalgamated here because the exact same laws apply in both.

3 Most notably New Zealand, Canada, and the United States of America as well as Northern Ireland and Ireland. While the legal framework in Scotland is different as a result of the *Burial and Cremation (Scotland) Act 2016*, the core themes raised here are equally relevant.

DOI: 10.4324/9781003304593-12

death studies to discuss how law's treatment of these disputes speaks to the materialities of death, and to reveal the familial and social significance of both funerals and memorials. In doing so, it highlights the role of law in (re)constructing and cementing the deceased's social identity, through the process of judicial decision making. The result is that the final decision on the contested funeral or memorial – through the medium of the law – becomes a public affirmation or recasting of certain familial relationships and intimate bonds with the deceased, and an obliteration of others.

Contested funerals

Case law reveals that funeral arrangements can trigger all sorts of disagreements amongst surviving relatives.[4] There is the fundamental question of whether to bury or cremate the deceased.[5] Then there is the type of funeral ceremony, where to hold it, and whether to incorporate specific religious or cultural elements.[6] A decision to bury inevitably raises the question of which grave, or perhaps which cemetery, churchyard, or burial ground;[7] sometimes the disagreement can be over which country.[8] Following cremation, there is the additional issue of what happens to the ashes: should they be interred or scattered (and where), or retained by one family member or divided between others?[9] For now, however, the focus is on funerals, and a clash of views that prevents this ritualised disposal of the dead from taking place.

Although ostensibly about the funeral, closer analysis shows that many of these disputes have their genesis in a range of issues that (re)surface on the deceased's passing.[10]

---

4 For an overview, see Heather Conway, *The Law and the Dead* (Abingdon: Routledge, 2016), ch 4. Of course, reported cases are only a snapshot; some sort of resolution will often be found before lawyers are engaged.

5 As in *Donahue v Morleys Funerals Pty Ltd* [2016] QSC 137 (de facto spouse's decision to cremate challenged by the deceased's mother). In *Re JS (Disposal of Body)* [2016] EWHC 2859 (Fam), separated parents fought over whether their teenage daughter should be cryogenically frozen, while new and emerging methods of bodily disposal (e.g., so-called 'water cremation' or Resomation[TM], and natural organic reduction or 'human composting') will trigger other conflicts of choice here.

6 See, e.g., *Saleh v Reichert* (1993) 104 DLR (4th) 384 (husband's decision to cremate his wife's remains, as per her instructions, challenged by the deceased's father who wanted burial in accordance with the Muslim faith in which she had been raised). Australian courts have dealt with numerous cases where non-adherence to Aboriginal traditions and death rituals have triggered conflict within families and the wider community: see, e.g., *Calma v Sesar* (1992) 106 FLR 446; *Reece v Little* [2009] WASC 30; *Dann v Office of the State Coroner* [2020] WASC 486; and *Frail v Shorey* [2021] NSWSC 122.

7 See, e.g., *Scotching v Birch* [2008] EWHC 844 (Ch) (mother who pleaded guilty to the unlawful killing of her son wanted to bury him in the local churchyard, close to the family home; boy's father – the couple were separated – insisted on a grave plot close to where he lived). See also *Kitchener v Magistrate Thomas* [2019] NSWSC 701 (deceased's mother insisting on burial in his Aboriginal homeland; de facto spouse (and mother of his children) wanting to bury the deceased close to where they had lived).

8 As in *Anstey v Mundle* [2016] EWHC 1073 (Ch) (deceased's daughters divided over burial in England or in Jamaica) and *Re Pangou (Deceased)* [2022] EWHC 147 (Ch) (deceased's long-term partner wanted burial in England, while his daughter wanted her father's body to be buried in France).

9 See, e.g., *Fessi v Whitmore* [1999] 1 FLR 767 and *Doherty v Doherty* [2006] QSC 257. The physical structure of ashes and their portability has 'enabled people to bring disputes … that would be inconceivable if the deceased was still in body form': Matthew Groves, "The Disposal of Human Ashes," *Journal of Law and Medicine* 12, no. 3 (2005): 270.

10 Heather Conway and John Stannard, "The Honours of Hades: Death, Emotion and the Law of Burial Disputes," *The University of New South Wales Law Journal* 34, no. 3 (2011): 860–97.

Death can bring out the worst in families who were already divided or prone to conflict; typical examples include siblings fighting over a dead parent's funeral arrangements (when old jealousies and childhood rivalries re-emerge) or separated parents fighting over a dead child.[11] The rise in second and blended families is also a significant factor here, with disputes between children from different relationships on the death of a parent, and tussles between children and their deceased parent's new spouse or partner.[12] Deeply held religious and cultural values can create conflict amongst the living over the observance of specific death rites.[13] More generally, the growth in non-traditional, more personalised funerals and memorials means a broader range of options for surviving relatives to quarrel over.[14]

Of course, underlying all these disputes is a complex – and somewhat volatile – emotional backdrop. Death produces a range of emotions, such as anger, hostility, shock, and despair, which manifest themselves through the grieving process.[15] Grief, however, is only one part of the picture, as death releases a host of other negative feelings within families such as jealously and simmering resentments linked to years of sibling rivalry,[16] or parental bitterness and hostility stemming from child custody disputes when the couple separated.[17] All of these sentiments play a central role when funeral disputes make their way into a courtroom. Such matters are both difficult and distressing for judges to deal with, as indicated by some passing observations in judgments.[18] Thus, the existence of an effective legal mechanism for deciding these cases has an important role to play beyond providing a means of solving the insoluble.

11 There are numerous examples of each. For feuding siblings, see, e.g., *Anstey v Mundle* [2016] EWHC 1073 (Ch); *McCredie v Batson* [2020] NSWSC 1913; and *Marinucci v Condo* [2020] VSC 613. For parental disputes over dead children, see *Fessi v Whitmore* [1999] 1 FLR 767; *Joseph v Dunn* [2007] WASC 238; *Re JS (Disposal of Body)* [2016] EWHC 2859 (Fam); and *Nayacakalou v Vincent* [2020] NSWSC 24.
12 See, e.g., *Burnes v Richards* (1993) 7 BPR 15, 104 and *Re Pangou (Deceased)* [2022] EWHC 147 (Ch).
13 See the cases cited at n. 6.
14 Modern funerals are increasingly about 'meaning-making' and celebrating the deceased's life through personalisation, secularisation, and increased consumer choice – see, e.g., Margaret Holloway, Susan Adamson, Vassos Argyrou, Peter Draper, and Daniel Mariau. "'Funerals Aren't Nice But It Couldn't Have Been Nicer'. The Makings of a Good Funeral," *Mortality* 18, no. 1 (2013): 30–53.
15 Seminal works include John Bowlby, "Processes of Mourning," *International Journal of Psycho-Analysis* 41 (1961): 317–40; Elisabeth Kübler-Ross, *On Death and Dying* (New York: Macmillan, 1969); and Colin Murray Parkes, *Bereavement: Studies of Grief in Adult Life* (London: Tavistock Press, 1972). For more recent authorities, see John Archer, *The Nature of Grief: The Evolution and Psychology of Reactions to Loss* (London: Routledge, 2003) and Leaat Granek, "Grief as Pathology: The Evolution of Grief Theory in Psychology from Freud to the Present," *History of Psychology* 13, no. 1 (2010): 46–73.
16 See Dorothy Rowe, *My Dearest Enemy, My Dangerous Friend: Making and Breaking Sibling Bonds* (Hove: Routledge, 2007) and Jeanne Safer, *Cain's Legacy: Liberating Siblings from a Lifetime of Rage, Shame, Secrecy, and Regret* (New York: Basic Books, 2012).
17 See, e.g., Robert E. Emery, *Renegotiating Family Relationships: Divorce, Child Custody, and Mediation* (New York: Guilford Press, 2011).
18 See the comments of Cronin J in *Derwen v Ling* [2008] FamCA [7] ('[t]his heart-rending tragedy affects everyone') and those of then Deputy Judge Sonia Proudman QC in *Hartshorne v Gardner* [2008] EWHC B3 (Ch), [2]–[3] (choosing between 'the earnest wishes of two grieving parents [about their dead child's funeral arrangements] requires the wisdom of Solomon, which I do not profess to have').

Courts in England and Wales, and in Australia, typically apply a clear order of entitlement based on succession law principles that favour the personal representatives.[19] The first point to note is that the deceased's own funeral preferences are not legally binding,[20] though these are an increasingly important reference point.[21] Instead, where the deceased made a will, the final say on the funeral arrangements lies with the executor.[22] For intestate deaths, the decision lies with the highest ranked next-of-kin according to the list of potential estate administrators. Much depends on the relevant intestacy statute, but in most instances a surviving spouse or civil partner takes priority, followed by the deceased's children, then parents, then sisters or brothers,[23] though individual Australian states also include cohabiting or de facto partners as a separate secondary category after surviving spouses or civil partners.[24] Delineating rights by a descending order of relational ties means, for example, that courts will favour a spouse over the deceased's parents or siblings where the two sides clash over funeral arrangements.[25] Of course, this hierarchy is ineffectual where the dispute involves feuding relatives within the same kinship cohort who have equal rights: for example, parents fighting over a dead child, or adult siblings fighting over a deceased parent.[26] In these circumstances, however, judges have devised a set of guiding principles to assist them in reaching a legal solution, incorporating things like the deceased's wishes, the needs of grieving relatives, the proposed timing of the funeral, and treating the dead with respect.[27]

This 'retreat to legal formalism'[28] serves two purposes. First, it allows judges to end the dispute by awarding 'custody' of the deceased to a particular individual who has the correlative legal right to make the funeral arrangements.[29] The court's sole function is to

---

19 Conway, *Law and the Dead*, 61–7. However, there are examples of judges departing from this legal framework and awarding control of the funeral to someone who is not the designated personal representative (i.e., the executor or highest-ranked kin under intestacy), either on the merits of the case and/or because the ranking is challenged in some way. See Conway, *Law and the Dead*, 100–4, and the more recent examples in *State of South Australia v Ken* [2021] SASC 10 and *Re Pangou (Deceased)* [2022] EWHC 147 (Ch). The point has also been made, at least in several Australian cases, that the personal representative rule is not absolute – see, e.g., *Re Ghosh* [2022] VSC 210.

20 *Williams v Williams* (1882) 20 Ch D 659.

21 See, e.g., *Burrows v HM Coroner for Preston* [2008]; *Donahue v Morleys Funerals Pty Ltd* [2016] QSC 137; and *Y v Z* [2018] EWHC 4026 (Ch).

22 See *Grandison v Nembhard* [1989] 4 BMLR 140 and *Kak v Kak (nee Boman)* [2020] NSWSC 140.

23 In England and Wales, see s. 46 of the *Administration of Estates Act 1925* and (more importantly) Rule 22 of the *Non-Contentions Probate Rules 1987*.

24 See, e.g., *Reece v Little* [2009] WASC 30 (de facto partner granted custody of the deceased's remains as the person entitled to seek letters of administration and consequent presumptive administrator under ss. 15 and 25 of the Administration Act 1903 (WA)).

25 See, e.g., *Threlfall v Threlfall* [2009] VSC 283 (coroner erred in releasing the deceased's body to his brother instead of his widow) and *Dann v Office of the State Coroner* [2020] WASC 486 (deceased's wife and mother of his 16-year-old son entitled to decide the funeral arrangements over the deceased's sister).

26 Similar issues arise where joint executors under a will disagree over funeral arrangements – see, e.g., *Leeburn v Derndorfer* [2004] VSC 172 (joint executor siblings under their father's will who clashed over his ashes).

27 Heather Conway, "'First Among Equals': Breaking the Deadlock in Parental and Sibling Funeral Disputes," *Liverpool Law Review* 39 (2018): 151–74. The same article explains how legislative solutions in other common law jurisdictions have resolved these disputes by applying blunt rules such as favouring the elder/eldest protagonist or majority rule.

28 Kieran McEvoy and Heather Conway, "The Dead, The Law, and the Politics of the Past," *Journal of Law and Society* 31, no. 4 (2004): 541.

29 In legal terms, that person has decision-making authority over the body, which carries with it a qualified and transient right to possession for funeral purposes only.

decide this matter, not to micro-manage the funeral.[30] As such, there is no need to unravel complicated family histories or make difficult subjective value judgments about the state of relations between the living and the dead: to do otherwise would be superfluous to the decision-making process, and unleash a Pandora's box of emotions on which the lid is already dangerously ajar.[31] Second, it allows a solution to be reached, and in a compressed timeframe. The dictates of public health combined with the fundamental tenets of human dignity and respect for the dead create an overwhelming sense of ensuring that the funeral takes place as quickly as possible.[32] However, granting control of the arrangements to one individual has lasting and very public consequences, as highlighted later in this chapter.

Contested memorials

Memorialisation can take many forms, and in recent years the proliferation of online memorial sites, Facebook memorials, and other forms of 'virtual commemoration' have re-shaped how the living remember the recently dead. These pose all sorts of complex legal issues that are beyond the scope of this chapter.[33] Instead, the focus here is on permanent, physical structures – the headstones, monuments, and commemorative plaques placed on individual graves in churchyards, burial grounds, and municipal cemeteries – and the resultant disputes that are triggered within families.[34] These can be about the design or siting of the memorial, but are more often about the wording that appears on a memorial as chosen by certain family members to the (deliberate) exclusion of others. For instance, biological parents who had re-established contact with their son or daughter might find themselves omitted from a memorial placed by adoptive parents on the child's grave.[35] A grieving widow may discover that she is not mentioned on a headstone erected by her in-laws, which describes the deceased as a 'dear son and brother and father'.[36] And in one

30 *ND v LD* [2019] EWHC 3639 (Fam). However, there have been isolated examples of judges imposing a range of directions about the funeral, usually to suppress the likelihood of further familial in-fighting – see, e.g., *McCredie v Batson* [2020] NSWSC 1913.

31 See, e.g., the comments of Debelle J in *Re Lochowiak (Deceased)* [1997] SASC 6301, [8] ('A court is … reluctant to enter into disputes of this kind which, clearly, involve emotional issues of a high degree'). This is not to suggest that what is occurring here is emotionless judging. The better approach – and one that is evident in numerous reported cases – is expressive empathy whereby judges acknowledge the emotional aspects of the dispute, and what has driven the parties to litigation. See Conway and Stannard, "The Honours of Hades."

32 There is a 'general public interest … that bodies of deceased persons be treated with respect and cremated or buried reasonably promptly and not be permitted unnecessarily to decompose before so doing': Gorton J in *Re Ghosh* [2022] VSC 210, [18].

33 For a flavour, see Tim Hutchings, "Wiring Death: Dying, Grieving and Remembering on the Internet," in *Emotion, Identity and Death: Mortality Across Disciplines*, ed. Douglas J. Davies and Chan-Wok Park (Farnham: Ashgate Publishing, 2012), 43–58 and Tony Walter, "New Mourners, Old Mourners: Online Memorial Culture as a Chapter in the History of Mourning," *New Review of Hypermedia and Multimedia* 21, no. 1–2 (2015): 10–24.

34 Issues may also arise where a proposed memorial does not comply with internal cemetery or churchyard regulations – including more transient memorials such as wind-chimes, teddy bears, football scarves, and other personal keepsakes that fall foul of 'graveyard aesthetics'. Here the dispute will be between surviving relatives and the regulatory body of the cemetery or churchyard. For an overview, see generally Conway, *Law and the Dead*, 215–8.

35 As occurred in *Smith v Tamworth City County Council* (1997) NSWLR 680.

36 As occurred in *Escott v Brikha* [2000] NSWSC 458. See also *Re Campbell (Judicial Review)* [2013] NIQB 32 (gravestone erected by the deceased's father referred to him as a 'much loved son

English case that attracted a lot of media attention in 2017, the court was asked to resolve a dispute between the deceased's children and their step-father when two separate memorials were placed on the same grave.[37] Susannah Allinson's cremated remains had been interred with those of her first husband Alan Matthewson (who died in 1978), and the couple's children had the existing headstone removed to add 'in loving memory of ... a dear wife, mother and nan' to Alan's inscription. While this was happening, the deceased's second husband, William Allinson, placed a second memorial on the grave – a flat tablet that described her as 'wife of Bill'.

Despite a much lower volume of reported case law than contested funerals, contested memorials are often triggered by the same family tensions, simmering feuds, and enduring estrangements that either come to the fore on death or, in this instance, emerge in its aftermath.[38] Such disputes are not as time sensitive as decisions about the funeral arrangements, though the emotional dynamics can be every bit as complex and the parties more entrenched in their views with the passage of time (even if the raw emotions of grief have subsided somewhat). Once again, there is a distinct legal rule to help judges navigate the dispute, and either allow the memorial to remain 'as is' or direct that changes be made. Subject to meeting churchyard or cemetery by-laws, or other regulatory frameworks taking precedence,[39] the final decision lies with the person who has the exclusive right of burial in the particular plot: that is, the person who purchased the grave and has basic decision-making authority over it.[40] This may not be the individual who would identify as the deceased's closest kin, as in the scenarios outlined above where the surviving spouses had no legal entitlements over the graves in question. In short, the exclusive right of burial carries with it the right to decide on the appearance of the grave and any headstone; any subsequent change in the otherwise permissible wording on the memorial requires the right-holder's consent. For instance, the family of Claire Morris – who was murdered in Scotland by her husband, Malcolm Webster, in a staged car accident in 1994 – were forced to ask his permission to change the wording on Claire's gravestone because the convicted killer had bought and paid for the burial plot and the memorial before his crimes had been exposed. The family were intending to change the inscription from 'Claire Webster' to the deceased's maiden name, and to remove Webster's tribute to his 'dear wife'.[41]

This, of course, is an extreme example. In the other cases mentioned here, the problem is of a more basic nature: what to do about a memorial which 'recognises a relationship

---

and brother' but omitted the deceased's wife) and *Wiebe v Bronstein* [2013] BCSC 1041 (deceased's same-sex partner challenged the memorial inscription chosen by the deceased's sister which referred to the deceased as a 'beloved son, brother, uncle and friend').

37 *Armitage: St John the Baptist* [2017] ECC Lic 1.

38 In some instances, the memorial dispute can be about 'reclaiming' the deceased. In the New Zealand case of *Bird v Bird* [2017] NZHC 1612, the deceased's will actually requested that the wording on his wife's headstone be amended to replace 'partner of Dick' with 'husband of Brian' despite the spouses having separated six years earlier.

39 For instance, the Church of England has very specific rules around churchyard burials and the style, content, and appearance of memorials and graves. This creates a distinct governance system and dispute resolution process for contested memorials – see, e.g., the discussion in *In re St Augustine's Churchyard, Droitwich Spa* [2016] 1 WLR 3365.

40 *Smith v Tamworth City County Council* (1997) NSWLR 680. Identical conclusions were reached in *Re Campbell (Judicial Review)* [2013] NIQB 32 and in *Boni v Larwood* [2014] SASC 185.

41 "Gravestone Needs Killer's Consent," *The Telegraph*, 3 June 2011, www.telegraph.co.uk/news/uknews/law-and-order/8552935/Gravestone-needs-killers-consent.html.

with some persons while deliberately remaining silent about other important relationships which are equally worthy of mention'.[42] Legal solutions have to be found, but, like contested funerals, the outcome has enduring and extremely public consequences, for reasons we now explore.

Materiality, law and the (re)construction of relationships between the living and the dead

The role of law in mediating contested funerals and memorials speaks to a core theme in death studies literature: the materialities of death.[43] Death and its rituals produce physical objects, one naturally occurring (the corpse) and one artificially created (the memorial), that are central to the funeral and the subsequent act of commemorating the deceased, but have now become sites of conflict. Neither of these things is a mere tangible item; most of us would challenge Nagel's assertion that a dead body may be viewed as something like 'a piece of furniture',[44] and a memorial is not simply a structure that records names and dates. Moreover, both the fate of the corpse through the medium of the funeral and the design and content of what marks its final resting place on earth play a pivotal role in the continuing relationships between bereaved families (and society more generally) and their dead, as discussed immediately below. Law must find a way of dealing with the object in question and mediating the contradictory claims and misguided assumptions that these disputes present. And while other chapters in this Handbook explore how the law attaches the dead to place,[45] what follows immediately below suggests a different type of situational positioning – one that focuses on a sense of place within the family itself, and openly attaches the dead to whichever individuals are deemed to have decision-making authority over the funeral or memorial.

Death and bereavement have been described as being 'both intensely private and personal while often simultaneously experienced and expressed collectively and publicly'; they are also 'intensified at certain sites ... and unfold in many others'.[46] Contested funerals and contested memorials capture these themes perfectly: they involve heightened feelings, experienced by individuals within a wider social grouping (that of the deceased's family or kinship circle, however defined) at the junction of what is inherently private yet profoundly public. In both situations, law acts as an internal dispute resolution

---

42 As summed up by The Chancellor, His Honour Judge Eyre QC, in *Armitage: St John the Baptist* [2017] ECC Lic 1, [23] when making his ruling on which of the two memorials should remain on the deceased's grave in the case outlined at text to n. 37. Stressing that the chosen memorial should not be used as an opportunity for settling old scores, it was decided that the second memorial would be removed when the deceased's children gave an undertaking to add new wording to the original headstone that reflected their mother's second marriage.

43 See, e.g., Jenny Hockey, Carol Komaromy and Kate Woodthorpe, eds., *The Matter of Death: Space, Place and Materiality* (Basingstoke, Palgrave Macmillan, 2010); Zahra Newby and Ruth Toulson, eds., *The Materiality of Mourning: Cross-disciplinary Perspectives* (Abingdon: Routledge, 2018).

44 Thomas Nagel, *Mortal Questions* (Cambridge: Cambridge University Press, 1979), 7. Contrast this with the discussion in Thorsten Benkel and Matthias Meitzler, "Materiality and the Body: Explorations at the End of Life," *Mortality* 24, no. 2 (2019): 231–46.

45 See, e.g., Chapters 8 and 10.

46 Avril Maddrell and James D. Sidaway, "Introduction: Bringing a Spatial Lens to Death, Dying, Mourning and Remembrance," in *Deathscapes: Spaces for Death, Dying and Remembrance*, ed. Avril Maddrell and James D. Sidaway (Farnham: Ashgate, 2010), 2.

mechanism within families. Judges have clear rules, allowing them to pronounce on the legal merits without getting too embroiled in messy family dynamics and emotionally laden narratives. Of course, one could argue that this approach is fundamentally flawed, given the centrality of such factors to the actual dispute; and that blunt succession or property law entitlements can never capture the nuances of individual contests or reflect the fact that a particular relative could have a stronger moral claim to decide the funeral arrangements or memorial content than the ultimate legal victor.[47] The content of the actual rules is also open to criticism. For instance, intestacy laws are often decried as 'privileging the nuclear family, to the exclusion of modern forms of associations and relationships'[48] in their articulation of next-of-kin. Extrapolating these rules on to funeral disputes creates the same problem: that is, an unduly narrow hierarchy of entitlement that does not align with contemporary family structures.[49]

However, the emphasis on familiar private law concepts of status, control, and the exercise of legitimate authority to the exclusion of all others has much wider consequences here, because both funerals and memorials are so intrinsically public. Funerals are not just about dealing with the dead, in a practical sense; they cement the deceased's place in the lives of family, friends, and community through a series of socially mandated and highly symbolic acts that frame the ritual in the minds of participants.[50] Moreover, as ceremonies that are 'personal in focus and societal in [their] consequences',[51] funerals are potent public statements about which surviving relatives were seemingly closest to the deceased in life. Those who make the final arrangements and position themselves as higher-ranking mourners as a result of family roles and psychodynamics[52] gain societal acknowledgement of their importance to the deceased.[53] A legal ruling on a contested funeral can therefore become a lasting and very public affirmation or recasting of certain relationships with the deceased. For example, allowing adoptive parents to decide a child's funeral arrangements allows them to permanently claim the child as their own, regardless of the role that biological parents may have latterly played in the deceased's life.[54] Parental disputes over a dead child can either

---

47 As in *Holtham v Arnold* [1986] 2 BMLR 123 where the deceased's estranged wife was allowed to cremate his remains, despite opposition from the deceased's long-term partner who wanted to bury him in accordance with what she claimed were his last wishes. (The estranged wife was the deceased's legal next-of-kin under English intestacy rules and was therefore entitled to custody of the remains). See also the outcomes in *Escott v Brikha* [2000] NSWSC 458 and *Re Campbell (Judicial Review)* [2013] NIQB 32, both mentioned at n. 36 (memorial wording that excluded the respective surviving widows was legally permissible).

48 See Shelly Kreiczer-Levy, "Big Data and the Modern Family," *Wisconsin Law Review* (2019): 349.

49 Additionally, the legal classification of next-of-kin may not reflect cultural notions of kinship, authority, and extended family ties in funeral disputes where the deceased was a member of a particular indigenous community – see, e.g., Prue Vines, "Consequences of Intestacy for Indigenous People: The Passing of Property and Burial Rights," *Australian Indigenous Legal Reporter* 8, no. 4 (2004): 1–10.

50 See, e.g., Thomas O'Rourke, Brian H. Spitzberg, and Annegret F. Hannawa, "The Good Funeral: Toward an Understanding of Funeral Participation and Satisfaction," *Death Studies* 35, no. 8 (2011): 729–50 and William G. Hoy, *Do Funerals Matter? The Purposes and Practices of Death Rituals in Global Perspective* (New York: Routledge, 2013).

51 David G. Mandelbaum, "Social Uses of Funeral Rites," in *Death and Identity*, ed. Robert Fulton (Bowie, MD: Charles Press, 1976), 338–60.

52 Harvey Peskin, "Who Has the Right to Mourn? Relational Deference and the Ranking of Grief," *Psychoanalytic Dialogues* 29, no. 4 (2019): 477–92.

53 Tanya K. Hernandez, "The Property of Death," *University of Pittsburgh Law Review* 60, (1999): 991.

54 See, e.g., *Buchanan v Milton* [1999] 2 FLR 844.

affirm the custodial or reinstate the non-custodial parent's right to 'have' for their child on a permanent basis, depending on who gets to decide the funeral arrangements.[55] And where surviving spouses or de facto partners clash with the deceased's parents and siblings, the outcome will elevate one side above the other in the funeral stakes.[56]

Memorials are also 'both intensely personal and manifestly public'.[57] They mark the physical location of an interred corpse or ashes, thereby creating a focal point for mourning and remembrance.[58] Yet, by denoting the deceased's life and passing in a particular way, memorials symbolise ongoing – and extremely public – narratives of association between the living and the dead.[59] The chosen inscription is a permanent and potent confirmation of the deceased's lifespan *and* most important relationships. Those who decide the wording, and are legally entitled to do so, cement their own ties and emotional attachments to the deceased. The resultant memorial creates a particular impression of who was closest to the deceased in life, and acts as a mode of 'identity (re)formation'[60] where other equally close – and higher-ranked relationships (both socially and legally) – are excluded from the narrative. Parents and siblings of a deceased son and brother omitting any reference to his widow on the grave marker is an excellent, if ultimately tragic, illustration of this. Compared to funerals, however, there are fewer options here – both legally and practically. Judges will occasionally circumvent the rules around funerals and allow someone else to make the arrangements;[61] the funeral is also an impending event that the 'losing' party can still attend and thereby gain recognition from the wider community as a close relative of the deceased. With contested memorials, the legal options are limited (the person with the exclusive right of burial tends to prevail), and the inscribed physical structure is already in place with no potentially redemptive public ceremony for the excluded party.

Conclusion

Both funerals and memorials are about the person who has died and his/her principal relationships in life. Although personal in content, they are public and permanent representations of the deceased's social identity as a much-loved spouse, partner, child, parent, sibling, etc. This makes them a frequent source of contention within families, triggering legal disputes that are highly charged and emotionally fraught. In the majority of cases, judges will apply a formalistic solution to end the current impasse, and while the

---

55 See respectively *Re JS (Disposal of Body)* [2016] EWHC 2859 (Fam) and *Burrows v Cramley* [2002] WASC 47.

56 This may be difficult for the deceased's family where, e.g., the deceased and their spouse or partner had informally separated or had a notoriously volatile relationship – see, e.g., *Dann v Office of the State Coroner* [2020] WASC 486 and *Jackamarra v Office of the State Coroner* [2021] WASC 301.

57 Tony Walter and Clare Gittings, "What Will the Neighbours Say? Reactions to Field and Garden Burial," in Hockey, Komaromy, and Woodthorpe, *The Matter of Death*, 172.

58 See, e.g., Anna Petersson, "The Production of a Memorial Place: Materialising Expressions of Grief," in Maddrell and Sidaway, *Deathscapes*, 141–159

59 See generally Kate Woodthorpe, "Private Grief in Public Spaces: Interpreting Memorialisation in the Contemporary Cemetery," in Hockey, Komaromy and Woodthorpe, *The Matter of Death*, 117–32.

60 Woodthorpe, "Private Grief," 122 and the sources cited therein.

61 See n. 19.

resultant 'winner-take-all outcome and consequential damage to close relationships'[62] will have a lasting impact within the family itself, this is only part of the overall picture.

It has been said that in 'decisions about funeral participation … familial relationships are being (re)constructed and displayed, or rejected and hidden' while the family itself (in whatever contemporary guise) 'is being used as a reference for attendees to judge the relationship(s) between the deceased, the organizer and other family members included within the funeral'.[63] Similar observations can be made about memorials: the chosen wording shows family ties being affirmed, recast, or concealed, and exhibited for all who view the headstone to witness and judge accordingly. In resolving contested funerals and memorials, the law plays an active role in (re)constructing and cementing the deceased's social identity by deciding who has the final say on the matter. This adds another layer of complexity to an experience that is already 'quite unpleasant and emotionally painful'[64] for those who are mourning the loss of a loved one. Of course, a case can be made for modifying the existing rules and moving away from strict succession and property law entitlements. For instance, one option might be to centralise the deceased's own wishes in contested funerals, and to supplement this with a modified list of close family members (more reflective of modern relationships) who have default decision-making powers if the deceased's wishes are unknown or wholly ambiguous.[65] Yet reformist zeal must always be tempered by a heavy dose of realism, and this is especially true of contested funerals and memorials. Whatever legal solution is applied will be 'hard to take for the losing party'[66] and will problematise the aftermath of the dispute – not just because they lose the right to decide the funeral arrangements or the wording on the memorial, but because that individual will have to live with the ramifications of what this (allegedly) says about their relationship with the deceased and in a very public sense. To the victor go the spoils; for the losing party, however, this aspect of the legal outcome – and its repercussions – may be just as hard to deal with in the long term.

Bibliography

Archer, John. *The Nature of Grief: The Evolution and Psychology of Reactions to Loss.* London: Routledge, 2003.

Benkel, Thorsten, and Matthias Meitzler. "Materiality and the Body: Explorations at the End of Life." *Mortality* 24, no. 2 (2019): 231–246.

Bowlby, John. "Processes of Mourning." *The International Journal of Psycho-Analysis* 42 (1961): 317–340.

---

62 Brian L. Josias, "Burying the Hatchet in Burial Disputes: Applying Alternative Dispute Resolution Techniques to Disputes Concerning the Interment of Bodies," *Notre Dame Law Review* 79, no. 3 (2004): 1166.

63 Kate Woodthorpe, "Family and Funerals: Taking a Relational Perspective," *Death Studies* 41, no. 9 (2017): 596.

64 Carla Sofka, "What Kind of Funeral? Identifying and Resolving Family Conflicts," *Generations* 28, no. 2 (2004): 21.

65 This approach has a number of advocates: see, e.g., Queensland Law Reform Commission, *A Review of the Law in Relation to the Final Disposal of a Dead Body*, Report No. 69 (December 2011); Remigius N. Nwabueze, "Legal Control of Burial Rights," *Cambridge Journal of International and Comparative Law* 2, no. 2 (2013): 196–226; Hernandez, "The Property of Death"; and Conway, *Law and the Dead*, ch. 5. For a recently enacted illustration, see ss. 65–6 of the *Burial and Cremation (Scotland) Act 2016* dealing with arrangements on the death of an adult and on the death of a child respectively.

66 As acknowledged by then Deputy Judge Sonia Proudman QC in *Hartshorne v Gardner* [2008] EWHC B3 (Ch), [2]– [3].

Conway, Heather. "'First Among Equals': Breaking the Deadlock in Parental and Sibling Funeral Disputes." *Liverpool Law Review* 39 (2018): 151–174.

Conway, Heather, and John Stannard. "The Honours of Hades: Death, Emotion and the Law of Burial Disputes." *The University of New South Wales Law Journal* 34, no. 3 (2011): 860–897.

Conway, Heather. *The Law and the Dead*. Abingdon: Routledge, 2016.

Emery, Robert E. *Renegotiating Family Relationships: Divorce, Child Custody, and Mediation*. New York: Guilford Press, 2011.

Finch, Janet, and Jennifer Mason. *Passing On: Kinship and Inheritance in England*. London: Routledge, 2013.

Gilding, Michael. "Reflexivity Over and Above Convention: The New Orthodoxy in the Sociology of Personal Life, Formerly Sociology of the Family." *The British Journal of Sociology* 61, no. 4 (2010): 757–777.

Granek, Leeat. "Grief as Pathology: The Evolution of Grief Theory in Psychology from Freud to the Present." *History of Psychology* 13, no. 1 (2010): 46–73.

Groves, Matthew. "The Disposal of Human Ashes." *Journal of Law and Medicine* 12, no. 3 (2005): 267–272.

Hernandez, Tanya K. "The Property of Death." *University of Pittsburgh Law Review* 60, (1999): 971–1028.

Hockey, Jenny, Carol Komaromy, and Kate Woodthorpe, eds. *The Matter of Death: Space, Place and Materiality*. Basingstoke: Palgrave Macmillan, 2010.

Holloway, Margaret, Susan Adamson, Vassos Argyrou, Peter Draper, and Daniel Mariau. "'Funerals Aren't Nice But It Couldn't Have Been Nicer'. The Makings of a Good Funeral." *Mortality* 18, no. 1 (2013): 30–53.

Hutchings, Tim. "Wiring Death: Dying, Grieving and Remembering on the Internet." In *Emotion, Identity and Death: Mortality Across Disciplines*, edited by Douglas J. Davies and Chan-Wok Park, 43–58. Farnham: Ashgate Publishing, 2012.

Hoy, William G. *Do Funerals Matter? The Purposes and Practices of Death Rituals in Global Perspective*. New York: Routledge, 2013.

Josias, Brian L. "Burying the Hatchet in Burial Disputes: Applying Alternative Dispute Resolution Techniques to Disputes Concerning the Interment of Bodies." *Notre Dame Law Review* 79, no. 3 (2004): 1141–1181.

Kreiczer-Levy, Shelly. "Big Data and the Modern Family." *Wisconsin Law Review* (2019): 349–372.

Kübler-Ross, Elizabeth. *On Death and Dying*. New York: Macmillan, 1969.

McEvoy, Kieran, and Heather Conway. "The Dead, the Law, and the Politics of the Past." *Journal of Law and Society* 31, no. 4 (2004): 539–562.

Maddrell, Avril, and James D. Sidaway, "Introduction: Bringing a Spatial Lens to Death, Dying, Mourning and Remembrance." In *Deathscapes: Spaces for Death, Dying and Remembrance*, edited by Avril Maddrell and James D. Sidaway, 1–16. Farnham: Ashgate, 2010.

Mandelbaum, David G. "Social Uses of Funeral Rites." In *Death and Identity*, edited by Robert Fulton, 338–360. Bowie, MD: Charles Press, 1976.

Nagel, Thomas. *Mortal Questions*. Cambridge: Cambridge University Press, 1979.

Newby, Zahra, and Ruth Toulson, eds. *The Materiality of Mourning: Cross-disciplinary Perspectives*. Abingdon: Routledge, 2018.

Nwabueze, Remigius N. "Legal Control of Burial Rights." *Cambridge International Law Journal* 2, no. 2 (2013): 196–226.

O'Rourke, Thomas, Brian H.Spitzberg, and Annegret F. Hannawa. "The Good Funeral: Toward an Understanding of Funeral Participation and Satisfaction." *Death Studies* 35, no. 8 (2011): 729–750.

Parkes, Colin Murray. *Bereavement: Studies of Grief in Adult Life*. London: Tavistock Press, 1972.

Peskin, Harvey. "Who Has the Right to Mourn? Relational Deference and the Ranking of Grief." *Psychoanalytic Dialogues* 29, no. 4 (2019): 477–492.

Petersson, Anna. "The Production of a Memorial Place: Materialising Expressions of Grief." In *Deathscapes: Spaces for Death, Dying and Remembrance*, edited by Avril Maddrell and James D. Sidaway, 14–159. Farnham: Ashgate, 2010.

Queensland Law Reform Commission. *A Review of the Law in Relation to the Final Disposal of a Dead Body*. Report No. 69, December 2011.

Rowe, Dorothy. *My Dearest Enemy, My Dangerous Friend: Making and Breaking Sibling Bonds*. Hove: Routledge, 2007.

Safer, Jeanne. *Cain's Legacy: Liberating Siblings from a Lifetime of Rage, Shame, Secrecy, and Regret.* New York: Basic Books, 2012.

Sofka, Carla. "What Kind of Funeral? Identifying and Resolving Family Conflicts." *Generations* 28, no. 2 (2004): 21–25.

Vines, Prue. "Consequences of Intestacy for Indigenous People: The Passing of Property and Burial Rights." *Australian Indigenous Law Reporter* 8, no. 4 (2004): 1–10.

Walter, Tony. "New Mourners, Old Mourners: Online Memorial Culture as a Chapter in the History of Mourning." *New Review of Hypermedia and Multimedia* 21, no. 1–2 (2015): 10–24.

Walter, Tony, and Clare Gittings. "What Will the Neighbours Say? Reactions to Field and Garden Burial." In *The Matter of Death: Space, Place and Materiality*, edited by Jenny Hockey, Carol Komaromy, and Kate Woodthorpe, 165–177. Basingstoke: Palgrave Macmillan, 2010.

Woodthorpe, Kate. "Private Grief in Public Spaces: Interpreting Memorialisation in the Contemporary Cemetery." In *The Matter of Death: Space, Place and Materiality*, edited by Jenny Hockey, Carol Komaromy, and Kate Woodthorpe, 117–132. Basingstoke: Palgrave Macmillan, 2010.

Woodthorpe, Kate. "Family and Funerals: Taking a Relational Perspective." *Death Studies* 41, no. 9 (2017): 592–601.

11

CARING FOR THE DEAD

The Role of Anatomical Pathology Technologists in Medico-legal Autopsies

Imogen Jones[1]

In the context of law, care ethics has been developed against a background of care for vulnerable living persons. In medicine, care ethics is most often invoked to understand the role of nurses. I develop this further by applying the ethics of care framework to understand what motivates the requirement for autopsies as part of some death investigations and the ways that the deceased body and the bereaved are treated during these investigations.

I argue that care is central to the relationships and identities of those who carry out and assist with the legally mandated post-mortem process. Yet, without consistent standards and agreed purpose, the treatment of deceased bodies, the experiences of the bereaved and the application of law will be inconsistent. I conclude that the value of care ought to be recognised, for both its practical and moral significance, and that care should be a key driver in the future development of death investigation.

Introduction

When a person dies unexpectedly in England and Wales, the law intervenes. There are good reasons for this legally mandated death investigation process, but the experience of the bereaved is, at least initially, often one of delay and disruption to 'normal' grief and body-disposal practices. The decision that there needs to be an invasive post-mortem (a term I use interchangeably with 'autopsy') can be particularly unsettling, not least because this involves invasive acts to the deceased body.

Both procedurally and temporally, an autopsy is only one small part of the much larger process of legal death investigation. Yet an autopsy is also the stage in which the deceased body itself is most involved, providing the focus for much of the disruption to what 'normally' happens when a person dies. How a body is treated before, during, and after an autopsy is therefore important in shaping the ethical and practical acceptability of medico-legal death investigation.

1 The research in this chapter was funded by British Academy/Leverhulme grant entitled 'Investigating Unexpected Death: Values and Attitudes in Coronial Autopsies' (SRG1819\191442).

DOI: 10.4324/9781003304593-13

Deceased bodies are not simply transferred from their place of death to the post-mortem room. Instead, they are sent to a mortuary, where they are kept until such time that they can be handed over to the next of kin[2] for disposal. This process is represented in the diagram below.

The time between arrival at the mortuary, autopsy, and release will vary depending on location and circumstance. Mortuaries are primarily staffed by anatomical pathology technologists (APTs). The APT role is broad and has been described by John Pitchers, an APT who chairs the Association of Anatomical Pathology Technologists, as follows:

> Anatomical Pathology Technologists do not have a protected scope of practice, meaning that staff can, perfectly legally, be employed in mortuaries on a low administrative or assistant grade, and be asked to complete tasks that are not appropriate … The only standards set out in this regard are those of the Human Tissue Authority (HTA), who require that 'all staff who are involved in mortuary duties are appropriately trained/qualified', but without defining what constitutes 'appropriate' training or qualification.[3]

Typical APT duties can include taking receipt of newly deceased persons (including identity checks), evisceration and reconstruction of the deceased, involvement in forensic examinations, maintaining bodies while at the mortuary, and handling contact with bereaved people and funeral directors.[4] APTs are, therefore, central to the physical treatment of a deceased body for the entire time that it remains in the mortuary, and this affects the way the bereaved experience this traumatic period.

I draw on data from semi-structured interviews conducted with APTs between 2019 and 2020.[5] These interviews were conducted at various locations across England and transcribed into an anonymised format. Thematic content analysis, with coding based on grounded theory, was used to analyse the transcripts. The data presented here reflect the

Figure 11.1 Diagram of medico-legal process

2 Or another legally nominated responsible person, such as an executor.
3 John Pitchers, email message to author, 7 December 2022. The HTA standards referred to are Human Tissue Authority, *Post-mortem Examination Licensing Standards and Guidance*, para. GQ3, (accessed 28 June 2023), https://content.hta.gov.uk/sites/default/files/2022-10/Post-mortem%20examination%20licensing%20standards%20and%20guidance_1.pdf.
4 The autopsy itself is carried out by a pathologist. In non-suspicious but unexpected/contentious death cases, which are the focus of this chapter, the pathologist will nearly always be a general pathologist. A general pathologist is a doctor who specialises in the causes and effects of disease, often with an emphasis on examining samples in a laboratory. They carry out the post-mortem as private fee-by-case work in addition to their primary job.
5 These will be supplemented in later publications by further post-COVID-19 interviews in 2023.

personal experiences of the interviewed APTs. These experiences are not generalisable to the entire profession but do provide useful insight into the work of this important group across varied sites.

I argue that we can use an ethics of care framework to understand the role and attitudes of APTs. I draw on Eva Kittay's concept of ethics of care[6] to understand the role that relationships of care play in practice and to provide a normative framework for evaluating relationships. As Leach Scully argued, 'the perspective of care is concerned not just with the fundamental relationality of moral behavior, but also the ethical consequences of the fact that power and vulnerability are unevenly distributed in human relationships, and especially in relationships of care'.[7]

We will see that care is not only central to the very nature of the APT role but also reflected in many APTs' attitudes and epistemological identity. The extent to which an ethic of care is embedded within the work of APTs will affect both the treatment of a deceased body and the experiences of the bereaved. This is delicate; there is a geographical lottery that pervades the death investigation system, whereby, among many decisions, coroners will have differing practices, including if and when they require an invasive post-mortem. The law provides a framework that affords significant latitude for interpretation and discretion.

Mortuaries licensed to carry out post-mortems must adhere to technical standards, but these standards do little to ensure that care is meaningfully provided. Instead, there is reliance on good faith, occupational cultures and local interpretations. There is little visibility of this work and no meaningful oversight of the (lack of) consistency across mortuaries. This reveals that care ethics are an ideal rather than a requirement in the treatment of the dead – and, I argue, by extension the living – during this early stage of a medico-legal death investigation.

To place my discussion of ethics of care and the work of APTs in context, I begin by briefly outlining the key legal frameworks. This includes those that determine whether and what type of post-mortem will take place, as well as the regulatory frameworks imposed by the *Human Tissue Act 2006* (UK) and HTA. Against this background, I develop an ethics of care in a new direction – one in which the person in receipt of the care need not be alive.

Legal frameworks

In this section, I break down the key legal frameworks that shape the ways in which a body is dealt with during the early stages of a non-suspicious[8] medico-legal death investigation in England and Wales. I conceptualise these frameworks as a kind of cascade, starting with the formal law and concluding with the occupational cultures that dominate practice within mortuaries. Each is crucial in understanding the experiences of both the deceased body and the bereaved.

---

6 Eva Kittay, *Learning from My Daughter: The Value and Care of Disabled Minds* (New York: Oxford University Press, 2019).
7 Jackie Leach Scully, "Naming the dead: DNA-based identification of historical remains as an act of care," *New Genetics and Society* 33, no. 3 (2014): 322, http://dx.doi.org/10.1080/14636778.2014.946002.
8 These represent the vast majority of medico-legal autopsies. For example, of the 84,599 medico-legal post-mortems carried out in 2021, only 2 per cent (1,880) were conducted by a Home Office registered forensic pathologist (HORFP).

The decision to autopsy: The Coroners and Justice Act 2009

The basic legal framework for medico-legal death investigation is provided for in the *Coroners and Justice Act 2009* (UK). The coronial duty to investigate is set out in section 1 of the Act. Under section 14, the coroner can order a post-mortem if they deem this necessary to discharge their duty to investigate. However, this decision alone tells us very little about what will happen to the body. A 'post-mortem' can mean many things. Among these are a CT scan, a minimally invasive post-mortem, an external examination only, a full invasive post-mortem, and everything between.[9] What links all of these is that the 'normal' process for certifying death and subsequent disposal of the body will be disrupted by a legally mandated process. The extent and nature of that disruption will depend not only on the type of post-mortem but on factors such as location, available resources, and time of year.

The statutory law found in the *Coroners and Justice Act 2009* is, of course, supplemented and clarified by common law. The decisions of coroners can be subject to judicial review, but there is no other formal route for appeal. This means that the lawfulness of the decision can be reviewed but the decision itself is not open to challenge.[10]

Regulation: The Human Tissue Act 2004

The *Human Tissue Act 2004* (UK) enacted a consent-based scheme for the use and retention of bodies and materials taken from them. However, under section 11 of the Act, coroners (or acts done for their purposes) are exempt from these consent requirements. This extends only so far as is necessary to discharge the duty to answer the questions posed in section 1 of the *Coroners and Justice Act 2009*. Retention of any material beyond this will not be legal without consent from the next of kin. However, as with the *Coroners and Justice Act 2009*, how this is operationalised is subject to a lottery. Some coroners will impose tight restrictions on the taking of samples, including toxicology, whereas others implement a system of trust in the judgement of the autopsy pathologist. Therefore, what is taken will again depend on the professionals involved at all levels, and the decision-making throughout the process is opaque.

Additionally, the ways in which mortuaries maintain and interact (*care for*, perhaps) with the deceased are also within the HTA's remit. Matters such as checking the deceased's identity and the body's condition and storage are regulated by the HTA. The framework set out in the guidance for the post-mortem sector[11] includes the respectful treatment of the body and body parts and ensuring that 'the dignity of the person,

---

9 See para. 136 of the *Coroners and Justice Act 2009* Explanatory Notes: 'The term "post-mortem examination" is not defined but it will include any examination made of the deceased including non-invasive examinations, for example, using Magnetic Resonance Imaging (MRI) scans' (accessed 20 August 2023), www.legislation.gov.uk/ukpga/2009/25/notes/division/5/1/1/1/14. To provide context for what this means in practice, the 'Coroner's Statistics 2021' noted, 'There were 9,150 post-mortems conducted using less-invasive techniques and 6,255 using only less-invasive techniques (such as Computerised Tomography [CT] scans) in 2021': Ministry of Justice, "Coroners Statistics 2021: England and Wales" (accessed 20 August 2023), www.gov.uk/government/statistics/coroners-statistics-2021/coroners-statistics-2021-england-and-wales.

10 See, e.g., *R ((1) Adath Yisroel Burial Society (2) Ita Cymerman) v HM Senior Coroner for Inner North London (Defendant) & Chief Coroner of England & Wales (Interested Party)* [2018] EWHC 969 (Admin).

11 Human Tissue Authority, *Post-mortem*, para 7(b).

whether living or deceased, is maintained'.[12] Mortuaries are subject to inspection by the HTA and can lose their licence to carry out licensable activities (such as post-mortems) if they fall short of the required standards.[13]

Professional frameworks: Qualifications, training, and professionalisation

APT is not a regulated profession and a person is not required to have any formal qualifications to work as an APT. However, since 2023, the Association of Anatomical Pathology Technologists has been approved by the Registration Authority to award RSciTech, RSci, and CSci registration.[14] These professional registrations are tied to qualifications (ranging from levels 3 to 7[15]) and experience as an APT. These qualifications aim to develop both technical competence and emotional sensitivities to the context of dealing with both deceased bodies and the bereaved. As such, we see treatment that protects 'dignity' and 'respect' is required. These are assessed primarily at the local level, and so meeting the standard will depend on local interpretations – for example, local interpretations of what is involved in 'dignified treatment' of the deceased.

Even when a professional qualification is undertaken by an APT, this is largely taught and assessed at the local level. Skills, expectations, and attitudes are heavily influenced by the beliefs and practices of those in leadership roles at a given mortuary. Resource availability and wider organisational structures – such as the relationship with a bereavement office (and who conducts viewings/interacts with the bereaved) – will also affect experiences.

Given the very basic frameworks provided by the *Coroners and Justice Act 2009* and HTA, and the optionality of professional qualifications, local culture is of central importance. Once the decision to order a post-mortem has been taken, local culture will have a much greater effect on the treatment of the body, and the experiences of the bereaved, than any formal law. Therefore, APTs' attitudes and practices are crucial. In the next section, I develop understanding of this by discussing the ways in which APTs understand their role in regard to the 'respectful' and 'dignified' treatment of the deceased (and, where relevant, the living).

Spaces of care: APTs and the deceased body

Each stage of the journey from death to disposal involves several decisions that have consequences for those that come later. By way of example, a doctor (increasingly a medical examiner[16]) will decide if a death needs to be referred to the coroner, following

12 Human Tissue Authority, *Post-mortem*, para 7(c).
13 The HTA provides detailed standard operating procedures for relevant areas of practice. Short-comings identified at inspection can be categorised as 'critical', 'major', or 'minor'. Each category prompts a requirement of remedy but within different timeframes. See Human Tissue Authority, *Post-mortem*, PFE2. In practice, licences are rarely removed, and the consequences of doing so are significant for the provision of post-mortem services. Therefore, it is a last resort.
14 Through licenced bodies, the Science Council admit to their registered scientists and science technicians who meet competence and conduct requirements and commit to Continuing Professional Development.
15 Levels 3 and 4 are focused on APT-specific skills. See Association of Anatomical Pathology Technologists, "Level 3 and 4 RSPH Diploma Courses & Resources" (accessed 21 August 2023), www.aaptuk.org/professional-support/level-3–4-diploma-courses–resources.
16 On the introduction of the national medical examiner system, see NHS England, "The national medical examiner system" (accessed 21 August 2023), www.england.nhs.uk/patient-safety/patient-safety-insight/national-medical-examiner.

which the coroner will decide if there needs to be an investigation and, if so, what is required for this. As outlined above, this may involve varying degrees of bodily deconstruction, retention of body parts, and associated delays. These are all putatively technical processes. Care is essential in softening the hardness of these 'scientific' procedures for the bereaved. This is because we are not talking about *just* bodies; rather, these bodies and their parts are somebody's body, and they are invariably also a living person's loved one. Yet we see the fragility of these processes when culture or resource allocations do not advance care as a priority. This leads to a lottery in how the deceased is treated and the weight given to the needs and experiences of the bereaved.

What is an ethic of care?

Ethics of care have been invoked by some feminist scholars as a way of understanding and valuing caring roles. Further, ethics of care have been developed as a normative moral framework of justice centred on care. This contrasts with traditional theories of justice that aspire to objectivity or are based on the idea that morality evolves from universal, abstract, or purely logical rules.[17]

Ethics of care was originally conceived as a gendered theory because of the way that these caring roles were – and are – typically performed by women. In her influential 1982 book *In a Different Voice*, Carol Gilligan claimed that Sigmund Freud's theory of psychoanalysis and Lawrence Kohlberg's theory of moral development were biased and male oriented.[18] In these dominant psychological accounts of human development, male development is taken as standard and female development is often judged as inferior. Gilligan argued that if women are 'more emotional' than men and pay more attention to relationships than rules, this is not a sign of them being less ethical but, rather, that they embody different values that are equally important to those displayed by men. While Gilligan may have deemed these differences to be 'natural' and associated with sex rather than gender, I argue that it is both possible and desirable to move beyond biologically assigned sex to instead thinking about the ethics of care as a framework that can help us to understand the importance of care in mediating law and navigating ethical thinking.[19]

As I noted in the introduction to this chapter, I advance and develop Kittay's definition of an ethic of care. This moves beyond questions of sex to developing a framework that recognises the relationality of care. Kittay argued that:

An ethics of care is one in which the embodied existence of each, in both our unique individuality and in our material connectedness to one another, is never

---

17 Maria Drakopoulou. "The Ethic of Care, Female Subjectivity and Feminist Legal Scholarship," *Feminist Legal Studies* 8 (2000): 199, https://doi.org/10.1023/A:1009266226936.
18 Carol Gilligan, *In a Different Voice* (Cambridge, MA: Harvard University Press, 1982).
19 This chapter is not the place for such debate, save to say that I do not dispute that the continued marginalisation of the value of care, and the dominance of women in caring roles, is very much a live issue. I take issue with any biological explanation and instead seek to consider the socialisation of women into these roles and the worrying lack of value assigned to them (and thus the labour and contribution of many women), while not excluding the possibility that men may also take on caring roles (and potentially face the same lack of recognition when they do so). The inverse, of course, is that we should not assume that women naturally wish to nurture others.

eclipsed. As such, it must be able to dignify each morally significant individual in his or her embodied existence.[20]

This articulation of an ethic of care thus requires an attitudinal shift from the self to the other and their needs and notes that caring exists in a relational context – caring arises from, and in, webs of (asymmetrical) relationships. Thus, we can invoke an ethic of care for its normative value – that is, providing a standard by which ethical judgements can be made.

There is also a practice of care, and this is where we tend to see the concept of ethic of care being used to describe and evaluate caring relationships. In the medical context, an ethic of care is often associated with nursing, and it is seldom applied to work with the dead. This is unsurprising if we consider the relationality at the core of Kittay's model. Embodied relationships are typically understood as existing between the living, and thus excluding the dead. There are three possible responses to this. First, we can note that we are talking about (bits of) bodies, and thus the embodiment of those living persons doing the caring is still engaged. Alternatively, we could take our lead from Marian Barnes, who has argued that not all forms of caregiving need be embodied, resulting in a shift from 'care giving' to 'taking care of'. This then allows care ethics to be extended, for example, to non-humans.[21]

I argue that there is a third possibility, whereby there is no need to look beyond bodies because, as I noted above, there are still (human) bodies engaged since relationships can exist with a deceased person. Although a body is not essential for social bonds to continue,[22] the presence of a body/bodily remains creates a different kind of relationship, whereby not only the embodiment of those who interact with the body is impacted, but there is also a physical body which, although dead, triggers a moral duty to care for it.

At its most basic level, death disrupts relationships. The medico-legal death investigation process amplifies this fracturing of the norm and adds further layers and types of relationships to mediate in addition to that between the deceased and the bereaved – for example, between the deceased and the community, and between the legal system and the bereaved. An ethic of care would advance an approach that seeks to repair these relationships via a process that recognises the value of, and need for, care for all parties.[23]

The problem of power

While relationships may exist with the dead, the dead do not have control over their body. They are, physically at least, powerless compared to those acting upon them. To understand why this need not be fatal to the application of an ethic of care in our context, we need to think more deeply about the importance not only of relationships but of attitudes within those relationships. Kittay argues that caring involves 'a positive, affective bond and investment in another's wellbeing'.[24] Jonathan Herring explains this in

20 Kittay, *Learning from My Daughter*, 171.
21 Marian Barnes, *Care in Everyday Life: An Ethic of Care in Practice* (Bristol: Bristol University Press, 2012).
22 Imogen Jones, "Objects of Crime: Bodies, Embodiment and Forensic Pathology," *Social & Legal Studies* 29, no. 5 (2020): 680, https://doi.org/10.1177/0964663919897957.
23 This draws on Leach Scully's use of ethic of care to understand the actions of the relatives of war dead. See Leach Scully, "Naming the Dead."
24 Eva Kittay, "The Ethics of Care, Dependence, and Disability", *Ratio Juris* 2, no. 1 (2011): 51–2, https://doi.org/10.1111/j.1467-9337.2010.00473.x.

Kantian terms. For Herring, those in ethical, caring relationships do not 'treat each other as objects but recognise each other as fellow human beings'.[25] Ethics of care upfronts the vulnerability of the deceased body to abuse or objectification. Concurrently, those providing the care benefit from recognising this interdependence – their bodies are also vulnerable, as are those of the living people that they depend on (and who depend on them). They have an obligation to care for the dead *as individuals* because they will eventually need someone to do this for them.

While we cannot interact with a deceased person in a traditional way, I argue that we can still perform care that is informed by the interests, needs, and views of the deceased person. Here, I am emphasising the value of care ethics in helping us to better understand actions and relationships, especially where there is an imbalance of power. Noting the normative value of care in decisions relating to the treatment of the deceased body/body parts, we can see that care can shape ethical decisions about treatment of the dead.

Drawing on Jones and Whitaker,[26] Simon Woods argues that 'the most appropriate attitude toward the dead body is to keep to the fore the idea that the body is "somebody's body", that it has both an identity and a biography, thus recognizing the deep connections between the living and the dead'. Doing this, he suggests, means that the body is no longer an object but rather somebody who is the subject of moral claims 'around care, respect, dignity and identity'.[27] In a similar vein, Jacki Leach Scully, in the context of the desire of kin to identify Second World War dead, suggests that language of care – from which she deduces the presence of an ethic of care – can be understood as 'treating the dead as still *mattering*' (italics original).[28] This, she states, is about more than memory – it is about caring for the now deceased person's life. Put another way, it is to treat them as 'somebody'.

Of course, we might also argue that it is still the living in the form of the bereaved who are the recipients of care. If we accept that the majority of the bereaved are both interested in and affected by the treatment of the bodies of their deceased loved ones, then treating the body in particular ways is an act of care for the bereaved. Finally, as will be shown later in this chapter, caring for the deceased body can be an act of self-care by APTs, providing a sense of professional authority while making the intolerable manageable and justifying the acts done.

We return then to the importance of attitude. Within a caring (job) role, I argue that this comes not only from the individual but is informed and developed in response to both formal rules and occupational cultures. In the next section, I draw on empirical data from my interviews with APTs to understand the importance of care in how these APTs articulate their role and consider how this affects the treatment of the deceased body. Whatever the cause of death, when placed against a backdrop of legally mandated autopsies, we see the importance of care as an ethical framework both for those working with the dead and for making the acts demanded by the law tolerable to the bereaved. To do this, I draw on two key examples: the ways in which bodies are stored and the important concept of viewability. Before this, however, I outline the importance of the concept of care to APTs when describing their role.

25 Jonathan Herring, "Ethics of Care and Disability Rights: Complementary or Contradictory?" in *Spaces of Care*, ed. Loraine Gelsthorpe, Perveez Mody, and Brian Sloan (London: Bloomsbury, 2020), 174.
26 D, Gareth Jones and Maja Whitaker, *Speaking for the Dead: The Human Body in Biology and Medicine* (London: Routledge, 2009): 40.
27 Simon Woods, "Death Duty – Caring for the Dead in the Context of Disaster," *New Genetics and Society* 33, no. 3 (2014): 342, https://doi.org/10.1080/14636778.2014.944260.
28 Leach Scully, "Naming the Dead," 313–32, 320.

Care and APT identity

Care is a well-established principle and function of health care. It means different things across contexts.[29] In the context of the dead, the APTs often drew an analogy between their role – and approach – and that of nurses dealing with the living. This was explained by APT 15 as follows:

> So people ask me what do I do, I just say, 'Well, kind of an nurse but for deceased'. Well, you're still looking after a person, you're still making sure they're clean, respectable, that they've got all their belongings, that they're cared for.

This was reinforced by APT 7 in their account of how they explained their work to nurses:

> So I get student nurses down and we do talks with them occasionally and what I will stress to them as well is just because a patient has died doesn't mean the care stops, so we will follow on that care throughout the entire state of the patient here so it's just basically like a ward transfer. So if we've done our job correctly, you shouldn't really be able to tell we've done anything at all.

This refusal to see the deceased as deserving less than the living was reflected in language, with many APTs insisting that the deceased was their 'patient':

> APT 1: [A]t the end of the day, you know, it was a person, you know? They're still your patient and you still have to provide the best care. So you wouldn't nurse somebody on a ward and leave them covered in vomit or things like that, would you? So it's the same sort of thing.
>
> APT 3: It's all about care after death. When someone dies, do you stop caring? No, you don't. We have to just, the way you're still respectful, you still treat them with, you know, with respect and it's a dignified approach but you just, it's got a slightly different take on it. You're not asking, 'Are you comfortable? Are you embarrassed? Are you ... ? Is this ... ?', you know? ... All those things you're ... you're still providing all of those things but it's in a slightly different format. So you still care, so I'm still here to care for people and, you know, provide ... care.

As such, these APTs understand the breadth of their role but have also formed a professional identity that highlights the moral value of their work. We can clearly see the normative importance of care in determining their assessment of decision-making frameworks. In the context of those deceased who will be the subject of a medico-legal autopsy, this gives them an important role:

---

29 See, e.g., the Care and Quality Commission's *Learning from Deaths* report. The report most traditionally/commonly equates care with 'treatment' but also opens with the following mission statement: 'Caring – treating everyone with dignity and respect. Care and Quality Commission, *Learning from Deaths: A Review of the First Year of NHS Trusts Implementing the National Guidance* (Gallowgate: Care and Quality Commission, 2019), www.cqc.org.uk/sites/default/files/20190315-LfD-Driving-Improvement-report-FINAL.pdf.

APT 4: I think that's why APTs are important because we are that link to that patient's care rather than just being an autopsy or pathology.

The above statement highlights the division of labour in non-suspicious death cases. Pathologists are not a homogenous group, and their views cannot be discussed at length here, but it is important to note that their function is limited to the autopsy and subsequent report and not the pre-/post-autopsy care of the deceased or bereaved.[30] If we accept that APTs consider care at these stages to be an important ethical duty, we can understand why they might imbue normative significance to their acts beyond 'just' the autopsy.

Storage

Storing deceased bodies is a technical necessity to slow decomposition and deterioration, both of which can interfere with efforts to accurately identify a cause of death. Here, we see various legal (e.g., section 1(b) of the *Coroners and Justice Act 2009*) and regulatory (e.g., the HTA guidance that bodies should be moved from refrigeration to freezer storage after 30 days[31]) requirements engaged. I return to this latter point when discussing 'viewability'. While preserving the condition of the body is important for the medico-legal process, this is not the only function served. The way bodies are stored is not only about the condition of bodies but also the social context in which they exist(ed).

As noted above, the role of APTs extends to the care of a body before and after autopsy, and sometimes to dealing with the family and viewings of the body. Unlike pathologists, APTs cannot avoid the social life of the now deceased person. In this context, many APTs felt a duty to care simultaneously for both the deceased and the bereaved by acknowledging the deceased as a person and adapting their practice accordingly. Thus, we find sentiments such as:

APT 2: I feel almost like when someone is here for a long time and they don't have family you almost take over that family role, because then everyone knows so and so who is in the freezer and has been in there for – we had that with a gentleman who was here when I first started; he was here for a good … I think over six months at that point and then he stayed for about another year after that; and we all knew his name and we all spoke about him like he was almost like just another member of the team or like a family member. I remember the day he went; I'll never forget that because it was kind of like, 'Oh, he's going', and we all sort of said goodbye and stuff, which really is … No, I think you almost take over that role in a way.

APT 15: People say to me if they've lost a loved one, 'You will check on my grandad or my dad, you'll tell them I love them, won't you?' I'll do it. They've asked me to do it and I'll do it, you know? And that's the difference.

APT 17: [S]ay my mum died and I wanted a teddy with her, it's no harm to us to do it, do you know what I mean? It's not exactly a problem, it's not a big task for us to do so … I don't know, if we can help someone out by doing that, then why not?

30 There will, of course, be exceptions, and there may be some contact at an inquest where one is held.
31 Human Tissue Authority, *Post-mortem*, PFE2 (c).

APT 4: [W]e say to our nurses, 'Nothing is a silly suggestion'. So, for example, we had one lady that said – she said, 'I know it sounds strange, but my husband is really scared of the dark', so we put a torch with him. And just that one little thing, if it helped her that little bit, then we will do things like that.

I argue that what we see here is the deceased body being viewed as a deceased person (or, as Woods put it, 'somebody's body'). Care is exercised by recognising that the now deceased person had preferences, needs, and vulnerabilities that are ethically relevant, and these inform APT behaviour. It does not matter whether the deceased themselves will benefit (we can imagine a range of views on this) because it is their *humanity* that triggers the duty to care. Acts of care are determined by both understanding what humans in general need and appreciating the individual personality of the now deceased person. This knowledge is gained by APTs through appreciating and valuing the relationships that the deceased had while alive.

Care is also extended to the bereaved, with whom APTs share living, embodied relationships. By agreeing to requests from the bereaved, APTs are able to reassure them about the treatment of their loved ones, who are viewed by the bereaved through the lens of their social life. I argue that it is here that we begin to appreciate the role of care in making tolerable the intolerable. By recognising the personhood of the deceased while simultaneously caring for the living, APTs can mitigate some of the effects of the disruption and distress caused by the death investigation process.

In my interviews with APTs, this was particularly pronounced in the self-reported views and practices of APTs who had direct contact with the bereaved. I hypothesise that this is not a coincidence, but rather that locating a body within a social context of the living creates a need to navigate the visible grief and needs of the still living – unlike the details in a coroner officer's report. This social context emphasises the continuing relational bonds the deceased person shared with the living, making their personhood impossible to ignore. This complex web of relationships and the caring acts that flow from them is even more profoundly reflected in the concept of making a body 'viewable'. It is this to which I now turn.

Viewability

In the context of the storage of deceased bodies, we have seen that APTs may go well beyond legal demands and be guided by an ethic of care, triggered by storing the body of a *person*. This is usually driven by the needs and requests of the bereaved but may exist even without the engagement of the bereaved because APTs view their duty to the deceased through a relational lens. The issue of viewability adds an additional layer because it demonstrates the cultural importance of external appearance. It also highlights how abstract concepts such as 'dignity' are often intrinsically linked to physical treatment and form. Our identity in both life and death is linked to our appearance, and this, in turn, frames physical – embodied – interactions between APTs, the deceased, and the bereaved. Ensuring viewability is, in short, an act of care to protect, or restore, physical appearance.

One issue covered in the HTA guidance relates to transferring a body from refrigeration to freezer storage, which the guidance states should be done after a maximum of 30 days. The HTA links this to the 'dignity' of the deceased,[32] which is, in turn, associated

---

32 Human Tissue Authority, *Post-mortem*, para 7(b).para 7(b). For discussion of what this means, see my (sometimes co-authored) blogs at 'Dead Bodies and the Law', https://deadbodiesandthelaw.wordpress.com/blog.

with storage that preserves the appearance of the deceased. Obviously, a body not stored at appropriate temperatures will deteriorate and decompose. Allowing this to happen is likely to cause distress to the bereaved and potentially render the body 'unviewable'.[33] But reducing the notion of viewability simply to storage temperatures fails to recognise the breadth of the work done by APTs to make a body, or person, 'viewable'. In the following section, I explore why 'viewability' matters to APTs and how their concern for this serves to make easier the disruption potentially wrought by unexpected death, including the autopsy process.

From my interviews with APTs, I found that issues of 'viewability' could typically be split into three sub-issues: general presentation/reconstruction post autopsy, decomposed bodies, and disfigured/fragmented bodies. I briefly discuss these examples below, demonstrating how viewability becomes a measure by which care is extended in all directions.

Viewing post autopsy

The invasive autopsy is necessarily destructive. It involves, among other things, the evisceration of the chest/abdominal cavity and the removal/dissection of major organs. While there are guidelines,[34] practice and extent vary according to pathologist/coroner preference and the material 'facts' of a death. The aforementioned major incision and removal of organs are common in most invasive post-mortems. These are major and invasive procedures that many would find undesirable but can be required by the coroner as part of their investigations.

Following the autopsy, the removed and dissected organs are contained within a plastic bag, then returned to the body (absent any retained samples) and the body stitched closed. This most basic form of reconstruction is important in concealing the destructive nature of the autopsy. We can safely assume that this reconstruction increases public acceptance of this medico-legal procedure, but it also matters because the physical body represents the person. This relational dimension is recognised by APTs and leads to common practices that extend beyond minimal reconstruction to caring for the body, both as a human independently deserving of dignified treatment and because of the needs of the bereaved:

> APT 9: [E]ven if the family are not going to see it, it is just a dignity for the person really, to be honest with you. I mean, we have had bodies down from [another mortuary] ... and they have left it all open. We would normally close it all up, just because of the funeral director and you are handling bodies and stuff really. It just looks nicer.
>
> APT 12: Respect for the deceased, yes. Just out of respect, simply for them. I don't do it in case the family want to see, because a lot – I say a lot, there is quite a few deceased that don't have families and they go for a social services funeral.

---

33 For legal discussion and potential implications of decomposition and visibility in the case of failure to properly store a body, see *Brennan and others v (1) City of Bradford Metropolitan District Council (2) Leeds Teaching Hospitals NHS Trust* [2021] 1 WLUK 429.

34 See Royal College of Pathologists, "What happens during a post mortem" and associated guidelines issued by the Royal College of Pathologists (accessed 21 August 2021), www.rcpath.org/discover-pathology/what-is-pathology/information-about-post-mortems-for-friends-and-relatives-/what-happens-during-a-post-mortem.html. Note that many pathologists do not routinely remove and examine brains.

APT 5: We're constantly thinking about the patient and the care of the patient and making sure that they're going to be presentable for their family afterwards. That they're going to be cleaned properly, that they're on dry sheets. And we're thinking about the bigger picture rather than the consultant that reports here, does what he's got to do, down tools and is off.

APT 4: We do a lot of teaching with the hospital because we know that some nurses have said to families, 'They're going to have an autopsy, you don't want to go see them after that', so we go to them and say, 'Why wouldn't they?' Because if anything, we've had a chance to wash them and comb their hair the way it would be and they look much more peaceful after the post-mortem. And it's hard to explain but it's nice that families have got that opportunity to come and do that and spend time with them, rather than wait for the funeral service.

Here, we see that care is linked to concepts such as respect (also used interchangeably with dignity by some APTs) and that care for physical appearance is considered a marker of this. Our external appearance is understood by APTs to be of intrinsic value to humans and to our sense of self, whether alive or dead. This is not least because it affects how we are perceived and remembered by others. It is also a caring act to not subject others to unnecessary trauma, or memory alteration, caused by seeing deconstructed bodies. Finally, these are acts of self-care by APTs. Unlike pathologists, APTs do not formally feed into legal decisions; thus, APTs' justification for involvement in autopsies is commonly framed around benefit to others and professional pride when successful in this.

Decomposition and trauma

The HTA guidelines recognise that bodies deteriorate with time and that the temperature of storage can delay this. However, bodies arrive at mortuaries in varying states of decomposition. Moreover, some traumatic deaths can result in the body itself being disrupted. For such cases, the APTs again linked viewability with the experiences of the bereaved and the belief that external presentation is a matter of dignity for the deceased person:

APT 6: [W]e will always try and put people back how they were, irrespective of how badly damaged they are … [regarding a patient whose head was crushed by a bus] it was important to me and it's important to all of us as technical staff that we do our absolute best for people and for the people's families.

APT 15: We just do the best we can even though we're not, we know they're not going to be viewed because they're not viewable. We still try and do your best just to patch them up.

APTs recognised that while it may not always be possible to completely reconstruct the body, the ability to 'view' in the sense of being with the body as a representation of the now deceased person often takes on cultural and emotional meaning. This leads to an emphasis on the presentation of the hands and face:

APT 14: They're not interested in the body, they're interested in hands and face. They're going to sit close to hand holding somebody's hand and then looking at the face. That's the main area. As long as everything else is back together and whole and clean and intact, then I think we've done a good job.

Care is, therefore, used as a mechanism to recognise that bodies matter, whether living or dead. By caring for the deceased body via reconstruction, APTs care for both the deceased person and the living. The two are not distinct; acts considered to protect the deceased are also understood to be in the interests of the bereaved. There is a clear sense in which the bodies and the bereaved are being 'cared for' – this care being an ethical imperative beyond legal requirements and aside from (but in full compliance with) the legal process. Especially when the bereaved are engaged, we can see how these acts of care by APTs soften the often-unbearable trauma of an unexpected death, the law's intervention, and the accompanying disruption to our bonds, relationships, and communities.

Conclusion

My focus in this chapter has been on the role of ethics of care in informing APTs' attitudes and actions when a medico-legal autopsy is required. I have demonstrated that care is considered an ethical duty and a description of the acts done. As is so often the case when dealing with death – and life – the webs of relationships and interests engaged are complex. I have argued that care can be extended to the dead body and deceased person while simultaneously serving the relationships of care with the living. To this extent, the analogy that interviewed APTs drew with the nursing profession highlights APTs' motivations and underscores the professionalism and need for this form of care.

While care itself is valuable, I argue that this ethic and the associated acts also facilitate the death investigation process. The formal law does not require particular types of reconstruction (beyond the basics), nor does it demand that the needs of the bereaved and the social and relational identity of the deceased inform practice. Yet, absent these, this stage of the death investigation process would inflict further harms, and this could, in time, lead to public mistrust of the legal process and those who administer it. The acceptability of the law and legal processes thus depends on the ethics of care that inform and motivate APTs.

Yet this status quo is fragile. The written law is imbued with discretion, leading to varied practices. APTs can only do so much – their influence is limited to their role, which is subordinate to the law, lawyers, and medics acting on the law's authority. Moreover, I argue that training and occupational culture are also forms of law, albeit not ones that we see publicly enforced. If we take the concept of 'viewability', for example, there is no objective standard as to what makes a body viewable. Therefore, this is a judgement call APTs must make. Thus, in some mortuaries, the bereaved may be advised against, but never prevented from, viewing, while in others, a stricter paternalistic approach may be taken. Similarly, the time and skills available to facilitate the more complex reconstruction of disrupted bodies vary significantly. This lottery – which exists in different forms throughout the entire coronial death investigation process – clearly affects the experiences of the bereaved, but we see how it can also determine the treatment of the deceased body.

The way we treat our deceased, and the bereaved, says much about our values as a society. We could do much worse than be led by an ethic of care in shaping practice, values, and the law.

There is still much to unpack in this area, and much to improve if we want to see greater consistency and recognition of the importance of ethics of care in dealing with the unexpected dead. But for now, I want to finish with the voice of APT 5, who powerfully threaded together why care matters to them:

They're not being dripped on or leaked on by other people. We're making sure that they are – we're monitoring them daily for any changes, physical changes, making sure they're not decomposing or changing overtly. It's not just about their physical appearance, it's about how – I think it's about how we would like to be treated if we were in that position … So, they're not just things, they're not just blocks of meat, they're not just dead bodies, they are people and they deserve the dignity and respect and privacy that people deserve.

Bibliography

Association of Anatomical Pathology Technologists. "Level 3 and 4 RSPH Diploma Courses & Resources." Accessed 21 August 2023, www.aaptuk.org/professional-support/level-3-4-diploma -courses–resources.

Barnes, Marian. *Care in Everyday Life: An Ethic of Care in Practice*. Bristol: Bristol University Press, 2012.

Care and Quality Commission. *Learning from Deaths: A Review of the First Year of NHS Trusts Implementing the National Guidance*. Gallowgate: Care and Quality Commission, 2019. www.cqc. org.uk/sites/default/files/20190315-LfD-Driving-Improvement-report-FINAL.pdf.

Drakopoulou, Maria. "The Ethic of Care, Female Subjectivity and Feminist Legal Scholarship." *Feminist Legal Studies* 8 (2000): 199–226. https://doi.org/10.1023/A:1009266226936.

Gilligan, Carol. *In a Different Voice*. Cambridge, MA: Harvard University Press, 1982.

Herring, Jonathan. "Ethics of Care and Disability Rights: Complementary or Contradictory?" In *Spaces of Care*, edited by Loraine Gelsthorpe, Perveez Mody, and Brian Sloan, 165–182. London: Bloomsbury, 2020.

Human Tissue Authority. *Post-mortem Examination Licensing Standards and Guidance*. Version 3. London: Human Tissue Authority, September 2022. https://content.hta.gov.uk/sites/default/files/ 2022-10/Post-mortem%20examination%20licensing%20standards%20and%20guidance_1.pdf.

Jones, D. Gareth, and Maja Whitaker. *Speaking for the Dead: The Human Body in Biology and Medicine*. London: Routledge, 2009.

Jones, Imogen. "Dead Bodies and the Law." Last modified 15 May 2023, https://deadbodiesandthelaw. wordpress.com/blog.

Jones, Imogen. "Objects of Crime: Bodies, Embodiment and Forensic Pathology". *Social & Legal Studies* 29, no. 5 (2020): 679–698. https://doi.org/10.1177/0964663919897957.

Kittay, Eva. "The Ethics of Care, Dependence, and Disability." *Ratio Juris* 2, no. 1 (2011): 39–58. http s://doi.org/10.1111/j.1467-9337.2010.00473.x.

Kittay, Eva. *Learning from My Daughter: The Value and Care of Disabled Minds*. New York: Oxford University Press, 2019.

Leach Scully, Jackie. "Naming the Dead: DNA-based Identification of Historical Remains as an Act of Care." *New Genetics and Society* 33, no. 3 (2014): 313–332. http://dx.doi.org/10.1080/14636778. 2014.946002.

Ministry of Justice. "Coroners Statistics 2021: England and Wales." Accessed 20 August 2023, www. gov.uk/government/statistics/coroners-statistics-2021/coroners-statistics-2021-england-and-wales.

NHS England. "The national medical examiner system." Accessed 21 August 2023, www.england.nhs. uk/patient-safety/patient-safety-insight/national-medical-examiner-system.

Royal College of Pathologists. "What happens during a post mortem." Accessed 21 August 2021, www.rcpath.org/discover-pathology/what-is-pathology/information-about-post-mortems-for- friends-and-relatives-/what-happens-during-a-post-mortem.html.

Woods, Simon. "Death Duty – Caring for the Dead in the Context of Disaster." *New Genetics and Society* 33, no. 3 (2014): 333–347. https://doi.org/10.1080/14636778.2014.944260.

12

SUBLIME EXECUTIONS AND MATERIAL AFFECTIONS

Law, Aesthetics, and the Death Penalty

Sabrina Gilani

Introduction

In its 2008 ruling in *Baze v. Rees*, [1] the Supreme Court of the United States asked us to put aside, for a moment, the centuries-long debate about the ethics of the death penalty, and to take as given two ideas: first, that punishment is, by its very nature, painful; and second, that states have the right to kill inmates. From there, the Court then confined its analysis more narrowly on the question of 'style': what should this death look like? Of course, the Court limited its inquiry to the very narrow parameters of death by lethal injection and ultimately ruled that a spectacular death would not amount to a cruel death unless it occurred with some regularity: 'an isolated mishap alone does not violate the Eighth Amendment'.[2] Nevertheless, what makes *Baze* unique is the clear implication that the death penalty's cruelty is an aesthetic experience, and the Court in this case was asking us to consider whether the killing in question was *to our taste*.

There has been much written about the aesthetics of killing and its connection to prevailing social passions and pressures. Some have written about how styles of killing expose underlying cultural anxieties associated with social modernisation and war.[3] Others report that the public fascination with killing for pleasure stems from the banalisation of the murdering body, the 'abnormal normality' of the serial killer.[4] Perhaps most controversially, De Quincey's work discusses how killing in life, like killing in art, once completed, should only be judged on the basis of its aesthetic, rather than moral, virtue. A close reading of De Quincey reveals a logic not entirely different from the one adopted by the Court in *Baze*:

1 *Baze v. Rees*, 553 U.S. 35 (2008).
2 *Francis v. Resweber*, 329 U.S. 459, 463–4 (1947).
3 Lisa Downing, "Beyond reasonable doubt: Aesthetic violence and motiveless murder in French decadent fiction," *French Studies* 58, no. 2 (2004): 189–203.
4 Lee Baxter, "The Aesthetic Simulation of Murder in Dexterland," *Monsters and the Monstrous* 1, no. 1 (2010): 75–92.

DOI: 10.4324/9781003304593-14

But suppose [a killing] is over and done, and what can you say of it ... A sad thing it was, no doubt, very sad; but we can't mend it. Therefore, let us make the best of a bad matter; and, as it is impossible to hammer anything out of it for moral purpose, let us treat it aesthetically, and see if it will turn to account in that way. Such is the logic of a sensible man; and what follows? We dry up our tears, and have the satisfaction, perhaps, to discover that a transaction which, morally considered, was shocking, and without a leg to stand upon, when tried by principles of Taste, turns out to be a very meritorious performance.[5]

Approaching killing from what Black has referred to as an 'aesthetic-critical perspective',[6] from the way the killing appears in sights, sounds, smells, and textures, produces a different ethical account to when it is approached as a morally charged event. The kind of embodied ethics that an aesthetic-critical perspective produces, treats the world-immersed body (and not the mind) as the principal site of meaning making, and sensations and feelings as integral to ethical decision making. An aesthetic-critical perspective reveals killing to be an interesting event. The greater its drama, its spectacularism, its monstrousness, the more attraction it holds for its spectators. Dramatic killing perpetuates a kind of 'delightful horror', and for Black, the fact that we find pleasure – as in desire, fascination, attraction – in an act that we also find morally repugnant exposes 'the supreme fiction' of our carefully constructed (moral) reality. 'Our aesthetic sensibilities,' he writes, '*often* conflict with our moral sense' and, as a result of this, we are more likely to reject the aesthetic 'as deceit and illusion, to the "truth" of moral rationalism'.[7]

This unease or conflict between the beautiful and good – aesthetic experience and moral sense – is also reflected in our systems of governance, and much has been written about how the theory and practice of law frequently idealises the rational and diminishes the sensual.[8] Modern legal theory and practice is often charged with adopting a disembodied subjectivity that disavows corporeal knowledge about the world as partial, subjective, and, for this reason, unreliable.[9] But more crucially, for many critical theorists, law rejects the sensual world while simultaneously directing its processes, procedures, and pronouncements to order it according to its own aesthetic sensibilities, law's *tastes*.[10] 'Law both *has* a sense and *is* a sense,' Nirta writes, '[...] law has never been outside the senses. Its way of making sense of the world is always premised on its sensorial immersion in the world itself.'[11]

This chapter examines how the law makes sense of the death penalty, but not in the usual way. Here, I expose the way its rules, procedures, processes, and pronouncements control how bodies encounter the execution chamber and the affections they form with

---

5 Thomas De Quincey, *On Murder Considered as One of the First Arts* (Richmond, UK: Alma Classics, 2016), 20–1.

6 Joel Black, *The Aesthetics of Murder* (Baltimore, MD: Johns Hopkins University Press, 1991).

7 Black, *The Aesthetics of Murder*, 4.

8 Caterina Nirta, "Introduction," in *Law and the Senses: Touch*, ed. Andrea Pavoni et al. (London: University of Westminster Press, 2020), 2–3.

9 Andrea Pavoni et al., eds., *Law and the Senses: Taste*. (London: University of Westminster Press, 2018).

10 Lionel Bently and Leo Flynn, eds., *Law and the Senses: Sensational Jurisprudence* (London: Pluto Press, 1996).

11 Nirta, "Introduction," 3.

its objects. In organising and ordering the material environment in which an execution takes place, the law is able to control 'what is seen and what can be said about it ... who has the ability to see and the talent to speak ... the properties of space and the possibilities of time'.[12] In 'stag[ing] itself affectively',[13] the law can engineer the kinds of affections that achieve the quiet, tranquil, orderly, timely death law requires in justification of state killing. Here, law's normative force remains largely concealed by aesthetics, so that what transpires in the death chamber (or not), dis/appears to us as the 'self-evident facts of sense perception'.[14] In turn, law's aesthetic design not only allows us to maintain the falsity of a kind of objective detachment from the law, but also prevents us from recognising how law constantly relies on the threat and risk of violence to cement itself as the 'voice' of reason; to achieve (like art that depicts extreme violence) 'some transcendent or nihilistic – but in any case, pre-aesthetic –"reality"'.[15]

Yet that does not mean that the materials and bodies upon which law exerts its rage for order are passive. The execution chamber, and the bodies within it, are unpredictable and do not always perform according to law's aesthetic design. Sometimes these bodies and objects intra-act to produce cacophonous and pungent deaths, deaths which invade sensory cavities in a way that exposes both the materiality of law and the normative force of the body. Spectacular death chamber scenes give rise to sensations, intensities, rhythms, vibrations, textures that produce a counter-aesthetic of death. We are alarmed by them largely because the law has engineered an atmosphere in which these activities have become implausible, *unthinkable*. But we are also fascinated by them because they present us with a different way of 'making sense' of the death penalty – where the sensible body possesses the power to overthrow law's translation of its rationality into an aesthetic, of 'thought-becoming-world'.[16] I refer to these sensual events as 'sublime executions', executions that strike spectating bodies by their sheer irresistible force. The sublime execution is a site not only of aesthetic upheaval but also of burgeoning political activity, for it literally dismembers law's (human) body, giving birth to a counter-aesthetic which moves us to devise alternate ways of living and dying.

The politics of aesthetics and the idea of the sublime

Any discussion of aesthetics must, necessarily, start with Kant, if for no other reason than the fact that almost every theory of the aesthetic draws from a *Critique of Judgment*, [17] and situates itself in relation to it. In *Critique of Judgment*, Kant sets out to distinguish aesthetic judgments, or judgments of taste, from moral judgments or judgments of good, and declares that while the latter is based on the faculties of reason and is cognitively driven, the former is motivated by the imagination and rooted in feelings of disinterested pleasure – pleasure that remains unconnected to both the object or scene's sensory or emotional appeal for the spectator or its pragmatic or practical use.[18] For

12 Jacques Rancière, *The Politics of Aesthetics*, ed. Gabriel Rockhill (London: Bloomsbury, 2004), 7–8.
13 Andreas Philippopoulos-Mihalopoulos, "Atmospheres of Law: Senses, Affects, Landscape," *Emotion, Space and Society* 7 (2013).
14 Rancière *The Politics of Aesthetics*, 7–8.
15 Black, *The Aesthetics of Murder*, 5.
16 Rancière *The Politics of Aesthetics*, 10.
17 Immanuel Kant, *Critique of Judgement*, trans. James Creed Meredith, ed. Nicholas Walker (Oxford: Oxford University Press, 2008).
18 Kant, *Critique of Judgement*, 37.

Kant, then, a beautiful object or scene is neither an object of desire nor an object of cognition. Rather, its beauty stems from the sensual pleasure that is derived from its simple observance – the 'feeling' that it gives its spectator. The 'beautiful' is libidinal; it depends on an encounter between an object or scene and the sensing subject (the viewer). But equally, this also means that, for Kant, aesthetic experience has both a conceptual and intuitive dimension. Our imagination must provide information (in time and space) – that which is experienced in the form of sensation – to our faculties of reason, which converts this information to a perception of pleasure or displeasure. Given the shared capacity for sensation that all humans have, our 'common sense', aesthetic judgments are universal. For Kant, there are objects and scenes from which every *body* derives pleasure.

Kant's idea that aesthetic judgments arise from disinterested pleasure is controversial. For some authors, aesthetics refers to a 'certain distribution of the sensible',[19] a 'regime of visibility and intelligibility ... which is inscribed in a reconfiguration of the categories of sensible experience and its interpretation'.[20] From this view, aesthetic experiences can be engineered and therefore political. They involve a 'delimitation of spaces and times, of the visible and invisible, of speech and noise, that simultaneously places the stakes of politics as a form of experience'.[21] In the work of other authors, aesthetic judgments cannot arise from disinterested pleasure because they are conditioned by one's social status.[22] There are some groups in society that have the power to determine what is pleasurable and vulgar for the rest of us. But also, our sense of something provides a kind of order or structure to that thing, a spatial and temporal logic to what is experienced, and this logic is socio-culturally driven. Much has been written about how our epistemological traditions privilege certain ways of knowing the world – for example, visual or auditory over gustatory accounts.[23] We are culturally conditioned to be visually drawn towards certain objects or elements of a scene, give certain meaning to its sonic activities, have preferences for its visual attributes over its aromas and textures. For this reason, these authors believe that it may be naïve to think that aesthetic evaluation comes about through a detachment from the social or is the product of disinterested pleasure.

An object or scene's aesthetic power stems from its affects, the sensation or feeling it produces in bodies, and which increase or diminish the body's powers to act. To the extent that these affections, or relations of affect, can be engineered, aesthetics become political. But, on the other hand, the affections that bodies form with the external world can also operate as a mode of political resistance and can thus drive social change. As Spinoza insists, we can never know beforehand what a body can do, what kinds of relations it will form when caught up in the motions, vibrations, textures, impulses, and rhythms of the world.[24] It is through affects that things in the world take material form,

19 Jacques Rancière "The Aesthetic Dimension: Aesthetics, Politics, Knowledge," *Critical Inquiry* 36, no. 1 (2009): 1.
20 Jacques Rancière, "Thinking Between Disciplines: An Aesthetics of Knowledge," *Parrhesia* 1, no. 1 (2006): 1.
21 Rancière *The Politics of Aesthetics*, 7–8.
22 Pierre Bourdieu, *Distinction: A Social-Critique of the Judgment of Taste* (London: Routledge, 2010).
23 Annemarie Mol, *Eating in Theory* (Durham, NC: Duke University Press, 2021); Jim Drobnick, *The Smell Culture Reader* (Oxford: Berg, 2006).
24 Baruch Spinoza, *Ethics: Treatise on the Emendation of the Intellect and Selected Letters*, trans. Samuel Shirley (Indianapolis, IN: Hackett Publishing, 1992).

lending themselves to 'dialogue and dialectic'.[25] Affects give bodies a sense that *something* is happening.

But the body is not just a passive recipient of sensory data. Merleau-Ponty argues that all human knowledge can be traced to perceptual experience: 'every sensation is spatial ... sensation is itself constitutive of a milieu of coexistence, that is, of space'.[26] Our senses create an integrated experience of the world, and position us, as subjects, within it. Bodies also give meaning to the world they sense, and we experience those meanings in the form of affects such as disgust, happiness, shame, fear. These sensations shape our actions and give us some direction about the rightness or wrongness of things happening in the world. Some authors have referred to this process as giving rise to a kind of 'visceral ethics',[27] what in everyday life we may refer to as a 'gut feeling' – sensations that make us aware that something is not quite right in the world. Authors like Bennett have even argued that bodies can be cultivated to espouse a kind of 'ethico-aesthetic sensibility',[28] positioning aesthetic experience as both coercive and emancipatory.

Although Kant may deny it, the connection between aesthetics and politics is also reflected in his own work, in particular in his theory of the sublime. Kant describes as sublime natural objects or scenes that captivate us in terms of their boundlessness, ethereality, and incomprehensibility – the depths of a dark sea, the infinite stretch of the night sky. The sublimity of these objects inheres in its capacity for disorder and otherness, to do 'violence to our imagination', and suspend our trust in reason and logic.[29] At the same time, however, sublime objects, unlike merely beautiful ones, are intimately connected to our faculty of reason because they make our mind *work harder* to make (rational) sense of it. Consequently, our attachment to the sublime can alternate between attraction and repulsion, delight and fear, wonderment and horror. The sublime forces us into a confrontation with the limits of human life and, indeed, human knowledge: 'the perceiving subject has the sense of being annihilated through the very encounter'.[30] An experience of the dynamical sublime – the kind of irresistible, wild, and spectacular force we encounter during a near-death experience for instance – has been described as a '*traumatic encounter* that cannot be retrieved and transcended ... because the boundaries between subject and object have dissolved: the latter is subjected to openness, to an absorption or total identification that briefly suspends the possibility of the subject'.[31] Sublimity is an aesthetic experience that holds us in thrall far more powerfully than the experience of beauty, precisely because it engenders fear of a thing that exists (by virtue of our sensory experience of it), but whose existence we cannot rationally explain. The sublime gives us a sense of the 'inhuman'.

For the purposes of this chapter, I describe sublime executions as aesthetic experiences that challenge the law's image of the death penalty as a kind of 'fatal slumber'. Sublime

25 Jean-François Lyotard, *The Inhuman: Reflections on Time*, trans. Geoffrey Bennington and Rachel Bowlby (Stanford, CA: Stanford University Press, 1991), 142.
26 Maurice Merleau-Ponty, *Phenomenology of Perception*, trans. Donald A. Landes (New York: Routledge, 2012), 230.
27 Elspeth Probyn, *Carnal Appetites: Food, Sex, Identities* (London: Routledge, 2000).
28 Jane Bennett, "'How is it, Then, That We Still Remain Barbarians?' Foucault, Schiller, and the Aestheticization of Ethics," *Political Theory* 24, no. 4 (1996): 655.
29 Immanuel Kant, *Critique of the Power of Judgment*, trans. Paul Guyer and Eric Matthews (Cambridge: Cambridge University Press, 2013), 128.
30 Jennifer Wawrzinek, "Sublime Politics," in *Ambiguous Subjects* (Amsterdam: Rodopi, 2008), 13.
31 Kiene Brillenburg Wurth, *Musically Sublime: Indeterminacy, Infinity, Irresolvability* (New York: Fordham University Press, 2009), 140.

executions strike the spectating body with force, collapsing the boundaries between the subjects and objects of punishment, and disorientating the spectator by simultaneously evoking a sense of delight and horror. In this instance, the spectator is both acutely aware of the otherness of the executed body, but also more sensibly aware of itself *as* a body. The otherness of the executed body infuses the spectator's own corporeal cavities, until 'one cannot be thought without the other'.[32] Sublime executions mark out the death chamber as a natural space of chaos and disorder, but, more importantly, they mark out the capacity of the inmate to inhere – in sights, smells, textures, sounds – in the body or being of the spectator.

Death affects and the time-spaces of state killing

In his notable lectures on the death penalty, Jacques Derrida explains how the logic of capital punishment rests on the state's ability to make 'cruelty disappear from the scene … in the sense of cancelling and the sense of making invisible, insensible, non-phenomenal, non-appearing, in the sense of "dissimulate"'.[33] This 'anaesthesial logic' enacts a death that appears fluid and serene, largely because the parts of it that aren't either are physically hidden from view or the law adopts measures to disguise them or make them otherwise imperceptible. Thus, this anaesthesial logic is dependent on a specific distribution of the senses, practices of soliciting and manipulating attention. To anaesthetise is to make something *appear to be* something it otherwise isn't. It requires a refocusing of our attention elsewhere, on other things, scenes, practices in our midst.

Apparently, the anaesthesial logic of the law appears in diverse forms, across many legal fields. Philippopoulos-Mihalopoulos writes about how private law propels itself through the solicitation and manipulation of the body's sensory experiences, increasing and diminishing the body's power to act. Referring to this as the 'aesthesic' significance of law, he insists that law's power depends on its ability to stage itself 'affectively',[34] using control-practices that 'regulat[e] the property of sensory stimulation'.[35] The lawscape controls bodies by engineering affective occurrences into a neatly designed aesthetic, or 'atmosphere'. He writes, '[t]he law determines an atmosphere by allowing certain sensory options to come forth while suppressing others' and this allows the law to 'guarantee specific sensory responses and anticipate affective responses'.[36] Consequently, sensations and feelings are not entirely interior to the body or personal to us. The law infuses itself into the most intimate aspects of lived experience, affecting how we come to know and respond to the world around us.

The execution chamber is a lawscape. Legal rules, processes, and procedures arrange and order its material environment to enact a killing that can be felt and thought as punishment. Thus, the execution chamber is not merely an instrument that puts into practice the words of law, the death *sentence*, but an affective architecture that materialises those words and gives them bodily presence. Through its infusion in the material

32 Wurth, *Musically Sublime: Indeterminacy, Infinity, Irresolvability*, 140.
33 Jacques Derrida, *The Death Penalty: Volume I*, trans. Peggy Kamuf (Chicago, IL: Chicago University Press, 2013), 48–9.
34 Andreas Philippopoulos-Mihalopoulos, "Law is a Stage: From Aesthetics to Affective Aestheses," in *Research Handbook on Critical Legal Theory*, ed. Emilios Christodoulidis, Ruth Dukes, and Marco Goldoni (Cheltenham: Edward Elgar, 2019).
35 Philippopoulos-Mihalopoulos, "Atmospheres of Law: Senses, Affects, Landscape," 35.
36 Philippopoulos-Mihalopoulos, "Atmospheres of Law: Senses, Affects, Landscape," 36.

environment, law's repressive force becomes less visible, less tangible. As Philippopoulos-Mihalopoulos explains:

> [T]he lawscape cannot have both space and law emerging at equal measure at the same time, for otherwise they would end up being intolerable: a legal city is the opposite of a *just* city, namely a city full of regulations, surveillance, punishment.[37]

As a room that has been designed to kill, the execution chamber's claim to justice relies on its appearance as a clinical, orderly, silent, timeless, passive, space; a space *devoid* of all the things that make law *law*. The chamber thus *de*materialises the normative thrust of law, abstracting ideas like cruelty and justice from their material moorings. Within its confines, cruelty becomes rationalised as something other than, something *beyond*, the straining, writhing, screaming, singed inmate-bodies, restrained, contained, caged in barred, monochromatic, and pungent places. Dematerialised, cruelty can be more easily construed as prolonged delays to an execution,[38] the intentional use of unnecessarily painful methods of killing,[39] modes of killing incapable of bringing about swift and certain death,[40] and lack of procedural safeguards protecting inmates from an arbitrary death.[41] These (anthropocentric) ways of defining cruelty do not only deny its sensual dimensions but impress upon us the idea that law is intellectually driven, that it has no *need* for the body. Cruelty and justice are dealt with as rational *a priori* concepts, that have universal meaning. But killing *is* an aesthetic experience, and while the courts may deny that there is a connection between aesthetics and ethics, or perhaps that this connection should inform legal decisions, the reality is that the law itself materialises in the form of aesthetic control. Law infuses the sensible 'fabric' of the execution chamber to transform killing into punishment, death into a peaceful slumber, all with the intent to make capital punishment a thinkable ideal.

The execution chamber is organised through a set of legal processes, procedures, and rules that engineer an atmosphere that is conducive to law's aesthetic of death. Soundproofing renders the chamber's sonic activities inaudible, unless the strategically placed microphones are switched on by prison personnel. By instructing that the microphones be activated at certain points of the execution process, legal rules predetermine what observers are permitted to hear and when. The same can be said about what is seen. During an execution, the chamber is itself only visible for a short time, curtained until the room and prisoner are prepped, and re-shielded as soon as the prisoner is pronounced dead. The death penalty for any prisoner can span decades; the preparation process on execution day can take hours from the time the prisoner leaves their holding cell to the time they are pronounced dead. Even witnesses can be seated several hours before the curtain to the chamber is drawn open. Yet only minutes of this entire process are made visible to the spectating public. The death penalty timeline is compressed for spectators, even more so when legal practitioners and judges debate its cruelty by reference to the seconds or minutes it takes a body to succumb to the lethal drugs or electrical shocks that have been

---

37 Philippopoulos-Mihalapoulos, "Atmospheres of Law: Senses, Affects, Landscape," 42.
38 *Lackey v. Texas*, 514 U.S. 1045 (1995).
39 *Glossip v. Gross*, 135 S. Ct. 2726 (2015).
40 *Re Kemmler*, 136 U.S. 436 (1890).
41 *Furman v. Georgia*, 408 U.S. 238 (1972).

administered. As the Court in *Provenzano* stated, the death *penalty* happens in the very limited time-space between when the first shocks (or drugs) are administered and the prisoner is declared deceased.[42]

During the visible parts of the process, the spectating body is controlled by rules that direct its attention towards certain scenes and objects and away from others. For instance, once an execution begins, many prison protocols require the lights in the witness box to be dimmed, sometimes turned off altogether, while the execution chamber itself remains lit.[43] Human interaction is inhibited by sequestering the different parties to the execution – the prisoner, prison personnel, and public spectators – in separate rooms, and the observers' attention is focused by using windows that frame the execution chamber, and in particular the prisoner, effectively putting them 'on show' for others. Some execution chambers are designed so that each of the different spectators – media personnel, victim's families, and prisoner's witnesses – are physically isolated from one another. Dividing spectators according to their perceived sympathies, and concealing their presence from one another using mirrored glass,[44] the material design of the execution suite maximises the affectual power of the execution itself by minimising the possibility of attention being diverted to individual or personal conflicts.

The spectating body's total immersion in the lawscape is maintained by securing all ports of exit with bolts, backed by rules that prohibit them from being opened before an execution is complete, even if its occupants become physically unwell.[45] The chamber's design, the sparsity of its interiors, where everything is presented as 'masculine, linear, white', and where every material 'has a function', helps to control what the spectators' eyes are drawn to, and preserve the 'banality' of the process. In a clinical setting, spectators start to feel more like observers to (rather than participants in) a killing.[46] The process is further normalised through its use of 'everyday' materials – designs characterised by their 'low budget medical undertones' – all of which help further conceal the execution's ritualistic function and its biopolitical significance.[47] The different ways in which each of these rules, processes, and procedures enable and constrain the material environment in which the death penalty is carried out anaesthetises spectators to how its enactment not only divests the criminalised body of life, but also deprives living bodies of the very capacities (to affect and be affected) that give life meaning.

Law delivers justice in the execution chamber by controlling the sensory experience of time. As Philippopoulos-Mihalopoulos states, justice requires a 'present calculation', in which law plays a significant part, '[a] just city ... has captured time itself, engraved it right *here*, onto the surface of its urban sprawl'.[48] Time's presence and passing is key to the law's definition of cruelty. Deaths that take too much of it, perch perilously close to becoming inhumane, and ones that take too little, while they may demonstrate the state's efficiency, risk giving the impression that justice may not have been done. Spectators to

---

42 *Provenzano v. Moore*, 744 So.2d 413 (FLA 1999).
43 Alan Blinder and Manny Fernandez, "Bearing Witness to Executions: Last Breaths and Lasting Impressions," *The New York Times*, 23 April 2017, www.nytimes.com/2017/04/23/us/bearing-witness-to-executions-last-breaths-and-lasting-impressions.html.
44 Raphael Sperry, "Death by Design: An Execution Chamber at San Quentin State Prison," *The Avery Review* 2 (2014): 1–5.
45 Blinder and Fernandez, "Bearing Witness to Executions: Last Breaths and Lasting Impressions."
46 Sperry, "Death by Design: An Execution Chamber at San Quentin State Prison."
47 Sperry, "Death by Design: An Execution Chamber at San Quentin State Prison."
48 Philippopoulos-Mihalopoulos, "Atmospheres of Law: Senses, Affects, Landscape."

an execution often want to get a sense of the inmate's suffering; a brisk death falls short of meeting the retributivist desires of those in support of the death penalty, and sometimes even those who are against it.[49] In essence, as Lyotard opines, modern or developmental efficiency promotes a culture in which 'to go fast is to forget fast'.[50]

During the process of state killing, time is materialised in numerous different forms. In photographs of death suites around the United States, the otherwise bare walls of the execution chambers and anterooms always contain a clock, often several of them.[51] The death sentence is prescribed to take place at a certain time, written on the death warrant, read at the outset of the execution, and based on which prison personnel have endured weeks of meticulous training. Time directs movement toward an end. In preparing for an execution, the prescribed protocols instruct the execution team to consistently check the chamber clocks to ensure they are functioning and the time they display is accurate and synchronised.[52] Finally, after the drugs are administered, the electrical shocks are given, and the appropriate amount of time has elapsed since any visible movement has been recorded, the inmate is checked for life by measuring their heart function to the steady beat of time. If no heartbeat is to be found, a time of death is recorded in both written and oral form. For the inmate, time *ends*.

A killing that takes more time than expected puts into motion a series of progressively more severe, frenzied measures: the use of longer electrical currents, the repeated checking of intravenous lines, the administration of additional doses of lethal drugs, and the drawing of curtains between the chamber and witness box to shield its occupants from a body that refuses to die *on time*. [53] Through these movements, witnesses become attuned to time, recognising that an inordinate amount of it has elapsed. Utterances like 'he has not expired'[54] remind spectators of the liminal status of the inmate, and impress upon observers the idea that a death sentence produces a body with a limited shelf-life; to 'not expire' is to outlive it. Time's presence and passing is sensed in the form of the sights, sounds, and textures the law either makes available or is unable to control.

For the spectators, each of these ways of making time creates the impression of an event that has a linear trajectory and is temporally delimited. The death penalty happens between the reading aloud of the death sentence and ends with the inmate's last breath. All events in between are perceived as moving towards that *one* end and, as I have argued elsewhere, this allows the law to limit its own analysis of cruelty to those very limited points in time.[55] Outside of its material and conceptual dimensions, time has no real meaning in terms of how bodies are lived, and for a society that has grown accustomed to temporality as a way in which the world comes to be *known*, duration becomes unbearable without something 'keeping time'. As one witness noted: '[B]efore the

---

49 "Arguments Against Capital Punishment," *BBC Online* (2014), www.bbc.co.uk/ethics/capitalpunishment/against_1.shtml.

50 Lyotard, *The Inhuman: Reflections on Time*, 3.

51 Jen Kirby, "Photos: A Haunting Look at America's Execution Chambers," *Intelligencer*, 16 May 2014, https://nymag.com/intelligencer/2014/05/haunting-photos-of-us-death-chambers.html.

52 "Execution Procedures: Standard Operating Procedures," Idaho Department of Corrections, 2021 (accessed 29 July 2020), https://dpic-cdn.org/production/documents/IdahoProtocol-3-30-2021.pdf.

53 Corinna Barrett Lain, "The Politics of Botched Executions," *University of Richmond Law Review* 49, no. 3 (2014).

54 "Botched Executions," Death Penalty Information Center, 2019, https://deathpenaltyinfo.org/executions/botched-executions.

55 Sabrina Gilani, "The Ethics of Capital Punishment and a Law of Affective Enchantment," *Social & Legal Studies* 32, no. 1 (2022), https://doi.org/10.1177/0964663922109493.

execution, we were in a room *without a clock*. It's a terrible experience. We were there, it seemed, like hours, while they were making sure [the inmate] didn't get a stay. We were all just miserable.'[56] In a room 'without a clock', time stands still; there is a sense that bodies and events are not only out of order, but at a standstill.

The lawscape exercises power by controlling the sensory experiences of the bodies operating within the execution suite. Through its manipulation of time and space, bodies are made to feel disoriented, inert, indifferent, passive, immobile. At the same time, however, it is important to note here that law does not colonise the execution chamber in absolute terms. The chamber remains a:

> manifold space, open to opportunities and controlled by compulsions, arranged by emotions and constrained by senses; it contains various orientations but not always prescribed directions; it is relational but accommodates different power balances between various bodies that circulate in it. It is not fully relational in that it allows for bodies to withdraw ontologically; it is reversible but cannot be easily controlled; and it is fully material ...[57]

The execution chamber can thus also function as a space of resistance. Every so often, it becomes a site of aesthetic upheaval, where law's seamless aesthetic of humane killing as 'just sleep then death'[58] is rattled by sights, sounds, smells, and textures that run counter to its design of how humans (should be made to) live and die.

The sublime execution and the executed body's thing-power

The death penalty does not always materialise in the form of a fatal slumber. In fact, it quite often explodes on to the scene in fits of spectacular rage and violence. These 'sublime executions' invade the sensory cavities of spectating bodies in textures, vibrations, impulses, waves, bringing forth a wonderous, affecting world, unlimited by human design. If the quiet, orderly, serene death of a 'successful' execution preserves a liberal political order commanded by a technologically agile human species capable of bending nature to 'human will',[59] then the bloody, deafening, pungent death of a sublime execution is one that brings us face to face with the squishy, messy, materiality of human existence, in all its unpredictable and astonishing glory. In the *Force of Things*, Bennett develops a material theory of the body, explaining how its form and experiences, everything that we treat as 'natural or real' about the body is informed by culture. 'The point is here,' she writes, 'that cultural forms are themselves material assemblages that *resist*.'[60] As 'protean flow[s] of matter-energy' that have, for the time being, congealed into relatively stable forms,[61] bodies are full of potentiality.

---

56 Blinder and Fernandez, "Bearing Witness to Executions: Last Breaths and Lasting Impressions."
57 Andreas Philippopoulos-Mihalapoulos, *Spatial Justice: Body, Landscape, Atmosphere* (Abingdon: Routledge, 2015), 16.
58 Dwight Conquergood, "Lethal Theatre: Performance, Punishment and the Death Penalty," *Theatre Journal* 54, no. 3 (2002): 364.
59 Jürgen Martschukat, "'The Art of Killing by Electricity': The Sublime and the Electric Chair," *Journal of American History* 89, no. 3 (2002), https://doi.org/10.2307/3092345.
60 Jane Bennett, "The Force of Things: Steps toward an Ecology of Matter," *Political Theory* 32, no. 3 (2004): 348.
61 Bennett, "The Force of Things: Steps toward an Ecology of Matter," 349.

A seamless lawscape, one in which law's normative force is fully dematerialised, rests on accurately predicting what (human and nonhuman) bodies will do. It is how the law anticipates the affections that will motivate (or inhibit) bodies to act in the manner desired by the law. However, in thinking about bodies using Bennett's analytic of 'thing-power materialism', it becomes possible to see that in every*thing* there remains an incorporeal hidden potential, a latent energy. The tiniest change in the material para-meters of the lawscape may trigger those dormant potentialities to produce the most volatile affects. Thinking about bodies in this way restores the executed body with live-liness and vitality. Indeed, this liveliness becomes horrifically apparent during a sublime execution, where sensibility operates as a 'law of the Other' and generates affects that signal a kind of ethico-aesthetic 'rupture'.[62]

The thing-power of the executed body is fully realised in two ways: first, in terms of the affections it generates between itself and spectating bodies; and second, in how it provokes a realignment of the lawscape, and forces the courts to step in and rationalise its spectacular affects. Here, the law reasserts its image of the executed body's otherness, ignoring any quali-ties and proclivities that could give it human form. When Clayton Lockett was being executed by lethal injection, many witnesses reported him struggling violently against his restraints, trying to sit up, and even speaking. Some spectators were even able to recall him distinctly muttering 'something is wrong', 'this shit is fucking with my mind', and 'the drugs are not working',[63] after prison personnel had already declared him unconscious. Thirty-four minutes into his execution, when Lockett remained alive despite all efforts, the attempt was called off, though no life-saving measures were taken, and the curtains were drawn to prevent observers from seeing the killing. Lockett died from cardiac arrest 43 minutes after the first lethal drug was injected into his body. Those present at Lockett's execution reported feeling panicked and alarmed, and one observer likened the scene in the execution chamber to a 'horror movie'.[64]

After Lockett's death, several inmates in Oklahoma petitioned for their executions to be stayed, arguing that an execution in which the prisoner was at risk of remaining conscious would amount to cruel and inhumane punishment.[65] The Court's ruling in *Glossip* focused exclusively on the activities of prison officials during Lockett's execution – examining the process by which the drugs were administered, the precautions taken to protect the inmate's well-being and dignity, and the future measures that would be adopted to prevent another 'accidental' infiltration of IV lines. There was no reference to Lockett's actions, movements, or speech. There was no consideration of the affective qualities of Lockett's death. Although it was the alarming sight of a talking, moving, communicating quasi-corpse that triggered the constitutional challenge in the first place, the courts treated the executed body as insensible: a body that was merely there as a passive and inert *recipient* of punishment. For authors like Edwards, this is a common feature of how the law manages the death penalty, by reinforcing the idea that the state is 'not killing a living person but redundantly killing a corpse – killing what has already been disqualified from life' by virtue of its criminal actions.[66]

---

62 Lyotard, *The Inhuman: Reflections on Time*.

63 Liliana Segura, "Will the Supreme Court Look Behind the Curtain of Lethal Injection?" *The Intercept*, 30 April 2015, https://theintercept.com/2015/04/30/lockettoneyearlater.

64 Katie Fretland, "Witness to Clayton Lockett Botched Execution 'Hated to See it Take so Long'," *The Guardian*, 30 December 2014, www.theguardian.com/us-news/2014/dec/30/clayton-lockett-execution-oklahoma-death-penalty-appeal.

65 *Glossip v. Gross*.

66 Erin E. Edwards, *The Modernist Corpse: Posthumanism and the Posthumous* (Minneapolis, MN: University of Minnesota Press, 2018), 77.

The sublime execution generates bodily encounters that allude to new and alternate possibilities of the human in the form of a kind of corpse-agency; dead or dying bodies that continue to act, communicate, and move. Some might say that the sublime execution operates as an incorporeal 'bloom-space' between spectating and corpse bodies:

> as excess, as autonomous, as impersonal, as the ineffable, as the ongoingness of process, as pedagogic-aesthetic ... as immanence of potential (futurity), the open, as a vibrant incoherence that circulates about zones of cliché and convention, as a gathering place of accumulated dispositions ... [the generative] affect as *promise*. [67]

If we are to think about the human as a body that is always in resistance, always on the verge of becoming other, then the sublime execution reproduces the human body as an object of desire. Berlant writes:

> [W]hen we talk about an object of desire, we are really talking about a cluster of promises we want someone or something to make to us and make possible for us. This cluster of promises could be embedded in a person, a thing, an institution, a text, a norm ... To phrase the 'object of desire' as a cluster of promises is to allow us to encounter what is incoherent or enigmatic in our attachments ... In other words, all attachments are optimistic. [68]

The sublime is the emergence of a set of surges that affect, and by their affects, give rise to what Berlant refers to as 'cruel optimism', 'a relation of attachment to compromised conditions of possibility whose realisation is divorced as either *im*possible, sheer fantasy, or *too* possible, and toxic'. [69] The sublime execution produces delightful *horror* precisely because it shows us the possibilities of human otherness. In a world where we have been told everything that makes us human ceases at death, what we encounter during a sublime execution is not only repulsive but also alluring. Here we encounter a death in which dead bodies communicate with living bodies, sometimes outside of the normal parameters of speech and gesture. Death unfolds in spurts, textures, intensities, impulses, and vibrations; it is not serene, calm, reticent, and it is not something that happens *to bodies*, but *with them*. The sublime execution exposes the relationship between ethics and aesthetics in the form of a corpse that no longer stands as passive matter, but an active, dare we say, agent (to the extent that it can affect and be affected).

Part of the terror the sublime execution triggers stems from our curiosity, and part of it from the sublime's oddity. Bodies in their everyday use bring about a kind of 'stale unaffecting familiarity'. [70] The broken, living-but-dead, communicating-but-lacking-agency, the mutilated and distorted, reeking executed body brings to the imagination a novel, liminal form of human existence. Our curiosity in other bodies stems from the existence of things that we normally do not encounter in ourselves, the insides of the body that we perceive as integral to the self but in many ways unavailable; the ways in

67 Melissa Gregg, Gregory J. Seigworth, and Sara Ahmed, *The Affect Theory Reader* (Durham, NC: Duke University Press, 2010), 9.
68 Lauren Berlant, "Cruel Optimism," in *The Affect Theory Reader*, ed. Melissa Gregg and Gregory J. Seigworth (Durham, NC: Duke University Press, 2010), 93.
69 Berlant, "Cruel Optimism," 94.
70 Edmund Burke, *On the Sublime and the Beautiful* (Good Press, 2020), 43.

which our bodies *could* exist, *do* exist, but are generally unavailable to our senses; the largely invisible ways in which we go on existing. Spectators are horrified by its affects, but also delighted by the body in pain because it brings a sense of relief and comfort in their own body's distance from it.

One could argue about law, as Lyotard has about the arts, that for much of the last century the law has not 'had the beautiful as [its] main concern, but something which has to do with the sublime'.[71] It is towards containing, restraining, preventing, and rejecting the sublime that the law is constantly directing itself. It is the *inhuman*, rather than the human, that captures law's attention and energies, because it has the potential to become *some*thing that defies law's ordering of time-space. When it comes to the death penalty, it is the sublime execution that generates ethical debate because it challenges the aesthetically natural state of the human form, as desired and demanded by law.

Conclusion

The constitutional legitimacy of the death penalty rests on whether the modes of killing being employed can bring about a quiet, unremarkable death. A death that materialises as a kind of fatal slumber. We are told by the courts that the punitive aspect of a death sentence is the death itself, and nothing more, and the different rules, processes, and procedures that are employed in executing the death penalty are directed at maintaining this very specific aesthetic of death that the law tells us is crucial to killing humanely. This chapter has examined how the law maintains this aesthetic by controlling the spectating body's sensory experience of the execution chamber. By mediating what spectators hear, see, touch, and smell in the execution chamber, the law is able to control how they come to *know* the death penalty. By permitting certain kinds of sensory experiences to come forth, while limiting or inhibiting others, the law engineers the kinds of affective occurrences it needs to sustain its image of how humans live and die.

For the most part, the death penalty triggers controversy *not* because it causes pain to inmates, but because every so often it gives its spectators the opportunity to sense that pain in visual, olfactoral, aural, and tangible form. The things that make the death penalty cruel lie dormant, waiting for the right conditions to make themselves known to other bodies in their midst. The sublime execution is an event in which the dormant cruelty of the death penalty springs forth, striking the spectating body in the form of powerful affects that astonish, awe, horrify, and fascinate. Here the executed body challenges our common perception of it as a mere 'object' of punishment. In generating a counter-aesthetic of death, it shows itself to be a powerful actor, having latent powers to transform punitive acts into torture, cruelty, and violence. In exercising its thing-power, the executed body produces affections that ensure that it is spoken and written about, thought, felt, debated, and adjudicated well after the law has declared it dead.

Bibliography

"Arguments against Capital Punishment." BBC Online, 2014. www.bbc.co.uk/ethics/capitalpunishm ent/against_1.shtml.

"Botched Executions." Death Penalty Information Center, 2019. https://deathpenaltyinfo.org/execu tions/botched-executions.

71 Lyotard, *The Inhuman: Reflections on Time*, 135.

"Execution Procedures: Standard Operating Procedures." Idaho Department of Corrections, 2021. http s://dpic-cdn.org/production/documents/IdahoProtocol-3-30-2021.pdf.

Baxter, Lee. "The Aesthetic Simulation of Murder in Dexterland." *Monsters and the Monstrous* 1, no. 1 (2010): 75–92.

Bennett, Jane. "The Force of Things: Steps toward an Ecology of Matter." *Political Theory* 32, no. 3 (2004): 347–372.

Bennett, Jane. "'How Is It, Then, That We Still Remain Barbarians?' Foucault, Schiller, and the Aestheticization of Ethics." *Political Theory* 24, no. 4 (1996): 653–672.

Bently, Lionel, and Leo Flynn, eds. *Law and the Senses: Sensational Jurisprudence.* London: Pluto Press, 1996.

Berlant, Lauren. "Cruel Optimism." In *The Affect Theory Reader*, edited by Melissa Gregg and Gregory J. Seigworth, 93–117. Durham, NC: Duke University Press, 2010.

Black, Joel. *The Aesthetics of Murder.* Baltimore, MD: Johns Hopkins University Press, 1991.

Blinder, Alan, and Manny Fernandez. "Bearing Witness to Executions: Last Breaths and Lasting Impressions." *The New York Times*, 23 April 2017. www.nytimes.com/2017/04/23/us/bearing-witness-to-executions-last-breaths-and-lasting-impressions.html.

Bourdieu, Pierre. *Distinction: A Social-Critique of the Judgment of Taste.* London: Routledge, 2010.

Burke, Edmund. *On the Sublime and the Beautiful.* Good Press, 2020.

Conquergood, Dwight. "Lethal Theatre: Performance, Punishment and the Death Penalty." *Theatre Journal* 54, no. 3 (2002): 339–367.

De Quincey, Thomas. *On Murder Considered as One of the First Arts.* Richmond, UK: Alma Classics, 2016.

Derrida, Jacques. *The Death Penalty: Volume I.* Translated by Peggy Kamuf. Chicago, IL: Chicago University Press, 2013.

Downing, Lisa. "Beyond Reasonable Doubt: Aesthetic Violence and Motiveless Murder in French Decadent Fiction." *French Studies* 58, no. 2 (2004): 189–203.

Drobnick, Jim. *The Smell Culture Reader.* Oxford: Berg, 2006.

Edwards, Erin E. *The Modernist Corpse: Posthumanism and the Posthumous.* Minneapolis: University of Minnesota Press, 2018.

Fretland, Katie. "Witness to Clayton Lockett Botched Execution 'Hated to See It Take So Long'." *The Guardian*, 31 December 2014. www.theguardian.com/us-news/2014/dec/30/clayton-lockett-execution-oklahoma-death-penalty-appeal.

Gilani, Sabrina. "The Ethics of Capital Punishment and a Law of Affective Enchantment." *Social & Legal Studies* 32, no. 1 (2022): 3–27. https://doi.org/10.1177/0964663922109493.

Gregg, Melissa, Gregory J. Seigworth, and Sara Ahmed. *The Affect Theory Reader.* Durham, NC: Duke University Press, 2010.

Kant, Immanuel. *Critique of Judgement.* Translated by James Creed Meredith. Edited by Nicholas Walker. Oxford: Oxford University Press, 2008.

Kant, Immanuel. *Critique of the Power of Judgment.* Translated by Paul Guyer and Eric Matthews. Cambridge: Cambridge University Press, 2013.

Kirby, Jen. "Photos: A Haunting Look at America's Execution Chambers." *Intelligencer*, 16 May 2014. https://nymag.com/intelligencer/2014/05/haunting-photos-of-us-death-chambers.html.

Lain, Corinna Barrett. "The Politics of Botched Executions." *University of Richmond Law Review* 49, no. 3 (2014): 825–844.

Lyotard, Jean-François. *The Inhuman: Reflections on Time.* Translated by Geoffrey Bennington and Rachel Bowlby. Stanford, CA: Stanford University Press, 1991.

Martschukat, Jürgen. "'The Art of Killing by Electricity': The Sublime and the Electric Chair." *Journal of American History* 89, no. 3 (2002): 900–921. https://doi.org/10.2307/3092345.

Merleau-Ponty, Maurice. *Phenomenology of Perception.* Translated by Donald A. Landes. New York: Routledge, 2012.

Mol, Annemarie. *Eating in Theory.* Durham, NC: Duke University Press, 2021.

Nirta, Caterina. "Introduction." In *Law and the Senses Series: Touch*, edited by Andrea Pavoni, Danilo Mandic, Caterina Nirta, and Andreas Philipopoulous-Mihalopoulos, 1–28. London: University of Westminster Press, 2020.

Pavoni, Andrea, Danilo Mandic, Caterina Nirta, and Andreas Philippopoulos-Mihalapoulos, eds. *Law and the Senses Series: Taste.* London: University of Westminster Press, 2018.

Philippopoulos-Mihalapoulos, Andreas. *Spatial Justice: Body, Landscape, Atmosphere*. Abingdon: Routledge, 2015.

Philippopoulos-Mihalapoulos, Andreas. "Law Is a Stage: From Aesthetics to Affective Aestheses." In *Research Handbook on Critical Legal Theory*, edited by Emilios Christodoulidis, Ruth Dukes, and Marco Goldoni, 201–222. Cheltenham: Edward Elgar, 2019.

Philippopoulos-Mihalapoulos, Andreas. "Atmospheres of Law: Senses, Affects, Landscape." *Emotion, Space and Society* 7 (2013): 35–44.

Probyn, Elspeth. *Carnal Appetites: Food, Sex, Identities*. London: Routledge, 2000.

Rancière, Jacques. *The Politics of Aesthetics*, edited by Gabriel Rockhill. London: Bloomsbury, 2004.

Rancière, Jacques. "The Aesthetic Dimension: Aesthetics, Politics, Knowledge." *Critical Inquiry* 36, no. 1 (2009): 1–19.

Rancière, Jacques. "Thinking between Disciplines: An Aesthetics of Knowledge." *Parrhesia*, no. 1 (2006): 1–12.

Segura, Liliana. "Will the Supreme Court Look Behind the Curtain of Lethal Injection?" *The Intercept*, 30 April 2015. https://theintercept.com/2015/04/30/lockettoneyearlater.

Sperry, Raphael. "Death by Design: An Execution Chamber at San Quentin State Prison." *The Avery Review* 2 (2014): 1–5.

Spinoza, Baruch. *Ethics: Treatise on the Emendation of the Intellect and Selected Letters*. Translated by Samuel Shirley. Indianapolis, IN: Hackett Publishing, 1992.

Wawrzinek, Jennifer. "Sublime Politics." In *Ambiguous Subjects*. Amsterdam: Rodopi, 2008.

Wurth, Kiene Brillenburg. *Musically Sublime: Indeterminacy, Infinity, Irresolvability*. New York: Fordham University Press, 2009.

PART 3

Contested Deaths

13

CORONIAL INVESTIGATIONS

Past Deaths and Future Lives

*Jessica Jacobson, Alexandra Murray, Hannah Rumble, and
Lorna Templeton*

Introduction

This chapter considers the interaction between law and death in the context of coroners'
investigations in England and Wales. Coroners are independent judicial office holders
with responsibility for investigating deaths suspected to be violent or unnatural, to have
occurred in custody or other form of state detention, or of unknown cause. Where
deemed necessary by the coroner, an investigation culminates in an inquest: a public
court hearing at which the coroner (occasionally sitting with a jury) hears written and/or
oral evidence in order to determine the facts of the death. Specifically, the inquest
addresses four questions: who died, how they died, when they died, and where the death
occurred. The hearing is inquisitorial, and the coroner is prohibited from apportioning
blame or commenting on any potential civil or criminal liability of a person or organisation. Designated 'interested persons' – including bereaved family members, anyone
whose act or omission may have contributed to the death, and others deemed by the
coroner to have 'sufficient interest'[1] – have certain participation rights, such as the right
to receive evidence and other information in advance of the inquest and to question
witnesses.

The role of the coroner in England and Wales is an ancient one, having originated in
the twelfth century. But it is also an evolving role, and the past two to three decades have
seen particularly rapid change in the legal and policy framework within which coronial
investigations are conducted. Our contention in this chapter is that recent changes to the
role and remit of the coroner can be understood, in part, as a gradual shift in focus from
past to future. This shift towards a future orientation is manifest most clearly in the
growing emphasis placed on the coroner's responsibility – a statutory duty under the
Coroners and Justice Act 2009 (UK) – to report to relevant bodies if they have concerns
about risk of future deaths and consider that actions should be taken to address such
risk. In other words, there is an expectation that the coronial investigation should ultimately help to *save lives*. Concern with the future is also implicit in policy and practice

---

1 *Coroners and Justice Act 2009* (UK), s. 47.

DOI: 10.4324/9781003304593-16

discourse, which places a high value on responsiveness to bereaved people's needs and thus suggests an ambition to help *reclaim lives* scarred by loss. This discourse is influenced by therapeutic jurisprudence – an approach to the law and legal scholarship that considers the ways in which the law itself can act as a 'therapeutic agent'.

We are not claiming that, in previous eras, coroners were not expected to – or did not in practice – look to the future in both senses noted here. Nor are we arguing that the core task of the coroner has departed from that of understanding how the deceased came to their death. Rather, the argument we are making is that recent reforms to the coronial jurisdiction have given future considerations greater prominence within the investigation and inquest process. Over the course of this chapter, we will describe the changes to coronial law and policy that together, in our view, comprise the shift towards a future orientation.

The chapter will also include consideration of some of the implications of this shift, with reference to available research and some emerging data from a study in which the authors and their co-investigators are currently engaged.[2] The study, *Voicing Loss*, is exploring the role of bereaved people in the coronial process, primarily through qualitative research involving coronial professionals (82 participants, including coroners, coroners' officers, lawyers, and providers of support services) and individuals who have experience of a coroner's investigation into the death of a family member since 2013 (89 participants).[3] While systematic analysis of the empirical data has not at the time of writing, been completed, an initial phase of data familiarisation, in the form of a close review of interview transcripts, has generated some preliminary insights. Among these is evidence suggesting that for many individuals who have been bereaved in tragic or contentious circumstances, there is a gap between *expectations* of the coronial process and what they *experience* in practice. One of the questions that arises from this (which we pose here but are not yet in a position to answer) is whether the growing emphasis on the coroner's role in 'saving' and 'reclaiming' lives might have the effect of reinforcing and even widening the gap between expectations and practical realities.

Saving lives

A preventive or public safety function has long been – albeit to varying extents – an important element of the coronial process. Over the course of the eighteenth and particularly the nineteenth century, the inquest evolved 'from a forum that was concerned with asserting and protecting the rights and privileges of the Crown, to a forum that, at least in theory, investigated deaths in the wider interests of society', and, as such, it became 'increasingly characterised as a source of public accountability for deaths at the hands of, for example, yeomanry cavalry, or in workhouses, prisons and orphanages'.[4]

---

2 The project team comprises the authors and co-investigators Dr Penny Cooper (Birkbeck, University of London) and Dr Camillia Kong (Queen Mary University of London).

3 The overarching aims of the study, which is funded by the Economic and Social Research Council (project reference ES/V002732/1), are to explore bereaved people's experiences in relation to their own inclusion and participation in the coronial process; surrounding legal, policy, and normative expectations; and potential ways for better supporting their inclusion and participation.

4 Sam McIntosh, "Taken Lives Matter: Open Justice and Recognition in Inquests into Deaths at the Hands of the State," *International Journal of Law in Context* 12, no. 2 (2016): 146. For a detailed history of the English inquest in the nineteenth and early twentieth century, see Ian Burney, *Bodies of Evidence: Medicine and the Politics of the English Inquest, 1830–1926* (Baltimore, MD: Johns Hopkins University Press, 2000).

Although many nineteenth-century coroners served the interests of the authorities, there were also those who maintained 'a focus on social welfare, inequality and public health', often supported or pushed in this direction by inquest jurors who 'were framed as active and central participants in the hearing'.[5]

However, the twentieth century saw a narrowing of the coroner's authority, along with efforts towards the professionalisation of the role, and a reduced role for the jury. The resultant 'modern inquest'[6] was a more technocratic process, focused on factual inquiry into the causes of death. In 1980, the *Coroners Act 1980* underlined this trend: it 'disposed of English coroners' historic ability to add "riders" or comments to coronial findings, removing the preventive aspect of the coroner's role'.[7] And yet, just four years later, Rule 43 of the Coroners Rules 1984 established a new, formalised process whereby coroners could take steps to prevent future deaths. Coroners were now told that they 'may' issue what became known as 'Rule 43 reports' where they believed 'action should be taken to prevent the recurrence of fatalities similar to that in respect of which the inquest is being held'. The scope of these reports was broadened by the Coroners (Amendment) Rules 2008, which specified that the risk to be addressed no longer had to pertain to 'similar' deaths. The amendments also stipulated that recipients of the reports must send a written response, copies of the report must be sent to interested persons, and the report and response 'may be published'. According to Ministry of Justice guidance, the intention was 'to give greater prominence and importance to coroner reports to improve public health and safety'.[8]

In 2009, the preventive role of the coroner was incorporated within primary legislation for the first time, under Schedule 5(7) of the *Coroners and Justice Act 2009* (with additional provisions in Regulations 28 and 29 of the Coroners (Investigations) Regulations 2013). Coroners 'must' now (no longer 'may') issue a report to relevent persons or organisations where an investigation has raised 'concern that circumstances creating a risk that other deaths will occur, or will continue to exist, in the future', and they believe 'action should be taken to prevent the occurrence or continuation of such circumstances, or to eliminate or reduce the risk of death created by such circumstances'. Recipients of the report are required to send a written response within 56 days, giving details of actions taken or proposed. An associated 'publication policy', subsequently issued by the Chief Coroner, states that reports and responses should be made accessible to the public unless there is 'a compelling reason' not to do so.[9] The statutory provisions for what are widely referred to as prevention of future death reports (PFDs) – also known as 'Regulation 28 reports' – are among a range of wider reforms introduced by the *Coroners and Justice Act*. These also include measures to strengthen and clarify the participation rights of bereaved family members and other 'interested persons' and the creation of the post of Chief Coroner 'to provide national oversight and leadership to coroners'.[10]

5   Edward Kirton-Darling, *Death, Family and the Law: The Contemporary Inquest in Context* (Bristol: Bristol University Press, 2022), 30, 32.
6   Kirton-Darling, *Death, Family and the Law*, 30, 32.
7   Jennifer Moore, *Coroners' Recommendations and the Promise of Saved Lives* (Cheltenham: Edward Elgar, 2016) 32.
8   Ministry of Justice, *Guidance for Coroners on Changes to Rule 43: Coroner Reports to Prevent Future Deaths* (London: MoJ, 2008), 4.
9   Chief Coroner, *Prevention of Future Deaths Reports: Publication Policy* (2021).
10 Ministry of Justice, *Post-Implementation Review of the Coroner Reforms in the Coroners and Justice Act 2009: Call for Evidence* (London: MoJ, 2015), 4.

In short, since Schedule 5 of the *Coroners and Justice Act* was implemented in 2013, coroners have had a statutory duty to concern themselves with the saving of future lives – even if the Chief Coroner's guidance on PFDs stipulates, citing case law, that 'PFDs are important, but they are "ancillary to the inquest procedure and not its mainspring"'.[11]

In addition to the introduction of PFDs, another facet of the contemporary coronial process that pushes in the direction of 'saving lives' is the provision for what are widely known as Article 2 inquests. Under Article 2 of the *European Convention on Human Rights* – incorporated into United Kingdom law by the *Human Rights Act 1998* – states have an obligation to protect the right to life and an associated 'procedural obligation' to ensure that there is an effective investigation into any deaths in which the state, or agents of the state, are implicated. The coronial investigation and inquest is the means by which this procedural obligation is fulfilled in England and Wales. Case law has established a wide scope for inquests concerned with potential breaches of Article 2. As expressed by Lord Bingham in the influential case of *Amin*, the purpose of such inquests is:

> to ensure so far as possible that the full facts are brought to light; that culpable and discreditable conduct is exposed and brought to public notice; that suspicion of deliberate wrongdoing (if unjustified) is allayed; that dangerous practices and procedures are rectified; and that those who have lost their relative may at least have the satisfaction of knowing that *lessons learned from his death may save the lives of others* [emphasis added].[12]

The wider scope of Article 2 inquests is given statutory force by Section 5(2) of the *Coroners and Justice Act*, which states that these inquests should not simply address the four factual questions of who, how, when, and where, but also look into 'in what circumstances the deceased came by his or her death'. Chief Coroner guidance on PFDs makes clear that there is a link, but not an essential one, between Article 2 inquests and the reports, stating that in such inquests, 'the PFD may complete the state's duty to inquire fully … but a PFD is not mandatory simply because an inquest is an Article 2 inquest'.[13]

Therapeutic jurisprudence and the goal of reclaiming lives

While some of the recent coronial reforms have focused on the coroner's role in prevention and public safety, another focus has been on the treatment of bereaved people within the investigation and inquest process. Indeed, a commitment to enhancing the status and role of bereaved people appears to have been a major driver of change, and the United Kingdom government has described 'putting the needs of bereaved people at the heart of the coroner system' as among the main aims – or even as *the* main aim – of the *Coroners and Justice Act*.[14] This was, at least in part, a response to a series of reviews and inquiries that highlighted failings in death investigations, including poor conduct towards families.[15] Policy

11 Chief Coroner, *Revised Chief Coroner's Guidance No.5: Reports to Prevent Future Deaths* (2020).
12 *R (Amin) v Secretary of State for the Home Department* [2003] UKHL 51.
13 Chief Coroner, *Guidance No.5*.
14 For example, Ministry of Justice, *Post-Implementation Review*, 4; Ministry of Justice, *Final Report: Review of Legal Aid for Inquests* (London: MoJ, 2019), 9.
15 See, e.g., N. Brodrick, *Report on the Committee on Death Certification and Coroners* (London: HMSO, 1971); Tom Luce, *Death Certification and Investigation in England, Wales and Northern Ireland: The Report of a Fundamental Review* (London: HMSO, 2003); Janet Smith, *The*

concerns with the needs of bereaved families should not be seen as distinct from the emphasis on prevention of future deaths; rather, there are close interconnections between the two developments – not least because of the value attached to the preventive coronial function by many bereaved people themselves, as found by many studies and reviews. The connection is made explicit in Chief Coroner guidance on PFDs, which notes that 'a bereaved family wants to be able to say: "His death was tragic and terrible, but at least it shouldn't happen to somebody else"'.[16] In the context of Article 2 inquests, in particular, it is widely recognised that bereaved family members can have an important part to play in ensuring that 'their loved ones' deaths were not in vain and that lessons are learnt for the future'.[17]

As noted above, the reforms focused on the bereaved family have included measures to enhance participation rights within the coronial process, such as the right to receive evidence in advance of inquest hearings and to question witnesses. A recent development is the removal, as of January 2022, of means testing for publicly funded legal representation for families attending Article 2 inquests.[18] But of most interest to us here is the extent to which coronial reforms are tacitly informed by notions of therapeutic jurisprudence – that is, concerns with how 'substantive rules, legal procedures, and the roles of lawyers and judges produce therapeutic or antitherapeutic consequences',[19] or, to put it more concisely, the (potential) operation of the law as a 'therapeutic agent'. This dimension of reform does not have as direct or concrete an orientation towards the future as the reforms that enhance the coroner's preventive role. Nevertheless, concern with the future is intrinsic to therapeutic principles; specifically, in this context, the future – 'reclaimed' – lives of bereaved individuals who could be harmed by antitherapeutic consequences of the coronial process or might benefit from therapeutic outcomes.

According to Freckelton, therapeutic jurisprudence has 'infused' processes of death investigation across the coronial jurisdictions of England and Wales, Australia, New Zealand, the United States of America, and Canada.[20] A number of studies, particularly from Australia, have examined the pertinence of therapeutic jurisprudence principles to the work of coroners. These studies note the influence of therapeutic approaches on practice, in a context in which legal decision-making necessarily involves encounters with 'raw and pressing emotions',[21] and make the case for further expansion of such approaches, as part of an 'ethic of care',[22] but also caution that the balance must be struck

Shipman Inquiry: Third Report: Death Certification and the Investigation of Deaths by Coroners (London: TSO, 2003).

16 Chief Coroner, *Guidance No.5.*
17 Sam McIntosh, "Fulfilling Their Purpose? Inquests, Article 2 and Next of Kin," *Public Law* 3 (2012).
18 Legal Aid Agency, "Civil News: Exceptional Case Funding for Families at Inquests", last modified 12 January 2022, www.gov.uk/government/news/civil-news-exceptional-case-funding-for-families-at-inquests.
19 D. B. Wexler and B.J. Winick, *Essays in Therapeutic Jurisprudence* (Durham, NC: Carolina Academic Press, 1991), 9981.
20 Ian Freckelton, "Death Investigation and Therapeutic Jurisprudence," in *The Methodology and Practice of Therapeutic Jurisprudence*, ed. Nigel Stobbs et al. (Durham, NC: Carolina Academic Press, 2019), 150.
21 Gordon Tait et al., "Decision-Making in a Death Investigation: Emotion, Families and the Coroner," *Journal of Law and Medicine* 23, no. 3 (106): 572.
22 Tait et al., "Decision-Making"; Michael King, "Non-Adversarial Justice and the Coroner's Court: A Proposed Therapeutic, Restorative, Problem-Solving Model," *Journal of Law and Medicine* 16, no. 3 (2008): 442–57; Belinda Carpenter et al., "Managing Families' Expectations in the Coronial Jurisdiction: Barriers to Enacting an Ethic of Care," *Journal of Law and Medicine* 29, no. 4 (2022): 1040–51.

'between rigorous, evidence-based decision-making ... and the achievement of collateral health-oriented objectives'.[23]

Terms and concepts suggestive of therapeutic jurisprudence make a regular appearance in recent policy discourse about coronial reforms in England and Wales. Such discourse highlights the importance of responsiveness and sensitivity to bereaved people's needs and presents bereaved people as recipients of a 'service' to which significant emotional weight is attached. This is evident, for example, in a 2004 Home Office 'position paper' on coronial reforms:

> Central to the changes we are proposing is the need to make the system sensitive to the needs of the bereaved and to provide a high standard of service in what are inevitably difficult circumstances. We will balance the need to put families at the heart of the system with the requirement for the service, acting independently and scrupulously, to find the answers to questions concerning a death and to provide accurate information for public health purposes.[24]

This Home Office paper appears to be the first formal policy document to articulate the aspiration to put bereaved people 'at the heart of the system'. Two years later, the Foreword to a draft Coroners Bill (which, in due course, was superseded by the Coroners and Justice Bill) opened with: 'Coroners have a vital task, giving certainty and reassurance to bereaved people, and meeting the public interest by determining the facts of deaths which are reported to them.'[25] The prominence given here to the task of providing 'certainty and reassurance' is notable. Similar language recurs in subsequent documents, such as the Explanatory Notes for the *Coroners and Justice Act*, which describe the purpose of the legislation as being 'to establish more effective, transparent and responsive justice and coroner services for victims, witnesses, bereaved families and the wider public'.[26] A consultation paper on the 'draft Charter' for bereaved people, which became the Ministry of Justice's *Guide to Coroner Services*, noted in its Foreword 'how distressing a coroner's investigation can be for those who are involved with and affected by it' and the intention that the Charter should 'improve what can be a bewildering process, by making the standards of service clearer'.[27] The first Chief Coroner to be appointed, Peter Thornton, echoed the language of responsiveness to family needs in a public lecture in 2012:

> It is natural justice, public justice and justice to be done in public, openly and transparently, for all to see, particularly the family. The family has now become, quite rightly, the focus for this public process, to give them answers, where that is possible. They are at the heart of the process.[28]

---

23 Ian Freckelton, "Death Investigation, the Coroner and Therapeutic Jurisprudence," *Journal of Law and Medicine* 15, no. 2 (2007): 248.

24 Home Office, *Reforming the Coroner and Death Certification Process* (London: Home Office, 2004), 12.

25 Department for Constitutional Affairs, *Coroner Reform: The Government's Draft Bill* (London: DCA, 2006), 3.

26 "Coroners and Justice Act 2009 Explanatory Notes," United Kingdom Government (accessed 22 June 2023), www.legislation.gov.uk/ukpga/2009/25/notes/division/3.

27 Ministry of Justice, *The Draft Charter for the Current Coroner Service* (London: Ministry of Justice, 2011), 3.

28 Cited in Kirton-Darling, *Death, Family and the Law*, 22.

Policy discourse has continued to reiterate the focus on the needs of bereaved people over the years since the implementation of the *Coroners and Justice Act*. The Foreword to a recent Ministry of Justice report on legal aid described the inquest as a process that 'can be traumatic for the bereaved family' but also 'important in helping them to understand and make sense of their loss'.[29] In 2021, the formal response to a report on the Coroner Service by the Justice Select Committee reiterated the government's continued commitment 'to supporting the bereaved and to make sure that inquests are as sympathetic to their needs as they can be'.[30] Also in 2021, practice guidance issued by the Chief Coroner about the use of 'pen portraits' in inquests placed a different kind of emphasis on family needs. The guidance stated:

> A number of recent inquests of national importance have used pen portraits to humanise the process and give dignity to the bereaved. It is a practice that can help the coroner to determine one of the four statutory questions, i.e. 'who' the deceased was.[31]

Here, there is not only an expectation that the antitherapeutic aspects of a coronial investigation – that is, distress and exacerbation of grief – can be *avoided* through sensitive and sympathetic treatment, but, with the reference to humanising proceedings and giving dignity to the bereaved, there is also a hint that *positive, therapeutic outcomes* might be achieved. (It is interesting to note also that the guidance links this – arguably somewhat disingenuously – to the coroner's role in addressing the factual question of 'who' died.) The potential for positive outcomes is considered in some of the above-cited research literature on therapeutic jurisprudence in death investigations. King, for example, refers to 'opportunity for closure' as an 'endpoint of the coronial process',[32] while Freckelton also argues that investigations can result in 'closure of grief and a perception that a constructive outcome has been extracted from tragedy by creating the conditions for healing and resolution'.[33] These ambitions for therapeutic jurisprudence in the coronial jurisdiction encompass an ideal of lives 'reclaimed' in the fullest sense – that is, by positing the possibility of recovery from grief, trauma, and loss.

The language of 'closure' and 'healing' generally does not feature in coronial policy documents in England and Wales. As demonstrated by the extracts presented above, these documents tend to promote the more modest goal of avoidance of harm. However, among the professionals interviewed for the *Voicing Loss* study, some did reference the potential for positive therapeutic outcomes, as in the following comments:

> Managing people's expectations, so that people get out of the process what they can, is fundamentally important. It being part of a process of catharsis, that's what I think is really important. ... [W]here they have a perception that something has gone wrong, it is their, quote unquote, day in court.
>
> *(Inquest lawyer; primarily represents state bodies)*

29 Ministry of Justice, *Review of Legal Aid*, 3.
30 House of Commons Justice Committee, *The Coroner Service: Government Response to the Committee's First Report* (London: House of Commons, 2021), 14.
31 Chief Coroner, *Guidance No. 41: Use of 'pen portrait' material* (2021), 1.
32 King, "Non-Adversarial Justice."
33 Ian Freckelton, "Minimising the Counter-Therapeutic Effects of Coronial Investigations: In Search of Balance," *QUT Review* 16, no. 3 (2016): 29.

The impact and power of an independent judicial holder and a public process in which people feel that the questions they have are put – even though they aren't necessarily answered in the way that they might want, and the findings of a judicial officer or jury that vindicate their concerns – is incredibly powerful and can really help them with their grieving process.

(Inquest lawyer; represents families)

The inquest should very much be that closure. I say 'closure' but very careful by that word. Because ... not everybody gets to that point of acceptance and the closure ... But hopefully, with the inquest, at least they go away knowing the facts and all the facts. ... Again, not like it, understand it or accept it, but have more information as to why their loved one is not with them, as opposed to that seed of doubt ... that can just eat away at them. ... [A]nd as I say, they have a voice. They are there, they are present, they are real. That's why the inquest, I think, empowers them.

(Coroner)

Expectations and realities

We have argued thus far that the legal and policy framework for coronial investigations and inquests has become increasingly future-oriented. Any assessment of the extent to which this shift is likely to be effective in terms of 'saving' or 'reclaiming' lives is far beyond the scope of this chapter. The narrower issue to which we turn in this final section is whether the shift risks reinforcing and even widening the gap between bereaved family members' expectations of the coronial process and what they experience in practice.

As Scott Bray and Martin have observed, 'Inquests can deliver justice, but they have also been known to stall, derail and dilute it; and ultimately those who are left to embrace the inquest's benefits, or bear its failings, are the bereaved'.[34] The evidence base on failings borne by bereaved people in England and Wales encompasses the formal reviews and inquiries into death investigations that have been referenced above. It also includes available academic research into bereaved people's experiences. This research has tended to focus on deaths of particular kinds, including suicides,[35] fatal accidents at work,[36] and road deaths.[37] The findings of these studies identify many aspects of the coronial process that bereaved people find difficult or distressing and can interfere with

34 Rebecca Scott Bray and Greg Martin, "Exploring Fatal Facts: Current Issues in Coronial Law, Policy and Practice," *International Journal of Law in Context* 12, no. 2 (2016): 136.
35 D. Harwood et al., "The Grief Experiences and Needs of Bereaved Relatives and Friends of Older People Dying Through Suicide," *Journal of Affective Disorders* 72 (2002): 185–94; Lucy Biddle, "Public Hazards or Private Tragedies? An Exploratory Study of the Effects of Coroners' Procedures on Those Bereaved by Suicide," *Social Science & Medicine* 56 (2003): 1033–45; Gordon Tait and Belinda Carpenter, "Suicide and the Therapeutic Coroner: Inquests, Governance and the Grieving Family," *International Journal for Crime, Justice and Social Democracy* 2, no. 3 (2013): 92–104; Marilyn Gregory, "Managing the Homicide–Suicide Inquest: The Practices of Coroners in One Region of England and Wales," *International Journal of Law, Crime and Justice* 42, no. 3 (2014): 237–50; A. Spillane et al., "How Suicide-Bereaved Family Members Experience the Inquest Process: A Qualitative Study Using Thematic Analysis," *International Journal of Qualitative Studies on Health and Well-being* 14, no. 1 (2019): 1563430.
36 Katy Snell and Steve Tombs, "'How Do You Get Your Voice Heard When No-One Will Let You?' Victimization at Work," *Criminology & Criminal Justice* 11, no. 3 (2011): 207–23; M. Ngo

grieving, such as delay, formality and complexity, poor treatment by professionals, and media coverage and associated invasions of privacy. Of particular significance is a body of work on death investigations into contentious deaths involving the police or other state actors. This includes research into the aftermath of deaths in custody.[38] Scraton's extensive work on official responses to the Hillsborough disaster considers how '[t]he suffering of bereavement and survival has been exacerbated by the continual torment of injustice embedded in the failures of formal inquiry and criminal justice'.[39] Hillsborough families' experiences, including of the two sets of inquests into the disaster (in 1990–1991 and 2014–2016), are also presented in Bishop James Jones's government-commissioned report, pointedly titled *The Patronising Disposition of Unaccountable Power*.[40]

The current *Voicing Loss* study provides an opportunity to explore experiences of individuals bereaved in a wide range of circumstances who have attended an inquest since implementation of relevant provisions of the *Coroners and Justice Act* in 2013. (Most prior empirical research predates this.) Such individuals have largely been recruited for the study via support services and networks engaged with bereaved people, with the result that the sample is skewed towards those who have sought support following bereavement in contentious or tragic circumstances. Nevertheless, the sample has sufficient diversity – particularly in terms of coroner's court attended, circumstances of death, and length and type of inquest – to generate important insights into those aspects of the inquest experience that bereaved people tend to find especially difficult or challenging. In this regard, from the preliminary review of the interview transcripts, it appears that (1) hopes and expectations of the coroner's preventive role often lead to particular frustrations and (2) many bereaved people perceive the coronial process to be far from responsive and sensitive to their needs.

Expectations and realities: Saving lives

One research participant, a bereaved sister, asserted in her interview, 'that's what all the families want: they want lessons to be learnt'. A coroner voiced his confidence that the service can meet this expectation: 'Ultimately, the real gift of the coroner ... [is to report on] whether or not something could have been done differently, which means that other people don't die in similar circumstances.'

Some bereaved participants had invested significant hope in the production of a PFD that would indeed help to 'save lives'. In around one-fifth of the cases, a report had been issued, but the *content* of the reports was the cause of some significant disappointment.

et al., "Bereaved Family Members' Views of the Value of Coronial Inquests into Fatal Work Incidents," *Omega – Journal of Death and Dying* 82, no. 3 (2021): 446–66.

37 Glennys Howarth, "Death on the Road: The Role of the English Coroners Court in the Social Construction of an Accident," in *The Aftermath of Road Accidents: Psychological, Social and Legal Consequences of Everyday Trauma*, ed. M. Mitchell (London: Routledge, 1997).

38 Philippa Tomczak, *Prison Suicide: What Happens Afterwards?* (Bristol: University of Bristol Press, 2018); Philippa Tomczak and Sue McAllister, "Prisoner Death Investigations: A Means for Improving Safety in Prisons and Societies?" *Journal of Social Welfare and Family Law* 43, no. 2, (2021): 212–30; Jo Easton, *Death in Custody: Inquests, Family Participation and State Accountability* (Bingley: Emerald, 2020).

39 Phil Scraton, "The Legacy of Hillsborough: Liberating Truth, Challenging Power," *Race and Class* 55, no. 2 (2013): 25.

40 James Jones, *'The Patronising Disposition of Unaccountable Power': A Report to Ensure the Pain and Suffering of the Hillsborough Families Is Not Repeated* (London: TSO, 2017).

Participants' descriptions included phrases such as 'lip-service', 'wishy-washy', 'skeletal', and 'not worth the paper they're written on'. But the strongest criticisms were reserved for what was perceived to be the poor or non-existent *impact* of PFDs on the authorities and services at which they were targeted:

> I thought the report was okay, yes. It's very succinct, it's very, very succinct. And the response was waffle. But the most important thing about those bloody responses is nobody checks to see that they've done it. They're required to submit a response, but there's no requirement that anyone checks that it has been done.
>
> *(Bereaved mother-in-law)*

> The coroner has no oversight and no quality control or no governance of the PFD that they issue. Therefore, they're meaningless. They're just a wish list, and that's why you then get really frustrated … If ever there's something that's failing to deliver what it says on the tin, it's that.
>
> *(Bereaved father)*

A bereaved mother vividly described her moment of realisation that a health trust was not going to respond to the PFDs in the way she had hoped:

> I realised that if I'm standing in the [health] trust's crisis centre, talking to the chief person when [my daughter] was alive, begging for their help to save her life: if they didn't listen to me then, they're not going to listen to me now she's dead, unless it impacts their funding or their job. They responded enough to secure that, but no more. It was at that point, when I read the responses to the reports, I thought, 'Enough. Enough', and I just let it go because I ran out of fight.

Perceptions of the limited impact of coroners' recommendations should be understood in their wider context. Despite the requirement, under the coroners' regulations, for recipients of PFDs to respond within 56 days, there are no sanctions for non-response. There are also no mechanisms for oversight of whether actions specified in PFDs or responses to them are implemented and with what effect. Inevitably, there are repercussions for the extent to which learning from coroners' investigations is shared and remedial actions are taken – as demonstrated by recent studies that have involved analysis of PFDs and submitted responses, particularly in the health field.[41]

Nevertheless, some bereaved participants in the *Voicing Loss* study reported positively regarding the preventive work of coroners. One bereaved parent said that a PFD had gone to a healthcare service identifying gaps in their guidance: 'And their response was basically, "Bugger me. Right, there's a gap; we've filled it now".' A bereaved father was highly impressed with the coroner's approach to tackling shortcomings in police practice:

41 Anthony Fox and Jessica Jacobson, "How Well Do Regulation 28 Reports Serve Future Public Health and Safety?" *Medicine, Science and the Law*, 61, no. 3 (2021): 186–92; H. S. France et al., "Preventable Deaths Involving Medicines: A Systematic Case Series of Coroners' Reports 2013–22," *Drug Safety* 46 (2023): 335–42; R. E. Ferner et al., "Preventing Future Deaths from Medicines: Responses to Coroners' Concerns in England and Wales," *Drug Safety* 42 (2019): 445–51.

Our lawyers were absolutely shocked that the coroner had been so critical, so direct, and picked up on every point which we'd highlighted ... it did push [the police force] to change their procedures ... We wanted ... the truth and to have some accountability and have some learning from [my son's] experience ... We couldn't have asked for anything better.

Expectations and realities: Reclaiming lives

We have argued above that aspects of coronial policy and practice in England and Wales suggest aspirations – broadly aligned with the principles of therapeutic jurisprudence – for a service that is genuinely responsive to the needs of bereaved people and even potentially transformative. That these are not impossible goals is suggested by comments from some *Voicing Loss* research participants. One bereaved mother described attendance at the inquest – with help and support from an experienced legal team – as 'almost therapy'. She went on to explain, 'I found peace in that inquest, strangely, which is probably surprising ... I found peace, because I could see everything, or pretty much everything was uncovered.' Another bereaved parent also spoke of being able to find a sense of 'peace' through the coronial process. This parent said that while the loss of their child had been 'devastating', their experience

would have been even worse had we not had some sort of acknowledgment and examination of what took place. Had that not taken place, I think we would have been even more devastated and lost ... If we hadn't had an inquest, I don't think we'd have ever been at peace.

Another mother emphasised how important the empathy shown by the coroner had been for her:

The Coroner was really kind and encouraging, recognising our grief, our distress and that this was a hard process ... We had a voice in this, and we were an active part. I think I felt, 'Gosh, somebody really did look into why she died and took that seriously'. I think it felt really respectful.

However, other participants recounted treatment during the coronial process that lacked compassion and sensitivity. Such treatment made them feel excluded from the investigation and inquest – in a variety of ways – rather than included and positioned 'at the heart', and ultimately *added to* rather than ameliorated their distress. Comments from research participants about harms arising from the coronial process itself include:

Other than my sister dying, the inquest was the worst experience ever.

(Bereaved sister)

You already feel like [the death is] your fault anyway ... It was one of the most hideous, utterly horrific and traumatic experiences of my life.

(Mother)

What you've done is you've introduced further trauma to people already traumatised.

(Father)

Reported experiences such as these indicate that even the relatively modest goal of avoiding antitherapeutic outcomes – let alone the more ambitious goal of achieving therapeutic outcomes – may be a long way from being achieved across much of the coronial service. The barriers to provision of a service that can help to 'reclaim lives' are likely to be many and varied. Among them, it seems, is a mismatch between expectations of an individualised, human-centred process and real-world experiences of proceedings that feel hurried and impersonal:

> I just found it cold. It's like a conveyor belt. We seemed to be in there, out there and they disposed of [my son] – of 30 years of life.
>
> *(Bereaved parent)*

> I felt like [my son's] life had to be rubber-stamped: 'Move on, next case'.
>
> *(Bereaved parent)*

> It's almost like, 'We're all very sorry it's happened, but we've just got to get through this process. Thanks very much, and see you later.'
>
> *(Bereaved parent)*

For some of the research participants, a related source of frustration and distress was that they felt the life and identity of the deceased were not properly reflected or accorded respect within the coronial process. One bereaved parent commented that her son's 'voice was lost in all of this', while another said that her son was treated as 'incidental ... It's sort of like, "Okay, he's dead. He's no longer important."' A bereaved sister argued forcefully that the inquest process had rendered her brother invisible:

> So, we witness [my brother] being stripped of everything before us, again, in death. That was quite something; I'll never be able to describe that. He suffered, he had a life so different to us because of [his health problems]. How is it possible that he could just be invisibilised?
>
> *(Bereaved sister)*

Conclusion

This chapter has described two aspects of a shift towards a future orientation in the work of the coroner in England and Wales. This shift is manifest, first, in the growing emphasis and statutory weight given to the coroner's preventive and public safety function, and second, in increasingly explicit policy commitments to meeting the needs of bereaved people during the coronial process. While the core purpose of coronial investigations and inquests remains *determination of the facts of past deaths*, consideration of *future lives* has thus become a more prominent part of the process.

Available research, along with emerging insights from the ongoing *Voicing Loss* study, suggests that there are tensions associated with this shift. Fulfilment of the coroner's preventive role appears to be hindered by systemic factors that limit the scope, reach, and impact of PFDs and can be a source of frustration to bereaved family members. Policy commitments to responsiveness to the needs of bereaved people, and to locating them 'at the heart' of the coronial process, may seem uncontentious, but there are questions to be asked about the extent to which these broad aspirations are being put into practice and with what effects. Arguably, as more is promised by the coronial service, the potential for disappointment and disillusion may grow if bereaved people feel that they are neither centrally included, nor treated with sufficient compassion or respect, nor party to a process that can help to save lives.

The implication of this is not that coroners should draw back from a preventive role, or that principles of therapeutic jurisprudence should *not* inform coronial policy and practice. But it does suggest that there is a pressing need for open, transparent debate about what the coronial process can and cannot realistically be expected to achieve in terms of both 'saving' and 'reclaiming' lives.

Bibliography

Biddle, Lucy. "Public Hazards or Private Tragedies? An Exploratory Study of the Effects of Coroners' Procedures on Those Bereaved by Suicide." *Social Science & Medicine* 56 (2003): 1033–1045.

Brodrick, N. *Report on the Committee on Death Certification and Coroners.* London: HMSO, 1971.

Burney, Ian. *Bodies of Evidence: Medicine and the Politics of the English Inquest, 1830–1926.* Baltimore, MD: Johns Hopkins University Press, 2000.

Carpenter, Belinda, Gordon Tait, and Stephanie Jowett. "Managing Families' Expectations in the Coronial Jurisdiction: Barriers to Enacting an Ethic of Care." *Journal of Law and Medicine* 29, no. 4 (2022): 1040–1051.

Chief Coroner. *Revised Chief Coroner's Guidance No.5: Reports to Prevent Future Deaths.* 2020.

Chief Coroner. *Prevention of Future Deaths Reports: Publication Policy.* 2021.

Chief Coroner. *Guidance No. 41: Use of 'Pen Portrait' Material.* 2021.

Department for Constitutional Affairs. *Coroner Reform: The Government's Draft Bill.* London: DCA, 2006.

Easton, Jo. *Death in Custody: Inquests, Family Participation and State Accountability.* Bingley: Emerald, 2020.

Ferner, R. E., T. Ahmad, and Z. Babatunde. "Preventing Future Deaths from Medicines: Responses to Coroners' Concerns in England and Wales." *Drug Safety* 42 (2019): 445–451.

Fox, Anthony, and Jessica Jacobson. "How Well Do Regulation 28 Reports Serve Future Public Health and Safety?" *Medicine, Science and the Law* 61, no. 3 (2021): 186–192.

France, H. S., J. K. Aronson, C. Heneghan, R. E. Ferner, A. R. Cox, and G. C. Richards. "Preventable Deaths Involving Medicines: A Systematic Case Series of Coroners' Reports 2013–22." *Drug Safety* 46 (2023): 335–342.

Freckelton, Ian. "Death Investigation, the Coroner and Therapeutic Jurisprudence." *Journal of Law and Medicine* 15, no. 2 (2007): 242–253.

Freckelton, Ian. "Death Investigation and Therapeutic Jurisprudence." In *The Methodology and Practice of Therapeutic Jurisprudence*, edited by Nigel Stobbs, Lorana Barels, and Michel Vols, 149–174. Durham, NC: Carolina Academic Press, 2019.

Freckelton, Ian. "Minimising the Counter-Therapeutic Effects of Coronial Investigations: In Search of Balance." *QUT Review* 16, no. 3 (2016): 4–29.

Gregory, Marilyn. "Managing the Homicide–Suicide Inquest: The Practices of Coroners in One Region of England and Wales." *International Journal of Law, Crime and Justice* 42, no. 3 (2014): 237–250.

Harwood, D., K. Hawton, T. Hope, and R. Jacoby. "The Grief Experiences and Needs of Bereaved Relatives and Friends of Older People Dying Through Suicide." *Journal of Affective Disorders* 72 (2002): 185–194.

Home Office. *Reforming the Coroner and Death Certification Process.* London: Home Office, 2004.

House of Commons Justice Select Committee. *The Coroner Service: Government Response to the Committee's First Report.* London: House of Commons, 2021.

Howarth, Glennys. "Death on the Road: The Role of the English Coroners Court in the Social Construction of an Accident." In *The Aftermath of Road Accidents: Psychological, Social and Legal Consequences of Everyday Trauma*, edited by M. Mitchell, 145–155. London: Routledge, 1997.

Jones, James. *'The Patronising Disposition of Unaccountable Power': A Report to Ensure the Pain and Suffering of the Hillsborough Families Is Not Repeated.* London: TSO, 2017.

King, Michael. "Non-Adversarial Justice and the Coroner's Court: A Proposed Therapeutic, Restorative, Problem-Solving Model." *Journal of Law and Medicine* 16, no. 3 (2008): 442–457.

Kirton-Darling, Edward. *Death, Family and the Law: The Contemporary Inquest in Context.* Bristol: Bristol University Press, 2022.

Luce, Tom. *Death Certification and Investigation in England, Wales and Northern Ireland: The Report of a Fundamental Review.* London: HMSO, 2003.

McIntosh, Sam. "Fulfilling Their Purpose? Inquests, Article 2 and Next of Kin." *Public Law* 3 (2012): 407–415.

McIntosh, Sam. "Taken Lives Matter: Open Justice and Recognition in Inquests into Deaths at the Hands of the State." *International Journal of Law in Context* 12, no. 2 (2016): 141–161.

Ministry of Justice. *Guidance for Coroners on Changes to Rule 43: Coroner Reports to Prevent Future Deaths.* London: Ministry of Justice, 2008.

Ministry of Justice. *The Draft Charter for the Current Coroner Service.* London: Ministry of Justice, 2011.

Ministry of Justice. *Post-Implementation Review of the Coroner Reforms in the Coroners and Justice Act 2009: Call for Evidence.* London: Ministry of Justice, 2015.

Ministry of Justice. *Final Report: Review of Legal Aid for Inquests.* London: Ministry of Justice, 2019.

Moore, Jennifer. *Coroners' Recommendations and the Promise of Saved Lives.* Cheltenham: Edward Elgar, 2016.

Ngo, M., L. R. Matthews, M. Quinlan, and P. Bohle. "Bereaved Family Members' Views of the Value of Coronial Inquests into Fatal Work Incidents." *Omega – Journal of Death and Dying* 82, no. 3 (2021): 446–466.

Scott Bray, Rebecca, and Greg Martin. "Exploring Fatal Facts: Current Issues in Coronial Law, Policy and Practice." *International Journal of Law in Context* 12, no. 2 (2016): 115–140.

Scraton, Phil. "The Legacy of Hillsborough: Liberating Truth, Challenging Power." *Race and Class* 55, no. 2 (2013): 1–27.

Smith, Janet. *The Shipman Inquiry: Third Report: Death Certification and the Investigation of Deaths by Coroners.* London: TSO, 2003.

Snell, Katy, and Steve Tombs. "'How Do You Get Your Voice Heard When No-One Will Let You?' Victimization at Work." *Criminology & Criminal Justice* 11, no. 3 (2011): 207–223.

Spillane, A., K. Matvienko-Sikar, C. Larkin, P. Corcoran, and E. Arensman. "How Suicide-Bereaved Family Members Experience the Inquest Process: A Qualitative Study Using Thematic Analysis." *International Journal of Qualitative Studies on Health and Well-being* 14, no. 1 (2019): 1563430.

Tait, Gordan, and Carpenter, Belinda. "Suicide and the Therapeutic Coroner: Inquests, Governance and the Grieving Family." *International Journal for Crime, Justice and Social Democracy* 2, no. 3 (2013): 92–104.

Tait, Gordon, Belinda Carpenter, Carol Quadrelli, and Michael Barnes. "Decision-Making in a Death Investigation: Emotion, Families and the Coroner." *Journal of Law and Medicine* 23, no. 3 (2016): 571–581.

Tomczak, Philippa. *Prison Suicide: What Happens Afterwards?* Bristol: University of Bristol Press, 2018.

Tomczak, Philippa, and Sue McAllister. "Prisoner Death Investigations: A Means for Improving Safety in Prisons and Societies?" *Journal of Social Welfare and Family Law* 43, no. 2 (2021): 212–230.

Wexler, D. B., and B. J. Winick. *Essays in Therapeutic Jurisprudence.* Durham, NC: Carolina Academic Press, 1991.

14

FEEDBACK LOOPS, VULNERABLE POPULATIONS, AND THE CORONIAL DETERMINATION OF SUICIDE

Belinda Carpenter, Ella Tait, and Claire Ferguson

Introduction

Across Australia, each of the six state and two territory governments operate a coronial court as an inquisitorial branch of the judiciary, investigating reportable deaths that occur in their jurisdiction. Alongside violent, unnatural, or suspicious deaths, deaths are reportable if the person's identity is unknown, the death was related to health care, or occurred in care or in custody or as a result of police operations.[1] In Queensland in 2021–2022, 6,044 deaths were reported to the coroner, representing 18 per cent of all deaths that occurred in Queensland during that time.[2] For most of the deaths reported to them, coroners' findings are based upon an administrative review of documentary evidence collected by police. However, a small selection of cases proceeds to a formal public hearing known as an inquest.[3] In Queensland in 2021–2022, 27 inquests were completed which represented 0.45 per cent of all reportable deaths.[4]

Inquests are the 'public face' of the coronial death investigation system,[5] and despite representing a small percentage of all deaths reported to coroners, inquest reports contain a wealth of information about the deceased and demonstrate how evidence is interpreted and prioritised by the coroner when reaching their finding. Inquests are legally required if the death occurred in custody or as the result of a police operation, or if the person died while in care. Inquests can also occur at the discretion of the coroner if, for example, it is considered in the public interest to do so or if there is doubt about the cause or circumstances of the death (e.g., determining whether the

---

1 Coroners Court Queensland, *State Coroners Guidelines* (2013), chapter 3.
2 Terry Ryan, *Coroners Court of Queensland 2021–22 Annual Report* (2022), 7.
3 Simon J. Walter, Lyndal Bugeja, Matthew J. Spittal, and David M. Studdart, "Factors predicting coroners' decisions to hold discretionary inquests," *Canadian Medical Association Journal* 184, no. 5 (2012): 521.
4 Ryan, *Annual Report*, 7.
5 *State Coroners Guidelines*, chapter 9.

DOI: 10.4324/9781003304593-17

death was a suicide or an accident).[6] Inquests are fact-finding exercises and are not bound by the rules of evidence.[7] Their inquisitorial approach is more akin to a Royal Commission than a criminal trial, but coroners are limited in their scope to how the death occurred as opposed to the broad circumstances surrounding the death.[8] It is suggested that the process of inquiry underpinning the inquest lends itself to the use of experts and research in order to test hypotheses, clarify opinions, and resolve uncertainties.[9]

This chapter is founded on the understanding that the boundaries of suicide are created by coroners and are thus influenced by organisational norms and concepts. In this way of thinking, observational categories – like death – are real-world things or events, while theoretical categories – like suicide – are the result of an imposition of an order on real-world things by an observer – like a coroner.[10] This sociological approach to suicide is influenced by the theorising of Douglas,[11] Atkinson,[12] and Taylor[13] and proceeds on four premises.

First, the incidence of suicide in mortality statistics reflects a governmental bureaucracy's definition of suicide rather than any insight into the phenomenon of suicide itself. Part of the reason for this was identified by Douglas,[14] who suggested that the moral stigma against suicide might motivate some families to want deaths of their loved ones to be categorised as something other than suicide. In such a scenario, the lower incidence of suicide in socially integrated people – central to Durkheim's theories – has more to do with successful familial lobbying of coroners than with a lower incidence of suicide in socially integrated individuals per se.

Second, a 'feedback loop' occurs in coronial determinations of suicide between researchers, experts, and coroners. In explorations of coronial determinations of suicide in England, Atkinson[15] theorised a symbiotic relationship between suicide research and coronial determinations, and proposed that academic explanations of suicide were nothing more than the 'formalised versions of the informal ones used by coroners' and that 'an acquaintance' with suicide research enabled coroners to feel more confident about the evidence required to infer intent.[16]

Third, coroners will only record a death as a suicide if the cues are consistent with general cultural assumptions circulating in society about why and how people kill

6 *State Coroners Guidelines*, chapter 9.2.
7 Ian Freckleton, "Inquest Law," in *The Inquest Handbook*, ed. Harry Selby (Sydney: Federation Press, 1998), 10.
8 Freckleton, "Inquest Law," 7.
9 Hugh Selby, "Introduction," in *The Inquest Handbook*, ed. Harry Selby (Sydney: Federation Press, 1998), xxi.
10 Barry Hindess, *The Use of Official Statistics in Sociology* (London: Macmillan, 1973), 19.
11 Jack Douglas, "The sociological analysis of social meanings of suicide," *Archives of European Sociology* 7 (1966): 249–75; Jack Douglas, *The Social Meaning of Suicide* (Princeton, NJ: Princeton University Press, 1967).
12 Maxwell J. Atkinson, "Societal reactions to suicide: The role of coroners' definitions," in *Images of Deviance*, ed. Stan Cohen (Harmondsworth: Penguin, 1971), 165–91; Maxwell J. Atkinson, *Discovering Suicide: Studies in the Social Organisation of Sudden Death* (London: Macmillan, 1978).
13 Steve Taylor, "Shorter Notices: Book Review," *Sociology* 17, no. 4 (1983): 599–600; Steve Taylor, *Durkheim and the Study of Suicide* (London: Macmillan. 1982); Steve Taylor, *Sociology and the Study of Suicide* (Doctoral Thesis, University of Leicester, 1978).
14 Jack Douglas, "The sociological analysis of social meanings of suicide," *Archives of European Sociology* 7 (1966): 249–75.
15 Atkinson, *Discovering Suicide*.
16 Atkinson, *Discovering Suicide*, 144, 172.

themselves. For coroners, certain types of deaths and certain evidence from the deceased's past together act as 'suicide cues' which enable coroners to construct a 'suicidal biography' and legitimise a suicide finding. But by making use of a range of material from the body, the scene, and the biography of the deceased to determine the circumstances of the death, coroners are not simply 'asking whether a particular death could have been a suicide but whether that particular person could have committed suicide'.[17]

Fourth, suicide findings by coroners, and thus official statistics, only include 'typical suicides' by people who are 'suicide prone.'[18] If a death is *really* a suicide, there must be evidence of abnormality, unhappiness, or disturbance, since 'the facts of the biography must match the facts of the death'.[19] Thus, using suicide statistics for research purposes does not lead to the discovery of factors associated with suicide but only those factors employed by officials to infer suicidal intent. Similarly, expert testimony derived from this suicide research can be nothing more than the elaborations of official (and general cultural) common-sense notions of suicide.[20]

Using these four premises, this chapter is interested in the procedures, processes, norms, and concepts involved in coronial decision making during an inquest into suspected suicide, and the particular role that expert testimony and suicide research play in these determinations. The implication of feedback loops between coroners, researchers, and experts in our knowledge of suicide in vulnerable populations will be a particular focus.

Literature review

To classify a death a suicide, the coroner needs to establish that the death is self-inflicted and intentional, and while the former is most often ascertained through a medical examination of the body, the latter is purely circumstantial and needs to be established from secondary evidence including witness reports, suicide notes, previous suicide attempts, testimonials, life crises, and lethality of modes of dying.[21] Considering this circumstantial evidence gathering, some deaths become 'routine suicides' where the evidence overwhelmingly points to suicidal intent. Carpenter et al.[22] established, for example, that certain methods of dying are suggestive to coroners of suicide, as are certain biographical details. An active method, such as hanging, is suggestive of suicide, as is the presence of a diagnosed mental illness. The existence of suicide cues, such as a note, also enable coroners to infer intent. Importantly, these ways of thinking about suicide align with the information from suicide researchers about individual risk factors for suicide, and coroners appear well versed in the scholarship relevant to suicide as a legal finding.[23]

17 Atkinson, *Discovering Suicide*, 172.
18 Taylor, *Sociology and the Study of Suicide*, 305.
19 Taylor, *Durkheim and the Study of Suicide*, 60, 85.
20 Taylor, "Shorter Notices: Book Review," 599.
21 Stephen Timmermans, "Suicide determination and the professional authority of medical examiners," *American Sociological Review* 70, no. 2 (2005): 317.
22 Belinda Carpenter, Bridget Weir, Stephanie Jowett, Gordon Tait, and Claire Ferguson, "Coronial determination of suicide: Insights from inquests," *Mortality* (2022): 1–17, https://doi.org/10.1080/13576275.2022.2114823.
23 Stephanie Jowett, Belinda Carpenter, and Gordon Tait, "Determining a suicide under Australian law," *UNSW Law Journal* 41, no. 2 (2018): 355–79.

However, research also indicates that suicide does not have the same meaning for all coroners, and it is unlikely that coroners follow the same rules in assigning particular cases to given categories.[24] In Australia, this is complicated by the lack of a clear definition of suicide in any of the legislative acts and a complicated civil standard of proof which invokes the Briginshaw principal within the balance of probabilities.[25] In the US, medical examiners readily admitted that suicide determinations differ between jurisdictions, and that this was due to consultation between law enforcement and district attorneys 'to ascertain the legal validity of the determinations'.[26] According to Timmermans,[27] this demonstrated that suicide findings were 'locally based and dependent on shifts in jurisprudence and personnel'. To assign a death to a particular category is therefore the result of negotiation and argument, and likely to involve certain idiosyncratic elements.

This process of negotiation is evident at the inquest which is 'structured to build consensus'[28] by bringing together experts, witnesses, and the grieving family to aid the coroner in identifying the circumstances in which a person has died. Inquests are positioned as neutral fact-finding missions, but inquests also produce facts, reconstructing the circumstances of a sudden and often unwitnessed death.[29] Experts are crucial 'to decipher the meanings of these clues' and produce 'objective knowledge about the end of life'.[30] In all of this, coroners continue their reconstruction of the story of the deceased by shaping the proceedings, by the questions they pose to experts, by emphasising or privileging certain expert accounts, and by the verdict they offer to the court.[31] In this way, coroners act as 'death work mediators', constructing information about the dead, editing and polishing it, and then publicly presenting the edited version.[32] In the inquest, 'multiple and criss-crossing' stories are presented, often in emotional accounts, and the coroner must create 'a story of the death' that is consistent within a 'limited number of possible legal verdicts'.[33] An identity is thus imposed on the deceased that is 'constructed [by the coroner] rather than self-constructing'.[34]

At the completion of an inquest, coroners have the capacity to make findings and recommendations aimed at preventing similar deaths from occurring in the future. While this is often cited as an important motivation for family involvement in the inquest,[35] these recommendations occur in a discursive space that relies heavily on expert

24 Stephanie Jowett, Belinda Carpenter, and Gordon Tait, "Determining a suicide under Australian law: A comparative study of coronial practice," *UNSW Law Journal*, 42, no. 2 (2019): 534–56.
25 See Jowett et al., "Determining a suicide under Australian law" (2018), 369, for a discussion of Briginshaw.
26 Timmermans, "Suicide determination," 329.
27 Timmermans, "Suicide Determination," 329.
28 David Aitken, "Investigating prison suicide: The politics of independent oversight," *Punishment and Society* 24, no. 3 (2022): 485.
29 Aitken, "Investigating Prison Suicide."
30 Aitken, "Investigating Prison Suicide," 478.
31 Susan Langer, "Distributed personhood and the transformation of agency: An anthropological perspective on inquests," in *The Matter of Death*, ed. Jenny Hockey (London: Palgrave Macmillan, 2010), 97.
32 Tony Walter, "Mediator Deathwork," *Death Studies* 29 (2005): 383.
33 Walter, "Mediator Deathwork," 396.
34 Walter, "Mediator Deathwork," 402.
35 Stephanie Dartnall, Jane Goodman-Delahunty, and Judith Gullifer, "Exploring family experiences of missing person inquests through the eyes of professionals and the lens of therapeutic jurisprudence," *Psychiatry, Psychology and the Law* 30, no. 5 (2023): 1–25.

knowledge from law and medicine.[36] Inquests thus acknowledge the personal dimensions of the deceased and their death, but they also transform the deceased through a narrative of the death created by the coroner.[37] While coronial recommendations can focus intense concern on a social issue, they often reproduce discursive constructions such as poor single mothers as bad parents.[38] In this way, the inquest can serve to 'reinforce stigma, myths and stereotypes' of vulnerable populations.[39] Judgements about the physical aspects of the death are thus constructed within a framework of socio-political evaluations, and the inquest is as much about social relationships as it is causes of death.[40]

Exploring possible feedback loops

To further understand suicide determinations by coroners, a study into the administrative formulation of the category of suicide itself was undertaken. The methodology of the study is summarised briefly below.[41]

Method

All inquests involving possible suicides from 2004 to 2018 were examined, with 130 relevant inquests identified for inclusion. Four experienced full-time coroners each conducted 20 or more of these inquests, accounting for 97 (75%) of those included. Of the 130 inquests identified, 98 (75.4%) were found by the coroner to be a suicide, 19 had an open or undetermined finding, and 13 were found to be not suicide. All relevant inquests were examined to determine patterns in coroners' use of expert testimony and suicide research, particularly in the context of vulnerable groups (such as Indigenous persons, a minor, an inmate, or a mental health patient). Expert evidence can come from witnesses who are independently commissioned by the coroner as well as from persons such as treating doctors. Only the expert testimony of independent experts was used in this study. The nature and purpose of the testimony and research used was assessed. For testimony, this included assessing whether the expert was to determine whether the deceased's death was a suicide; whether the deceased had received adequate care from the hospital or treating team; and/or the specific cause of death. If suicide research was used by the coroner, it was assessed whether this scholarship discussed: suicide statistics and causes; reducing suicide risk; and/or the treatment of patients. Each inquest was qualitatively analysed using a deductive thematic analysis. We explored the inquests to determine the similarities and differences in the ways in which coroners engaged with expertise in coronial investigations into suspected suicide in different population types. To protect the anonymity of involved parties, all public inquests have been de-identified to the extent possible, prior to publication.[42]

36 Mandy Gray, "Pathologizing Indigenous Suicide: Examining the Inquest into the Deaths of C.J. and C.B. at the Manitoba Youth Centre," *Studies in Social Justice* 10, no. 1 (2016): 80.
37 Langer, "Distributed personhood," 95.
38 Kamal Kramar, "Coroners Interested Advocacy: Understanding Wrongful Accusations and Convictions," *Canadian Journal of Criminology and Criminal Justice* 48, no. 5 (2006): 811–30.
39 Gray, "Pathologizing Indigenous Suicide," 81.
40 Lindsay Prior, "The good, the bad and the unnatural: A study of coroner's decisions in Northern Ireland," *The Sociological Review* 33, no. 1 (1985): 64–90.
41 For a full description of the method, see Carpenter et al., "Coronial determination of suicide."
42 This publicly available research was gathered in 2019 as part of ARC Discovery project 150101402 and was approved by QUT Ethics – project ID 1116.

Findings

The purpose of this discussion is twofold: to provide a descriptive snapshot of the 130 inquests, by identifying the different ways in which expert testimony and suicide research are utilised in the inquests of vulnerable and non-vulnerable populations; and to more deeply engage with the inquests into Indigenous peoples, those in custody, and those in mental health facilities to demonstrate thematically the different ways in which suicide research and testimony are utilised. Following this, a detailed discussion of the feedback loop evidenced in these inquests is presented.

Descriptive analysis

Table 14.1 demonstrates that coroners utilised independent expert testimony and/or research in just over half of all inquests into suspected suicide (57%). Of those inquests, testimony was the most utilised, followed by a combination of testimony and research. Table 14.1 also demonstrates that most deceased who were the subject of an inquest into a suspected suicide were members of vulnerable populations (74%). Given the requirement for mandatory inquests of those who died in custody, because of issues arising from a police operation, or when a death in care raises issues about that care, this finding is expected. However, Table 14.1 also demonstrates that inquests into non-vulnerable populations were less likely to utilise independent expert testimony and/or suicide research to aid coroners in their decision making than inquests investigating the suspected suicide of vulnerable populations (56% vs. 39% respectively used neither form of expertise).

Table 14.2 demonstrates that coroners most often relied upon independent expert testimony in inquests into the suspected suicide of mental health patients and were less likely to rely on suicide research in these inquests. In contrast, use of a combination of

Table 14.1 Utilising research and testimony in vulnerable vs non-vulnerable populations

Population	Testimony n (%)	Research n (%)	Testimony and research n (%)	Neither n (%)	Total n (%)
Vulnerable	28 (29)	8 (8)	23 (24)	37 (39)	96 (74)
Not Vulnerable	7 (21)	2 (6)	6 (18)	19 (56)	34 (26)
Total	35 (27)	10 (8)	29 (22)	56 (43)	130 (100)

Table 14.2 Vulnerable population type, and use of research and testimony

Vulnerable population	Research	Testimony	Research and testimony	Neither	Total
Indigenous	4	-	6	6	16
Minors	–	3	3	3	9
Inmates, inc. police	6	4	11	29	50
Mental health patients	–	24	4	6	34

Note that some deceased appear in more than one category, and thus have been counted more than once (e.g., Indigenous inmate, Indigenous minor).

research and testimony, or research alone, appeared more often in all other vulnerable populations. Finally, those dying in custody or during a police operation were least likely have research or testimony utilised in their inquest proceedings.

Table 14.3 demonstrates that most of the independent expert testimony was utilised to determine adequacy of care for mental health patients.

Table 14.4 demonstrates that most of the research relied on by the coroner was on the causes and prevalence of suicide, as opposed to suicide prevention or suicide treatment, and was most utilised by coroners in the inquests into Indigenous peoples.

Table 14.3 Vulnerable population and type of testimony

Vulnerable population	Total	Suicide determination	Adequacy of care	Other
Not vulnerable	34	9	2	1
Indigenous	16	3	3	–
Minors	9	5	1	–
Inmates	50	9	7	1
Mental health patients	34	2	25	1

Note that some deceased appear in more than one category, and thus have been counted more than once (e.g., Indigenous inmate, Indigenous minor).

Table 14.4 Vulnerable population and type of research

Vulnerable population	Total	Causes and prevalence	Suicide prevention	Suicide treatment
Not vulnerable	34	6	1	3
Indigenous	16	8	2	1
Minors	9	3	2	–
Inmates	50	14	11	1
Mental health patients	34	4	2	2

Note that some deceased appear in more than one category, and thus have been counted more than once (e.g., Indigenous inmate, Indigenous minor).

These preliminary findings indicate different ways in which coroners make use of independent expert testimony and suicide research, which may be contingent upon the deceased's position – or not – in a vulnerable population considered susceptible to suicide. The subsequent qualitative findings further explore this suggestion of a variable feedback loop in the coronial determination of suicide with a focus on mental health patients, Indigenous people, and those in custody.

Thematic analysis

THE ROLE OF RESEARCH IN INQUESTS INTO THE SUSPECTED SUICIDE OF VULNERABLE POPULATIONS

The following excerpts reveal that research relied upon by coroners in inquests into the suspected suicide of Indigenous peoples was focused on their over-representation in suicide statistics, and the difficulty of preventing their suicide[43] – so much so that

43 Emphasis has been added to key themes in each excerpt.

recommendations from inquests were considered futile. Similarly, research relied upon in the inquests of those in custody reiterated their over-representation in suicide statistics, and how difficult such suicides are to predict or prevent. In contrast, research relied upon in inquests into suspected suicide of mental health patients was most often focused on prevention and treatment.

INDIGENOUS PEOPLE

The issue of suicide among Indigenous Australians has been studied at length. The facts revealed by those studies are alarming. For example, in one analysis it was demonstrated that the rate of suicide among Aboriginal men is twice that of the general population. When it is realised that Australia has one of the worst rates of suicide among the general population in the world, the magnitude of Aboriginal suicide is drawn sharply into focus ... **Regrettably, after reviewing the evidence presented in this case and having considered the literature that is readily available to me, I have come to the conclusion that Indigenous suicide is too complex a question for me to make meaningful preventative recommendations about.**

(Inquest 8)

The data relating to suicides indicates that there has been no reduction in suicide rates in recent years. Rates have remained relatively static. At the national level, suicide accounted for 2,520 deaths in 2013 at a standardised death rate of 10.7 per 100,000 people compared to the 2011 rate of 9.9 per 100,000 ... **Across Australia, young Indigenous Australians up to age 24 years are 5.2 times more likely to die due to intentional self-harm than other young people in the same age range.**

(Inquest 29)

He was a young male South Sea Islander. Research describes rates of suicide in Pacific Island countries as among the highest in the world. There is also American research identifying Pacific Islander youth at higher risk of depression suicidal behaviours, although no Australia specific research was cited ... Notably, [deceased] was a male who suicided in a post separation period following the breakdown of a personal relationship, which is a known high risk category of suicide occurring.

(Inquest 64)

Research utilised by coroners at inquests determines that Indigenous people are 'suicide prone.' It identifies an over-representation of this vulnerable population, their higher risk, and the limitations of prevention programmes in this 'complex' situation. The hopelessness, helplessness, and inevitability of suicide in this vulnerable population is thus made evident.

IN CUSTODY

Suicide is by far the single biggest cause of death among prisoners accounting for 46% of all prison deaths. In raw numbers, in the period 1980 to 2005, 520 prisoners took their own lives while the second most common cause of death was natural causes which accounted for 403 deaths. Prisons are viewed by many as dangerous places, yet in the same period homicide caused only one tenth as many deaths as suicide. Hanging is by far the most common mechanism by which prisoners take their own lives accounting for 90% of all cases. Research has consistently shown that **suicide in many cases is an impulsive action**.

(Inquest 42)

As this case demonstrates, it is impossible to identify with precision those prisoners who might take their own lives. Of the 552 suicides that have occurred in Australian jails since 1980, 90% have been hangings. Therefore, if gaol suicides are to be minimised, it is essential all prisoners are kept in cells that do not have hanging points.

(Inquest 43)

It is an accepted principle that prisoners should receive health care equivalent to that available in their community, without discrimination based on their legal situation. **Rates of the major mental illnesses, such as schizophrenia and depression, are between three and five times higher in offender populations than those expected in the general community.** Prison provides an opportunity for these health issues to be addressed. It is clearly not possible for those responsible for providing mental health services to prisoners to maintain adequate levels of service delivery within current resources in the face of the recent growth in prisoner numbers.

(Inquest 68)

For those in custody, research relied upon in the inquest supports the idea that this vulnerable population is also 'suicide prone'. Over-representation in suicide statistics is linked to an over-representation of mental illness, but prevention is largely focused on the removal of opportunities for self-harm, such as hanging points, rather than mental health support. This is justified by coroners due to the lack of resourcing, the overabundance of inmates, and the unpredictability of this vulnerable population.

MENTAL HEALTH PATIENTS

Firstly, as to environmental hazards: Issues related to the environment and access to means of suicide were identified by the Committee in 11 of 23 inpatient suicides and 1 of 7 unexpected deaths. In 8 of the 23 inpatient suicides the Committee identified structural issues relevant to the suicide including 4 cases where the patient jumped from the hospital car park. **In the prevention of suicide,** important environmental issues include the structure of wards and nearby facilities such as car parks and railway stations, access to the means of suicide such as hanging points and ligatures, and security in inpatient wards.

(Inquest 21)

Research has shown consistently there is a strong link between suicidality and mental illness, particularly those who are impacted by affective disorders such as major depression or bipolar disorder, schizophrenia and alcohol and other substance use disorders. **Effective treatment reduces the risk of suicide in those cases.**

(Inquest 56)

In contrast, the research used by coroners into inquests of mental health patients is only focused on prevention, adequacy of care, and lessons learnt. This is a population where suicide prevention is framed as certainly possible, and inquests seek to understand the failures that led to the death. This is not the case when inquests investigate the suspected suicide of Indigenous people or those in custody, where the difficulty, or impossibility of preventing the suicide is more the focus.

Independent expert testimony in the inquests of Indigenous peoples suspected of dying through suicide suggests that suicide is always a possibility, despite the lack of usual cues that would serve to indicate intent in others. In the inquests into suspected suicide of those in custody, expert testimony indicates not only the impulsivity evident in such suicides but also the risk factor of imprisonment itself. In contrast, the expert testimony in inquests of mental health patients suspected of dying by suicide is focused on the adequacy of care and treatment and the insight that inquests can offer suicide prevention in the future.

INDIGENOUS PEOPLE

> [Independent expert] considered that the [youth's] death was preceded by anger as a result of the argument with his older sister and intoxication from a combination of alcohol and illicit substances. Both factors have been found to increase the risk of suicide, particularly in young men. [Independent expert] considered that [youth's] suicide appeared to **be purely impulsive, which can occur as a result of the loss of the normal process of inhibition produced by both alcohol and inhaled solvents.** [Independent expert] considered there is no evidence that [youth] was experiencing suicidal ideation prior to his death and that his cousin's suicide was not sufficiently proximate to have played a significant role.
>
> *(Inquest 27)*

> The strange location of the incident, the manual dexterity that would be required to execute it and the use of an unusual ligature could raise some concerns as to whether the [child] was the sole author of his own demise. **I was assisted in resolving these doubts by the expert evidence of [independent expert], a psychiatrist with extensive experience in attending to mental health patients in Indigenous communities and a leading scholar in suicidology** ... He suggested the exposure of children to the unhappy fact of adult Aboriginal suicides in Aboriginal communities has led to an increase in child suicide. In that regard it is noteworthy that there had been a very large number of suicides in [community] in the years leading up to the [child's] death. **Against that background it is not as surprising as it may have first seemed that a [child] would commit suicide.**
>
> *(Inquest 1)*

Once again, the expert testimony relied upon by coroners in the inquests of suspected suicide of Indigenous people supports an inevitability of suicide, the lack of risk factors or cues, and the difficulty of prevention.

IN CUSTODY

> **A number of expert witnesses gave evidence to this inquest that [the inmate's] mental state made him susceptible to poorly controlled impulsivity.** It is not the case that if obvious opportunities to commit suicide are removed, all potential victims will find another way. Studies have shown that the placing of even minimal barriers will discourage numerous attempters. In prison this is even easier to effect as prisoners have such limited access to other means – this is why hanging is so often the method used: it is almost the only mechanism available.
>
> *(Inquest 42)*

> Overall I accept the proposition by [independent expert] that [deceased] received a good standard of mental health care, and possibly of a higher standard than he might have accessed had he not been incarcerated. **It cannot however be overlooked that incarceration itself is a circumstance documented to elevate the risk of suicide.**
>
> *(Inquest 48)*

> [Independent expert's] evidence was that [deceased's] case was complex and difficult, and his medical conditions placed him at risk of an aspiration event. **It was also clear that his will to live had fluctuated after he was faced with the prospect of an additional prison term for [further] offences.** This had led to a suicide attempt and subsequent refusal of food and medication.
>
> *(Inquest 71)*

For those in custody, expert testimony is utilised to explain the suicide, rather than to prevent it, and such explanations focus on poor impulse control, access to hanging points, and the burden of imprisonment on mental health, such that imprisonment itself becomes a key risk factor.

MENTAL HEALTH PATIENTS

> [Independent expert] was provided with all of the investigation material and prepared a report. She was asked to address a series of issues, **which centred on whether the deceased's treatment was appropriate and whether staff acted appropriately.**
>
> *(Inquest 41)*

> Expert opinion is that even absent any communication about a request, strong, persistent or otherwise for a hospital admission, the clinical picture warranted more aggressive action including an admission. **Her reasons for advancing this proposition have been discussed and I accept them.**
>
> *(Inquest 23)*

[Independent expert] engaged by the court to conduct an expert review of clinical management noted there is emerging literature demonstrating that risk assessment is of very little or no value whereas active treatment of mental illness is of value and has been proven to reduce suicide rates. **She considered [deceased's] deteriorating mental state, was noted by medical staff and responded to appropriately, with an increase in observations and the addition of an antidepressant.**

(Inquest 34)

Expert testimony in the inquests of mental health patients is utilised by coroners to seek out the gaps in care, treatment, and diagnosis that may have prevented the suicide.

These brief excerpts from inquests into the suspected suicide of three vulnerable populations reveal patterns in the use of research and testimony. To summarise, it was discovered that the theme of suicide prevention was most often utilised in the inquests of mental health patients, while the impulsivity of suicide in Indigenous peoples was most noted. Finally, inquests into inmates most often identified the risk that imprisonment itself posed in the suicide of the incarcerated. Together, these findings suggest a feedback loop between coroners, experts, and researchers that perpetuates disparate understandings of suicide depending upon the vulnerable population. For Indigenous people, research and testimony suggest suicide is often inevitable, and unable to be prevented. For those in custody, imprisonment itself is a key factor in the difficulty of suicide prevention, which is otherwise unpredictable. For mental health patients, however, there is always more to learn to prevent and treat suicide in the future.

Discussion

According to Prior, not only is medical, legal, and sociological evidence fused in an exercise of power within the coroner's court, but the 'dominance of suicide by sociological studies of unnatural deaths has created a legacy of misunderstanding about sudden death which has been hard to overcome'.[44] Such misunderstandings suggest a causal link between suicide and personal or social disorganisation, which was perpetuated by Durkheim,[45] given the associations he discovered between suicide and social integration. This created a tradition of connecting suicide to the moral weakness of social groups, enabling social characteristics associated with suicide rates to be positioned as characteristics which caused people to die by suicide. This positioning has produced a 'distinct social profile' of those who die by suicide, which have subsequently been used by coroners as 'cues' to classify unnatural deaths, and by researchers and experts as the raw data from which to draw their conclusions.

In research on coronial determinations of suicide, Tait et al.[46] found conventional and ill-informed ideas about Indigenous life and culture enabled coroners to situate Indigenous suicide as more understandable given their social and material deprivation. He also identified that coroners understood Indigenous suicide to be intrinsically different to non-Indigenous suicide and that this gave them permission to make disparate determinations. For example, alcohol was viewed by coroners as a protective factor for non-Indigenous

---

44 Prior, "The good, the bad and the unnatural," 71–2.
45 Emile Durkheim, *Suicide: A Study in Sociology* (London: Routledge and Kegan Paul, 1952 [1897]).
46 Gordon Tait, Belinda Carpenter, and Stephanie Jowett, "Coronial Practice, Indigeneity and Suicide," *International Journal of Environmental Research and Public Health* 15, no. 4 (2018).

suicides, but as a risk factor for Indigenous suicides, and therefore coroners were less likely to make a finding of suicide when non-Indigenous people were affected by alcohol, but more likely to make a finding when Indigenous people were affected. Similarly, in an analysis of four inquests into the suspected suicide of 45 Indigenous people in the Kimberly region of Western Australia, Carpenter et al.[47] discovered a medicalised discourse focusing on the sick Aboriginal body, a welfare/paternalistic discourse positioning Indigenous people as failing citizens and likely to indulge in risky behaviours, and a deficit discourse of Indigenous dysfunction. The pathologising narrative of these inquests has also been identified by Gray[48] and Razack.[49] All suggest that the inquest constructs Indigeneity itself as a suicide risk.

In contrast, mental health patients are investigated to determine if their care and treatment was adequate, and if their suicide was preventable. For mental health patients, the suicide risk resides in the hospital, in the doctors and nurses, and in the drug regime. Prevailing Western understandings conceptualise suicide as the result of mental illness, and much of our knowledge of suicide, and its treatment and prevention, comes from the disciplines of psychology and psychiatry. This has entrenched 'psycho-centrism' as the singular view of knowledge production, which 'diagnoses social problems and human struggles as innate pathologies of the individual'.[50] As a consequence, the related assumptions that suicide is pathological (suicide only occurs in the mentally ill) and individual (the risk of suicide can be located in the interior of a single subject) dominate research, clinical practice, and inquest narratives.[51] It is thus not surprising, given the unassailable belief in the truth of this first claim, that the only substantive discussions about suicide of mental health patients in inquests relate to the adequacy of drug regimes, access to cutting-edge treatments, or appropriate supervision, for it is these that form the 'principal line of defence' in the risk management of suicide.[52] Similarly, the strongly individualised understanding of suicide, as intentional and self-inflicted, positions suicide as a private and individual act, the result of a 'psychological or psychiatric disturbance', and/or an 'internal bodily pathology'.[53] In clinical practice and in the inquest, symptoms of the illness are accessible through the 'expert reading of a mental health professional'.[54]

Interestingly, such narratives and expertise are often missing from the inquests into the suicide of Indigenous people and those who suicide in custody, with such deaths conceptualised in 'sacrificial terms: as the wasteful loss of human life for a supposed gain in some public good'.[55] In the inquest, behaviours that lead to imprisonment are also considered to make prisoners vulnerable to suicide. These include adverse life events,

---

47 Belinda Carpenter, Megan Harris, Stephanie Jowett, Gordon Tait, and Rebecca Scott-Bray, "Coronial Inquests, Indigenous Suicide and the Colonial Narrative," *Critical Criminology* 29, no. 3 (2021): 527–45.

48 Gray, "Pathologizing Indigenous Suicide."

49 Shereen Razack, *Dying from Improvement: Inquests and Inquiries into Indigenous Deaths in Custody* (Toronto: University of Toronto Press, 2015).

50 Gray, "Pathologizing Indigenous Suicide," 81.

51 Ian Marsh, "Critiquing contemporary suicidology," in *Critical Suicidology: Transforming Suicide Research and Prevention for the 21st Century*, ed. Jennifer White, Ian Marsh, Michael Kral, and Jennifer Morris (Vancouver: UBC Press, 2016), 16–7.

52 Marsh, "Critiquing contemporary suicidology," 18.

53 Marsh, "Critiquing contemporary suicidology," 22.

54 Marsh, "Critiquing contemporary suicidology," 20.

55 Ian Loader, "A Question of Sacrifice: The Deep Structure of Deaths in Police Custody," *Social and Legal Studies* 29, no. 3 (2020): 403.

negative interpersonal relationships, social and economic disadvantage, alcohol and drug addiction, poor educational and employment history, low self-esteem, and poor problem-solving ability. The disadvantage, marginalisation, and vulnerability of the majority of prison inmates, alongside the challenges of imprisonment, suggest to Liebling that 'the prison population is carefully selected to be at risk of suicide'.[56] Focused on acute health care, energy is directed to containment and treatment, reinforcing a pathological approach reminiscent of the approach to mental health patients.[57] However, in prison, this psychiatric paradigm is inclined to perceive inmate distress as 'irrational and mean-ingless', 'manipulative and aggressive', or 'psychopathic'.[58] The link between vulner-ability to imprisonment and vulnerability to suicide suggests that the demands made on inmates by imprisonment not only exceed the resources available but also perpetuate a narrative of impulsivity rather than illness. This is supported by the focus in inquests on hanging points, or access to belts and sheets, as the means to prevent suicide, as opposed to failures in clinical diagnosis and treatment. The contrast between this focus and that seen in mental health patients is stark, despite significant overlap in the populations, and speaks to the importance of context in the feedback loops between coroners and experts.

Conclusion

The coronial jurisdiction has a mandate on bad deaths: the sudden, unexpected, or vio-lent. Inquests must investigate the bad deaths of vulnerable people in care and custody, and have the discretion to investigate others, 'in the public interest'. Inquests can also resolve doubt about cause and circumstance. This chapter has demonstrated that cor-oners are more likely to rely on independent experts' testimony and research when the deceased is a member of a vulnerable population suspected of dying by suicide. More-over, these external experts are used in varying ways depending on the populations under investigation. Inquests of mental health patients are most likely to rely on the expert testimony of medical doctors and psychiatrists, and are most interested in determining not if the death was due to suicide but whether it could have been prevented.

The dominance of the psy-disciplines in clinical, professional, and academic research, and the relationship between mental illness and suicide, is well established. The resultant pathologising and individualising narrative of suicide was most evident in the inquests of mental health patients but was also apparent in the inquests of Indigenous people and those in custody. However, outside of care settings it took a different form. Unlike the focus on prevention and adequate treatment in the mental health inquests, those investi-gating deaths of Indigenous people or those in custody instead sought answers to the cause and circumstance of the death, to determine whether it was suicide. Here, the inquests did not find the answer in the mental health of the deceased but rather in the impact of imprisonment or in the risk of Indigeneity itself.

This chapter began with the premise that suicide findings by coroners occur in a dis-cursive space that is filled with assumptions about the biography of people who die by suicide and common-sense understandings of the causes of suicide. These are dominated

56 Alison Liebling, "Vulnerability and Prison Suicide," *The British Journal of Criminology* 35, no. 2 (1995): 181.
57 Nick deViggiani, "Unhealthy prisons: Exploring structural determinants of prison health," *Sociology of Health and Illness* 29, no. 1 (2007): 115–35.
58 Liebling, "Vulnerability and Prison Suicide," 181.

by the psychology and psychiatry disciplines, but they are also historical, social, and cultural. The research presented in this chapter supports the premise that a feedback loop operates between coronial findings at inquest and expert testimony and suicide research, producing knowledge about suicide that supports the vulnerability of certain populations to such a death.

Bibliography

Aitken, David. "Investigating prison suicide: The politics of independent oversight." *Punishment and Society* 24, no. 3 (2022): 477–497.

Atkinson, J. Maxwell. *Discovering Suicide: Studies in the Social Organisation of Sudden Death.* London: Macmillan, 1978.

Atkinson, J. Maxwell. "Societal reactions to suicide: The role of coroners' definitions." In *Images of Deviance*, edited by Stan Cohen, 165–191. Harmondsworth: Penguin, 1971.

Carpenter, Belinda, Bridget Weir, Stephanie Jowett, Gordon Tait, and Claire Ferguson. "Coronial determination of suicide: Insights from inquests." *Mortality* (2022): 1–17. https://doi.org/10.1080/13576275.2022.2114823.

Carpenter, Belinda, Megan Harris, Stephanie Jowett, Gordon Tait, and Rebecca Bray Scott. "Coronial Inquests, Indigenous Suicide and the Colonial Narrative." *Critical Criminology* 29, no. 3 (2021): 527–545.

Coroners Court Queensland. *State Coroners Guidelines* (2013). www.courts.qld.gov.au/__data/assets/pdf_file/0013/206122/osc-state-coroners-guidelines-chapter-3.pdf.

Dartnall, Stephanie, Jane Goodman-Delahunty, and Judith Gullifer. "Exploring family experiences of missing person inquests through the eyes of professionals and the lens of therapeutic jurisprudence." *Psychiatry, Psychology and the Law* 30, no. 5 (2023): 1–25. https://doi.org/10.1080/13218719.2022.2085208.

deViggiani, Nick. "Unhealthy prisons: Exploring structural determinants of prison health." *Sociology of Health and Illness*. 29, no. 1 (2007): 115–135. https://doi.org/10.1111/j.1467-9566.2007.00474.x.

Douglas, Jack. "The sociological analysis of social meanings of suicide." *Archives of European Sociology* 7 (1966): 249–275.

Douglas, Jack. *The Social Meaning of Suicide*. Princeton, NJPrinceton University Press, 1967.

Durkheim, Emile. *Suicide: A Study in Sociology*. London: Routledge and Kegan Paul, 1952 [1897].

Freckleton, Ian. "Inquest Law." In *The Inquest Handbook*, edited by Hugh Selby, 1–10. Sydney: Federation Press, 1998.

Gray, Mandy. "Pathologizing Indigenous Suicide: Examining the Inquest into the Deaths of C.J. and C.B. at the Manitoba Youth Centre." *Studies in Social Justice*. 10, no. 1 (2016): 8–94. https://doi.org/10.26522/ssj.v10i1.1327.

Hindess, Barry. *The Use of Official Statistics in Sociology*. London: Macmillan, 1973.

Jowett, Stephanie, Belinda Carpenter, and Gordon Tait,. "Determining a suicide under Australian law: A comparative study of coronial practice." *UNSW Law Journal* 42, no. 2 (2019): 534–556. https://doi.org/10.53637/YMWD9017.

Jowett, Stephanie, Belinda Carpenter, and Gordon Tait. "Determining a suicide under Australia law." *UNSW Law Journal* 41, no. 2 (2018): 355–379.

Kramar, Kamal. "Coroners Interested Advocacy: Understanding Wrongful Accusations and Convictions." *Canadian Journal of Criminology and Criminal Justice* 48, no. 5 (2006): 811–830. https://doi.org/10.3138/cjccj.48.5.803.

Langer, Susan. "Distributed personhood and the transformation of agency: An anthropological perspective on inquests." In *The Matter of Death*, edited by Jenny Hockey, 85–99. London: Palgrave Macmillan2010.

Liebling, Alison. "Vulnerability and Prison Suicide." *The British Journal of Criminology* 35, no. 2 (1995): 173–187. https://doi.org/10.1093/oxfordjournals.bjc.a048492.

Loader, Ian. "A Question of Sacrifice: The Deep Structure of Deaths in Police Custody." *Social and Legal Studies* 29, no. 3 (2020): 401–420. https://doi.org/10.1177/0964663919874111.

Marsh, Ian. "Critiquing contemporary suicidology." In *Critical Suicidology: Transforming Suicide Research and Prevention for the 21st Century*, edited by Jennifer White, Ian Marsh, Michael Kral, and Jennifer Morris, 15–31. Vancouver: UBC Press, 2016.

Prior, Lindsay. "The good, the bad and the unnatural: A study of coroner's decisions in Northern Ireland." *The Sociological Review* 33, no. 1 (1985): 64–90. https://doi.org/10.1111/j.1467-954X.1985.tb00788.x.

Razack, Shereen. *Dying from Improvement: Inquests and Inquiries into Indigenous Deaths in Custody.* Toronto: University of Toronto Press, 2015.

Ryan, Terry. *Coroners Court of Queensland 2021–2022 Annual Report* (2022). www.courts.qld.gov. au/__data/assets/pdf_file/0018/750051/osc-ar-2021-2022.pdf.

Selby, Hugh. "Introduction." In *The Inquest Handbook*, edited by Harry Selby, v–xxiii. Sydney: Federation Press, 1998.

Tait, Gordon, Belinda Carpenter, and Stephanie Jowett. "Coronial Practice, Indigeneity and Suicide," *International Journal of Environmental Research and Public Health* 15, no. 4 (2018). https://doi.org/10.3390/ijerph15040765.

Taylor, Steve. *Sociology and the Study of Suicide*. Doctoral Thesis, University of Leicester. 1978.

Taylor, Steve. *Durkheim and the Study of Suicide*. London: Macmillan, 1982.

Taylor, Steve. "Shorter Notices: Book Review." *Sociology* 17, no. 4 (1983): 599–600.

Timmermans, Stephen. "Suicide determination and the professional authority of medical examiners." *American Sociological Review* 70, no. 2 (2005): 311–333. https://doi.org/10.1177/000312240507000206.

Walter, Tony. "Mediator Deathwork." *Death Studies* 29, no. 5 (2005): 383–412. https://doi.org/10.1080/07481180590932508.

Walter, Simon J., Lyndal Bugeja, Matthew J. Spittal, and David M. Studdart. "Factors predicting coroners' decisions to hold discretionary inquests." *Canadian Medical Association Journal* 184, no. 5 (2012): 521–528. https://doi.org/10.1503/cmaj.110865.

15

ACCOUNT-GIVING AND THE JUSTIFICATION OF RACIAL VIOLENCE IN INQUESTS OF BLACK PEOPLE KILLED BY POLICE

Carson Cole Arthur

Introduction

There is death and then there is its representation. One may say 'a', 'the', or 'simply' *death*. While 'a' or 'the' death denote an event, 'simply' death is the otherness of death. The event of death and the event of its representation are not identical but are inter-twined. If the former is a temporal point or period when life ends or comes to an end, then the latter is the knowledge-production of this passing or killing as a particular type of a death, which is a particular type of an event. The main focus of this chapter is on the representation of a 'death in police custody' where the deceased was a black person.[1] However, instead of highlighting and identifying the 'misrepresentation' of this event, such as the racial prejudicial views of police officers involved, I explore how racial vio-lence is inherent in the modes of narrativisation that the police officers engaged in when they provided an account and explanation of this event. Thus, this chapter's focus is not simply on representation (what is communicated) but self-representation (how an expla-nation is understood to be spoken and heard). I argue that the ethical framework of accountability in the Coroner's Court is a structure for the production of facts that serve to justify racial violence. Reading and examining the court transcripts of the inquest of Olaseni Lewis, killed by police in a mental health hospital in London in 2010, I will explore how the event of providing an account of this death was of more concern to the investigation than the death itself.

---

1 I write 'black' or 'blackness' in lowercase. This is because to capitalise the sociality and meta-physics of 'black' and 'blackness' would be to infer an absoluteness to the term and concept, which, following a *black mysticism*, goes against my perspective that *blackness* is ungraspable and immeasurable. Fred Moten, "Blackness and Nothingness (Mysticism in the Flesh)," *South Atlantic Quarterly* 112, no. 4 (2013): 737; Calvin Warren, *Ontological Terror: Blackness, Nihi-lism, and Emancipation* (Durham, NC: Duke University Press, 2018).

DOI: 10.4324/9781003304593-18

A 'death in police custody' is not *the* death that happened under police custodianship but the representation. This is not merely to make the seemingly obvious temporal distinction of then and now, of death and its subsequent narrative. On the contrary, these two temporal periods are entangled with one another, and it is this aporia or ambiguity that gives police officers space to rewrite and rearticulate reasoning and rationale. Further, in England and Wales, 'death in police custody' is not simply a category defined by the regulatory body, the Independent Office for Police Conduct (IOPC), but, narratologically speaking, it is also an ethical framework for police officers to provide explanations for their decisions and actions. I argue the governing principle and model for this ethical framework is accountability. However, it is crucial we distinguish *accountability* from *account-giving* while also recognising what is indistinguishable between the two. Accountability is not merely a political discursive value, as certain criminologists would have it.[2] More so, as I explore in this chapter, accountability is an episteme – a model for knowledge-production. In the Coroner's Court and the inquest process, accountability is a model for the mediation of facts, underpinning the ostensible fact-finding mission. However, this is mediated through the mode of account-giving – a performative and narrative process, as provided by the police officer. From account-giving, a representation and event are produced. A particular type of event that I will discuss is the concept of a *situation* – the very 'putting into place' of an event, for facts to be found. When an event is situated and provided context, the death of a black person is seemingly resolved based on pathological descriptions and a logic of causality[3] for the purpose of justifying their death. Yet this representation, this situation, requires a self-presence, whereby a police officer explains their (cognitive) understanding of the texts (voiced and written) that they provide to the court.

In the next section, I will further discuss the categorisation of 'deaths in police custody' as defined by the IOPC for England and Wales and challenge the alternative categories that criminology has come up with, explaining what I believe to be their limitations. From reflecting on how terms such as 'murder' and 'killing' also have their theoretical-conceptual limitations in the study of the deaths of black people, I move on to a brief overview of how black scholars have used different articulations of the notion of 'social death' to argue that, socially and ontologically, a black person is already always dead as inscribed by colonialism and modernity. Noting the lack of consideration for narrative in these studies on social death, I begin to explicate that this rendering of blackness as already always dead is constituted and instituted through speech/writing. Put another way, as I will argue, an event (e.g., a situation) is produced to contain and maintain racial violence within the situatedness and contextualisation of a spoken/written narrative. To elaborate on my use of the terms 'narrative' and 'narrativisation', I discuss the in/distinguishability of accountability and account-giving. I then move to focus on the inquest of Olaseni Lewis. Based on my deconstructive reading of the Coroner's Court's transcript, I provide examples of account-giving and the mediation of facts where descriptions of violence were attributed to blackness by the police officers involved. My intention is also to show how the account-giving of a police officer entails that they explain to the court how they 'read' and understand past statements.

2 David Baker, *Deaths After Police Contact* (London: Palgrave Macmillan, 2016); Ian Loader, "A Question of Sacrifice: The Deep Structure of Deaths in Police Custody," *Social & Legal Studies* 29, no. 3 (2020): 401.

3 Denise Ferreira da Silva, "Towards a Critique of the Socio-logos of Justice: The Analytics of Raciality and the Production of Universality," *Social Identities* 7, no. 3 (2001): 421.

Naming death and the dead

As I touched on above, 'deaths in police custody' is both a category and paradigm. 'Deaths in police custody' immediately contextualises a death as belonging to the societal issue of policing. It is formalised as such for it to be investigated, mainly and purposely for the IOPC, following a complaint procedure system. According to IOPC guidance:

> Under the Police Reform Act 2002, forces in England and Wales have a statutory duty to refer to the IOPC any complaint or incident involving a death which has occurred during or following police contact, and where there is an allegation or indication that the police contact, be it direct or indirect, contributed to the death.[4]

Thus, the concept of legal duty is bound up with 'deaths in police custody'.

The main categories and sub-categories of 'deaths in police custody' focus on the encounter of a police officer and a member of the public.[5] It is delimiting as a concept for criminological and sociological study as it is concerned with the isolated event of the encounter rather than the wider socio-political and cultural conditions that give rise to the encounter in the first place. It also seeks to isolate the event of a death from the investigation. However, to be investigated, the categorisation of a 'death in police custody' posits death within issues of police conduct, which makes it very hard for it to be considered a political issue related to the policing of black people in England and Wales.

Although Baker rephrases 'deaths in police custody' to 'deaths after police contact', he nevertheless follows the logic of the original category that places or rather situates a death according to a causality. A death happens *after* police 'contact' for Baker, as opposed to the police creating the conditions for death to occur. Conforming to a traditional police studies view, deaths after police contact is premised on the idea that the public's relation ultimately comes down to a 'police–citizen' encounter.[6] Like the IOPC, this perspective is also delimiting because it follows and reifies the notion that there is a good and bad practice of police and that this is measurable; that one can, for example, determine the proportionality of the use of force.

Arguably, whether 'deaths in police custody' or 'deaths after police contact', the terms 'deaths' or 'death' are used neutrally, mitigating the violence and injustice of the event. A more accurate term may be 'killing', 'murder', or 'extrajudicial' where force was used by the police. However, we should be cautious with these terms, given the carceral logic implicated within them.[7] Indeed, there is little evidence to suggest that state prosecution

---

4 Independent Office for Police Conduct, "Deaths During or Following Police Contact. Annual Report Guidance," accessed 4 January 2024, https://webarchive.nationalarchives.gov.uk/ukgwa/20220916120054/https://policeconduct.gov.uk/sites/default/files/Documents/statistics/Guidance_IOPC_Annual_Death_Report.pdf.

5 The IOPC disaggregate 'deaths in police custody' with the sub-categories of 'Road traffic fatalities', 'Fatal shootings', 'Deaths in or following police custody', 'Apparent suicides following police custody', and 'Other deaths following police contact'. The benefit for the IOPC is that deaths can be counted and allocated to these sub-categories based on criteria for quantitative analysis. On the basis of its remit, the IOPC investigates a death to establish whether a police officer has conducted themselves according to professional practice.

6 Geoffrey P. Alpert and Roger G. Dunham, *Understanding Police Use of Force: Officers, Suspects, and Reciprocity* (Cambridge: Cambridge University Press, 2004).

7 See Ashon T. Crawley, "Of Forgiveness," *Los Angeles Review of Books*, 25 February 2020, https://lareviewofbooks.org/article/of-forgiveness.

reduces police killings or violence. In regard to 'extrajudicial killings', when appropriated from countries ruled by a military dictatorship and applied to so-called liberal democratic countries, this term risks erasing transnational political differences. Moreover, 'extra-judicial' presupposes and maintains the idea that police can be within the law, just as they can also be above or exceed the law. A view commonly held by civil liberties orga-nisations and procedural justice theorists is that when police 'abuse' what they are legally authorised to do, they go against the public interest, breaking trust and damaging their relations with society. However, police or legal institutions more broadly are always excessive, for this is what makes them the law; that is to say, *law* is police and *police* is law.[8] While 'killing' emphasises the 'graphic' violence meted out, I contend that with removing the term 'death', what is forfeited is the tensive relationship death has with the status of *life*. Killing implies not just a carceral logic but a criminological logic, in the sense that motive and intention are demanded from this term.[9] By extension, there are thus connotations with issues of cruelty or brutality, which can have the counterintuitive effect of making 'killing' a principally moral issue rather than a political one. There are different reasons and strategies for using these terms, but each has certain limitations, especially if we are trying to attend to the onto-epistemological violence that undergirds racial violence. The terms 'killing', 'murder', and 'death' can slip and conform to a lib-eral notion of the police (i.e., for the public good) and sometimes be used to support the notion that black people have been 'dehumanised'. However, this moral humanism appeals to the ideality of humanity and does not consider that a black person has died or is killed because they were never regarded as human in the first place.[10] Thus, it is not that they were dehumanised; instead, it is that they were ontologically determined as non-human or non-being.[11]

Already always dead

To underscore the predetermination of blackness as death, Ferreira da Silva notes that a black person is always already dead, not simply due to the social relations of racial sub-jugation but due to a scientific and metaphysical logic.[12] For Ferreira da Silva, the death of a black person is irreducible to the social, for they are figured within the metaphysical dimension of transcendental thought. Put another way, for Ferreira da Silva, a black person is brought 'before the law' as already dead. It is not cultural difference or unconscious bias that perpetrates racial violence but the scene of thought and reason that violates a black person.

8 Jacques Derrida, "Force of Law: The 'Mystical Foundation of Authority'," in *Acts of Religion*, ed. Jacques Derrida and Gil Anidjar (London: Routledge, 2002), 230–98; Petero (petals) Kalulé and James (Tia) Trafford, "Unforming Police: The Impossibility of abolition," Critical Legal Thinking, December 1, 2020, https://criticallegalthinking.com/2020/12/01/unforming-poli ce-the-impossibility-of-abolition.
9 Jacques Derrida, *Death Penalty: Volume 2* (Chicago, IL: University of Chicago Press, 2017).
10 There are numerous black scholars who argue this in their own ways. Of particular note is Zakiyyah Iman Jackson, *Becoming Human* (New York: New York University Press, 2020), which sharply points out that even if we were to accept the terms, humanising is in itself dehu-manising for black people.
11 Warren, *Ontological Terror*.
12 Denise Ferreira da Silva, "Scene of Nature," in *Searching for Contemporary Legal Thought*, ed. Justin Desautels-Stein and Christopher Tomlins (Cambridge: Cambridge University Press, 2017), 275–89.

The *scene of nature* provides the ground or the setting for the *social event*, another term Ferreira da Silva conceptualises to explain how the death of a black person is resolved by legal institutions in terms of a racial event, and thus represented as being the natural order of things due to the pathologisation of a black person. This pathologisation seeks to explain that a black person is the cause of their own death. A black person does not merely embody death but is ontologically determined as dead or death. Through sociological or rather social logics,[13] the *social* of the *social event* functions to remove the death (or killing) of a black person from any connection to a political or criminal act. Based on social logics and pathological descriptions, through the social event, the death of a black person is rendered as a natural event.[14]

If a black person is already dead, how is this inscribed and repeated? To draw this out further, if there is a moral script – as Ferreira da Silva suggests, a moral text where blackness is (under)written as causative of death – what are the tools and modes by which this text is written? I argue one such mode is account-giving. As a performative and narrative mode, account-giving inscribes and ascribes anti-black violence through the representation of the social event. Attending to the textuality of account-giving moves us to consider how what produces the social event is a *situating* of decisions and actions. This situating functions to bring an event into an understanding, whereby an event is put into place, a representation is presented to the self, and where facts are founded to be found. Put another way, through the *situe*, a text is put into a context, and contextualised, for it to be read; however, this notion of (pure) reading 'after' writing or account-giving is a phantasy, for a text is always in the process of being written and voiced.

Accountability and account-giving

According to Baker, where there are multiple agencies involved in a death in custody, the different conceptualisations of accountability create interpretative conflict, leading him to call accountability a relational concept.[15] Thus, on the level of governmentality, for Baker, the value of accountability is inextricably linked to other measures and concepts such as consensus and legitimacy. Yet accountability is also synonymous with the concepts of answerability and responsibility, and it is precisely this homology that makes the conceptualisation of accountability resplendent with duplicity. As McKernan points out, the concept of accountability is frequently exchanged with answerability and responsibility, along with rationality and transparency.[16] When accountability is considered as an intersubjective relation, in which a calculative demand constricts how a subject provides an account, issues of morals and ethics arise, as certain critical accounting studies scholars have addressed.[17] As a result, with its obligation on a

---

13 Ferreira da Silva, "Towards a Critique."
14 Ferreira da Silva explains the social event in terms of tragedy, yet this is based on the view that tragedy is separate from law.
15 Baker, *Deaths After Police Contact.*
16 John Francis McKernan, "Accountability as Aporia, Testimony, and Gift," *Critical Perspectives on Accounting* 23, no. 3 (2012): 258.
17 Richard Boland, "Accounting and the Interpretive Act," *Accounting, Organizations and Society* 18, no. 2–3 (1993): 125; Stephen Darwall, "Taking Account of Character and Being an Accountable Person," *Oxford Studies in Normative Ethics* 6 (2016): 12; Peter Miller, "Accounting for the Calculating Self," in *Globalisation in Practice*, ed. Nigel Thrift, Adam Tickell, Steve Woolgar,

subject to account, to calculate, and to judge, accountability 'may undermine responsibility' to a certain extent.[18]

However, what is not considered, and is an even more pressing issue, is the interchangeability of *accountability* with *accounting* or rather *account-giving*. Too often accountability eclipses account-giving – and yet part of accountability's structure is for it to efface its performative and narrative aspects. Under the ethical imperative to be accountable or follow a professional procedure, the methods and modes for account-giving are forgotten, yet they are never completely erased; in the Coroner's Court, police officers cannot do without the writings and media of account-giving because they need them in order to provide explanations and reasons.

Account-giving is the providing of an explanation towards a justification. This is provided through language and speech; however, it is not a simple verbalisation of a statement. Account-giving is similar to testimony, for its principle conditionality is the *possibility* of fiction and mistakenness.[19] However, account-giving is more structured by a self-reflexivity and self-referentiality within its narrativisation.[20] In regard to investigations and inquests of deaths in police custody, accountability is the ethical framework that structures account-giving, with its principles and procedures of decision making contributing to justifications of the use of force on the premise of public 'safety'. What is important to underscore is that accountability is not simply an element but a governing epistemological structure – the dimension within which elements of decision making are active and, moreover, within which a narrative is mediated through account-giving.

Account-giving reflexively speaks of its very own conditions, possibilities, and *abilities* to account within and part of its narrative. It provides facts and provides for how it has the *capacity* to provide facts. It is not sufficient to speak of a fact but also necessary to speak of how one hears themselves speak of this fact. Account-giving requires a display of understanding from the subject on what they are cognised to within this providing. Moreover, a subject, or rather a self, can only account for itself. In short, one accounts for oneself. In a more general sense, only the person who has been assigned to a duty can speak of their decisions and actions related to that duty during an event under investigation. Put another way, a self cannot, or should not, account for another/the other. Yet the self is an other to itself in account-giving.[21]

Account-giving must give the impression that facts are exterior to its narrative. I argue that in inquests of deaths in police custody, particularly deaths of black people, this is

and William H. Rupp (Oxford: Oxford University Press, 2014), 236; Teri Shearer, "Ethics and Accountability: From the For-Itself to the For-the-Other," *Accounting, Organizations and Society* 27, no. 6 (2002): 541.

18 McKernan, "Accountability as Aporia," 262.

19 Carson Cole Arthur, "Make Believe: Police Accountability, Lying and Anti-Blackness in the Inquest of Sean Rigg," *Crime, Media, Culture* 19, no. 3 (2023): 362. https://doi.org/10.1177/17416590221131552; Jacques Derrida, *Demeure: Fiction and Testimony* (Stanford, CA: Stanford University Press, 2000).

20 Account-giving seeks to be reducibly a narrative, yet its narrativisation betrays this presumption. That is, while it may not sacrifice, it does not simply account, for it requires to demonstrate how it comes to narrate and understand both the narrative and its process of narrativisation. Put another way, the mediation of facts requires a conscious recognition of import. In the finding (found-ing) of a fact, the finding is just as important as, if not more important than, the 'fact' itself, whereby *finding* affirms and affirmed by *facticity*.

21 See Cathrine Bjørnholt Michaelsen, *Remains of a Self: Solitude in the Aftermath of Psychoanalysis and Deconstruction* (Lanham, MD: Rowman & Littlefield, 2021).

attempted with the narrative positionality of a situation. This situation puts into place an event – a placing that is always implicated with a replacing of an event.[22] Neither inferior nor superior to an event, a situation places decisions and actions in order to be found and accounted for.[23] The purpose of its construction is to maintain a logic of cause and effect. The narrative of the situation, that arranges cause and effect, supports a police officer in their account-giving insofar that it provides structure in which decisions and actions can be placed, contextualised, and understood. A common phrase in the inquest of Olaseni Lewis that officers either stated or evoked was that they were put into a situation not of their own making.

The inquest of Seni Lewis

Twenty-three-year-old Olaseni ('Seni') Lewis was killed on 31 August 2010 from restraint that lasted for over 40 minutes by 11 Metropolitan Police Service officers at Bethlem Royal Hospital (part of the South London and Maudsley NHS Mental Health Trust).[24] After carrying out a procedure called a cell extraction, which they had attempted for over half an hour, it was only after all officers exited the seclusion room that they noticed from an adjacent observation room that Lewis was unconscious.[25] They entered and performed CPR, with delays in retrieving a defibrillator. The London Ambulance Service eventually arrived to take over. Lewis was 'eventually pronounced dead on 3 September 2010'. The inquest, in 2017, concluded that:

> the Hospital Trust failed to meet training targets, that there was a lack of communication between police and medical staff, that the restraint was prolonged[,] disproportionate and unreasonable, that police failed to follow their training to administer basic life support, and that medical staff failed to respond to the medical emergency.[26]

Later that year, six police officers involved in Lewis' death were 'cleared of any misconduct at a Metropolitan Police disciplinary hearing'.[27]

22 This notion of the (re)placing of place in regard to touch is explored in Jacques Derrida, *On Touching, Jean-Luc Nancy* (Stanford, CA: Stanford University Press, 2005); Jean-Luc Nancy, *Corpus* (New York: Fordham University Press, 2008).
23 My thinking on situation draws slightly from Badiou, though it does not entirely adopt his sense of the concept. For Badiou, an event comes out from a situation; the situation is structured on a void or an absent cause of a truth. My interest is less in upholding an absolute idea of an event, nor do I follow Badiou that the truth and knowledge are oppositional. Rather, my intention is to attend to the eventfulness of the event and how this contextualises black social death as simply a 'social' death. For more on the philosophy of the eventfulness of the event, see François Raffoul, *Thinking the Event* (Bloomington: Indiana University Press, 2020).
24 INQUEST, "Inquest Opens into the Death of Olaseni Lewis Following Police Restraint at Bethlem Royal Hospital in August 2010," accessed 4 January 2024, www.inquest.org.uk/olaseni-lewis-inquest-opening.
25 Although his family prefer the first name Seni to be used, I use his last name, not with the intention to depersonalise him, but rather to denote specifically the *representation* (of Seni) within the police officers' account-giving.
26 South London Coroner's Court, "Inquest Touching the Death of Olaseni Lewis. Report to Prevent Future Deaths," accessed 4 January 2024, www.judiciary.uk/wp-content/uploads/2017/07/Olaseni-Lewis-2017-0205.pdf.
27 INQUEST, "Officers Cleared by Met of Gross Misconduct Following the Restraint Death of Olaseni Lewis," accessed 4 January 2024, www.inquest.org.uk/olaseni-lewis-officers-cleared.

Lewis's family 'brought him to hospital after he started to exhibit uncharacteristically odd and agitated behaviour'.[28] He was eventually transferred to Bethlem Royal Hospital. At this hospital, on the night of 31 August 2010, staff called the police after Lewis kicked a door, apparently causing damage to it. The first group of officers numbered five. They were requested to control Lewis and decided to move him to a seclusion room. In the first period of restraint, the five officers attempted a cell extraction – a procedure where officers force a detainee into a cell and then exit, with the detainee left locked inside alone. This attempt failed, with Lewis managing to reach the door before it was closed behind him. Officers pushed Lewis back into the seclusion room and restrained him for a second attempt.

Although some of the five officers had previously been called to mental health hospitals to assist with patients, it was nevertheless unusual for the police to be managing someone with mental health issues within a hospital setting. At the inquest, this was emphasised by the police officers to maintain the notion that the police should be the last resort for mental health emergencies and, further, that they were put into a situation not of their making and not within their role as police. This view influenced how officers described the events.

The situation concerned a problem–solution nexus: the problem that presented was to control Lewis, and the solution (assumed, as this was requested by hospital staff) was to detain or 'secure' Lewis in a seclusion room. This problem–solution nexus was symmetrical to the linearity of cause and effect. According to this logic, so long as there was no resistance, there would be no cause for police officers to use force. Relatedly, this situation was seemingly 'contingent' or subject to change. Such was the dynamism occurring within the situation.

Police officers described the situation at Bethlem Royal Hospital and with Lewis in terms of a dynamism (altering over course of time) and momentum (force). The situation here was subject not just to events at the time of death but also its subsequent accounts; that is, the putting into place and its explanatation were processed through repeated account-giving.

During the first attempt to move Lewis to the seclusion room, according to Police Constable (PC) Smith, Lewis's resistance was not expected. For the police, the situation immediately changed from escorting a voluntary Lewis to forcing Lewis into the seclusion room against his will. Following a logic of causality, this change reflected the dynamism that constituted the (police) situation – far from being a medical emergency, as the officers maintained in their account-giving at the inquest. This pivotal moment came down to a decision, an action, but also a word, bound up within a narrative.

PC Smith used the word 'push' in his previous statement, yet he was less inclined to call the action a 'push' at the inquest due to his concern at how it may be interpreted. As PC Smith expressed:

> Yes, it is a push and I don't want it sound like a push [*sic*], like we shoved him in like that [indicates]. It was controlled, in the sense that we were under each arm and we were pushing him as such, but it wasn't just a kind of letting – push him and see where he ends up.
>
> *(Day 16, p. 63)*[29]

28 INQUEST, "Inquest Opens."

29 Day and page number correspond to the Microsoft Word document of the transcript of the inquest of Olaseni Lewis, which was held at Croydon Coroner's Court, 6 February–9 May 2017. The jury recorded a 'narrative conclusion'. A transcript of the inquest was produced by the court and provided to the 'interested parties' of the inquest, including the legal representatives and the Lewis family (Chief Coroner's Guidance No. 4 ss 6 and 10). The transcripts have been provided to me by the lawyers of Lewis's family with their permission.

The Coroner directed PC Smith to not be preoccupied with what the court thought he was saying and instead speak from memory. According to PC Smith, the push (or pushing) was purposely done. PC Smith did not want to create the impression that the officers were not in control of the situation, yet he, as with the other officers at the inquest, attributed force not just to their actions but included Lewis. Indeed, in their account-giving, Lewis was described as the source of this force. Yet, according to the officers, it was supposedly undecidable how much Lewis was struggling. The narrative PC Smith related was one in which he, the other officers and Lewis were all taken by the force of the situation, of its momentum. His push was the build-up and built into a momentum that took all of them forwards, further into the situation. According to PC Aldridge, the dynamism of the situation altered his sense of time, and he claimed to be unable to say for certain the order of events because of this.

Considering the police felt compelled to attempt the cell extraction again, after Lewis reached the door, this reflected that while the situation had changed, the aim and objective were unmoved and remained the same. The officers placed handcuffs and leg restraints on Lewis and continued to physically restrain him. Lewis was unresponsive to a baton strike from one officer and the triggering of a pressure point by another. This suggests Lewis was experiencing Acute Behavioural Disorder (ABD) and required medical attention, but the officers carried on in their attempt to restrain and isolate Lewis. Instead of seeking medical professionals, the officers focused more on preventing positional asphyxia, so they claimed. 'Positional asphyxia' is a term that specifically relates to the risks of restraint; it describes the position a subject is put in when they are placed on their stomach, with their face down to the ground, or on their side. This weight, in addition to the weight on top of them from the restraint and downward pressure from being faced to the ground, reduces clear airway passage and can cause death if in this position for a prolonged period of time, especially if the subject is overweight, has alcohol or drugs in their body, or is experiencing a 'mental health crisis'. ABD describes behaviour with high levels of energy as innate and unique to the person who displays these signs, whereas positional asphyxia names a position the police should avoid having a person in.

One of the officers called for backup. Another group of six officers arrived soon after and switched roles with the original five. The police were committed to the situation, to accomplish the cell extraction; apparently, they could not leave Lewis as he was. According to them, this could have been a risk to his life and others, as they claimed he was resisting them and thus displayed violence. In some sense, Lewis was paradoxically in an inescapable position: he continued to try to escape – to resist and break free from the officers – yet there was no break, as PC Boyle expressed. Lewis's resistance was constant throughout, PC Boyle claimed. The only time it was safe to remove the mechanical restraints, withdraw physical restraint, and leave Lewis was when he stopped moving, and the police officers were no longer *moved* by his body, his corporeality, his ('super-human') force (day 19, p. 214).

Like many other deaths of black people in police custody, Lewis's death was related to issues such as race, policing, and mental health.[30] One of the many items the inquest examined was the police duty to prevent positional asphyxia, especially where the subject is suffering from ABD. Although police officers were asked if race was a factor in their

---

30 Eddie Bruce-Jones, "Mental Health and Death in Custody: The Angiolini Review," *Race & Class* 62, no. 3 (2021): 7.

treatment towards Lewis (which they all denied), the court did not examine and challenge the term ABD (also known as excited delirium) for its racial pathologisation.[31]

Accepting ABD as a term, for the use of it as a reference, the court examined the officers' assessment according to the police guidance at the time of Lewis's death. The officers in general maintained that although they may not have been fully aware or conscious of ABD, they were more focused on preventing positional asphyxia. The more the officers were challenged on ABD, the more they reiterated their defence that they were restraining Lewis to stop him from putting himself into positional asphyxia.

One of PC Boyle's previous statements read: 'I was aware of Lewis suffering from excited delirium.' The Lewis family's counsel examined PC Boyle on this during the inquest; PC Boyle insisted that the sentence was 'poorly written' and incorrectly worded and did not express what he intended to mean (day 19, pp. 217–25). The issue then became what this sentence actually meant and how it was supposed to be read. Yet, through this 'reading', a speaking and a writing would provide context. As PC Boyle explained, he basically used the wrong word; instead of 'aware', he meant 'conscious', yet he used this term to describe being cognised of a possibility, not necessarily perceptible to a reality. That is, this sentence from his previous statement was 'not to convey that I thought Mr Lewis was suffering from positional asphyxia. It's – I was conscious of it and I was trying to prevent that from happening. It's just poorly written' (day 19, p. 225). Put another way, according to PC Boyle, he was trying to prevent positional asphyxia from happening, not that he thought positional asphyxia had happened and thus needed to be stopped.

The Lewis family's counsel stressed the point that had PC Boyle been aware of ABD, he would have known that continuing the restraint would be a risk to Lewis's life. The strategy was to read the statement back to PC Boyle and suggest he was aware of the risk based on what he himself had written. However, in the inquest, the statement could not be merely read verbatim. The Coroner's Court required a 'reading' be given, but one in which it was heard what PC Boyle understood the meaning of his statement to be. Further into PC Boyle's examination by the Lewis family's counsel, the officer's counsel interjected and made the family's counsel read the sentence after the one in question: 'Due to this fact we continually attempted to move Lewis onto his left side to enable him to continue to breathe easily' (day 19, p. 225). The assumption then, seemingly accepted by the Coroner, was that the 'poorly written' sentence now made sense. The sentence that followed evoked the preventive rather than determinative. The contextualisation or situatedness altered the meaning of the previously cited sentence, seemingly making awareness and consciousness interchangeable, and positional asphyxia and ABD reconcilable. This apparently new context was produced paradoxically in reference to an old or pre-existent context: a pre-text – for the death of Seni Lewis.

Conclusion

The social event of the death of a black person in police custody is produced through a narrativisation (account-giving) that puts into place this event, exterior from account-giving; however, the two are invariably interrelated. The pathologicalisation of a black person, which aims to make the event of their death (or killing) a genre of a racial/urban

---

31 Sherene Razack, *Dying from Improvement: Inquests and Inquiries into Indigenous Deaths in Custody* (Toronto: University of Toronto Press, 2015).

event (i.e., explainable in terms of cultural difference), is produced not merely from a European self-determinate being of whiteness but a self-reflexivity within this sovereign being. The legal authority that determines the pathology and violence of blackness (that attributes cause to a black person) operates from a self-reflexivity, whereby legal authority presents to itself and puts into place an event.

Cell extraction is a procedure for the removal of police officers from a cell with a prisoner left locked inside. It typifies how officers acted towards Lewis: an object or thing to be disposed and placed in a self-contained room. Considered as a metaphysical operation, cell extraction is also a type of *situation*: the placing of an object, or rather an event, with the self attempting to be exterior to this placement. Yet, regarding the death and inquest of Seni Lewis, with this attempted cell extraction, officers were – as they claimed in their account-giving at the inquest – brought *into* the 'use of force': both the physical restraints (on one level) and the cause and effect of death (on another level). This procedure generated a force, a force that remained and increased over the course of events, and pulled officers back in as quickly as it had pulled them out, if only momentarily. Even if Lewis was resisting, as the police claimed, and thus working against them, he was, nevertheless, in the procedure, the situation, with them all; and in some respects, Lewis could be described as not simply embodying this force but, moreover, his body was *the* force.[32]

Lewis was described by officers in terms of forcing them into a situation. Racist, more specifically anti-black, pathologisation reduced blackness to resistance and violence, and thus the cause of death. This was narrated in the inquest, but what 'properly' established this narrative was the self-representation of the account-giving; that is, an account was not simply given but heard to have been given. Understanding and meaning-making (intentionality) formed part of the narrativisation. Thus, the production of an event, the putting into place of a situation, and providing context for meaning and resolution, was exercised through account-giving – a method of consciousness and writing, as structured by the episteme of accountability. In the Coroner's Court, this episteme is of an ethical framework that, rather than investigating a death, investigates its knowledge and knowing of a death towards its production as an event. We cannot entirely separate the two. Yet it is precisely the indeterminacy of the experience of death and the event(-ing) of death that hold and sustain anti-black and racial violence.

Bibliography

Alpert, Geoffrey P., and Roger G. Dunham. *Understanding Police Use of Force: Officers, Suspects, and Reciprocity*. Cambridge: Cambridge University Press, 2004.

Arthur, Carson Cole. "Make Believe: Police Accountability, Lying and Anti-Blackness in the Inquest of Sean Rigg." *Crime, Media, Culture* 19, no. 3 (2023): 362–379. https://doi.org/10.1177/17416590221131552.

Baker, David. *Deaths After Police Contact*. London: Palgrave Macmillan, 2016.

Barrett, Lindon. *Seeing Double: Blackness and Value*. Cambridge: Cambridge University Press, 1999.

Boland, Richard. "Accounting and the Interpretive Act." *Accounting, Organizations and Society* 18, no. 2–3 (1993): 125–146.

Bruce-Jones, Eddie. "Mental Health and Death in Custody: The Angiolini Review." *Race & Class* 62, no. 3 (2021): 7–17.

---

32 On the relation of blackness and force, see Lindon Barrett, *Seeing Double: Blackness and Value* (Cambridge: Cambridge University Press, 1999).

Crawley, Ashon T. "Of Forgiveness." *Los Angeles Review of Books*, 25 February 2020. https://larevie wofbooks.org/article/of-forgiveness/.

Darwall, Stephen. "Taking Account of Character and Being an Accountable Person." *Oxford Studies in Normative Ethics* 6 (2016): 12–36.

Derrida, Jacques. *Demeure: Fiction and Testimony*. Stanford, CA: Stanford University Press, 2000.

Derrida, Jacques. "Force of Law: The 'Mystical Foundation of Authority'." In *Acts of Religion*, edited by Jacques Derrida and Gil Anidjar, 230–298. London: Routledge, 2002.

Derrida, Jacques. *On Touching, Jean-Luc Nancy*. Stanford, CA: Stanford University Press, 2005.

Derrida, Jacques. *Death Penalty: Volume 2*. Chicago, IL: University of Chicago Press, 2017.

Ferreira da Silva, Denise. "Towards a Critique of the Socio-logos of Justice: The Analytics of Raciality and the Production of Universality." *Social Identities* 7, no. 3 (2001): 421–454.

Ferreira da Silva, Denise. "Scene of Nature." In *Searching for Contemporary Legal Thought*, edited by Justin Desautels-Stein and Christopher Tomlins, 275–289. Cambridge: Cambridge University Press, 2017.

Jackson, Zakiyyah Iman. *Becoming Human*. New York: New York University Press, 2020.

Kalulé, Petero, and James Trafford. "Unforming Police: The Impossibility of Abolition." *Critical Legal Thinking*, 1 December 2020. https://criticallegalthinking.com/2020/12/01/unforming-poli ce-the-impossibility-of-abolition.

Loader, Ian. "A Question of Sacrifice: The Deep Structure of Deaths in Police Custody." *Social & Legal Studies* 29, no. 3 (2020): 401–420.

Independent Office for Police Conduct. "Deaths During or Following Police Contact. Annual Report Guidance." Accessed 4 January 2024. https://webarchive.nationalarchives.gov.uk/ukgwa/ 20181001115207/https://www.policeconduct.gov.uk/sites/default/files/Documents/statistics/Guida nce_IOPC_Annual_Death_Report.pdf.

INQUEST. "Inquest Opens into the Death of Olaseni Lewis Following Police Restraint at Bethlem Royal Hospital in August 2010." Accessed 4 January 2024. www.inquest.org.uk/olaseni-lewi s-inquest-opening.

INQUEST. "Officers Cleared by Met of Gross Misconduct Following the Restraint Death of Olaseni Lewis." Accessed 4 January 2024. www.inquest.org.uk/olaseni-lewis-officers-cleared.

Nancy, Jean-Luc. *Corpus*. New York: Fordham University Press, 2008.

McKernan, John Francis. "Accountability as Aporia, Testimony, and Gift." *Critical Perspectives on Accounting* 23, no. 3 (2012): 258–278.

Michaelsen, Cathrine Bjørnholt. *Remains of a Self: Solitude in the Aftermath of Psychoanalysis and Deconstruction*. Lanham, MD: Rowman & Littlefield, 2021.

Miller, Peter. "Accounting for the Calculating Self." In *Globalisation in Practice*, edited by Nigel Thrift, Adam Tickell, Steve Woolgar, and William H. Rupp, 236–241. Oxford: Oxford University Press, 2014.

Moten, Fred. "Blackness and Nothingness (Mysticism in the Flesh)." *South Atlantic Quarterly* 112, no. 4 (2013): 737–780.

Raffoul, François. *Thinking the Event*. Bloomington: Indiana University Press, 2020.

Razack, Sherene. *Dying from Improvement: Inquests and Inquiries into Indigenous Deaths in Custody*. Toronto: University of Toronto Press, 2015.

Shearer, Teri. "Ethics and Accountability: From the For-Itself to the For-the-Other." *Accounting, Organizations and Society* 27, no. 6 (2002): 541–573.

South London Coroner's Court. "Inquest Touching the Death of Olaseni Lewis. Report to Prevent Future Deaths." Accessed 4 January 2024. www.judiciary.uk/wp-content/uploads/2017/07/Olaseni-Lewis-2017-0205.pdf.

Warren, Calvin. "Black Mysticism: Fred Moten's Phenomenology of (Black) Spirit." *Zeitschrift für Anglistik und Amerikanistik* 65, no. 2 (2017): 219–229.

Warren, Calvin. *Ontological Terror: Blackness, Nihilism, and Emancipation*. Durham, NC: Duke University Press, 2018.

16

CONTESTED DEATH AND THE CORONIAL JURISDICTION

Rebecca Scott Bray

Introduction

In September 2022, the inquest into the death of 19-year-old Warlpiri young man Kumanjayi Walker commenced in Alice Springs, in the Northern Territory, Australia. The inquest followed the April 2022 acquittal of police constable Zachary Rolfe for the murder of Kumanjayi Walker. Kumanjayi Walker's inquest bears all the hallmarks of the contemporary inquest in the digital age. It was live-streamed from the Alice Springs courthouse, with transcripts, rulings and orders, image evidence, and documents posted online each day. The daily witness list was published, along with court sitting times and days, and, significantly, the inquest was translated into local Warlpiri language. Not only was the inquest accessible to community and publics with its online presence, but it also reflected community concerns via its scope, which considered whether systemic racism played a part in Kumajayi Walker's death. This scope acknowledges the significance of colonisation and its impact on the lives and deaths of First Nations peoples in Australia's criminal legal systems. Notwithstanding the inquest's digital innovations, unparalleled in Australian coronial practice, this was not the first inquest to examine such issues within scope. Over the past five years, a number of Australian inquests into the deaths of First Nations peoples have included issues of racism in scope, including inquests into the deaths of Yorta Yorta woman Tanya Day and Gunditjmara, Dja Dja Wurrung, Wiradjuri, and Yorta Yorta woman Veronica Nelson in Victoria, or of unconscious bias, such as the inquest into the death of Wiradjuri woman Naomi Williams in New South Wales. These inquests, and others, highlight how coronial investigations into contested deaths, such as those in custody or in care, are critical moments where scrutiny of the state's relationship to and with its citizens is changing.

Coronial fact-finding is officially conceived of as a narrow exercise that does not 'address general political problems about power, values, interests and resources'.[1] Dominic Aitken surmises that independent oversight bodies, such as coroners, 'avoid more difficult questions', including about 'the meaning of pain in punishment'.[2] Instead,

---

1 Dominic Aitken, "Investigating Prison Suicides: The Politics of Independent Oversight," *Punishment & Society* 24, no. 3 (2022): 493.
2 Aitken, "Investigating Prison Suicides," 493.

deaths are dealt with on a case-by-case basis. It is in this sense, Aitken argues, that coronial investigations are examples of depoliticisation. When a contested death occurs, such
as a death in custody, attention is deflected away from those running prisons, for example, and 'onto depoliticised bodies comprised of independent professionals'.[3] Depoliticisation denotes 'efforts to dial down the ideological content of political questions', where
'value-laden policy questions' are recast as 'technical challenges'.[4] According to this
schema, in the case of deaths in custody, coronial investigations are not about examining
the intractability of the prison estate and the carceral agenda, but concern individual fact-
finding about the 'how' of a specific death leaving the broader 'why' untouched.[5] However, these fatal events expose normative death-making state practices, which, in the case
of incarceration – with its litany of fatal risks around restraint, suicide, health disparities,
and so on – 'require us to think about ... not only *how* we punish, but *why*'.[6] This
chapter argues that despite inquests' depoliticised status, this does not tell the complete
story of coronership in contemporary society.

This chapter contends that some contemporary cases highlight a moment of political
imagination in death investigation, where the tussle between how the state sees itself in
relation to its citizens and non-citizens, and how the coronial process sees fit to intervene
in that relationship is evident. This is a potentially transformative moment, advanced by
the complexion of open justice in a digital age, a structured rights-based era and strong
community advocacy. The contention is that the digitalisation of death politics enabled
by the open justice principle has led to new 'death democracies' which challenge both
coroners and conventional policy ideas about not only vulnerability and marginalisation,
but also inquest matters such as scope, evidence, findings, inquest commentary, and participation. Drawing on contemporary case studies of contested deaths in custody, the
chapter explores how coronial scrutiny of contentious deaths spills out of the inquest
space and is contemporaneously interrogated by communities and across digital media, to
the effect that understandings about 'contested' deaths in the coronial jurisdiction are
being tested and expanded. These challenges reflect a critical community of practice
around deaths that enjoins bereaved communities, advocates, non-state actors, and others
such as journalists, who resist established narratives and push coronial practice into new
realms. Here, coronial openness and scrutiny are underwritten by revised scope and a
deeper understanding of the political life of death, signalling the emergent possibility of a
more responsive coronial jurisdiction.

Open justice in coronial courts

The focus of this chapter is on Australian coronial inquests: inquisitorial, public, fact-
finding hearings that aim to ascertain the identity of the person who died, the time and
place, and the cause and circumstances of their sudden, unexpected, or unnatural death,
often referred to as the 'who, where, when, what, and how' of fatality. Coronial jurisdictions globally have attempted to modernise coronial law and practice, seeking to
address systemic delays, upgrade forensic medical practices, recognise the rights and role
of families, respect cultural and religious beliefs and practices, elevate the preventive

---

3 Aitken, "Investigating Prison Suicides," 492.
4 Aitken, "Investigating Prison Suicides," 491.
5 Aitken, "Investigating Prison Suicides," 493.
6 Aitken, "Investigating Prison Suicides," 493, emphasis in original.

principle, and centre the importance of communication with the public. This latter aim reconciles the evolving publicity of and engagement with coronial courts aligned with the open justice principle, which now takes effect within a digitally literate culture. The open justice principle, plainly stated, is the principle that the administration of justice must take place in public, affording access, transparency, and public awareness and scrutiny, which contributes to public confidence in the courts, such that '[t]he security of securities is publicity'.[7]

Research around open justice largely accounts for trial practices in civil or criminal courts, not inquests in coroners' courts. Coronial researchers have argued that open justice in inquests should be understood very differently to how it is applied to civil and criminal justice contexts, where it is typically considered a procedural principle and an instrumental aid to ensuring a fair trial.[8] Observing UK coroners' inquests, Sam McIntosh argues that open justice in inquests is less associated with ensuring fair and proficient conduct than with 'a need for accountability regarding *the subject matter under investigation*'.[9] This need is necessarily contextualised by inquests being non-retributive and non-compensatory, unlike fora such as criminal courts. McIntosh argues that open justice as traditionally conceived is too narrow for inquests – we must also consider 'the practice of openness as manifested *through* inquests'.[10] This entails reflecting on when an inquest is held, inquest scope, and its openness to public participation.

Commenting specifically on use-of-force deaths, McIntosh emphasises that learning about the circumstances of death is not merely a taken-for-granted presumptive right for families and the public, but is a part of the core scrutiny and accountability purposes of inquests into contested deaths that underwrite openness in coronial contexts.[11] This means that scrutiny of and accountability for deaths in contested circumstances intrinsically require openness. Central to this is recognition of individuals as rights bearers and valued community members who suffer harm following contested deaths, such as deaths at the hands of the state, and considering the ways in which families and their communities are recognised as having 'enhanced' interests in the inquest process, as well as appreciating the additional harms that accrue when the state inadequately responds to a death.[12] The broader public too have different but important interests in inquests, underpinned by a right to scrutinise the exercise of fatal state power and 'the right to participate as an informed citizenry in wider debates about the use of force by the state'.[13] As McIntosh correctly asserts:

> If we are to reflect upon and engage with related questions – about how, for example, we recruit, train and oversee our police forces; about the implications of routinely arming the police with tasers or firearms; about the conditions and staffing levels in our prisons; and about the realities of how the criminal justice system manages the vulnerable, the mentally ill and those with drug dependencies – we need to be properly informed about them.[14]

7 *Scott v Scott* [1913] A.C. 417, at 477–8 (Lord Shaw).
8 Sam McIntosh, "Taken Lives Matter: Open Justice and Recognition in Inquests into Deaths at the Hands of the State," *International Journal of Law in Context* 12, no. 2 (2016): 144.
9 McIntosh, "Taken Lives Matter," 144, emphasis in original.
10 McIntosh, "Taken Lives Matter," 142, emphasis in original.
11 McIntosh, "Taken Lives Matter," 144.
12 McIntosh, "Taken Lives Matter," 151–2.
13 McIntosh, "Taken Lives Matter," 151–2.
14 McIntosh, "Taken Lives Matter," 152.

For McIntosh, however, the link between openness and justice in these fatal contexts is not reducible to the traditional court–media relationship, but engages participatory rights in democratic societies.

Drawing on recognition theory to explore the significance of openness in inquests, McIntosh notes that they can adequately respond to state-related deaths in a rights-based era, given that inquests are public and produce official and public narratives about how someone died, with a reasonably broad scope. Families can attend and participate, representing their interests and also the interests of their community and the wider public.[15] McIntosh acknowledges concerns about whether these interests are adequately recognised in practice, or are in fact misrecognised and cause further harm, nevertheless proposing there are tangible benefits for an approach to *justice as recognition* in the coronial context. For example, framing recognition seriously in the coronial context can reinforce the need for greater legal aid for families, tackle systemic issues such as inquest delays, and support more radical reform such as supporting the role of human rights interveners at inquest.[16] Before returning to the implications of this for death investigation in expanding digital cultures across differing political landscapes, the chapter considers the distinctiveness of coronial evolution in Australia.

Tracking different jurisdictional rites around rights

McIntosh is parsing issues in the context of use-of-force death investigation in England and Wales, a jurisdiction bound by the European Convention on Human Rights (ECHR) obligations through the *Human Rights Act 1998* (UK) (HRA). Significant influence has come from Article 2, the right to life, and human rights litigation has determined what the ECHR requires of death investigations following 'Article 2' cases, such as deaths in custody, from defining the purposes of Article 2 death investigations,[17] the investigative conduct required,[18] to clarifying approaches to considering 'how' a person died, and what the ECHR requires of verdict, judgment, findings, or recommendations.[19] Human rights litigation highlights how accountability is imagined in a rights-based era, where not only human rights breaches are scrutinised, but also death investigation processes themselves, impacting how contested deaths are defined, and how they are investigated.

The evolving trajectory for death investigation of contested cases differs in Australia. In distinction to the UK, the absence of a European-style human rights framework means Australia takes an ad hoc approach to human rights recognition, including in terms of formal systemic scrutiny. Australia is a signatory to human rights treaties,[20] but only three out of eight jurisdictions in Australia give some local effect to human rights,[21]

15 McIntosh, "Taken Lives Matter," 158.
16 McIntosh, "Taken Lives Matter," 158. See also Rebecca Scott Bray, "Death Investigation, Coroners' Inquests and Human Rights," in *The Routledge International Handbook of Criminology and Human Rights*, ed. Leanne Weber, Elaine Fishwich, and Marinella Marmo (Abingdon: Routledge, 2017).
17 *Jordan v United Kingdom* (2003) 37 EHRR 2 [105]; *R (Amin) v Secretary of State for the Home Department* [20], [31].
18 See, e.g., *Jordan v United Kingdom* [105–109]; *R (Amin) v Secretary of State for the Home Department*; *Edwards v United Kingdom* [69–73].
19 *R (Middleton) v HM Coroner for West Somerset*.
20 *International Covenant on Civil and Political Rights* (ICCPR) and the *International Covenant on Economic, Social and Cultural Rights* (ICESCR).
21 Those jurisdictions are the Australian Capital Territory, Victoria, and Queensland: *Human Rights Act 2004* (ACT); *Charter of Human Rights and Responsibilities Act 2006* (Vic); *Human Rights Act 2019* (Qld).

which provide for rights-protecting legislative scrutiny and require that public authorities act consistently with human rights. These instruments lack the ECHR's 'array of teeth' with respect to effective enforcement of obligations and breach remedies.[22]

It has been argued that despite this, Australian coronial law and practice is 'fashioned and influenced by considerations that are respectful of human rights',[23] evidenced by reform provisions concerning post-mortem examination practices, acknowledgement of cultural concerns, and the rights and role of families in the coronial process, including objections to coroner's decisions, matters not comparatively legislated for in UK coronial law. Further, Australia's focus on death prevention is, in principle, faithful to right-to-life obligations. Those obligations demand an independent inquiry into deaths[24] and the capacity for lessons learned through an enshrined preventive principle guiding the recommendatory role.[25] And, as a matter of standard practice, Australian coronial fact-finding in contested death cases echoes ECHR obligations as determined by the courts. Following *R (Middleton) v HM Coroner for West Somerset*, Article 2 inquests must take a broad approach to the question of 'how' the deceased died, interpreting it as 'by what means and in what circumstances',[26] a decision which recognised the limitations of traditional short-form verdicts, and how narrative conclusions provide greater scope for juries to express the surrounding circumstances of a death.[27] In Australia, it is established that the phrase 'how the death occurred' should be given the broad construction of 'by what means and in what circumstances the death occurred'.[28] Correspondingly, a narrative findings style with robust contextual fact-finding has long been a common feature of Australian coronial practice and is much more discursive than the most extensive UK narrative conclusions.

In addition to Charter responsibilities increasingly addressed in coronial findings in specific jurisdictions, human rights find effect in Australian coronial practice in other ways, including via human rights interveners in inquests: what McIntosh refers to as an aspect of 'radical reform' offered through a justice-as-recognition approach to contested death investigation.[29] Interveners are granted leave to appear as interested parties to assist the coroner with a range of matters, including identifying human rights issues, understanding the relationship between those rights and the circumstances of death, and appreciating state obligations with respect to the implementation and protection of human rights, with interveners making submissions on matters such as inquest scope and coronial recommendations with often effective outcomes.[30] This move towards a more

---

22 Ian Freckelton and Simon McGregor, "Coronial Law and Practice: A Human Rights Perspective," *Journal of Law and Medicine* 21, no. 3 (2014): 587.
23 Freckelton and McGregor, "Coronial Law and Practice," 599.
24 *Jordan v United Kingdom* [105–109].
25 *R (Amin) v Secretary of State for the Home Department*, [31]. See Scott Bray, "Death Investigation."
26 *Coroners and Justice Act 2009* (UK) s. 5(2).
27 *R (Middleton) v HM Coroner for West Somerset* [35]. *R (Ali Zaki Mousa) v Secretary of State for Defence (No 2)* [148]–[149], [221].
28 *Conway v Jerram* (2010) 78 NSWLR 371; *Atkinson v Morrow* [2005] QSC 92; *Atkinson v Morrow* [2005] QCA 353.
29 McIntosh, "Taken Lives Matter," 158.
30 See, for instance, Inquest into the death of Mulrunji Doomadgee; Inquest into the death of Elder Ward; Inquest into the death of Tyler Cassidy. See Jonathon Hunyor, "Disgrace: The Death of Mr Ward," *Indigenous Law Bulletin* 7, no. 15 (2009): 3–8; Jonathon Hunyor, "Human Rights in Coronial Inquests," *Australian Indigenous Law Review* 12, no. 2 (2008): 64–74; Freckelton and McGregor, "Coronial Law and Practice."

rights-responsive jurisdiction has been enabled by human rights stakeholders, who have the capacity to shape the coronial process by movement lawyering in the coronial space, which, in the Australian settler-colonial context, is textured by Indigenous sovereignty and self-determination.

Australian coronial law and practice developed far from the metropole, and coronial death investigation proceeded in the context of invasion, dispossession, settler-colonial violence, and genocide of sovereign peoples.[31] Examining inquest records into Aboriginal deaths involving the Queensland Police, Mark Finnane and Jonathan Richards document substantial inquest industry but little accountability for deaths. Amanda Nettlebeck and Robert Foster similarly conclude that inquests were an instrument of colonial governance and, by their ineffectiveness as an accountability process, evidence that 'securing the interests of settlers was the first task of the rule of law'.[32] Death investigation was difficult; fatal violence was concealed, and views of the body so central to the inquest (*super visum corporis*) were prevented by deliberate destruction, such as through the burning of bodies. Juries were difficult to assemble in remote areas, and regional expanse meant that police magistrates and justices of the peace conducted inquiries in a coroner's absence.[33] The police were central to the administrative power of death investigation, and this reliance on police work continued subsequent to the development of juristic and medico-legal expertise.

The pivotal relationship between coroners and police has been criticised and still remains firmly under the spotlight. Most notably, it was scrutinised by the Royal Commission into Aboriginal Deaths in Custody (RCIADIC), which was established in 1987 to investigate Aboriginal custodial deaths and sought recognition of, and greater expectations for, the coroner's role in death prevention following Indigenous deaths in custody, and the call for an enshrined legislative response in respect of these duties.[34] The RCIADIC's 1991 *National Report*, revealed 'the pervasive and troubling failure' of the coronial system in every Australian state and territory to uncover the circumstances of Aboriginal deaths in custody.[35] It also highlighted the limitations of coronial legislation, including the inadequacy of statutory provisions around coronial recommendations which accorded them low priority, hence marginalising their preventive potential.[36] The RCIADIC noted issues with the exercise of coronial powers; that the prescribed coronial fact-finding task in deaths in custody was of 'narrow focus', a 'tunnel vision' which meant that coronial investigations into deaths in custody excluded a consideration of wider issues in inquest

---

31 Mark Finnane and Jonathan Richards, "'You'll Get Nothing Out of It'? The Inquest, Police and Aboriginal Deaths in Colonial Queensland," *Australian Historical Studies* 35, no. 123 (2004): 91, 105; see also Marc Trabsky, *Law and the Dead: Technology. Relations and Institutions* (Abingdon: Routledge, 2019).

32 Amanda Nettelbeck and Robert Foster, "Colonial Judiciaries, Aboriginal Protection and South Australia's Policy of Punishing 'with Exemplary Severity'." *Australian Historical Studies* 41, no. 3 (2010): 331.

33 Lee Butterworth, "What Good is a Coroner? The Transformation of the Queensland Office of Coroner 1859–1959", Doctoral Thesis, Griffith University, 2012.

34 Mark Thomas, Nigel Stobbs, and Geraldine Mackenzie, "'What Really Happened' Versus 'What We Can Prove': Tension Between the Roles of Coroner and DPP in Queensland," *Indigenous Law Bulletin* 6, no. 24 (2006): 7.

35 Ray Watterson, Penny Brown, and John McKenzie, "Coronial Recommendations and the Prevention of Indigenous Death," *Australian Indigenous Law Review* 12, no. 2 (2008): 6.

36 Royal Commission into Aboriginal Deaths in Custody (RCIADIC), *National Report, Vol. 1* (1991) [4.5.87]–[4.5.89].

scope, such as the quality of custodial care, treatment, and supervision of the person prior to their death.[37] The RCIADIC was notable for the attention it brought to the Australian coronial process and the issue of Indigenous death prevention, including through inquest scope.

For Indigenous deaths in custody, specific histories are petitioned around social and legal injustice, policing, and incarceration in the context of invasion.[38] Following the insufficiencies established by RCIADIC, these determining histories are slowly receiving greater attention in Australian coronial courts via expanded inquest scope; however, this has not been an untroubled trajectory. A key example is the inquest into the preventable death of 22-year-old Yamatji woman Ms Dhu, who died in custody in Western Australia (WA) in 2014 after being arrested for unpaid fines following trivial offences. In her findings into the death of Ms Dhu, the WA State Coroner acknowledged the relationship of historical context to the inquest's scope, referring to the RCIADIC's recommendations to expand the coronial inquiry beyond cause of death to address underlying factors.[39] However, instead of accounting for underlying causes of death and the structural context of Indigenous disadvantage, the coroner narrowed her focus to Ms Dhu's personal history.[40] Comments about institutional racism are found in the conclusion to her 165-page findings but fail to contextualise its origins and, importantly, its persistence.[41] The coroner did not, as Elyse Methven identifies, trace the direct line of flight from trivial offences to Ms Dhu's death in custody following disproportionate policing of Indigenous peoples.[42] And the coronial technique of seeing, reading, and declaring Ms Dhu's death as naturalised ultimately undermined the impact that a finding of 'inhumane' conduct on the part of police and below-standard medical treatment might otherwise have effected, with its serious corollary for addressing the prevention of avoidable death in the context of right-to-life breaches. In Ms Dhu's case, despite exhortations around expanded scope and historical context, the coronial court failed to realise critical scrutiny of the state's relationship to its citizens.[43]

Contested deaths and the digitalisation of death politics

What Ms Dhu's inquest did catalyse were transformative media justice practices in Australia around contested deaths. Ms Dhu's inquest proceeded in 2015–2016 at the same time as the inquest into the deaths arising from the Lindt Café siege in Sydney; however, it was only the latter that had a discrete Coroner's Court webpage, televised opening

---

37 RCIADIC, "National Report," [4.5.83]–[4.5.84].

38 Rebecca Scott Bray, "Death Scene Jurisprudence: The Social Life of Coronial Facts," *Griffith Law Review* 19, no. 3 (2010): 567–92; Chris Cunneen, "Aboriginal Deaths in Custody: A Continuing Systematic Abuse," *Social Justice* 33, no. 4 (106) (2006): 42.

39 Watterson, Brown, and McKenzie, "Coronial Recommendations," 6; Western Australia Coroners Court, *Inquest into the Death of Ms Dhu, Inquest 11020–14* (2016): 8.

40 Western Australia Coroners Court, *Inquest into the Death of Ms Dhu*, 161; Pauline Klippmark and Karen Crawley, "Justice for Ms Dhu: Accounting for Indigenous Deaths in Custody in Australia," *Social & Legal Studies* 27, no. 6 (2018): 695–715.

41 Aileen Moreton-Robinson, *The White Possessive: Property, Power, and Indigenous Sovereignty* (Minneapolis: University of Minnesota Press, 2015).

42 Elyse Methven, "A Death Sentence for Swearing: The Fatal Consequences of the Failure to Decriminalise Offensive Language," *Griffith Law Review* 29, no. 1 (2020): 73–90.

43 Suvendrini Perera and Joseph Pugliese, "What the Law Saw: Repertoires of Violence and Regimes of Impunity," 30 December (2016): 1–11, paper on file with author.

remarks of each hearing segment, and published inquest material. These aspects are what are commonly associated with the high watermark of open justice in contemporary courts, which has heralded online access to inquests, including websites that publish coronial findings and recommendations, practice notes, law sheets, jurisdictional information and, in some cases, standalone inquest websites.[44] However, even where jurisdictions support online access to coronial information, in addition to the more recent development of live-streaming in the COVID-19 era, these aspects of coronial publicity and openness are not enough; public scrutiny is also important.[45] Arguably, the shape of public scrutiny in the digital age has changed considerably. While previously integral to facilitating scrutiny of courts, media now play an instrumental role in 'mediated quasi-interaction'[46] of the public in court cases due to declining publics in courtrooms, smaller galleries, and the emergence of a new media ecology enabling rolling reportage through live blogs and social media accounts.[47] However, the implications for contested deaths stretch well beyond this. Returning to Ms Dhu's inquest, *Guardian* journalists live-tweeting and reporting from court sought up-to-date statistics about the number of Indigenous deaths in custody since the RCIADIC. Upon discovering a 'vague figure',[48] in 2018 they created the *Deaths Inside* database to provide a real-time, online, searchable database that complemented the *Guardian*'s reporting on related issues, including, for example, prone restraint and incarceration. Significantly, this initiative was in light of Australia's extant programme to monitor deaths in custody – the Australian Institute of Criminology's (AIC) *National Deaths in Custody Program* (NDICP) – which was established in 1992 following a RCIADIC recommendation. Subsequent to *Deaths Inside*, scrutiny officially fell on the AICs NDICP at the Commonwealth's Parliamentary Joint Committee on Law Enforcement,[49] and, in 2023 the AIC introduced a real-time monitoring dashboard as part of the NDICP.[50]

Such media initiatives also offer a corrective to mainstream media reporting following the deaths of First Nations peoples in custody. The history of media reporting on Indigenous peoples was an issue specifically addressed by the RCIADIC and led to material changes in Australian journalism.[51] Chris Cunneen recounts that while the RCIADIC

44 Including the Jean Charles de Menezes inquest in 2008 and the 7/7 inquests in 2010–2011. See Rebecca Scott Bray, "Paradoxical Justice: The Case of Ian Tomlinson," *Journal of Law and Medicine* 21, no. 2 (2013): 447–72.

45 Leslie J. Moran, "Mass-Mediated 'Open Justice': Court and Judicial Reports in the Press in England and Wales," *Legal Studies* 34, no. 1 (2014): 144. McIntosh, "Taken Lives Matter."

46 Moran, "Mass-Mediated 'Open Justice'," 144, citing John B. Thompson.

47 Lieve Gies, "'My Name Is Raffaele Sollecito and Not Amanda Marie Knox': Marginalisation and Media Justice," in *Transmedia Crime Stories: The Trial of Amanda Knox and Raffaele Sollecito in the Globalised Media Sphere*, ed. Lieve Gies and Maria Bortoluzzi (London: Palgrave Macmillan, 2016), 226; Chris Greer and Eugene McLaughlin, "The Ian Tomlinson inquest was justice seen to be done," *The Guardian*, 4 May, 2011, www.theguardian.com/commentisfree/2011/may/03/ian-tomlinson-inquest-live-blogging. See also Rebecca Scott Bray, "Paradoxical Justice: The Case of Ian Tomlinson."

48 Calla Wahlquist, Nick Evershed, and Lorena Allam, "We Examined Every Indigenous Death in Custody Since 2008: This is Why," *The Guardian*, 28 August 2018, www.theguardian.com/australia-news/2018/aug/28/we-examined-every-indigenous-death-in-custody-since-2008-this-is-why.

49 Commonwealth of Australia, Parliamentary Joint Committee on Law Enforcement, *Summary Report of the 24 June 2020 Public Hearing on the Australian Institute of Criminology's National Deaths in Custody Program* (October), 2020.

50 See Australian Institute of Criminology, "Deaths in Custody Monitoring Program," www.aic.gov.au/statistics/deaths-custody-australia.

51 Chris Cunneen, "Indigenous People, Resistance and Racialised Criminality," in *Media, Crime and Racism*, ed. Monish Bhatia, Scott Poynting, and Waqas Tufail (Cham: Palgrave Macmillan, 2018).

acknowledged the significant role of investigative journalism in questioning the deaths of Indigenous people in custody and state responses to them, including its role in the RCIADIC's establishment, it also emphasised that the 'progressive role' of the media was 'overshadowed by more problematic approaches', where Indigenous people were criminalised or simply ignored.[52] Since the RCIADIC, the development of Indigenous media has 'provided a powerful source in questioning misinformation within the mainstream media portrayal'[53] but this has not signalled an end to representations of racialised criminality.[54] Journalism has often worked to 'entrench and extend the violence of settler colonialism'.[55] And, despite persistent Indigenous resistance to police brutality in Australia evident in national protests, Yuin scholar Amanda Porter details how the mainstream media resort to moral panics about this resistance rather than tackling racial politics.[56] Correspondingly, other digital tools, such as social media, enter a complicated landscape of representational politics around contested deaths.

Ms Dhu's inquest was one of the first in Australia to highlight that if the public right to access the courts is aided by the media, contemporarily this right is further structured by new forms of access which include social media contemporaneously transmitting details about inquests in a rights-based era of scrutiny. Contested coronial cases now progress in the context of changing media practices where inquests are scrutinised and evidence is reproduced and discussed in social media, via podcasts and online fora among community groups, advocates, non-government organisations, and the public, often in concert with real-time engagement with coronial proceedings. Another key example includes the inquest into the death of Yorta Yorta woman Tanya Day. In December 2017, Tanya Day was asleep on a train to Melbourne to visit her pregnant daughter when police arrested her for being intoxicated, despite the RCIADIC recommending abolishing the offence due to its discriminatory effect on the policing of Indigenous people. Tanya Day died in hospital 17 days after sustaining critical head injuries from falling in the police cell. The 2019 inquest into her death was live-tweeted by the *Guardian*, including *Guardian* journalists who had live-tweeted Ms Dhu's inquest and developed the *Deaths Inside* database, Indigenous media, and a community of Indigenous legal practitioners, academics, activists, writers, and supporters. These tweets were re-tweeted by a wider community, prioritising Indigenous voices that added broader context around colonialism and policing, and deaths in custody, in addition to analysing techniques of inquest such as the language used in court, witness demeanour, lawyers' re-narration of events, legal tactics, and broader observations about the idiosyncrasies of inquest process and RCIADIC recommendations.

Such inquests highlight how social media has facilitated a reshaping of coronial court reporting by traditional media and journalists, but, importantly, also by the bereaved and

52 Cunneen, "Indigenous People," 279. See also Wendy Bacon, "A Case Study in Ethical Failure: Twenty Years of Media Coverage of Aboriginal Deaths in Custody," *Pacific Journalism Review* 11, no. 2 (2005): 17–41; Bonita Mason, "Reporting Black Lives Matters: Deaths in Custody Journalism in Australia," *Pacific Journalism Review* 26, no. 2 (2020): 202–20.

53 Amanda Porter, "Riotous or Righteous Behaviour? Representations of Subaltern Resistance in the Australian Mainstream Media," *Current Issues in Criminal Justice* 26, no. 3 (2015): 299.

54 Cunneen, "Indigenous People."

55 David Nolan, Alanna Myers, Kerry McCallum, and Jack Latimore, "Reckoning with Investigative Journalism and Indigenous News in Australia," in *Investigative Journalism in Changing Times: Australian and Anglo-American Reporting*, ed. Caryn Coatney (Abingdon: Routledge, 2022), 69.

56 Porter, "Riotous or Righteous Behaviour?"

their communities, who use social media to translate, analyse, and contest the work of coroners and even exert pressure to enact reform. Ideally, formally, what is seen to flow from this practice is justice being seen to be done, transparency, public awareness, and scrutiny, which are all supposed to contribute to boosting public confidence in the courts. Yet these ideas are usually thought of, theorised, discussed, and assessed with reference to criminal courts, including the core idea that open justice is 'synonymous with the notion of a fair and accurate trial'.[57] For coronial cases, however, these facets are emerging as fundamentally disruptive and corrective; they challenge the limitations of the jurisdiction and contest official narratives not only about death but also the inquest process itself. The consequence is that the democratisation of the media ecology around contested death is resisting established narratives around fatality and its investigation, and reshaping public participation in inquests. The digitalisation of death politics carries added significance for contested cases by enlivening participatory rights on issues of grave public importance, and documenting resistance to conventional framings, where systemic racism and structural violence supplant individual vulnerability and marginalisation. The following discussion highlights how the new media ecology is contributing to change concerning Australian coronial courts at the very time when the politics of death and death investigation is publicly entangled with issues that have implications for addressing the 'underlying factors, structures and practices' around 'Indigenous disadvantage' following settler-colonialism;[58] those issues being Indigenous sovereignty, self-determination, and treaty and constitutional recognition on the political stage.

Coronial activism

Returning to McIntosh, state-related deaths are circumstances in which 'the basic nature of the state/citizen relationship is called into question',[59] and it is axiomatic that inquests following state-related deaths necessarily are of social and political importance.[60] To posit otherwise means 'the legitimacy of the state's monopoly on the use of force, and its social exercise, are brought into question',[61] and participatory rights in democratic societies are undermined. If openness is an intrinsic requirement in the scrutiny of and accountability for deaths in contested circumstances, and if the public needs to be 'properly informed'[62] about policing and prisons through such processes so as to be able to effectively scrutinise the fatal exercise of state power, then contemporary coronial practice and responses to it are illuminating some critical issues.

First, in terms of inquests into contested deaths and new media practices, the question arises as to whether coronership *does in fact* 'properly' inform the public about policing practices and the prison estate. The language coroners use in their voluminous findings following contested deaths is instructive in how publics are informed about custodial practices and their outcomes. Coroners draw a line of flight from institutional practices

---

57 Linda Mulcahy, *Legal Architecture: Justice, Due Process and the Place of Law* (Abingdon: Routledge, 2011), 85.
58 Watterson, Brown and McKenzie, "Coronial Recommendations," cited in Western Australia Coroners Court, *Inquest into the Death of Ms Dhu*, 8.
59 McIntosh, 'Taken Lives Matter," 151.
60 See Ian Freckelton and David Ranson, *Death Investigation and the Coroner's Inquest* (South Melbourne: Oxford University Press, 2006), 224.
61 McIntosh, 'Taken Lives Matter," 152.
62 McIntosh, 'Taken Lives Matter," 152.

to fatal outcomes through determining causation. Despite increasing attempts by coroners to respect and 'humanise' the deceased, researchers detail how Indigenous deaths in custody regularly are characterised as 'timely' or 'tragic' and, therefore, 'naturalised', such that effective scrutiny is displaced from carceral practices.[63] Gomeroi scholar Alison Whittaker has analysed Australian coronial findings following Indigenous deaths in custody to reveal how the conduct of police or prison officers is described by coroners as 'unnecessary', the use of force 'unfortunate' but 'never causative'.[64]

Here is coronial language that glosses over custodial conduct, diminishes its place in the causative chain, or otherwise buries causative conduct within a range of 'naturalised' factors rather than state violence, evacuating accountability following the deaths of First Nations people in custody.[65] Furthermore, family submissions at inquests into deaths of First Nations people in custody demonstrate the importance of coronial language and its effects, such as the inquest submission of Tanya Day's family in the Victorian jurisdiction.[66] In a submission that spoke in Tanya Day's voice and, in centring her, resisted the typical framing of legal submissions, Tanya Day's family clearly outlined the significance of language and how it makes meaning of death.[67] These critical submissions and research highlight the importance and impact of coroners' findings, and illuminate how the deaths of First Nations people in custody are interpreted and officially registered by the coronial system.[68]

If there remain serious concerns around whether coronership 'properly' informs the public about policing practices and the prison estate, the corollary is *what else* is being exposed in contemporary open justice around coronial fact-finding following contested death? Part of this necessarily involves recognising that if Indigenous deaths in custody petition specific socio-legal legacies, then so too does coronership. Coronial courts are a well-documented part of the circuitry of death injustice following Indigenous deaths in custody.[69] This is placed in the context of not only questions around causative findings, language use, and lack of accountability, but also disproportionate contact of First

63 See Sherene H. Razack, "Timely Deaths: Medicalizing the Deaths of Aboriginal People in Police Custody," *Law, Culture and the Humanities* 9, no. 2 (2013): 352–74.

64 Alison Whittaker, "'Dragged Like a Dead Kangaroo': Why Language Matters for Deaths in Custody," *The Guardian*, 8 September 2018, www.theguardian.com/commentisfree/2018/sep/07/dragged-like-a-dead-kangaroo-why-language-matters-for-deaths-in-custody.

65 A key example here is the death of Dunghutti man David Dungay Jr: Coroners Court of NSW, *Inquest into the Death of David Dungay* (2015/381722). See Alison Whittaker, "Despite 432 Indigenous Deaths in Custody Since 1991, No One Has Ever Been Convicted. Racist Silence and Complicity Are to Blame," *The Conversation*, 3 June 2020, https://theconversation.com/despite-432-indigenous-deaths-in-custody-since-1991-no-one-has-ever-been-convicted-racist-silence-and-complicity-are-to-blame-139873. See also Whittaker, "'Dragged Like a Dead Kangaroo'."

66 Available at: www.hrlc.org.au/news/2019/11/10/family-of-tanya-day-call-for-police-accountability.

67 *Inquest into the Death of Tanya Day: Submissions by Belinda Day/Stevens, Warren Stevens, Apryl Watson and Kimberly Watson, the Children of Tanya Day* (2019), 6, www.hrlc.org.au/news/2019/11/10/family-of-tanya-day-call-for-police-accountability.

68 Whittaker, "'Dragged Like a Dead Kangaroo'."

69 See the submission of families and advocates to: New South Wales Parliament, Legislative Council, *Select Committee on the High Level of First Nations People in Custody and Oversight and Review of Deaths in Custody*, Chair: Hon Adam Searle MLC. NSW, (April) 2021, www.parliament.nsw.gov.au/committees/listofcommittees/Pages/committee-details.aspx?pk=266#tab-submissions; New South Wales Parliament, Legislative Council, *Select Committee on Coronial Jurisdiction in New South Wales*, Chair: Hon Adam Searle MLC, NSW, (April) 2022, www.parliament.nsw.gov.au/committees/listofcommittees/Pages/committee-details.aspx?pk=273#tab-submissions.

Nations peoples with the coronial system, in addition to lack of cultural safety when in contact.[70] Increasingly, the new media ecology is ensuring that not only policing and prisons, but inquests, coronial practices, and coronial decision making are also being drafted in for scrutiny in light of this history.

Second, then, and relatedly, is the question of who constitutes the 'public' of coronial processes, and the nature and quality of their interests. It is clear that coronership needs to address different publics, with diverse experiences and interests. In the case of the contested deaths of First Nations peoples, such interests are nested in sovereignty. In a period when Australians voted on amending the Constitution to establish an Indigenous Voice to Parliament, and public debate referenced the significance of truth-telling and treaty, and the need to finally, fully, address the recommendations of the RCIADIC, it is no coincidence that these issues find some expression both inside and outside of coronial courts. The New South Wales (NSW) State Coroner has, for example, repeatedly referenced the Uluru Statement from the Heart in coronial findings, made public commitments to addressing Indigenous deaths in custody, and declared the importance of Indigenous self-determination.[71] Both Victoria and NSW have developed practice notes on death investigation processes following Indigenous deaths in custody, and introduced First Nations liaison in coronial process.[72] Added to this is the expansion of inquest scope to consider systemic racism, which has evolved since Ms Dhu's inquest and been shaped by critical communities of practice. Recent examples include the inquests into the deaths of Tanya Day and Veronica Nelson in the Charter jurisdiction of Victoria, and the inquest into the death of Kumanjayi Walker in the Northern Territory.

The strength of determining contexts is therefore gradually receiving increased recognition in coronial courts; however, progress is slow and, as Craig Longman and Alison Whittaker have identified, inconsistent.[73] NSW coroners have commented on background factors regarding the deaths in custody of Indigenous people, citing research findings concerning the incarceration rate of First Nations people and the structural disadvantage underpinning disproportionate incarceration, in addition to referring to the RCIADIC. And while some coroners recognise the significance of settler-colonialism and its ongoing violence against Indigenous peoples, until recently they largely relegated this history to the background, which undermines the force of determining contexts and their relevance

---

70 Fiona Allison and Chris Cunneen, "Coroners Courts and Death Investigations," in *Australian Courts: Controversies, Challenges and Change*, ed. Marg Camilleri and Alistair Harkness (Cham: Springer International Publishing, 2023); George Newhouse, Daniel Ghezelbash and Alison Whittaker, "The Experience of Aboriginal and Torres Strait Islander Participants in Australia's Coronial Inquest System: Reflections from the Front Line," *International Journal for Crime, Justice and Social Democracy* 9, no. 4 (2020): 76–89.

71 Michaela Whitbourn, "'Unfinished Business': Top Coroner's Call to Action on Indigenous Deaths in Custody," *The Sydney Morning Herald*, 12 April 2021, www.smh.com.au/national/nsw/unfi nished-business-top-coroner-s-call-to-action-on-indigenous-deaths-in-custody-20210408-p57hml.htm l; Natassia Chrysanthos, "More Must Be Done After Record Indigenous Deaths in Custody, Says Coroner," *The Sydney Morning Herald*, 28 September 2022, www.smh.com.au/national/nsw/m ore-must-be-done-after-record-indigenous-deaths-in-custody-says-coroner-20220921-p5bjws.html.

72 See Victorian State Coroner, *Practice Direction 6 of 2020: Indigenous Deaths in Custody;* New South Wales State Coroner, State Coroner's Protocol, *First Nations Protocol: Supplementary arrangements applicable to section 23 deaths involving First Nations Peoples.*

73 Craig Longman and Alison Whittaker, "Practitioner Perspective: Chasing Professionalism – The Practitioner Role in Responding to First Nations Deaths in Custody," in *Australian Courts: Controversies, Challenges and Change*, ed. Marg Camilleri and Alistair Harkness (Cham: Springer International Publishing, 2023), 267.

to the scope of inquests and thus the facts of death.[74] In McIntosh's framing of contested death inquests, this constitutes misrecognition, and therefore harm.[75]

The question arises, then, about the politics around recognition in the context of death investigation. Taking critical aim at inquests as sites of apology and reparation, Sherene Razack suggests that 'transparency and virtue' – which arguably also undergird open justice in contested death contexts – are a part of the way 'the settler state pursues its legitimacy in law'.[76] As Razack observes, citing Elizabeth Povinelli, such work can highlight 'the cunning of recognition',[77] where what is actually being performed is repentance 'alongside continuing dispossession'.[78] Assessing how effectively recognition operates when the investigatory scope is drawn is one way of ascertaining how adept coroners are at tackling determining contexts, because a corollary of this effectiveness is how findings about vulnerability and disadvantage move away from individualistic approaches to structural understandings.[79] Another way is through gauging the nature and quality of participatory rights. The role and place of the bereaved in coronial investigations is an issue that has been subject to growing attention and research, and it has been observed in inquires and reviews of coronial systems that bereaved families and communities do not have specific rights when it comes to engagement with coronial process.[80] By comparison, victims of crime are typically afforded rights with respect to their engagement with the criminal justice process by way of a victims of crime charter. There is increasing debate about whether and to what extent coronial investigations do, can, or should accommodate families, and the nature and quality of participatory rights in inquests is an important consideration, not least because, as McIntosh observes, the bereaved and their communities have enhanced interests in inquests following state-related deaths.[81] Yet these issues need to be parsed more finely in the context of critical Indigenous thought and lived experience of the coronial system. As Indigenous legal scholars have identified in relation to Aboriginal and Torres Strait Islander families and communities, effective inquest participation is limited.[82] In the context of such harm, acts of refusal depose the coronial politics of recognition, such as when 27-year-old Gunggari man Steven Lee Nixon-McKellar's family withdrew from making a family statement at his inquest, declaring that they would not edit or amend their statement following objections from police.[83] These concerns articulate with wider political concerns around sovereignty and self-determination, and

---

74 Phil Scraton, "Policing with Contempt: The Degrading of Truth and Denial of Justice in the Aftermath of the Hillsborough Disaster," *Journal of Law and Society* 26, no. 3 (1999): 274.

75 McIntosh, "Taken Lives Matter."

76 Sherene H. Razack, "Both Sorry and Happy: Inquests into Indigenous Deaths in Custody," in *The Routledge International Handbook on Decolonizing Justice*, ed. Chris Cunneen, Antje Deckert, Amanda Porter, Juan Tauri, and Robert Webb (London: Routledge, 2023), 252.

77 Razack, "Both Sorry and Happy," 252.

78 Razack, "Both Sorry and Happy," 252.

79 Allison and Cunneen, "Coroners Courts."

80 See JUSTICE, *When Things Go Wrong: The Response of the Justice System* (London, 2020) Chair: Sir Robert Owen, 2; Phil Scraton and Gillian McNaull, *Death Investigation, Coroners' Inquests and the Rights of the Bereaved*, Irish Council for Civil Liberties, 2021; House of Commons Justice Committee, *The Coroner Service*, First Report of Session 2021–22, HC 68 (27 May 2021), 20–21.

81 McIntosh, "Taken Lives Matter," 153. See also Edward Kirton-Darling, *Death, Family and the Law: The Contemporary Inquest in Context* (Bristol: Bristol University Press, 2022).

82 Newhouse, Ghezelbash, and Whittaker, "The Experience of Aboriginal and Torres Strait Islander Participants."

83 Callan Morse, "Mum Frustrated as Inquest Statement is Rejected," *National Indigenous Times*, 26 September 2023, https://nit.com.au/26-09-2023/7820/mum-frustrated-as-inquest-statement-is-re

cannot be siloed.[84] What the digital age reveals, through social media's micro-engagements with coronial inquests, is just how often resistance emerges in coronial courts: to questions, evidence, policies, and the coronial process itself; matters which do not reach the coronial finding record and would slip from view but for the memory of community, both physical and, now, online.

Finally, the notion that a preventable death in custody can be narrowed to fact-finding and denuded of its terror is a concern that families and communities of those who have died or been killed in custody repeatedly call out. Inquests are not neutral spaces, and the political work of inquests is also on clear view. As coronial scholars have identified, death investigations form a key part of the political life of contested death.[85] Coroners do more than find facts; they re-narrate death, perform coronial history, and contribute to death's archive, conducting much broader socio-legal work than mere fact-finding, and in all of this, the horror of premature and preventable death prevails. In the digital age, when scrutiny of contested deaths is spilling outside of the inquest space, and reflecting the critical community of practice around deaths that enjoins bereaved communities, advocates, and non-state actors, there is visible resistance to established coronial language and narratives, and sustained efforts to push coronial practice into newer realms with a deeper understanding of the political life of death that includes coronership itself. There is evidence to suggest, *cautiously*, that coronial law, practice and coronership are transforming. To this end, it was significant when Victorian coroner Simon McGregor delivered his findings into the preventable death in custody of Gunditjmara, Dja Dja Wurrung, Wiradjuri, and Yorta Yorta woman Veronica Nelson in early 2023, and repeatedly uttered the word 'carceral'.[86]

Bibliography

Aitken, Dominic. "Investigating Prison Suicides: The Politics of Independent Oversight." *Punishment & Society* 24, no. 3 (2022): 477–497.

Allison, Fiona, and Chris Cunneen. "Coroners Courts and Death Investigations." In *Australian Courts: Controversies, Challenges and Change*, edited by Marg Camilleri and Alistair Harkness, 247–268. Cham: Springer International Publishing, 2023.

Arthur, Carson Cole. "Make Believe: Police Accountability, Lying and Anti-Blackness in the Inquest of Sean Rigg." *Crime, Media, Culture* 19, no. 3 (2023): 362–379.

Australian Institute of Criminology. "Deaths in Custody Monitoring Program." Accessed 20 September 2023. www.aic.gov.au/statistics/deaths-custody-australia.

jected. See Audra Simpson, "The Ruse of Consent and the Anatomy of 'Refusal': Cases from Indigenous North America and Australia," *Postcolonial Studies* 20, no. 1 (2017).

84 Glen S. Coulthard, "Subject of Empire: Indigenous Peoples and the 'Politics of Recognition' in Canada," *Contemporary Political Theory* 6 (2007).

85 Phil Scraton, and Kathryn Chadwick, *In the Arms of the Law: Coroner's Inquests and Deaths in Custody* (London: Pluto Press, 1987); Sherene Razack, *Dying from Improvement: Inquests and Inquiries into Indigenous Deaths in Custody* (Toronto: University of Toronto Press, 2015); Whittaker, "'Dragged Like a Dead Kangaroo'."; Travis Hay, "Foreclosing Accountability: The Limited Scope of the Seven Youth Inquest in Thunder Bay, Ontario," *Canadian Review of Social Policy* 78 (2018); Lindsay McCabe and Allen George, "Improving Indigenous Family Engagement with the Coronial System in New South Wales," *Alternative Law Journal* 46, no. 3 (2021); Carson Cole Arthur, "Make Believe: Police Accountability, Lying and Anti-Blackness in the Inquest of Sean Rigg," *Crime, Media, Culture* 19, no. 3 (2023).

86 Coroners Court of Victoria, *Finding into Death with Inquest, Inquest into the Passing of Veronica Nelson, COR2020 0021* (2023).

Bacon, Wendy. "A Case Study in Ethical Failure: Twenty Years of Media Coverage of Aboriginal Deaths in Custody." *Pacific Journalism Review* 11, no. 2 (2005): 17–41.

Butterworth, Lee. *What Good is a Coroner? The Transformation of the Queensland Office of Coroner 1859–1959.* Doctoral Thesis, Griffith University, 2012.

Chrysanthos, Natassia. "More Must Be Done After Record Indigenous Deaths in Custody, Says Coroner." *The Sydney Morning Herald*, 28 September 2022. www.smh.com.au/national/nsw/more-m ust-be-done-after-record-indigenous-deaths-in-custody-says-coroner-20220921-p5bjws.html.

Commonwealth of Australia, Parliamentary Joint Committee on Law Enforcement. *Summary Report of the 24 June 2020 Public Hearing on the Australian Institute of Criminology's National Deaths in Custody Program* (October), 2020.

Coulthard, Glen. S. "Subject of Empire: Indigenous Peoples and the 'Politics of Recognition' in Canada." *Contemporary Political Theory* 6 (2007): 437–460.

Cunneen, Chris. *Conflict, Politics and Crime: Aboriginal Communities and the Police.* Crows Nest, NSW: Allen and Unwin, 2001.

Cunneen, Chris. "Indigenous People, Resistance and Racialised Criminality." In *Media, Crime and Racism*, edited by Monish Bhatia, Scott Poynting, and Waqas Tufail, 277–299. Cham: Palgrave Macmillan, 2018.

Cunneen, Chris. "Aboriginal Deaths in Custody: A Continuing Systematic Abuse." *Social Justice* 33, no. 4 (106) (2006): 37–51.

Finnane, Mark, and Jonathan Richards. "'You'll Get Nothing Out of It'? The Inquest, Police and Aboriginal Deaths in Colonial Queensland." *Australian Historical Studies* 35, no. 123 (2004): 84–105.

Freckelton, Ian, and David Ranson. *Death Investigation and the Coroner's Inquest.* South Melbourne: Oxford University Press, 2006.

Freckelton, Ian, and Simon McGregor. "Coronial Law and Practice: A Human Rights Perspective." *Journal of Law and Medicine* 21, no. 3 (2014): 584–601.

Gies, Lieve. "'My Name Is Raffaele Sollecito and Not Amanda Marie Knox': Marginalisation and Media Justice." In *Transmedia Crime Stories: The Trial of Amanda Knox and Raffaele Sollecito in the Globalised Media Sphere*, edited by Lieve Gies and Maria Bortoluzzi, 211–230. London: Palgrave Macmillan, 2016.

Greer, Chris, and Eugene McLaughlin. "The Ian Tomlinson inquest was justice seen to be done." *The Guardian*, 4 May 2011. www.theguardian.com/commentisfree/2011/may/03/ian-tomlinson-in quest-live-blogging.

Hay, Travis. "Foreclosing Accountability: The Limited Scope of the Seven Youth Inquest in Thunder Bay, Ontario." *Canadian Review of Social Policy* 78 (2018): 1–24.

House of Commons Justice Committee. The Coroner Service, First Report of Session 2021–2022. HC 68, 27 May 2021.

Hunyor, Jonathon. "Disgrace: The Death of Mr Ward." *Indigenous Law Bulletin* 7, no. 15 (2009): 3–8.

Hunyor, Jonathon. "Human Rights in Coronial Inquests." *Australian Indigenous Law Review* 12, no. 2 (2008): 64–74.

Inquest into the Death of Tanya Day: Submissions by Belinda Day/Stevens, Warren Stevens, Apryl Watson and Kimberly Watson, the Children of Tanya Day (2019), 6. Available at: www.hrlc.org. au/news/2019/11/10/family-of-tanya-day-call-for-police-accountability.

JUSTICE. *When Things Go Wrong: The Response of the Justice System.* Chair: Sir Robert Owen. London, 2020.

Kirton-Darling, Edward. *Death, Family and the Law: The Contemporary Inquest in Context.* Bristol: Bristol University Press, 2022.

Klippmark, Pauline, and Karen Crawley. "Justice for Ms Dhu: Accounting for Indigenous Deaths in Custody in Australia." *Social & Legal Studies* 27, no. 6 (2018): 695–715.

Longman, Craig, and Alison Whittaker. "Practitioner Perspective: Chasing Professionalism – The Practitioner Role in Responding to First Nations Deaths in Custody." In *Australian Courts: Controversies, Challenges and Change*, edited by Marg Camilleri and Alistair Harkness, 264–268. Cham: Springer International Publishing, 2023.

Mason, Bonita. "Reporting Black Lives Matters: Deaths in Custody Journalism in Australia." *Pacific Journalism Review* 26, no. 2 (2020): 202–220.

McCabe, Lindsay, and Allen George. "Improving Indigenous Family Engagement with the Coronial System in New South Wales." *Alternative Law Journal* 46, no. 3 (2021): 212–218.

McDonald, David, and Chris Cunneen. "Aboriginal Incarceration and Deaths in Custody: Looking Back and Looking Forward." *Current Issues in Criminal Justice* 9, no. 1 (1997): 5–20.

McIntosh, Sam. "Taken Lives Matter: Open Justice and Recognition in Inquests into Deaths at the Hands of the State." *International Journal of Law in Context* 12, no. 2 (2016): 141–161.

Methven, Elyse. "A Death Sentence for Swearing: The Fatal Consequences of the Failure to Decriminalise Offensive Language." *Griffith Law Review* 29, no. 1 (2020): 73–90.

Moran, Leslie J. "Mass-Mediated 'Open Justice': Court and Judicial Reports in the Press in England and Wales." *Legal Studies* 34, no. 1 (2014): 143–166.

Moreton-Robinson, Aileen. *The White Possessive: Property, Power, and Indigenous Sovereignty*. Minneapolis: University of Minnesota Press, 2015.

Morse, Callan. "Mum Frustrated as Inquest Statement is Rejected." *National Indigenous Times*, 26 September 2023. https://nit.com.au/26-09-2023/7820/mum-frustrated-as-inquest-statement-is-rejected.

Mulcahy, Linda. *Legal Architecture: Justice, Due Process and the Place of Law*. Abingdon: Routledge, 2011.

Nettelbeck, Amanda, and Robert Foster. "Colonial Judiciaries, Aboriginal Protection and South Australia's Policy of Punishing 'with Exemplary Severity'." *Australian Historical Studies* 41, no. 3 (2010): 319–336.

Newhouse, George, Daniel Ghezelbash, and Alison Whittaker. "The Experience of Aboriginal and Torres Strait Islander Participants in Australia's Coronial Inquest System: Reflections from the Front Line." *International Journal for Crime, Justice and Social Democracy* 9, no. 4 (2020): 76–89.

New South Wales Parliament. Legislative Council. *Select Committee on the High Level of First Nations People in Custody and Oversight and Review of Deaths in Custody*. Chair: Hon Adam Searle MLC. NSW, (April) 2021. www.parliament.nsw.gov.au/committees/listofcommittees/Pages/committee-details.aspx?pk=266#tab-submissions.

New South Wales Parliament. Legislative Council. *Select Committee on Coronial Jurisdiction in New South Wales*. Chair: Hon Adam Searle MLC. NSW, (April) 2022. www.parliament.nsw.gov.au/committees/listofcommittees/Pages/committee-details.aspx?pk=273#tab-submissions.

Nolan, David, Alanna Myers, Kerry McCallum, and Jack Latimore. "Reckoning with Investigative Journalism and Indigenous News in Australia". In *Investigative Journalism in Changing Times: Australian and Anglo-American Reporting*, edited by Caryn Coatney, 63–83. Abingdon: Routledge, 2022.

Perera, Suvendrini, and Joseph Pugliese. "What the Law Saw: Repertoires of Violence and Regimes of Impunity." 30 December 2016, 1–11. Accessed 10 September 2019. rapbs.org/wp-content/uploads/2016/12/What-the-law-saw.pdf.

Porter, Amanda. "Riotous or Righteous Behaviour? Representations of Subaltern Resistance in the Australian Mainstream Media." *Current Issues in Criminal Justice* 26, no. 3 (2015): 289–304.

Razack, Sherene H. "Timely Deaths: Medicalizing the Deaths of Aboriginal People in Police Custody." *Law, Culture and the Humanities* 9, no. 2 (2013): 352–374.

Razack, Sherene. *Dying from Improvement: Inquests and Inquiries into Indigenous Deaths in Custody*. Toronto: University of Toronto Press, 2015.

Razack, Sherene H. "Both Sorry and Happy: Inquests into Indigenous Deaths in Custody." In *The Routledge International Handbook on Decolonizing Justice*, edited by Chris Cunneen, Antje Deckert, Amanda Porter, Juan Tauri, and Robert Webb, 247–255. London: Routledge, 2023.

Royal Commission into Aboriginal Deaths in Custody. *National Report, Vol. 1*, 1991.

Scott Bray, Rebecca. "Death Scene Jurisprudence: The Social Life of Coronial Facts." *Griffith Law Review* 19, no. 3 (2010): 567–592.

Scott Bray, Rebecca. "Paradoxical Justice: The Case of Ian Tomlinson." *Journal of Law and Medicine* 21, no. 2 (2013): 447–472.

Scott Bray, Rebecca. "Death Investigation, Coroners' Inquests and Human Rights." In *The Routledge International Handbook of Criminology and Human Rights*, edited by Leanne Weber, Elaine Fishwich, and Marinella Marmo, 172–182. Abingdon: Routledge, 2017.

Scraton, Phil, and Gillian McNaull. *Death Investigation, Coroners' Inquests and the Rights of the Bereaved*. Irish Council for Civil Liberties, 2021.

Scraton, Phil, and Kathryn Chadwick. *In the Arms of the Law: Coroner's Inquests and Deaths in Custody*. London: Pluto Press, 1987.

Scraton, Phil. "Policing with Contempt: The Degrading of Truth and Denial of Justice in the Aftermath of the Hillsborough Disaster." *Journal of Law and Society* 26, no. 3 (1999): 273–297.

Simpson, Audra. "The Ruse of Consent and the Anatomy of 'Refusal': Cases from Indigenous North America and Australia." *Postcolonial Studies* 20, no. 1 (2017): 18–33.

Thomas, Mark, Nigel Stobbs, and Geraldine Mackenzie. "'What Really Happened' Versus 'What We Can Prove': Tension Between the Roles of Coroner and DPP in Queensland." *Indigenous Law Bulletin* 6, no. 24 (2006): 6–10.

Trabsky, Marc. *Law and the Dead: Technology. Relations and Institutions*. Abingdon: Routledge, 2019.

Victorian Parliamentary Law Reform Committee. *Coroners Act 1985: Final Report* (2006).

Wahlquist, Calla, Nick Evershed, and Lorena Allam. "We Examined Every Indigenous Death in Custody Since 2008: This is Why." *The Guardian*, 28 August 2018. www.theguardian.com/australia-news/2018/aug/28/we-examined-every-indigenous-death-in-custody-since-2008-this-is-why.

Watterson, Ray, Penny Brown, and John McKenzie. "Coronial Recommendations and the Prevention of Indigenous Death." *Australian Indigenous Law Review* 12, no. 2 (2008): 4–26.

Whitbourn, Michaela. "'Unfinished Business': Top Coroner's Call to Action on Indigenous Deaths in Custody." *The Sydney Morning Herald*, 12 April 2021. www.smh.com.au/national/nsw/unfinished-business-top-coroner-s-call-to-action-on-indigenous-deaths-in-custody-20210408-p57hml.html.

Whittaker, Alison. "Despite 432 Indigenous Deaths in Custody Since 1991, No One Has Ever Been Convicted. Racist Silence and Complicity Are to Blame." The Conversation, 3 June 2020. https://theconversation.com/despite-432-indigenous-deaths-in-custody-since-1991-no-one-has-ever-been-convicted-racist-silence-and-complicity-are-to-blame-139873.

Whittaker, Alison. "'Dragged Like a Dead Kangaroo': Why Language Matters for Deaths in Custody." *The Guardian*, 8 September 2018. www.theguardian.com/commentisfree/2018/sep/07/dragged-like-a-dead-kangaroo-why-language-matters-for-deaths-in-custody.

Whittaker, Alison. "The Unbearable Witness, Seeing: A Case for Indigenous Methodologies in Australian Soft Law." *Pandora's Box* 2018 (2018): 23–35.

17

CONTESTED DEATHS AND THE PUBLIC INQUIRY IN HEALTHCARE

Where the Norm Becomes the Exception

Hamish Robertson, David J. Carter, and Joanne Travaglia[1]

Introduction

In 2008, *The Special Commission of Inquiry, Acute Care Services in NSW Public Hospitals*, also known as the Garling Inquiry, named after Commissioner Peter Garling SC who led the inquiry, visited 61 hospitals, received more than 1,200 written submissions and heard from 628 witnesses regarding the quality and safety of the New South Wales (NSW) public health system.[2] Commissioner Garling concluded his inquiry by making 139 recommendations. He characterised the health system as 'a paradox', as 'one of the better public healthcare systems in the developed world' and yet on the 'brink' of catastrophic crisis and failure.[3] For Commissioner Garling, the parlous state of the NSW health system was best understood as the fruit of a unique and defined period of crisis, with his most prominent frame being that 'even the best systems are not immune from crises and the public health system has entered one such period now'.[4]

The Garling Inquiry followed two deaths at Sydney's Royal North Shore Hospital (RNSH) which gave rise to widespread public and media attention. In November 2005,

1 We acknowledge the contribution of Professor Joanne Travaglia to this work prior to her untimely death. This chapter, and so much of our intellectual endeavour, is influenced by Jo and her commitment to justice for those harmed by the health system. The authors disclosed receipt of the following financial support for the research, authorship, and/or publication of this article: This work was supported by a National Health and Medical Research Council Early Career Fellowship [grant number 1156520]. The contents are solely the responsibility of the individual author and does not reflect the views of NHMRC.
2 Peter Garling, *Final Report of the Special Commission of Inquiry Acute Care Services in NSW Public Hospitals*, 27 November 2008 (accessed 1 December 2023) 1, www.dpc.nsw.gov.au/__da ta/assets/pdf_file/0003/34194/Overview_-_Special_Commission_Of_Inquiry_Into_Acute_Care_Ser vices_In_New_South_Wales_Public_Hospitals.pdf.
3 Garling, *Final Report*, 2.
4 Garling, *Final Report*, 2.

DOI: 10.4324/9781003304593-20

16-year-old Vanessa Anderson was admitted to RNSH after sustaining a head injury from a golf ball. Her admission was plagued by a combination of what the Inquiry described as almost every conceivable error or omission by hospital staff.[5] Ms Anderson was administered an excess amount of opiate medication following a misreading of medication orders which caused respiratory arrest and her death. Several factors were identified by the hospital, Coroner and eventually the Garling Inquiry, including an absence of hospital-wide pain management guidelines; an absence of inter-team lines of responsibility; clinician inexperience; and poor notes and record-keeping, as contributing to Ms Anderson's death.

Ms Anderson's case was followed by another highly publicised incident in September 2007, when Jana Horska, then 14 weeks pregnant, presented to the RNSH Emergency Department. Ms Horska was triaged for medical review and treatment within one hour. Ms Horska did not receive medical treatment and, after two hours of acute pain, suffered a miscarriage in the emergency department toilets. The miscarriage suffered by Ms Horska prompted staff from other hospitals to share accounts of similar events, which they attributed to a chronic lack of funding, staffing and beds.[6]

Despite the significant failures of the health system and individuals involved in the treatment of Anderson and Horska, the final report handed down by Commissioner Garling was greeted with almost universal support by all key stakeholders within the NSW healthcare system. NSW Minister for Health, Hon. John Della Bosca, called it a 'landmark report'[7] that would significantly improve the way healthcare was delivered. Professor Goulston, spokesperson for the Hospital Reform Group, said that senior clinicians were 'very confident' that Commissioner Garling's report brought with it the potential for change: 'We support 100 per cent the whole report. We think it's an extraordinary thing.'[8]

Despite this early welcome and support, merely one year later, the 'feel-good moment'[9] of agreement between medical practitioners, nurses, government, and others was reported to 'have already passed'.[10] Professor Goulston's observations at that time reflect this significant shift from the confidence that marked his earlier commentary:

> People are getting cynical … I think the morale overall is low and even lower than it used to be. People feel that the Garling report was thorough and exposed all the problems and the issues, but I think the response has not been genuinely accepted by the bulk of clinicians in the workplace as achieving a significant change.[11]

No longer would this landmark public inquiry bring about change. Instead, cynicism, lack of clinician acceptance and plummeting morale was now the order of the day.

5 Garling, *Final Report*, 16.
6 Isabelle Oderberg, "Years after Jana's horror story made headlines, the system is still letting women down," *The Sydney Morning Herald*, 16 April 2023, www.smh.com.au/lifestyle/health-a nd-wellness/years-after-jana-s-horror-story-made-headlines-the-system-is-still-letting-wom en-down-20230411-p5czmu.html.
7 Natasha Wallace and Alexandra Smith, "Public Hospitals on 'Brink of Collapse'," *The Sydney Morning Herald*, 28 November 2008, www.smh.com.au/national/public-hospitals-on-brink-of-collapse-20081128-gdt4kb.html.
8 Wallace and Smith, "Public Hospitals."
9 Wallace and Smith, "Public Hospitals."
10 Julie Robotham and Natasha Wallace, "Heartbreak Hospitals," *Sydney Morning Herald*, 21 November 2009, www.smh.com.au/national/heartbreak-hospitals-20091120-iqv4.html.
11 Robotham and Wallace, "Heartbreak Hospitals."

This was not the first nor the last 'landmark' public inquiry that aimed to understand and advance solutions to 'iatrogenic' deaths – a form of highly contested death, caused by the application of healthcare, rather than an underlying disease or injury. Nor was it the first public inquiry regarding the quality and safety of healthcare that would be received so positively and then, shortly afterwards, so negatively. Instead, within the healthcare context, public inquiries proliferate, and so too does the pattern of positive reception followed quickly by rejection, dissention and continued quality and safety failures. The landmark *Mid Staffordshire NHS Foundation Trust Public Inquiry*, [12] in the United Kingdom, chaired by Robert Francis QC, followed the same pattern. Commonly known as the 'Mid Staffs scandal', the Inquiry reported there had been at least 400 unnecessary deaths between 2005 and 2008 due to 'appalling' standards of care.[13] In 2017, Francis claimed in a manner similar to the flow of events regarding the reception of the Garling Inquiry – some four years after his inquiry – that conditions in the NHS 'sound familiar' to those that existed during the Mid-Staffordshire scandal:[14]

> We've got a virtual storm of financial pressures, increased demand, difficulties finding staffing, and pressure on the service to continue delivering. And some of that sounds quite familiar – as it was, those were the conditions pertaining at the time of Mid Staffordshire.[15]

Given the failure of these forms of public inquiry to force sustained improvement in the quality and safety of healthcare, and prevention of such contested iatrogenic deaths from occurring again at a similar scale, it is tempting to conclude that the inquiry form itself is a failure and its instrumental effectiveness as an 'intervention' proven faulty. Alternatively, this failure to achieve the changes inquiries call for could be laid squarely at the feet of health services and those who fund and operate them, making it a problem of implementation rather than diagnosis. Neither of these views are something we wish to counter or resolve here. Instead, we wish to draw into the conversation the place of inquiries themselves in governing contested iatrogenic deaths, for it seems that despite their paradoxical character and failure – either as a mechanism of diagnosis or an intervention designed to effect change – their continued proliferation tells us that they must be productive for someone or for some purpose.

With their continued use within healthcare to govern contested deaths of this type, what do public inquiries into healthcare quality and safety produce and for whom? In short, we believe that public inquiries construct iatrogenic harm and death in healthcare as *exceptional*

12 Commission for Healthcare Audit and Inspection (the 'Healthcare Commission'), *Investigation into Mid Staffordshire NHS Foundation Trust* (London: Commission for Healthcare Audit and Inspection, 2009).

13 Robert Francis, *Independent Inquiry into Care Provided by Mid Staffordshire NHS Foundation Trust January 2005–March 2009 Volume 1* (London: The Stationery Office, 2010), 352.

14 The events at Mid Staffordshire NHS Foundation Trust resulted in several inquiries and reviews. The last of these, the second Francis Inquiry in 2013 found that 'between 2005 and 2009, hundreds of patients [most of them elderly] may have died needlessly and countless more suffered appalling violations of their dignity at the Mid Staffordshire NHS Foundation Trust': David Holmes, "Mid Staffordshire scandal highlights NHS cultural crisis," *The Lancet* 381, no. 9866 (2013): 521–2. The Inquiry produced 290 recommendations for the NHS.

15 Jamie Grierson, "NHS Hasn't Improved Enough since Mid Staffs, Says Inquiry Lawyer," *The Guardian*, 13 February 2017, www.theguardian.com/society/2017/feb/12/nhs-improve-enough-mid-staffs-inquiry-lawyer.

rather than the *norm* that it indeed is. They do so primarily by framing healthcare harm as local and specific in time, space, and culture. Additionally, their effect is generally to grant medical power/knowledge[16] continued dominance over contested iatrogenic deaths through their work as a technique and practice of jurisdiction,[17] even when medicine/medical power is one of the very causes of the harm and death that inquiries are empowered to investigate. This perverse outcome ultimately re-asserts and embeds the power of medicine over its own healthcare quality and safety failures and the contested deaths that result.

Iatrogenic harm and contested death

Most research shows that at least 10 per cent of hospital admissions are associated with an 'adverse event'[18] in which a person is harmed.[19] Although not without controversy, various studies conclude that many such episodes are preventable, hence providing justi-fication for review and corrective action across healthcare systems.[20] Unfortunately, these rates of iatrogenic harm, established during the 1990s and 2000s, have not improved in

16 Michel Foucault, *Power/Knowledge: Selected Interviews and Other Writings, 1972–1977* (New York: Pantheon Books, 1980); Paula Rowland, *Power/Knowledge, Identity and Patient Safety: Intersections of Patient Safety and Professional Practice Discourses in a Canadian Acute Care Hospital*, Doctoral Thesis, Fielding Graduate University, 2013.

17 Shaunnagh Dorsett and Shaun McVeigh, "Questions of Jurisdiction," in *Jurisprudence of Jur-isdiction*, ed. Shaun McVeigh (Abingdon: Routledge-Cavendish, 2006); Shaunnagh Dorsett and Shaun McVeigh, *Jurisdiction* (Abingdon: Routledge, 2012).

18 The healthcare quality and safety movement and associated clinical and research disciplines have developed its own vocabulary. *Adverse events* (AEs) are defined as incidents 'in which harm resulted to a person receiving health care' and *iatrogenic* pertains to 'arising from or associated with healthcare rather than the underlying disease of injury', whilst maintaining various legal and ordinary language definitions is understood within quality and safety writing to include 'disease, injury, suffering, disability and death'; William Runciman, "Shared meanings: Preferred terms and definitions for safety and quality concepts," *The Medical Journal of Australia* 184, no. 10 (2006): 41–3. See also R. M. Wilson, W. B. Runciman, R. W. Gibberd, B. T. Harrison, L. Newby and J. D. Hamilton, "The Quality in Australian Health Care Study," *The Medicine Journal of Australia* 163, no. 9 (1995): 458.

19 William Runciman and J. Moller, *Iatrogenic Injury in Australia* (Adelaide: Australian Patient Safety Foundation, 2001); these rates are now regarded as consistent across both advanced and developing healthcare systems. See Angus Corbett, Jo Travaglia, and Jeffrey Braithwaite, "The Role of Individual Diligence in Improving Safety," *Journal of Health Organization and Man-agement* 25, no. 3 (2011): 247–60; John D. Hamilton, Robert W Gibberd, and Bernadette T Harrison, "After the quality in Australian health care study, what happened?" *The Medical Journal of Australia* 201, no. 1 (2014): 23; R. M. Wilson, P. Michel, S. Olsen, R. W. Gibberd, C. Vincent, R. El-Assady, O. Rasslan et al., "Patient safety in developing countries: Retrospective estimation of scale and nature of harm to patients in hospital," *BMJ* 2012, no. 344 (2012): e832 for an accounting of these rates and their calculation.

20 The 1994–95 Australian QAHCS study reported, 'Preventability was not strongly associated with age, sex or insurance status, nor was it associated with the level of disability, except for death (in which 70% of Adverse Events showed high preventability). Only 1.2% of AEs in the "no pre-ventability" category resulted in death, compared with 4.1% in the "low preventability" category and 6.5% in the "high preventability" category. Some of this association between preventability and death could be ascribed to outcome bias'; Wilson et al., "The Quality in Australian Health Care Study." The QAHCS study also reported 51 per cent preventability across all AEs; see also Runciman and Moller, *Iatrogenic Injury*, 22. The QAHCS results were reinterpreted at this point where 'all adverse events were re-classified as to whether they fell into one of two categories, "potentially preventable", or "not preventable with current medical knowledge" rather than using the six-point scale in the QAHCS, it was found that 80% of adverse events fell into

the aggregate, despite their preventability having drawn significant investment, activity, and attention.[21]

Iatrogenic deaths are contested deaths. The first way in which they are contested is the historical and ongoing contestation of the very existence and nature of iatrogenic death itself. There has been a long and contested history of the recognition of the existence and particularly the scale of iatrogenic death marked by a resistance to the acceptance of their preventability. Early attempts to establish, define, and understand iatrogenic deaths were highly contested across the globe,[22] 'discovered'[23] as 'an unexpected by-product'[24] of government-backed inquiries into the sustainability of civil liability and of medical indemnity insurance systems. The second way in which these deaths are contested is more straightforward: the deaths at the heart of these matters are subject to contestation by families, patient safety advocates, and activists, which, in the cases of public inquiries we engage with here, lead to more widespread attention and contestation in the public sphere. A persistent form of response to these contested deaths alleged to have been caused by breaches of patient safety has been the use of public inquiries.

The role of inquiries in relation to contested iatrogenic deaths

One response to the persistence of the contested deaths that are produced by iatrogenic harm is the use of public inquiries into specific events. Inquiries into health and social care have a long history in common law jurisdictions. The United Kingdom,[25] New Zealand,[26] Canada,[27] and Australia[28] each have turned to inquiries to examine the causes of iatrogenic death. Patient safety inquiries have been defined as the 'retrospective examination of events or circumstances,

potentially preventable categories'; W. B. Runciman, M. J. Edmonds, M. Pradhan, "Setting priorities for patient safety," *BMJ Quality & Safety* 11, no. 3 (2002): 224–9.

21 Jeffrey Braithwaite, Robert L. Wears, and Erik Hollnagel, "Resilient health care: Turning patient safety on its head," *International Journal for Quality in Health Care* 27, no.5 (2015): 418–20; Robert L. Wears, Kathleen M. Sutcliffe, and Eric Van Rite, "Patient Safety: A Brief but Spirited History," in *Patient Safety: Perspectives on Evidence, Information and Knowledge Transfer*, ed. Lorri Zipperer (London: Routledge, 2016), 49–68.

22 David J. Carter, *Responsibility for Iatrogenic Death in Australian Criminal Law*, Doctoral Thesis, University of Technology Sydney, 2017, 109–56; David J. Carter, "Responsibility for Iatrogenic Death in Australian Criminal Law," *Journal and Proceedings of the Royal Society of New South Wales* 152, no. 471/472 (2019): 140–2; Joanne Travaglia, "Disturbing the Doxa of Patient Safety: Comment on 'False Dawns' and New Horizons in Patient Safety Research and Practice," *International Journal of Health Policy and Management* 7, no. 9 (2018): 867.

23 Corbett, Travaglia, and Braithwaite, "The Role of Individual Diligence," 247–60; Wears, Sutcliffe, and Van Rite, "Patient Safety," 3–22.

24 Carter, *Responsibility for Iatrogenic Death*, 113.

25 The Bristol Royal Infirmary Inquiry, *Learning from Bristol: The Report of the Public Inquiry into Children's Heart Surgery at the Bristol Royal Infirmary 1984–1995* (Bristol: Bristol Royal Infirmary Inquiry, 2001).

26 New Zealand Committee of Inquiry into Allegations Concerning the Treatment of Cervical Cancer at National Women's Hospital, *Report of Inquiry into Allegations Concerning the Treatment of Cervical Cancer at National Women's Hospital and into Other Related Matters* (Auckland: Government Printing Office, New Zealand Government, 1988).

27 Associate Chief Justice Murray Sinclair, *Report of the Manitoba Pediatric Cardiac Surgery Inquest* (Winnipeg: Manitoba Provincial Court, 1994).

28 Neil Douglas, Kathleen Fahy, and Jeffrey Robinson, *Final Report of the Inquiry into Obstetric and Gynaecological Services at King Edward Memorial Hospital 1990–2000* (Perth: State Law Publishing, 2001); Garling, *Final Report*, 6.

specially established to find out what happened, understand why, and learn from the experiences of all those involved'.[29] These inquiries have investigated major breakdowns in health systems and the aftermath of specific healthcare 'disasters', reviewed government services and departments, addressed issues of significant public concern and, sometimes, all of the above.

Amongst these patient safety inquiries, there are a set of public inquiries that have come to be regarded as landmark events in the history of the use of this mechanism of contested death investigation in common law jurisdictions. These include the Bristol Royal Infirmary Inquiry and Gosport Hospital Inquiry in the United Kingdom, the Cartwright Inquiry in New Zealand, and the King Edward Memorial Hospital Inquiry and Garling Inquiry in Australia. We provide an overview of these inquiries and the contested deaths at the heart of each here.

The Bristol Royal Infirmary Inquiry was initiated after 16-month-old Joshua Loveday died on the operating table during cardiac surgery. In the years before the infant's death, healthcare professionals had expressed concern over aspects of the Bristol unit's performance. Following the incident, three practitioners were de-registered by the General Medical Council. The Inquiry found that clinicians were 'too easily persuaded that their poor results were a run of bad luck' and condemned the unit's practice of explaining away poor outcomes.[30]

The New Zealand Committee of Inquiry into Allegations Concerning the Treatment of Cervical Cancer at National Women's Hospital, led by former Governor General Silvia Cartwright ('the Cartwright Inquiry'), followed an article published in *Metro Magazine* in 1987 which alleged a failure by Dr Herbert Green to adequately treat patients with cervical carcinoma (CIS). In 1966, Dr Green was granted permission to conduct research, in which he attempted to prove that CIS is not a pre-malignant disease.[31] The article alleged that Dr Green withheld standard care for cervical CIS patients in the furtherance of his research. The Inquiry concluded the National Women's Hospital failed to treat a 'significant number' of cervical CIS patients to 'generally accepted standards over a period of years'.[32] It attributed this failure, in part, to the hospital's failure to stop Dr Green's trial and treat patients when signs of risk emerged.

On Australian shores, the Inquiry into the King Edward Memorial Hospital ('the Douglas Inquiry') was commissioned to inquire into the provision of obstetric and gynaecological services between 1990 and 2000. The Inquiry came after the recently appointed Chief Executive expressed concerns surrounding the hospital's clinical quality management system. Over 18 months, the Inquiry accessed information from over 1,600 patient records. It identified a 'lack of active involvement in important safety and quality issues at board and hospital management levels', 'unclear lines of authority, responsibility and lack of accountability for clinical care', and a need for '"safety nets" to protect patients and support staff'.[33]

29 Kieran Walshe, *Inquiries: Learning from Failure in the NHS* (London: Nuffield Trust, 2003); Kieran Walshe, "Gosport deaths: Lethal failures in care will happen again," *British Medical Journal* 362 (2018): k2931.

30 The Bristol Royal Infirmary Inquiry, *Learning from Bristol*, 248 [4].

31 Silvia Rose Cartwright, *The Report of the Committee of Inquiry into Allegations Concerning the Treatment of Cervical Cancer at National Women's Hospital and into Other Related Matters* (Auckland, New Zealand, July 1988), 21.

32 Cartwright, *Treatment of Cervical Cancer*, 210.

33 The Australian Council for Safety and Quality in Health Care, *Lessons from the Inquiry into Obstetrics and Gynaecological Services at King Edward Memorial Hospital 1990–2000* (The Australian Council for Safety and Quality in Health Care, July 2002), 6, www.safetyandquality.

Finally, in the United Kingdom in 2018, the Gosport Hospital Inquiry found that 456 patients died after opioids were administered without appropriate clinical justification between May 1988 and April 2000.[34] The inquiry indicated that there may have been a further 200 deaths produced by iatrogenic means in the hospital and health service, bringing the overall total of deaths to approximately 650 patients dying as a consequence of the maladministration of opioids. The inquiry found that 'there was a disregard for human life and a culture of shortening the lives of a large number of patients' and referred to Gosport as an 'an institutionalised regime' of prescribing and administering dangerous doses of opiods that caused death. The Chair of the Panel, the Right Reverend James Jones, summarised the findings:

> [D]uring a certain period at Gosport War Memorial Hospital, there was a disregard for human life and a culture of shortening the lives of a large number of patients … [W]hen relatives complained about the safety of patients and the appropriateness of their care, they were consistently let down by those in authority – both individuals and institutions.[35]

While all of these inquiries begin with instances of iatrogenic harm and resulting death, inquiries take a variety of forms. They take on a number of legal forms, including coronial inquests, internal reviews, independent commissions of inquiry established by standing or special powers by parliaments. Despite variation in their legal form, there is a set of shared features of these inquiries and a number of authors have developed analysis and their own typologies of inquiries. Scott Prasser proposes 11 key features of public inquiries, including that they are non-permanent, established, and appointed by the executive, are independent of government, and produce a report, but remain advisory and cannot action their proposals. Prasser further classifies public inquiries into those that are inquisitorial/investigatory or policy advisory committees.[36] Graham Gibbs and Christopher Hall argue that such inquiries can take either a more or less inquisitorial approach, the latter being 'more confessional, enabling witnesses to describe their perspectives and experiences'.[37] So too does Alastair Stark's work on the post-crisis inquiry name the form of inquiry that engages with contested iatrogenic death that we are interested in here.

In all cases, we see what Louis Blom-Cooper describes as the *inquiry process*, which consists of four separate strands which have:

> [the] combined function of revealing the culmination of culpability or blameworthiness and the examination of strictures of public institutions and agencies. The four are: (1) to establish the facts; (2) to identify individuals' culpability; (3) to survey the arrangements that led to the scandal, disaster or abuse; and (4) to

gov.au/sites/default/files/migrated/king_edward.pdf; see also Douglas, Fahy, and Robinson, "Inquiry into Obstetric and Gynaecological Services."

34 Gosport Independent Panel, *Return to an Address of the Honourable the House of Commons Dated 20 June 2018 for Gosport War Memorial Hospital: The Report of the Gosport Independent Panel* (2018), www.gosportpanel.independent.gov.uk.

35 Gosport Independent Panel, *Return to an Address*.

36 Scott Prasser, *Royal Commissions and Public Inquiries in Australia* (LexisNexis Butterworths, 2006).

37 Graham Gibbs and Christopher Hall, "The research potential of testimony from public inquiry websites," *Children & Society* 21, no. 1 (2007): 70. Gibbs and Hall label these two approaches the 'public inquiry' or the 'Commission' respectively.

provide the symbolic purpose of holding up to obloquy the particular event that induced the crisis of public confidence.[38]

Gregory Inwood and Carolyn Johns also claim that two of the primary functions of inquiries are governance and policy making.[39]

These views on the function of inquiries can be aided by insights from a more critical perspective. Hilgartner, for example, argues that 'public inquiries have the potential to contain disasters within durable narrative frames, recreating the collective experience of a manageable world by fixing cause, focusing blame, meting out justice, taking strong action'.[40] Elliott and McGuinness take this further. To them:

> At one, idealised, extreme the public inquiry represents a panacea, an opportunity for remedying such misfortune. Alternatively, the public inquiry may offer little more than a placebo, creating the impression that remedies are being evaluated until the incident under investigation slips from the public consciousness.[41]

It is this process of narrative containment that we take up later in this chapter.

Despite these more critical views on the function of inquiries, public inquiries proliferate. They have been held in areas of public concern across most industries and policy domains over the past two centuries and show no signs of becoming redundant, or even superseded, as a mechanism for dealing with 'exceptional' or 'extraordinary' cases. Usefully, the proliferation of such inquiries means that there is now an expanding historical record of the ways in which this mechanism of addressing and resolving purportedly exceptional circumstances has been utilised alongside assessments of their outcomes. For example, the Garling Inquiry introduced earlier in this chapter was the last in a series of three held in quick succession in NSW, following a coronial investigation into the death of Vanessa Anne Anderson at Royal North Shore Hospital.[42] So too were other major inquiries in contested iatrogenic deaths occurring in the same period. The Walker Special Commission of Inquiry into Campbelltown and Camden Hospitals was conducted in 2003,[43] sparked as a result of whistleblowing by hospital staff.[44] A NSW Parliament Joint Select Committee (chaired by the Revd Hon. Fred Nile) examined the quality of care also provided by Royal North Shore Hospital to Jana Horska, who experienced a miscarriage in that hospital's emergency department toilets.[45] Each of these were sparked by public unease towards cases

---

38 Louis Blom-Cooper, *Public Inquiries: Wrong Route on Bloody Sunday* (Oxford: Bloomsbury Publishing, 2017), 4.

39 Gregory J. Inwood and Carolyn M. Johns, "Commissions of inquiry and policy change: Comparative analysis and future research frontiers," *Canadian Public Administration* 59, no. 3 (2016): 382–404.

40 Stephen Hilgartner, "Overflow and Containment in the Aftermath of Disaster," *Social Studies of Science* 37, no. 1 (2007): 155.

41 Dominic Elliott and Martina McGuinness, "Public inquiry: Panacea or placebo?" *Journal of Contingencies & Crisis Management* 10, no. 1 (2002): 14.

42 Garling, *Final Report*, 6.

43 Bret Walker, *Final Report of the Special Commission of Inquiry into Campbelltown Camden Hospitals* (Sydney: NSW Government Special Commission of Inquiry into Campbelltown Camden Hospitals, 2004).

44 Megan-Jane Johnstone, "Patient safety, ethics and whistleblowing: A nursing response to the events at the Campbelltown and Camden Hospitals," *Australian Health Review* 28, no. 1 (2004): 13–9.

45 NSW Legislative Council, *Legislative Council Joint Select Committee Inquiry into Royal North Shore Hospital* (Sydney: NSW Government, 2007); Anthony P. Joseph and Stephen N. Hunyor,

of poor-quality care in Sydney public hospitals alone. The Garling Inquiry was typical both in its process and its outcomes.[46] It resulted in the restructuring of the NSW 'Area Health Services' into 'Local Health Districts' and the establishment of several 'pillars', including the Clinical Excellence Commission, the Agency for Clinical Innovation, and the Bureau of Health Information. Commissioner Garling's language in his final report was direct about the seriousness of the crisis he observed in the public health system: 'We are,' he wrote, 'on the brink of seeing whether the public system can survive and flourish or whether it will become a relic of better times.'[47] For Commissioner Garling, a 'new culture' needed to take root 'which sees the patient's needs as the paramount central concern of the system and not the convenience of the clinicians and administrators'.[48] Despite this action and rhetoric, the attempts at reducing errors in healthcare have had limited impact overall,[49] and inquiries continued to flourish.[50] As a consequence of this lengthening and deepening historical timeline of repeated public inquiries into contested iatrogenic death, we take this opportunity to 'inquire on inquiries' as a mechanism, process, and performance.

The exception or the norm? Constructing contested iatrogenic deaths as local, specific, and time-limited

Part of the rationale for inquiries is that they are a response to a situation so exceptional that a public reckoning is required.[51] These are 'post-crisis inquiries' that are established in the aftermath of disaster.[52] However, as the title of this chapter suggests, we propose that such post-crisis inquiries continue to be so relied upon because they resolve the contested iatrogenic death by rendering the norm of patient harm as exceptional in both time and space when, in actuality, iatrogenic harm and death are a remarkably consistent result of the application of healthcare over time.

The primary basis for our claim is empirical. Despite years of inquiries as well as health system efforts directed at harm reduction, the rate of harm remains constant across time, affecting approximately 10–16 per cent of hospital admissions. This has not

"The Royal North Shore Hospital inquiry: An analysis of the recommendations and the implications for quality and safety in Australian public hospitals," *Medical Journal of Australia* 188, no. 8 (2008): 469–72.

46 Don Hindle, Jeffrey Braithwaite, Jo Travaglia, and R. Iedema, *Patient Safety: A Comparative Analysis of Eight Inquiries in Six Countries* (Sydney: Centre for Clinical Governance Research, University of New South Wales, 2006).

47 Peter Garling, *Final Report*, 4.

48 Garling, *Final Report*, 3.

49 Russell Mannion and Jeffrey Braithwaite, "False dawns and new horizons in patient safety research and practice," *International Journal of Health Policy & Management* 6, no. 12 (2017): 685.

50 Jason Dominiczak and Lara Khansa, "Principles of automation for patient safety in intensive care: Learning from aviation," *The Joint Commission Journal on Quality & Patient Safety* 44, no. 6 (2018): 366–71; Chi Huynh, Ian C. Wong, Jo Correa-West, David Terry, and Suzanne McCarthy, "Paediatric patient safety and the need for aviation black box thinking to learn from and prevent medication errors," *Paediatric Drugs* 19, no. 2 (2017): 99–105; Aline C. Stolk-Vos, Marion H. Heres, Jasper Kesteloo, Dick Verburg, Frans Hiddema, Desiree A. Lie, and Dirk F. de Korne, "Is there a role for the use of aviation assessment instruments in surgical training preparation? A feasibility study," *Postgraduate Medical Journal* 93, no. 1095 (2017): 20–4.

51 Hilgartner, "Overflow and Containment," 153–8; Geoffrey Howe, "The management of public inquiries," *The Political Quarterly* 70, no. 3 (1999): 294–304.

52 Alastair Stark, "New institutionalism, critical junctures and post-crisis policy reform," *Australian Journal of Political Science* 53, no. 1 (2018): 24–39.

changed materially in at least 50 years.[53] Healthcare-related harm and death is, in this way, a norm rather than an exception.

Despite the constancy of healthcare harm, inquiries can be seen in social science terms as 'placing' events in a narrative frame of exceptionalism. Rather than acknowledge patient death as a norm, inquiries by their very nature and use of various narrative and rhetorical practices continue to frame healthcare-related deaths as exceptional – that is, as local, specific, and time-limited. In the case of the Garling Inquiry, for example, Commissioner Garling's framing of the health system in NSW as 'a very good health system' which was simply in 'crisis'[54] represents harm as time and geographically specific to a period of crisis. This, despite all evidence indicating that the so-called 'crisis' is in fact nothing like an exception, but instead its opposite. Rather than a 'crisis' within a 'very good health system', iatrogenic deaths are ubiquitous and persistent across time, not limited just to particular jurisdictions or hospitals and not unique in any material sense. As Hindle et al. show in their extensive examination of the findings of inquiries into patient safety, the causes of patient harm are unexceptional and the findings of patient safety inquiries are uniform across both time and space in the healthcare context.[55]

There is also an associated discourse that supports this notion of exceptionalism, produced by the rhetorical framing device frequently used within healthcare inquiries to reframe contested iatrogenic deaths: 'so this doesn't happen to anyone else'. This device is used in two main ways: first, by patients and others who make contributions to the call for and conduct of inquiries, and, second, by the inquiries and governments themselves to justify an inquiry's conduct and findings. While used in these two distinct but related ways, the effect remains the same: rather than acknowledge the historically repetitive nature and continuity of these contested deaths and their resulting inquiries, most parties involved in the inquiry process tend to focus on its exceptional nature. 'Never again' fails to account for the long timeline of such inquiries and for the fact that any particular inquiry is only exceptional until the next one occurs.

As for the use of this rhetorical strategy by patients and others, individuals who call attention to the problems of a particular health service by contesting the deaths produced by it frequently do so for years prior to the establishment of a formal inquiry process. By the time a formal inquiry emerges, the harms have usually multiplied to a 'sufficient' level to force a systemic, government, or public response.[56] Thus, the temporal specificity of the inquiry process serves by its own *in extremis* nature to conceal the slow response of healthcare systems and other legal authorities (e.g., police), and the deeper history of harms that preceded a specific inquiry event. Instead of a long series of contested iatrogenic deaths culminating in the inquiry process, we often receive a contraction of harms that are effectively bundled into the timeframe of inquiries and their responses. Afterwards, business largely 'returns to normal' since systemic change may be encouraged through inquiries but rarely negates the fundamental nature of the healthcare system and its structural outcomes – until the next time. As Nedwick and Danbury reflect on the

---

53 The Health Foundation, *Evidence Scan: Levels of Harm* (London: The Health Foundation, 2011); Braithwaite, Wears, and Hollnagel, "Resilient health care," 418–20; Wears, Sutcliffe, and Van Rite, "Patient safety," 49–68.

54 Garling, *Final Report*, 6.

55 Hindle, Braithwaite, Travaglia, and Iedema, *Patient Safety*.

56 The Bristol Royal Infirmary Inquiry, *Learning from Bristol*, 248; Janet Smith, *The Shipman Inquiry* (London: The Stationery Office, 2004); Gosport Independent Panel, *Return to an Address*.

links between the 2001 Bristol Royal Infirmary Inquiry and the Francis Inquiry into Mid-Staffordshire held over a decade later, there is a 'gap' between them:

> Speaking of the public response to the deaths of children at the Bristol Royal Infirmary before 2001, the BMJ commented that the NHS would be 'all changed, changed utterly'. Today, two inquiries into the Mid Staffordshire Foundation Trust suggest nothing changed at all.[57]

Embedding and (re)asserting the power of medicine over its own failure

One effect of inquiries' ability to construct contested iatrogenic deaths as exceptional is the (re)embedding and (re)assertion of control of medicine over its own harms. Mannion and Braithwaite note that medical professionals first rejected but have now 'embraced' the patient safety movement.[58] This renders visible medicine's own failure (s) to deliver healthcare of sufficient quality and safety, and failures to respond to this limitation. This embrace has been read in a variety of ways; however, a critical stream within patient safety now sees it as a mechanism for control of the patient safety agenda – control by appropriation. Regarding medical dominance, Travaglia notes how the World Health Organization's first *Patient Safety Curriculum Guide*, published in 2009, was produced for medical schools.[59] Given that there are more than double the number of nurses compared to doctors worldwide, the rationale was clearly not prioritised on the basis of workforce numbers or patient encounters. The second Curriculum Guide, published in 2011, was entitled 'Multi-Professional' – in other words, 'everyone else'.[60] So too does a recent comparison of patient and regulators' views on quality, for example, conclude that:

> [t]he predominant clinical approach taken by regulators does not match the patients' perspective of what is relevant for healthcare quality ... patients seem to be more tolerant of what they perceive to be clinical or management errors than of perceived relational deficiencies in care providers. If regulators want to give patients a voice, they should expand their horizon beyond the medical framework.[61]

This expansion and prioritisation of voices outside of the medical framework has yet to fully emerge. Within the specific context of healthcare safety inquiries, one reason for this is the mobilisation of broader claims to virtue in the unit, the team, the profession, or the system as a response to inquiries and their precipitating events. The claim that 'no one willingly does harm' is offered up with regularity during many less severe forms of

---

57 Christopher Newdick and Christopher Danbury, "Culture, compassion and clinical neglect: Probity in the NHS after Mid Staffordshire," *Journal of Medical Ethics* 41, no. 12 (2015): 956.
58 Mannion and Braithwaite, "False dawns," 685.
59 Travaglia, "Comment on 'False Dawns'," 867.
60 Travaglia, "Comment on 'False Dawns'," 867.
61 Renee Bouwman, Manja Bomhoff, Paul Robben, and Roland, Friele, "Is there a mismatch between the perspectives of patients and regulators on healthcare quality? A survey study," *Journal of Patient Safety* 17, no. 7 (2021): 473–82; David J. Carter, James Brown, and Carla Saunders, "Understanding Public Expectations of Healthcare Quality and Safety Regulation in Australia," *Journal of Law & Medicine* 25, no. 2 (2018): 408–28.

incident investigation, as well as larger-scale public inquiries.[62] The working out of these claims within the investigation of contested death and, as we claim, within the context of large-scale public inquiries generates a (perhaps deliberate) confusion of act and intentionality. In our view, this is a form of dissociative practice on the part of health professionals. They are deeply wedded to an *ideology* of innocence, even though they observe errors, deliberate or not, on a daily basis. This generalised claim to virtue inhibits a more reasoned approach to the harms that do occur, a resistance to their early amelioration, and an inability to internalise the knowledge inquiries produce in promoting consistent, enduring change for the better.

Taken together, these processes result in a form of 'utopian duplication' within the domain of healthcare, a term taken from the work of Foucault in his work on prison reform. For Foucault, as is well known, the 'failure' of prisons to stem the tide of criminal activity has seen the prison '[offer itself] as its own remedy: the reactivation of the penitentiary techniques as the only means of overcoming their perpetual failure'.[63] Similarly, justified criticism of medicine's production of widespread and intractable patient harm leads to reform programmes that simply restore the goals, ideals, structures, and dominance of medicine, its ways of working and thinking, and, with it, the medical profession.

Contested deaths and the healthcare system – The need for a sociological critique of inquiries

Given the continuing need for a systemic response to supposedly exceptional events in the healthcare system, the time is ripe for a new sociological critique not only of particular inquiries or inquiries in general, but of the nature of the inquiry mechanism and process specifically within the healthcare quality and safety domain as it engages with contested iatrogenic death.

There is now an expanding field of literature addressing the idea that societies do not simply respond to harms but that they may actually generate a wide variety of harmful outcomes for their citizens and others.[64] Legal scholar Pemberton writes about the concept of 'harmful societies', or zemiology,[65] an idea emerging from and intended to extend the analytical impact of critical criminological and legal theory. This is, at least in part, because critical criminological and legal theory has also identified the fact that crime and the criminal justice system have different impacts on different social groups. Those who fear crime the most, for example, are often least affected by it. In addition, the scope of what is *criminal* differs across time, space, and socio-political regimes. In this sense, such theorists reprise Hulsman's personal and professional observation that 'crime' lacks any firm ontological basis.[66] This idea connects, we believe, rather neatly with the

---

62 Travaglia, "Comment on 'False Dawn'," 867.

63 Michael Foucault, *Discipline and Punish: The Birth of the Prison* (New York: Vintage Books, 1977).

64 Steve Tombs, "Harmful societies," *Criminal Justice Matters* 101, no. 1 (2015): 36–7; Paddy Hillyard and Steve Tombs, "Social harm and zemiology," in *The Oxford Handbook of Criminology*, ed. Alison Liebling, Shadd Maruna, and Lesley McAra (Oxford: Oxford University Press, 2017), 284–305.

65 Simon A. Pemberton, *Harmful Societies: Understanding Social Harm* (Bristol: Policy Press, 2016).

66 Louk H. Hulsman, "Critical criminology and the concept of crime," *Contemporary Crises* 10, no. 1 (1986): 63–80.

mechanistic nature of inquiries as formal responses which 'exceptionalise' contested deaths that exhibit recurrent and specific patterns by making the everyday seem abnormal and unique.

Foucault's investigations of social institutions, such as prisons and hospitals, are highly relevant to a broadening critical sociology of inquiries, while his doctoral supervisor, Canguilhem, also developed and explored the twin concepts of the normal and the pathological in medicine,[67] though this notion has strayed far outside of medical boundaries to an idea with social power and influence in its own right. The pervasiveness of this distinction between the normal and the pathological can even be seen as one that the inquiry form has internalised. Specifically, iatrogenic death, a normal output of a complex and poorly governed system, is characterised as pathological: a distinctive and infrequent deviation from the norm. This is problematic in view of the history of iatrogenic harm and death, the inquiries which investigate them, their recurrent nature, and the stability of the particular social groups who are harmed.

A key observation we make in this chapter is that the social groups most frequently, and repeatedly, harmed in healthcare environments, are the same ones across time. This includes groups who are socially or economically vulnerable, the elderly, and people who are living with a mental illness. Given this, we need to consider the regulatory power of hospitals and their ancillary sub-systems to mediate and differentially distribute the (poor) quality of care provided to different social groups. The health sciences represent a product and system of social ordering and, therefore, those at risk in them are those whose harms are most often tolerated by society. This differential distribution of death between different social, racialised, or other groupings is the hallmark of the operation of biopower as it abandons particular groups through a greater exposure to death.[68] As critical sociology and critical legal theory suggest, there is a point at which systems do not produce exceptions but instead the outcomes they were *designed* to produce. In other words, inquiries form a mechanism not so much for improvement or change as re-establishing the equilibrium of a system used to and confident in the outcomes it so consistently shows.

Conclusion

It might be that public inquiries are a failed mechanism for investigating and preventing contested deaths in healthcare environments, as major adverse events and ongoing iatrogenic harm and death continue to occur at regular intervals around the globe. However, beyond their failure to effectively arrest the rate of iatrogenic death, inquiries must also be seen as producing *something* and productive for some purpose. As such, these broader productive effects of the public inquiry into healthcare-related death need to be considered and analysed in a more wide-ranging sociological and critical legal context than has been the case to date. Do inquiries, for instance, generate sustained change, and if so, where, how, and for whom? Why, if the same groups continue to be harmed at regular intervals by health systems and professionals, is this the case, and what change might we make to these seemingly inevitable outcomes?

67 Georges Canguilhem, *The Normal and the Pathological* (New York: Zone Books, 1989).
68 Ben Golder, "The Distribution of Death: Notes towards a Bio-Political Theory of Criminal Law," in *New Critical Legal Thinking: Law and the Political*, ed. Matthew Stone, Illan Rua Wall, and Costas Douzinas (London: Taylor & Francis, 2012), 91–111; Achille Mbembe, "Necropolitics," *Public Culture* 15, no. 1 (2003): 17.

Current academic modalities and specialties seem inadequate for understanding the scope and complexity of events that produce social harms, especially in the context of formalised responses, such as healthcare inquiries. We have thus suggested that inquiries and the evidence and knowledge they produce have a highly generalisable nature, yet each inquiry tends to be treated on its own narrowly specific terms, as though it inherently lacks generalisability. This is an issue for a critical and sociologically informed examination of inquiries. Accordingly, combining *critical* perspectives from sociology, history, and law may improve both the outcomes of individual inquiries and their ability to ameliorate, if not prevent, future large-scale failures in patient safety.

Bibliography

Blom-Cooper, Louis. *Public Inquiries: Wrong Route on Bloody Sunday*. Oxford: Bloomsbury Publishing, 2017.

Bouwman, Renee, Manja Bomhoff, Paul Robben, and Roland Friele "Is there a mismatch between the perspectives of patients and regulators on healthcare quality? A survey study." *Journal of Patient Safety* 17, no. 7 (2021): 473–482. https://doi.org/10.1097/PTS.0000000000000413.

Braithwaite, Jeffrey, Robert L. Wears, and Erik Hollnagel. "Resilient health care: Turning patient safety on its head." *International Journal for Quality in Health Care* 27, no. 5 (2015): 418–420. https://doi.org/10.1093/intqhc/mzv063.

Canguilhem, Georges. *The Normal and the Pathological*. New York: Zone Books, 1989.

Carter, David J. *Responsibility for Iatrogenic Death in Australian Criminal Law*. Doctoral Thesis, University of Technology Sydney, 2017.

Carter, David J. "Responsibility for Iatrogenic Death in Australian Criminal Law." *Journal and Proceedings of the Royal Society of New South Wales* 152, no. 471/472 (2019): 140–142.

Carter, David J., James Brown, and Carla Saunders. "Understanding Public Expectations of Healthcare Quality and Safety Regulation in Australia." *Journal of Law & Medicine* 25, no. 2 (2018): 408–428.

Cartwright, Silvia Rose. *The Report of the Committee of Inquiry into Allegations Concerning the Treatment of Cervical Cancer at National Women's Hospital and into Other Related Matters*. Auckland, New Zealand, July 1988.

Commission for Healthcare Audit and Inspection. *Investigation into Mid Staffordshire NHS Foundation Trust*. London: Commission for Healthcare Audit and Inspection, 2009.

Corbett, Angus, Jo Travaglia, and Jeffrey Braithwaite. "The Role of Individual Diligence in Improving Safety." *Journal of Health Organization & Management* 25, no. 3 (2011): 247–260. https://doi.org/10.1108/14777261111143518.

Dominiczak, Jason, and Lara Khansa. "Principles of automation for patient safety in intensive care: Learning from aviation." *The Joint Commission Journal on Quality & Patient Safety* 44, no. 6 (2018): 366–371. https://doi.org/10.1016/j.jcjq.2017.11.008.

Dorsett, Shaunnagh, and Shaun McVeigh. "Questions of Jurisdiction." In *Jurisprudence of Jurisdiction*, edited by Shaun McVeigh. Abingdon: Routledge-Cavendish, 2006.

Dorsett, Shaunnagh, and Shaun McVeigh. *Jurisdiction*. Abingdon: Routledge, 2012.

Douglas, Neil, Kathleen Fahy, and Jeffrey Robinson. *Final Report of the Inquiry into Obstetric and Gynaecological Services at King Edward Memorial Hospital 1990–2000*. Perth: Western Australian Government Inquiry into Obstetric Gynaecological Services at King Edward Memorial Hospital, 2001.

Elliott, Dominic, and Martina McGuinness. "Public inquiry: Panacea or placebo?" *Journal of Contingencies & Crisis Management* 10, no. 1 (2002): 14–25. https://doi.org/10.1111/1468-5973.00177.

Foucault, Michel. *Power/Knowledge: Selected Interviews and Other Writings, 1972–1977*. New York: Pantheon Books, 1980.

Foucault, Michael. *Discipline and Punish: The Birth of the Prison*. New York: Vintage Books, 1977.

Francis, Robert. *Independent Inquiry into Care Provided by Mid Staffordshire NHS Foundation Trust January 2005–March 2009 Volume 1*. London: The Stationery Office, 2010.

Garling, Peter. *Final Report of the Special Commission of Inquiry, Acute Care Services in NSW Public Hospitals*. Sydney: NSW Department of Premier and Cabinet, 2008.

Garling, Peter. *Final Report of the Special Commission of Inquiry, Acute Care Services in NSW Public Hospitals: Overview report*. Sydney: NSW Department of Premier and Cabinet, 2008.

Gibbs, Graham, and Christopher Hall. "The research potential of testimony from public inquiry websites." *Children & Society* 21, no. 1 (2007).

Golder, Ben. "The Distribution of Death: Notes towards a Bio-Political Theory of Criminal Law." In *New Critical Legal Thinking: Law and the Political*, edited by Matthew Stone, Illan RuaWall, and Costas Douzinas, 91–111. London: Taylor & Francis, 2012.

Gosport Independent Panel. *Return to an Address of the Honourable the House of Commons Dated 20 June 2018 for Gosport War Memorial Hospital: The Report of the Gosport Independent Panel*, 2018. www.gosportpanel.independent.gov.uk.

Grierson, Jamie. "NHS Hasn't Improved Enough since Mid Staffs, Says Inquiry Lawyer." *The Guardian*, 13 February 2017. www.theguardian.com/society/2017/feb/12/nhs-improve-enough-mid-staffs-inquiry-lawyer.

Hamilton, John D., Robert W. Gibberd, and Bernadette T. Harrison. "After the quality in Australian health care study, what happened?" *The Medical Journal of Australia* 201, no. 1 (2014): 23. https://doi.org/10.5694/mja14.00615.

Hilgartner, Stephen. "Overflow and Containment in the Aftermath of Disaster." *Social Studies of Science* 37, no. 1 (2007): 153–158. https://doi.org/10.1177/0306312706069439.

Hillyard, Paddy, and Steve Tombs. "Social harm and zemiology." In *The Oxford Handbook of Criminology*, edited by Alison Liebling, Shadd Maruna and Lesley McAra, 284–305. Oxford: Oxford University Press, 2017.

Hindle, Don, Jeffrey Braithwaite, Jo Travaglia, and R. Iedema. *Patient Safety: A Comparative Analysis of Eight Inquiries in Six Countries*. Sydney: Centre for Clinical Governance Research, University of New South Wales, 2006.

Holmes, David. "Mid Staffordshire scandal highlights NHS cultural crisis." *The Lancet* 381, no. 9866 (2013): 521–522. https://doi.org/10.1016/S0140-6736(13)60264-0.

Howe, Geoffrey. "The management of public inquiries." *The Political Quarterly* 70, no. 3 (1999): 294–304. https://doi.org/10.1111/1467-923X.00232.

Hulsman, Louk H. "Critical criminology and the concept of crime." *Contemporary Crises* 10, no. 1 (1986): 63–80. https://doi.org/10.1007/BF00728496.

Huynh, Chi, Ian C. Wong, Jo Correa-West, David Terry, and Suzanne McCarthy. "Paediatric patient safety and the need for aviation black box thinking to learn from and prevent medication errors." *Paediatric Drugs* 19, no. 2 (2017): 99–105. https://doi.org/10.1007/s40272-017-0214-8.

Inwood, Gregory J., and Carolyn M. Johns. "Commissions of inquiry and policy change: Comparative analysis and future research frontiers." *Canadian Public Administration* 59, no. 3 (2016): 382–404. https://doi.org/10.1111/capa.12177.

Johnstone, Megan-Jane. "Patient safety, ethics and whistleblowing: A nursing response to the events at the Campbelltown and Camden Hospitals." *Australian Health Review* 28, no. 1 (2004): 13–19. https://doi.org/10.1071/AH040013.

Joseph, Anthony P., and Stephen N. Hunyor. "The Royal North Shore Hospital inquiry: An analysis of the recommendations and the implications for quality and safety in Australian public hospitals." *Medical Journal of Australia* 188, no. 8 (2008): 469–472. https://doi.org/10.5694/j.1326-5377.2008.tb01720.x.

Mannion, Russell, and Jeffrey Braithwaite. "False dawns and new horizons in patient safety research and practice." *International Journal of Health Policy & Management* 6, no. 12 (2017): 685–689. https://doi.org/10.15171/ijhpm.2017.115.

Mbembe, Achille. "Necropolitics." *Public Culture* 15, no. 1 (2003): 11–40. https://doi.org/10.1215/08992363-15-1-11.

New Zealand Committee of Inquiry into Allegations Concerning the Treatment of Cervical Cancer at National Women's Hospital. *Report of Inquiry into Allegations Concerning the Treatment of Cervical Cancer at National Women's Hospital and into Other Related Matters*. Auckland: Government Printing Office, New Zealand Government, 1988.

Newdick, Christopher, and Christopher Danbury. "Culture, compassion and clinical neglect: Probity in the NHS after Mid Staffordshire." *Journal of Medical Ethics* 41, no. 12 (2015): 956–962. http://dx.doi.org/10.1136/medethics-2012-101048.

NSW Legislative Council. *Legislative Council Joint Select Committee Inquiry into Royal North Shore Hospital*. Sydney: NSW Government, 2007.

Oderberg, Isabelle. "Years after Jana's horror story made headlines, the system is still letting women down." *The Sydney Morning Herald*, 16 April 2023. www.smh.com.au/lifestyle/health-and-well

ness/years-after-jana-s-horror-story-made-headlines-the-system-is-still-letting-wom en-down-20230411-p5czmu.html.

Pemberton, Simon A. *Harmful Societies: Understanding Social Harm.* Bristol: Policy Press, 2016.

Prasser, Scott. *Royal Commissions and Public Inquiries in Australia.* LexisNexis Butterworths, 2006.

Robotham, J., and N. Wallace. "Heartbreak Hospitals." *Sydney Morning Herald,* 21 November 2009. www.smh.com.au/national/heartbreak-hospitals-20091120-iqv4.html.

Rowland, Paula. *Power/Knowledge, Identity and Patient Safety: Intersections of Patient Safety and Professional Practice Discourses in a Canadian Acute Care Hospital.* Doctoral Thesis, Fielding Graduate University, 2013.

Runciman, William. "Shared meanings: Preferred terms and definitions for safety and quality concepts." *The Medical Journal of Australia* 184, no. 10 (2006): 41–43. https://doi.org/10.5694/j. 1326-5377.2006.tb00360.x.

Runciman, William, and J. Moller. *Iatrogenic Injury in Australia.* Adelaide: Australian Patient Safety Foundation, 2001.

Runciman, W. B., M. J. Edmonds, and M. Pradhan. "Setting priorities for patient safety." *BMJ Quality & Safety* 11, no. 3 (2002): 224–229.

Sinclair, Murray. *Report of the Manitoba Pediatric Cardiac Surgery Inquest.* Winnipeg: Manitoba Provincial Court, 1994.

Smith, Janet. *The Shipman Inquiry.* London: The Stationery Office, 2004.

Stark, Alastair. "New institutionalism, critical junctures and post-crisis policy reform." *Australian Journal of Political Science* 53, no. 1 (2018): 24–39. https://doi.org/10.1080/10361146.2017.1409335.

Stolk-Vos, Aline C., Marion H. Heres, Jasper Kesteloo, Dick Verburg, Frans Hiddema, Desiree A. Lie and Dirk F. de Korne. "Is there a role for the use of aviation assessment instruments in surgical training preparation? A feasibility study." *Postgraduate Medical Journal* 93, no. 1095 (2017): 20–24. https://doi.org/10.1136/postgradmedj-2016-133984.

The Australian Council for Safety and Quality in Health Care. *Lessons from the Inquiry into Obstetrics and Gynaecological Services at King Edward Memorial Hospital 1990–2000.* Canberra: The Australian Council for Safety and Quality in Health Care, 2002. www.safetyandquality.gov.au/sites/ default/files/migrated/king_edward.pdf.

The Bristol Royal Infirmary Inquiry. *The Report of the Public Inquiry into Children's Heart Surgery at the Bristol Royal Infirmary 1984–1995.* Bristol: Bristol Royal Infirmary Inquiry, 2001.

The Health Foundation. *Evidence Scan: Levels of Harm.* London: The Health Foundation, 2011.

Tombs, Steve. "Harmful societies." *Criminal Justice Matters* 101, no. 1 (2015): 36–37. https://doi.org/ 10.1080/09627251.2015.1080945.

Travaglia, Joanne. "Disturbing the Doxa of Patient Safety: Comment on 'False Dawns and New Horizons in Patient Safety Research and Practice'." *International Journal of Health Policy & Management* 7, no. 9 (2018): 867–869. https://doi.org/10.15171/ijhpm.2018.26.

Walker, Bret. *Final Report of the Special Commission of Inquiry into Campbelltown Camden Hospitals.* Sydney: NSW Government Special Commission of Inquiry into Campbelltown Camden Hospitals, 2004.

Wallace, Natasha, and Alexandra Smith. "Public Hospitals on 'Brink of Collapse'." *The Sydney Morning Herald,* 28 November 2008. www.smh.com.au/national/public-hospitals-on-brink-of-collap se-20081128-gdt4kb.html.

Walshe, Kieran. *Inquiries: Learning from Failure in the NHS.* London: Nuffield Trust, 2003. www. nuffieldtrust.org.uk/sites/default/files/2017-01/inquiries-learning-from-failure-nhs-web-final.pdf.

Walshe, Kieran. "Gosport deaths: Lethal failures in care will happen again." *British Medical Journal* 362 (2018): k2931. https://doi.org/10.1136/bmj.k2931.

Wears, Robert L., Kathleen M.Sutcliffe, and Eric Van Rite. "Patient Safety: A Brief but Spirited History." In *Patient Safety: Perspectives on Evidence, Information and Knowledge Transfer,* edited by Lorri Zipperer, 49–68. London: Routledge, 2016.

Wilson, R. M., P. Michel, S. Olsen, R. W. Gibberd, C. Vincent, R. El-Assady, O. Rasslanet al. "Patient safety in developing countries: Retrospective estimation of scale and nature of harm to patients in hospital." *BMJ 2012,* no. 344 (2012): e832. https://doi.org/10.1136/bmj.e832.

Wilson, R. M., W. B. Runciman, R. W. Gibberd, B. T. Harrison, L. Newby and J. D. Hamilton. "The Quality in Australian Health Care Study." *The Medicine Journal of Australia* 163, no. 9 (1995): 458–471. https://doi.org/10.5694/j.1326-5377.1995.tb124691.x.

18

THE RIGHT TO LIFE AND LEARNING LESSONS FROM DEATH

Stuart Wallace

Introduction

Contested deaths in England and Wales are often the subject of inquests, and a common denominator in these cases is that something has gone wrong and someone has died as a result. The most natural response to such contested deaths is to try to determine what went wrong and ensure that it does not happen again. The state plays a central role in this process through conducting inquests. Inquests are a pivotal part of the system to investigate deaths in England and Wales.[1] A coroner must hold an inquest where they have reason to suspect that a deceased person died a violent or unnatural death,[2] where the cause of death is unknown, or if the deceased died while in custody or state detention. Inquests are limited to examining who the deceased was and how, when, and where the deceased came by their death.[3] However, investigating and determining the facts is only part of the process. I would argue that correcting the mistakes and learning lessons from the death is equally important to, if not more important than, the investigation itself. In England and Wales, coroners issue prevention of future death reports (PFDs) following inquests where their investigation gives rise to a concern that preventable future deaths will occur and that action should be taken to forestall that outcome. In 2022 to 2023 alone, coroners issued 409 PFDs across England and Wales.[4] Yet, as the United Kingdom Parliament's Justice Committee has observed, 'there is no follow-up to see if coroners' reports have had the desired impact'.[5]

In this chapter, I argue that the state has an obligation to learn lessons from avoidable deaths and try to ensure they do not happen again. I explore the current system in cor-onial law of issuing PFDs and identify weaknesses in the system that mean PFDs are not acted upon after they have been issued. I then examine the proposal from the non-

---

1 *R (Middleton) v West Somerset Coroner* [2004] UKHL 10, [20].
2 *Coroners and Justice Act 2009*, ss. 1 and 6.
3 *Coroners and Justice Act 2009*, s. 5(1).
4 Courts and Tribunals Judiciary, "Prevention of Future Death Reports." Accessed 5 June 2023, www.judiciary.uk/?s=&pfd_report_type=&post_type=pfd&order=relevance.
5 House of Commons Justice Committee, *The Coroner Service* (HC 68), 2021, 4.

DOI: 10.4324/9781003304593-21

governmental organisation INQUEST to establish a body to ensure PFDs are tracked and implemented in practice. I consider what effective tracking and implementation requires, drawing on lessons from other industries, and consider the functions that such a body would need to perform to effectively track and implement PFDs.

Legal obligations to prevent future deaths under international human rights law

Article 2 of the *European Convention on Human Rights* (ECHR) contains obligations to respect, protect, and fulfil the right to life. These obligations are interconnected and designed to ensure comprehensive protection. The state must refrain from arbitrarily depriving people of their life, effectively investigate loss of life or life-threatening injuries,[6] protect people from avoidable loss of life where threats to life are foreseeable,[7] and put in place effective legal and administrative frameworks to effectively deter threats to the right to life.[8]

The underlying purpose of the different obligations is important because it speaks to a deeper obligation. In *R (Amin) v Secretary of State for the Home Department*, Lord Justice Bingham observed that the purposes underpinning the obligation to investigate are clear:

> to ensure so far as possible that the full facts are brought to light; that culpable and discreditable conduct is exposed and brought to public notice; that suspicion of deliberate wrongdoing (if unjustified) is allayed; that dangerous practices and procedures are rectified; and that those who have lost their relative may at least have the satisfaction of knowing that lessons learned from his death may save the lives of others.[9]

This element of learning from mistakes is repeated over and over in the jurisprudence. The Court of Appeal observed in *R (Lewis) v HM Coroner for the Mid and North Division of the County of Shropshire* that the objective of the obligation to investigate is to learn lessons for the future.[10] In *R (Sacker) v West Yorkshire Coroner*, the House of Lords observed that investigative mechanisms like inquests have 'a vital part to play in the correction of mistakes and the search for improvements'.[11] There are repeated references to learning lessons for the future; it is seen as central to the protection of the right to life.

The investigative obligation and the obligation to establish an administrative framework that protects the right to life are also linked. According to the European Court of Human Rights (ECtHR), the purpose of the investigation is, in part, to ensure that the administrative framework set up to protect the right to life is properly implemented and any problems with it are identified.[12] The ECtHR refers to ensuring 'adequate protection "by law" safeguarding the right to life and deterring similar life-endangering conduct in

---

6 *McCann and Others v United Kingdom* (1996) 21 EHRR 97, [161].
7 *Osman v United Kingdom* (2000) 29 EHRR 245, [115].
8 *Makaratzis v Greece* (2005) 41 EHRR 49, [57].
9 *R (Amin) v Home Secretary* [2003] UKHL 51, [31].
10 *R (Lewis) v HM Coroner for the Mid and North Division of the County of Shropshire* [2009] EWCA Civ 1403, [11].
11 *R (Sacker) v West Yorkshire Coroner* [2004] UKHL 11, [11]. See also *R (Letts) v Lord Chancellor* [2015] EWHC 402 (Admin), [63].
12 *Oneryildiz v Turkey* (2005) 41 EHRR 20, [91], [94].

future'.[13] In *Lopes de Sousa v Portugal*, a case concerning medical negligence, the court observed that:

> the States' obligation to regulate must be understood in a broader sense which includes the duty to ensure the effective functioning of that regulatory framework. The regulatory duties thus encompass necessary measures to ensure implementation, including supervision and enforcement.[14]

The House of Lords links these investigation and administrative framework obligations in *R (Sacker) v West Yorkshire Coroner*:

> There must be a rigorous examination in public of the operation at every level of the systems and procedures which are designed to prevent self-harm and to save lives.[15]

Thus, to protect the right to life effectively, the systems that protect lives, including the regulatory framework, must function effectively.

Taken together, these statements speak to a deeper obligation of the state under Article 2. An obligation to identify problems with the regulatory framework of the state, correct mistakes, and deter similar life-endangering conduct in future, or, put simply, to learn lessons. The underlying aim of consistent, incremental improvement is entirely consistent with the ECHR's overarching goal of providing rights protection that is practical and effective and not theoretical and illusory.[16] This deeper obligation is integral to the different aspects of protecting the right to life, but in practice, in England and Wales at least, it is often overlooked. While the state often goes to great lengths through inquests, police investigations, public inquiries, etc. to determine what caused a death, very little effort is expended to learn from the death and ensure it does not happen again. This process is largely overlooked but must be addressed if victims are to have the consolation of knowing that lessons will be learned from the death of their loved one and others will not suffer the same fate. In the next section, I explore how the current coronial system attempts to learn from deaths.

Recommendations arising from inquests

The obligation to investigate is triggered once a death or life-threatening injury is brought to the state's attention.[17] Unsurprisingly, the type of investigation required varies depending on the circumstances. A person dying of natural causes in old age will warrant a very limited, if any, investigation, while a mass shooting or terrorist attack will often demand a massive investigation spanning government departments and lasting a very long time. What is surprising – and central to this entire chapter – is the degree of variation in what happens *after* the investigation and how the state responds to and follows up on recommendations to prevent future deaths. Here, the circumstances of one's death have a huge impact. In some cases, for example, where fatalities arise from an aviation accident,

13 *Oneryildiz v Turkey* (2005) 41 EHRR 20, [118].
14 *Lopes de Sousa v Portugal* (2018) 66 EHRR 28.
15 *R (Sacker) v West Yorkshire Coroner* [2004] UKHL 11, [11].
16 See, among many authorities, *Airey v Ireland* (1979) 2 EHRR 305, [24].
17 *Ergi v Turkey* (2001) 32 EHRR 18, [82].

a great deal of energy and resources are expended to ensure deaths arising from similar circumstances are prevented. In other cases, very little is done to ensure deaths arising from similar circumstances are prevented. In this section, I focus on and critique the process by which recommendations to prevent future deaths are made at inquests.

Inquests

Inquests are a pivotal part of the system to investigate deaths in England and Wales.[18] A coroner must hold an inquest where they have reason to suspect that a deceased person died a violent or unnatural death,[19] where the cause of death is unknown, or if the deceased died while in custody or state detention. Inquests are limited by law to examining who the deceased was and how, when, and where the deceased came by their death.[20]

The *Coroners and Justice Act 2009* imposes a duty on coroners to make reports where the coroner believes that action should be taken to prevent future deaths.[21] These are commonly known as 'prevention of future death reports' or PFDs.[22] Reports are made to 'a person, organisation, local authority or government department or agency' who the coroner believes may have the power to take action to reduce the risk of death arising from similar circumstances.[23] Coroners issue hundreds of PFDs each year.[24] The reports are sent to the Chief Coroner 'and every interested person who in the coroner's opinion should receive it'.[25]

The addressee of the report, who the coroner believes has the power to take action to reduce the risk of death arising in similar circumstances, is under a duty to respond to a PFD and must respond within 56 days of the date on which the report is sent.[26] The response should include details of any action that has been taken or is proposed to be taken in response to the PFD and a timetable for this. Alternatively, an explanation as to why no action is proposed can be sent.[27] On receipt of a response, the coroner who completed the PFD must send a copy of the response to the Chief Coroner and any interested persons who, in the coroner's opinion, should receive it or other persons who may find it useful or of interest.[28] The Chief Coroner can publish a copy of the response or a summary of it.[29] The United Kingdom Ministry of Justice publishes most PFDs and responses to them on its website.[30] However, as the House of Commons Justice Select Committee observed, 'The information published is the bare minimum and is difficult to search and analyse'.[31] This makes it difficult to identify any recurring issues and hampers efforts to follow up.

18 *R (Middleton) v West Somerset Coroner* [2004] UKHL 10, [20].

19 *Coroners and Justice Act 2009*, ss. 1 and 6.

20 *Coroners and Justice Act 2009*, s. 5(1).

21 *Coroners and Justice Act 2009*, Schedule 5, para. 7.

22 *Coroners (Investigations) Regulations 2013*, Part 7.

23 *Coroners and Justice Act 2009*, Schedule 5, para. 7(1).

24 Courts and Tribunals Judiciary, "Revised Chief Coroner's Guidance No.5 Reports to Prevent Future Deaths," published 20 November 2020, www.judiciary.uk/guidance-and-resources/revi sed-chief-coroners-guidance-no-5-reports-to-prevent-future-deathsi.

25 *The Coroners (Investigations) Regulations 2013*, s. 28(4)(a).

26 *The Coroners (Investigations) Regulations 2013*, s. 29(4).

27 *The Coroners (Investigations) Regulations 2013*, s. 29(3).

28 *The Coroners (Investigations) Regulations 2013*, s. 29(6).

29 *The Coroners (Investigations) Regulations 2013*, s. 29(7).

30 Courts and Tribunals Judiciary, "Prevention of Future Death Reports."

31 House of Commons Justice Committee, "Coroner Service," 53.

Prevention of future death recommendations

Cross and Garnham contend that PFDs are an extremely important part of discharging the state's obligation to investigate under the right to life.[32] Failure to issue a PFD could amount to a breach of Article 2 of the ECHR.[33] Given the importance of PFDs in the process of protecting the right to life, it is puzzling that so little attention is given to following up on recommendations after they are issued. As the Chief Coroner observed in 2021:

> PFD reports are an extremely valuable part of the armoury of coroners. The responses are equally important, but we need to make sure that we don't let those lessons fall between different stools and that we follow them through.[34]

A PFD raises concerns and recommends that action should be taken, but not what that action should be.[35] The latter is a matter for the person or organisation to whom the PFD is directed. Lady Justice Hallett stated:

> [I]t is neither necessary, nor appropriate, for a coroner making a report [...] to identify the necessary remedial action. As is apparent from the final words of rule 43(1), the coroner's function is to identify points of concern, not to pre-scribe solutions.[36]

Thus, it is left to the party receiving the recommendation to determine how to act. In *Re Clegg*, the court stated that

> a coroner cannot be expected to do more than to make general recommendations and that it must, at the end of the day, be for the National Health Service to give detailed consideration to how their recommendations should be implemented.[37]

There is no detailed assessment of whether the recommendations are implemented. The Chief Coroner has alluded to having a role in following up PFDs:

> [T]he Chief Coroner should have a role in taking some reports (and responses) further. Therefore, from time to time the Chief Coroner makes an assessment of areas of concern, whether from single or multiple reports, and may advise action

---

32 The importance of PFDs has been emphasised by Parliament by placing the rules originally con-tained in the Coroners Rules 1984 into statute, in the *Coroners and Justice Act 2009*: Caroline Cross and Neil Garnham, eds. *The Inquest Book: The Law of Coroners and Inquests.* (Oxford; Portland, OR: Hart Publishing, 2016).

33 *R (Lewis) v HM Coroner for the Mid and North Division of the County of Shropshire* [2009] EWCA Civ 1403, [38].

34 House of Commons Justice Committee, *Coroner Service*; House of Commons Justice Committee, "Oral Evidence," 17 November 2020, Q153, https://committees.parliament.uk/oralevidence/1235/html.

35 Courts and Tribunals Judiciary, "Revised Chief Coroner's Guidance No.5."

36 Heather Hallett, "Coroner's Inquests into the London Bombings of the 7 July 2005: Concluding Remarks," Judicial Communications Office, published 6 May 2011. https://sris.aviationreporting.eu/safety-recommendations. https://webarchive.nationalarchives.gov.uk/ukgwa/20120216072447mp_/http://7julyinquests.independent.gov.uk/hearing_transcripts/06052011am.htm.

37 *Re Clegg* (1996) 161 JP 521 (DC).

where appropriate. He may consult on areas of concern and where feasible recommend action, whether by way of advice to government or an organisation or individual, or where necessary by recommending a change in the law. These recommendations may also be published.[38]

This role is vaguely defined at best, and it is unclear how much capacity the Chief Coroner's office has to do this. What happens after a PFD is issued represents a central weakness in the entire system protecting the right to life in England and Wales. There is a duty to report and respond to reports, but nothing else: no tracking of the addressee's response and no evaluation of whether appropriate actions have been taken. As the House of Commons Justice Select Committee observed in a report on the Coroner Service:

> There is no process to follow-up whether actions promised at inquests or in responses to prevention of future death reports are put into effect [...] There is a lack of a proper central hub to properly monitor such reports and to follow them up and to try and secure change.[39]

The committee described the system as 'under-developed' and a 'missed opportunity'.[40] The British government itself acknowledged that there was 'more that can be done' to ensure PFDs actively contribute to improvements in public safety.[41] The committee recommended establishing an independent office to report on emerging issues and follow up on actions promised in response to a PFD. It was suggested that the proposed Coroner Service Inspectorate could undertake this task,[42] but linking this task specifically to a Coroner Service Inspectorate could be problematic because the issues surrounding following up on recommendations to prevent future deaths are not germane to the Coroner Service. There are also problems with following up on recommendations from public inquiries, and several public inquiries have emerged from inquests concerning extremely serious issues.[43] If an office established to follow up on recommendations was linked exclusively to inquests, it could miss extremely important recommendations arising from public inquiries. As such, there is a case for a more free-standing body not limited exclusively to a specific investigatory mechanism. In the next section, I consider what that body might look like and the functions it would need to perform.

Tracking and implementing recommendations

The non-governmental organisation INQUEST has been campaigning for many years for the need to track and follow up recommendations to prevent future deaths from inquests

---

38 Courts and Tribunals Judiciary, "Revised Chief Coroner's Guidance No.5."
39 House of Commons Justice Committee, Coroner Service, 50–1.
40 House of Commons Justice Committee, Coroner Service, 53.
41 House of Commons Justice Committee, Coroner Service, Appendix: Government Response.
42 House of Commons Justice Committee, Coroner Service, 53.
43 The *Coroners and Justice Act 2009*, Schedule 1, makes specific provision for inquests to be converted into public inquiries. Several inquests have been converted to public inquiries, including the inquest into the death of Alexander Litvinenko, see *R (Litvinenko) v Secretary of State for the Home Department* [2014] EWHC 194 (Admin), [14]; the inquest into the death of Azelle Rodney, see Christopher Holland, *The Executive Summary of the Azelle Rodney Inquiry Report* (HC 551), 3; and the inquest into the death of Anthony Grainger, see Thomas Teague, *Report into the Death of Anthony Grainger* (HC 2354), 2.

and public inquiries.[44] INQUEST has proposed the creation of '[a] new, independent, public body with a duty to collate, analyse and monitor recommendations and their implementation arising from post death investigations, inquiries and inquests'.[45] This body, described as a National Oversight Mechanism, would respond to the state's legal obligations to learn lessons from deaths. The campaign has received support from the Justice Select Committee, the Joint Committee on Human Rights, and several other parties.[46]

The need for such a body is well recognised, but as a minister from the Ministry of Justice acknowledged in 2021, 'how one goes about doing that effectively is a subject for legitimate discussion'.[47] In this section, I draw on lessons from other sectors to explore this issue, arguing that a National Oversight Mechanism should have responsibility for the collation of data, tracking the implementation of recommendations, evaluating the responses of addressees, responding to non-implementation, and analysing data to identify systemic problems.

Collation of data

The first objective of the National Oversight Mechanism should be the collation of recommendations by creating a database for PFD recommendations. The benefits of creating a single, accessible source of information to keep track of recommendations and the status of implementation are clear. If we cannot quickly and easily establish what the recommendations are, we cannot track implementation. Collating this type of data is common in other sectors. In the context of civil aviation, which has an excellent record of incremental safety improvement,[48] the system of investigating air accidents also involves the collection and collation of all investigation reports in a centralised database.[49] The database, run by the European Union Commission, is called the Safety Recommendations Information System and collates both the safety recommendations issued and actions taken in response to them from across the European Union.[50] According to the European Commission, the increased transparency and publicity provide 'strong incentives for their addressees to effectively react' to the recommendations made.[51]

Currently, in England and Wales, the Chief Coroner publishes PFDs on the Courts and Tribunal website, but this lacks the functionality of a database and pales in comparison to the resources available in other jurisdictions. The Australian National Coronial

44 INQUEST, "INQUEST calls for new mechanism for oversight on recommendations in response to the Grenfell Tower Inquiry," published 30 October 2019, www.inquest.org.uk/grenfell-phase1.
45 INQUEST, "Inquest Campaigns," published 2 August 2022, www.inquest.org.uk/Pages/Category/campaigns.
46 Home Office, *Report of the Independent Review of Deaths and Serious Incidents in Police Custody* (London: Home Office, 2017), 229; Joint Committee on Human Rights, "Mental Health and Deaths in Prison: Interim Report" (HC 893), 2017, 10; House of Commons Justice Committee, "Coroner Service," 53.
47 House of Commons Justice Committee, "Coroner Service"; House of Commons Justice Committee, "Oral Evidence," Q179.
48 Statistics show there is one fatality for every 287 million passengers carried by United Kingdom civil aviation operators, compared with a one in 17,000 chance of being killed in a road accident: Civil Aviation Authority, *Annual Safety Review 2022*, accessed 8 July 2024, www.caa.co.uk/publication/download/20660.
49 Council Regulation (EU) 996/2010, Article 18(5).
50 European Central Repository of Safety Recommendations, "Safety Recommendations.".
51 European Commission, *Commission Staff Working Document on the Implementation of Regulation (EU) No 996/2010*, 6.

Information System, for example, provides a fully indexed repository of coronial data from Australia and New Zealand, including the outcomes of inquests and other contextual details, which makes tracking recommendations much more straightforward.[52] It is understood that the Office of the Chief Coroner in England and Wales is 'exploring ways in which publication of the reports may be enhanced and made easier to research and digest'[53] and has made some recent improvements. Creating a more structured resource would allow interested parties to gain insights into deaths much more quickly than under the current system.[54] It could also facilitate the wider dissemination of PFDs to coroners and other parties who can effect change and may help to identify systemic problems sooner.[55]

Clear responsibility for tracking implementation

The second objective of the National Oversight Mechanism must be establishing a system of responsibility for tracking implementation that is directly linked to a database. In other sectors, recommendations are tracked automatically and responsibility for doing this is clear. In civil aviation, for example, domestic aviation authorities investigate civil aircraft accidents and issue safety recommendations with the intention of preventing accidents and incidents in future.[56] Similar to PFDs, these are sent to relevant parties, including manufacturers, who are obligated to respond within 90 days to explain what actions they have taken and the timescales for completion.[57] The addressees are obligated to monitor the progress of action taken in response to the recommendations.[58] The safety investigation authority evaluates the adequacy of the response and can follow up with the addressee to request that their response and proposed actions be reviewed.[59]

A central weakness of the PFD system is an absence of ownership over recommendations. At inquests, there is no designated party charged with ongoing monitoring or follow-up on implementation of recommendations.[60] The closest analogue is a loosely defined role for the Chief Coroner 'in taking some reports (and responses) further ... from time to time'.[61] This appears to be ad hoc and inconsistent. Identifying a responsible party for tracking implementation would close this feedback loop and overcome the current disconnect between issuing recommendations and tracking implementation.

Response evaluation

The third objective of the National Oversight Mechanism must be evaluating the adequacy of responses to recommendations. Civil aviation investigation authorities classify the

---

52 National Coronial Information System, "Explanatory Notes."
53 Office of the Chief Coroner, *Report of the Chief Coroner to the Lord Chancellor: Seventh Annual Report*, 27.
54 Leary et al., "A Thematic Analysis."
55 Home Office, *Report of the Independent Review*, 229.
56 Regulation (EU) No 996/2010, Article 2(15).
57 Regulation (EU) No 996/2010, Article 18.
58 Regulation (EU) No 996/2010, Article 18.
59 Regulation (EU) No 996/2010, Article 18.
60 Home Office, *Report of the Independent Review*, 229.
61 Courts and Tribunals Judiciary, "Revised Chief Coroner's Guidance No.5," 62.

responses to their safety recommendations as either 'not adequate', 'partially adequate', or 'adequate'.[62] They offer clear feedback to addressees on progress towards implementation. There is no similar system following inquests. In fact, coroners are actively discouraged from identifying remedial actions because it is not considered appropriate for them to do so.[63] This may rightly be considered inconsistent with the role of the coroner,[64] but the absence of any other party to fulfil this role is clearly problematic. A key challenge for any National Oversight Mechanism will be developing the capacity to evaluate responses across the breadth and complexity of coronial investigations. Coroners deal with a huge range of issues, from emergency medical response procedures to building regulations; evaluating responses to recommendations across these diverse fields will require a range of expertise.

There are lessons to be learned from other systems. The Committee of Ministers at the Council of Europe, for example, supervises the implementation of judgments made by the ECtHR.[65] This involves states submitting action plans to the committee outlining how they will remedy issues arising from ECtHR judgments.[66] These judgments cover everything from torture to violations of freedom of assembly across the legal systems of 46 member states. There is scope for victims to input on whether the issue has been resolved, and in 2021, the committee closed over 1,100 cases.[67] The committee also does this on a relatively modest annual budget of approximately €6 million.[68] The system is far from perfect,[69] but it illustrates that it is possible for a body to supervise the implementation of recommendations across a wide range of activities. The process of evaluating responses could also engage different select committees in parliament, which have expertise in discrete areas but can also call on experts to give evidence where needed to help evaluate responses.

Responses to non-implementation

The fourth objective of the National Oversight Mechanism must be the creation of an effective response to non-implementation of recommendations. While there is a duty on the addressee of a PFD to respond,[70] there are no consequences for not implementing recommendations, which must be addressed. First, where public authorities are addressees of PFD recommendations, there should be a statutory duty to report on the implementation of recommendations at regular intervals. This has been proposed in the context of implementation of public inquiry recommendations and

---

62 European Co-ordination Centre for Accident and Incident Reporting Systems, "What is a Safety Recommendation", accessed 5 June 2023, https://aviationreporting.eu/en/safety-recommendations.
63 Hallett, "Coroner's Inquests."
64 House of Commons Justice Committee, *Coroner Service*; House of Commons Justice Committee, "Oral Evidence," Q153.
65 D. J. Harris, M. O'Boyle, Ed Bates, and Carla Buckley, *Harris, O'Boyle & Warbrick: Law of the European Convention on Human Rights*, 4th ed. (Oxford: Oxford University Press, 2018), 184.
66 Harris et al., *Harris, O'Boyle & Warbrick*, 187.
67 Committee of Ministers of the Council of Europe, *Annual Report 2021* (Strasbourg: Council of Europe, 2022), 44.
68 Council of Europe, *Council of Europe Programme and Budget 2022–2025* (Strasbourg: Council of Europe, 2021), 31.
69 Harris et al., *Harris, O'Boyle & Warbrick*, 201; Steven Greer, "Protocol 14 and the Future of the European Court of Human Rights," *Public Law* [2005]: 83–106, 92–3.
70 *The Coroners (Investigations) Regulations 2013*, s. 29(4).

should be applied in the context of PFDs too.[71] Second, when recommendations are not acted upon for whatever reason, the addressee should be obligated to explain why the recommendation is not being acted on. Finally, there should be a system to notify higher authorities of non-implementation of recommendations. This will necessarily be context specific, but notifying the Chief Coroner, government ministers, and parliamentary select committees would help to raise awareness and potentially prompt further action.

Analysis

The final objective of the National Oversight Mechanism should be the analysis of data it has collected to identify systemic problems arising from PFDs. Official analyses of these reports are extremely limited, with the Chief Coroner taking an ad hoc approach to 'identify particular trends' of concern to the country in their annual reports.[72] The 2017 annual report, for example, contained some thematic analysis of deaths in custody.[73] The Office of the Chief Coroner analysed ten PFDs to identify any common themes and discovered issues with emergency medical responses and lack of awareness of procedures among prison officers. There are over 4,000 PFDs in the records, so looking at ten to identify systemic problems is limited at best. The Chief Coroner would like to do more work like this, but the office is not properly resourced to carry it out.[74]

Empirical studies of coronial data in Australia have been used to identify systemic patient safety concerns.[75] There have also been some pioneering studies of PFDs by independent researchers in the UK. Leary et al., for example, conducted a thematic analysis of PFDs in healthcare contexts, looking at over 700 PFDs filed over three years that identified more than 3,000 concerns.[76] Their analysis identified 36 PFDs in which coroners expressed concerns about issuing repeated PFDs to the same institutions for similar issues.[77] They concluded that '[i]f PFDs were used as a source of data for patient safety in a systematic way it might be possible to avoid deaths'[78] and there was a 'substantial opportunity for learning from PFD reports'.[79] Clearly the information in PFDs remains a largely untapped resource that could contribute significantly to public safety and the prevention of avoidable deaths if properly utilised.

71 House of Commons Public Administration Select Committee, "Government by Inquiry" (HC 51-I), 2005, 52; House of Lords Select Committee on the Inquiries Act 2005, *The Inquiries Act 2005: Post-Legislative Scrutiny* (HL 143), 2014, 85.

72 House of Commons Justice Committee, *Coroner Service*; "House of Commons Justice Committee", "Oral Evidence", Q153.

73 Office of the Chief Coroner, *Report of the Chief Coroner to the Lord Chancellor: Fifth Annual Report*, 18–9.

74 Home Office, *Report of the Independent Review*, 229.

75 See, e.g., Val Pudney and Carol Grech, "Benefit of Hindsight: Systematic Analysis of Coronial Inquest Data to Inform Patient Safety in Hospitals," *Australian Health Review* 40, no. 4 (2016): 371–7.

76 Leary et al., "Thematic Analysis," 16.

77 Leary et al., "Thematic Analysis," 16.

78 Leary et al., "Thematic Analysis," 19.

79 Leary et al., "Thematic Analysis," 20.

Conclusion

The United Kingdom rightly expends significant resources to investigate loss of life in various circumstances. Hundreds of PFDs are issued in England and Wales each year with the potential to prevent avoidable deaths in future. Yet all of this effort is in vain if, after having identified problems that lead to avoidable deaths, we do not act to ensure they do not happen again. This is exactly what is happening in the coronial system today. There is no follow-up to determine whether any action has been taken, no checks on implementation, and no consequences for doing nothing in the face of an identified risk. This is the missing link in the protection of the right to life within the United Kingdom and it is imperative that action is taken to address it.

Currently, there are huge disparities in the consequences of our deaths – disparities that lack any clear justification. Why should a death arising from a civil aviation accident set in motion a huge investigation that will result in safety recommendations to various parties that are followed up and evaluated, but a death arising from a road accident lead to an inquest, a PFD, and nothing else? There is no reason why the outcomes should be so disparate, and the system currently in place contains a gaping void of responsibility for following up on PFD recommendations and ensuring lessons are learned.

This chapter has highlighted the problems we face in learning from deaths that are the subject of inquests. The problem is widely acknowledged and calls to address it date back decades. The chapter explored how different bodies handle recommendations to prevent future deaths and what we can learn from them. The weaknesses in the coronial system are clear. There is a need to collate and catalogue recommendations. There need to be clear lines of responsibility for tracking the implementation of recommendations and evaluations of the responses. There also need to be responses and escalations where non-implementation of recommendations occurs. Finally, there needs to be some capacity to analyse the recommendations emerging from these sources to identify systemic problems and try to address them. Until such a time as a National Oversight Mechanism (like that proposed by INQUEST) is created to fulfil this role, preventable deaths will continue to occur.

Bibliography

Civil Aviation Authority. *Annual Safety Review 2022*. Accessed 8 July 2024. www.caa.co.uk/publica tion/download/20660.

Committee of Ministers of the Council of Europe. *Annual Report 2021*. Strasbourg: Council of Europe, 2022.

Council of Europe. *Council of Europe Programme and Budget 2022–2025*. Strasbourg: Council of Europe, 2021.

Courts and Tribunals Judiciary. "Prevention of Future Death Reports." Accessed 5 June 2023. www. judiciary.uk/?s=&pfd_report_type=&post_type=pfd&order=relevance.

Courts and Tribunals Judiciary. "Revised Chief Coroner's Guidance No.5 Reports to Prevent Future Deaths." Published 20 November 2020. www.judiciary.uk/guidance-and-resources/revised-chief-cor oners-guidance-no-5-reports-to-prevent-future-deathsi.

Cross, Caroline, and Neil Garnham, eds. *The Inquest Book: The Law of Coroners and Inquests*. Oxford; Portland, OR: Hart Publishing, 2016.

European Central Repository of Safety Recommendations. "Safety Recommendations." Published 31 May 2023. https://sris.aviationreporting.eu/safety-recommendations.

European Commission. *Commission Staff Working Document on the Implementation of Regulation (EU) No 996/2010 on the Investigation and Prevention of Accidents and Incidents in Civil Aviation*. Brussels: European Commission, 2016.

European Co-ordination Centre for Accident and Incident Reporting Systems. "What is a Safety Recommendation." Accessed 5 June 2023. https://aviationreporting.eu/en/safety-recommendations.

Greer, Steven. "Protocol 14 and the Future of the European Court of Human Rights." *Public Law* [2005]: 83–106.

Hallett, Heather. "Coroner's Inquests into the London Bombings of the 7 July 2005: Concluding Remarks." Judicial Communications Office. Published 6 May 2011. https://webarchive.nationalarchives.gov.uk/ukgwa/20120216072447mp_/http://7julyinquests.independent.gov.uk/hearing_transcripts/06052011am.htm.

Harris, D. J., M. O'Boyle, Ed Bates, and Carla Buckley. *Harris, O'Boyle & Warbrick: Law of the European Convention on Human Rights.* 4th ed. Oxford: Oxford University Press, 2018.

Holland, Christopher. *The Executive Summary of the Azelle Rodney Inquiry Report* (HC 551). 2013.

Home Office. *Report of the Independent Review of Deaths and Serious Incidents in Police Custody.* London: Home Office, 2017.

House of Commons Justice Committee. "Oral Evidence." 17 November 2020, Q153, https://committees.parliament.uk/oralevidence/1235/html.

House of Commons Justice Committee. *The Coroner Service* (HC 68). 2021.

House of Commons Public Administration Select Committee. *Government by Inquiry* (HC 51-I). 2005.

House of Lords Select Committee on the Inquiries Act 2005. *The Inquiries Act 2005: Post-Legislative Scrutiny* (HL 143). 2014.

INQUEST. "INQUEST calls for new mechanism for oversight on recommendations in response to the Grenfell Tower Inquiry". Published 30 October 2019. www.inquest.org.uk/grenfell-phase1.

INQUEST. "Inquest Campaigns." Published 2 August 2022. www.inquest.org.uk/Pages/Category/campaigns.

Joint Committee on Human Rights. *Mental Health and Deaths in Prison: Interim Report* (HC 893). 2017.

Leary, Alison, David Bushe, Crystal Oldman, Jessica Lawler and Geoffrey Punshon. "A Thematic Analysis of the Prevention of Future Deaths Reports in Healthcare from HM Coroners in England and Wales 2016–2019." *Journal of Patient Safety and Risk Management* 26, no. 1 (February 2021): 14–21. https://doi.org/10.1177/2516043521992651.

National Coronial Information System. "Explanatory Notes." Published 31 May 2023. www.ncis.org.au/about-the-data/explanatory-notes.

Office of the Chief Coroner. *Report of the Chief Coroner to the Lord Chancellor: Fifth Annual Report: 2017–2018.* London: Her Majesty's Stationery Office, 2018.

Office of the Chief Coroner. *Report of the Chief Coroner to the Lord Chancellor: Seventh Annual Report: 2019–2020.* London: Her Majesty's Stationery Office, 2020.

Pudney, Val, and Carol Grech. "Benefit of Hindsight: Systematic Analysis of Coronial Inquest Data to Inform Patient Safety in Hospitals." *Australian Health Review* 40, no. 4 (2016): 371–377. https://doi.org/10.1071/AH15020.

Teague, Thomas. *Report into the Death of Anthony Grainger* (HC 2354). 2019.

PART 4

Posthumous Harms

19

AMBIVALENT PARALLELS IN REGISTRATION AND CERTIFICATION OF (LIVE) BIRTH, STILLBIRTH, AND MISCARRIAGE

Karolina Kuberska and Sheelagh McGuinness

Introduction

Decades of historical, anthropological, and socio-legal research have demonstrated that the foetus not only has an extremely complex ontological status but is also charged with a powerful potential that affects the way society deals with it and its material forms. This is particularly salient in the case of pregnancy loss, where matters of disposal and requirements for registration (or lack thereof) shape the material, social, and legal spaces occupied by this kind of experience.[1] Research has shown that certain practices around pregnancy loss in England mirror more formal legal expectations accompanying death, such as funerals and registration, although the parallels are fraught with ambivalence.[2]

Pregnancy loss is a relatively common reproductive event, with 20–25 per cent of all pregnancies ending in a miscarriage.[3] In the United Kingdom (UK), people who experience pregnancy loss can obtain psychological or material support from third-sector organisations, such as the Miscarriage Association or Tommy's (among others). Various pregnancy loss-focused third-sector organisations have pushed to increase the social, scientific, medical, and political visibility of reproductive loss[4] via advocacy work and

---

1 Karolina Kuberska et al., "Death before Birth: Liminal Bodies and Legal Frameworks," in *A Jurisprudence of the Body*, ed. Chris Dietz, Mitchell Travis, and Michael Thompson (Basingstoke: Palgrave Macmillan, 2020), 149–78.

2 Karolina Kuberska, "Unwitnessed Ceremonies: Funeral Services for Pre-24-Week Pregnancy Losses in England," in *Navigating Miscarriage: Social, Medical, and Conceptual Perspectives*, ed. Susie Kilshaw and Katie Borg (New York: Berghahn, 2020), 247–76; Aimee Middlemiss, "Pregnancy Remains, Infant Remains, or the Corpse of a Child? The Incoherent Governance of the Dead Foetal Body in England," *Mortality* 26, no. 3 (2021): 299–315, https://doi.org/10.1080/13576275.2020.1787365.

3 Miscarriage Association, "Background Information," 2022 (accessed 14 November 2023), www.miscarriageassociation.org.uk/media-queries/background-information.

DOI: 10.4324/9781003304593-23

political lobbying to move away from treating miscarriage as a low-priority issue.[5] These efforts, to some extent underpinned by an assumption that reproductive losses are experienced as a form of bereavement, have included lobbying for paid bereavement leave following miscarriage[6] and creating a miscarriage register and certification system.[7] As a result, there is a growing recognition of the bereavement that a miscarriage may cause.[8]

This chapter focuses on the bureaucratic space that certificates of miscarriage both belong and do not belong to, with a specific focus on England. In England and Wales, pregnancy loss is currently governed by legal frameworks that characterise the foetus differentially by reference to gestational stages. Foetal death from the first day of the 24th week onwards of pregnancy is classified as stillbirth, requiring the issuing of a stillbirth certificate by a medical professional and a formal registration of the stillborn baby.[9] Conversely, foetal death occurring before or on 23 weeks and six days of pregnancy is classified as miscarriage and does not require legal registration. The lack of requirement for miscarriage registration is an area of contention in the UK (and elsewhere), as demonstrated by the range of efforts to institute some kind of formal-yet-optional recognition of pre-24-week pregnancy loss, from multiple petitions to offer official 'certification' for pre-24-week losses,[10] to centring the mission of third-sector organisations around formal recognition of such losses.[11] While the Westminster government's official position not to introduce a register of miscarriages remains unchanged, the 2022 Women's Health Strategy for England included a commitment to providing 'pregnancy loss certificates' in England, with the caveat that they will not be legal documents.[12]

4 Sarah Earle et al., "Conceptualizing Reproductive Loss: A Social Sciences Perspective," *Human Fertility* 11, no. 4 (2008): 259–62, https://doi.org/10.1080/14647270802298272.

5 Sarah Elizabeth Cox, "Changing the Miscarriage Story," *British Journal of Midwifery* 30, no. 7 (2022): 211–2, https://doi.org/10.12968/bjom.2022.30.7.366; Sands UK, "Sands: Our Strategy 2022–2025. Saving Babies' Lives. Supporting Bereaved Families," 2022 (accessed 12 December 2023), https://sands.org.uk/sites/default/files/Sands_Strategy_2022-2025.pdf; Sands UK, "Sands' Poll Results Summary in Response to Pregnancy Loss Review," 2018 (accessed 12 December 2023), https://sands.org.uk/sites/default/files/Sands%27%20poll%20results%20summary%20in%20response%20to%20Pregnancy%20Loss%20Review.pdf; Saying Goodbye, "About Saying Goodbye – Support for Miscarriage and Baby and Infant Loss | Saying Goodbye," 2022 (accessed 12 December 2023), www.sayinggoodbye.org/about.

6 Aimee Louise Middlemiss et al., "Employment Leave for Early Pregnancy Endings: A Biopolitical Reproductive Governance Analysis in England and Wales," *Gender, Work & Organization* 31, no. 1 (2023): 75–91, https://doi.org/10.1111/gwao.13055.

7 Cox, "Changing the Miscarriage Story"; UK Parliament, "Paid Miscarriage Leave," Hansard, 17 March 2022, https://hansard.parliament.uk//commons/2022-03-17/debates/6B765FDF-1BE3-4F82-A60B-4D79579F4CEA/PaidMiscarriageLeave.

8 Danielle Fuller et al., *Death before Birth: Preliminary Project Findings for Meeting with Representatives of the Department of Health and Social Care* (Birmingham/Bristol: University of Birmingham/University of Bristol, 2018).

9 Catherine Fairbairn, "Registration of Stillbirth", Briefing paper, House of Commons, 1 February 2018, www.parliament.uk/globalassets/documents/commons-library/Registration-of-stillbirth-SN05595.pdf; "Still-Birth (Definition) Act 1992" (accessed 6 December 2023), www.legislation.gov.uk/ukpga/1992/29/section/1.

10 See, e.g., Sarah Henderson, "Allow Registered Birth Certificates for Children Born from 20 Weeks," Change.org, 14 January 2017, www.change.org/p/department-of-health-uk-allow-registered-birth-certificates-for-children-born-from-20-weeks.

11 Saying Goodbye, "About Saying Goodbye – Support for Miscarriage and Baby and Infant Loss | Saying Goodbye."

Further details of what this process would entail were published in the Government Response to the Pregnancy Loss Review (PLR) in July 2023[13] and are discussed in detail later in this chapter. Throughout this chapter, we describe this as a system of 'certification' as the details announced to date do not include provision for registration in a formal sense nor do they detail whether there will be a government repository that records the issued certificates. The primary focus instead is on the certificate to be made available to parents in recognition of their loss while not being a legal document.

We start with an examination of the practices and consequences of formal registration and certification processes that are associated with death, birth, and stillbirth.[14] Consideration of these practices gives rise to two intertwined but distinct ways in which registration and subsequent issuing of a certificate (i.e., certification) operate. First, registration and certification have certain tangible material benefits often deemed consequent to certification but, in fact, more accurately understood as consequent to the status that registration is a marker of. Registration of birth, death, or stillbirth is often the mechanism through which access to parental leave and certain benefits (e.g., child benefits or funeral benefits) is mediated. The process of accessing these benefits often requires evidentiary proof, in the form of a certificate, that the relevant event (e.g., live birth or stillbirth) happened. Second, there is a less tangible – although no less important – symbolic function of registration and certification. For many, registration and certification is importantly linked to recognition.[15] In the contexts of births, deaths, and stillbirth, the process can operate as an acknowledgement of existence or of a certain relationship status being bestowed on an individual or individuals.[16] In the sphere of reproductive loss, registration has been emphasised as an important moment of recognition of both the experience of pregnancy and parenthood; the certificate also acts as an important and tangible piece of evidence of the birth, or, more profoundly, the existence of the person/entity who never had the chance to 'live'.[17] The certificate exists in the world and can be pointed to as proof of what happened and who existed. As such, registration and certification have both material and symbolic values that, when teased

12 Department of Health & Social Care (DHSC), "Women's Health Strategy for England," Policy paper, 30 August 2022, www.gov.uk/government/publications/womens-health-strategy-for-england/womens-health-strategy-for-england.

13 Department of Health & Social Care (DHSC), "Government Response to the Independent Pregnancy Loss Review: Care and Support When Baby Loss Occurs before 24 Weeks' Gestation", Policy paper, 22 July 2023, www.gov.uk/government/publications/government-response-to-the-independent-pregnancy-loss-review/government-response-to-the-independent-pregnancy-loss-review-care-and-support-when-baby-loss-occurs-before-24-weeks-gestation.

14 Andrew Bainham, "What Is the Point of Birth Registration?" *Child and Family Law Quarterly* 20, no. 4 (2008): 449–74; Gayle Davis, "Stillbirth Registration and Perceptions of Infant Death, 1900–60: The Scottish Case in National Context," *The Economic History Review* 62, no. 3 (2009): 629–54, https://doi.org/10.1111/j.1468-0289.2009.00478.x.

15 Fuller et al., *Death before Birth*.

16 Edward Higgs, *Life, Death and Statistics: Civil Registration, Censuses and the Work of the General Register Office, 1836–1952* (Hatfield: Local Population Studies, 2004); Simon Szreter, "The Right of Registration: Development, Identity Registration, and Social Security – A Historical Perspective," *World Development* 35, no. 1 (2007): 67–86, https://doi.org/10.1016/j.worlddev.2006.09.004.

17 Laura Griffin, "Certifying Pregnancy Loss in Australia: Registration, Recognition, and the Colonial State," *Australian Feminist Law Journal* 43, no. 2 (2017): 211–30, https://doi.org/10.1080/13200968.2018.1425079; Carol Sanger, "'The Birth of Death': Stillborn Birth Certificates and the Problem for Law," *California Law Review* 100 (2012): 269.

out, (1) highlight the the ambivalent parallels between the 'formal' and 'informal' processes; and (2) highlight the limitations of proposals to extend 'certification' to pre-24-week pregnancy losses. Although not the focus of this chapter, many of the concerns we raise about these proposals in the sphere of reproductive loss are also relevant to the ad hoc and piecemeal evolution of the law on birth registration.[18]

This chapter is underpinned by the research conducted for an interdisciplinary project, 'Death before Birth: Understanding, informing and supporting choices made by people who have experienced miscarriage, termination and stillbirth' (2016–2018).[19] The project's goals included determining the socio-medical and legal contexts in which decisions about the disposal of the remains of pregnancy following miscarriage, termination, and stillbirth are made and investigating how professionals in England interpret guidance on the disposal of pregnancy remains. The research demonstrated a consistent discrepancy between guidance and routine praxis around the disposal of pre-24-week pregnancy remains, where the most commonly used options parallel traditional funeral rituals with limited evidence of other options being routinely offered.[20] Just as importantly, the research highlighted multiple parallels in the lived experiences of bereavement following different types of pregnancy losses, challenging the division imposed by differences in legal classification and reaffirming the lack of correlation between the type of pregnancy loss and the intensity of grief and bereavement experienced, while also emphasising that not all experiences of reproductive loss are experienced as a bereavement.[21] The research evidenced a diversity of experiences of perceived 'loss' following miscarriage, which may correlate with gestational stage of pregnancy, but was often influenced by a range of other factors, and as such emphasised policy accommodating this breadth of views and needs. In this chapter, we consider the extent to which the proposed extension of 'certification' practices will cater to the needs of bereaved individuals and the limitations of these proposals. It will be important that the rollout of any policy in this area avoid the imposition of particular homogenising scripts on individual needs and be responsive to the diversity of personal experience.

The chapter starts with an overview of pregnancy loss in England, paying particular attention to the distinction in the support offered to those who experience miscarriage as opposed to stillbirth. Although both types of loss fall within the broad understanding of reproductive loss, there is a chasm between how they are treated at the legal and policy levels.[22] In narrowing our focus to the particular challenges posed by registration practices, we contrast the expectations of registration in the contexts of birth, death, and

---

18 Julie McCandless, "Reforming Birth Registration Law in England and Wales?" *Reproductive Biomedicine & Society Online* 4 (2017): 52–8, https://doi.org/10.1016/j.rbms.2017.07.001.

19 This project was funded by the Economic and Social Research Council, UK (ref: ES/N008359/1).

20 Kuberska et al., "Death before Birth"; Sheelagh McGuinness, Karolina Kuberska, and Louise Austin, "Report to the Human Tissue Authority on Disposal of Pregnancy Remains (Less Than 24 Weeks' Gestational Stage)" (School of Law, University of Bristol, 2017).

21 Fuller et al., *Death before Birth*; Karolina Kuberska and Sarah Turner, "The Presence of Absence: Tensions and Frictions of Pregnancy Losses – An Introduction," *Women's Studies International Forum* 74 (2019): 91–3, https://doi.org/10.1016/j.wsif.2019.03.009.

22 Kuberska et al., "Death before Birth"; Middlemiss, "Pregnancy Remains, Infant Remains, or the Corpse of a Child?"; Lucy K. Smith et al., "Parents' Experiences of Care Following the Loss of a Baby at the Margins between Miscarriage, Stillbirth and Neonatal Death: A UK Qualitative Study," *BJOG: An International Journal of Obstetrics & Gynaecology* 127, no. 7 (2020): 868–74, https://doi.org/10.1111/1471-0528.16113.

stillbirth with the absence of state-mandated processes regarding miscarriage. In doing so, we provide an overview of some of the informal processes that have been developed by support organisations in this area. We also give an overview of the recently introduced 'certificate of baby loss' service. These certificates are responsive to the needs of those who experience miscarriage as a form of bereavement and are very much geared towards the symbolic value that 'certification' has. Specifically, the certificates of support organisations may be found lacking in the extent to which they are not embedded in the bureaucratic spaces that procedurally link certificates with registers of events, such as births and stillbirths. Simultaneously, it could be argued that the government system does embed 'certification' processes within these bureaucratic processes to some extent as clear steps are taken to ensure that the process is delineated, as evidenced in the following statement:

> The certificate will provide official recognition of the pre-24-week pregnancy loss, but it will not be a legal document. The certificate will not provide evidence of the parents' identity, or entitlement to any statutory maternity or bereavement benefits.[23]

In this chapter, we use 'miscarriage certificates' and 'certificates of miscarriage' interchangeably to refer to documents recognising pre-24-week pregnancy losses. However, these documents are also referred to as 'pregnancy loss certificates' or 'baby loss certificates', drawing attention to various aspects of the experience as well as presenting different social framing: from the focus on the event to the focus on the subject of pregnancy. We argue that certificates of miscarriages parallel birth and stillbirth certificates in an ambivalent way. While a certificate of miscarriage constitutes a document aiming to recognise the experience of miscarriage, the document does not refer to a formal register of that event, in which space would be assigned to preserve a record of that pregnancy outcome. Nor does the certificate mediate access to material benefits, as in the case of other certificates. Understood in this way, certificates of miscarriage parallel just one aspect of a much broader infrastructure which governs registration and certification of stillbirth, birth, and death. Certificates of miscarriage may provide a certain level of recognition, but they should not be divorced from the wider system of welfare supports which individuals may need, such as bereavement leave.

Birth, death, pregnancy loss, and the law

To understand the significance of 'certification' for those who experience reproductive loss, it is important to first consider the general purpose of the practice of birth and death registration and the legal framework in which it arose.[24] In providing an overview of the origins of the civil registration system in England, we highlight some of the key concerns that underpinned the development of this system, from the protection of property rights to the promotion of public health.[25] This can then be contrasted with the motivations of those who wish for increased levels of registration and certification in cases of

23 Zoe Clark-Coates and Samantha Collinge, "The Independent Pregnancy Loss Review – Care and Support When Baby Loss Occurs before 24 Weeks Gestation" (London, July 2023) (accessed 8 August 2023), https://assets.publishing.service.gov.uk/government/uploads/system/uploads/atta chment_data/file/1172417/Pregnancy-Loss-Review-web-accessible.pdf.
24 Higgs, *Life, Death and Statistics*.
25 Higgs, *Life, Death and Statistics*.

reproductive loss, and miscarriage in particular, which is succinctly summarised in the Government Response to the PLR as follows: 'The purpose of issuing a certificate is to provide comfort and help parents validate their loss.'[26] It is our aim in this section to begin to unpick some of the mismatch that exists between the contemporary interpretations of registration and certification in terms of recognition and acknowledgement versus their more formal origins and functions.

Since the origins of the civil registration system, there has been a widening of understandings of registration from concerns about inheritance and lineage in the case of birth registration to a more public health focus.[27] Stillbirth registration followed a slightly different path, initially focusing on suspicion of undetected abortion and infanticide to later public and maternal health concerns.[28] More recent calls are based on a presumption that certificates are mechanisms for recognition (of parenthood or existence). Understanding this shift is key to evaluating policy and practice in this area.

Understanding the registration system for births and stillbirths

The current registration system requires all births and deaths in England and Wales to be formally registered and a certificate to be issued. This system of civil registration arose from the enactment of the *Births and Deaths Registration Act 1836*.[29] While there are many different views on the aims and objectives of this system,[30] prominent among these were the protection of property rights (reliant on bloodline inheritance)[31] and the monitoring of the 'health of the nation' by the state.[32] It was not until the early 1920s that a similar statutory requirement was introduced for stillbirths.[33] Following the *Births and Deaths Registration Act 1926*, stillbirths began to be formally recorded in England and Wales. This legislation emerged in response to the pressing maternal health crisis, particularly concerns about 'wastage' and suspicions that at least some stillbirths were, in fact, murder of neonates to conceal illegitimate births. Some commentators have noted that the surveillance aim may have had priority over the public health aim given that the cause of stillbirth was not formally recorded until much later in 1960.[34]

---

26 DHSC, "Government Response to the Independent Pregnancy Loss Review."
27 Higgs, *Life, Death and Statistics*.
28 Davis, "Stillbirth Registration and Perceptions of Infant Death, 1900–60"; Nadja Durbach, "Dead or Alive? Stillbirth Registration, Premature Babies, and the Definition of Life in England and Wales, 1836–1960," *Bulletin of the History of Medicine* 94, no. 1 (2020): 64–90, https://doi.org/10.1353/bhm.2020.0002.
29 Higgs, *Life, Death and Statistics*.
30 Simon Szreter, "Introduction: The GRO and the Historians," *Social History of Medicine* 4, no. 3 (1991): 401–14, https://doi.org/10.1093/shm/4.3.401.
31 Bainham, "What Is the Point of Birth Registration?"
32 Edward Higgs, "A Cuckoo in the Nest? The Origins of Civil Registration and State Medical Statistics in England and Wales," *Continuity and Change* 11, no. 1 (1996): 115–34, https://doi.org/10.1017/S0268416000003118.
33 Davis, "Stillbirth Registration and Perceptions of Infant Death, 1900–60"; Simon Szreter and Keith Breckenridge, "Recognition and Registration: The Infrastructure of Personhood in World History," in *Registration and Recognition: Documenting the Person in World History*, ed. Keith Breckenridge and Simon Szreter (Oxford: Oxford University Press, 2012), https://doi.org/10.5871/bacad/9780197265314.003.0001.
34 Davis, "Stillbirth Registration and Perceptions of Infant Death, 1900–60"; Durbach, "Dead or Alive?"

The *Births and Deaths Registration Act 1953* (England and Wales) as amended by the *Stillbirth (Definition) Act 1992* (UK) and the *Registration of Births and Deaths Regulations 1987* (England and Wales) contains the framework for registering births, deaths, and stillbirths in England and Wales. In accordance with this framework, all live births must be registered within 42 days of occurrence in accordance with very specific rules.[35] Once a birth is registered, a birth certificate is issued, which contains, among other items, the child's name, sex, date and place of birth, mother's name, and father's name (if provided). Similarly, there are very specific rules about registering death, with restrictions on who can do so and when this must take place.[36] Importantly, to register a death, a medical certificate of cause of death, completed and signed by a doctor, must be provided. Once death is registered, a death certificate is issued, which contains the deceased person's name, sex, and date and place of death. The process for registering a stillbirth combines elements of both birth and death registration.[37] All stillbirths must be registered within 42 days (as with a birth) and the registrar must be provided with a medical cause of stillbirth certificate (similar to death registration). Once stillbirth is registered, a certificate is provided, which, like a birth certificate, contains the baby's name (if provided) and the names of the parents. As for both birth and death certificates, the date and place of stillbirth is recorded. There are no such mandatory registration and certification requirements for miscarriage.

In recent years, pregnancy loss in England has been subject to increased scrutiny and attention at the legal and policy levels. Groupings such as the All-Party Parliamentary Group (APPG) on Baby Loss (established in 2016) have created a political space to shine a light on the needs of those who have experienced child death and reproductive loss. Sands (the Stillbirth and Neonatal Death Charity) is the secretariat for this APPG, which aims to 'develop policy that supports families dealing with the grief and loss of a baby, and to raise awareness of what more can be done by the government, Parliament or other agencies to help those affected'.[38] Although not historically a core focus of Sands' activity, miscarriage is now included within the ambit of the charity's bereavement care work. Each year, during Baby Loss Awareness Week, the APPG facilitates a parliamentary debate addressing issues such as bereavement care in hospitals, parental leave following the death of a child, and the staffing crisis in maternal healthcare.[39] The policy gains associated with these debates have been significant in meeting the needs of those who experience reproductive loss. For example, in March 2022, there was a 'Backbench Business debate' on the introduction of paid miscarriage leave.[40] The debate was introduced by Angela Crawley MP who also introduced a Private Member's Bill on the same topic,

35 GOV.UK, "Register a Birth" (accessed 8 August 2023), www.gov.uk/register-birth.
36 GOV.UK, "What to Do after Someone Dies" (accessed 8 August 2023), www.gov.uk/after-a-death.
37 GOV.UK, "Register a Stillbirth" (accessed 8 August 2023), www.gov.uk/register-stillbirth.
38 UK Parliament, "Register Of All-Party Parliamentary Groups as at 9 February 2022: Baby Loss," 9 February 2022, https://publications.parliament.uk/pa/cm/cmallparty/220209/baby-loss.htm.
39 Anastasia Lewis, Elizabeth Rough, and Tom Powell, "Baby Loss and Safe Staffing in Maternity Care," 12 December 2022, https://commonslibrary.parliament.uk/research-briefings/cdp-2022-0174; Nikki Sutherland et al., "Baby Loss Awareness Week," 12 December 2022, https://commonslibrary.parliament.uk/research-briefings/cdp-2021-0154; UK Parliament, "Baby Loss: Covid-19," Hansard, 5 November 2020, https://hansard.parliament.uk/commons/2020-11-05/debates/3E96A149-3A14-4D24-98B0-5DF83448BFA3/BabyLossCovid-19.
40 UK Parliament, "Paid Miscarriage Leave"; Andy Powell and Fintan Codd, "Debate Pack: Introduction of Paid Miscarriage Leave," 16 March 2022, https://researchbriefings.files.parliament.uk/documents/CDP-2022-0060/CDP-2022-0060.pdf.

which had its first reading in July 2022, but was subsequently prorogued.[41] This activity also illustrates that miscarriage, at a political and policy level, is increasingly discursively narrated through the lens of grief and bereavement.[42]

In addition to debates on quality of care and employment leave, attention has also been given to whether there should be a formal process for registering and certifying pregnancy loss.[43] Several popular petitions have called for lowering the gestational threshold for registration of stillbirth, including one on the Change.org platform to 'allow registered birth certificates for children born from 20 weeks' that has over 350,000 supporters[44] and a government petition to 'amend the Births and Deaths Registration Act 1953 to include all pregnancy loss' that closed early due to the UK 2017 general election.[45] In addition, well-established third-sector organisations such as Tommy's, the Miscarriage Association, and Sands have worked tirelessly to respond to the gaps in the support provided to those who experience miscarriage, including through the development of informal certificates of loss that can be provided to women during their clinical care. These organisations work closely with medical organisations to improve all aspects of care, including bereavement care in the clinical context. The impact of this work is evidenced in the Royal College of Obstetricians and Gynaecologists' 'Good Practice Guide: Registration of Stillbirths and Certification for Pregnancy Loss before 24 Weeks of Gestation', which states:

> NHS trusts are encouraged to develop a system of hospital-based commemorative certification for fetuses that are not classified as stillbirths. This would provide women or couples with a certificate recording their pregnancy loss before 24 weeks of gestation. However, not all women or couples will want this certificate following a pregnancy loss.[46]

It is worth noting the fact that the title of this document distinguishes between the registration and certification processes. The guide goes on to provide a copy of Sands' 'generic certificate' as a model that can be adapted to the local context. In parallel, there has also been considerable advocacy work taking place in the political sphere aimed at transforming approaches to registration and certification.

Since 2014, Tim Loughton MP has been at the forefront of calling for parliamentary reforms of stillbirth registration and the need to design a system of registration and certification that is more reflective of the experience of reproductive loss (both miscarriage and stillbirth). Loughton has been critical of the extent to which the law focuses on what

41 UK Parliament, "Miscarriage Leave Bill – Parliamentary Bills," Hansard, 2 November 2023, https://bills.parliament.uk/bills/3312.

42 Danielle Fuller and Karolina Kuberska, "Outside the (Memory) Box: How Unpredictable Objects Disrupt the Discourse of Bereavement in Narratives of Pregnancy Loss," *Mortality* 27, no. 1 (2022): 1–17, https://doi.org/10.1080/13576275.2020.1783221.

43 Cox, "Changing the Miscarriage Story"; Griffin, "Certifying Pregnancy Loss in Australia"; Sanger, "The Birth of Death".

44 Henderson, "Allow Registered Birth Certificates for Children Born from 20 Weeks."

45 Petitions – UK Government and Parliament, "Amend the Births and Deaths Registration Act 1953 to Include All Pregnancy Loss", Petitions – UK Government and Parliament (accessed 12 December 2022), https://petition.parliament.uk/archived/petitions/187027.

46 Royal College of Obstetricians and Gynaecologists (RCOG), "Registration of Stillbirths and Certification for Pregnancy Loss before 24 Weeks of Gestation," Good Practice No. 4, January 2005, www.rcog.org.uk/media/030jxnk5/goodpractice4registrationstillbirth2005.pdf.

he perceives to be arbitrary gestational limits rather than recognition of the birthing experience. His first attempt to reform the law in this area came in 2013/2014, with the introduction of a Private Member's Bill whose purpose was to allow for the registration of 'babies stillborn' prior to 24 weeks' gestation.[47] That Bill did not progress, but Loughton returned to the issue with his 'Civil Partnerships, Marriages and Deaths (Registration etc.) Bill', which sought to address what he perceived as the arbitrariness of the legislative cliff edge between stillbirth and miscarriage. He illustrated this with the following story:

> One particularly stark example was a woman who had given birth to stillborn twins delayed [*sic*] either side of the 24-week threshold. One was registered as stillborn, recognised in the eyes of the state, while the other, born just before 24 weeks, did not exist. That cannot be right, and we can and must do better.[48]

This argument frames pregnancy loss using criteria that are fundamentally different from the ones currently used in law (experience of birth rather than gestational age), highlighting a preference for foregrounding subjective experiences of losses over a more objective criterion such as gestational stage.

This Bill was a wide-ranging piece of legislation that contained proposals to amend the law in a range of areas, including the extension of civil partnerships to heterosexual couples. In the area of reproductive loss, the Bill contained amendments to extend the jurisdiction of the coroner to include stillbirth investigations and a proposal to lower the threshold for stillbirth registration. Clause 3(1) proposed that the law be amended to 'require or permit the registration of pregnancy losses which cannot be registered as still-births under the Births and Deaths Registration Act 1953'. In the Bill's second reading, Loughton explained this latter proposal as changing:

> the definition of a stillborn child in the Births and Deaths Registration Act 1953 to include the formal recording of a child who is stillborn in the usual way but before the current threshold of 24 weeks' gestation.[49]

Again, this discourse stretches the meaning of 'stillborn' to include miscarriages, shows a preference for individual subjective experience as a criterion for state recognition of pregnancy loss, and is driven (potentially understandably) by the desire to respond to the needs of bereaved parents at the expense of considering the wider consequences or coherence of the law. It also did not determine what it means to be 'stillborn in the usual way'.

It is clear from the form of words quoted here that Loughton saw registration as having a symbolic value and as an important process of state recognition. For Loughton, such recognition should attach to the subjective experience of 'giving birth' as the threshold for registration rather than, for example, the gestational age at physical separation or birth weight. This is similar to arguments developed by Carol Sanger in her critical appraisal of the evolution of law in this area. Sanger described how technological and cultural advances now mean that social birth, in Euro-American contexts, takes place

---

47 Fairbairn, "Registration of Stillbirth."
48 UK Parliament, "Civil Partnerships, Marriages and Deaths (Registration Etc.) Bill," Hansard, 2 Febuary 2018, https://hansard.parliament.uk//commons/2018-02-02/debates/E9121077-9E81-44A8-BBD D-AC8F4DDF0444/CivilPartnershipsMarriagesAndDeaths(RegistrationEtc)Bill.
49 UK Parliament, "Civil Partnerships, Marriages and Deaths (Registration Etc.) Bill."

much earlier than biological birth.[50] The social life of the foetus is firmly embedded in cultural practices surrounding pregnancy and has led to increased personification of the foetus.[51] Sanger noted that reforms to the law in this area are often perceived as compassionate responses to the needs of bereaved families; however, she cautioned about the unintended consequences of such reforms.[52] It is undoubtedly the case that we must be mindful of the unintended consequences that Sanger highlights, but we should be equally cautious not to separate the needs of those accessing abortion care from those experiencing other sorts of reproductive loss. Often this binary relies on stereotypes of 'wanted' and 'unwanted' pregnancies, and 'intended' and 'unintended' pregnancy outcomes, that does not reflect the diversity and complexity of experience in this area.

Ultimately, the *Civil Partnerships, Marriages and Deaths (Registration etc) Act 2019* (UK) was enacted but did not amend the law on stillbirth registration. Instead, section 3 of the Act contains a significantly watered-down proposal placing an obligation on the Secretary of State for Health and Social Care to:

> make arrangements for the preparation of a report on whether, and if so how, the law ought to be changed to require or permit the registration of pregnancy losses which cannot be registered as still-births under the Births and Deaths Registration Act 1953.

This obligation was met by the PLR (launched by then–Secretary of State for Health and Social Care Jeremy Hunt), whose goal was 'to consider whether the law should be changed to allow registration of pregnancy losses that take place before gestation of 24 weeks'.[53] The PLR was chaired by Zoë Clark-Coates, who established the bereavement charity Saying Goodbye, and Samantha Collinge, a bereavement midwife. The PLR's terms of reference were 'to consider whether the law should be changed to allow registration of pregnancy losses that take place before gestation of 24 weeks', and its membership included bereaved individuals, medical professionals, researchers working in the area, and people working in relevant support groups. The PLR's report and subsequent government response were published in July 2023. Chapter 8 of the PLR's report set out the review's findings on certification of miscarriage, which led to Recommendation 61:

> In recognition of a life lost, the government must ensure that an official certificate is available to anyone who requests one after experiencing any loss pre-24 weeks' gestation. The certificate must:
>
> - be backdate-able with no cut-off point so people with a historic loss may also access this long-requested recognition
> - be available to anyone regardless of the type of loss they have experienced. Parents must have the option to be able to supply evidence of the loss, but this should not be mandatory

---

50 Sanger, "The Birth of Death".
51 Janelle S. Taylor, "The Public Life of the Fetal Sonogram and the Work of the Sonographer," *Journal of Diagnostic Medical Sonography* 18, no. 6 (2002): 367–79, https://doi.org/10.1177/8756479302238392.
52 Sanger, "The Birth of Death".
53 GOV.UK, "Pregnancy Loss Review Group" (accessed 12 December 2023), www.gov.uk/government/groups/pregnancy-loss-review-group.

- contain wording that is adaptable (including an option to add a baby's name) as it is vital that parents are able to choose the language they prefer
- be available as a download or as a hard copy. The certificate needs to be accessible by all, not just by people with access to a computer
- be available to both parents

To ensure the certificates remain credible, the applicant should be required to provide identity verification.

The certificates will not be legal certificates, but will be official government-issued ones, and should look official, rather than just commemorative, as it is crucial to families that they have official recognition of their loss.

We will continue to partner with the government to design and deliver this as quickly as possible.[54]

The recommendations on certification had been widely trailed in the preceding years and, as noted earlier, were formally endorsed in the Women's Health Strategy for England published in July 2022 (a year before the PLR's report). The strategy stated it would ensure that all those who go through the loss of a pregnancy before 24 weeks could, if they wish, be issued a certificate in recognition of their experience.[55] Certification was thus, unsurprisingly, one of the 'immediate actions' in the Government Response to the PLR, which announced that a new 'certificate of baby loss' service would be rolled out during Baby Loss Awareness Week (9–15 October) 2023.[56] Key features include (1) certificate issuance being voluntary; (2) medical verification not being required for certification, so as to be inclusive of historic losses; and (3) '[t]he certificate will provide official recognition of the pre-24-week pregnancy loss, but it will not be a legal document. The certificate will not provide evidence of the parents' identity, or entitlement to any statutory maternity or bereavement benefits.'[57] To better understand the tension inhering in miscarriage certification, we return to the symbolic and material values that certification is understood as having.

Challenges: Ambivalent parallels

Improvements in the provision of bereavement care following pregnancy loss have been shown to translate into less trauma and better ability to deal with the experience – for parents and healthcare staff.[58] Bereavement care following pregnancy loss includes options for making memories (e.g., hand- and foot-prints), creating opportunities and spaces for parents to see and spend time with the baby, and memento photography.[59]

54 Clark-Coates and Collinge, "The Independent Pregnancy Loss Review."
55 DHSC, "Women's Health Strategy for England."
56 At the time of writing, December 2023, this still has not happened.
57 DHSC, "Government Response to the Independent Pregnancy Loss Review."
58 Bethany Atkins et al., "Stillbirth: Prevention and Supportive Bereavement Care," *BMJ Medicine* 2, no. 1 (2023), https://doi.org/10.1136/bmjmed-2022-000262.
59 Fuller and Kuberska, "Outside the (Memory) Box"; Abigail McNiven, "(Re)Collections: Engaging Feminist Geography with Embodied and Relational Experiences of Pregnancy Losses" (Doctoral Thesis, Durham University, 2014), http://etheses.dur.ac.uk/10786; Sands UK, *Pregnancy Loss and the Death of a Baby: Guidelines for Professionals, 4th Edition* (London, 2016).

Additional routine bereavement care also includes disposal of the remains of the pregnancy, often handled by the hospital in collaboration with a local funeral home or a crematorium, organised in a way that follows the preferences of the parents, often resembling services for people who lived and died.[60] Acknowledging the parallels in the effects that miscarriages and stillbirth have on individual persons has been key in shaping bereavement care pathways centred on the experiences of those who have lost a pregnancy. A closer focus on the phenomenon of certificates of miscarriage brings into sharp relief the ambivalences in how these documents acknowledge the loss while failing to occupy the legal bureaucratic space they attempt to mirror.

Pregnancy loss certificates in the UK

The use of certificates of miscarriage has been increasing in the UK in recent decades. Currently, the National Bereavement Care Pathway and the Miscarriage Association recommend that certificates should be offered to those experiencing miscarriage. As previously noted, a similar recommendation was made in the Royal College of Obstetricians and Gynaecologists' 'Good Practice Guide' as early as 2005.[61] Variations of informal certificates are offered to parents by numerous hospital care teams to acknowledge the pre-24-week pregnancy loss.[62] Some pregnancy loss charities in the UK have template certificates that they offer to hospitals.[63] The aim of this kind of certificate is to mark the loss and serve as a personal (rather than official) proof of their experience and their baby's existence. An analysis of National Health Services (NHS) trust documentation relevant to bereavement care following pregnancy loss from 2016 to 2017 has shown a variation in practice around offering certificates for miscarriage and the form these certificates take, especially in wording.[64] The lack of uniformity in the design and wording of miscarriage certificates highlights their informal character and also the fact that not all those who experience miscarriage will want a certificate or indeed to be offered such a certificate. Many miscarriage certificates in the UK use the official NHS trust–headed papers, but some feature images of flowers (especially snowdrops or forget-me-nots) and/or a decorative border, which distinguishes them from undecorated official documents. Such miscarriage certificate documents embody a striking paradox. On the one hand, their aesthetic designs are meant to manifest kindness and warmth in the recognition of pre-24-week pregnancy loss. On the other hand, this design further distinguishes the certificates of miscarriage from the starkness of official stillbirth certificates.

While the new 'official' certificates are to be welcomed, it is clear these certificates will be largely symbolic in nature. This perpetuates the gap between the expectations of what these documents can achieve and what the law affords. In a context such as England and

60 Kuberska, "Unwitnessed Ceremonies"; Middlemiss, "Pregnancy Remains, Infant Remains, or the Corpse of a Child?"
61 RCOG, "Registration of Stillbirths and Certification for Pregnancy Loss before 24 Weeks of Gestation."
62 Fuller et al., *Death before Birth*.
63 Miscarriage Association, "Certification" (accessed 9 December 2022), www.miscarriageassociation.org.uk/information/for-health-professionals/certification; Miscarriage Association, "Sample Certificates to Mark Pregnancy Loss before 24 Weeks of Pregnancy" (accessed 9 December 2022), www.miscarriageassociation.org.uk/wp-content/uploads/2016/09/Certificate-Examples-2017.pdf.
64 Fuller et al., *Death before Birth*.

Wales, miscarriage certificates are not mandatory and do not come with the statutory entitlements (e.g., parental leave, as is provided in the case of stillbirth). While 'official' miscarriage certificates may be a welcome step towards recognising pregnancy loss as a potentially important personal life event, ultimately, although they resemble documents issued for life events that require formal registration (such as births, stillbirths, and deaths), the miscarriage certificates do not refer to a central register (contrary to certificates for those other life events). Nor will the miscarriage certificates bring with them the more formal material responses indicative of other life events (e.g., leave from employment or welfare supports). Finally, it will be interesting to see how bereaved families respond to miscarriage certificates when they are abstracted from the bereavement support context – official miscarriage certificates will be applied for online or over the phone, and no details have been given on whether parents will be signposted to other sorts of support during this process.

The purpose of informal certificates of miscarriage

Recognition of the significance and effects that pregnancy loss can have on those who experience it is one of the major themes in the research on and advocacy around pregnancy loss and miscarriage in particular. At an immediate level, this recognition can manifest through empathetic care from healthcare practitioners or through interactions with other people that acknowledge the event in accordance with the views of the individual. At a higher level, recognition of pregnancy loss can be manifested via local policies and guidelines that offer all those experiencing pregnancy loss opportunities, if they want them, to say goodbye to the baby via memory making, funeral options, and/or paid compassionate leave. Finally, formal recognition would include an official record of the event, with the names of those involved and other details such as the time and place of the event. Certificates of events recorded in formal registers are a proof of a kind of life event that the state recognises.

Certificates of miscarriage may record a range of information that is somewhat similar to the information included on a stillbirth certificate. Currently, the information on informal certificates of miscarriage is often recorded by a healthcare professional, and certificates may also be signed and dated. What certificates of miscarriages aim to do is create additional parallels between pre-24-week pregnancy losses (which are not registered) and post-24-week pregnancy losses, or stillbirths, which require formal registration. So while miscarriage certificates do not carry the weight of the certificates issued for births and stillbirths, the introduction of government-issued miscarriage certificates can be seen to form part of a spectrum of (ambivalent) recognition. At one end of the spectrum is a miscarriage certificate with a purported aim to 'provide comfort and help parents validate their loss',[65] and at the other end are birth and death certificates where the focus of the recognition is not on parental experience but rather the formal attribution of state recognition to an entity. Nonetheless, calls abound for birth registration to also be more responsive to the needs of parents and pay due attention to the ways in which registration practices are important to family experience and identity.[66]

65 DHSC, "Government Response to the Independent Pregnancy Loss Review."
66 Liam Davis, "The Evolution of Birth Registration in England and Wales and Its Place in Contemporary Law and Society," *The Modern Law Review* 87, no. 2 (2024): 317–42, https://doi.org/10.1111/1468-2230.12836.

Miscarriage certificates point to a theoretical status in the formal register of live births and stillbirths and to the entitlements that obtaining this status could grant them, from a formal recognition of their existence to material support received by those whose babies were stillborn or born alive.

The fundamental informality of miscarriage certificates – or their ability to only symbolise recognition to a limited audience rather than grant access to material support, such as paid leave – is obscured by their material form and the way they are produced: in good faith, respectfully, by a healthcare professional, another person (e.g., an individual in a third-sector organisation) or local artist. Pregnancy has been conceptualised as a forward-moving liminal state that pregnancy loss disrupts in fundamental ways, positioning the person in an inescapable variation of that liminality: no longer pregnant but not a parent.[67] The invisibility of this type of liminality resulting from a miscarriage, further reinforced by marginalisation of pregnancy loss in mainstream reproductive scripts, is what is challenged by work around pregnancy loss awareness and support.[68] Recognition relies on familiarity; in the absence of first-hand experiences, it must rely on empathy emerging from parallel experiences.

Regarding funerals for pre-24-week pregnancy losses in the UK, the most common routine arrangements resemble traditional funeral ceremonies – including music, orders of service, and even a person leading the ceremony.[69] Where they differ from ceremonies for people who lived and died is in the fact that the pregnancy remains are often put in a shared coffin, there is no registration of the pregnancy remains as individuals, and the ceremonies are often unattended. Importantly, those who organise and carry out these ceremonies – funerary industry professionals, bereavement midwives, and/or members of hospital chaplaincy teams – all emphasise the importance of making these events resemble funerals for people who lived and died, highlighting the parallels in experiences of bereavement with a view to offering a way of saying goodbye to a baby that can only be recognised in a limited way.

We observe similar parallels in the practices around certification. While death (of either a foetus or living person) causes an absence, those who stay alive summon materiality that can testify to the past existence of those who died and to reorder their social world.[70] Certificates of miscarriage may be tools for summoning materiality in that they resemble certificates that testify to the existence of those who are also recorded in formal registers. Ultimately, however, the power of miscarriage certificates is symbolic without consequent material support. Research suggests that these certificates matter a great deal to some people as an important symbol to recognise the existence of their child and their status as a parent. They also reveal the unequal status of pregnancy losses on either side

67 Linda L. Layne, *Motherhood Lost: A Feminist Account of Pregnancy Loss in America* (New York: Routledge, 2013); Alison Reiheld, "'The Event That Was Nothing': Miscarriage as a Liminal Event," *Journal of Social Philosophy* 46, no. 1 (2015): 9–26, https://doi.org/10.1111/josp.12084.
68 See, e.g., Kuberska and Turner, "The Presence of Absence"; Olga Kuchinskaya and Lisa S. Parker, "'Recurrent Losers Unite': Online Forums, Evidence-Based Activism, and Pregnancy Loss," *Social Science & Medicine* 216 (2018): 74–80, https://doi.org/10.1016/j.socscimed.2018.09.014; Erica van der Sijpt, "Navigating Reproductive Losses," in *The Routledge Handbook of Anthropology and Reproduction*, ed. Sallie Han and Cecília Tomori (London: Routledge, 2021).
69 Kuberska, "Unwitnessed Ceremonies."
70 Jenny Hockey, Carol Komaromy, and Kate Woodthorpe, eds., *The Matter of Death: Space, Place and Materiality* (Basingstoke: Palgrave Macmillan, 2010).

of the 24-week pregnancy threshold. However, we must be careful that they do not also serve to homogenise the experience of loss prior to 24 weeks in ways that may be at odds with experiences within this group. In a sea of parallels found in bereavement care and practices, the lack of parallel stands out here.

Conclusion

In this chapter, we have critiqued recent attempts to extend 'certification' practices to miscarriage on several levels, specifically attempting to understand the significance of a process of certification disentangled from registration. While the original purpose of the English registration system primarily involved property rights, inheritance, and welfare protections, it evolved to include public health concerns, and this, in turn, prompted the formalisation of stillbirth registration. 'Vital registrations' became an important tool for monitoring the overall health of the nation, as these demographic indicators were used as a shorthand for quality of life.[71] This framework for vital registrations remains in use to this day and, as such, it is important to acknowledge its origins in presenting a critical overview of current practices and the challenges of changing them. Registration and certification practices in the context of reproductive loss are further complicated by the way in which part of the origin story of stillbirth registration involved suspicion, as Davis summarised:

> There was a more significant concern that some stillbirths were in fact cases of infanticide, and the 'stillbirth' label merely a convenient classification to avoid suspicion. Through the late nineteenth and early twentieth centuries, there was widespread social concern over the issue of infanticide.[72]

These factors go some way to explaining why formal processes are often mismatched with parental expectations.

The landscape of recognition, guidelines, and available support for those experiencing miscarriage is changing in England. Despite managing to generate some interest and favourable responses from members of the government, no changes to law have been made. This is reflective of the finding that while most parents welcome having a choice to register a miscarriage, they do not think it should be mandated.[73] Importantly, the Women's Health Strategy for England did not commit to creating a formal record of miscarriage, only recommending that certificates of miscarriage be provided to those who request them.[74] This gives rise to a paradoxical situation in which the only pre-24-week pregnancy endings formally recorded by the state are those resulting from the termination of a pregnancy in accordance with the *Abortion Act 1967* (UK).

Moving away from the formal processes to a consideration of extending certification practices, we wished to highlight that there is a danger in the extent to which this symbolic move of providing miscarriage certificates may come at the cost of more tangible material support that bereaved people need or improving scientific and medical understandings in this area. Cynically, it may be viewed as an easy win in a policy context. A

71 Higgs, *Life, Death and Statistics.*
72 Davis, "Stillbirth Registration and Perceptions of Infant Death, 1900–60," 632.
73 Clark-Coates and Collinge, "The Independent Pregnancy Loss Review"; Sands UK, "Sands' Poll Results Summary in Response to Pregnancy Loss Review."
74 DHSC, "Women's Health Strategy for England."

full appreciation of the procedural idiosyncrasies of the registration system is only sensible when we consider the origins of the framework. Changing who or what is recorded in the civil registration system is not simply a matter of being able to produce more nuanced statistics; it is a matter of who or what deserves special space in this record of a nation. It is in this context that we critique the efforts towards enabling registration and certification of miscarriages in England.

The power of bureaucracies lies not in their effectiveness but in the fact that they can be benevolent or violent.[75] In the case of pregnancy loss in the UK, the gestational age of the dead pregnancy determines its recognition by the state as an existence worth recording, issuing a certificate for, and supporting through statutory entitlements. Old enough and the baby becomes registered as stillborn; otherwise, parents must hitherto rely on their baby being recognised by those willing to do the emotional labour of acknowledging the loss. By amplifying parallels with officially recognised pregnancy losses, certificates of miscarriage may be argued to attempt to cut across this divide by highlighting the criterion of meaning of the pregnancy to those who lost it. In that process, a space is being carved out for a new kind of dead: those currently invisible to the state.

Acknowledgement

Karolina Kuberska is supported by the Health Foundation's grant to the University of Cambridge for The Healthcare Improvement Studies Institute.

The Open Access version of this chapter has been funded by UKRI, grant number ES-N008359, https://deathbeforebirthproject.wordpress.com/. The research materials described in this article have been deposited with the UK Data Service (SN 853488) 10.5255/UKDA-SN-853488.

Bibliography

Atkins, Bethany, Lindsay Kindinger, Muhammad Pradhiki Mahindra, Zoe Moatti, and Dimitrios Siassakos. "Stillbirth: Prevention and Supportive Bereavement Care". *BMJ Medicine* 2, no. 1 (2023). https://doi.org/10.1136/bmjmed-2022-000262.

Bainham, Andrew. "What Is the Point of Birth Registration?" *Child and Family Law Quarterly* 20, no. 4 (2008): 449–474.

Clark-Coates, Zoë, and Samantha Collinge. *The Independent Pregnancy Loss Review – Care and Support When Baby Loss Occurs before 24 Weeks Gestation*. London: HMSO, July 2023. Accessed 8 August 2023, https://assets.publishing.service.gov.uk/government/uploads/system/uploads/attachment_data/file/1172417/Pregnancy-Loss-Review-web-accessible.pdf.

Cox, Sarah Elizabeth. "Changing the Miscarriage Story." *British Journal of Midwifery* 30, no. 7 (2022): 211–212. https://doi.org/10.12968/bjom.2022.30.7.366.

Davis, Gayle. "Stillbirth Registration and Perceptions of Infant Death, 1900–60: The Scottish Case in National Context." *The Economic History Review* 62, no. 3 (2009): 629–654. https://doi.org/10.1111/j.1468-0289.2009.00478.x.

Davis, Liam. "The Evolution of Birth Registration in England and Wales and Its Place in Contemporary Law and Society." *The Modern Law Review* 87, no. 2 (2024): 317–342. https://doi.org/10.1111/1468-2230.12836.

Department of Health & Social Care. "Government Response to the Independent Pregnancy Loss Review: Care and Support When Baby Loss Occurs before 24 Weeks' Gestation." Policy paper, 22 July 2023. www.gov.uk/government/publications/government-response-to-the-independent-pregna

---

75 David Graeber, *The Utopia of Rules: On Technology, Stupidity, and the Secret Joys of Bureaucracy* (New York: Melville House, 2015).

ncy-loss-review/government-response-to-the-independent-pregnancy-loss-review-care-and-support-when-baby-loss-occurs-before-24-weeks-gestation.

Department of Health & Social Care. "Women's Health Strategy for England." Policy paper, 30 August 2022. www.gov.uk/government/publications/womens-health-strategy-for-england/womens-health-stra tegy-for-england.

Durbach, Nadja. "Dead or Alive? Stillbirth Registration, Premature Babies, and the Definition of Life in England and Wales, 1836–1960." *Bulletin of the History of Medicine* 94, no. 1 (2020): 64–90. http s://doi.org/10.1353/bhm.2020.0002.

Earle, Sarah, Pam Foley, Carol Komaromy, and Cathy Lloyd. "Conceptualizing Reproductive Loss: A Social Sciences Perspective." *Human Fertility* 11, no. 4 (2008): 259–262. https://doi.org/10.1080/14647270802298272.

Fairbairn, Catherine. "Registration of Stillbirth." Briefing paper. House of Commons, 1 February 2018. www.parliament.uk/globalassets/documents/commons-library/Registration-of-stillbirth-SN05595.pdf.

Fuller, Danielle, and Karolina Kuberska. "Outside the (Memory) Box: How Unpredictable Objects Disrupt the Discourse of Bereavement in Narratives of Pregnancy Loss." *Mortality* 27, no. 1 (2022): 1–17. https://doi.org/10.1080/13576275.2020.1783221.

Fuller, Danielle, Sheelagh McGuinness, Jeannette Littlemore, Karolina Kuberska, Sarah Turner, and Meera Burgess. *Death before Birth: Preliminary Project Findings for Meeting with Representatives of the Department of Health and Social Care*. Birmingham/Bristol: University of Birmingham/University of Bristol, 2018.

GOV.UK. "Pregnancy Loss Review Group." Accessed 12 December 2023. www.gov.uk/government/groups/pregnancy-loss-review-group.

GOV.UK. "Register a Birth." Accessed 8 August 2023. www.gov.uk/register-birth.

GOV.UK. "Register a Stillbirth." Accessed 8 August 2023. www.gov.uk/register-stillbirth.

GOV.UK. "What to Do after Someone Dies." Accessed 8 August 2023. www.gov.uk/after-a-death.

Graeber, David. *The Utopia of Rules: On Technology, Stupidity, and the Secret Joys of Bureaucracy*. New York: Melville House, 2015.

Griffin, Laura. "Certifying Pregnancy Loss in Australia: Registration, Recognition, and the Colonial State." *Australian Feminist Law Journal* 43, no. 2 (2017): 211–230. https://doi.org/10.1080/13200968.2018.1425079.

Henderson, Sarah. "Allow Registered Birth Certificates for Children Born from 20 Weeks." Change. org, 14 January 2017, www.change.org/p/department-of-health-uk-allow-registered-birth-certifica tes-for-children-born-from-20-weeks.

Higgs, Edward. "A Cuckoo in the Nest? The Origins of Civil Registration and State Medical Statistics in England and Wales." *Continuity and Change* 11, no. 1 (1996): 115–134. https://doi.org/10.1017/S0268416000003118.

Higgs, Edward. *Life, Death and Statistics: Civil Registration, Censuses and the Work of the General Register Office, 1836–1952*. Hatfield: Local Population Studies, 2004.

Hockey, Jenny, Carol Komaromy, and Kate Woodthorpe, eds. *The Matter of Death: Space, Place and Materiality*. Basingstoke: Palgrave Macmillan, 2010.

Kuberska, Karolina. "Unwitnessed Ceremonies: Funeral Services for Pre-24-Week Pregnancy Losses in England." In *Navigating Miscarriage: Social, Medical, and Conceptual Perspectives*, edited by Susie Kilshaw and Katie Borg, 247–276. New York: Berghahn, 2020.

Kuberska, Karolina, Danielle Fuller, Jeannette Littlemore, Sheelagh McGuinness, and Sarah Turner. "Death before Birth: Liminal Bodies and Legal Frameworks." In *A Jurisprudence of the Body*, edited by Chris Dietz, Mitchell Travis, and Michael Thomson, 149–178. Basingstoke: Palgrave Macmillan, 2020.

Kuberska, Karolina, and Sarah Turner. "The Presence of Absence: Tensions and Frictions of Pregnancy Losses – An Introduction." *Women's Studies International Forum* 74 (2019): 91–93. https://doi.org/10.1016/j.wsif.2019.03.009.

Kuchinskaya, Olga, and Lisa S.Parker. "'Recurrent Losers Unite': Online Forums, Evidence-Based Activism, and Pregnancy Loss." *Social Science & Medicine* 216 (2018): 74–80. https://doi.org/10.1016/j.socscimed.2018.09.014.

Layne, Linda L. *Motherhood Lost: A Feminist Account of Pregnancy Loss in America*. New York: Routledge, 2013.

Lewis, Anastasia, Elizabeth Rough, and Tom Powell. "Baby Loss and Safe Staffing in Maternity Care." 21 October 2022. https://commonslibrary.parliament.uk/research-briefings/cdp-2022-0174.

McCandless, Julie. "Reforming Birth Registration Law in England and Wales?" *Reproductive Biomedicine & Society Online* 4 (2017): 52–58. https://doi.org/10.1016/j.rbms.2017.07.001.

McGuinness, Sheelagh, Karolina Kuberska, and Louise Austin. "Report to the Human Tissue Authority on Disposal of Pregnancy Remains (Less Than 24 Weeks' Gestational Stage)." School of Law, University of Bristol, 2017.

McNiven, Abigail. *(Re)Collections: Engaging Feminist Geography with Embodied and Relational Experiences of Pregnancy Losses.* Doctoral Thesis, Durham University, 2014. http://etheses.dur.ac. uk/10786.

Middlemiss, Aimee. "Pregnancy Remains, Infant Remains, or the Corpse of a Child? The Incoherent Governance of the Dead Foetal Body in England." *Mortality* 26, no. 3 (2021): 299–315. https://doi. org/10.1080/13576275.2020.1787365.

Middlemiss, Aimee Louise, Ilaria Boncori, Joanna Brewis, Julie Davies, and Victoria Louise Newton. "Employment Leave for Early Pregnancy Endings: A Biopolitical Reproductive Governance Analysis in England and Wales." *Gender, Work & Organization* 31, no. 1 (2023): 75–91. https://doi.org/10. 1111/gwao.13055.

Miscarriage Association. "Background Information." Accessed 14 November 2023. www.miscarriagea ssociation.org.uk/media-queries/background-information.

Miscarriage Association. "Certification." Accessed 9 December 2022. www.miscarriageassociation.org. uk/information/for-health-professionals/certification/.

Miscarriage Association. "Sample Certificates to Mark Pregnancy Loss before 24 Weeks of Pregnancy." Accessed 9 December 2022. www.miscarriageassociation.org.uk/wp-content/uploads/2016/ 09/Certificate-Examples-2017.pdf.

Petitions – UK Government and Parliament. "Amend the Births and Deaths Registration Act 1953 to Include All Pregnancy Loss." Accessed 12 December 2023, https://petition.parliament.uk/archived/p etitions/187027.

Powell, Andy, and Fintan Codd. "Debate Pack: Introduction of Paid Miscarriage Leave." 16 March 2022. https://researchbriefings.files.parliament.uk/documents/CDP-2022-0060/CDP-2022-0060.pdf.

Royal College of Obstetricians and Gynaecologists. "Registration of Stillbirths and Certification for Pregnancy Loss before 24 Weeks of Gestation". Good Practice No. 4, January 2005. www.rcog.org. uk/media/030jxnk5/goodpractice4registrationstillbirth2005.pdf.

Reiheld, Alison. "'The Event That Was Nothing': Miscarriage as a Liminal Event." *Journal of Social Philosophy* 46, no. 1 (2015): 9–26. https://doi.org/10.1111/josp.12084.

Sands UK. *Pregnancy Loss and the Death of a Baby: Guidelines for Professionals, 4th Edition.* London: Sands, 2016.

Sands UK. "Sands: Our Strategy 2022–2025. Saving Babies' Lives. Supporting Bereaved Families." Accessed 12 December 2023. https://sands.org.uk/sites/default/files/Sands_Strategy_2022-2025.pdf.

Sands UK. "Sands' Poll Results Summary in Response to Pregnancy Loss Review." Accessed 12 December 2023. https://sands.org.uk/sites/default/files/Sands%27%20poll%20results%20summary% 20in%20response%20to%20Pregnancy%20Loss%20Review.pdf.

Sanger, Carol. "'The Birth of Death': Stillborn Birth Certificates and the Problem for Law." *California Law Review* 100 (2012): 269.

Saying Goodbye. "About Saying Goodbye – Support for Miscarriage and Baby and Infant Loss | Saying Goodbye." Accessed 12 December 2023. www.sayinggoodbye.org/about.

Smith, Lucy K., Joanne Dickens, Ruth Bender Atik, Charlotte Bevan, Jane Fisher, and Lisa Hinton. "Parents' Experiences of Care Following the Loss of a Baby at the Margins between Miscarriage, Stillbirth and Neonatal Death: A UK Qualitative Study." *BJOG: An International Journal of Obstetrics & Gynaecology* 127, no. 7 (2020): 868–874. https://doi.org/10.1111/1471-0528.16113.

Sutherland, Nikki, Rachael Harker, Sarah Barber, and Tom Powell. "Baby Loss Awareness Week." Accessed 12 December 2023. https://commonslibrary.parliament.uk/research-briefings/cdp-2021-0154.

Szreter, Simon. "Introduction: The GRO and the Historians." *Social History of Medicine* 4, no. 3 (1991): 401–414. https://doi.org/10.1093/shm/4.3.401.

Szreter, Simon. "The Right of Registration: Development, Identity Registration, and Social Security – A Historical Perspective." *World Development* 35, no. 1 (2007): 67–86. https://doi.org/10.1016/j. worlddev.2006.09.004.

Szreter, Simon, and Keith Breckenridge. "Recognition and Registration: The Infrastructure of Personhood in World History." In *Registration and Recognition: Documenting the Person in World History*, edited by Keith Breckenridge and Simon Szreter, Oxford: Oxford University Press, 2012. https://doi.org/10.5871/bacad/9780197265314.003.0001.

Taylor, Janelle S. "The Public Life of the Fetal Sonogram and the Work of the Sonographer." *Journal of Diagnostic Medical Sonography* 18, no. 6 (2002): 367–379. https://doi.org/10.1177/8756479302238392.

UK Parliament. "Baby Loss: Covid-19." Hansard, 5 November 2020. https://hansard.parliament.uk//commons/2020-11-05/debates/3E96A149-3A14-4D24-98B0-5DF83448BFA3/BabyLossCovid-19.

UK Parliament. "Civil Partnerships, Marriages and Deaths (Registration Etc.) Bill." Hansard, 2 February 2018. https://hansard.parliament.uk//commons/2018-02-02/debates/E9121077-9E81-44A8-BBDD-AC8F4DDF0444/CivilPartnershipsMarriagesAndDeaths(RegistrationEtc)Bill.

UK Parliament. "Miscarriage Leave Bill – Parliamentary Bills." Hansard, 2 November 2023. https://bills.parliament.uk/bills/3312.

UK Parliament. "Paid Miscarriage Leave." Hansard, 17 March 2022. https://hansard.parliament.uk//commons/2022-03-17/debates/6B765FDF-1BE3-4F82-A60B-4D79579F4CEA/PaidMiscarriageLeave.

UK Parliament. "Register Of All-Party Parliamentary Groups as at 9 February 2022: Baby Loss." 9 February 2022. https://publications.parliament.uk/pa/cm/cmallparty/220209/baby-loss.htm.

Van der Sijpt, Erica. "Navigating Reproductive Losses." In *The Routledge Handbook of Anthropology and Reproduction*, edited by Sallie Han and Cecília Tomori. London: Routledge, 2021.

20

POSTHUMOUS PHOTOGRAPHIC IMAGES

Remigius N. Nwabueze[1]

Introduction

This chapter pertinently considers the 'materiality' of death images through examining the significance of images in creating and reinforcing one's identity and personality, and through an analysis of the impact of the publication of death images on memory and privacy. Symbolically, a photographic image is a powerful thing. In the hands of the subject of the image, it is a tool to construct their identity and personality. It empowers them to control the public's perception and visualisation of their physical identity, upon which the evaluation of their character may depend and their social acceptability conditioned. Therefore, the decision to publish or withhold publication of a photographic image is an important one for the subject of that image, and hence unauthorised publication of a photographic image potentially harms the subject as it egregiously takes away the image subject's right to control public's perception of their identity and personality. In part, this rationalises the court's damnation of an image publisher in damages for breach of privacy,[2] at least when the images related to a living person.[3] What about the dead subject of a photographic image, especially an embarrassing death image? Does the legal protection accorded to a living subject of a photographic image vanish upon death? Can the dead, like the living, suffer a photographic harm posthumously via death images? Who is the subject of that harm? Can survivors suffer a legally recognisable harm from unauthorised publication of a dead relative's image?

These questions have become timely and are likely to continue to engage the public's imagination for a much longer time in the future, not least because of the Internet and

---

1 This work is generously funded by the Leverhulme Trust under its Major Research Project grant in relation to the project titled 'Modern Technologies, Privacy Law and the Dead' (RPG-2020-048).

2 The contours of the relevant privacy action, misuse of private information, have been mapped and examined in several cases including those below, and *ZXC v Bloomberg LP* [2020] EWCA Civ 611, paras 40–48; *Sicri v Associated Newspapers Ltd.* [2020] EWHC 3541, paras 65–77.

3 *Campbell v MGN* [2004] 2 A.C. 457; *Douglas V Hello! Ltd. (No. 3)* [2008] A.C. 1; *Murray v Express Newspapers* [2009] Ch. 481; *AMP v Persons Unknown* [2011] EWHC 3454 (TCC); *R (Wood) v Commissioner of Police of the Metropolis* [2010] 1 WLR 123; *Weller v Associated Newspapers Ltd.* [2016] 1 WLR 1541.

DOI: 10.4324/9781003304593-24

diffusion of smartphone usages which have made the taking and dissemination of death images ubiquitous.[4] *Collins* is a recent and paradigmatic case which provoked the public's outcry over unauthorised taking and dissemination of death images by police offers who were assigned to protect a London park murder crime scene in which the brutally murdered and naked bodies of the Smallman sisters lay. Instead, the officers took images of the double murder victims' naked bodies and shared the images with their colleagues and friends on their WhatsApp group chats. They were charged, convicted, and given custodial sentences for the common law offence of misconduct in public office. Some of the observations of the Court of Appeal in *Collins* have important resonances for civil liability. For instance, the Court of Appeal accepted that, just as in the case of a living subject of an image, the unauthorised publication of a death image undermines survivors' control powers over a loved one's death image, causing 'their loss of control of the treatment of those for whom they grieve'.[5] As the *Collins* court further observed, death images damage a family's dignity and respect, noting that 'in relation to images of the dead in particular, the act of creating, accessing or copying such images, if unauthorised, will amount to a failure to accord dignity and respect to those who have died and their families'.[6] But on what legal, doctrinal, theoretical, and philosophical grounds can such photographic harm be vindicated? This chapter attempts to answer these questions using a mix of theoretical, philosophical, historical, and doctrinal methods of analysis.

Photographic *harm* to the dead

The italicisation and deployment of *harm* in the subheading above is markedly deliberate, particularly in its reflexivity of the philosophical and regulatory question of harm as the basis of interference with an individual's conduct. The question, therefore, is whether an unauthorised publisher of a death image could, by that publication, harm or wrong the dead,[7] the subject of that image. Whether the dead, being non-sentient, could suffer a photographic harm is a pertinent question that requires analysis regardless of the justiciability of that harm; that is, regardless of one's view on the kindred question of whether the dead has a sufficient standing or legal personality to sue, or have an action brought on their behalf, in relation to an unauthorised publication of a death image. This latter question is addressed in the subsection below.

Arguably, a publisher's freedom to publish a death image without consent depends, in part, on whether the non-living subject of that image could be harmed or wronged by the publication. If such a harm or wrong is possible, then its vindication, subject to the recognition of the dead's legal personality analysed below, would require, amongst other things, the bringing of a relevant legal action against the publisher on behalf of the dead by their legal representatives. To put it differently in Mill's terminology, the wrong, if at all, of a death image would entail some regulatory or coercive interference with the

---

4 A point recently underscored by the Court of Appeal in *R v Collins, Lewis & Jaffer* [2022] EWCA Crim 742, para 12; Clay Clavert, "A Familial Right over Death Images: Critiquing the Internet-Propelled Emergence of a Nascent Constitutional Right that Preserves Happy Memories and Emotions," *Hastings Constitutional Law Quarterly* 40, no. 3 (2013): 475.

5 *R v Collins, Lewis & Jaffer* [2022] EWCA Crim 742, para 11.

6 *R v Collins, Lewis & Jaffer* [2022] EWCA Crim 742 para 13; also para 66.

7 'Harm' and 'wrong' are not interchangeable and imply different orders of legal injury – a harmful conduct might not be legally wrongful, so they are used loosely here.

freedom, independence, or sovereignty of the publisher.[8] Mill developed the framework of *harm to others* as a regulatory criterion and fundamental condition for interference with the *individuality* of another person.[9] Of course, Mill's libertarian thesis above – the autonomy, independence, and sovereignty of an individual – focused on the *living* individual. Mill put this beyond peradventure, observing that 'this doctrine is meant to apply only to human beings in the maturity of their faculties. We are not speaking of children or of young persons below the age which the law may fix as that of manhood or womanhood.'[10] Therefore, Mill was certainly not concerned with any question of harm to the dead (photographic or otherwise), nor the potential use of a concept of harm to the dead as a legitimate basis of interference with an individual's conduct towards a corpse.

But could Mill's theoretical and philosophical framework of *harm to others* apply to the dead analogically? Could harm to the dead be a basis of interfering with an individual's conduct, such as the taking and publication of an intrusive death image? Some post-Mill(ian) philosophers think so, at least impliedly, in that they approach the issue from the related question of whether posthumous interests exist and, if so, how should those interests be protected? Put differently, can the dead be harmed posthumously? The literature on this issue is extensive and cannot be fully examined in a work of this scope.[11] It suffices to say that, apart from the question of whether the dead can have conscious experience of a posthumous harm,[12] the extant literature on posthumous interests and harm focuses on identifying the interest-bearer or the subject of harm, if any. For instance, although Sperling rejected the idea that the dead could qualify as a *person*, [13] he nonetheless argued in support of the existence of certain posthumous interests, particularly 'the interest in the recognition of one's symbolic existence'.[14] Sperling further argued that the dead's interest in the recognition of their symbolic existence could be harmed, in that 'when tied to the concept of interests, harm is conceived as the thwarting, setting back, or defeating of an interest'.[15] In the same vein, Boonin postulated that frustration of a person's interest or desire (such as a lifelong project in which the person has invested time and money) could harm the person, in the sense of making things worse for them or making their life go less well, and that the frustrating act could

---

8 John Stuart Mill, *On Liberty* (with Introduction by G Himmelfarb; first published 1859) (London: Penguin Books, 1974).

9 Mill, *On Liberty*, 68–9.

10 Mill, *On Liberty*, 69.

11 A part of that literature is referenced below, including Joel Feinberg, "The Rights of Animals and Unborn Generations," in *Philosophy and Environmental Crisis*, ed. William Blackstone (Athens: University of Georgia Press, 1974), 43–68; Barbara Baum Levenbook, "Harming Someone after His Death," *Ethics* 94, no. 3 (1984): 407–19; George Pitcher, "The Misfortunes of the Dead," *American Philosophical Quarterly* 21, no. 2 (1984): 183–8; Dorothy Grover, "Posthumous Harm," *Philosophical Quarterly* 39, no. 156 (1989): 334; Steven Luper "Posthumous Harm," *American Philosophical Quarterly* 41, no. 1 (2004): 63; James Stacey Taylor, "The Myth of Posthumous Harm," *American Philosophical Quarterly* 42, no. 4 (2005): 311.

12 Such as a posthumous defamatory statement against the dead or, as in our case, the publication of an embarrassing or intrusive death image. The literature on posthumous harm generally accepts that conscious experience of harm is not a necessary ingredient for the existence of posthumous harm; for instance, Derek Parfit, *Reasons and Persons* (New York: Oxford University Press, 1984).

13 Daniel Sperling, *Posthumous Interests: Legal and Ethical Perspectives* (Cambridge: Cambridge University Press, 2008), 5.

14 Sperling, *Posthumous Interests*, 9; also, 40–1.

15 Sperling, *Posthumous Interests*, 10.

still be harmful even if the act takes place after the person is dead.[16] To have an *interest*, according to Feinberg, is to have a *stake* in something, to stand to gain or lose from the outcome of something.[17] Therefore, 'posthumous harm occurs when the deceased's interest is thwarted at a time subsequent to his death'.[18]

The crux of the matter, however, lies in identifying the interest-bearer, the subject of the posthumous interest, the *person* who is harmed by the thwarting or frustration of an interest or desire. Is it the post-mortem person – the lifeless physical corpse, the ante-mortem person – the person who is now a corpse, or somebody else, such as heirs or survivors?[19] For, as Partridge observed, 'without an interest bearer, such talk (about posthumous interests) is senseless'.[20] Furthermore, Partridge argued that Feinberg's defence of posthumous interests was unsustainable, because such interests lack an interest-bearer. Feinberg famously addressed that issue, building on Pitcher's framework,[21] by identifying the bearer of a posthumous interest as the *antemortem* person. This person, according to Feinberg, was, whilst alive, the subject of an interest that was all along going to be defeated:

> The ante-mortem person was harmed in being the subject of interests that were going to be defeated whether he knew it or not. It does not become 'retroactively true' that as the subject of doomed interests he is in a harmed state; rather it was true all along.[22]

In other words, the occurrence of a posthumous event or harm makes it true or evident that the antemortem person was harmed by it during their lifetime.[23] Callahan, however, provides a trenchant refutation of Feinberg's defence of the antemortem person as the subject of posthumous interests. She argued that only the living can have or bear interests, including interests alleged to be posthumous in nature, and that 'the interests a person had before death only survive *as interests* if they are carried on by living interests bearers'.[24] Furthermore, Callahan argued that Feinberg was mistaken in positing the antemortem person as the subject of a posthumous harm, because that approach implausibly identifies a wrongdoer long before the commission of a wrongful act, and a victim of wrong at a time when no affliction had been meted out to them. On Feinberg's hypothesis, Callahan observed, a person not yet born at the time the antemortem person died could nevertheless be considered to have posthumously harmed the antemortem person so long as it is now true or obvious that the harm was inevitable; that is, so long as the occurrence of the harm was true all along. Callan considered this proposition untenable, querying:

---

16 David Boonin, *Dead Wrong: The Ethics of Posthumous Harm* (Oxford: Oxford University Press, 2019).

17 Joel Feinberg, "Harm and Self-Interest," in *Law, Morality and Society: Essays in Honour of H. L. A. Hart*, ed. Peter Hacker and Joseph Raz (Oxford: Clarendon Press, 1977), 285–86.

18 Feinberg, "Harm and Self-Interest," 308.

19 Callahan argues in favour of heirs or survivors as the proper bearers or subjects of alleged posthumous interests: Joan Callahan, "On Harming the Dead," *Ethics* 97 (1987): 341.

20 Ernest Partridge, "Posthumous Interests and Posthumous Respect," *Ethics* 91, no. 2 (1981): 247.

21 Pitcher had earlier signposted the antemortem person as the subject of a posthumous interest: Pitcher, "The Misfortunes of the Dead."

22 Joel Feinberg, *Harm to Others* (New York: Oxford University Press, 1984), 91.

23 Taylor, "The Myth of Posthumous Harm," 314.

24 Callahan, "On Harming the Dead," 344. Italics in the original.

For what now shall we say of a person who will later perform an action productive of posthumous harm? It seems that we must say that he is, long before *doing* something, already responsible for placing the antemortem Smith or A in a harmed state. Even worse, it can surely turn out on this view that our would-be agent is responsible for harming another even before he is born, just as long as it is now true that he will perform the act.[25]

Therefore, Callahan argued that accepting Feinberg's thesis on the antemortem person as the subject of a posthumous harm would induce an acceptance of the (Christian) doctrine of original sin,[26] or the theory of human immortality,[27] both of which she could not subscribe to.

Furthermore, funerary rites and mortuary culture could support the idea that the dead might be harmed posthumously. For instance, in discussing death and funerary rituals in England and Wales, Richardson observed:

> The significance of the human corpse in popular death culture at the time of the Anatomy Act [1832] seems to have been coloured by a prevailing belief in the existence of a strong tie between body and personality/soul for an undefined period of time after death. This belief underpinned the central role of the corpse in popular funerary ritual, and gained added power from confusion and ambiguity concerning both the definition of death and the spiritual status of the corpse. The result was an uncertain balance between solicitude towards the corpse and fear of it.[28]

In some other cultures, such as the Native Hawaiians in the USA, the dead are even regarded as continuing to exist after death, and thus could have actions maintained in their name and on their behalf to vindicate their interests. Amongst the Native Hawaiians, therefore, the dead could be harmed by a posthumous event. For instance, the claimants in *Na Iwi O Na Kapuna O Mokapu v Dalton* were Native Hawaiian remains that had been disinterred from the Mokapu Peninsula and placed under the curatorial custody of the Bishop Museum by the US Secretary of the Department of Navy for the purpose of inventory and repatriation under the Native American Graves Protection and Repatriation Act (NAGPRA).[29] The claimant-human remains alleged, amongst other breaches of NAGPRA, that the additional research done on them (the remains), by the museum-defendant as a part of its inventory process, desecrated them (the remains) and thereby inflicted an *injury* on them. The defendant successfully applied for a summary judgment, partly on the basis that the remains lacked legal standing. Nonetheless, Ezra J. made pertinent observations regarding the Native Hawaiians' conceptualisation of the dead as a 'being' capable of suffering posthumous harm:

---

25 Callahan, "On Harming the Dead,"345. Italics in the original.

26 Callahan, "On Harming the Dead," 345. *Bible* (New International Version), Psalm 51:5: 'Surely I was sinful at birth, sinful from the time my mother conceived me.'

27 Callahan, "On Harming the Dead," 348.

28 Ruth Richardson, *Death, Dissection and the Destitute* (London: Routledge and Kegan Paul, 1988), 7. Gittings made a similar observation regarding the 'perceived continuity of life and death': Clare Gittings, *Death, Burial and the Individual in Early Modern England* (London: Croom Helm, 1984), 35.

29 *Na Iwi O Na Kapuna O Mokapu v Dalton*, 894 F. Supp. 1397 (1995).

The complaint … lists the Na Iwi, or the Mokapu remains, as plaintiffs. The Na Iwi purportedly brought this action by and through their alleged guardian, the Native Hawaiian organisation Hui Malama … the Mokapu remains were intended as plaintiffs in their own right. Hui Malama asserts that according to Hawaiian custom, human remains are spiritual beings that possess all of the traits of a living person. The Federal Defendant's physical examination of the remains was, they contend, a violation and desecration of the remains. As a result, the remains have allegedly suffered an injury to their spiritual well-being and have standing to bring suit.[30]

As highlighted above, Ezra J. dismissed the claimant's contention, holding that 'neither the provisions of NAGPRA nor the common law afford standing to the Mokapu remains'.[31] Surely, Ezra J.'s analysis was based on common law and statutory provisions on the matter, rather than on any social, anthropological, or philosophical view of the moral personality of human remains in Native Hawaiian worldview.

All of the above is not to say for certain that the dead can suffer posthumous harm, particularly the photographic harm of the unauthorised publication of a death image. Indeed, no such absolute claim can be made on the issue of posthumous harm, for as Partridge pointedly cautioned, 'plausible, well-considered arguments can be presented to support either affirmative or negative answers to these questions (on posthumous interests and harm) … these questions seem to be such that no answer can put us fully at ease'.[32] Therefore, the aim here is to underscore the plausibility of a view in defence of the existence of posthumous photographic harm. To the extent that such a harm to the dead is plausible, it reinforces the argument in the section below that English and Welsh common law generally or broadly recognises the legal personality of the dead, and that such a recognition is very well historically grounded. It must, however, be stated at the outset that the attribution of legal personality relies very much on legal fictions,[33] and thus is not conditioned on the dead's susceptibility to posthumous harm.

Not so long with the *person* of the dead

If the dead could be harmed by a death image, and if a death image constitutes a legal injury, do the dead have the necessary legal personality to justify the bringing of an action in their name in order to remedy the injury? As highlighted in the introduction above, there has been a long-standing preanalytical doctrinal assumption that English and Welsh common law interdicts personhood at the moment of death, thereby marking the cessation or withdrawal of a deceased person's legal personality and their ability to have actions brought or defended on their behalf. Therefore, it is said that *actio personalis moritur cum persona*; that is, a personal right of action ceases with the death of either or both parties to an action or potential action. And yet an analyst searches in vain for the clear provenance or authority for such a remarkable pretheoretic doctrine.

30 *Na Iwi O Na Kapuna O Mokapu v Dalton*, 894 F. Supp. 1397, 1406 (1995).
31 *Na Iwi O Na Kapuna O Mokapu v Dalton*, 894 F. Supp. 1397 (1995).
32 Partridge, "Posthumous Interests and Posthumous Respect," 243.
33 Margaret Davies and Ngaire Naffine, *Are Persons Property? Legal Debates About Property and Personality* (Aldershot: Ashgate Publishing Ltd., 2001), 51–69.

Historically, the view that legal personality ends with death in England and Wales has been traced by the legal historian Goudy to an obfuscatory Latin reference to Roman law made by a thirteenth-century English jurist, Bracton, who purportedly inferred from Roman law that legal personality ends with death in England as well.[34] But Goudy argued that the *actio personalis* doctrine itself was 'not taken from the Roman Law nor from any mediaeval civilian; indeed to a Roman lawyer or a Civilian it would have sounded non-sensical'.[35] Consequently, Goudy concluded that the *actio personalis* doctrine 'came into our law owing to the misunderstanding by Bracton of the Roman Law, his inaccurate use of its language, and the consequently erroneous doctrine adopted by Fitzherbert and others'.[36] In the same vein, Winfield accused Bracton of inflicting the *actio personalis* doctrine on English law, arguing that the doctrine would not 'have been mentioned at all but for an injustice that has been done by Bracton'.[37] Winfield considered it incomprehensible that 'Bracton's successors twisted this [Bracton's] quotation into actio personalis moritur cum persona.'[38] It was not the first time in English legal history that an established rule of common law on a matter had been engendered by an erroneous interpretation of law made by a leading legal authority. For instance, the court in *Haynes Case* considered whether the defendant could be convicted of theft (then characterised as larceny) of shrouds which had been used to wrap some dead bodies.[39] The defendant had unlawfully disinterred some dead bodies for the sole purpose of taking the shrouds in which they were wrapped; he intended to sell the shrouds. The defendant's conviction, however, depended on whether the shrouds could be owned, and by whom? If the shrouds were in the legal ownership of nobody, then the charge of larceny was bound to fail. To resolve this issue of ownership, the court held that the shrouds were not capable of being owned by the deceased persons with whose bodies they were wrapped, because 'the dead body is not capable of it ... a dead body being but a lump of earth hath no capacity'.[40] Rather, the 'property in the sheets remain in the owners, that is, in him who had property therein, when the dead body was wrapped therewith'.[41] Thus, the court was clearly not concerned with the proprietary status of a corpse in *Haynes Case*; and yet Coke, the leading writer on English law in the seventeenth century, erroneously interpreted *Haynes Case* to mean that dead bodies were not capable of being property: 'The burial of the cadaver (that is, *caro data vermibus*) is *nullius in bonis*, and belongs to Ecclesiastical cognisance.'[42] This no-property rule for dead bodies thus established erroneously by Coke was endorsed by Blackstone, another common law legal icon, who observed that 'though the heir has a property interest in the monuments and escutcheons of his

---

34 Henry Goudy, "Two Ancient Brocards," in *Essays in Legal History Read Before the International Congress of Historical Studies Held in London in 1913*, ed. Paul Vinogradoff (London: Oxford University Press, 1913), 222–3.
35 Goudy, "Two Ancient Brocards," 216.
36 Goudy, "Two Ancient Brocards," 227.
37 Percy Henry Winfield, "Death as Affecting Liability in Tort," *Columbia Law Review* 29, no. 3 (1929): 241.
38 Winfield, "Death as Affecting Liability in Tort," 241.
39 *Haynes Case* [1614] 77 ER 1389.
40 *Haynes Case* [1614] 77 ER 1389.
41 *Haynes Case* [1614] 77 ER 1389. For a fuller discussion of this case, Ngaire Naffine, "But a Lump of Earth? The Legal Status of the Corpse," in *Courting Death: The Law of Mortality*, ed. Desmond Manderson (London: Pluto Press, 1999), 95–110.
42 Edward Coke, *Institutes of the Laws of England* Part 111 (London: Thames Baset, 1680), 110.

ancestors, he has none in their bodies or ashes'.[43] Despite the dubious origin of the no-property rule for cadavers and body parts, it has become an established part of the common law in England and Wales, and a standard regulatory and analytical framework for examining issues relating to unauthorised interreferences with dead bodies.[44] This prompted the observation of Rose LJ in *R v Kelly* that:

> however questionable the historical origins of the principle, it has now been the common law for 150 years at least that neither a corpse nor parts of a corpse are in themselves and without more capable of being property protected by rights.[45]

Therefore, in relation to *actio personalis* rule, the echoes from *Haynes'* historiography resound. Notwithstanding its dubious origin and erroneous importation into English law by Bracton, the *actio personalis* doctrine became a part of the common law. The *actio personalis* doctrine was most clearly judicially recognised (but not applied) for the first time in an English court in *Pinchon's Case*, decided in the seventeenth century.[46] Equally, the doctrine gained its first statutory recognition via the Common Law Procedure Act 1833, s. 2, which provided for the transmissibility of certain causes of action.

In contrast to *Haynes'* objectification of a corpse, the common law practically repudiated the *actio personalis* doctrine by recognising the legal personality and right of the dead, through their legal representatives, to sue or be sued upon in various areas of private law. In the realm of property law, for instance, the *actio personalis* rule did not apply. Actual or potential proprietary causes of action were never defeated by the death of either or both parties to a case at common law.[47] In contractual actions as well, common law did not recognise, nor enforced, the *actio personalis* doctrine.[48] Furthermore, the *actio personalis* rule was never applied to a claim that sought to enforce a statutory right or obligation of a dead person, regardless of whether the death occurred during the pendency of the suit or before the commencement of the action.[49] It was only in the field of tort law that the *actio personalis* doctrine prevailed.[50] Whatever remained of the *actio personalis* doctrine at common law was statutorily eroded by s. 1(1) of the Law Reform (Miscellaneous Provisions) Act 1934. Having regard to the phrase 'causes of action subsisting', delineated in the Act above, it is arguable that an unauthorised publication of a death image, arising as it does after the death of the photographic subject, is not a cause of action *subsisting* at the time of death, and therefore, is not transmissible under the 1934 Act. Whilst this argument is strong, it can only mean that a cause of action based on unauthorised publication of a death image is not covered by the transmission rule of the 1934 Act; not that such a cause of action is necessarily non-

---

43 William Blackstone, *Commentaries on the Laws of England Volume 11: Of the Rights of Things* (Chicago, IL: University of Chicago Press, 1979), 429 – reprint of the 1st ed. 1765–69. Also, Sir James Stephen, *A Digest of the Criminal Law* (London: Macmillan, 5th edn, 1894), 252 (Art 318).

44 Remigius Nnamdi Nwabueze, "Regulation of Bodily Parts: Understanding Bodily Parts as a Duplex," *International Journal of Law in Context* 15, no. 4 (2019): 515.

45 *R v Kelly* [1999] Q.B. 621, 630.

46 *Pinchon's Case* [1611] 77 E.R. 859.

47 *Sackvill's Case* [1558] 73 E.R. 385; *Williams v Keinshame* [1558] 73 E.R. 384

48 *Airey v Airey* [1958] 2 Q.B. 300, 307; *Pinchon's Case* [1611] 77 E.R. 859, 863, 865–6.

49 *Peebles v Oswaldtwistle Urban District Council* [1896] 2 Q.B. 159; *Darlington v Roscoe & Sons Ltd.* [1907] 1 K.B. 219; *Andrews (Deceased) v Lewisham & Guy Mental Health NHS Trust* [2000] I.C.R. 707.

50 *Higgins v Butcher* [1606] Yelv. 89.

transmissible. This issue would necessarily be decided on first principles. In view of common law's liberality in recognising the legal personality or standing of a deceased person, as highlighted above, I suggest that courts should equally recognise that a post-death accrued cause of action, such as an authorised publication of a death image, is actionable and transmissible.

In sum, the *actio personalis* doctrine trenches on an illegitimate origin, and contrary to unanalysed modern assumptions regarding the historical strength of its application, the doctrine never really made its way into the English and Welsh courts until the seventeenth century. More importantly, the courts largely ignored the doctrine and refused to apply it in various areas of private and statutory law right up to the twentieth century when the doctrine was almost annihilated by the 1934 Act. All this is to say that common law broadly or generally recognised the legal personality and standing of the dead. I suggest, therefore, that the dead, through their legal representatives, should be able to maintain actions for photographic violations. In the event that prospect of legal change becomes unattainable, attention should now be focused on the legal fortunes of survivors below.

Shock and trauma of published death images

Unauthorised publication of a death image, particularly an embarrassing death image, would certainly inflict some damage on survivors, but the damage is most likely to be mental or psychiatric in nature, rather than physical or financial harm. This has considerable repercussions for the availability of legal redress for harm resulting from such publications considering the historical reluctance of the courts to grant tort compensation for mental harm that is unaccompanied by physical or financial damage.[51] Mental harm resulting from a published devastating death image is arguably more damaging than (or at least as damaging as) physical or financial harm. The additional distress, and intrusion upon grief, that such publications inflict on survivors are beyond quibble.[52] Take, for instance, the US Supreme Court case of *National Archives and Records Admin. v Favish*,[53] where, pursuant to the Freedom of Information Act (FOIA), Favish sought disclosures of death-scene photographs of a suicide victim, Vincent Foster, Jr., who was the deputy counsel to President Clinton. In a unanimous judgment withholding the disclosures of death-scene photographs of Foster's body pursuant to the privacy exemption of the FOIA, Kennedy J. delineated the mental distress such a disclosure would pose for Foster's family which called for protection:

> In a sworn declaration with the District Court, Foster's sister, Sheila Foster Anthony, stated that the family had been harassed by, and deluged with requests from, '[p]olitical and commercial opportunists' who sought to profit from Foster's suicide. In particular, she was 'horrified and devastated by [a] photograph [already] leaked to the press.' ... '[E]very time I see it,' Sheila Foster Anthony wrote, 'I have nightmares and heart-pounding insomnia as I visualize how he

51 William Vaughan Horton Rogers, *Winfield & Jolowicz on Tort*, 18th ed. (London: Sweet & Maxwell, 2010), 259–60; Werdner Page Keeton, et al., eds., *Prosser & Keeton on the Law of Torts*, 5th ed. (St. Paul, MN: West Publishing Co., 2001), 54–7.

52 "Emiliano Sala death images: Pair face prison over accessing mortuary footage," *Sky News*, 9 August 2019, https://news.sky.com/story/pair-admit-accessing-emiliano-sala-death-images-11780818 (accessed on 14 December 2022).

53 *National Archives and Records Admin. v Favish*, 541 U.S. 157 (2004).

must have spent his last few minutes and seconds of his life.' She opposed the disclosures of the disputed pictures because 'I fear that the release of [additional] photographs certainly would set off another round of intense scrutiny by the media. Undoubtedly, the photographs would be placed on the Internet for world consumption. Once again my family would be the focus of conceivably unsavory and distasteful media coverage.'[54]

A court would be hard pressed to deny protection against the infliction of such mental damage, a matter to which the law of tort beckons. After shaking off the historic shackles preventing redress for mental harm, imposed by the Privy Council in *Victorian Ry Commissioners v Coultas*,[55] the courts now grant compensation for mental injury occasioned by intentional[56] as well as negligent[57] conduct.

The use of an intentional tort action to vindicate mental harm caused by the publication of a death image poses some doctrinal difficulties. Take, for instance, the tort's requirement that the impugned conduct must be intentional which, on the surface, might appear to be easily provable by a claimant-survivor since the act of publishing a death image is, by definition, always intentional. However, the requisite intention is not so much about the intentionality of the publication itself as it is about the defendant's intention to inflict mental harm on the claimant-survivor by virtue of the publication. In short, the intent must be to harm the claimant, or be directed towards the claimant; nothing less will do. Accordingly, the Supreme Court observed in *Rhodes v OPO*:

> The conduct element requires words or conduct directed towards the claimant for which there is no justification or reasonable excuse, and the burden of proof is on the claimant ... We agree with the approach of the Court of Appeal in regarding the tort as confined to those towards whom the relevant words or conduct were directed, but they may be a group ... In the present case the Court of Appeal treated the publication of the book as conduct directed towards the claimant and considered that the question of justification had therefore to be judged vis-à-vis him. In this respect we consider that they erred.[58]

Cases will be rare in which a claimant-survivor can scale this elemental hurdle, because most death images are published for sheer feral joy, in pursuit of voyeurism,[59] or driven by morbid curiosity,[60] but hardly to pointedly inflict mental distress on a claimant-survivor. For instance, in *Collins* the Court of Appeal observed that 'Collins (who was 56 years old) had acted from morbid and gratuitous curiosity',[61] and the trial judge similarly observed:

---

54 *National Archives and Records Admin. v Favish*, 541 U.S. 157, 167 (2004).
55 *Victorian Ry Commissioners v Coultas* [1888] 13 App. Cas. 222. Also, the House of Lords in *Lynch v Knight* [1861] 9 H.L.C. 577 at 590 (Lord Wensleydale).
56 *Wilkinson v Downton* [1897] 2 Q.B. 57; *Rhodes v OPO* [2015] UKSC 32.
57 *Dulieu v White* [1901] 2 K.B. 669; *Janvier v Sweeney* [1919] 2 K.B. 316; *Alcock v CC South Yorkshire* [1992] 1 A.C. 310.
58 *Rhodes v OPO* [2015] UKSC 32, para. 74.
59 Calvert, "A Familial Right over Death Images."
60 "CCTV pair who watched Emiliano Sala mortuary footage jailed," *The Telegraph*, 23 September 2019, www.telegraph.co.uk/news/2019/09/23/cctv-boss-employee-jailed-emiliano-sala-mortuary-fo otage-judge (accessed on 14 December 2022).
61 *R v Collins, Lewis & Jaffer* [2022] EWCA Crim 742, para 22

[T]he defendants' conduct was 'appalling and inexplicable'. They had wholly disregarded the privacy of the two women and their families by taking images and passing them to others, for what could only have been a 'cheap thrill, kudos, a kick or some form of bragging rights'...[62]

Furthermore, not every type of mental distress or damage suffices for this tort – the mental damage alleged, unless accompanied by physical harm, which is hardly the case, must approximate to a recognisable psychiatric illness.[63] The distress survivors suffer from the publication of a death image might not be able to meet this threshold of psychiatric damage.

A claimant-survivor may fare better with the alternative cause of action for negligent infliction of mental distress, because it does not require a survivor or victim of mental distress to be the direct focus of the defendant's act of publishing a death image, provided the survivor-claimant is within the zone of harm foreseeable from the defendant's conduct. Other requirements for the existence of a duty of care would also need to be satisfied.[64] Even then, two significant issues arise for consideration. First, like the action for intentional infliction of mental distress, is a claimant in an action for negligent infliction of mental distress arising from published death images required to show that his or her mental injury is consistent with a recognisable psychiatric illness?[65] Second, does *Alcock*'s control mechanism, developed in the context of secondary victims of an accident, apply to a potential negligent action in relation to mental distress suffered in connection with published death images? Why the issues above, relating to proof of psychiatric injury and satisfaction of *Alcock*'s control mechanism, have been very much discussed in the cases, only a handful of those cases relate to dead bodies, some of which are examined below.

Turning to the first issue above, *AB v Leeds Teaching Hospital NHS* may be relevant,[66] where parents of autopsied children allegedly suffered mental distress upon the revelation that the defendants non-consensually removed, retained, and used various body parts of their children. The parents sued in negligence. Gage J, however, found as a fact that the claimant-parents suffered a recognisable psychiatric illness in the form of adjustment disorder; thus, it is not clear the direction the case would have taken if the parents' mental distress had failed to rise to the psychiatric level of adjustment disorder. But the question seems to have been answered in the negative by the Court of Appeal in *Owens v Liverpool Corporation*,[67] where a tramcar negligently driven by the defendant's servant collided with, and damaged, a hearse leading a funeral procession, causing the coffin in the hearse containing the dead body of the claimants' relative to be overturned. The claimants, who were in a carriage following the hearse, witnessed the accident (or its immediate aftermath) and thereby suffered various degrees of nervous shock. Although the nervous shock or mental distress suffered by the claimants was not accompanied by any physical injury, nor was there any suggestion that the mental damage suffered by the

---

62 *R v Collins, Lewis & Jaffer* [2022] EWCA Crim 742, para 51.

63 *Wong v Parkside Health NHS Trust* [2001] EWCA Civ 1721; *Rhodes v OPO* [2015] UKSC 32, para 73; Rogers, *Winfield & Jolowicz on Tort*, 143–4.

64 *Caparo Industries Plc v Dickman* [1990] 2 A.C. 605.

65 Rogers firmly observed that, in a negligence action for the infliction of mental distress, 'There must be some recognisable and acknowledged psychiatric illness'; Rogers, *Winfield & Jolowicz on Tort*, 260.

66 *AB v Leeds Teaching Hospital NHS* [2005] 2 W.L.R. 358.

67 *Owens v Liverpool Corporation* [1939] 1 K.B. 394.

claimants rose to the level of a recognisable psychiatric illness,[68] the Court of Appeal upheld the trial court's finding that the claimants had suffered a compensable injury by way of nervous shock.[69] Whilst *Owens* remains good law, as it has not been overruled, though doubted by Lord Oliver in *Alcock*, Rogers described the outcome in *Owens* as 'strange',[70] because of the absence of a recognisable psychiatric injury. Nonetheless, *Owens* is consistent with the approach in some US jurisdictions, where the courts award damages for negligent mishandling or mistreatment of a dead body resulting in severe mental distress unaccompanied by physical injury, nor resulting in psychiatric illness, provided the negligent conduct itself was extremely outrageous.[71]

On the second issue above, the former House of Lords held in *Alcock* that a claimant (secondary victim) who suffered nervous shock because of an accident involving a third party (primary victim) must, amongst other things, satisfy certain control mechanisms:

a   A close tie of love and affection with the primary victim;

b   The claimant must establish proximity to the accident in time and space; and

c   The claimant must have directly perceived the accident, not being merely informed of it by third parties.

As highlighted above, however, *Alcock* involved a terrible accident to primary (human) victims, some football fans and spectators at the Hillsborough football stadium's disaster of 1989, as a result of which some of them died or were seriously injured. Considering the context of *Alcock*, therefore, the question is whether *Alcock's* control mechanism equally applies to cases of shock arising from an interference with a dead body? Rogers answered this question in the negative, observing that such cases, typified by *Owens*, 'do not fall within *Alcock* since no "third person" was endangered'.[72] This suggests that where the endangerment was to a corpse, a non-person, then the shock suffered by a claimant thereof was not legally compensable. In *Owens*, however, the Court of Appeal clearly rejected a distinction between mental distress suffered from an apprehension of injury to a human being and that suffered from fear of damage to a corpse, or a non-human being, such as a dog. Therefore, on the issue of whether 'in a claim for damages for shock, there must in every case be apprehension of injury to some human being',[73] MacKinnon LJ observed that 'On principle we think that the right to recover damages for mental shock caused by the negligence of a defendant is not limited to cases in which apprehension as to human safety is involved'.[74] Consequently, it is most likely that when the question arises, *Alcock's* control mechanism would be considered applicable to nervous shock arising from an interference with a dead body. This conclusion is even more justified having regard to the doubts expressed by both MacKinnon LJ in *Owens* and

---

68 Indeed, the Court of Appeal doubted that, had it been the trial court, it would have found that the claimants suffered injury in the first place: 'we entertain considerable doubt whether we should have arrived at his (trial judge) conclusions as to injury being sustained by the plaintiffs, or as to its extent'; *Owens v Liverpool Corporation* [1939] 1 K.B. 398.

69 *Owens v Liverpool Corporation* [1939] 1 K.B. 398.

70 Rogers, *Winfield & Jolowicz on Tort*, 275 (footnote 736).

71 Keeton, *Prosser & Keeton on the Law of Torts*, 64. See also, Remigius Nnamdi Nwabueze, "Biotechnology and the New Property Regime in Human Bodies and Body Parts," *Loyola of Los Angeles International & Comparative Law Review* 24, no. 1 (2002): 29–30.

72 Rogers, *Winfield & Jolowicz on Tort*, 275 (footnote 736).

73 *Owens v Liverpool Corporation* [1939] 1 K.B. 399.

74 *Owens v Liverpool Corporation* [1939] 1 K.B. 400.

Lord Oliver in *Alcock* as to the reality of the existence of the injury alleged in *Owens*. However, it appears that the three *Alcock* factors above can, in the nature of things, be relatively easily satisfied by survivors alleging mental distress in connection with published death images of a loved one. Nonetheless, the difficulties above associated with the actions for intentional and negligent infliction of mental distress compel the consideration of a novel action for the enforcement of a familial right to privacy, something outside the scope of this chapter.

Conclusion

Diffusion of smartphone usages and the Internet have made death images ubiquitous, creating an enduring and worrying sociolegal problems of immense proportions which raise questions about the plausibility of posthumous photographic harm, the existence of legal personality of the dead, and the nature and scope of legal redress available to survivors. I argue that, philosophically and theoretically, the dead, as an antemortem person, can suffer photographic harm posthumously. Also, that historically, the *actio personalis* rule is not an accurate reflection of the common law, which has always recognised the legal personality of the dead, something that was impliedly put on a statutory basis by the 1934 Act relating to the transmissibility of actions. Consequently, it is possible to bring a privacy action in the name of a deceased person in relation to a misuse of death images. Furthermore, I argue that survivors can vindicate the mental harm they suffered from misuse of a relative's death image through the tort actions for intentional and negligent infliction of nervous shock.

Bibliography

Blackstone, William. *Commentaries on the Laws of England Volume 11: Of the Rights of Things.* Chicago, IL: University of Chicago Press, 1979.
Blackstone, William. *Philosophy and Environmental Crisis.* Athens: University of Georgia Press, 1974.
Boonin, David. *Dead Wrong: The Ethics of Posthumous Harm.* Oxford: Oxford University Press, 2019.
Callahan, Joan. "On Harming the Dead." *Ethics* 97 (1987): 341–352.
Clavert, Clay. "A Familial Right over Death Images: Critiquing the Internet-Propelled Emergence of a Nascent Constitutional Right that Preserves Happy Memories and Emotions." *Hastings Constitutional Law Quarterly* 40, no. 3 (2013).
Coke, Edward. *Institutes of the Laws of England Part 111.* London: Thames Baset, 1680.
Davies, Margaret, and Ngaire Naffine. *Are Persons Property? Legal Debates About Property and Personality.* Aldershot: Ashgate, 2001.
Feinberg, Joel. "Harm and Self-Interest." In *Law, Morality and Society: Essays in Honour of H. L. A. Hart*, edited by Peter Hacker and Joseph Raz, 285–286. Oxford: Clarendon Press, 1977.
Feinberg, Joel. *Harm to Others.* New York: Oxford University Press, 1984.
Feinberg, Joel. "The Rights of Animals and Unborn Generations," in *Philosophy and Environmental Crisis*, ed. William Blackstone, 43–68. Athens: University of Georgia Press, 1974.
Gittings, Clare. *Death, Burial and the Individual in Early Modern England.* London: Croom Helm, 1984.
Goudy, Henry. "Two Ancient Brocards." In *Essays in Legal History Read Before the International Congress of Historical Studies Held in London in 1913*, edited by Paul Vinogradoff. London: Oxford University Press, 1913.
Grover, Dorothy. "Posthumous Harm." *Philosophical Quarterly* 39, no. 156 (1989): 334–353.
Hacker, Peter, and Joseph Raz. *Law, Morality and Society: Essays in Honour of H. L. A. Hart.* Oxford: Clarendon Press, 1977.

Keeton, Werdner Page. *Prosser & Keeton on the Law of Torts*, 5th ed. St. Paul, MN: West Publishing Co., 2001.

Levenbook, Barbara Baum. "Harming Someone after His Death." *Ethics* 94, no. 3 (1984): 407–419.

Luper, Steven. "Posthumous Harm." *American Philosophical Quarterly* 41, no. 1 (2004): 63–72.

Manderson, Desmond. *Courting Death: The Law of Mortality*. London: Pluto Press, 1999.

Mill, John Stuart. *On Liberty* (with Introduction by G. Himmelfarb; first published 1859). London: Penguin Books, 1974.

Naffine, Ngaire. "But a Lump of Earth? The Legal Status of the Corpse." In *Courting Death: The Law of Mortality*, edited by Desmond Manderson. London: Pluto Press, 1999.

Nwabueze, Remigius Nnamdi. "Biotechnology and the New Property Regime in Human Bodies and Body Parts." *Loyola of Los Angeles International & Comparative Law Review* 24, no. 1 (2002): 19–64.

Nwabueze, Remigius Nnamdi. "Regulation of Bodily Parts: Understanding Bodily Parts as a Duplex." *International Journal of Law in Context* 15, no. 4 (2019): 515–535.

Parfit, Derek. *Reasons and Persons*. New York: Oxford University Press, 1984.

Partridge, Ernest. "Posthumous Interests and Posthumous Respect." *Ethics* 91, no. 2 (1981): 243–264.

Pitcher, George. "The Misfortunes of the Dead." *American Philosophical Quarterly* 21, no. 2 (1984): 183–188.

Richardson, Ruth. *Death, Dissection and the Destitute*. London: Routledge and Kegan Paul, 1988.

Rogers, William Vaughan Horton. *Winfield & Jolowicz on Tort*, 18th ed. London: Sweet & Maxwell, 2010.

Sperling, Daniel. *Posthumous Interests: Legal and Ethical Perspectives*. Cambridge: Cambridge University Press, 2008.

Stephen, James. *A Digest of the Criminal Law*, 5th ed. London: Macmillan, 1894.

Taylor, James Stacey. "The Myth of Posthumous Harm." *American Philosophical Quarterly* 42, no. 4 (2005): 311–322.

Winfield, Percy Henry. "Death as Affecting Liability in Tort." *Columbia Law Review* 29, no. 3 (1929): 239–254.

21

WHEN BIRTH AND DEATH COLLIDE

Maternal Infanticide and the Illusive Born Alive Rule

Emma Milne

Introduction

There is a basic principle in English and Welsh criminal law: one cannot be a victim of homicide until they have achieved a living, independent existence from their biological mother and thus become a reasonable creature in *rerum natura* (in existence).[1] In other words, an infant must be born alive to become a full legal subject and so protected under the criminal law as any other living person. This, one would suppose, would end the debate regarding the criminal liability of any person, including a pregnant woman, who ends the life of a foetus: as the foetus is not a reasonable creature in existence, it does not have legal personality and so no homicide offence has been committed. However, as this chapter outlines, when the law surrounding birth collides with the criminal law surrounding death, the level of debate is substantial, and the application of the law blurs the lines between life and death – particularly when a 'deviant' woman is at the centre of the case.

The nature of cases where a child dies in suspicious circumstances around the time of birth – prior to labour, during labour, or after achieving live birth – means that women are overwhelmingly the main suspects in these cases. Women bear the burden of pregnancy in terms of the physical capacity but also in terms of the stigma and hardships that characterise a pregnancy if it is deemed to be 'unauthorised' by the society in which she lives. For example, historically, and still today in many communities, to be pregnant outside of the confines of marriage is stigmatised, often with the woman presented as morally and sexually deviant, regardless of the context of how she became pregnant. Today, women are regularly chastised for failing to meet social standards of 'good' motherhood, an unachievable standard of behaviour that requires a woman to put the needs and wellbeing of her child, including her unborn

---

1 Edward Coke, *The Fourth Part of the Institutes of the Laws of England: Concerning the Jurisdiction of Courts.* 6th ed. (London: Printed by W. Rawlins, for Thomas Basset at the George near St. Dunstans Church in Fleet-street, 1644 [1681]), 50–1.

DOI: 10.4324/9781003304593-25

child, before her own.[2] Consequently, when considering the impacts of the legal responses to the suspicious death of a child around the time of birth, it is almost certainly the criminalisation of women that lies at the centre of the debate.

The laws and cases analysed in this chapter form but one example of the wider regulation and control of women's bodies evident around the world. The United States offers a clear example, with abortion almost completely unavailable in many states since *Dobbs v. Jackson Women's Health Organization*[3] overturned *Roe v. Wade*[4] and *Planned Parenthood v. Casey*.[5] Consequently, 40 million women live in US states that are hostile to abortion.[6] In Latin America, women are imprisoned for abortions and for experiencing miscarriages.[7] In European countries such as Poland and Northern Ireland, abortion continues to be difficult to access.[8] Beyond abortion, women report power, control, and coercion being exerted over their bodies during pregnancy and childbirth,[9] and women are forced to use long-acting reversible contraception.[10] Together, this paints a clear picture that women do not enjoy the freedom of bodily autonomy and the right to control their bodies that men do. This is the context in which the analysis presented in this chapter sits.

This chapter illustrates the tension between birth and death within criminal law and the impacts on vulnerable women by first outlining the significant history of the criminal law in this area and the construction of a 'menu' of offences available to prosecute accused women. The chapter then demonstrates how contemporary applications of the law manipulate the born alive rule and so blur the boundary between birth and death.

A mishmash of overlapping offences

On 14 April 1675, an unmarried woman, who is not named in the court record, was tried at the Old Bailey for 'the Murthering of her Bastard-child'.[11] As it was determined that she could not prove with the testimony of one witness that the child had been born dead, the law allowed for her to 'suffer Death as in case of Murther'.[12] Fifty years earlier, in

---

2 Emma Milne, *Criminal Justice Responses to Maternal Filicide: Judging the Failed Mother* (Bingley: Emerald Publishing, 2021).

3 597 US 19-1392 (2022).

4 410 US 113 (1973).

5 505 US 833 (1992).

6 Guttmacher Institute, "Roe v. Wade Overturned: Our Latest Resources" (accessed 25 May 2023), www.guttmacher.org/abortion-rights-supreme-court.

7 Rivers-Moore, Megan, "In Latin America, not only abortions but miscarriages can lead to jail time," *The Conversation*, 4 January 2022, https://theconversation.com/in-latin-america-not-only-abortions-but-miscarriages-can-lead-to-jail-time-173719.

8 Abortion Support Network. "Get Help – I'm in Northern Ireland" (accessed 25 May 2023), www.asn.org.uk/get-help-ni; Amnesty International. "Poland: Regression on Abortion Access Harms Women," 26 January 2022, www.amnesty.org/en/latest/news/2022/01/poland-regression-on-abortion-access-harms-women.

9 Camilla Pickles and Jonathan Herring, eds., *Childbirth, Vulnerability and Law: Exploring Issues of Violence and Control* (Abingdon: Routledge, 2020).

10 Flavin, Jeanne. *Our Bodies, Our Crimes: The Policing of Women's Reproduction in America* (New York: New York University Press, 2009).

11 Old Bailey Online. "Trial of Woman (T16750414-3)" 1675 (accessed 5 September 2020), www.oldbaileyonline.org/browse.jsp?id=t16750414-3-off10&div=t16750414-3#highlight.

12 Parliament Papers, 1624 21 Jac 1 c27, cited in Anne-Marie Kilday, *A History of Infanticide in Britain, C.1600 to the Present* (Basingstoke: Palgrave Macmillan, 2013), 17–8.

1624, Parliament had introduced an Act that reversed the burden of proving live birth of a newborn child if the mother was unmarried and suspected of causing their death. Prior to the change, to convict any person of the murder of a newborn child, the Crown had first to prove that the child had been born alive and then that they had been killed. Such a requirement, understandably, proved a challenge during the seventeenth century.

The legal change developed in the context of longstanding concerns about the financial burden of the 'undeserving' poor. One group deemed to unduly take advantage of Parish support was unmarried women and their 'bastard' children. During the late Elizabethan and early Jacobean periods, numerous pieces of legislation were enacted with the aim of reducing the financial burden of illegitimacy, which resulted in unmarried women facing fines and imprisonment for pregnancy.[13] The aim of these laws was to discourage women from becoming pregnant outside of marriage. Scholars have argued, and it was believed at the time, that these changes resulted in an increase in the number of unmarried women who killed their illegitimate children following birth and then claimed the child was stillborn to escape both the stigma and shame of an illegitimate child and punishment under the poor laws.[14] Amending the evidential burden of proof of live birth to secure a murder conviction was deemed to offer further disincentive to unmarried women to 'fornicate'. No longer could women hide their 'shame' through a secret birth, killing the baby, and then claiming it had been born dead.

By the turn of the nineteenth century, the 1624 Act had long fallen out of favour within legal and political circles, who considered it to dissuade juries from convicting suspected unmarried women of murder due to the perceived harshness of the law.[15] Consequently, Lord Ellenborough, the Lord Chief Justice, repealed the Jacobean statute, so placing unmarried women on an equal legal basis with all others tried for the murder of a new-born child. However, within the same legislation, Ellenborough created a new criminal offence, concealment of birth (hereafter 'concealment').[16] Originally proposed as a new capital offence, concealment criminalised the secret disposal of the dead body of a baby to hide the fact that they had been born.[17] The crime could only be committed by unmarried women, and the offence operated as an alternative verdict that a jury could select if they found a woman not guilty of murder. Consequently, the offence acted as a catch-all for cases of newborn child murder by unmarried women: if the Crown could prove live birth and unlawful killing by the mother, then she could be convicted of murder, but if one or both of these elements could not be proven, then she could be convicted of concealment. Changes were made to the draft Bill as it passed through Parliament, resulting in the maximum penalty for concealment being two years of penal servitude, with or without hard labour.

The 1624 Act and the offence of concealment provide our first examples of the born alive rule being worked around to achieve the desired legal outcome: criminalisation of 'deviant' women. The former changed the law so that evidence to satisfy the born alive rule was not needed, and the latter created a new offence that did not rely on the born

---

13 Mark Jackson. *New-Born Child Murder: Women, Illegitimacy and the Courts in Eighteenth-Century England* (Manchester: Manchester University Press, 1996).

14 Jackson, *New-Born Child Murder*; Peter Charles Hoffer, and N. E. H. Hull. *Murdering Mothers: Infanticide in England and New England, 1558–1803* (New York: New York University Press, 1981).

15 Jackson, *New-Born Child Murder*.

16 *Malicious Shooting or Stabbing Act 1803*. Also known as the Lord Ellenborough's Act.

17 Emma Milne, "Concealment of Birth: Time to Repeal a 200-Year-Old 'Convenient Stop-Gap'?" *Feminist Legal Studies* 27, no. 2 (2019): 139–62.

alive rule to be satisfied – so long as the body and birth of the child were concealed, then it did not matter if the child died in utero, during labour, or after live birth had been completed. Both workarounds only applied to unmarried women who were suspected of killing newborn children, thus suggesting that the true 'crime' being targeted was illicit sex and a subsequent pregnancy – their 'deviance'.[18] In reality, during the early modern period and over the eighteenth and into the nineteenth centuries, concealed pregnancy, giving birth alone, and then disposing of the body of a dead newborn child was not an uncommon practice for married couples.[19] If the aim was to protect the life of foetuses/ newborn children, then one would imagine that the law would criminalise all women who gave birth alone, resulting in the death of the child, as well as all people who concealed the body of a dead newborn child. Only in 1874 did failure to register a live born child become a crime,[20] while it was not until 1927 that the public were required to register stillbirths.[21] Prior to this, there was no legal requirement to declare the death of a newborn infant, unless you were a woman suspected of killing their illegitimate child. In which case, failure to declare could have resulted in conviction of concealment (at best) and potentially murder.

During the 1800s, further legislation was enacted to control and regulate women's pregnancies – notably, the creation of the statute offence of procuring a miscarriage in 1803. Rather than being designed to protect foetuses, McLaren has argued that the wording of this statute indicates that the law targeted those who provided abortions, thus being designed to protect women from being killed in the process of an abortion gone wrong: 'thereby to murder, or thereby to cause and procure the Miscarriage of any Woman'.[22] Such an interpretation of this law is supported by evidence that the criminalisation of abortion was codified as a means through which medical men were able to exert their influence and control as a process of recognition of their role as professionals.[23] Prior to the nineteenth century, abortion was a common law offence when committed post-quickening (the first time a woman feels the foetus move, approximately 15 to 17 gestational weeks). Mostly regarded as a matter for the ecclesiastic courts, the law was infrequently, inconsistently, and sporadically applied, implying a tolerance of the practice of ending a pregnancy;[24] that it was not seen as a moral or legal wrong; and that, prior to the nineteenth century, abortion played an important role in the regulation of fertility.[25] Further, Spivack argues that any concern for the 'criminality' of abortion in secular and ecclesiastic courts during the early modern period occurred in the context of a wider focus on illegitimacy and sex outside of the confines of marriage: abortion

---

18 Milne, "Concealment of Birth"; Milne, *Criminal Justice*.
19 Laura Gowing. "Secret Births and Infanticide in Seventeenth-Century England," *Past & Present* 156, no. 1 (1997): 87–115; Elizabeth Rapaport, "Mad Women and Desperate Girls: Infanticide and Child Murder in Law and Myth," *Fordham Urban Law Journal* 33, no. 2 (2006): 527–71.
20 *Registration of Births and Deaths Act 1874* (UK), s. 1.
21 *Births and Deaths Registration Act 1926* (UK).
22 Angus McLaren, *Reproductive Rituals: The Perception of Fertility in England from the Sixteenth Century to the Nineteenth Century* (London: Methuen, 1984).
23 John Keown, *Abortion, Doctors and the Law: Some Aspects of the Legal Regulation of Abortion in England from 1803 to 1982* (Cambridge: Cambridge University Press, 1988).
24 Colin Francome, *Abortion Practice in Britain and the United States* (London: Allen & Unwin, 1986); Bernard M. Dickens, *Abortion and the Law* (London: Macgibbon & Kee, 1966); Keown, *Abortion*.
25 Angus McLaren, *Reproductive Rituals*.

facilitated both, by allowing the unwanted product of the 'immoral' sexual act to be eradicated prior to spontaneous birth.[26]

Regardless of the historical tolerance for abortion as a means of contraception, in 1861, the offence of procuring a miscarriage was extended to include women who self-aborted at any point in their pregnancy.[27] Scholars generally agree, as with previous iterations of the offence, that the purpose of the law was to condemn or prevent harm from coming to pregnant women, although it is also argued that the prevention of the intentional destruction of foetal life was also a key element of the law.[28] As there was no parliamentary debate about this aspect of the 1861 Act, it is hard to say for certain, but scholars such as Williams argue that the former purpose – protection of pregnant women – was of most importance, as the concern was not for the unborn child but for the injury done to women as a result of the actions of unskilled abortion providers.[29] Importantly, the law, which is still in force today, criminalises the ending of a pregnancy rather than specifically the killing of a foetus.[30] A woman will still commit the offence if she ends her pregnancy, resulting in the child being born alive. The distinction between ending a pregnancy and killing a foetus is important, as will become clear later in this chapter when we look at how procuring a miscarriage is used today to dodge the born alive rule.

In contrast to procuring a miscarriage, the offence of child destruction, enacted in 1929, does criminalise the ending of the life of a foetus.[31] Also still in force today, the offence was created to close a legal loophole. During the late nineteenth and early twentieth centuries, parliamentarians, legal commentators, and doctors were concerned that women who wished to kill a newborn child would wait until their labour started naturally, so they would not be committing the offence of procuring a miscarriage, and then would kill the child before it had been fully delivered, so not committing the offence of murder as the child was not a reasonable creature in *rerum natura* when killed.[32] As a consequence, the new offence criminalised any person who 'with intent to destroy the life of a child capable of being born alive, by any wilful act causes a child to die before it has an existence independent of its mother'. The offence was punishable by life imprisonment. While at the time of enactment, life imprisonment was a lesser punishment than a person would face if they were convicted of murder, the punishment for which was death, it was a punishment equivalent to the offence of infanticide, created in 1922, which is discussed below.[33] Child destruction continues to exist as a criminal offence today, and the punishment has not changed. Therefore, the offence now has the same tariff as murder – life imprisonment – although it is not a mandatory sentence.

---

26 Carla Spivack, "To Bring Down the Flowers: The Cultural Context of Abortion Law in Early Modern England," *William & Mary Journal of Women and the Law* 14, no. 1 (2007): 107–52.

27 *Offences Against the Person Act 1861*, s. 58.

28 Dickens, *Abortion and the Law*; Keown, *Abortion*.

29 Glanville Llewelyn Williams, *The Sanctity of Life and the Criminal Law* (London: Faber and Faber, 1958).

30 Milne, *Criminal Justice*; E. C. Romanis, "Artificial Womb Technology and the Choice to Gestate *Ex Utero*: Is Partial Ectogenesis the Business of the Criminal Law?" *Medical Law Review* 28, no. 2 (2020): 342–74.

31 *Infant Life (Preservation) Act 1929* (UK), s. 1.

32 Donna Cooper Graves, "'… in a Frenzy While Raving Mad': Physicians and Parliamentarians Define Infanticide in Victorian England," in *Killing Infants: Studies in the Worldwide Practice of Infanticide*, ed. Brigitte H. Bechtold and Donna Cooper Graves (Lewiston: Edwin Mellen Press, 2006), 111–36.

33 *Infanticide Act 1922* (UK), s. 1.

The offence of procuring a miscarriage, if considered in light of the intentions of Parliament when it enacted the final version of the offence, which is still in force today, does not appear to work around the born alive rule. In 1861, Parliament was mostly concerned with the unintentional killing of a woman while an abortion was being performed. Conversely, child destruction could be perceived as a workaround as it allows a woman to be convicted of an offence for which she could be imprisoned for life if she killed a child prior to them becoming a legal person. For those supporting the enactment of the two offences, the envisaged woman to be convicted of the crimes was pregnant outside of marriage, killing an illegitimate child. Thus, again we see the prioritisation of the criminalisation of 'deviant' women over the legal rule of when personhood begins. Further, contemporary applications of both the child destruction and procuring a miscarriage offences demonstrate, to a far greater extent, how they can be used as workarounds the born alive rule, as examined later in this chapter.

There is limited evidence that women in the late nineteenth and early twentieth centuries were *actually* intentionally killing children who were in the process of being born, but the panic about this loophole occurred in the context of widespread concern that unmarried women who killed newborn children were not facing justice due to growing public sympathies for the plight of the accused. As illustrated in Higginbotham's examination of cases from the Old Bailey heard between 1839 and 1906, even in cases where there was clear evidence that violence had been inflicted upon the child, juries were finding women not guilty of murder, very often stating that they were unconvinced by the evidence that the child was born alive.[34] Instead, these women were convicted of concealment or acquitted. For the small number of women who were convicted, a sentence of death would be duly handed down by the judge, with full awareness that it would be commuted by the Home Secretary. No woman was executed for murdering her infant after 1849, and the last execution of a woman for newborn child murder was in 1832.[35] The failure to convict a woman of murdering her newborn child, or the commuting of her death sentence if a conviction was obtained, was so common that the judiciary dubbed it the 'black-cap farce', as judges donned the black cap to sentence someone to death, knowing the process was a sham, or the 'solemn mockery'. Indeed, Davies argued in his 1937 review, 'Child-Killing in English Law':

> The widespread dislike of the application of the law of murder in all its severity to cases of infanticides by mothers led to such a divorce between law and public opinion that prisoners, witnesses, counsel, juries and even many of H.M.'s judges, conspired to defeat the law.[36]

The ability for the law to be defeated through a manipulation of the born alive rule was considered unacceptable by consecutive governments. Consequently, numerous attempts were made to reform the law of homicide over the late nineteenth and early twentieth centuries.[37] Yet it was not until 1922 that the offence of infanticide was created, allowing

34 Ann R, Higginbotham, "'Sin of the Age': Infanticide and Illegitimacy in Victorian London," *Victorian Studies* 3, no. 3 (1989): 319–37.

35 Martin J. Wiener, *Men of Blood: Violence, Manliness and Criminal Justice in Victorian England* (Cambridge: Cambridge University Press, 2004), 124–5.

36 D. Seaborne Davies, "Child-Killing in English Law," *Modern Law Review* 1, no. 3 (1937): 203–23.

37 For further details, see Davies, "Child-Killing in English Law" (1937); D. Seaborne. Davies, "Child-Killing in English Law," *The Modern Law Review* 1, no. 4 (1938): 269–87. Tony Ward, "The Sad Subject of Infanticide: Law, Medicine and Child Murder, 1860–1938," *Social & Legal*

for juries to convict women of a homicide offence but without the mandatory death penalty being applied.

The offence/partial defence of infanticide enacted in 1922 was only available to women who killed a newborn child if, at the time of the killing, 'the balance of her mind was disturbed by reason of her not having fully recovered from the effect of giving birth to the child'. While the legislation may read as a psychiatric offence/defence, it was widely understood that the disturbance of mind experienced by women was not a form of insanity, or any mental illness that would now be captured under the partial defence of diminished responsibility.[38] Instead, an infanticidal woman's disturbance of the balance of the mind was understood to be temporary, caused by the stress of the solo birth and the context of illegitimate pregnancy.[39] Her behaviour was understood to be more closely aligned with a temporary losing of her mind due to the specific context, rather than being caused by mental ill-health or insanity, and her act of violence was seen as more akin to provocation.[40] This understanding is significant, as the basis of the *Infanticide Act 1922* was mostly to prevent the judges facing the solemn mockery and increase the number of convictions, as Davies argues:

> If we survey the history of the reform, the appropriate title for the Act was not the 'Infanticide Act' or the 'Mentally Disturbed Mothers (Protection) Act', but the 'Judges (Protection against the Solemn Mockery) Act'. ... The main argument advanced time and again by the Judges who played so prominent a part in obtaining its enactment was that it would reduce the opportunities for the staging of the 'solemn mockery', so distasteful to the Judges themselves and so disgracefully tending to bring into disregard the most solemn and awful function which a Judge can be called upon to discharge.[41]

The outcome of the *Infanticide Act 1922* was to provide leniency for women, but, in reality, this was simply formalising the leniency already provided through case outcomes.

As a further example of the understanding of the mental state of accused women, consider the reform of the *Infanticide Act* proposed in 1936. This drew on a statute mooted by Lord Ashbourne in 1909 to provide mitigation for women 'of provocation to a mother's mental stress consequent upon "distress and despair arising from solicitude for her child or extreme poverty or other causes"'.[42] The Bill failed to progress to law due to the 'disturbance surrounding the Abdication [of Edward VIII]'.[43] Instead, the *Infanticide Act* was re-enacted in 1938 to include women who killed their infants aged up to one year. In including these cases, women who experienced 'puerperal' or 'lactation' psychosis, killing an infant that was older than a newborn, could be included in the remit of the Act. Insanity was not considered an appropriate outcome for these women, and so they lacked the protection from the gallows afforded to their sisters who killed newborn children. As Davies argued, the expansion of infanticide was again to prevent the solemn

    Studies 8, no. 2 (1999): 163–80; Karen Brennan, "Social Norms and the Law in Responding to Infanticide," *Legal Studies* 38, no. 3 (2018): 480–99.
38 *Homicide Act 1957* (UK), s. 2.
39 Ward, "Sad Subject."
40 Davies, "Child-Killing in English Law" (1938).
41 Davies, "Child-Killing in English Law" (1938), 284–85.
42 Davies, "Child-Killing in English Law" (1938), 286.
43 Davies, "Child-Killing in English Law" (1938), 286.

mockery that judges faced when sentencing a woman to death after she had killed an infant aged one month.[44] Consequently, rather than seeing the *Infanticide Act* as a law of leniency, we need to interpret it as a way of ensuring women were convicted of a homicide offence, rather than a lesser offence or no offence at all, and of relieving judges of the sham of declaring that convicted women would be executed. Consequently, the *Infanticide Act* removed a workaround for the born alive rule that had been created by judges and juries to allow them to find women not guilty of murder.

Working around the born alive rule in the twenty-first century

Much as in the long history of infant killing and the criminal law, contemporary applications of the aforementioned offences demonstrate similar conflicts between birth and death. In theory, there is a clear line that demarks birth, which thus has a substantive implication for whether a person is a victim of homicide: not born alive equals no homicide, born alive equals potential homicide. However, the 'menu' of criminal offences available for prosecutors to select from if a child is suspected to have been killed around the time of birth and the applications of these offences reveal that the demarcation of live birth, and the relevant legal consequences, is not as clear as suggested.[45] All of the offences outlined above still exist today: murder, infanticide, child destruction, procuring a miscarriage, and concealment of birth. Examination of applications of these offences in the contemporary period, especially procuring a miscarriage and concealment of birth, illustrates that the criminalisation of women continues to be a priority, and thus the born alive rule has a similar level of fluidity in criminal law today as it had in the past.

As argued above, procuring a miscarriage criminalises the ending of a pregnancy rather than the ending of the life of a foetus. And yet, in the two cases that had concluded by the time of writing this chapter, where women were suspected of ending their pregnancies by taking abortion medication they obtained outside of approved abortion providers,[46] the discussion of their culpability focused on the harm they caused to their foetuses, rather than the 'crime' of ending their pregnancies. In Hayley's[47] case, her actions were not seen as the ending of a pregnancy but as the killing of a foetus. Several times during Hayley's sentencing hearing, the judge equated her actions to homicide:

> This is not charged as murder, and I would be wrong to treat it as such, as a matter of law. Equally it is not manslaughter, nor is it akin to it, because the termination here was deliberately caused with a view to terminating the life of an unborn child. It is not akin to causing death by dangerous driving either, with its maximum sentence of 14 years, but once again I have to bear in mind the nature of the calculated intentionality here. As matters stand in English law, none of those offences could be committed in relation to an unborn child, but the seriousness of the criminality here is that, at whatever stage life can be said to begin, the child in the womb was so near to birth that in my judgment all

---

44 Davies, "Child-Killing in English Law" (1938), 286.
45 Milne, *Criminal Justice*.
46 At the time of writing (May 2023), there are several women accused of procuring a miscarriage whose cases are pending outcomes.
47 I have used pseudonyms for the women whose cases are discussed here. For a discussion of the ethics of anonymising these cases, see Milne, *Criminal Justice*, 17.

right thinking people would consider this offence more serious than that of unintentional manslaughter or any offence on the calendar other than murder.

(Judge's remarks during Hayley's sentencing)[48]

In both Hayley and Sophie's cases, the foetus was referred to as a 'child', being noted by the prosecution as having been named. Further, in Sophie's case, the prosecution argued that it was Sophie's action of taking the abortifacients that led to the death of the foetus – a point that should arguably be irrelevant when considering the behaviour the offence criminalises:

PROSECUTION: The conclusion was that it was very likely he was still born. My Lord, I won't go into the details of the post-mortem.

JUDGE: No.

PROSECUTION: Save to say that the cause of death was antenatal foetal hypoxia, and that was the consequence of the self-administration of misoprostol.

JUDGE: Yes.

PROSECUTION: There was no indication that there was any naturally occurring trigger for labour or delivery, and at that gestation a normally formed foetus, which he was otherwise, would be expected to survive with appropriate and timely medical treatment.

(Sophie, prosecution opening)[49]

While both Hayley and Sophie were convicted of an offence that criminalises the ending of a pregnancy, it is clear that the focus was on the 'killing' of a foetus.

Looking at examples of cases concerning concealment of birth, similar language about the women's culpability is evident. As I have argued elsewhere, concealment continues to be used to facilitate convictions when it is suspected women have killed their live born infants, but the decomposed state of the body means it is impossible to determine whether the child was born alive or the subsequent cause of death.[50] For example, in Lily's case, the judge summarised the suspicions during sentencing:

There has been a veiled suggestion in the case, and I put it no higher than that, that there may have been something suspicious about the birth and your subsequent behaviour. You were never charge [*sic*] of course with any homicide, but what can be said is that you were already the mother of three children and you have cared for children subsequently and cared well, and I dismiss any suggestion, veiled or otherwise, that there was something sinister about your birth of the child and procuring its birth.

(Judge's remarks during Lily's sentencing)[51]

---

48 Quotation obtained from the court transcript of Hayley's sentencing hearing. See Milne, *Criminal Justice* for full details of the research.

49 Quotation obtained from the court transcript of Sophie's sentencing hearing. See Milne, *Criminal Justice* for full details of the research.

50 Milne, "Concealment of Birth"; Milne, *Criminal Justice*.

51 Quotation obtained from the court transcript of Lily's sentencing hearing. See Milne, *Criminal Justice* for full details of the research.

But more than this, as Sally's case illustrates, concealment is also being used in cases where concern is raised about the woman's behaviour while pregnant, especially their failure to mitigate risk faced by the foetus,[52] or the actions or inactions of the pregnant woman that put the foetus at risk. The judge's remarks when sentencing Sally focused on Sally's behaviour while pregnant that had the potential to cause harm to the foetus, and provide the clearest example of such judgments:

> [W]hilst the circumstances and reasons for the stillborn births will never fully be able to be established, your chaotic lifestyle choices, including alcohol abuse and promiscuity at the time of your pregnancies was such as to put the good health of any unborn child at risk.
>
> *(Judge's remarks during Sally's sentencing)*[53]

Similar sentiments were voiced during Imogen's trial in relation to her failure to prepare for the birth of the child:

> We shall never know whether his life might have been saved had you sought proper medical attention at the time of his birth. Many would describe your conduct as wicked. You wanted to conceal your pregnancy. You wanted to conceal the birth and the death of your son. Your conduct was truly deplorable.
>
> *(Judge's remarks during Imogen's sentencing)*[54]

The suggestion, in both Sally's and Imogen's cases, is that the women, through their actions or inactions while pregnant, bore some responsibility for the death of the foe-tuses/babies. As there is neither the evidence to support this belief nor the scope within the law to capture such behaviour as criminal offences, these comments remain extra-neous to their convictions. Nevertheless, the inclusion of these comments does indicate that the women's 'failure' to ensure the survival of their foetuses and to safeguard the wellbeing of their 'children' were considered key elements of their criminal conduct, even if not specifically the behaviour they were criminalised for.

The examples of the applications of procuring a miscarriage and concealment out-lined here, and explored further elsewhere,[55] lead to the conclusion that while Eng-land and Wales does not formally have foetal protection laws and, in fact, maintains the born alive rule, in reality, women are subject to criminal sanctions if they are suspected to have harmed their foetuses and failed to act as responsible pregnant women and 'good' mothers.[56] As in the past, the born alive rule would appear to be a legal principle to be overcome or got around to arrive at the desired legal outcome: punishment of 'deviant' women. Historically, the deviance punished was becoming

---

52 Milne, *Criminal Justice*; Lealle Ruhl, "Liberal Governance and Prenatal Care: Risk and Regula-tion in Pregnancy," *Economy and Society* 28, no. 1 (1999): 95–117; Deborah Lupton, *The Social Worlds of the Unborn* (Basingstoke: Palgrave Macmillan, 2013).

53 Quotation obtained from the court transcript of Sally's sentencing hearing. See Milne, *Criminal Justice* for full details of the research.

54 Quotation obtained from the court transcript of Imogen's sentencing hearing. See Milne, *Crim-inal Justice* for full details of the research.

55 Milne, *Criminal Justice*.

56 Milne, *Criminal Justice*.

pregnant outside of marriage. Today, the deviance punished is not adhering to the ideals of motherhood.[57]

The concern these cases raise, in terms of undermining the born alive rule, is amplified when we consider the nature of the cases and the experiences of women captured by the applications of offences on the 'menu'. Women who conceal their pregnancy from the world, often also denying it to themselves, are incredibly vulnerable. They are living in abusive situations, experience poverty, and have limited social support. The pregnancy causes them a crisis, and it is a crisis that they cannot see a way out of. So, they hide the pregnancy and either take steps to end it themselves, or are surprised by the labour and delivery, which they also conceal from the world. No woman goes through this experience unless she is in crisis – a reality that the criminal justice system fails to see or consider.[58]

Conclusion: The temporality of death

Criminal law and criminal justice responses to the death of a child around the time of birth in contemporary England and Wales illustrate the significance of the interaction between the criminal law, birth, and death. The cases examined in this chapter demonstrate the temporality of death when it collides with birth. The strict principle of the born alive rule should dictate whether a legal person has been killed or if the 'victim' is instead a non-legal subject and, thus, no homicide has transpired. In the strictest sense of the law, none of the women whose cases have been examined in this chapter were convicted of homicide offences. And yet the language utilised during their sentencing hearings and the culpability that is described point to a different reality and understanding of their conduct. Consequently, these cases indicate that when birth and death come together, and when the suspect is a 'deviant' woman (historically she is unmarried and today she is a 'bad' mother), then the existence of the distinguishing line drawn between live birth and the period prior to birth seems to vanish in favour of holding the woman responsible for the death. Further, in these cases, both death and birth are created or constructed in a way that allows for the outcome of punishment. The malleability of birth and death in this way reveals that while being born and dying might be considered fixed phenomena, in the context of the criminal law they are far more fluid concepts.

The nature of cases of suspected foetal/infant killing means it is almost certainly a woman who will be implicated in the death of a child around the time of birth. She may have 'assistance' from someone else, so a man might be involved, but this is rare due to the contexts that lead women to the scenario of a crisis pregnancy and subsequent death of a child. Consequently, the interaction between birth and death in the context of the law highlights yet another example of the sexism embedded within the structures of the criminal law.[59] The harms experienced by women, which directly impact on their conduct while pregnant – male abuse that is not effectively sanctioned by the state, and poverty and lack of social support that are not relieved by the state – are never

57 Emma Milne, "Putting the Fetus First – Legal Regulation, Motherhood, and Pregnancy," *Michigan Journal of Gender & Law* 27, no. 1 (2020): 149–211; Milne, *Criminal Justice*.
58 Milne, *Criminal Justice*.
59 Robin West, "Jurisprudence and Gender," *University of Chicago Law* Review 55, no. 1 (1988): 1–72; Ngaire Naffine, *Law and the Sexes: Explorations in Feminist Jurisprudence* (Sydney: Allen & Unwin, 1990).

considered the basis of their 'offending'. Instead, it is her, and her failing as a 'mother', and her 'deviance' as a woman that are to blame, and thus need to be punished under the criminal law.[60]

Bibliography

Amnesty International. "Poland: Regression on Abortion Access Harms Women," 26 January 2022. www.amnesty.org/en/latest/news/2022/01/poland-regression-on-abortion-access-harms-women.

Abortion Support Network. "Get Help – I'm in Northern Ireland." Accessed 25 May 2023. www.asn.org.uk/get-help-ni.

Brennan, Karen. "Social Norms and the Law in Responding to Infanticide." *Legal Studies* 38, no. 3 (2018): 480–499. https://doi.org/10.1017/lst.2017.20.

Coke, Edward. *The Fourth Part of the Institutes of the Laws of England: Concerning the Jurisdiction of Courts*. 6th ed. London: Printed by W. Rawlins, for Thomas Basset at the George near St. Dunstans Church in Fleet-street, 1644 [1681].

Davies, D. Seaborne. "Child-Killing in English Law." *The Modern Law Review* 1, no. 4 (1938): 269–287. https://doi.org/10.1111/j.1468-2230.1937.tb00025.x.

Davies, D. Seaborne. "Child-Killing in English Law." *Modern Law Review* 1, no. 3 (1937): 203–223. https://doi.org/10.1111/j.1468-2230.1937.tb00018.x.

Dickens, Bernard M. *Abortion and the Law*. London: Macgibbon & Kee, 1966.

Flavin, Jeanne. *Our Bodies, Our Crimes: The Policing of Women's Reproduction in America*. New York: New York University Press, 2009.

Francome, Colin. *Abortion Practice in Britain and the United States*. London: Allen & Unwin, 1986.

Gowing, Laura. "Secret Births and Infanticide in Seventeenth-Century England." *Past & Present* 156, no. 1 (1997): 87–115. https://doi.org/10.1093/past/156.1.87.

Graves, Donna Cooper. "'… in a Frenzy While Raving Mad': Physicians and Parliamentarians Define Infanticide in Victorian England." In *Killing Infants: Studies in the Worldwide Practice of Infanticide*, edited by Brigitte H. Bechtold and Donna Cooper Graves, 111–136. Lewiston: Edwin Mellen Press, 2006.

Guttmacher Institute. "Roe v. Wade Overturned: Our Latest Resources." Accessed 25 May 2023. www.guttmacher.org/abortion-rights-supreme-court.

Higginbotham, Ann R. "'Sin of the Age': Infanticide and Illegitimacy in Victorian London." *Victorian Studies* 3, no. 3 (1989): 319–337.

Hoffer, Peter Charles, and N. E. H. Hull. *Murdering Mothers: Infanticide in England and New England, 1558–1803*. New York: New York University Press, 1981.

Jackson, Mark. *New-Born Child Murder: Women, Illegitimacy and the Courts in Eighteenth-Century England*. Manchester: Manchester University Press, 1996.

Keown, John. *Abortion, Doctors and the Law: Some Aspects of the Legal Regulation of Abortion in England from 1803 to 1982*. Cambridge: Cambridge University Press, 1988.

Kilday, Anne-Marie. *A History of Infanticide in Britain, C.1600 to the Present*. Basingstoke: Palgrave Macmillan, 2013.

Lupton, Deborah. *The Social Worlds of the Unborn*. Basingstoke: Palgrave Macmillan, 2013.

McLaren, Angus. *Reproductive Rituals: The Perception of Fertility in England from the Sixteenth Century to the Nineteenth Century*. London: Methuen, 1984.

Milne, Emma. "Concealment of Birth: Time to Repeal a 200-Year-Old 'Convenient Stop-Gap'?" *Feminist Legal Studies* 27, no. 2 (2019): 139–162. https://doi.org/10.1007/s10691-019-09401-6.

Milne, Emma. *Criminal Justice Responses to Maternal Filicide: Judging the Failed Mother*. Bingley: Emerald Publishing, 2021. doi:doi:10.1108/978-1-83909-620-420211009.

Milne, Emma. "Putting the Fetus First – Legal Regulation, Motherhood, and Pregnancy." *Michigan Journal of Gender & Law* 27, no. 1 (2020): 149–211. https://doi.org/10.36641/mjgl.27.1.putting.

Naffine, Ngaire. *Law and the Sexes: Explorations in Feminist Jurisprudence*. Sydney: Allen & Unwin, 1990.

Old Bailey Online. "Trial of Woman (T16750414-3)," 1675. Accessed 5 September 2020. www.oldbaileyonline.org/browse.jsp?id=t16750414-3-off10&div=t16750414-3#highlight.

60 Milne, *Criminal Justice*.

Pickles, Camilla, and Jonathan Herring, eds. *Childbirth, Vulnerability and Law: Exploring Issues of Violence and Control*. Abingdon: Routledge, 2020.

Rapaport, Elizabeth. "Mad Women and Desperate Girls: Infanticide and Child Murder in Law and Myth." *Fordham Urban Law Journal* 33, no. 2 (2006): 527–571.

Rivers-Moore, Megan. "In Latin America, not only abortions but miscarriages can lead to jail time". *The Conversation*, 4 January 2022. https://theconversation.com/in-latin-america-not-only-abortions-but-miscarriages-can-lead-to-jail-time-173719.

Romanis, E. C. "Artificial Womb Technology and the Choice to Gestate *Ex Utero*: Is Partial Ectogenesis the Business of the Criminal Law?" *Medical Law Review* 28, no. 2 (2020): 342–374. https://doi.org/10.1093/medlaw/fwz037.

Ruhl, Lealle. "Liberal Governance and Prenatal Care: Risk and Regulation in Pregnancy." *Economy and Society* 28, no. 1 (1999): 95–117. https://doi.org/10.1080/03085149900000026.

Spivack, Carla. "To Bring Down the Flowers: The Cultural Context of Abortion Law in Early Modern England." *William & Mary Journal of Women and the Law* 14, no. 1 (2007): 107–152.

Ward, Tony. "The Sad Subject of Infanticide: Law, Medicine and Child Murder, 1860–1938." *Social & Legal Studies* 8, no. 2 (1999): 163–180. https://doi.org/10.1177/096466399900800201.

West, Robin. "Jurisprudence and Gender." *University of Chicago Law Review* 55, no. 1 (1988): 1–72. https://doi.org/10.2307/1599769.

Wiener, Martin J. *Men of Blood: Violence, Manliness and Criminal Justice in Victorian England* Cambridge: Cambridge University Press, 2004.

Williams, Glanville Llewelyn. *The Sanctity of Life and the Criminal Law*. London: Faber and Faber, 1958.

22

CORPORATE HOMICIDE

Penny Crofts[1] and Honni van Rijswijk

Introduction

People can be killed by corporations as employees, consumers, and/or as part of the general public. Many such deaths are preventable and unnecessary, frequently arising due to the pursuit of profit above all else. Although fatalities due to corporate conduct vastly exceed homicides committed by individuals, deaths caused by corporations tend not to be regarded as unlawful homicides or crimes of violence.[2] A central theme of this chapter is that criminal law reflects and reinforces biases that prevent the law from even conceiving of corporations as responsible subjects, let alone attributing culpability for homicide.[3] Law not only fails to prosecute but enables and systematises death caused by corporations as an acceptable or allowable cost of doing business.[4] Law continues to justify the assumption that high levels of risk are a necessary part of capitalist endeavours. Rather than aiming to secure the protection of workers and members of the public, law effectively protects corporations from the consequences of their violence.[5] Consequently, we need to acknowledge the routine horror of corporate homicide – that is, the legal and social acceptance of a proliferation of ongoing, massive harms as banal and everyday.[6]

1 Penny's research for this chapter is funded by an Australian Research Council Grant entitled 'Rethinking organisational culpability: Criminal Law, Horror and Philosophy' (DE180100577).

2 Steve Tombs, "Violence, Safety Crimes and Criminology," *British Journal of Criminology* 47, no. 4 (2007): 531; Steve Tombs and David Whyte, *The Corporate Criminal: Why Corporations Must Be Abolished* (London: Taylor & Francis, 2015); Rory O'Neill, Simon Pickvance, and Andrew Watterson, "Burying the Evidence: How Great Britain is Prolonging the Occupational Cancer Epidemic," *International Journal of Occupational and Environmental Health* 13, no. 4 (2007), https://doi.org/10.1179/oeh.2007.13.4.428.
3 Celia Wells, *Corporations and Criminal Responsibility*, 2nd ed. (Oxford: Oxford University Press, 2001), 1.
4 Marc Trabsky and Jacinthe Flore, "Prescription Medicines and Economies of Death," in *Evil Corporations: Law, Culpability and Regulation*, ed. Penny Crofts (London: Routledge, 2024).
5 Harry J. Glasbeek, "The Corporation as a Legally Created Site of Irresponsibility," in *International Handbook of White-Collar and Corporate Crime*, ed. Henry Pontell and Gilbert Geis (New York: Springer, 2007).
6 Penny Crofts and Honni van Rijswijk, "The Nightmare on Elm Street: The Failure and Responsibility of Those in Authority," in *ReFocus: The Films of Wes Craven*, ed. Calum Waddell (Edinburgh: Edinburgh University Press, 2023).

Instead of using criminal frameworks, most jurisdictions have conceptualised corporate violence as health and safety offences, with some jurisdictions introducing corporate or industrial manslaughter offences. Even the latter regimes vastly underestimate the number of people killed by corporations.

Critical criminologist David Whyte asserts:

> After taking into account studies from across disciplines and after treating official data with the necessary analytical revision, at least 50,000 people die every year as a result of working in the United Kingdom alone. That's more than 1,000 a week. And, according to established research by the restrained UK safety watchdog, the Health and Safety Executive (HSE), as many as three-quarters of those workers are killed because of criminal breaches of the law. Put differently, the number of people criminally killed by their employer *every week* in the United Kingdom is roughly comparable to the number killed by interpersonal murder *every year*. Globally, there are many times more people killed by illness and injury at work and by the toxic environmental consequences of profit-making every year than are killed in wars and conflicts. And yet, studies of safety crimes are few and far between, and are dwarfed by the burgeoning literature in terrorism and political violence studies, or indeed the literature on war crimes.[7]

The scale of routine killing by corporations is incalculable and incomprehensible. For example, approximately 90,000 people globally die from asbestos-related diseases each year. As of 16 June 2023, the Mesothelioma Center's homepage listed that an estimated 125 million people worldwide remain at risk of occupational exposure to asbestos.[8] Likewise, the opioid epidemic was caused by corporations through deceptive conduct:

> Since the late 1990s, pharmaceutical companies have continuously downplayed the addictive nature of opioids. Out of 700,000 overdose deaths, roughly 68% are due to overdoses involving opioids. Approximately 130 individuals die each day from opioids.[9]

This excess of corporate slayings has not led to charges of homicides for the corporations that produced these dangerous products.

The next section articulates some of the ways in which law's individualistic bias manifests in a failure to regard corporations as responsible for homicides. The second section ('Not a criminal legal subject') highlights the historical obstacles to applying existing homicide offences to corporations. The third section ('The symbolic recognition of killer corporations') then considers the symbolic recognition of corporations as killers in industrial manslaughter offences, and the chapter concludes by considering the limits

---

7 David Whyte, "Still Dying for a Living," *The British Journal of Criminology* 53, no. 6 (2013): 1206–7, https://doi.org/10.1093/bjc/azt058.
8 Michelle Whitmer, "Asbestos Facts and Statistics," The Mesothelioma Center. Last modified 16 June 2023, www.asbestos.com/asbestos/statistics-facts.
9 Kristen S. Jones, "The Opioid Epidemic: Product Liability or One Hell of a Nuisance? Symposium: The Opioid Crisis: An Epidemic Explained," *Mississippi College Law Review* 39, no. 1 (2021): 33.

of occupational health and safety regulations, where the official records of corporate homicides are most likely to be relegated.

Individualistic bias

Crime is a construct, with no ontological reality. Criminal legal doctrine was historically constructed around the archetypal legal subject – the responsible human being.[10] This has resulted in an 'individualistic bias'[11] that manifests in a myriad of ways to ensure that corporations are extremely unlikely to be criminally prosecuted for existing homicide offences. This individualistic bias is revealed in the ways the criminal law fails to properly view the corporation as a criminal legal subject – as seen in the way law deals with industrial manslaughter and in regulatory regimes that fail to protect people from corporate harm.

Individualistic bias is epitomised in many legal definitions of homicide as 'the killing of one person by another'. This definition reflects and reinforces the assumptions (and preferences) of the criminal law for singularity – of one person killing one victim. There are, of course, cases of multiple victims (e.g., mass murder) and examples of multiple perpetrators (dealt with under the complex legal doctrine of group agency such as complicity and accessorial liability). However, on a purely pragmatic level, corporations are capable of causing harm on an 'industrial scale'[12] that greatly exceeds the capacity of individual perpetrators. This excessive capacity of corporations to cause harm results in difficulties in even accounting for and recording the resulting fatalities. A common response to corporate harms – including homicides – is a 'language of estimation and approximation'.[13] Crofts has argued this is because there are 'too many harmed, too many losses to calculate accurately' and difficulties 'in terms of which harms are counted, or when to stop counting'.[14] These difficulties of calculation are exacerbated by the capacity of corporate fatalities to transcend state borders, with different methodologies and choices made in different jurisdictions. Accordingly, there is even contestation in the foundational statistics as to what counts and does not count as a corporate homicide.

Law's ethos of individualism means that despite the vast harms caused by corporations, the law's focus is on interpersonal violence. We have simplistic understandings of action and intention, which means we assume that corporations are not criminal and/or violent.[15] When corporations kill, there is a perceived lack of agency and, consequently, of legal prosecution, with media and inquiries preferring to use the lexicon of accident, tragedy, disaster, or event, rather than the language of crime. Such language reinforces and reflects the idea that corporations are not responsible moral or legal agents and that they lack the intention to kill. Deaths are expressed in the passive voice, as a 'shortening'

---

10 Ngaire Naffine, "Our Legal Lives as Men, Women and Persons," *Legal Studies* 11, no.4 (2016).

11 Wells, *Corporations and Criminal Responsibility*, 1.

12 Garry Slapper,. "Corporate Homicide, Corporate Social Responsibility, and Human Rights," in *The Handbook of Homicide*, ed. Fiona Brookman, Edward R. Maguire, and Mike Maguire, 213 (Wiley and Sons, 2017).

13 Penny Crofts, "The Horror of Corporate Harms," *Australian Journal of Corporate Law* 38, no. 1 (2022): 25

14 Crofts, "The Horror," 30.

15 Steve Tombs and David Whyte, "A Deadly Consensus: Worker Safety and Regulatory Degradation Under New Labour," *The British Journal of Criminology* 50, no. 1 (2010): 542, https://doi.org/10.1093/BJC%2FAZP063.

of life,[16] as though there is no responsible agent that has exercised choices across time that led to those deaths.[17] This reflects and produces a 'charade of non-violence',[18] rendering victims of corporate violence as invisible. However, the bulk of industrial deaths are eminently preventable and unnecessary, often resulting from long-term choices by corporations to run risks, avoid compliance, and prioritise profit.[19] In many cases, inquiries have demonstrated that corporations had knowledge of these risks many years prior to the general public and governments.

Law's ethos of individualism leads to a failure to criminalise corporate homicides and reinforces the idea that deaths are an unfortunate cost of doing business. Corporations are legally constructed as occupying a very privileged position – they are able to cause mass deaths through deliberate or negligent decision making while also having such consequences explained away as unforeseen mishaps.[20] This externalising of harms is inscribed in the principle of limited liability, whereby investors are only liable for what they have invested, rather than for the harms or losses that they have actually caused.[21] Corporate personhood, limited liability and the corporate veil are key legal privileges granted to corporations under capitalist law.[22] Corporate personhood established the corporation as an autonomous legal entity, independent of those who own and control it; limited liability limits the legal jeopardy for the actual owners and controllers of a corporate entity; and the corporate veil represents the barrier so constructed through these double artifices. The corporate veil is thus the basis for the corporation as a structure of violent irresponsibility.[23]

While corporations are on notice for foreseeable risks in the area(s) in which they have chosen to operate, they are not held accountable for failure to prevent those risks. This lack of agency goes hand in hand with the responsibilisation of individuals (whether as workers or consumers) for the risks run, caused and realised by corporations. Deaths at work are frequently blamed on inexperienced, unskilled workers.[24] There is a long history of blaming individuals, particularly workers, for injuries and fatalities at work – assuming that such incidents are accidents, a regrettable but unavoidable part of the routine cost of capitalist production.[25] The agency and blameworthiness of corporations for workplace deaths is thus reframed, denying or obscuring corporate violence.[26] Quinlan studied the mining industry in five countries over 25 years and considered worker behaviour in the context of financial and other pressures. He argued that the

---

16 Gosport Independent Panel, *Gosport War Memorial Hospital* (2018). The Report uses the term 'shortening of life' throughout, e.g., vii, viii, 11, 77.

17 Jasmine Hebert, Steven Bittle, and Steve Tombs, "Obscuring Corporate Violence: Corporate Manslaughter in Action," *The Howard Journal of Crime and Justice* 58, no. 4 (2019): 559, https://doi.org/10.1111/hojo.12345.

18 Rene Girard, *Sacrifice* (East Lansing, MI: Michigan State University Press, 2011), 5.

19 Slapper, "Corporate Homicide," 215; Penny Crofts, "Aliens: Legal Conceptions of the Corporate Invasion," *Law and Literature* 34, no. 3 (2021), https://doi.org/10.1080/1535685X.2020.1862521.

20 Hebert, Bittle, and Tombs, "Obscuring Corporate Violence," 559.

21 Gregg Barak, *Unchecked Corporate Power: Why the Crimes of Multinational Corporations Are Routinized Away and What We Can Do about It* (London: Routledge, 2017).

22 Tombs and Whyte, *The Corporate Criminal*.

23 Hebert, Bittle, and Tombs, "Obscuring Corporate Violence," 566.

24 Bobbie Oliver, ""No Place for Tourists": Deaths on Western Australian Construction Sites," *Labour History* 119, no. 1 (2020): 115–42, https://doi.org/10.3828/jlh.2020.21.

25 Slapper, "Corporate Homicide"; Glasbeek, "The Corporation."

26 Hebert, Bittle, and Tombs, "Obscuring Corporate Violence," 559.

responsibilisation of workers is compounded by the broader shift to the use of precarious workers who fear job loss, are afraid to raise safety as an issue, and are inadequately trained.[27] To redress this problem, Oliver argued that the emphasis should be on safe places, not safe individuals.[28]

The model of criminal culpability has as its pinnacle the concept of intentional wrongdoing. As Reiman has effectively illustrated, intentionality tends to assume an individual sentience. So what of a corporate employer that does not positively intend harm but rather fails to maintain and invest in safety? Take the mining executive who:

> wanted to harm to no-one in particular, but he knew his acts were likely to harm someone – and *once someone is harmed, the victim is someone in particular*. There is no moral basis for treating one-on-one harm as criminal and indirect harm as merely regulatory. [Emphasis original][29]

This kind of brutal indifference is at least as culpable as intention, and ought to be treated as such by the criminal justice system. There is another way in which intentionality is complicated when it comes to corporate violence: such violence is generally unintended, except in the sense that in the intended pursuit of maximising profits above all else, people die because proper responsibility has not been taken. Reiman argued that corporations and their employees are just as responsible as the street criminals who are targeted by criminal law because the injuries and deaths are caused purposely, knowingly, recklessly, and/or negligently, and our laws allow for persons to be held culpable in these instances. In fact, corporate actors are potentially more culpable because, as Reiman concludes, perpetrators of intentional, one-on-one harm are less likely to represent some generalised threat to others, in contrast to the aforementioned mining executive.[30]

We can adopt different approaches to conceptualising mens rea in organisations. We can, of course, attribute culpability to individuals – those who knowingly and intentionally choose to do wrong by using the rational choice model of organisational action, which views organisational outcomes as the result of strategic decisions.[31] For example, in the infamous case of the Ford Pinto car, top Ford executives chose to keep the Pinto on the market despite knowing it was a fire trap and would catch fire if someone crashed into the rear of the vehicle on the basis of an amoral cost–benefit analysis: the cost of the required redesign was less than the quantified cost of human life in damages for accidents if the redesign was not done – an act that has been characterised as 'sensible bloodshed'.[32] Alternatively, this conduct can be reframed as not due to specific calculations but a consequence of institutionally embedded cultures of unreflective action (e.g., institutional rewards for not knowing, the use of plausible deniability, and the diffusion of

---

27 Michael Quinlan, *Ten Pathways to Death and Disaster: Learning from Fatal Incidents in Mines and Other High Hazard Workplaces* (Annandale: Federation Press, 2014).

28 Oliver, "No Place for Tourists."

29 Jeffrey Reiman, *The Rich Get Richer and the Poor Get Prison: Ideology, Class and Criminal Justice*, 7th ed. (Boston, MA: Allyn and Bacon, 2003), 67–70.

30 Reiman, *The Rich Get Richer*.

31 Matthew Lee and Jeannine Gailey, "Attributing Responsibility for Organizational Wrongdoing," in *International Handbook of White-Collar and Corporate Crime*, ed. Henry Pontell and Gilbert Geis (New York: Springer, 2007).

32 Matthew Lee and David Ermann, "Pinto 'Madness' as a Flawed Landmark Narrative: An Organization and Network Analysis," *Social Problems* 46, no.1 (1999): 42.

responsibility). Corporations may prioritise maintaining the company over the need to secure the health and wellbeing of workers who are otherwise sacrificed.[33] This naturalises corporate deaths, which are thus not only 'accidents waiting to happen' but killings waiting to happen.[34] These deaths are a product of a system that falls short of legal requirements to ensure workers' safety.[35]

This violence is compounded by the symbiotic partnership of corporations and the state. For example, Ken and Leon analysed pork meatpacking corporations during the COVID-19 pandemic, finding that 318 meatpacking and processing workers in the United States died due to COVID-19 in 2020.[36] They argued that the corporate–state nexus

> places workers' illnesses and deaths in a necropolitical framework that demands attention to the state's tacit approval of inhumane working conditions, use of law to keep packing plants open, and attempts to limit the liability of corporations for any deaths or illnesses they have caused.[37]

Not a criminal legal subject

Corporations have long been regarded as legal persons,[38] but what this means in different legal contexts remains a matter of debate.[39] Historically, courts and treatise writers pointed to procedural obstacles to justify early opposition to applying criminal law to corporations, such as the requirement that an accused be present in court or that serious felonies such as murder required imprisonment.[40] However, even when these procedural impediments were removed, courts cited earlier precedent disavowing corporate criminal liability. This was demonstrated in the first attempted prosecution of a company for manslaughter in the United Kingdom (UK) in the 1920s. During a miners' strike, an unemployed miner was electrocuted by a fence put up to protect the mining company's property. The Miners' Federation supported a private prosecution brought by the deceased's brother, and the company employed the best lawyers of the day to challenge the indictment. At a court of assize, Justice Finlay held that it was not possible to prosecute a company for a serious offence such as manslaughter, partly on the grounds that a corporation could not be imprisoned.[41] This explanation was a colloquial furphy because the offence of manslaughter was punishable with a fine.

But even after the legislature and courts had (reluctantly) recognised corporations as criminal legal subjects, difficulties arose in applying criminal legal doctrine primarily constructed around the archetypal legal subject – that is, the responsible human being – to corporations.[42] Criminal legal doctrine requires that an accused's

33 Hebert, Bittle, and Tombs, "Obscuring Corporate Violence," 569.
34 Hebert, Bittle, and Tombs, "Obscuring Corporate Violence," 563.
35 Tombs and Whyte, "Deadly Consensus."
36 Ivy Ken and Kenneth Sebastian Leon, "Necropolitical Governance and State-Corporate Harms: COVID-19 and the US Pork Packing Industry," *Journal of White Collar and Corporate Crime* 3, no. 2 (2022): 76.
37 Ken and Leon, "Necropolitical Governance," 76.
38 Eric W. Orts, *Business Persons: A Legal Theory of the Firm* (Oxford: Oxford University Press, 2013).
39 See, e.g., debates about whether corporations are entitled to human rights: Elizabeth Pollman, "Corporate Law and Theory in Hobby Lobby," in *The Rise of Corporate Religious Liberty*, ed. Micah Schmartzman, Chad Flanders, and Zoe Robinson (Oxford: Oxford University Press, 2016).
40 Wells, *Corporations and Criminal Responsibility*, 93.
41 *R v Cory Bros Ltd* [1927] 1 KB 810.
42 Naffine, "Our Legal Lives."

acts or omissions are simultaneously accompanied by fault – an almost impossible requirement vis-à-vis large corporations due to the diffusion of responsibility.[43] This has been exacerbated by a refusal by many to conceptualise the corporation over and above its individual members. A particular obstacle to criminal liability was the assertion that corporations could not commit offences that required mens rea because it was assumed they were not moral beings. This was famously expressed by Edward Thurlow, 1st Baron Thurlow: 'Did you ever expect a corporation to have a conscience, when it has no soul to be damned, and no body to be kicked?'[44]

This construction of corporations as lacking the capacity for mens rea is problematic for criminal law because it is a system of blaming – and our current system of blaming (which is necessarily contingent) claims to focus on whether or not an accused was subjectively culpable – that is, had the intention or knowledge to commit the offence.[45] An ongoing question is whether and how a corporation can be said to have intention or knowledge. How can a corporation be blameworthy in the absence of, or in addition to, individuals being at fault? Legal approaches to corporate intention can be split into nominalist and realist camps. Nominalists believe that corporations can only act and think through the individuals that make up the corporation. On this basis, the mens rea of a corporation can only be established by ascertaining whether a (specific) member of the corporation had mens rea. In contrast, realists assert that a corporation is more than the sum of its parts, and it is possible to ascertain a corporation's intention and knowledge through its practices and procedures.[46]

Currently, the dominant approaches in the UK, the United States, and Australia are nominalist. The United States has developed principles of vicarious liability, whereby a corporation is liable for the actions and intentions of its members. This approach is simultaneously too broad and too narrow – inculpating corporations for the actions and intentions of rogue employees and exculpating corporations for systemic failures.[47] Starting with *Tesco*,[48] the UK and Australia have developed the identification doctrine, requiring that:

> The person who acts is not speaking or acting for the company. He is acting as the company and his mind which directs his acts is the mind of the company. If it is a guilty mind then that guilt is the guilt of the company.[49]

43 Ernest Lim, "A Critique of Corporate Attribution: 'Directing Mind and Will' and Corporate Objectives," *Journal of Business Law* 3, no. 3 (2013).

44 Quoted in John Coffee Jr., "No Soul to Damn: No Body to Kick: An Unscandalised Inquiry into the Problem of Corporate Punishment," *Michigan Law Review* 79 (1981): 386.

45 George Fletcher, *Rethinking Criminal Law* (Boston, MA: Little Brown, 1978); Penny Crofts, *Wickedness and Crime: Laws of Homicide and Malice* (London and New York: Routledge, 2013).

46 Vicky Comino, "'Culture' is Key – An Analysis of Culture-Focused Techniques and Tools in the Regulation of Corporations and Financial Institutions," *Australian Business Law Review* 49, no. 1 (2021); Elise Bant, "The Culpable Corporate Mind: Taxonomy and Synthesis," in *The Culpable Corporate Mind*, ed. Elise Bant (Oxford: Hart, 2023); Peter A. French, *Collective and Corporate Responsibility* (New York: Columbia University Press, 1984); Mihailis E. Diamantis, "Corporate Criminal Minds," *Notre Dame Law Review* 91, no. 5 (2016): 2049–90; Crofts, "Aliens."

47 Joshua D. Greenberg and Ellen C. Brotman. "Strict Vicarious Criminal Liability for Corporations and Corporate Executives: Stretching the Boundaries of Criminalization," *American Criminal Law Review* 51, no. 1 (2014).

48 *Tesco Supermarkets Ltd v Nattrass* [1972] AC 153.

49 *Tesco Supermarkets Ltd v Nattrass* [1972] AC 153, [1971] UKHL 1, 3 (Lord Reid).

Under this doctrine, criminal liability can exist solely where a person in the organisation who was sufficiently senior to represent the 'directing mind' of the company is proved to have the requisite knowledge and fault required for the offence.[50] Identification doctrine has created its own set of difficulties, including identifying the directing mind and then working out what it knew and when.[51]

These difficulties are apparent in the lack of prosecution of corporations for homicides and the lack of success of those rare prosecutions that do go ahead, which, in turn, further discourages prosecution. Corporations could (and should) be prosecuted for common law involuntary manslaughter offences – whether manslaughter by criminal negligence or manslaughter by unlawful and dangerous act. But the individualistic bias operates here too.

Two rare prosecutions in the 1990s demonstrate (manufactured) problems in applying existing manslaughter offences to large corporations. The first is *R v P&O European Ferries (Dover) Ltd* (1991),[52] in which P&O was charged with manslaughter after 192 passengers and crew drowned. The roll-on/roll-off ferry *Herald of Free Enterprise* capsized in March 1987 after it left Zeebrugge harbour with its bow doors open. The assistant bosun responsible for shutting the doors had fallen asleep, and the chief officer responsible for ensuring the doors were shut did not do so. The subsequent government report was critical of the ship's crew for failing to ensure the doors were shut and extended this criticism to the company:

> [A] full investigation into the circumstances of the disaster leads inexorably to the conclusion that the underlying or cardinal faults lay higher up in the company. All concerned in management, from the members of the Board of Directors down to the junior superintendents, were guilty of fault in that all must be regarded as sharing responsibility for the failure of management.[53]

The company's safety policy was very poor – crew worked long shifts, there were no door indicator lights on the bridge, and there had been previous incidents of the company's ships going to sea with doors open.[54] Despite this, Justice Turner directed acquittals before the prosecution could finish presenting its case, on the basis that no one person in senior management was individually criminally culpable. This was an application of identification doctrine, whereby a corporation can be liable for criminal offences with a fault component only if a senior manager of the company was individually criminally culpable.[55] Justice Turner refused to conceptualise collective responsibility, for example, by aggregating (or combining) evidence from the number of incidents of recklessness, neglect, or negligence caused by various individuals.[56] This meant the

---

50 *R v HM Coroner for East Kent; Ex parte Spooner (Herald of Free Enterprise/Zeebrugge Ferry Disaster)* (1987) 88 Cr App Rep 10 (DC), 16.
51 Lim, "A Critique of Corporate Attribution."
52 *R v P & O European Ferries (Dover) Ltd* (1991) 93 Cr App Rep 72.
53 Justice Sheen, *The Merchant Shipping Act of 1894: MV Herald of Free Enterprise – Report of the Court No. 8-74* (London: Department of Transport, 1987), para. 14.1.
54 Sheen, *The Merchant Shipping Act of 1894.*
55 *Tesco Supermarkets Ltd v Nattrass* [1972] AC 153.
56 At the time of the charges, negligent manslaughter required recklessness – which could either involve a recognition of a risk or a failure to give any thought to the possibility of there being any such risk: *R v Seymour* (1983) 2 AC 493.

prosecution had to prove that a P&O company director either knew about or ignored an obvious and serious risk that the vessel would sail with her bow doors open. Despite the Sheen Inquiry finding that 'from top to bottom the body corporate was infected with the disease of sloppiness',[57] P&O was acquitted of manslaughter.

The second case was in 1999, in which Great Western Trains (GWT) was prosecuted for the manslaughter of seven passengers in the Southall rail crash of 1997. In that case, a GWT train ran through red lights and crashed into a goods unit while the driver was allegedly packing his bag ready for the train's arrival in Paddington. Here, too, the judge directed acquittals. But unlike in the P&O case, the Attorney General referred the legal issues to the Court of Appeal,[58] on the basis that GWT's procedures permitted a high-speed train with a malfunctioning automatic warning system (AWS) to be driven by one person. Although an effective AWS had been promised after previous crashes, there was no AWS used in the train in question because the driver had not been trained to operate such a system. The company pleaded guilty to a breach of the *Health and Safety Work Act 1974* (UK), for encouraging drivers to depart on time even if safety devices were not working. However, it was more difficult to establish guilt for manslaughter. The prosecution sought to argue that there was no need to prove an individual director's negligence; rather, it should be sufficient to prove that the company's management policies had resulted in the failure to have a proper warning system, which led to the crash. The trial judge ruled that a corporation can only be convicted via the guilt of a human being with which it could be identified, and the case collapsed. The Attorney General referred the question to the Court of Appeal to determine if this finding was correct. The Court of Appeal held that the narrow identification doctrine from *Tesco* still applied, stating that 'unless an identified individual's conduct, characterisable as gross negligence, can be attributed to the company the company is not, in the present state of the common law, liable for manslaughter'.[59]

Both the P&O and GWT cases highlight the impact of the individualistic bias expressed in identification doctrine, whereby a corporation can only be at fault through its senior members. As Wells argued, *Tesco* 'relies on an outdated and shallow theory of organizational behaviour in assuming that only directors make decisions'[60] and fails to capture the 'corporateness of their conduct'.[61] This belies the diffusion of responsibility in large corporations and the extent to which this common law focus may encourage senior management to ensure plausible deniability. The only corporations successfully prosecuted for common law manslaughter offences have been small companies – where it is easy to identify the directing mind and what it knew.[62] For example, in *R v Kite* [1996] 2 Cr App R (S) 295, two instructors took eight children and two teachers canoeing. The canoe capsized and four children died. The instructors were reported to be 'totally incompetent'. The managing director and the company (OLL Ltd) were charged with four counts of manslaughter. It was a small company, and it was clear that Peter Kite, the company director, was the directing mind *and* was aware of the serious and obvious risk. OLL Ltd was fined £60,000 and Peter Kite was sentenced to three years'

---

57 Sheen, *The Merchant Shipping Act of 1894*, para. 14.1.
58 *Attorney General's Reference (No. 2 of 1999)* [2000] EWCA Crim 91.
59 *Attorney General's Reference (No. 2 of 1999)* [2000] EWCA Crim 91, 191 (Lady Justice of Appeal Rose).
60 Wells, *Corporations and Criminal Responsibility*, 114.
61 Wells, *Corporations and Criminal Responsibility*, 114.
62 *R v Kite and others* (1994); *R v Jackson Transport (Ossett) Ltd* (1996).

imprisonment. In contrast, the larger a corporation, the more complex its organisational and decision-making structures, the more capable it is of causing systemic harms, and the less likely it is for the prosecution to identify the 'directing mind' and then prove that it had the necessary mens rea.

The individualistic bias is also expressed in the failure to prosecute corporations for unlawful and dangerous act manslaughter. As the name of this offence specifies, it requires an unlawful act that is objectively dangerous and caused death(s).[63] In an early case, Justice Field confined the 'unlawful act' to those acts that are subject to criminal punishment and not simply to civil liability.[64] On that basis, regulatory offences that cause death cannot form the foundational offence for unlawful and dangerous act manslaughter.[65] The archetypal offence here is interpersonal – specifically, an assault in a barroom brawl where an accused inadvertently kills someone.[66] But this reflects the tendency to minimise the harms and violence of corporations. Breaches of health and safety are far more likely to be 'dangerous' in the sense of 'likely to injure another person'.[67] As Justice Simpson stated in a case where an accused illegally engaged in street racing that killed two victims, what should matter is whether the act was (a) a breach of laws (including so-called regulatory laws such as traffic laws) and (b) 'dangerous, and sufficiently dangerous to justify the application of the criminal law'.[68] Most corporations kill by breaching statutory duties such as occupational health and safety or environmental laws.[69] But the idea of using breaches of these laws as the basis for unlawful and dangerous act manslaughter is not even raised, despite these breaches having a greater capacity for causing greater harms to a greater number of people. For example, in both the abovementioned P&O and GWT cases, the corporations had long histories of breaches of safety that could have formed the foundational offences for unlawful and dangerous act manslaughter.[70]

The symbolic recognition of killer corporations: Industrial manslaughter offences

In response to massive 'disasters' and the failure to prosecute corporations under existing homicide offences, despite evidence of repeated and prolonged breaches of existing legal duties by corporations in the pursuit of profit, many jurisdictions have introduced industrial manslaughter offences. For example, in the UK, law reform was provoked by a series of 'accidents', including the Clapham Rail train crash in 1988, which killed 35 people; the Hillsborough disaster in 1989, which killed 96 people; the King's Cross London Underground fire in 1987, which killed 31 people; the Piper Alpha oil platform explosion in 1988, which killed 167 people; the sinking of the *Marchioness* on the River

---

63 *Wilson v The Queen* (1992) 174 CLR 313.

64 *R v Franklin* (1883) 15 Cox CC 163.

65 See also *R v Pullman* (1991) 25 NSWLR 89, which held that regulatory offences such as breaches of traffic laws could not form the basis for unlawful and dangerous act manslaughter.

66 See e.g. *Wilson v The Queen* (1992) 174 CLR 313.

67 *R v Larkin* [1943] KB 174; 1 All ER 217, 219.

68 *R v Borkowski* [2009] NSWCCA 102, [3].

69 Frank Pearce and Steve Tombs, *Toxic Capitalism: Corporate Crime and the Chemical Industry*, 1st ed. (London: Routledge, 1998), 152–4.

70 See also Thalia Anthony and Penny Crofts, "The Dreamworld Deaths: Corporate Crime and the Slumber of Law," *Current Issues in Criminal Justice* 36, no. 2 (2024): 197–218.

Thames in 1989, which killed 51 people; and the sinking of the *Herald of Free Enterprise*, which killed 188 people. Public inquiries found that systemic failures in management and accountability caused the disasters and loss of life. Despite these findings, none of the companies were successfully prosecuted for gross negligence manslaughter. In response to a series of multiple-fatality 'disasters' in the 1990s, the Law Commission proposed a new law on corporate manslaughter in 1996. Yet it was not until 2008 that the *Corporate Manslaughter and Corporate Homicide Act 2007* (UK) came into force.[71]

There tends to be a great deal of opposition to introducing industrial manslaughter offences, and where these are proposed, there is generally significant tinkering to reduce the potential reach of the offences. For example, in the UK, despite attempts to bypass the limits of identification doctrine, the new corporate manslaughter offence still relies on proof of individual agency – that is, the fatality must be caused by a gross breach of a relevant duty of care owed by the corporation or organisation to the deceased, where the way in which the activities of the organisation were managed or organised by senior management was a substantial element in that breach. Despite such reforms, there continues to be a lack of prosecutions for homicides; at most, corporations may be prosecuted for breach of duty.[72] In the decade since the *Corporate Manslaughter and Corporate Homicide Act 2007* was passed, there have been only 25 convictions for corporate manslaughter and a handful of acquittals and dismissals.[73]

Many jurisdictions have recognised the possibility of killer corporations in specific industrial manslaughter offences, but for the vast majority of corporate homicides, this has not translated into prosecutions. Here, too, lies another explanation for the individualistic bias in perceptions of violence and crime: states are reluctant to develop criminal principles that could potentially apply to governments. The *Corporate Manslaughter and Corporate Homicide Act 2007* can be applied to government agencies.[74] For example, the Crown Office and Procurator Fiscal Service confirmed in March 2023 that it had instructed Police Scotland to investigate the Scottish Prison Service for corporate responsibility, including corporate homicide, over the restraint-related death of a man, Allan Marshall, in prison in 2015. Marshall died in March 2015, four days after being violently restrained by up to 17 prison officers in HMP Edinburgh. The Crown Office and Procurator Fiscal Service determined soon after the death that no criminal proceedings were warranted and granted to all those involved in Marshall's restraint immunity from prosecution from any action related to this. In 2019, a Fatal Accident Inquiry (the Scottish system for investigating deaths) found that the prison officers testifying about the restraint were 'mutually and consistently dishonest'. The Lord Advocate for Scotland

---

71 Some jurisdictions have introduced a specific offence of industrial manslaughter; for example, the Australian Capital Territory via the *Crimes Act 1900* (ACT) pt 2A (introduced by the *Crimes (Industrial Manslaughter) Amendment Act 2003* (ACT) s 2).

72 Anthony and Crofts, "Dreamworld Deaths."

73 Victoria Roper, "The Corporate Manslaughter and Corporate Homicide Act 2007 – A 10 Year Review." *The Journal of Criminal Law* 82, no. 1 (2018): 48–75.

74 In 2016, the NHS Trust was charged with manslaughter after the victim, Cappuccini, never woke up from anaesthetic following an emergency caesarean section at Tunbridge Wells Hospital in Kent. The prosecutors argued that if one or both doctors was found to be grossly negligent, then the NHS Trust employed someone it knew or should have known was not suitably qualified or trained. However, the trial judge directed the jury to acquit on the basis that there was no case to answer: Peter Walker, "NHS Caesarean Death: Landmark Corporate Manslaughter Trial Collapses," *The Guardian*, 29 January 2016, www.theguardian.com/society/2016/jan/28/frances-capp uccini-caesarean-death-trial-collapses.

acknowledged that the original investigation was inadequate and conducted a comprehensive review. As a result, the Lord Advocate concluded that there were grounds for investigation into the civil and criminal liability of the Prison Service. Due to legal immunity, individual officers could not be prosecuted for their involvement.

Routine homicide within regulatory regimes

In the absence of criminal law, corporate homicides are most likely to be recorded under health and safety regimes – although they are also apparent in records of environmental harms, dangerous products, etc.[75] Regulation takes place in a neoliberal environment touting individual responsibility and small government. Only a small subset of deaths are investigated by health and safety regulators, and then a small number of those investigations may lead to convictions for safety offences.[76] Many offences are regarded and recorded as breaches of occupational health and safety rather than as homicides.[77] The International Labour Organization has reported that over 2.78 million people die annually as a result of occupational illnesses and accidents at work and some 374 million non-fatal work-related injuries occur each year.[78] Most governments monitor deaths at work under the category of occupational or workplace health and safety, although many health and safety crimes are 'invisible'[79] and attract no regulatory or criminal justice attention. Workplace fatalities may give rise to investigations by police and the relevant government safety authority. Deaths may also lead to a coronial inquiry to make findings and recommendations to prevent similar deaths from occurring in the future.[80] Jurisdictions differ as to whether bystanders and/or commuter deaths (worker fatalities travelling to or from work) are included in the statistics.[81] In most jurisdictions, employers conducting business have a statutory duty to ensure the safety of their workers and others in the workplace.[82] Various workplaces are regarded as particularly dangerous, including construction sites, transportation, mining, suppliers and users of hazardous chemicals, forestry, and fishing. For example, at construction sites, most fatalities are from falls while working at heights, being hit by falling objects, being hit or trapped between stationary and/or moving objects, and vehicle incidents.[83] The costs of occupational illness and accidents at work are estimated at 4 per cent of global gross domestic product annually. The International Labour Organization describes the human cost of

---

75 Tombs and Whyte, *The Corporate Criminal*.
76 Steve Tombs, "The UK's Corporate Killing Law: Un/Fit for Purpose?" *Criminology and Criminal Justice* 18, no. 4 (2018): 489, https://doi.org/10.1177/1748895817725559.
77 For example, Ardent Pty Ltd was prosecuted for three breach of duty offences in response to four homicides: Anthony and Crofts, "Dreamworld Deaths."
78 International Labour Organization, *Quick Guide on Sources and Uses of Statistics on Occupational Safety and Health*. Switzerland: ILO, https://ilostat.ilo.org/pdf/quick-guide-on-sources-and-uses-of-statistics-on-occupational-safety-and-health.
79 Tombs, "Violence," 532.
80 Lynda R. Matthews et al., "Bereaved Families and the Coronial Response to Traumatic Workplace Fatalities: Organizational Perspectives," *Death Studies* 40, no. 3 (2016), https://doi.org/10.1080/07481187.2015.1115787.
81 For example, Safe Work Australia includes the fatalities of bystanders but does not include commuter deaths in its fatality statistics.
82 For example, the *Work Health and Safety Act 2011* (NSW) s. 19.
83 Cameron O'Neill, Vinod Gopaldasani, and Robyn Coman, "Factors that influence the effective use of safe work method statements for high-risk construction work in Australia – A literature review," *Safety Science* 147 (2022): 105628, https://doi.org/10.1016/j.ssci.2021.105628.

occupational safety and health deficits as 'vast and unacceptable'.[84] These figures do not include the thousands of people who die from conditions like asbestosis and mesothelioma that stem from their employment but take many years to kill.[85]

Most corporate homicides arise from corporations' failure(s) to comply with standards – health and safety, environmental, etc. – over long periods of time. Despite such behaviour signifying ongoing decisions and omissions, deaths are labelled as 'accidents'.[86] For example, in July 1988, the Piper Alpha oil platform (operated by Occidental Petroleum) exploded, killing 165 of the 226 workers on board. Two rescue workers also died. At the time of the explosion, Piper Alpha was producing 10 per cent of the North Sea's annual oil and gas output. It transpired that Occidental Petroleum, a multinational Texan company, had failed to follow maintenance or safety procedures and that this had caused the explosion. Multiple management failures had contributed to the disaster – the focus was on continuing production rather than safety. The safety valve of Pump A had been removed for maintenance. When Pump B was blocked, the control room staff restarted Pump A to ensure that production continued; a breakdown in communication meant those staff were unaware that Pump A was out of commission. Within moments, Pump A leaked gas, which exploded when it ignited. It was regarded as one of the biggest failures in the management of safety regulation to ever occur in the UK.[87] A breakdown in communication led to the use of machinery that was under maintenance, and a valve had not been fully tightened. Many of the employees were unfamiliar with the layout of the platform and had not been properly trained on emergency procedures. The safety systems on the platform were, at best, inadequate. The rescue arrangements were also inadequate; for example, the standby vessel was unsuitable for rescuing survivors. Lord Cullen blamed the owners for 'adopting a superficial attitude to the risk of major hazards'.[88] In short, there were no acceptable practices in place to respond to foreseeable dangers inherent in oil and gas production. The company had previously been prosecuted for breaches of health and safety, yet the regulator's inspection platform's health and safety and maintenance procedures was superficial. Despite clearly failing in its duty of care to workers, Occidental Petroleum escaped any criminal sanctions for the death. The company was instead subjected to fines for its breach of health and safety regulations.

Conclusion

The law tends not to regard corporate homicides as violence.[89] Individualistic bias means that law does not perceive deaths caused by corporations as homicides. Law does not see corporations as agents who cause death, instead tending to label homicides by corporations as 'disasters', 'tragedies', or 'accidents', as though there was no controlling agent. Acts of recklessness, such as employers cutting back on basic maintenance, training, or the replacement of hardware and software, combine with an intensification of work and employees' subservience to power to create more dangerous conditions.[90] This is

84 International Labor Organization, *Quick Guide*, 5.
85 Slapper, "Corporate Homicide."
86 Hebert, Bittle, and Tombs, "Obscuring Corporate Violence," 558.
87 Kenneth Miller, "Piper Alpha and the Cullen Report," *Industrial Law Journal* 20, no. 3 (1991).
88 Miller, "Piper Alpha," 182.
89 Michael Levi and Mike Maguire, "Violent Crime," in *Oxford Handbook of Criminology*, ed. Mike Maguire, Rod Morgan, and Robert Reiner (Oxford: Oxford University Press, 2002).
90 Tombs, "Violence," 543.

exacerbated by the fact that regulatory frameworks are increasingly becoming influenced by free market models, accompanied by a reduction in regulatory funding and powers.[91] The lack of criminal prosecution of corporations reflects corporate power to define and influence definitions and enforcement of criminal law. Rather than corporate offending being seen as the quotidian and pervasive phenomenon that it truly is, it is characterised as 'relatively marginal and aberrant rather than widespread and routine'.[92] Paradoxically, it is simultaneously seen as avoidable and preventable yet entirely routine and allowable harm. It is truly horrific that the law – and we as a society – do not see these deaths as criminal. Unlike the spectacle of an event, these are cases of slow-burning horror.

Bibliography

Anthony, Thalia, and Penny Crofts. "The Dreamworld Deaths: Corporate Crime and the Slumber of Law." *Current Issues in Criminal Justice* 36, no. 2 (2024): 197–218.

Bant, Elise. "The Culpable Corporate Mind: Taxonomy and Synthesis." In *The Culpable Corporate Mind*, edited by Elise Bant, 3–36. Oxford: Hart, 2023.

Barak, Gregg. *Unchecked Corporate Power: Why the Crimes of Multinational Corporations Are Routinized Away and What We Can Do about It*. London: Routledge, 2017.

Coffee Jr., John. "No Soul to Damn: No Body to Kick: An Unscandalised Inquiry into the Problem of Corporate Punishment." *Michigan Law Review* 79 (1981): 386–459.

Comino, Vicky. "'Culture' is Key – An Analysis of Culture-Focused Techniques and Tools in the Regulation of Corporations and Financial Institutions." *Australian Business Law Review* 49, no. 1 (2021): 6–25.

Crofts, Penny, and Honni van Rijswijk. "The Nightmare on Elm Street: The Failure and Responsibility of Those in Authority." In *ReFocus: The Films of Wes Craven*, edited by Calum Waddell, 102–117. Edinburgh: Edinburgh University Press, 2023.

Crofts, Penny. "Aliens: Legal Conceptions of the Corporate Invasion." *Law and Literature* 34, no. 3 (2021): 387–415. https://doi.org/10.1080/1535685X.2020.1862521.

Crofts, Penny. "The Horror of Corporate Harms." *Australian Journal of Corporate Law* 38, no. 1 (2022): 23–45.

Crofts, Penny. *Wickedness and Crime: Laws of Homicide and Malice*. London and New York: Routledge, 2013.

Diamantis, Mihailis E. "Corporate Criminal Minds." *Notre Dame Law Review* 91, no. 5 (2016): 2049–2090.

Fletcher, George. *Rethinking Criminal Law*. Boston, MA: Little Brown, 1978.

French, Peter A. *Collective and Corporate Responsibility*. New York: Columbia University Press, 1984.

Girard, Rene. *Sacrifice*. East Lansing, MI: Michigan State University Press, 2011.

Glasbeek, Harry J. "The Corporation as a Legally Created Site of Irresponsibility." In *International Handbook of White-Collar and Corporate Crime*, edited by Henry Pontell and Gilbert Geis, 248–278. New York: Springer, 2007.

Gosport Independent Panel. *Gosport War Memorial Hospital: The Report of the Gosport Independent Panel*. United Kingdom: House of Commons, 2018. www.gosportpanel.independent.gov.uk/panel-report.

Greenberg, Joshua D., and Ellen C. Brotman. "Strict Vicarious Criminal Liability for Corporations and Corporate Executives: Stretching the Boundaries of Criminalization." *American Criminal Law Review* 51, no. 1 (2014): 79–98.

Hebert, Jasmine, Steven Bittle, and Steve Tombs. "Obscuring Corporate Violence: Corporate Manslaughter in Action." *The Howard Journal of Crime and Justice* 58, no. 4 (2019): 554–579. https://doi.org/10.1111/hojo.12345.

---

91 Tombs and Whyte, "Deadly Consensus."
92 Tombs and Whyte, "Deadly Consensus," 49.

International Labour Organization. *Quick Guide on Sources and Uses of Statistics on Occupational Safety and Health*. Switzerland: International Labour Organization, 2020. https://ilostat.ilo.org/pdf/quick-guide-on-sources-and-uses-of-statistics-on-occupational-safety-and-health.

Jones, Kristen S. "The Opioid Epidemic: Product Liability or One Hell of a Nuisance? Symposium: The Opioid Crisis: An Epidemic Explained." *Mississippi College Law Review* 39, no. 1 (2021): 32–79.

Ken, Ivy, and Kenneth Sebastian Leon, "Necropolitical Governance and State-Corporate Harms: COVID-19 and the US Pork Packing Industry." *Journal of White Collar and Corporate Crime* 3, no. 2 (2022): 76–89.

Lee, Matthew, and David Ermann. "Pinto 'Madness' as a Flawed Landmark Narrative: An Organization and Network Analysis." *Social Problems* 46, no. 1 (1999): 30–47.

Lee, Matthew, and Jeannine Gailey. "Attributing Responsibility for Organizational Wrongdoing." In *International Handbook of White-Collar and Corporate Crime*, edited by Henry Pontell and Gilbert Geis, 51–77. New York: Springer, 2007.

Levi, Michael, and Mike Maguire. "Violent Crime." In *Oxford Handbook of Criminology*, edited by Mike Maguire, Rod Morgan, and Robert Reiner, 795–843. Oxford: Oxford University Press, 2002.

Lim, Ernest. "A Critique of Corporate Attribution: 'Directing Mind and Will' and Corporate Objectives." *Journal of Business Law* 3, no. 3 (2013): 333–353.

Matthews, Lynda R., Scott J. Fitzpatrick, Michael G. Quinlan, Mark Ngo, and Philip Bohle. "Bereaved Families and the Coronial Response to Traumatic Workplace Fatalities: Organizational Perspectives." *Death Studies* 40, no. 3 (2016): 191–200. https://doi.org/10.1080/07481187.2015.1115787.

Miller, Kenneth. "Piper Alpha and the Cullen Report." *Industrial Law Journal* 20, no. 3 (1991): 176–187.

Naffine, Ngaire. "Our Legal Lives as Men, Women and Persons." *Legal Studies* 24 11, no. 4 (2004): 621–642.

O'Neill, Cameron, Vinod Gopaldasani, and Robyn Coman. "Factors that influence the effective use of safe work method statements for high-risk construction work in Australia – A literature review." *Safety Science* 147 (2022): 105628. https://doi.org/10.1016/j.ssci.2021.105628.

O'Neill, Rory, Simon Pickvance, and Andrew Watterson. "Burying the Evidence: How Great Britain is Prolonging the Occupational Cancer Epidemic." *International Journal of Occupational and Environmental Health* 13, no. 4 (2007): 428–436. https://doi.org/10.1179/oeh.2007.13.4.428.

Oliver, Bobbie. "'No Place for Tourists': Deaths on Western Australian Construction Sites." *Labour History* 119, no. 1 (2020): 115–142. https://doi.org/10.3828/jlh.2020.21.

Orts, Eric W. *Business Persons: A Legal Theory of the Firm*. Oxford: Oxford University Press, 2013.

Pearce, Frank, and Steve Tombs. *Toxic Capitalism: Corporate Crime and the Chemical Industry*. 1st ed. London: Routledge, 1998.

Pollman, Elizabeth. "Corporate Law and Theory in Hobby Lobby." In *The Rise of Corporate Religious Liberty*, edited by Micah Schmartzman, Chad Flanders, and Zoe Robinson, 149–171. Oxford: Oxford University Press, 2016.

Quinlan, Michael. *Ten Pathways to Death and Disaster: Learning from Fatal Incidents in Mines and Other High Hazard Workplaces*. Annandale: Federation Press, 2014.

Reiman, Jeffrey. *The Rich Get Richer and the Poor Get Prison: Ideology, Class and Criminal Justice*. 7th ed. Boston, MA: Allyn and Bacon, 2003.

Roper, Victoria. "The Corporate Manslaughter and Corporate Homicide Act 2007 – A 10 Year Review." *The Journal of Criminal Law* 82, no. 1 (2018): 48–75.

Sheen, Justice. *The Merchant Shipping Act of 1894: MV Herald of Free Enterprise – Report of the Court No. 8074*. London: Department of Transport, 1987.

Slapper, Garry. "Corporate Homicide, Corporate Social Responsibility, and Human Rights." In *The Handbook of Homicide*, edited by Fiona Brookman, Edward R. Maguire, and Mike Maguire, 213–230. Wiley and Sons, 2017.

Tombs, Steve, and David Whyte. *The Corporate Criminal: Why Corporations Must Be Abolished*. London: Taylor & Francis, 2015.

Tombs, Steve, and David Whyte. "A Deadly Consensus: Worker Safety and Regulatory Degradation Under New Labour." *The British Journal of Criminology* 50, no. 1 (2010): 46–65. https://doi.org/10.1093/BJC%2FAZP063.

Tombs, Steve. "The UK's Corporate Killing Law: Un/Fit for Purpose?" *Criminology and Criminal Justice* 18, no. 4 (2018): 488–507. https://doi.org/10.1177/1748895817725559.

Tombs, Steve. "Violence, Safety Crimes and Criminology." *British Journal of Criminology* 47, no. 4 (2007): 531–550.

Trabsky, Marc, and Jacinthe Flore. "Prescription Medicines and Economies of Death." In *Evil Corporations: Law, Culpability and Regulation*, edited by Penny Crofts, 78–90. London: Routledge, 2024.

Walker, Peter. "NHS Caesarean Death: Landmark Corporate Manslaughter Trial Collapses." *The Guardian*, 29 January 2016. www.theguardian.com/society/2016/jan/28/frances-cappuccini-caesarean-death-trial-collapses.

Wells, Celia. *Corporations and Criminal Responsibility*. 2nd ed. Oxford: Oxford University Press, 2001.

Whitmer, Michelle. "Asbestos Facts and Statistics." The Mesothelioma Center. Last modified 16 June 2023, www.asbestos.com/asbestos/statistics-facts.

Whyte, David. "Still Dying for a Living." *The British Journal of Criminology* 53, no. 6 (2013): 1206–1211. https://doi.org/10.1093/bjc/azt058.

23

KILLING AS AN OPERATION OF THE CIVIL LAW

Two Examples of Roman Jurisprudence

Edward Mussawir

Introduction

The civil law, like the criminal law, sometimes understands death as a harm that may have been avoided, were it not for the wrongful act that is said to have caused it. According to this view, the act of causing death is an externality that the law can seek only either to denounce or to ratify, if not, of course – as the law sometimes does with other kinds of acts – to *rescind* or *annul* it. It falls typically outside that class of acts which the modern civil law tradition has come to call 'juridical': acts such as to transfer ownership, to enter or terminate a contract, to bequeath, to institute a will, to marry, to adopt, and so on, through which one creates or shapes definite legal relations. To kill: this is not, supposedly, a transaction the meaning of which can be comprehended in the positive legal effects that are intended by it.

Of course, the notion of an avoidability of harm – integral to the civil law – does not automatically provide the thought about death with its deepest roots. For that reason, the technicality of the lawyerly imagination of it – the steadfast attention toward the structure of accusation, obligation, causation, reparation, and so on – can seem ill-equipped sometimes to deal even with the most basic human responses to irrevocable loss. The law steers resolutely clear both of the spiritual and of the merely sentimental.[1] In the common law tradition, as in others, personal actions were thought strictly to be extinguished along with the person him or herself, in such a way that the recognition of actions for 'wrongful death' were the result of twentieth-century statutory modifications which extended relief beyond the person herself in favour of the dependents and family members.[2] And even

---

1 See especially Yan Thomas, "Res Religiosae: On the categories of religion and commerce in Roman law," in *Law, Anthropology and the Constitution of the Social*, ed. Alain Pottage and Martha Mundy (Cambridge University Press, 2004), 40–72. Thomas's study attends to the depth and originality of juridical thought in its relation to religion by situating the dead within a legal regime of 'things' and temporal management of estates.

2 See Wex S. Malone, "The Genesis of Wrongful Death," *Stanford Law Review* 17 (1965): 1044. Malone ties the exclusion of actions for 'wrongful death' in the common law tradition to two historical maxims: (1) the idea that all personal actions die with the person (*actio personalis moritur cum persona*); and (2) that 'the death of a human being was not regarded as giving rise

---

DOI: 10.4324/9781003304593-27

there, the law also gave a narrow view to the sort of loss that the death represented. In itself, of course, death remained a form of damage that could not be remedied. But the losses that law did recognise were limited to the secondary quantifiable, pecuniary dimensions, leaving emotion out of the equation.

It seems less likely still that any deeper thoughts about death would be capable of being found in the evaluations that the civil law makes about acts of killing as such. Death, in this connection, seems only to add to the seriousness of the consequences of an act already understood to be wrongful rather than to change anything significant in its juridical composition. With the act of killing, the legal mind, at first glance, struggles to go very far past the regime of a definite sanction. To kill, in other words, is usually to act against the law. It is understood within a purely negative – that is to say, 'less-than-perfect' – operation of legal order.[3]

However, it is precisely on this unlikely terrain of the civil law, as I would like to argue in this chapter, that some of the examples of law's deeper contemplation of death are presented. It is not, from my perspective at least, in that area that considers the act of killing most routinely – namely in the law of homicide – that we find the development of a reflection on killing as a positive juridical operation. In that area, as mentioned, the law is interested in killing only in so far as it may constitute a transgression – that is, negatively, ignoring in this way any of its possible constitutive legal functions. While death on its own may frequently change the juridical qualification of an unlawful act – for example, from one classified as an 'assault' to one classified as 'manslaughter' or 'murder' in certain criminal jurisdictions – it doesn't necessarily change anything fundamental in the relation that the act of killing itself maintains with an essentially negative frame of prohibition. So too, while questions about what constitutes a justified or unjustified killing have been complex and enduring enough to occupy the minds of legal thinkers in many different eras, those questions have also at the same time been circumscribed by the same problematic of transgression/exoneration, leaving any further consideration of the creative dimensions of the legal act out of the picture.

It is for that same reason also that the broader and more obvious areas of the civil law that concern themselves with killing, namely in relation to torts or delicts where death forms part of the alleged damage or loss, don't always provide the most fertile ground. Again, the act that is there imagined to end a life can be brought into a straightforward relation to the wrong as it is conceived by the law: a relation between wrongful act and fatal harm that requires no further effort of the jurist to conceptualise in order to bring under pre-existing juridical forms designed to compensate for injury.

to any cause of action at common law on behalf of a living person who was injured by reason of the death'.

3 Yan Thomas explains that the Roman jurists – namely Ulpian in the opening to his *Rules* – designated as 'less-than-perfect' those laws that fell somewhere between 'perfect' and 'imperfect' law. Perfect laws were those whose mode of action was to automatically annul or rescind that which resisted them. These laws were effective without the need of a penalty for non-compliance. The act was, in so far as it was contrary to the law, struck by non-existence. Imperfect laws were, on the contrary, those which had a content but no force. Every law that thus required the force of a penalty to be effective was characterised as 'less-than-perfect'. Yan Thomas, "Sanctio: les défences de la loi," *L'ecrit du temps* 19 (1988): 70–1. For the relevant text of Ulpian's *Rules* see John Thomas Abdy and Bryan Walker, eds., *The Commentaries of Gaius and the Rules of Ulpian*, trans. John Thomas Abdy and Bryan Walker (Cambridge: Cambridge University Press, 1874), 355–6.

The better examples are to be found in more isolated places: in particular, in those where killing is not the central object of the proceedings nor the primary matter for legal consideration but where the argumentation of the case brings it indirectly to the fore. In these places, death sometimes lends the starkness of its limits to the technical configurations of legal action: a figure against which the necessary plasticity of the juridical formulations can occasionally be realised. It finds thereby a surer route into the deeper meditations of the jurist. There can be little depth, for instance, to the thought of law that links death solely and straightforwardly to the concept of victimhood: the result of some injustice. Lawyers show us instead, in certain examples of their thinking, an effort to reconcile it not just with the frame of legal order but with the imperative mood in which definite relations are activated and instituted on the terrain of the law.

In this chapter, I would like to illustrate just two examples. These examples are drawn from the classical Roman jurisprudence preserved in Justinian's Digest. The first is a fragment from the work of the jurist Paul concerned with the institution of heirs. The so-called 'right of life and death' (*ius vitae necisque*) is invoked at the close of this passage in order to figure the instantaneousness of the relation of inheritance when it concerns 'own heirs' (*sui heredes*). The act of killing finds itself figured here as a decisive operation for the imagination of a fundamental institution of the civil law. The second example is from Ulpian's account of a civil action called the 'action on poverty' (*actio de pauperie*). This was an action brought by an injured party against the owner of a four-footed animal that had caused harm. In a fragment that has perplexed many Romanists, Ulpian relates a case-example supposedly showing why the action cannot be sustained for beasts that are 'wild by nature'. The reference that the jurist makes to the killing of the animal at the close of this passage, neglected by most commentators, has an important significance for understanding the complexity of the juristic work in question.

In each of these examples, the act of killing (represented by the Latin verb *occidere* [4]) serves as a constructive hypothesis in aid of the mental effort of the jurist and adds an unexpected final emphasis to the logic of the legal argumentation. My approach to each case here is to unravel the casuistic dimensions that underlie the work and in doing so hopefully to explain the resort to a figure (killing) in the lawyers' deliberations over their civil law. Together, the two cases provide a glimpse of the ways that lawyers – in the Roman legal tradition in particular – have not entirely neglected to imagine killing as an operation with distinct legal effect and how they have also not thereby neglected to bring death into connection with the depth and originality of their thought.

Right of life and death

The problem: the inheritance of 'own heirs'

When the classical jurist Paul responds to the problem of describing in Roman law the formal instantaneousness of the institution of inheritance under the civil law – the task of

---

4 The verb *occidere* (to kill) is thought to have had a core verbal meaning in the context of Roman civil law: a meaning which realises its specificity especially by way of certain statutory distinctions, between an *actio legis Aquiliae* and an *actio in factum*, for instance, in which the terms *occidere* (a direct act of killing) and *mortis causam praestare [or praebere]* (providing the cause of death) were used to formulaically conceptualise kinds of precipitation of death. See especially Dieter Nörr, "Causam Mortis Praebere," in *The Legal Mind: Essays for Tony Honoré*, ed. Neil MacCormick and Peter Birks (Oxford: Clarendon Press, 1986), 203–17; N. H. Andrews, "'Occidere' and the Lex Aquilia," *Cambridge Law Journal* 46, no. 2 (1987): 315–29.

ensuring that strictly no gap in time is imagined between the death of the father and the succession of his own heirs (*sui heredes*) – he puts it in this way:

> In the case of own heirs (*sui heredes*), it is more clearly evident that the continuation of ownership leads to this, that no inheritance is regarded as having taken place, as if they (own heirs) were already owners, being thought of as in some sense owners even in the lifetime of the father. And so a son-in-power (*filiusfamilias*) is even called the same as a head of the household (*paterfamilias*) with the addition only of a qualification which makes a distinction between the person who fathers and the person who is fathered. Therefore, after the death of the father they are not regarded as taking up an inheritance, but rather get free power of administration of the property. For this reason, even if they have not been instituted heirs, they are owners; and *it is no objection to say that it is permissible to disinherit them, because it was also permissible to kill them.* [5]

What is the meaning of this fragment? And what, in particular, is the meaning of the enigmatic reference in the final few words to this act of killing?

There is no mistaking the reference. Paul, a jurist of the second and third centuries CE, was drawing a connection in the last phrase to a very ancient legal power/right: the 'power of life and death' (*vitae necisque potestas*) that Roman fathers were said to have held over their sons from the very beginning of the city of Rome itself: from the decree – according to Dionysius of Halicarnassus – of their first king and law-giver Romulus, roughly a millennium before Paul was composing his legal treatise *On Sabinus*. [6] Supposedly, Roman fathers held a power and a right to kill their sons (or grandsons, etc,. if they had succeeded to the position of son), not just while those sons were in their infanthood, but even as adults: for as long as they themselves lived. This is taken, not only in Paul's fragment but in the juristic literature more broadly, as a quintessential norm of Roman legal order, and one of its main premises. Paternal power (*patria potestas*) was an absolute, not a conditional, relation.

Now, the intrigue regarding the right itself – fascinating as it may be for the historians and sociologists – is not the main object of Paul's work. [7] The evidence for the historical exercise of such a 'right of life and death', after all – as Yan Thomas reminds us – is

---

5 Digest 28.2.11. Paul, *Sabinus*, book 2. Alan Watson, ed., *The Digest of Justinian Vol. 2* (University of Pennsylvania Press, 1985), 362–3. Emphasis added.

6 Dionysius of Halicarnassus, *Roman Antiquities Vol. 1*, trans. Earnest Carey (Loeb Classical Library Edition, 1937 [1st century BCE]), at 387–9 [2.26.4–6].

7 For modern commentary on this power, see Yan Thomas, "Vitae necisque potestas: le pére, la cité, la mort," in *Du châtiment dans la cité. Supplices corporels et peine de mort dans le monde antique* (École Française de Rome, 1984), 499–548; William V. Harris, "Roman Father's Power of Life and Death," in *Studies in Roman Law: In Memory of A. Arthur Schiller*, ed. Roger S. Bagnall and William V. Harris (Leiden: E. J. Brill, 1986), 81–95; Giorgio Agamben, "*Vitae necisque potestas*," in *Homo Sacer: Sovereign Power and Bare Life* (Stanford, CA: Stanford University Press, 1998), chapter 4; Raymond Westbrook, "Vitae Necisque Potestas," *Historia: Zeitschrift für Alte Geschichte* 48, no. 2 (1999): 203–23; Brent D. Shaw, "Raising and Killing Children: Two Roman Myths," *Mnemosyne* 54, no. 1 (2001): 31–77; Bruce W. Frier and Thomas A. McGinn, "The Power of Life and Death," in *Casebook on Roman Family Law*, chapter 3 (Oxford University Press, 2003), 191–210; Bé Breij, "Vitae Necisque Potestas in Roman Declamation," *Advances in the History of Rhetoric* 9, no. 1 (2006): 55–79.

rather more obscure than its purely legal conceptual existence.[8] Whether fathers really were the tyrants with respect to their own sons as this right implies is beside the point. There is as much doubt over its meaning in everyday Roman family life as there is certainty and absoluteness in its juridical conception.

In Paul's fragment, it is invoked with another intellectual aim entirely: to help resolve a difficulty in the more complex jurisprudence concerning succession. Since the passage is divorced from its original casuistic context, that intellectual aim is not immediately apparent. Thomas indeed tells us that this 'remarkable' fragment of Paul's has been either unduly denigrated by a 'hyper-positivist and imprudent interpolationist critique' that attempted to read into its denial of 'inheritance' to *sui heredes* certain doctrinal heresies, or else conscripted to the task of reconstructing the primitive sociology of 'a kind of inter-generational indivisibility of the "joint family"'.[9] These were, in his view, to ignore the narrow juridical significance of the figures at play and thus to set things on the wrong path. 'Paul strives quite simply to justify, in the language and with the ideas of his time,' Thomas says, 'a mechanism which dates back undoubtedly to a very early age, but which was nonetheless not easy to make clear'[10]: the succession of *sui heredes*, of individuals who were not just intestate heirs but individuals whose very existence took precedence over the testamentary provisions that failed to contemplate them. What was the technical difficulty that forced the jurist to stretch this juridical figure all the way up to this other one: a right to kill? What was the specific problem in the civil law regarding succession that this particular 'right to kill' was recruited to address in the mind of the lawyer? And what does it tell us about the lawyerly reflection on killing as a civil juristic function?

The context: the legal hypothesis of a death

Consider the following case. A son of the family father, whose wife is expecting a child, is condemned to death. Ordinarily, in the classical period of Roman law in question, such a condemned individual, after the magistrate's sentence but before their execution, would lose their civil status. They would become a slave by penalty – a *servus poenae* – losing with that status all their testamentary powers and entitlements and rights of inheritance.[11] Suppose, however, that this condemned son has petitioned the emperor for a reprieve which, if granted, would restore him to his former position. His father meanwhile decides to institute a will. This will first disinherits the condemned son, and second institutes an extraneous heir to his estate: a person of the father's choosing who was not already part of the agnatic family (the father's descendants). The expected grandchild is not mentioned at all. The will passes over this unborn individual. Now, before the son has had his petition determined or his sentence carried out, the father-testator dies. The instituted heir is called to the estate. While he is in the process of deciding whether to take up the inheritance under the father's will, the daughter-in-law gives birth to the male grandchild (son of the condemned son). The question is this: how to interpret the father's will and administer the transactions relating to the father's estate in the interim period

8 Thomas, "Vitae necisque potestas."
9 Yan Thomas, "L'enfant à naître et l'« héritier sien »: sujet de pouvoir et sujet de vie en droit romain," *Annales. Histoire, Sciences Sociales* 62, no. 1 (2007): 48.
10 Thomas, "L'enfant à naître," 54.
11 Digest 48.19.17 pr. Marcian, *Institutes*, book 1. Watson, *The Digest of Justinian Vol. 4*, 364.

until the son's fate is finally determined? Does the newborn grandchild have a legitimate claim to the estate? Does his birth break the grandfather's will, shutting out the extraneous heir? Or is it possible for the extraneous heir to rely unencumbered on the terms of the will that instituted him solely as heir, as if the grandchild did not exist?

The difficulty relates to the position of 'own heirs' (*sui heredes*) with regard to the Roman law of succession: a difficulty that is heightened by the uncertainty over the condemned son's civil status. The *sui heredes* are not defined by the closeness of their biological or kinship relation to the deceased whose estate is in question, but by the paternal power that ties them to their dying male progenitor, whose estate they automatically enter into upon the father's death: whether or not they are instituted as heirs, whether or not the father even knew about them, and whether or not they even wish to take up the inheritance. Even if the inheritance involves debts more than profits, the *sui heredes* (unlike an instituted heir) are not in a position to refuse it. Contemporaries to the one who – being their nearest male ancestor – had *patria potestas* over them, they succeed automatically. The Roman casuistry indeed goes to some effort to emphasise the extent of this relation of power that ensures a continuous line of succession. It was concerned with such problems as what happened when a natural gap came to separate the time of the father's death from that of the birth of a member of the next generation. By means of certain fictions, the jurists affirm that even a child born within ten months after the father's death can be deemed to come under his power. The birth of such a posthumous child, if that child had not been provided for in his testament, namely by being either instituted as heir or disinherited, will break the will. It is the same for a grandson who, when born, will be under the power of his grandfather. The testator must therefore think in advance and make precautions, since even the clearest testamentary intentions may be subverted in this way by the accidental birth of a son – or a grandson born to a son who died during the lifetime of the father – who the law brings under that testator's posthumously extended paternal power whether he had wished it or not.

The explanation: killing annuls the juristic ambivalence of death

In the case at hand, then, two different answers to the question of entitlement to the patrimony appear to be activated depending on the ultimate fate – like Schrödinger's cat – of the condemned son. If, after the emperor has considered his petition, this son's condemnation is confirmed, he will not have been *sui heredes* at the time of his father's death. He will have been a slave. It is the grandchild in that case who, when born, is born into that position of *suus*, even if his birth occurs after the death of his grandfather. This birth now breaks the testament in which that grandchild was passed over and in which the extraneous heir was instituted. The claim of the extraneous heir fails. However, what if the outcome of the petition is the reverse? What if the son is eventually granted his reprieve by the emperor and is restored to his civil status and rights? The testament will then apparently remain valid. The disherison of the son will be effective and the grandchild – not being a *suus heres* since the son stands in his way – will have had no reason to have been mentioned in the will.

Of course, the law cannot simply wait and see. Despite the ambivalence between these two positions, which are effectively held in suspense until the fate of the son is known, a definite decision must be reached. The instituted heir has come to claim the inheritance. His argument: that the fiction of an early death of the condemned son should not strike down the validity of the father's will. At the time of the father's death, he argues, neither the son nor the grandson was in a condition to accept the estate. The father's testamentary intention should therefore be considered clear. Regardless of the fate of the condemned son, he is to be disinherited. I (the extraneous heir) am clearly instituted in his place. This is the only thing that the father should be required to have turned his mind to in making the will. And it is a step too far to consider the birth of the grandson to retrospectively alter that certainty and therefore to prevent me – at least provisionally – from taking full possession of what the will entitles me to, when the only thing that calls it into question is the ambivalent and presumptive status of the condemned.

Paul's fragment seems to be responding to an argument like this when its explanation of the succession of *sui heredes* ends with reference to the father's right to kill. The *sui heredes*, Paul says, were to succeed to the estate even if they had not been instituted heirs. Their being *sui* is determined not by testament but by the operation of *patria potestas*. It is as if there is a unity in the person of the father and that of the son, such that the son isn't thought strictly to take up the inheritance. In fact, no inheritance seems to take place, simply a relation of power that is passing away in the one who is dying at the very instant in which it is emerging in those others who – by strict operation of the civil law – were considered to be under his power. Paul therefore, in order to emphasise the point, goes as far as saying that the *sui heredes* are thus considered sort of like owners already during the lifetime of the father. And he explains – to respond to the objection of the instituted heir that the father's testament which indeed disinherited the son (as *suus heres*) could very well have done the same, if he had turned his mind to it, for the grandchild – that the fact that the father may very well disinherit either of them is no argument against this position, since he also had (insofar as they were under his power) a right to kill them.

We see here the act of killing acquiring in the thought underlying the case, something of a distinct jurisprudential outline. Killing describes neither a transgression of the law to which a sanction attaches nor an exception from such a sanction, but an operation in which one is invited to imagine only its strict juridical function. Put it this way: the death of the son is, with regard to the question of succession, not a fact but a legal hypothesis. To the uncertainty that this hypothetical death introduces – in particular with regard to the meaning of the father's will – the jurist opposes the certainty of a right (of the highest order and antiquity) that itself had operated less in reality than also by hypothesis: the *ius vitae necisque*, the father's right of life and death. The son is condemned to death. If the time of his legal death is to strictly determine the validity or invalidity of his father's will, where else does one need to look but to this right that the father himself had with respect to the death of his son, to bring it forward or to push it back, and thus to properly ensure the certainty over the trajectory of his own patrimony?

Jurisprudence in this way – just as with the doctrine of *postliminium* which fictionalises the time of death of those fallen into captivity in order to repair gaps created with regard to succession by their loss of status – holds on to conceptions of death that are uniquely its own. These conceptions aren't make-believe. What they show on the contrary, as Thomas indeed suggests, is that law is something more than a 'flat mirror' to social reality.[12] They are the products and the necessary contours of thinking with law and which give rise to their own depth. If the son, condemned to death, is either to survive and return redeemed and restored to his rights, or alternatively if he remains condemned and is thus considered not to have been in existence at all during the period of

12 Thomas, "L'enfant à naître," 62.

his condemnation, all of these radical contingencies are made to return in Paul's fragment to the one figure: that of the *paterfamilias* in control and full management of his own estate. What limit can be imagined to the legal means by which that estate can be precisely passed on in one form or another? The act of testamentary inheritance and disinheritance can, evidently, be ambiguous, misinterpreted, defective. The act of killing, however, cannot. So while it may have been in the father's power to disinherit the grandson along with the son, it was also technically within his legal power (as father) to turn what remained only a hypothesis of the son's death into an unalterable and unambiguous reality.

Action on poverty

The problem: civil liability for harm done by a bear

Take a second example. In a title of the Digest dealing with the scope of a certain civil action originally provided under the Twelve Tables (451 BCE), the classical jurist Ulpian provides an elaboration that has perplexed many modern interpreters. The action in question is one called the *actio de pauperie* (action on poverty) that gave a person a right to claim from another in relation to harm that had been caused to them by a four-footed animal (*quadrupedes*), usually domestic livestock, and required that the animal itself, which had 'committed *pauperies*' (*pauperiem fecisse*) – meaning damage done without any legal wrong on the part of the doer – be handed over to the injured party or alternatively that monetary recompense be offered to compensate for the loss.

Having explained, somewhat nebulously, that the action lies whenever a wild animal (*fera*), being stirred 'against nature' (*contra naturam*), gave '*pauperies*'; the text suggests that the action cannot be invoked for beasts (*bestiis*) that are 'wild by nature' (*naturalem feritatem*). And Ulpian provides the following illustration:

> Therefore if a bear breaks loose and so causes harm, its former owner cannot be sued because he ceased to be owner as soon as the wild animal escaped. *Accordingly, if I kill the bear, the body is mine.* [13]

What is meant by this illustration and in particular the final phrase in which the 'killing' of the animal in question comes to apparently figure in a rationale for the exclusion of wild beasts from the scope of the action?

As mentioned, this particular fragment has given rise to some controversy over its meaning. The main reasons are not difficult to see. Instead of clarifying the general rule about the exclusion of wild animals from the scope of the *actio de pauperie*, the passage in fact seems unnecessarily to complicate it. One would expect the example to demonstrate the generality of the rule. However, by entertaining an issue regarding an escaping bear, it instead seems to have the opposite effect. It raises the question of the possibility of an action against the owner of a wild animal that had *not* escaped in such a way, but which had remained within the person's possession. Was that situation covered or not? Was the *actio de pauperie* ever meant to cover wild animals like bears? We don't seem to have a clear answer. Some of the modern commentators thought that the text must have

---

13 Digest 9.1.1.10. Ulpian, *Edict*, book 18. Watson, *The Digest of Justinian Vol. 1*, 276. Emphasis added.

been interpolated, either through conscious alteration by Justinian's compilers or perhaps by a more simple omission of a key step in the logic. Franz Haymann thought, for instance, that the inauthenticity of the general rule could be proven since the classical material elsewhere referred only to *quadrupes*, without a distinction between wild and domestic animals.[14] Others such as Ashton-Cross focused on the meaning of the requirement that the animal act 'against nature' (*contra naturam*) which the glossators interpreted as being against the nature of the species, so that only a tame and not a wild beast could act *contra naturam* when it caused harm.[15] Tony Honoré, applying this view, thought then that it was likely that a simple step in the reasoning had gone missing in the fragment in question, explaining the awkwardness of the conjunction. It was likely, in his view, that the jurist had in fact originally intended to state not a definitive reason for why wild beasts are excluded from the action but 'another reason' – that is, in addition to the fact that they don't act 'against their nature' by exhibiting ferocity. That additional reason was the fact that when they escape, they also are no longer considered to have an owner.[16]

Now few, if any, of the commentators on this fragment consider the reference to the *killing* of the animal as such to be of particular importance. It is as though this killing were nothing more than an additional emphasis placed on the basic point that ownership in the bear was lost as soon as it escaped without adding anything critical in answer to the problem of the scope of the *actio de pauperie* or to the problem of reconciling the general rule with the particular example.

The problem is compounded by the fact that the Digest fragment – as with the previous example discussed above – is apparently missing the procedural context of the case itself to which it must have originally constituted a response. Without this associated casuistry, the fragment is easily reduced to a single piece in an otherwise purely didactic puzzle: one which assumes the certainty of a doctrinal position at any historical point in time and seeks only to retrieve this certainty through a critique of the sources through which it is revealed.

The context: a claim 'against' or 'according to' nature?

In a recent work, Nadja El Beheiri helpfully reconstructs some of the unwritten procedural aspects to the case in question. 'Our case deals,' she conjectures, 'with an animal on private property, perhaps a dancing bear...'

> We can imagine that our *dominus* did not have a large number of animals nor
> much experience in handling them, since the creature escaped and caused

---

14 Franz Haymann, "Textkritische Studien zum römischen Obligationenrecht," *Zeitschrift der Savigny-Stiftung für Rechtsgeschichte [Romanistische Abtheilung]* 42, no. 1 (1921): 357–93.

15 D. I. C. Ashton-Cross, "Liability in Roman Law for Damage Caused by Animals," *Cambridge Law Journal* 11, no. 3 (1953): 395–403. On the question of the 'nature' of animals in the context of Ulpian's work on the *actio de pauperie* as an investigation into the relation of Roman law and Greek philosophy, see especially Joseph Meleze-Modrzejewski, "Ulpien et la nature des animaux," in *La filosofia greca e il diritto romano. Colloquio italo-francese Roma, 14–17 aprile 1973* (Rome, 1976), 177–99.

16 Tony Honoré, "Liability for Animals: Ulpian and the Compilers," in *Satura Roberto Feenstra sexagesimum quintum annum aetatis complenti ab alumnis collegis amicis oblata* (Universitaires Fribourg, 1985), 239–50.

damage. It seems that the one who killed the animal was the injured person who demands to keep – perhaps as a trophy or compensation – the remains. If the noxal system of the *actio de pauperie* could be applied to the case, the answer to the question about whether the hunter can keep the body of the animal would be negative. If we accept Ulpian's solution that with the flight of the animal the property is extinguished, the hunter would have acquired the domain according to the rules applied to hunting. The conjuncture is that it was precisely this singular condition of the animal that would have led to the question whether the bear could be treated within the scope of the *actio de pauperie*. [17]

El Beheiri hits upon a critical feature here: the context of a hunt. It is this that touches at least more directly on the meaning of the '*contra naturam*' that Ulpian inscribes as a feature of the pauperian action – the requirement for the animal to have acted 'against nature' – and consequently, as I hope to explain, also the meaning behind the killing of the bear. In the first place, this *contra naturam* of the pauperian action can be understood not as suggesting that the action of the animal must be 'contrary to' the nature of the particular species of animal in question, as the glossators seemed to have thought,[18] nor that it is against 'natural law' as some transgression of a universal moral order derived from 'nature', but rather that its wildness arises in a context that is 'against' a special juridical state, one that borrows the name 'nature'. The phrases 'against nature' (*contra naturam*) and 'according to nature' (*secundum naturam*), for instance, are sometimes used by the classical jurists to emphasise certain institutional arrangements. Slavery, as the famous statement of Florentinus has it, for example, is an institution of the law of peoples, by which someone is subject to the dominion of another 'against nature' (*contra naturam*).[19] While, on the other hand, a text of Paul explains that 'according to nature' (*secundum naturam*), 'to whomever the advantages of a thing follow, the disadvantages of that thing also follow'.[20] Nature doesn't describe here some transcendent or original or primal order, but an institutional diagram 'according to' which or 'against' which specific legal relations are constructed. The jurist can thus oppose this institution called 'nature' – by which, for instance, a hunter may acquire a right over the wild animal she has perhaps chased and wounded, ahead of other pursuers who may step in at the last minute – to other institutional arrangements like those called 'public' which rely on other constructions or conventional transactions.[21]

---

17 Nadja El Beheiri, "Actio de Pauperie: El Caso Del Oso Escapado. Un Análisis en Clave Fenomenológica," *Revista de Estudios Histórico-Jurídicos [Sección derecho romano]* 43 (2021): 39–55, at 42–3.

18 Azo of Bologna had quite simply glossed Justinian's text, at the '*contra naturam*' of D. 9.1.1.7, with the explanation: 'namely of its own kind' (*scilicet sui generis*). See Milena Polojac, "Actio de Pauperie: Anthropomorphism and rationalism," *Fundamina* 18, no. 2 (2012): 119–44, at 134.

19 Digest 1.5.4.1. Florentinus, *Institutes*, book 9. Watson, *The Digest of Justinian Vol. 1*, 15.

20 Digest 50.17.10. Paul, *Sabinus*, book 3. Watson, *The Digest of Justinian Vol. 4*, 471.

21 Ulpian says, in a different context, that the relation of parental piety between a slave mother and her son who have become free together should be preserved 'according to nature' (Digest 37.15.1.1); that is, according to a different institutional regime than the one that imagines that same relation, when it is between citizens, not as 'natural' but as 'public'. See Yan Thomas, "Imago Naturae: note sur la institutionnalité de la nature à Rome," in *Collection de l'École Française de Rome 147, Théologie et Droit dans la Science Politique de L'État Moderne* (École Française de Rome, 1991), 207.

The case in question is situated in this way, as El Beheiri suggests, somewhere between two schemes of 'nature'. On the one hand, a scheme 'according to nature': one which structures the law on acquisitive prescription, the rules of acquiring things that did not, immediately prior to this acquisition, belong to anyone else. On the other hand, a scheme constructed upon what is 'against nature', in which an animal which is owned, by its own action, undoes the relation that made it an acquirable 'good' and subjects it to a procedure that requires the reverse: its surrender.[22]

There is a dispute between two parties. The first (the 'hunter') has, in encountering the escaped bear, probably been injured by it, perhaps in her attempt to capture it. The second, a former owner of the bear from whom it had escaped. However, rather than the hunter having already killed the animal, as El Beheiri pictures, I think it far more likely the jurist imagines both parties as having claims to the living bear as their own: the former owner perhaps because he had not intended to relinquish his ownership of it when it escaped; the hunter either on the basis of an acquisitive prescription (as the first taker of an animal) or alternatively on the basis of the *actio de pauperie* itself (as the victim of 'pauperies'). The final reference to the killing of the animal is far from an inessential detail here but an important and decisive clue. Possibly before instigating an action, the hunter seeks an opinion of the jurist. The 'hunter' has little interest in the bear itself which perhaps represents negligible value to her. She prefers monetary compensation for the injury. The former owner probably wants to claim the return of the bear, which was perhaps part of his business. The question, I think, is likely to have been put in this way: if I (the hunter) were to bring suit under the *actio de pauperie* against the former owner, and then let's say I kill the bear, would the action succeed based on the former owner's pleading (i.e., that he remained the owner of the animal)? And would I then – with the termination of the animal – be entitled to the damages? Or would the whole action fail for want of a proper object?

The explanation: killing as a juridical operation on the proceedings

To understand the jurist's response to this question, it's necessary to first consider something of the peculiar grammar of the noxal action. Normally, even in Roman law, a civil action seeks reparation as compensation for harm which is to be paid by the one who was at fault or who did the wrongful act that caused it. The fault is what gives rise to a right to claim reparation. With the *actio de pauperie*, on the other hand, wherever there is fault, the legal action is *excluded*. It deals, counterintuitively perhaps, only with matters where fault is missing. The harm (*noxia*) consequently is not the result of a delict but, as Ulpian says, 'constitutes the delict itself'.[23] And, rather than reparation principally remedying the harm, the doer of the harm (*noxa*) – that is, the animal – must itself be offered as the reparation (noxal surrender). What this means is that the reparation is not simply a quantifiable thing but indeed a *living* thing. The right of action subsists only for as long as the animal is alive. Ulpian indeed explains that if the animal should die before joinder of issue (*litem contestatam*), the pauperian action 'dies with it', and affirms that the reparation, noxal surrender, involves the handing over of the live animal, not a dead

---

22 This arrangement explains the etymology of 'pauperies' which Alan Watson linked to the idea of 'lack of productivity'. Alan Watson, "The Original Meaning of Pauperies," *Révue Internationale des Droits de l'Antiquité* 17 (1970): 365.

23 Digest 9.1.1.1. Ulpian, *Edict*, book 18. Watson, *The Digest of Justinian Vol. 1*, 276.

one.[24] This appears to be a structural element of the action. The text of the Digest is explicit in this regard. A noxal remedy will be denied to a defendant who pleads before the magistrate that the animal does not belong to him if it is later proven that it in fact does.[25] In that case, the action is successful for the full amount of damages: a defendant cannot later take advantage of surrendering an animal he had earlier claimed he didn't own. And Ulpian goes further still when he emphasises that if the animal were to be killed by a third party after joinder of issue – since an action would lie for the owner of the animal against that third party under the *lex Aquilia* (a separate basis of reparation) for the unlawful damage of the loss of his power to surrender it (alive) – the whole matter will be converted to one dealt with under that law (the *lex Aquilia*). Technically speaking, action under the *actio de pauperie* would cease along with the life of the beast; however, the involvement of the third party allows a particular value of damages under the *lex Aquilia* to effectively stand in for the noxal surrender. Finally, as if to emphasise the point, Ulpian indeed also mentions at Digest 9.1.1.17 that the *actio de pauperie* survives the death of the litigants, just as surely as it doesn't survive the death of the animal. We can see here the procedural importance of the hypothetical death of the bear and how it decisively connects the general rule with the example. Far from confusing the general rule, the example takes us to the most favourable situation that the jurist can imagine for a pauperian action subsisting for a 'wild' animal: precisely the situation where one party is led to swear, to his own advantage, to have remained the owner of it. But even in this singularly favourable scenario, Ulpian demonstrates that the pauperian action will fail. The rationalisation is not simply that, where the animal escapes, the former owner loses ownership, and with it the liability. We must imagine that ownership is still precisely in contestation between these parties and that it calls into question a whole conjunction of two sets of institutional relations 'according to' and 'against' nature. Even in the provisionality that that conjunction implies, the wild animal is considered to 'return' to nature before it can be imagined to be surrendered as 'against' it. This is why, far from holding open the possibility of a transformation of the proceedings to the hunter's advantage, the act of killing the bear actually forecloses it. According to one scheme, the killing of the wild animal only ensures the certainty of its acquisition; according to the other, the impossibility of its surrender.

This killing, one might say, is invoked as an act whose consequences touch purely on the juridical relations in question. It has no meaning here other than as what we would call a juridical act: a formal procedural step in a civil action whose institutional limits happen to be coextensive with the life of an animal; a means by which this precise legal relation alone is purportedly realised. And it is brought in this way into much sharper connection with the originality of the thought that takes hold of it. As in the previous example discussed, the jurist treats the positive limits placed upon a life by an act of killing not as limits beyond which lies an unknown or transcendent realm, but those which – in response to the legal case – may serve as an apparatus for testing also the limits of an institution.

Conclusion

I know of few places where the juristic side to the act of killing is contemplated with such clear-headedness as it is in these examples. Abstracted both from the idea of

24 Digest 9.1.1.13 and Digest 9.1.1.14. Ulpian, *Edict*, book 18. Watson, *The Digest of Justinian Vol. 1*, 277.
25 Digest 9.1.1.15. Ulpian, *Edict*, book 18. Watson, *The Digest of Justinian Vol. 1*, 277.

transgression and indeed from any concept of harm or wrongfulness, killing – an act that wilfully configures the limits of a life – comes also to lend its positivity and sharpness to institutions of the civil law, to the objects of legal action and legal contemplation, those whose positive limits sometimes require precise formulation by lawyers.

The examples which I've introduced in this chapter are by no means representative of the way the act of killing or of causing death is typically imagined in the ordinary configurations of the civil law. It is not at the centre after all but at the extremes that we come to glimpse the necessary relation in which thinking enters into connection with legal order. It may not be unusual for the limits of certain civil legal actions to be tied to the limits of the life of real individuals. In such circumstances, death sometimes irreversibly transforms the claims, the statuses, the transactions, and so on, just as certainly as it extinguishes the lives of those who pursue them. It remains there an external fact upon which the law draws certain normative consequences. But if one looks a little further, one encounters cases in which death is only the hypothesis according to which a particular juridical view of the world can alone be affirmed or denied. The positive formulation of the law cannot, in these places, be left entirely to the contingency of facts that lie outside of it. Instead, it demands recourse to the figure of a postulated procedural decision.

If there seems to be a sober, even cold, rationality to the acts of killing in these fragments – acts that, as the analysis has shown, are mentioned without any apparent motive other than the subtle technical-procedural manoeuvres that they seemingly represent for a testator or litigant in the context of possible civil action – it is all the more a sign that the legal mind there resists the temptation to abandon death, and loss more generally, to the realm of a purely sentimental and ultimately transcendental contemplation. The depth and originality of juridical thought resists an imagination of killing purely as transgression and of death as a 'beyond' to the world of legal relations. To kill is sometimes to perform a precise juridical operation.

Bibliography

Abdy, John Thomas, and Bryan Walker, eds. *The Commentaries of Gaius and the Rules of Ulpian.* Translated by John Thomas Abdy and Bryan Walker. Cambridge University Press, 1874.

Agamben, Giorgio. "*Vitae necisque potestas.*" In *Homo Sacer: Sovereign Power and Bare Life.* Stanford, CA: Stanford University Press, 1998.

Andrews, N. H. "'*Occidere*' and the *Lex Aquilia.*" *Cambridge Law Journal* 46, no. 2 (1987): 315–329.

Ashton-Cross, D. I. C. "Liability in Roman Law for Damage Caused by Animals." *Cambridge Law Journal* 11, no. 3 (1953): 395–403.

El Beheiri, Nadja. "Actio de Pauperie: El Caso Del Oso Escapado. Un Análisis en Clave Fenomenológica." *Revista de Estudios Histórico-Jurídicos* [*Sección derecho romano*] 43 (2021): 39–55.

Breij, Bé. "Vitae Necisque Potestas in Roman Declamation." *Advances in the History of Rhetoric* 9, no. 1 (2006): 55–79.

Dionysius of Halicarnassus. *Roman Antiquities Vol. 1.* Translated by Earnest Carey. Loeb Classical Library Edition, 1937 [1st century BCE].

Frier, Bruce W., and Thomas A. McGinn. "The Power of Life and Death." In *Casebook on Roman Family Law*, 191–210. Oxford University Press, 2003.

Harris, William V. "Roman Father's Power of Life and Death." In *Studies in Roman Law: In Memory of A. Arthur Schiller*, edited by Roger S. Bagnall and William V. Harris, 81–95. Leiden: E. J. Brill, 1986.

Haymann, Franz. "Textkritische Studien zum römischen Obligationenrecht." *Zeitschrift der Savigny-Stiftung für Rechtsgeschichte* [*Romanistische Abtheilung*] 42, no. 1 (1921): 357–393.

Honoré, Tony. "Liability for Animals: Ulpian and the Compilers." In *Satura Roberto Feenstra sexagesimum quintum annum aetatis complenti ab alumnis collegis amicis oblata*, 239–250. Universitaires Fribourg, 1985.

Malone, Wex S. "The Genesis of Wrongful Death." *Stanford Law Review* 17, no. 6 (1965): 1043–1076.

Meleze-Modrzejewski, Joseph. "Ulpien et la nature des animaux." In *La filosofia greca e il diritto romano. Colloquio italo-francese Roma, 14–17 aprile 1973*, 177–199. Rome, 1976.

Nörr, Dieter. "Causam Mortis Praebere." In *The Legal Mind: Essays for Tony Honoré*, edited by Neil MacCormick and Peter Birks, 203–217. Oxford: Clarendon Press, 1986.

Polojac, Milena. "Actio de Pauperie: Anthropomorphism and rationalism" *Fundamina* 18, no. 2 (2012): 119–144.

Shaw, Brent D. "Raising and Killing Children: Two Roman Myths." *Mnemosyne* 54, no. 1 (2001): 31–77.

Thomas, Yan. "Vitae necisque potestas: le pére, la cité, la mort." In *Du châtiment dans la cité. Supplices corporels et peine de mort dans le monde antique*, 499–548. École Française de Rome, 1984.

Thomas, Yan. "Sanctio: les défences de la loi." *L'ecrit du temps* 19 (1988): 61–84.

Thomas, Yan. "Imago Naturae: note sur la institutionnalité de la nature à Rome." In *Collection de l'École Française de Rome 147, Théologie et Droit dans la Science Politique de L'État Moderne*, 201–227. École Française de Rome, 1991.

Thomas, Yan. "Res Religiosae: On the categories of religion and commerce in Roman law." In *Law, Anthropology and the Constitution of the Social*, edited by Alain Pottage and Martha Mundy, 40–72. Cambridge University Press, 2004.

Thomas, Yan. "L'enfant à naître et l'« héritier sien »: sujet de pouvoir et sujet de vie en droit romain." *Annales. Histoire, Sciences Sociales* 62, no. 1 (2007): 29–68.

Watson, Alan. "The Original Meaning of Pauperies." *Révue Internationale des Droits de l'Antiquité* 17 (1970): 357–367. https://digitalcommons.law.uga.edu/fac_artchop/391.

Watson, Alan, ed. *The Digest of Justinian Vols 1–4*. University of Pennsylvania Press, 1985.

Westbrook, Raymond. "Vitae Necisque Potestas." *Historia: Zeitschrift für Alte Geschichte* 48, no. 2 (1999): 203–223.

24

DEATH AND THE CHALLENGES OF DISTANT AFFECTIVITY

Liminal Narratives at the International Criminal Court

Caroline Fournet and Adina-Loredana Nistor

Introduction

> So you are free and I hope you can forget, continue to forget everything
> about what happened to you. Thank you very much.[1]

As witnesses conclude their testimonies before international criminal courts and tribunals, they are often urged to forget what they have testified about. Forget what they saw, felt, experienced. Forget the death and the trauma.[2] Yet the crimes they witnessed – and survived – are, by definition, 'unimaginable atrocities that deeply shock the conscience of *humanity*' (emphasis added).[3] Following the creation of *ad hoc* international tribunals to prosecute atrocities committed in the Second World War and later following the dissolution of Yugoslavia and the Rwandan genocide, the International Criminal Court (ICC) was established as a permanent court, embodying a continuous aspiration to (potentially) deliver justice to victims worldwide. It was created to adjudicate the most serious human rights violations, such as genocide, crimes against humanity, war crimes, and aggression. 'Humanity', the concept that unites regardless of differences, is prominently invoked on the ICC's website; borrowing the words of former United Nations Secretary-General Kofi Annan, the pledge is made to serve 'the cause of all humanity'. Far from being incidental, such express references to 'humanity' aptly illustrate the global endeavour of the ICC to prosecute international crimes – an endeavour that, in the context of the present research, seems intrinsically paradoxical. Indeed, ample sociological

---

1 *Prosecutor v Dominic Ongwen*, ICC-02/04–01/15, Trial Chamber IX, Trial Transcript (10 November 2015), 5.
2 Suzanne Leontine Schot, *Testimonial Evidence of Traumatised Witnesses in Trials of International Crimes: Striking a Balance in the Interest of Fair Proceedings and Accurate Fact-finding* (Doctoral Thesis, University of Groningen, 2019), 247–53.
3 United Nations Diplomatic Conference of Plenipotentiaries on the Establishment of an International Criminal Court. *Rome Statute of the International Criminal Court*. U.N. Doc. A/Conf. 183/9, 17 July 1998 (entered into force 1 July 2022), Preamble, 1.

DOI: 10.4324/9781003304593-28

and anthropological research has shown that death as a social phenomenon is defined according to culture,[4] which maps a mosaic of practices and beliefs,[5] whether the dead are individualised, sacralised, intimately celebrated, or publicly commemorated. How can a forum whose raison d'être is to prosecute atrocities – and thus death – hold global ambitions that, by definition, override distinct cultural considerations? This paradox is at the core of this chapter, which explores death narratives at the ICC.

Rather expectedly, the concept of death permeates the definitions of most international crimes. Yet it is rarely explicitly mentioned in the text of international criminal law – the Rome Statute of the ICC. Aside from two war crimes expressly referring to death as the outcome of criminal acts (articles 8(2)(b)(vii) and 8(2)(b)(x)), death otherwise appears under the guise of other concepts that admittedly reflect the 'unimaginable atrocities' mentioned in the Rome Statute, such as 'killing' or 'physical destruction' in the definition of genocide (article 6) and 'murder' or 'extermination' in the definition of crimes against humanity (articles 7(1)(a) and 7(1)(b)). This textual aspect has practical consequences and raises the question of whether the ICC depicts death in a way that may contribute to 'the production of highly visible spectacles of horrific violence'.[6] How then – if at all – do these 'highly visible spectacles' enter the realm of international criminal justice via the judgments issued by the ICC? This chapter addresses this exact question. Based on a meticulous analysis of completed ICC cases (trial and appeals judgments), this chapter explores how the ICC narrates death, and attempts to identify a distinct approach taken by the ICC.

While the constraints of legal jargon reduce personal experiences to facts that need to be proven, the analysis of the ICC's judgments reveals that the ICC's death narratives occur in different scenarios, depending on each trial. This chapter uncovers that the initial distance, created through a terminology stripped of emotion, is later reduced and sometimes completely dissolved by the personal accounts of the victim-witnesses – which are often reproduced verbatim in the judgments. Once this layering becomes an obvious pattern, other patterns emerge: the legal definitions and criteria to be met are only devoid of emotion at first glance. As the reading of the judgments progresses, they can be seen more as metonyms that 'substitute a name of something for the name of a related thing'.[7] These words therefore stand for individual accounts of materialised tragedies. While the demands of international justice supersede cultural sensitivities, this chapter demonstrates how *the intimate* is introduced into the judicial, or, in other words, how *the personal* is introduced into *the austere*, to produce (consciously or unconsciously) what Bens calls 'the affective life of international criminal justice'. Bens' book opens with an introduction aptly titled 'Affect, Emotion, and the Law' and a reflection on *The Gift*, a substantial sculpture that faces the ICC's building, 'based on salt crystals found in tears and in the water of the nearby sea', meant to 'symbolise the universal expression of the emotions of

4 Alexander Paul Isiko, "The Socio-cultural Perspectives of the Bakonzo of Uganda about Death," *Journal of Humanities and Social Science* 24, no. 4 (2017): 57.
5 Ruth McManus, "The Sociology of Death and Dying," in *The Cambridge Handbook of Sociology: Specialty and Interdisciplinary Studies*, ed. Kathleen Odell Korgen (Cambridge: Cambridge University Press, 2017), 256–62.
6 Randle C. DeFalco, *Invisible Atrocities: The Aesthetic Biases of International Criminal Justice* (Cambridge: Cambridge University Press, 2022), 2.
7 Antonius C. G. M. Robben and Alexander Laban Hinton, *Perpetrators: Encountering Humanity's Dark Side* (Stanford, CA: Stanford University Press, 2023), 133.

joy and sorrow and the sea that connects all continents'.[8] This reflection is accompanied by a picture of the sculpture, reproduced in Figure 24.1.[9]

In this judicial context not devoid of all sentiments, the potential effects of the unpredictability of emotions on the fairness of proceedings and defendants' rights could be raised. While such analysis would go beyond the scope of the present research, this chapter nonetheless shows how the Trial Chambers oscillate between a dispassionate and emotionally distant narrative based on factual – even graphic – recollections of events (sometimes accompanied by corroborating scientific evidence) and more personalised, almost emphatic, depictions that rest on individualised accounts of the occurrence of death and, where possible, identification of the victims. Other times, the two narratives overlap, and the forensic evidence is strengthened by the sociocultural context in which the crimes were committed. At this point, the dead body becomes a 'discursive vehicle' through which violence represents a 'meaningful cultural expression'[10] that needs to be deciphered in the courtroom. Simultaneously, the body is a witness that can 'testify' to the violence it was subjected to ante and post mortem,[11] and as such, it can reveal a pattern in the criminal modus operandi.[12]

Figure 24.1 International Criminal Court, The Hague, Netherlands. Photo taken by the authors.

8 Jonas Bens, *The Sentimental Court: The Affective Life of International Criminal Justice* (Cambridge: Cambridge University Press, 2022), 1–2.
9 International Criminal Court, The Hague, Netherlands. Photo taken by authors.
10 Nigel Eltringham, "Display, concealment and 'culture': The disposal of bodies in the 1994 Rwandan genocide," in *Human Remains and Mass Violence: Methodological Approaches*, ed. Jean-Marc Dreyfus and Élisabeth Anstett (Manchester: Manchester University Press, 2015), 166.
11 See Clyde Snow as cited in Eric Stover, *The Graves: Srebrenica and Vukovar* (New York: Scalo, 199), 94.
12 See Caroline Fournet. "The human body: Victim, witness and evidence of mass violence," in *Human Remains and Mass Violence: Methodological Approaches*, ed. Jean-Marc Dreyfus and Élisabeth Anstett (Manchester: Manchester University Press, 2015), 57, 68.

Prior to any analysis, however, it must be acknowledged that conducting this research was not devoid of personal biases. Due to word limits restricting the scope and length of this chapter, it was impossible to explore all the death accounts in the case law of the ICC. Therefore, certain extracts of judgments were selected as illustrative of more general trends. This sampling approach is perhaps best demonstrated in the first section of this chapter ('Keeping death at a distance'), which focuses on factual and forensic narratives. There is, however, no denying that for the subsequent sections – which address how reports of lethal sexual violence, children's deaths, and the identification of dead victims contribute to reducing, if not altogether breaking, the judicial emotional distance – the authors' personal biases and emotional responses might have influenced the selection of extracts.

Keeping death at a distance: Dispassionate narratives of factual accounts and the forensic lens

This research identified two main ways in which death has been introduced in a rational, scientific, and perhaps sanitised way into ICC proceedings. The first way relates to body counts, where death is either reduced or amplified through numbers and the use of a specific terminology behind which individual deaths disappear. For instance, the *Katanga* judgment mentioned that 'approximately 200 civilians' died during the battle of Bogoro,[13] while the *Ntaganda* judgment reported that 'many people were killed' in a 'massacre'.[14] The second way is through the judicial resort to a forensic lens with express references to (expert) testimonies related to ballistics, weaponry, trauma, forensic archaeology, anthropology, and/or pathology to determine the most plausible causes of death and infer the date of the death and of the burial. The following sections map the way in which the ICC's judgments have addressed death through the filter of a strictly legal approach that remains both anonymous and detached. This distance should not be systematically read in a negative light; to the contrary, it may contribute to achieving the goals of international criminal justice: to assess the guilt or innocence of the accused, based on solid evidence presented in a way that respects fairness of proceedings and the principle of equality of arms.[15]

Factual accounts and the quantification of death: The body as a number

Perhaps unsurprisingly, considering that (international) criminal law judgments have to be dispassionate accounts of the perpetrated acts, the Trial Chambers of the ICC generally recount death in a very factual manner. As a preliminary remark, it should be noted that death is largely absent from the judgments issued against Lubanga and Al Mahdi, being either swiftly mentioned or reduced to side remarks in footnotes. This absence may be due to the crimes for which the defendants stood trial, namely, child soldiering (Lubanga) and destruction of cultural property (Al Mahdi), which do not entail systematic death.[16] However, those two cases are exceptions, and the destruction

---

13 *Prosecutor v Germain Katanga*, ICC-01/04-01/07, Trial Chamber II, Judgment (7 March 2014), para. 835.
14 *Prosecutor v Bosco Ntaganda*, ICC-01/04-02/06, Trial Chamber VI, Judgment (8 July 2019), para. 448.
15 United Nations, *Rome Statute of the International Criminal Court*, article 67.
16 See *Prosecutor v Thomas Lubanga Dyilo*, ICC-01/04-01/06, Trial Chamber I, Judgment (14 March 2012). See also *Prosecutor v Ahmad Al Faqi Al Mahdi*, ICC-01/12-01/15, Trial Chamber VIII, Judgment (27 September 2016).

of human life is prominent in the other judgments issued by the ICC. Yet, even then, death is usually anonymous. This anonymity can be partly justified by the legal requirements to not divulge witnesses' identities and to ensure their protection,[17] and partly by the massive and systematic nature of international crimes themselves, which erases individuality and concentrates on the approximate overall number of 'many'. As a result, the judgments tend to unemotionally focus on the sequence of events, the number of victims, and the cause and manner of their death.[18]

The following extracts from the *Ntaganda* judgment provide apt illustrations of how ICC judgments can depict death in atrocious circumstances while remaining devoid of emotion. For instance, with respect to an assault on the governor's residence, the judgment reported that '[m]any people were killed in the residence alone – mostly women and children, mainly "non-natives" or Lendu, who had tried to escape the fighting. Witnesses described the scene as "macabre" or a "massacre". Many of the bodies had gunshot wounds.'[19] With respect to an assault on Kilo, the judgment related that 'the UPC/FPLC ... began going after the Lendu in the village, killing some of them. The bodies of those killed were thrown into mass graves, some of which had been previously dug by those who were later killed.'[20]

The Trial Chamber also gave factual accounts of the *ratissage* operations, an expression which encapsulated the way in which Union des Patriotes Congolais (UPC)/Force Patriotique pour la Libération du Congo (FPLC) soldiers searched 'houses for any remaining soldiers'; killed civilians, 'some of them inside their homes'; and 'also raped women'.[21] Perhaps even more illustrative is the following paragraph narrating the unbearable in a very factual fashion:

> On or about the day the UPC/FPLC left Kobu, and the following day, people came to Kobu-Wadza to see what had happened. Bodies of those killed were discovered in the banana field. There were bodies of men, women, and children, including babies. Some bodies were naked. Some sticks and pounders were lying amongst the corpses, but no other weapons. Some bodies, but not all, had been tied up. Some looked like they had been beaten to death. Some bodies had slit throats, and some had been decapitated. Some had other knife cuts. Some looked like they had been killed by machete. Some had been disembowelled. Some were missing their genitals and some looked like their genitals had been perforated with sticks. The body of at least one woman looked like she had had a baby cut out of her. At least one corpse had bullet wounds around the mouth. The heads of some bodies had been crushed.[22]

The *Ongwen* judgment is equally replete with such accounts, as exemplified by the following extract:

> In the course of the attack, LRA fighters killed civilians by shooting, burning and/or beating them. The attackers killed at least 28 civilian residents of the

17 See, e.g., United Nations, *Rome Statute of the International Criminal Court*, article 68.
18 See, e.g., *Katanga* (Trial Judgment), paras 464, 516, 858–70.
19 *Ntaganda* (Trial Judgment), para. 448.
20 *Ntaganda* (Trial Judgment), para. 543.
21 *Ntaganda* (Trial Judgment), para. 464. See also paras 526, 665.
22 *Ntaganda* (Trial Judgment), para. 633.

camp. In other instances, killings were not fully carried out by the LRA fighters because of independent circumstances. Survivors returning the next morning found bodies strewn throughout the camp, including children. Some bodies were burnt or had the backs of their heads smashed, others had been shot. Dead bodies were found inside houses, at doorsteps and among the remains of burnt huts. These civilians were killed by LRA fighters. One of Dominic Ongwen's subordinate commanders intruded into a house with over 10 inhabitants, forced several to carry looted goods and then closed the door and set fire to the house with the remaining inhabitants inside.[23]

These detached accounts notwithstanding, death is at times recounted through the voices of witnesses, admittedly providing for more individualised accounts, even where the need to protect the witness required the anonymity of both the witness and the victim(s).[24] In the *Bemba Gombo* judgment, a detailed account of the death of the victim was made via the testimony of P69:

> The day after their arrival in PK12, when the MLC was the only armed group in and around PK12, two armed soldiers, speaking Lingala and wearing army uniforms, raided P69's house. The 'Banyamulengués' demanded money from his sister, who had a large amount of money tied around her waist. When she refused, the MLC soldiers threw her to the ground and took the money. She continued to resist, so one shot her in the head, killing her. The witness 'saw the brain of [his] sister … as if an animal's skull had been hit'.[25]

In the *Ongwen* judgment, perhaps further blurring the line between detachment and individualisation, the judges explicitly referred on several occasions to witnesses' in-court testimonies to narrate death:

> P-0187 testified that some bodies were not recovered soon after the attack, some bodies were found in the bush, many months after the attack. She stated, 'the bodies were discovered like luggage which had been abandoned'. Similarly, camp resident P-0024 testified that some of the dead bodies were never recovered, others were burned in the houses, and some remained in the bush. She stated that for some deceased their bodies were been [*sic*] eaten by dogs.[26]

In some instances, the Trial Chamber has directly reproduced/quoted the words used by witnesses to describe the death of victims. Regarding the killing of civilians by the Lord's Resistance Army (LRA) in Abok, the Trial Chamber turned to the testimony of LDU officer D-0065, who:

> testified about the LRA's actions during the attack: [The LRA] had already burnt houses in the camp. Some people were being pushed in the fire that was

23 *Prosecutor v Dominic Ongwen*, ICC-02/04-01/15, Trial Chamber IX, Judgment (4 February 2021), para. 1925.
24 See United Nations, *Rome Statute of the International Criminal Court*, article 68.
25 *Prosecutor v Jean-Pierre Bemba Gombo*, ICC-01/05-01/08, Trial Chamber III, Judgment (21 March 2016), para. 496.
26 *Ongwen* (Trial Judgment), para. 1752.

burning; they would be shot and pushed in the fire. Others were being shot from the houses, others were abducted when – [the LRA] took them alive, but they were killed on the way. Others were abducted and taken into the bush and have never returned up to now.[27]

The account of death in a judgment is occasionally given via the voice of the defendant. The *Katanga* judgment recalled the words of Germain Katanga, who described the aftermath of the battle in Nyakunde as a 'disaster',[28] adding that 'the people ... struggled to grow vegetables in Nyakunde because of the human skulls' (translation). He also confirmed that civilians, including women and children, had been killed.[29] Not all mentions of death are translated, however, and, at times, the Trial Chambers reproduce local expressions without translating them, which – just as in the case of the legal terminology where 'killing' or 'murder' could stand in for detailed and gruesome depictions of atrocities – seem to serve as metonyms that encompass extreme violence and suffering. For instance, in the *Ntaganda* case, it is in a foonote that the Trial Chamber reproduced the explanations given by witness P-0963 as to the meaning of the expression '*kupiga na kuchaji*', which stood as an 'instruction ... "to drive all the Lendus out"' but which contained a hidden – and more violent – dimension. As clarified by the witness, this 'was a tribal war, and the purpose was to drive out the Lendu, or *eliminate all of them*, loot their possessions, their various goods, possessions, financial means, occupy their houses' (emphasis added).[30] 'Driving the Lendus out' thus meant eliminating them.

It is difficult to determine whether this express use of local language to designate methods of killing reduces the emotional distance. What seems clearer, however, is that it attempts to bridge a geographical and cultural gap by capturing the reality of the crimes perpetrated in a way that no other language could, while striking a balance with the scientific evidentiary language diffused throughout judgments.

Distance through rationalisation: The forensic narrative and the body as evidence

ICC judges have supported their factual accounts with forensic evidence when it is available, thus arguably adding another layer of distance via the use of scientific jargon within the narrative, since forensic evidence is presented to the judges by in-court expert testimonies.[31] This was particularly the case in the *Ntaganda* judgment, in which the judges used the evidence presented by forensic experts to corroborate witnesses' accounts.

For instance, regarding the 2014 exhumation of 14 bodies in Kobu related to a massacre in the nearby banana field, forensic evidence showed that 'exhumed bodies in Kobu died from blunt force trauma'.[32] This was corroborated by 'witnesses who saw bodies in the banana field together with sticks lying amongst the corpses, and testified that some people looked like they had been beaten to death, and that the heads of some bodies had been crushed'[33]

27 *Ongwen* (Trial Judgment), para. 1932.
28 *Katanga* (Trial Judgment), para. 558.
29 *Katanga* (Trial Judgment), para. 1687.
30 *Ntaganda* (Trial Judgment), fn. 1188.
31 See Caroline Fournet, "Forensic Evidence in Atrocity Trials: A Risky Sampling Strategy?" *Journal of Forensic and Legal Medicine* 69 (2020): 101852.
32 *Ntaganda* (Trial Judgment), fn. 1971.
33 *Ntaganda* (Trial Judgment), fn. 1971.

and by witnesses who 'testified that they saw bodies with slit throats knife cuts, and who looked like they had been killed by machete, as well as decapitated bodies'.[34] Engaging with forensic knowledge and terminology, the Trial Chamber particularly noted forensic pathology expert 'Dr Martrille's evidence that cutting trauma can leave no trace on the bones, including that if a throat is slit, it may not be visible on the skeleton' and forensic pathology and genetics expert 'Dr Uhlin-Hansen's evidence that sharp injuries by, for instance, a knife or a machete may cut large blood vessels without hitting the bones'.[35] Ultimately, the Trial Chamber found 'that the only reasonable conclusion is that pounders were used to kill people'.[36]

Regarding the deaths of victims in Sayo[37] and the 2014 exhumation of two bodies in Tchudja, the Trial Chamber also resorted to forensic evidence to corroborate witnesses' testimonies, thereby offering a narrative that mixed witnesses' accounts and scientific jargon; for example:

> Expert evidence corroborates P-0100's account of the burial of his wife and is consistent regarding the burial of his young son: two bodies, one of an adult and one of a subadult, in a single grave were exhumed in Tchudja (TCH1) ... Dr Congram (P-0420) testified that two bodies exhumed in Tchudja had been laid out respectfully, indicating a measure of care, which the Chamber notes is consistent with P-0100's testimony that the family members had been brought there for burial.[38]

The *Ntaganda* judgment is not an isolated instance. The *Bemba Gombo* judgment had previously made connections between witnesses' testimony and the outcomes of the scientific analyses – both forensic and ballistic – conducted. This was notably the case regarding the testimony of witness P87, which was narrated in particular detail:

> At daybreak, P87 returned to the house with a neighbour and together they discovered her 'brother's' dead body. She noted three bullet wounds on her 'brother's' chest and blood on his body and on the floor. She also noted large injuries on his back.[39]
>
> P87 and several neighbours later buried her 'brother'. A body was exhumed from the grave where P87's 'brother' was said to have been buried. Forensic analysis of bone and dental samples concluded that it was the body of P87's 'brother'. An autopsy uncovered three chest injuries consistent with gunshot wounds.[40]

Immediately turning to a more scientific and technical language, the Trial Chamber then specified that:

> crime scene analysis also corroborates P87's account of the killing, concluding that a bullet most probably went through the body of P87's 'brother', through

34 *Ntaganda* (Trial Judgment), fn. 1971.
35 *Ntaganda* (Trial Judgment), fn. 1971.
36 *Ntaganda* (Trial Judgment), fn. 1972.
37 *Ntaganda* (Trial Judgment), para. 1466.
38 *Ntaganda* (Trial Judgment), fn. 2020.
39 *Bemba Gombo* (Trial Judgment), para. 476.
40 *Bemba Gombo* (Trial Judgment), para. 477.

the door, and into the next room. An analysis of two bullets discovered by the victim's father showed that they were fired from the same weapon, likely an AK47. The direction of fire was consistent with P87's account, either a horizontal shot at a standing victim or a descending shot at a kneeling victim.[41]

The *Ongwen* judgment also featured such scientific accounts; for instance, it is via the 'comprehensive and detailed' evidence provided by government pathologist Martin Kalyemenya that the judgment considered the victims of the May 2004 attack on the Lukodi internally displaced persons camp.[42]

Sometimes the forensic findings are corroborated by the sociocultural context in which the crimes took place. For example, in *Ntaganda*, the Trial Chamber noted:

> the conclusions of Dr Derek Congram (P-0420) that the graves he examined differed from routine burial custom, suggesting that the circumstances of burial were irregular and were indicative of multiple people dying at or around the same time (P-0420: T-123, pages 27, 67, and 113 to 114), which the Chamber considers to be consistent with the eyewitness testimonies that 'bodies were buried in shallow graves, communally, and quickly'.[43]

Details concerning burial practices among the affected communities, even if only briefly mentioned in the judgment, were amply addressed during the trial, giving the judges the opportunity to better grasp the context of the commission of the crimes.

Death taboos: Narrating the unbearable

The elderly, women, and children are generally considered the most vulnerable groups[44] subjected to the highest risk of victimisation during conflict, particularly in societies where gender equality is low.[45] As the following sections highlight, this increased vulnerability pierces through ICC judgments, notably – though not exclusively – when death is accompanied by sexual violence or when children and babies are targeted.

Sexual violence and death: Killing the spirit before killing the body

Several instances of death that ensued following acts of sexual violence were reported in the *Ntaganda* judgment. On various occasions, the judgment relied on witnesses' testimonies according to which the rapists intended to kill their victims, as in the case of witness P-0018, who testified in court of her own rape[46] and of the rape and killing of her sister-in-law:

---

41 *Bemba Gombo* (Trial Judgment), para. 478.
42 *Ongwen* (Trial Judgment), para. 553.
43 *Ntaganda* (Trial Judgment), fn. 2021.
44 See Charli R. Carpenter, "'Women, Children and Other Vulnerable Groups': Gender, Strategic Frames and the Protection of Civilians as a Transnational Issue," *International Studies Quarterly* 49, no. 2 (2005): 295–334, https://doi.org/10.1111/j.0020-8833.2005.00346.x.
45 See Jan van Dijk, "The Criminal Victimization of Children and Women in International Perspective", in *Women and Children as Victims and Offenders: Background, Prevention and Reintegration. Suggestions for Succeeding Generations (Volume 1)*, ed. Helmut Kury, Sławomir Redo, and Evelyn Shea (Switzerland: Springer, 2016), 405–27.
46 *Ntaganda* (Trial Judgment), para. 601.

P-0018 was in a position to conclude from the circumstances that her sister-in-law was raped and shot, and thus [the Chamber] finds her evidence credible in this regard ... The Chamber therefore finds that the only reasonable conclusion, on the basis of the specific circumstances described by the witness, is that her sister-in-law was raped and killed.[47]

These reports also included instances when victims were male, as per the testimony of P-0019:

The named UPC/FPLC commander told her that she and others were not human beings, but 'beasts or animals', and 'hostages'. P-0019 testified that she felt 'as if [she] were dead'. P-0019 also saw other women being raped inside and outside the house, including with sticks. P-0019 further witnessed UPC/FPLC soldiers anally penetrate men with their penises or by using 'bits of wood'. Following the rapes, the men 'suffered a great deal' and then they died.[48]

Aside from the feeling of death expressed by the victims, the *Katanga* judges themselves highlighted that the suffering was so intolerable that the victims would have preferred to be killed:

The six armed men undressed her, assaulted her, threatened her with death and then twice forcibly penetrated her vagina as she begged them to leave her alone. These acts were repeated when the same group of combatants forced her into a place where she was held against her will and where she was further hit and raped, even though she asked them to kill her rather than treat her in that manner.[49]

These sections of the judgments are particularly difficult to read, even though – or perhaps because – they generally remain factual and devoid of any sentiment. Relying on the testimony of P-0853, the judgment asserted:

Sexual violence took place in Bambu during the course of the Second Operation. P-0863 testified that the Lendu militia forced him to bury the body of a Lendu woman. He explained that the woman's pagne was ripped and that he observed mutilations of her genitals and between her thighs, as if a sharp object had been introduced 'into her female genitalia'. He further testified to having seen dried semen on her thighs. On the basis of the latter, P-0863 concluded that this woman had been raped.[50]

Admittedly going one step further on the scale of the unbearable is the account of Nadège's death in the *Ntaganda* judgment. Expressly named therein, Nadège, a girl 'who was around nine years old at the time, and who was taken to training at Lingo camp, was raped; P-0758 explained that there was pus coming out of Nadège's vagina and that,

---

47 *Ntaganda* (Trial Judgment), fn. 1863. See also para. 600.
48 *Ntaganda* (Trial Judgment), para. 623.
49 *Katanga* (Trial Judgment), para. 993.
50 *Ntaganda* (Trial Judgment), para. 588.

as a result, she died'.[51] Nadège is not the only victim to be named in an ICC judgment, and the mere fact of this personalisation by name and (young) age, even if devoid of any affect, contributes to bridging the emotional gap.

Further breaking the distance: Babies and children as victims of atrocities

Notwithstanding their generally factual and dispassionate accounts, the Trial Chambers of the ICC seem to always specify when babies and/or children are among the victims, thereby emphasising the particular vulnerability of these victims while admittedly adopting a more emotional approach.

In the *Katanga* judgment, the Trial Chamber notably referred to the testimonies of P-353, who '[a]mong the many victims she saw being killed ... remembered *two four-year-old children* who were hacked with machetes' (emphasis added);[52] of P-268, who 'saw, in front of his uncle's house close to a school, the *corpse of a two-year-old child* lying on the ground who had been shot and hacked to pieces by machete' (emphasis added);[53] and of P-161, who:

> said that he heard that the attackers had killed one of his sons, *aged four years*, and one of his daughters and one of his nephews, *both aged six years*, by machete whilst they were fleeing. He further stated that his older sister's *three young children* were killed by machete alongside their mother, who was shot dead, and a woman who was with them (emphasis added).[54]

The judgment also reproduced the testimony of P-287, who:

> stated that after the attackers entered the house, they wounded her child with a spear and shot at her ... They forced her to part from her child by striking her on the back with a machete ... Shortly thereafter, she heard a gunshot. Even though she did not see anything, she is convinced that her child, whom she has never seen since, was killed at that time.[55]

Perhaps even more horrific is the recollection of the testimony of V-2, who recounted how she 'felt a machete strike her and saw that her child had been savagely killed'.[56] The Trial Chamber found that 'V-2's baby, killed by machete, and the two-year-old child seen by P-268, shot dead and chopped to pieces by machete, were killed by Lendu'.[57]

In a similar vein, in the *Ongwen* judgment, the Trial Chamber specified when babies or children were among the victims. Recounting one particular massacre by the LRA, the Trial Chamber stated, '[m]any civilians were shot as they ran away from the LRA. Among the victims were elderly civilians, *children*, a pregnant woman as well as women carrying *babies* tied to their back' (emphasis added).[58] Recounting another attack led by

---

51 *Ntaganda* (Trial Judgment), para. 410.
52 *Katanga* (Trial Judgment), para. 330. See also para. 826.
53 *Katanga* (Trial Judgment), para. 814.
54 *Katanga* (Trial Judgment), para. 816.
55 *Katanga* (Trial Judgment), para. 822.
56 *Katanga* (Trial Judgment), para. 344. See also para. 814.
57 *Katanga* (Trial Judgment), para. 867.
58 *Ongwen* (Trial Judgment), para. 167.

the LRA, the judgment specified, 'Survivors returning the next morning found bodies strewn throughout the camp, *including children*' (emphasis added).[59]

The *Ongwen* Trial Chamber also resorted to witnesses' accounts, poignantly referring to 'camp resident P-0187's general testimony about the LRA's killing of children in the camp':[60]

> P-0187 testified: Some were hit. Some children were put in a polythene bag and beaten to death. Some were locked inside and burnt inside. Others were put in a bag and they were thrown in the bush. So many of them – some of them disappeared and they were never found. Others were found in the morning.[61]

The Trial Chamber also cited the testimony of P-0024, who testified that 'a child who was taken by the LRA and thrown away in the bush during the course of the retreat died and the dead body was never recovered'.[62] Interestingly, the Trial Chamber also recalled the testimony of LRA fighter P-0379, who testified as to the age of the victim – a key point for the characterisation of the war crime of conscripting or enlisting children under the age of 15 years into the national armed forces or using them to participate actively in hostilities:[63]

> [H]e saw a very young boy, who appeared to be a rebel, who was shot around the shoulders and on his head and was dead and it appeared he had been holding bubble gum in his hand but it fell next to him. While P-0379 does not explicitly estimate the age of the 'very young boy' that he saw, the description that he gave makes it plain that he spoke of a child below the age of 15. The Chamber thus notes P-0379's evidence as corroborative of the other evidence in relation to the participation of children under 15 years old in the LRA attack on Pajule IDP [internally displaced persons] camp on 10 October 2003.[64]

What is perhaps unexpected in this extract is the specification that the deceased child was seemingly 'holding bubble gum in his hand' – a detail that again contributes to breaking the distance while highlighting the horror of the crime perpetrated simply by recalling the ordinary humanness of the victim. According to Turok-Squire, 'this gum is part of a scene mixing the seen with the imagined'.[65] In the judgment, the event was still unfolding – the young boy was not described as holding the gum; rather, it is 'imagined to have been held in the boy's palm'.[66] The snippet therefore recreates 'the gum's journey to the ground as if it definitely happened: "but it fell next to him"'. Material details abound, and they bring some life to otherwise dry and anonymised accounts and foster a sense of empathy. Among 'estimates of huge numbers of people being attacked and long lists of the dead', such details bring into the courtroom fragments of 'complex individual lives unravelling within a war'.

59 *Ongwen* (Trial Judgment), para. 197.
60 *Ongwen* (Trial Judgment), para. 1750.
61 *Ongwen* (Trial Judgment), para. 1750.
62 *Ongwen* (Trial Judgment), para. 1753.
63 United Nations, *Rome Statute of the International Criminal Court*, articles 8(2)(b)(xxvi) and 8(2)(e)(vii).
64 *Ongwen* (Trial Judgment), para. 1239.
65 Ruby Lindiwe Turok-Squire, "A Judgment Like a Spiderweb: Catching Dominic Ongwen in the Language of the International Criminal Court," *Journal of International Criminal Law* 3, no. 1 (2022): 70.
66 Turok-Squire, "A Judgment," 71.

Reducing the distance: Not just a dead body

The previous sections have highlighted that in the austere setting of the ICC, what becomes relevant is often the fact that the death of *one individual* was part of a larger destruction. Words such as 'mass scale', 'mass graves', and 'numerous civilians' are key in qualifying the deaths not only as crimes but as atrocities. Death is, therefore, an abstraction that relates to faceless and unknown victims. Rather than being individualised, the victims are enumerated under generic categories: civilians, children, elderly, women. Yet individual accounts at times suspend the legal jargon and break the distance. The voices of those who were directly involved in these narratives of death pierce through, with their exact words sometimes directly quoted. These poignant fragments interrupt the dry and cold legal statements and considerations to reveal the affective and the personal.

As shown by the factual and scientific narratives explored above, death at the ICC has generally been treated in a rather anonymous fashion. Symptomatically, in the case against Jean-Pierre Bemba Gombo, the Pre-Trial Chamber found that 'in case of mass crimes, it may be impractical to insist on a high degree of specificity. In this respect, it is not necessary for the Prosecutor to demonstrate, for each individual killing, the identity of the victim and the direct perpetrator.'[67]

Similarly, in the *Ntaganda* judgment, the Trial Chamber held that 'it is not necessary for the Prosecution to prove the specific identity of the victim or the perpetrator'.[68] However, this did not stop the same Trial Chamber from narrating in detail the individual circumstances of the death of an anonymous victim, a woman 'wearing rags' who 'was unarmed at the time she came to the health centre seeking treatment for her approximately two-year-old child'.[69] The judgment notably reported the testimony of witness P-0017, who 'saw the body of the woman in front of the health centre and heard a child crying inside the centre, while on the way back, once the attack had finished, the child was also lying dead in front of the health centre'.[70] This specification notwithstanding, the Trial Chamber did not depart from the legalistic language when it concluded that it was 'satisfied that woman was a civilian not actively taking part in hostilities at the time when she was killed'.[71]

In some instances, the Trial Chamber named the victim, such as Abbé Boniface Bwanalonga, whose death was addressed at several points in the judgment.[72] He was described in the judgment as 'a Lendu man of advanced age ... serving as a Catholic priest at the Mongbwalu parish',[73] who had been brought to the Appartements camp 'for interrogation shortly after the takeover of Mongbwalu'.[74] Bosco Ntaganda was charged with 'the murder of Priest Boniface Bwanalonga by way of shooting him several times in the head with a revolver behind his apartment in Kilo-Moto'.[75]

---

67 *Prosecutor v Jean-Pierre Bemba Gombo*, ICC-01/05-01–08, Pre-Trial Chamber II, Decision Pursuant to Article 61(7)(a) and (b) of the Rome Statute on the Charges of the Prosecutor against Jean-Pierre Bemba Gombo, 15 June 2009, paras 133–4.
68 *Ntaganda* (Trial Judgment), para. 862.
69 *Ntaganda* (Trial Judgment), para. 888.
70 *Ntaganda* (Trial Judgment), fn. 1482. See also fn. 1480.
71 *Ntaganda* (Trial Judgment), para. 888.
72 See, e.g., *Ntaganda* (Trial Judgment), paras 241, 533.
73 *Ntaganda* (Trial Judgment), para. 529.
74 *Ntaganda* (Trial Judgment), fn. 617.
75 *Ntaganda* (Trial Judgment), para. 734.

Perhaps marking a turning point in the death narrative at the ICC, the most recent judgment issued by the ICC expressly cited – where available – the victims' names. In the *Ongwen* judgment, the Trial Chamber named the victims[76] and explicitly 'discusse[d] the evidence related to the LRA's killing and attempted killing of specific individuals within the camp',[77] all of whom are named and the specific circumstances of their deaths described.[78] The Trial Chamber did not divulge the rationale behind this approach, and reaching definitive conclusions as to the judges' intention here would be pure speculation. What seems clear, however, is that these more individualised narratives contribute to breaking the (emotional) distance created by purely factual and/or scientific accounts.

Conclusion

Criminal law, as Bens writes, 'is about ascribing legal significance to actual events that have occurred'.[79] As legal truth is being construed throughout judicial proceedings and as each party puts forward its own narrative, a '"plausible" version of past events' is being established and, ultimately, the judges 'apply legal significance to this plausible past'.[80]

As this chapter has revealed, this plausibility is primarily obtained through a dis-passionate, factual, and forensic approach. This approach hinges on precision, time frames, and numbers, even when these remain in the undefined realm of 'many' or 'numerous'. Nevertheless, plausibility is not only construed through statistics and cold facts but also through another dimension that is never explicitly mentioned and can only be inferred: the realm of emotions. This emotional dimension is at times conspicuous in the language being used. In the *Ongwen* judgment, the Trial Chamber described the evi-dence as 'so shocking',[81] the crimes as 'evil committed',[82] the facts as 'horrors',[83] and the perpetrator – through the voice of one of his victims – as 'the worst when it came to young girls'.[84] Such characterisations reflect the 'unimaginable atrocities' the ICC has pledged to prosecute and admittedly produce the 'highly visible spectacles of horrific violence'[85] mentioned in the introduction to this chapter.

The concept of death is omnipresent and multidimensional in the ICC's judgments. It is captured in the necessary references to the definitions of international crimes as embodied in the stern language of the Rome Statute, with its list of lethal acts, such as physical destruction, killing, murder, and extermination. It is apparent in the forensic accounts and reports that detail the causes, manners, and circumstances of the deaths in question. It manifests in the excerpts of witnesses and victims' testimonies, which, when directly reproduced/quoted, preserve the first-person narrative. And yet the urge to forget sometimes asked of witnesses contradicts the collective promise – if not duty – to 'never forget' and humanity's pledge to *never* permit such atrocities to be repeated. The ICC becomes a vault where such stories of horror are kept, hidden in plain sight, in countless

---

76 *Ongwen* (Trial Judgment), paras 16–9, 171, 175, 183–4, 187–8, 198, 1593, 1597–608.
77 *Ongwen* (Trial Judgment), para. 1947.
78 *Ongwen* (Trial Judgment), paras 1948–57.
79 Bens, *The Sentimental Court*, 80.
80 Bens, *The Sentimental Court*, 81.
81 *Ongwen* (Trial Judgment), para. 314.
82 *Ongwen* (Trial Judgment), para. 2722.
83 *Ongwen* (Trial Judgment), para. 2040.
84 *Ongwen* (Trial Judgment), para. 2040.
85 DeFalco, *Invisible Atrocities*, 2.

pages of transcripts and hours of trial hearings; an oral history of 'unimaginable atrocities' that is judicially translated into judgments. It is inside the walls of this vault, within this space of temporal atemporality, that witnesses' voices are heard. And when these individual voices pierce through, they may well be the voice of all humanity.

Bibliography

Bens, Jonas. *The Sentimental Court: The Affective Life of International Criminal Justice*. Cambridge: Cambridge University Press, 2022.

Carpenter, R. Charli. "'Women, Children and Other Vulnerable Groups': Gender, Strategic Frames and the Protection of Civilians as a Transnational Issue." *International Studies Quarterly* 49, no. 2 (2005): 295–334. https://doi.org/10.1111/j.0020-8833.2005.00346.x.

DeFalco, Randle C. *Invisible Atrocities: The Aesthetic Biases of International Criminal Justice*. Cambridge: Cambridge University Press, 2022.

Eltringham, Nigel. "Display, concealment and 'culture': The disposal of bodies in the 1994 Rwandan genocide." In *Human Remains and Mass Violence: Methodological Approaches*, edited by Jean-Marc Dreyfus and Élisabeth Anstett, 161–180. Manchester: Manchester University Press, 2015.

Fournet, Caroline. "Forensic Evidence in Atrocity Trials: A Risky Sampling Strategy?" *Journal of Forensic and Legal Medicine* 69 (2020): 101852. https://doi.org/10.1016/j.jflm.2019.07.008.

Fournet, Caroline. "The human body: Victim, witness and evidence of mass violence." In *Human Remains and Mass Violence: Methodological Approaches*, edited by Jean-Marc Dreyfus and Élisabeth Anstett, 56–80. Manchester: Manchester University Press, 2015.

International Criminal Court. "How the Court Works." Accessed 31 August 2023. www.icc-cpi.int/about/how-the-court-works.

Isiko, Alexander Paul. "The Socio-cultural Perspectives of the Bakonzo of Uganda about Death." *Journal of Humanities and Social Science* 24, no. 4 (2017): 57–68. https://doi.org/10.9790/0837-2404055768.

McManus, Ruth. "The Sociology of Death and Dying." In *The Cambridge Handbook of Sociology: Specialty and Interdisciplinary Studies*, edited by Kathleen Odell Korgen, 256–262. Cambridge: Cambridge University Press, 2017.

Robben, Antonius C. G. M., and Alexander Laban Hinton. *Perpetrators: Encountering Humanity's Dark Side*. Stanford, CA: Stanford University Press, 2023.

Schot, Suzanne Leontine. *Testimonial Evidence of Traumatised Witnesses in Trials of International Crimes: Striking a Balance in the Interest of Fair Proceedings and Accurate Fact-finding*. Doctoral Thesis, University of Groningen, 2019.

Stover, Eric. *The Graves: Srebrenica and Vukovar*. New York: Scalo, 1998.

Turok-Squire, Ruby Lindiwe. "A Judgment Like a Spiderweb: Catching Dominic Ongwen in the Language of the International Criminal Court." *Journal of International Criminal Law* 3, no. 1 (2022): 54–93. https://doi.org/10.22034/JICL.2022.144820.

van Dijk, Jan. "The Criminal Victimization of Children and Women in International Perspective." In *Women and Children as Victims and Offenders: Background, Prevention and Reintegration. Suggestions for Succeeding Generations (Volume 1)*, edited by Helmut Kury, Sławomir Redo, and Evelyn Shea, 405–427. Switzerland: Springer, 2016.

INDEX